EUROPEAN LIBRARIES AND THE INTERNET

EUROPEAN LIBRARIES AND THE INTERNET

Copyright and Extended Collective Licences

Rán Tryggvadóttir

intersentia
Cambridge – Antwerp – Portland

KU LEUVEN CITIP
CENTRE FOR IT & IP LAW

Intersentia Ltd
Sheraton House | Castle Park
Cambridge | CB3 0AX | United Kingdom
Tel.: +44 1223 370 170 | Fax: +44 1223 370 169
Email: mail@intersentia.co.uk
www.intersentia.com | www.intersentia.co.uk

Distribution for the UK and Ireland:
NBN International
Airport Business Centre, 10 Thornbury Road
Plymouth, PL6 7 PP
United Kingdom
Tel.: +44 1752 202 301 | Fax: +44 1752 202 331
Email: orders@nbninternational.com

Distribution for Europe and all other countries:
Intersentia Publishing nv
Groenstraat 31
2640 Mortsel
Belgium
Tel.: +32 3 680 15 50 | Fax: +32 3 658 71 21
Email: mail@intersentia.be

Distribution for the USA and Canada:
Independent Publishers Group
Order Department
814 North Franklin Street
Chicago, IL60610
USA
Tel.: +1 800 888 4741 (toll free) | Fax: +1312 337 5985
Email: orders@jpgbook.com

ISBN 978-1-78068-674-5
ISBN 978-1-78068-712-4 (pdf)
D/2018/7849/74
NUR 827

British Library Cataloguing in Publication Data. A catalogue record for this book is available from the British Library.

To my mother, the librarian and booklover, who inspired me to start,
and to my granddaughter, who inspired me to finish.

ACKNOWLEDGEMENTS

This book is based on my PhD thesis which I successfully defended at KULeuven, Belgium, on December 1st, 2017. The following are my acknowledgements for the final version of my thesis:

It is with a deep sense of gratitude that I sit down and write these lines of acknowledgement. Writing a PhD can be a very lonely affair, especially as an external researcher, which I was for most of the time. However, I have had the good fortune to be surrounded by wonderful people wherever I have been, who have helped me enjoy this journey, both highs and lows.

I would first like to thank my supervisor Professor Marie-Christine Janssens, Head of Unit of the Centre for IT & IP Law, KU Leuven, for her continuous support and helpful advice throughout the journey, from near and far, in person and over Skype. Then I would like to thank my supervisory committee: Professor Geertrui Van Overwalle and Professor Lucie Guibault. Professor Van Overwalle was very encouraging in the early stages of my work and inspired me to go outside my comfort zone and design the only graph in the work. Professor Lucie Guibault has been a valuable inspiration and source of expertise in the area of access to the cultural heritage. She has not always agreed with my approach, but her comments have been most helpful and guided me to the end. As I was an external student for much of the time I had less of an opportunity to collaborate with my fellow PhD researchers at the Centre. However, all of them have been very helpful when I have needed advice, practical or theoretical. In particular I would like to thank Esther van Zimmeren, who was finishing her PhD when I was starting, Christine Frison, Arina Gorbatyuk and Amandine Leonard. I would also like to thank the administrative staff at the Centre for IT & IP Law, KU Leuven, in particular Linda Mees and Shuki Tang.

I had the good fortune to be a visiting scholar at Columbia Law School for two years during my research. That provided me with invaluable facilities and the opportunity to interact with fellow researchers. I am very grateful to Professor Jane Ginsburg for sponsoring me and for the time she took answering my questions. I am also very grateful to the numerous visiting scholars I met and who all helped me in one way or another, in particular: Irina Eidsvold Tøien,

Associate Professor at the Norwegian Business School, Vigjilenca Abazi, Associate Professor, Maastrict Univeristy, Professor Christina Ramberg, University of Stockholm, Professor Christina D. Tvarnø, Copenhagen Business School, Dr. Şeyda Emek, Policy Officer at the German Federal Ministry of the Interior, Tamsin Phillipa Paige, Research Associate at the University of New South Wales, Canberra at the Australian Defence Force Academy and Frank S. Giaoui, PhD candidate at Sorbonne Law School and Columbia Law School.

I also owe thanks to several people who have taken the time to discuss my topic, answered my questions in e-mails and provided me with valuable information. First in this group I would like to thank Helge Sønneland, former Director General of the Norwegian Ministry of Culture, who has a keen interest in the subject of my research and has generously given me his time and always been willing to assist in any way; Jerker Rydén, Chief Legal Adviser of the Swedish National Library, for his enthusiastic approach to cross-border licensing via extended collective licences and willingness to answer and discuss the subject on several occasions; Hege Døssland, Head of Department, Licensing, Kopinor, Norway, who has always answered my e-mails and provided me with valuable insights into the practical side of licensing; Jón Vilberg Guðjónsson, Director of the Department of Legal Affairs at the Icelandic Ministry of Education, Science and Culture, who has provided valuable support throughout the research; Anna Vuopala, Government Counsellor at the Ministry of Education and Culture, Finland, who provided much valuable information about Finnish practice; Jukka Liedes, Chairman of the Finnish Copyright Society and former Director, responsible for i.a. the national copyright policy, Ministry of Education and Culture, Finland, who has on several occasions given me very useful insights; Bengt O. Hermansen, Deputy Director General of the Norwegian Ministry of Culture, Department of Media and Copyright; Professor Ole-Andreas Rognstad, University of Oslo; Professor Jan Rosén, University of Stockholm; Professor Severine Dusollier, Sciences Po Law School; Olav Stokkmo, former Secretary General of IFRRO; Grímur Jóhannsson, Senior Officer, EFTA; Professor Annette Kur, Max Planck Institute for Innovation and Competition; June M. Besek, Executive Director and lecturer in law, Kernochan Center for Law, Media and the Arts, Columbia Law School; Dr. Katharina Schöneborn, German National Library, Digital Services; Tommi Nilsson, Executive Director of Kuvasto, Finland; Dr. Matthías Pálsson, Counsellor at the Directorate for Legal and Executive Affairs, Ministry of Foreign Affairs, Iceland; Högni Kristjánsson, College Member, EFTA Surveillance Authority; Associate Professor Rebecca Giblin, Monash University; Professor Tomas A. Lipinski, School of Information Studies, University of Wisconsin; Eleonora Rosati, Associate Professor at University of Southamton; Dr. Johan Axhamn, University of Stockholm; Matej Gera, LL.M., PhD Researcher, Centre for Intellectual Property Policy & Management, Bournemouth University; Judith Bannister, Senior Lecturer, Adelaide Law School.

I would also like to thank all my friends who have supported me, in particular my informal PhD group of mature PhD candidates at various stages of the journey, who have provided invaluable moral support at times: Dr. Brynja Ingadóttir, Dr. Ásthildur Björg Jónsdóttir, Dr. Þórunn Scheving Elíasdóttir, Margrét Vala Kristjánsdóttir, Associate Professor at Reykjavík University and PhD candidate at University of Oslo, Svala Ísfeld Ólafsdóttir, Associate Professor at Reykjavík University and PhD candidate at University of Iceland, Kristrún Heimisdóttir, PhD candidate at Columbia Law School, Elísabet Þórðardóttir, PhD candidate at the University of Iceland, Svana Helen Björnsdóttir CEO of Stiki and PhD candidate at Reykjavík University, Helga Kristín Auðunsdóttir, Assistant Professor, Bifröst University, and PhD candidate at Fordham Law School, New York. My various running and walking partners: Eva Ingólf, Bergdís, Vala, María Kristín J. and María Kristín G., Blanca, Tawney. My good and supporting neighbours in New York Roa Lynn and Bernard Kripkee and many more people who have made my life pleasant and fun the last few years.

Finally, I would like to thank my family for endless inspiration and support. My mother, the librarian, who taught me to love books and libraries, my father, who taught me never to take short-cuts when writing, my brothers, who have given me a healthy bounce of competitiveness and my sons, who have taught me about unconditional love. Last but not least, my beloved husband, Nick, without whom I would not have finished this project. His loving support, practical and emotional, glimmers through every line of this book.

FOREWORD

This is the second book to be published in the newly established series launched by the KU Leuven Centre for IT & IP Law (CiTiP). As was the case with the first book[1], this publication is very timely as the European legislator is in the process of discussing possible new provisions as regards extended collective licenses (ECL) in its forthcoming new Directive on Copyright in the Digital Single Market.[2] The mechanism of ECL has for many decades been successfully applied in a number of European Member States, most notably in Nordic countries. Yet, and despite the assurance in paragraph 18 of the Information Society Directive preamble stating that "this Directive is without prejudice to the agreements in the Member States concerning the management of rights such as extended collective licensing", the application of ECLs remains controversial in certain areas of copyright law.

New provisions need a clear and well-argued understanding. That is precisely what the author seeks – and successfully accomplishes in this book, that contains the results of the doctoral research that the author carried out at CiTiP in the period 2012–2017. With her Nordic (Icelandic) background as well as a residence in Brussels for many years, the author of this book was the right person in the right place to research the topic of ECL. The research is driven by the author's concern that libraries should continue to fulfil their role of custodians of the cultural heritage in the online digital environment. The book provides valuable insights into the many challenges libraries encounter. Its ultimate goal is to propose a legal environment in which libraries are able to make works from their collections available online with cross-border effect.

The book reads as a novel. The author takes the reader on a journey through the legal framework of exclusive copyrights, looking for answers in the system of exceptions and limitations to these rights, ploughing through problems of international private law that arise because of the cross-border dimension of online use as well as the territorial nature of copyright and flying over the landscape set by the different laws on ECL in the Nordic countries. At the core of this exploratory expedition lies an in-depth and rigorous quest for answers as

1 Niels Vandezande, *Virtual Currencies: A Legal Framework*, KU Leuven Centre for IT & IP Law Series, Intersentia, 2018.

2 Proposal for a Directive of the European Parliament and of the Council on copyright in the Digital Single Market, COM(2016)593.

regards the compatibility of ECL agreements with the EU and international legal copyright framework.

As all the mentioned legal issues are presented and analyzed in a thoroughly structured manner I am certain that this book will constitute a useful tool. It will certainly help specialists in copyright to better understand the system of extended collective licensing. The author concludes that the ECL system can address the need to make in-copyright works available in a way that affords flexibility and legal certainty to users, such as libraries, and is at the same time not unacceptably intrusive on the exclusive rights of rightholders.

Certainly, it will not convince everyone and I can already hear some reservations. The conclusions, which specify the 'hybrid' nature of the extension effect of the ECL system are indeed complex, but they certainly have merit and are very valuable in the discussion over the nature of an extended collective license. Indisputably, the book adds some useful pieces to the jigsaw puzzle of European copyright law in a period when European copyright law is under construction.

For me personally, it has been a rewarding experience and a true pleasure to serve as the promotor of this research.

Prof. dr. Marie-Christine Janssens
Head of Unit KU Leuven Centre for IT & IP law (CiTiP)

5 September 2018

CONTENTS

ACRONYMS AND ABBREVIATIONS

ALAI	Association Littéraire et Artistique Internationale
ALRC	Australian Law Reform Commission
ARROW	Accessible Registries of Rights Information and Orphan Works
ASA	Amended Settlement Agreement (USA)
BA	The Norwegian Bokhylla Agreement
CDPA	Copyright and Designs Patents Act (UK)
CEIPI	Centre for International Intellectual Property Studies, University of Strasbourg, France
CISAC	International Confederation of Societies of Authors and Composers, France
CJEU	Court of Justice of the European Union (formerly the European Court of Justice, ECJ)
CMO	Collecting Management Organisation
CNA	Competent National Authority
CRPR	Copyright and Rights in Performances (Extended Collective Licensing) Regulations (SI 2014/2588) (UK)
CULT	EP Committee on Culture and Education
DCA	Danish Copyright Act
DLF	Digital Library Federation
DSM proposal or DSMP	*Proposal for a Directive of the European Parliament and of the Council on copyright in the Digital Single Market,* COM(2016) 593 final.
EBLIDA	European Bureau of Library, Information and Documentation Associations
ECL	Extended Collective Licences
EEA	European Economic Area
EFTA	European Free Trade Association
EIPR	European Intellectual Property Review
EP	European Parliament
ERR Act	Enterprise and Regulatory Reform Act 2013 (UK)
EU	European Union
EUIPO	European Union Intellectual Property Office
FA	Framework Agreement (used for the German "Rahmenvertrag zur Nutzung von vergriffenen Werken in Büchern")
FCA	Finnish Copyright Act

FCIP	The French Code of Intellectual Property
FNGA	Finnish National Gallery Agreement
FSA	The First Settlement Agreement (Google, USA)
GCA	The German Copyright Act
GCAA	The German Copyright Administration Act
GDPR	General Data Protection Regulation
HLG	High Level Expert Group on Digital Libraries
ICA	Icelandic Copyright Act
IFLA	International Federation of Library Associations and Institutions
IFRRO	International Federation of Reproduction Rights Organisations
IIC	International Review of Industrial Property and Competition Law
IMCO	EP Committee on the Internal Market and Consumer Protection
IPO	Intellectual Property Office (UK)
IPRs	Intellectual Property Rights
IPQ	Intellectual Property Quarterly (Sweet & Maxwell, UK)
ITRE	EP Committee on Industry, Research and Energy
IVIR	Instituut voor Informatierecht (Institute for Information Law, University of Amsterdam, The Netherlands)
JIPITEC	Journal of Intellectual Property, Information Technology and E-Commerce Law
MoU	Memorandum of Understanding
NCA	Norwegian Copyright Act
NCB	Nordisk Copyright Bureau
NIR	Nordiskt Immateriellt Rättsskydd (Nordic Intellectual Property Law Review)
NNL	Norwegian National Library
NNLA	The Norwegian National Library Agreement for delivery of digital copies to end-users
OBR	Online Broadcasting Regulation: Regulation of the European Parliament and of the Council laying down rules on the exercise of copyright and related rights applicable to certain online transmissions of broadcasting organisations and retransmissions of television and radio programmes, COM(2016) 594 final, 14 September 2016.
PP	Portability Proposal: COM(2015) 627, *Proposal for a Regulation of the European Parliament and of the Council on ensuring the cross-border portability of online content services in the internal market*, 9 Dec 2015.
REPROBEL	The Belgian RRO
RIDA	Revue Internationale du Droit d'Auteur (France)
RROs	Reproduction Rights Organisations
SCA	Swedish Copyright Act

SDNY	Southern District of New York (Court)
SNL	Swedish National Library
SOFIA	Société Française des Intérêts des Auteurs de l'Ecrit (The French CMO for text)
TEU	Treaty on European Union
TFEU	Treaty on the functioning of the European Union
TORB	Tijdschrift voor onderwijsrecht en onderwijsbeleid (Belgian Journal of Education Law and Education Policy)
TRIPs	Agreement on the Trade-Related Aspects of Intellectual Property Rights of 15 April 1994 (WTO)
UNESCO	United Nations Educational, Scientific and Cultural Organization
USCO	United States Copyright Office
VG Bild-Kunst	Verwertungsgesellschaft Bild-Kunst (The German CMO for images)
VG-Wort	Verwertungsgesellschaft WORT (The German CMO for text)
VIP Treaty	The Marrakesh Treaty to Facilitate Access to Published Works for Persons Who Are Blind, Visually Impaired or Otherwise Print Disabled
WCT	WIPO Copyright Treaty
WIPO	World Intellectual Property Organization
WPPT	WIPO Performances and Phonograms Treaty
WTO	World Trade Organization
ZUM	Zeitschrift für Urheber- und Medienrecht (Germany)

CHAPTER 1
INTRODUCTION

...the capabilities of digital technology are not dictated by the copyright framework, and neither are the problems caused by digital technology in any sense solved by the copyright system.[1]

1.1. DIGITAL LIBRARIES AND COPYRIGHT

1. Few would dispute the importance of preserving and providing access to the cultural heritage. From the great Library of Alexandria through the monastic and courtly libraries and the university repositories of learning, libraries have played a central role in this endeavour. The significance of this task has not diminished in the digital age, but the digital revolution has radically changed how information is preserved and made available and, hence, the way libraries work. At the same time as digital technology has provided powerful new tools to reproduce and disseminate works it has transformed the demands and expectations of users[2].[3] Today much information and many works are only available in digital form. More and more people go online in search of information and entertainment, while there has been a marked decline in the use of physical libraries.[4] Users'[5] default assumption has become "that all content can and should be available to them in digital form, without the necessity of going to a physical library"[6] and if content is "not found on the Web, it effectively does not exist".[7]

---

1 IPO, ©the way ahead: A Strategy for Copyright in the Digital Age, October 2009, p. 22.

2 The term user refers here to end-users, i.e. natural persons, see further fn. 35.

3 Estelle Derclaye (ed), *Copyright and Cultural Heritage; preservation and access to works in a digital world* (Edward Elgar Publishing, 2010) 233; Nadine Klass and Hajo Rupp, 'EUROPEANA, ARROW and Orphan Works: Bringing Europe's Cultural Heritage Online' in Irini Stamatoudi and Paul Torremans (eds), *EU Copyright Law; A Commentary* (2014) 950.

4 UCL, *Information behaviour of the researcher of the future, a ciber briefing paper, Study conducted for the JISC and the British Library,* (11 January 2008) 7; Department for Culture Media and Sport, *Empower, Inform, Enrich,* (November 2009) 5; David Baker and Wendy Evans, 'Digital Libraries economics: the environment' in David Baker and Wendy Evans (eds), *Digital library economics: an academic perspective* (Chandos, 2009) 7.

5 See fn. 2.

6 Lynne Brindley, Dame, 'Foreword, Digital Libraries economics: an introduction' in David Baker and Wendy Evans (eds), *Digital library economics: an academic perspective* (Chandos, 2009) xv; June M. Besek, 'The development of digital libraries in the United States' in Lionel Bently, Uma Suthersanen and Paul Torremans (eds), *Global Copyright; Three Hundred Years since the Statute of Anne, from 1709 to Cyberspace* (Edward Elgar, 2010) 208.

7 Lynne Brindley, Dame, 'Phoenixes in the internet era – the changing role of libraries' in Lionel Bently, Uma Suthersanen and Paul Torremans (eds), *Global Copyright: Three Hundred*

2. Furthermore, the powerful tools of digitisation are by no means only in the hands of the recognised preservers of the cultural heritage. Google was instrumental in bringing the written word, and in particular books, squarely into the digital world with its Book Search Project based on mass digitisation of the world's literary heritage.[8] Google's initiative has been described as one "of the most significant developments in the history of books, as well perhaps [as] in the history of copyright".[9] The mass digitisation has enabled search engines like Google to engage in important aspects of library's roles.[10] Accessing digital content is one of the most popular online activities, and concerns to a very large extent copyright protected works.[11] Tools for such access abound, but they often ignore copyright law.[12]

3. The implications of these developments for libraries are stark. If libraries are not to become obsolete they will have to become digital and be able to provide the same services in the digital environment as in the analogue world.[13] In order to become digital libraries will have to overcome several challenges. Not only must they be equipped with the costly technology required to digitize and preserve works digitally[14], but libraries also will have to make sure they operate

---

Years Since the Statute of Anne, from 1709 to Cyberspace (2nd edn, Edward Elgar, 2010) 178; Tim Padfield, 'Preserving and accessing our cultural heritage – issues for cultural sector institutions: archives, libraries, museums and galleries' in Estelle Derclaye (ed), *Copyright and Cultural Heritage; Preservation and Access to Works in a Digital World* (Edward Elgar Publishing, 2010) 209; SEC(2006) 1075, *Commission Recommendation on the digitisation and online accessibility of cultural material and digital preservation – Impact assessment*, (24.08.2006) 10; European Commission, *Report on the responses to the Public Consultation on the Review of the EU Copyright Rules*, (July 2014) 50.

8 See discussion on the Google Book Search Project in Ch. 2.3.

9 Pamela Samuelson, 'Google Book Search and the future of Books in Cyberspace', 2010, (5), Minnesota Law Review, 1308–1374, 1308.

10 Besek, Digital libraries, 2010, 208; Jerker Rydén, 'Are digital national libraries a vision or a utopia?', 2016, Lov&Data, 14–17, 14–15.

11 SWD(2015) 100 final, *Commission Staff Working Document: A Digital Single Market Strategy for Europe – Analysis and Evidence, accompanying the document: Communication from the Commission to the European Parliament, the Council, the European Economic and Social Committee and the Committee of the Regions*, (6.5.2015) 25.

12 WIPO, *Making International IP Law: an interview with Francis Gurry* (2014) 4. In 2012 27% of EU internet users accessed illegal sites at least once a month, cf. SEC(2012) 680, *Debat d'orientation sur le contenu dans l'economie numerique – Note de cadrage diffusée sous l'autorité de M. le PRESIDENT*, (28 November 2012) Annex.

13 Lucie Guibault, 'The nature and scope of limitations and exceptions to copyright and neighbouring rights with regard to general interest missions for the transmission of knowledge: prospects for their adaptation to the digital environment', 2003, (October-December), e-Copyright Bulletin, 21; C-174/15 *Opinion of Advocate General Szpunar in Vereniging Openbare Bibliotheken v Stichting Leenrecht* ECLI:EU:C:2016:459, CJEU, 16 June 2016 par. 1–3; Rydén, Are digital, 2016, 14.

14 In fact a considerable amount of digitisation in libraries has been done under "public-private-partnership" agreements because of the cost, such as with Google, cf. Maurizio Borghi and Stavroula Karapapa, *Copyright and Mass Digitization* (OUP, 2013), 104.

within the legal framework.[15] Libraries are obliged to respect copyright but this can create a conflict with their role of preserving the cultural heritage and promoting access to works which are still under copyright in the digital age.[16]

Before the advent of digital technology, libraries acquired copyrighted works in tangible hard copies. Those copies were then preserved in their original form and access was granted on the premises or by lending. Today libraries often handle works that are born digital and, in many cases, have never existed in hard tangible copy.[17] In addition, there is a demand to digitize analogue works, either for preservation purposes or to save space or to make them available on-line.[18] These demands create a tension with copyright law[19] and constitute a huge challenge for libraries and other cultural heritage institutions when it comes to digital use because of the massive volume of in-copyright works. The problem is compounded by the territorial nature of copyright, which generally means that the exercise of the exclusive rights afforded by copyright in one country is geographically restricted to that country, unless the rights are specifically recognised in another country.[20] For digital libraries which want to put in-copyright works online, the principle of territoriality is usually understood to oblige them to obtain licences from rightholders[21] for each country where

15 Tanya Aplin, 'A global digital register for the preservation and access to cultural heritage: problems, challenges and possibilities' in Estelle Derclaye (ed), *Copyright and Cultural Heritage; Preservation and Access to Works in a Digital World* (Edward Elgar Publishing, 2010) 4; Allard Ringnalda, 'Orphan Works, Mass Rights Clearance, and Online Libraries: The Flaws of the Draft Orphan Works Directive and Extended Collective Licensing as a Solution', 2011, (1), Medien und Recht International, 3–11, 4–5; C-174/15 – VOB, AG opinion, par. 87.

16 Klass and Rupp, EUROPEANA… 2014, 962, 967; SEC(2011) 615 final, *Impact Assessment on the Cross-Border Online Access to Orphan Works; Commission Staff Working accompanying the document Proposal for a Directive of the European Parliament and of the Council on certain permitted uses of orphan works*, (24.5.2011) 22.

17 Library of Congress and others, *International Study on the Impact of Copyright Law on Digital Preservation*, (July 2008) 6; Rydén, Are digital, 2016, 14.

18 COM(2008) 466, *Green Paper; Copyright in the Knowledge Economy*, (16.07.2008) 7.

19 Aplin, A global digital register, 2010, 4; Padfield, Preserving and accessing our cultural heritage, 2010, 208–209; Besek, Digital libraries, 2010, 190.

20 Paul Goldstein and Bernt Hugenholtz, *International Copyright; Principles, Law, and Practice* (3 edn, Oxford University Press, 2013), 95; Paul Torremans, 'Copyright Territoriality in a Borderless Online Environment' in Johan Axhamn (ed), *Copyright in a Borderless Online Environment* (Norstedts Juridik 2012) 25; Rita Matulionyte, 'Enforcing Copyright Infringement Online; In Search of Balanced Private International Rules', 2015, (2), JIPITEC, 132–145, 138; Alexander Peukert, 'Territoriality and Extraterritoriality in Intellectual Property Law' in G. Handl and J. Zekoll (eds), *Beyond Territoriality: Transnational Legal Authority in an Age of Globalization, Queen Mary Studies in International Law* (Brill Academic Publishing, 2011) 1–2 (cited page-numbers refer to the ssrn version); *Joseph Beuys Werke, I ZR 24/92* IIC 1995, 26(4), 573–578, German Federal Court of Justice (BGH), 575.

21 Unless specifically mentioned otherwise the term rightholder will be used here in the same way as under Art. 3(c) of Directive 2014/26/EU of the European Parliament and of the Council of 26 February 2014 on collective management of copyright and related rights and multi-territorial licensing of rights in musical works for online use in the internal market, hereafter the CMO Directive, which states that 'rightholder' means any person or entity, other than a collective management organisation, that holds a copyright or related right or, under an agreement for the exploitation of rights or by law, is entitled to a share of the rights revenue.

they make a work available online.[22] This is a major obstacle to making Europe's cultural heritage available and easily accessible.

4. Lack of a comprehensive legal framework and of legal solutions to enable libraries to become fully digital creates a danger of a 20th century "black hole" where "cultural material from before 1900 is accessible on the web, but very little material from the more recent past"[23], at least not legally.[24] Thus the digital library Europeana, which was partly established as the European response to the Google book project[25], mainly offers access to out-of-copyright works.[26]

5. There are several copyright issues that affect libraries and their role of preserving and disseminating the cultural heritage. The largest copyright challenge for digital libraries is the process of identification of rightholders of copyright and clearance of rights, i.e. obtaining authorisation or licences for use of in-copyright works.[27] Stakeholders do not agree how best to facilitate libraries in preserving and disseminating the cultural heritage. Some advocate the establishment of legal exceptions whereas others maintain licences are the

---

22 Johan Axhamn and Lucie Guibault, *Cross-border extended collective licensing: a solution to online dissemination of Europe's cultural heritage?*, (August 2011) 19; Mireille van Eechoud and others, *Harmonizing European Copyright Law: The Challenges of Better Lawmaking* (Kluwer Law International, 2009), 309; Jean-François Canat, Lucie Guibault and Elisabeth Logeais, *Study on copyright limitations and exceptions for museums*, (April 30, 2015) 28. This is a similar position as with online music providers, e.g. Spotify and such services.

23 COM(2008) 513 final, *Communication from the Commission to the European Parliament, the Council, the European Economic and Social Committee and the Committee of the Regions on Europe's cultural heritage at the click of a mouse: Progress on the digitisation and online accessibility of cultural material and digital preservation across the EU*, (11.8.2008) 3; COM(2009) 440 final, *Communication from the Commission to the European Parliament, the Council, the European Economic and Social Committee and the Committee of the Regions: Europeana – next steps*, (28.8.2009) 5; COM(2011) 287 final, *Communication from the Commission to the European Parliament, the Council, the European Economic and Social Committee and the Committee of the Regions; A Single Market for Intellectual Property Rights boosting creativity and innovation to provide economic growth, high quality jobs and first class products and services in Europe*, (24.5.2011) 6.

24 There are more books available for sale on Amazon.com from the year 1850 than the year 1950, cf. Armin Talke, 'Verwaiste und vergriffene Werke – Kommt das 20. Jahrhundert endlich in die Digitale Bibliothek?', 2013, LIBREAS Library Ideas, 131–144, 132.

25 COM(2005) 465, *Communication from the Commission to the European Parliament, the Council, the European Economic and Social Committee and the Committee of the Regions on i2010: Digital Libraries*, (30.09.2005); María Iglesias, 'Digital libraries: any step forward?', 2008, (5), Auteurs & Média, 345–363; SEC(2011) 615 final, Impact Assessment, 2011, 6–7.

26 See Ch. 2.4.1.

27 Barbara Stratton, *Seeking New Landscapes: A rights clearance study in the context of mass digitisation of 140 books published between 1870 and 2010*, 4. See also discussion in SEC(2007) 1710, *Commission Staff Working Document accompanying the Communication from the Commission to the European Parliament, the Council, the European Economic and Social Committee and the Committee of the Regions on Creative Content Online in the Single Market* (03.01.2008) 22–29; SWD(2016) 301 final, *Commission staff working document: Impact Assessment on the modernisation of EU copyright rules, Part I*, (14 September 2016) 65–69.

solution.[28] A couple of instruments have been adopted in the EU to facilitate the use of in-copyright works for digital libraries, such as the Orphan Works Directive[29] of 2012 and the Memorandum of Understanding on Out-of-Commerce Works in 2011.[30] However, neither these nor the current exceptions for libraries in the InfoSoc Directive[31] have fully enabled libraries to fill the "black hole".

6. In my work I have concentrated on online use by libraries of in-copyright works in their collections, especially use which is not territorially limited[32] within Europe, or more specifically within the European Economic Area (EEA)[33], and how such use is affected by copyright. Thus I do not attempt to cover all copyright issues relevant for libraries.[34] The aim is to explore options in relation to the legal framework which could allow libraries to operate in the digital world where they would provide access to works online while maintaining the necessary balance of rights and obligations between rightholders and users.[35]

There are two main approaches to providing a legal basis for online use by libraries. One approach entails introducing further limitations and exceptions,

---

28 European Commission, Report on the responses, 2014, 49–53.

29 Directive 2012/28/EU of the European Parliament and of the Council of 25 October 2012 on certain permitted uses of orphan works, hereafter the "Orphan Works Directive" or OWD.

30 Memorandum of Understanding on Key Principles on the Digitisation and Making Available of Out-of-Commerce Works of 20 September 2011, hereafter the "MoU on out-of-commerce works" or simply the MoU.

31 Directive 2001/29/EC of the European Parliament and of the Council of 22 May 2001 on the harmonisation of certain aspects of copyright and related rights in the information society, hereafter the "InfoSoc Directive".

32 Distinct from e-lending or consultation on the premises of libraries or through closed networks, which usually do not include cross-border use.

33 The Agreement on the European Economic Area (EEA Agreement), which entered into force on 1 January 1994 (OJ No L 1, 3.1.1994, 3.), brings together the 28 Members of the European Union (EU) and three European Free Trade Association (EFTA) countries – Iceland, Liechtenstein and Norway – in a single internal market, referred to as the "Internal Market." All new EU legislation of EEA relevance is dynamically incorporated into the Agreement and therefore applies throughout the EEA. In the following where I refer to the EU it applies to the whole of the EEA unless otherwise specified. I will not be discussing the potential effects on the subject of the thesis of the UK leaving the EU.

34 Issues regarding the preservation of digitally born material, e-lending and text and data mining, to name a few areas which are highly relevant for libraries and are affected by copyright, are not dealt with here specifically except when relevant for online availability. Neither are related areas pertaining to the online use of works, such as the EU legislation on privacy and data protection and on the reuse of public sector information discussed.

35 The term user is defined in Art. 3(k) CMO Directive, as "any person or entity that is carrying out acts subject to the authorisation of rightholders, remuneration of rightholders or payment of compensation to rightholders and is not acting in the capacity of a consumer". Here, it will mainly be used to refer to libraries carrying out acts under exceptions or authorisation by rightholders. Libraries are middle-users and their use is usually intended to benefit end-users, who would be considered consumers under the terminology of the COM Directive, cf. Lucie Guibault and Stef van Gompel, 'Collective Management in the European Union' in Daniel Gervais (ed), *Collective Management of Copyright and Related Rights* (3 edn, Wolters Kluwer, 2016) 144. Care will be taken to distinguish, when appropriate, between these two types of users.

as was done in the Orphan Works Directive 2012[36]; the other entails promoting collective licensing with legislative support as advocated by stakeholders in the 2011 MoU. The latter seems currently to be the approach preferred by the European Commission[37, 38] at least with regard to use of out-of-commerce works.

My starting assumption is that, given the impact of online use on the internet even just within Europe, licensing is a more appropriate and flexible tool than exceptions for online use of in-copyright works. Obtaining individual licences for the use of in-copyright works held by libraries is complicated, time-consuming and costly, in particular for cross-border use.[39] Thus individual licensing is not a practical solution for libraries except for the use of a few well defined works. Even collective licensing does not fully solve the licensing issue because no collective management organisation (CMO) has mandates from all rightholders in a given field.[40] Hence, I propose that the solution is to be found through collective licences with legislative support, in particular the system of extended collective licences (ECL).

---

36 See discussion in e.g. European Commission, Report on the responses, 2014, 43–46, 50; Paul Torremans, 'Archiving exceptions: where are we and where do we need to go?' in Estelle Derclaye (ed), *Copyright and Cultural Heritage; Preservation and Access to Works in a Digital World* (Edward Elgar Publishing, 2010) 118; see also European Parliament, *Resolution of 9 July 2015 on the implementation of Directive 2001/29/EC of the European Parliament and of the Council of 22 May 2001 on the harmonisation of certain aspects of copyright and related rights in the information society (2014/2256(INI))* item 51. In Australia it was recommended in April 2016 that all uses of orphan works and out-of-commerce works should be allowed under a fair use clause, cf. Australian Government Productivity Commission, *Intellectual Property Arrangements; Draft Report*, (April 2016) 121–163; Discussion Paper from the 4th Europeana Licensing Workshop in Luxembourg, 26th and 27th of November 2015 which suggested such exception with an opt-out option.

37 Hereafter "Commission".

38 Recital (40) InfoSoc Directive; COM(2011) 287 final, IPR Strategy, 2011, 13; 2011/711/EU, *Commission Recommendation on the digitisation and online accessibility of cultural material and digital preservation*, (27 October 2011) Art. 6; SWD(2016) 301 final, IA Part I, 2016, 69–71; COM(2016) 593 final, *Proposal for a Directive of the European Parliament and of the Council on copyright in the Digital Single Market*, (14 September 2016) Art. 7–9, hereafter the DSM proposal or DSMP.

39 Lucie Guibault, 'Cultural Heritage Online? Settle It in the Country of Origin of the Work', 2015, (3), JIPITEC, 173–191, 173; Julian Boulanger and others, *Assessing the economic impacts of adapting certain limitations and exceptions to copyright and related rights in the EU – Analysis of specific policy options*, (May 2014) 13–14, 17, 20; Axhamn and Guibault, Cross-border ECL, 2011, 70; COM(2007) 836 final, *Communication from the Commission to the European Parliament, the Council, the European Economic and Social Committee and the Committee of the Regions on Creative Content Online in the Single Market*, (03.01.2008) 23; Gregor Langus, Daminen Neven and Sophie Poukens, *Economic Analysis of the Territoriality of the Making Available Right in the EU*, (March 2014) 2; Thomas Dreier and others, 'Museen, Bibliotheken und Archive in der Europäischen Union; Plädoyer für die Schaffung des notwendigen urheberrechtlichen Freiraums', 2012, ZUM, 273–281, 280; Maurizio Borghi, Kris Erickson and Marcella Favale, 'With Enough Eyeballs All Searches Are Diligent: Mobilizing the Crowd in Copyright Clearance for Mass Digitization', 2016, (1), Chicago-Kent Journal of Intellectual Property, 135–166, 149.

40 SWD(2016) 301 final, IA Part I, 2016, 67–68.

1.2. DIGITAL LIBRARIES AND EXTENDED COLLECTIVE LICENCES

7. An extended collective licence is a licence for a specific use of in-copyright works in a specified field based on an agreement that a CMO makes with a user, such as a library, and which is extended to rightholders that are not members of the CMO, often called outsiders. The legal effect of the extension is made possible by a provision in a copyright act. The scope and applicability of the ECL is based on the agreement. The system of ECL was developed in the Nordic countries[41] in the early sixties for situations where there was a public interest need for mass use of copyright protected works, such as for use by broadcasting stations, and where it was impractical to individually negotiate with rightholders or even CMOs because of non-represented rightholders, i.a. because it was impossible or difficult to predict beforehand which works would be used under the collective agreement. The ECL system is generally well accepted in all the Nordic countries and has functioned well since its introduction[42], first for analogue uses but later also for digital uses. Thus the question has been posed of whether the system could be used elsewhere and, in particular, for digital use of works.[43]

---

41 In this research the term "Nordic countries" refers to Denmark, Finland, Iceland, Norway and Sweden.

42 Ds 2003:35, *Upphovsrätten i informationssamhället – genomförande av direktiv 2001/29/EG, m.m.*, 277; Thomas Riis and Jens Schovsbo, 'Extended Collective Licenses and the Nordic Experience: It's a Hybrid but is it a VOLVO or a Lemon?', 2010, (4), Columbia Journal of Law and the Arts, 471, 496 to 497; Ole-Andreas Rognstad, 'Avtalelisens som nordisk løsningmodell – Noen refleksjoner, særlig knyttet til avtalelisensens legitimitet i utlandet', 2012, NIR, 620, 621; Rán Tryggvadóttir, 'Digital libraries, the Nordic system of extended collective licenses and cross-border use', 2014, (5), Auteurs & Media, 314–325, 316; Dinusha Mendis and Victoria Stobo, 'Extended Collective Licensing in the UK – One Year On: A Review of the Law and a Look Ahead to the Future', 2016, (4), EIPR, 208–220, 208.

43 Robin Kerremans, Katleen Janssen and Peggy Valcke, 'Collective solutions for cultural collections online: Search and select!', 2011, (9), Journal of Intellectual Property Law & Practice, 647–648; Pamela Samuelson, 'Legislative Alternatives to the Google Book Settlement', 2011, (4), Colum JL & Arts 697, 709 ff; Ringnalda, Orphan Works, 2011, *op.cit.*; Stef van Gompel and P. Bernt Hugenholtz, 'The Orphan Works Problem: The Copyright Conundrum of Digitizing Large-Scale Audiovisual Archives, and How to Solve It', 2010, (1), Popular Communication – The International Journal of Media and Culture, 61–71, 65 ff; Stef van Gompel, 'Unlocking the Potential of Pre-Existing Content: How to Address the Issue of Orphan Works in Europe?', 2007, (6), International Review of Industrial Property and Competition Law (IIC), 669–702, 687 ff.; Daniel Gervais, *Collective Management of Copyright and Neighbouring Rights in Canada: An International Perspective*, (August 2001) 38–45, 89; Daniel Gervais, 'Collective Mangement of Copyright: Theory and Practice in the Digital Age' in Daniel Gervais (ed), *Collective management of Copyright and Related Rights* (2nd edn, Kluwer Law International, 2010) 21 ff.; Ian Hargreaves, *Digital Opportunity; A Review of Intellectual Property and Growth*, (May 2011) 37–38; Jia Wang, 'Should China adopt an extended licensing system to facilitate collective copyright administration: preliminary thoughts', 2010, (6), EIPR, 283–289; Silke von Lewinski, 'Certain Legal Problems Related to the Making Available of Literary and Artistic Works and other Protected Subject Matter through Digital Networks', 2005, UNESCO e-copyright Bulletin 15; Jane Ginsburg, 'Fair Use for Free, or Permitted-but-paid', 2014, (3), Berkeley Technology Law Journal, 1383–1446, 38.

The increased international interest in the Nordic ECL systems has resulted in various studies and articles on the system.[44] Some of these have come to the conclusion that the ECL system is not necessarily fit for export and many have highlighted the apparent lack of legal basis for cross-border use.[45] Others have concluded that ECL agreements could have cross-border effect in online use.[46] However, there is no in-depth study so far of the cross-border use of ECLs by libraries or other ECL users. If the system of ECL is to provide the necessary legal certainty to enable digital libraries to use works online it is of paramount importance that ECLs can have cross-border effect and this, therefore, was the focal point of my research upon which this book is based.

8. Online cross-border use often has worldwide implications and European cultural heritage is also important as a world heritage. Nevertheless, using ECLs as a solution for cross-border online use requires a certain infrastructure that might currently only be applicable within Europe. Thus it seemed prudent to limit the research geographically, e.g. to the European Economic Area (EEA). I argue that ECL system is an optimal solution for mass use of works due to the

---

44 Riis and Schovsbo, ECLs, 2010, *op.cit.*; Jukka Liedes, *Memorandum on the Extended Collective Licence*, (April 2010); Norwegian Research Center for Computers and Law, Christian Rydning, 'Extended collective licenses: the compatibility of the Nordic solution with the international conventions and EC law', (Oslo University 2010); Alain Strowel, 'The European "Extended Collective Licensing" Model', 2011, (4), Columbia Journal of Law & the Arts 665; Axhamn and Guibault, Cross-border ECL, 2011, *op.cit.*; Rognstad, Avtalelisens, 2012, *op.cit.*; Thomas Riis and Jens Schovsbo, 'Extended Collective Licenses in Action', 2012, (8), International Review Of Intellectual Property And Competition Law (IIC), 930–950; Felix Trumpke, 'The Extended Collective License – A Matter of Exclusivity?', 2012, (3), NIR 264; Anna Vuopala, *Extended Collective Licensing – A solution for facilitating licensing of works through Europeana, including orphans?*, (January 2013); Jan Rosén, 'The Nordic Extended Collective Licensing Model as a Mechanism for Simplified Rights Clearance for Legitimate Online Services' in Johan Axhamn (ed), *Copyright in a Borderless Online Environment* (2012); IPO, *Government response to the technical consultation on draft secondary legislation for extended collective licensing (ECL) schemes*, (2014); Tryggvadóttir, Digital libraries, 2014, *op.cit.*; Lucie Guibault, *D5.4: Report on the effectiveness of licensing systems for clearing content for Europeana use*, (30 March 2015); Guibault, Cultural, 2015, *op.cit.*; Matej Gera, 'Extended collective licensing under the new Slovak Copyright Act', 2016, (3), Journal of Intellectual Property Law & Practice, 170–171; Max-Planck-Institute für Innovation und Wettbewerb, Felix Trumpke, 'Exklusivität und Kollectivierung: Das skandinavische Modell der Erweiterten Kollektiven Lizenz (Extended Collective Licensing)', (PhD, 2015).

45 Riis and Schovsbo, ECLs, 2010, 497–498; COM(2011) 289 final, *Proposal for a Directive of the European Parliament and of the Council on certain permitted uses of orphan works*, (24.05.2011) 3; SEC(2011) 615 final, Impact Assessment, 2011, 27; Strowel, The European, 2011, 667, 669; Manon A.A. Oostveen and Lucie Guibault, *Summary report on IPR issues faced by Europeana and its partners*, 11; Rosén, The Nordic ECL Model, 2012, 84; Prop. 2012/13:141, *Regeringens proposition: Förbättrade möjligheter till licensiering af upphovsrätt*, (7 March 2013) 29.

46 Guibault, Cultural, 2015, 190–191; Marie-Christine Janssens and Rán Tryggvadóttir, 'Facilitating access to orphan and out-of-commerce works to make Europe's cultural resources available to the broader public' in Irini Stamatoudi (ed), *Copyright and the Digital Agenda for Europe: Current Challenges for the Future* (Sakkoulas Publications, 2015) 90–91; Tryggvadóttir, Digital libraries, 2014, 323–325; Vuopala, Extended, 2013, 27–28; Liedes, Memorandum, 2010, 17; Martin Kyst, 'Aftalelicens – Quo Vadis?', 2009, (1), NIR, 44, 52.

flexibility and legal certainty it offers for users, such as libraries. The fact that ECL agreements are based on negotiations between CMOs representative of a substantial number of rightholders on the one hand, and the users on the other increases the likelihood of a mutually beneficial agreement. I argue that the inherent restriction of the outsider's right is an exception that must fulfil international norms. My analysis of the system leads me to conclude that ECL agreements under the Nordic system in most cases pass the three-step test. I, however, furthermore suggest that ECL agreements that fulfil international norms could, due to the hybrid nature of the system, also be seen as an arrangement of management of rights; this would be consistent with the position taken in relevant EU legislation. This position can affect i.a. the choice of applicable laws in disputes regarding the online use under ECL agreements of works accessible in other countries within the EU, as the issue might consequently be dealt with under the Rome I Regulation[47] on contractual obligations. This could in many cases lead to the applicable laws being the law of the country of origin. Thus I suggest that a national ECL agreement, if it fulfils international norms and if the negotiating CMO is representative of substantial numbers of rightholders and has the relevant territorial mandates, can enable national libraries to make works from their collection, which have a relevant connection to the country concerned, available with cross-border effect, at least within the EEA, without specific legislation to that effect. However, legislation recognising the cross-border effect of ECL agreements would create more legal certainty.

Nevertheless, I am of the opinion that the ECL system will not solve all copyright issues for libraries, not even with regard to online cross-border use of in-copyright works from their collections. Thus a mixture of solutions, including exceptions, should be available for libraries to fully function in the digital age, fulfilling their purpose of preserving and giving access to the cultural heritage.

9. The book is split into three parts. In **Part I** (chapters two, three and four) I discuss the exclusive rights and exceptions relevant for the online use by libraries. In **Part II** (chapters five, six and seven) I concentrate on collective licensing with legislative support for online use by libraries, in particular the system of ECL. In **Part III** (chapters eight, nine, ten and eleven) I discuss the territoriality of copyright and online use with cross-border effect by libraries. In chapter 12 I sum up and set out my conclusion.

47 Regulation (EC) No 593/2008 of the European Parliament and of the Council of 17 June 2008 on the law applicable to contractual obligations (Rome I).

PART I

EXCLUSIVE RIGHTS AND EXCEPTIONS RELEVANT FOR THE CROSS-BORDER ONLINE USE OF LIBRARIES

CHAPTER 2
DEFINITIONS AND DEVELOPMENTS

Libraries are one of civilisation's most ancient institutions, predating by several centuries the invention of paper and the emergence of books as we know them today. In the 15th century, they successfully adapted to, and benefited from, the invention of printing and it was to the libraries that the law of copyright, which emerged in the 18th century, had to adjust. Today we are witnessing a new, digital revolution, and one may wonder whether libraries will be able to survive this new shift in circumstances.[48]

10. In this chapter I will, first, define libraries and digital libraries for the purposes of this book, second, discuss briefly copyright and how it pertains to libraries and, finally, give a short overview of developments in Europe with regard to digital libraries.

2.1. LIBRARIES

11. Traditionally the term library was used solely for a physical collection of books, archives and manuscripts.[49] However, in the latter half of the 20th century the word "library" began to refer to collections of material other than books, such as audiovisual media.[50] Today the ordinary meaning of library extends to works other than books[51] as can be seen in this dictionary definition: "a place in which literary, musical, artistic, or reference materials (as books, manuscripts, recordings, or films) are kept for use but not for sale."[52] Libraries are thus highly diverse, but most often they have a public-service mission of preserving and

48 C-174/15 – VOB, AG opinion, par. 1.

49 Talke, Verwaiste und vergriffene Werke, 2013, 132.

50 The International Federation of Library Associations and Institutions (IFLA), *Guidelines for Audiovisual and Multimedia Materials in Libraries and other Institutions*, (March 2004).

51 Michel M. Walter and Silke von Lewinski (eds), *European Copyright Law, A Commentary* (Oxford University Press 2010) 1036; Besek, Digital libraries, 2010, 187; J.A.L. Sterling, *World Copyright Law* (Trevor Cook ed, 4 edn, 2015), 635.

52 <www.merriam-webster.com/dictionary/library>, last viewed 29 June 2017. There are other categories of works to be found in some libraries than mentioned in this definition, such as video-games or computer games. In fact the term library is often used "to denote a collection of any kind", cf. Besek, Digital libraries, 2010, 187.

making their collection accessible to a wide range of users. Their role and typical function is hence to collect, preserve, archive and disseminate information.[53]

Today's buzzword when discussing digitisation and access to collections of institutions such as libraries is "cultural heritage". However, the term does not have a clear definition. To begin with the term culture is hard to define. The word heritage has a very wide application which for the purpose of legislative and policy analyses is not definite enough.[54] The subject matter of this book is primarily the digitisation of and online access to in-copyright works in the collections of libraries. The majority of those works are literary works. Hence, when the term "cultural heritage" is used here it mainly refers to such works.

12. The term "digital library" did not come into general usage until the mid-1990s whereas in the early 1990's "... the term 'electronic library' was being used to describe an organised and networked collection of materials in electronic form".[55] Today, there are several definitions of digital libraries originating from different environments.[56] The systems that the term is used for range from digital object and metadata repositories, reference-linking systems, archives and content administration systems (mainly developed by industry) through to complex systems that integrate advanced digital library services (mainly developed in research environments). As there is no agreement on what a digital library is or its functions it has been suggested that the term is "overloaded" with a resulting lack of interoperability and duplication of efforts.[57] Furthermore, librarian scholars have suggested that too much emphasis has been put on the technical side of the definition of digital libraries and that digital libraries must first and foremost be defined by their library qualities.[58] This is particularly true with regard to copyright. Thus in the US the Section 108 Study Group recommended that in order for a library to be eligible for copyright exceptions it had i.a. to possess "a public service mission, employing trained library or archives staff,

---

53 Art. 2.2.1 IFLA Statutes, available at <www.ifla.org/files/assets/hq/ifla-statutes-en.pdf>, last viewed 29 June 2017; Kenneth Crews, *Study on Copyright Limitations and Exceptions for Libraries and Archives*, (26 April 2008) 31; Lucie Guibault, 'Evaluating Directive 2001/29/EC in the Light of Digital Public Domain' in Melanie Dulong de Rosnay and Juan Carlos De Martin (eds), *The Digital Public Domain: Foundations for an Open Culture* (Open Book Publishers, 2008) 65; Klass and Rupp, EUROPEANA... 2014, 950; Dreier and others, Museen, Bibliotheken, 2012, 274.

54 COM (2007) 242, *Communication from the Commission to the European Parliament, the Council, the European Economic and Social Committee and the Committee of the Regions on a European agenda for culture in a globalizing world*, (10.5.2007) 3; Klass and Rupp, EUROPEANA... 2014, 947; Janet Blake, 'On defining the cultural heritage', 2000, International and Comparative Law Quarterly, 61–85, 67–68.

55 Reg Carr, 'A history of digital library economics' in David Baker and Wendy Evans (eds), *Digital library economics: an academic perspective* (Chandos, 2009) 57–58.

56 Baker and Evans, Digital Libraries, 2009, 4–5.

57 Delos, *The DELOS Digital Library Reference Model Foundations for Digital Libraries*, 13.

58 Baker and Evans, Digital Libraries, 2009, 5–6.

providing professional services normally associated with libraries and archives, and possessing a collection comprising lawfully acquired and/or licensed materials."[59]

13. The central question is, however, what the role of libraries should be in the internet age or even whether they have a role any longer.[60] Clearly a very important role for digital libraries is to preserve the digital heritage which is under threat.[61] Another important function for digital libraries could be the authentication of digital works. Digital works are easily manipulated, unlike physical objects, and hence it becomes an important issue which version of a digital work is the original and authentic.[62]

Preservation and authentication aside the principal issue is how digital libraries will promote access to the cultural heritage when "competition" for access to digital information is so fierce. How will they do it better or differently than other providers, such as Google?[63] Derek Law, an experienced academic in library and information technology matters, maintains that "... a key benefit of digital library collections will be the value we add to the products we acquire in order to make them more useful." In his view it is sufficient to make them relevant for local communities. However, he points out that libraries have always seen themselves as part of a global system. "Creating collections of local relevance but making them available globally is in the spirit of this tradition and in turn guarantees that the local users have access to a rich and global set of resources."[64] This vision of global access to collections is not viable, however, without taking territorial aspects of copyright into consideration, except for works that are in the public domain.

14. It seems likely then that the role of libraries in the digital world will remain the same as in the analogue world, i.e. the preservation of and providing access to the cultural heritage. Both these activities are copyright relevant, especially in the digital environment, as they comprise acts of reproduction and communication to the public which fall under the exclusive right of copyright holders. Preservation is usually defined as the act of making a copy in anticipation of the loss of a work from e.g. deterioration, electronic damage or theft; thus a copy is made before the loss of the work in order to ensure it

---

59 The Section 108 Study Group, *The Section 108 Study Group Report*, 34; Besek, Digital libraries, 2010, 188.

60 Brindley, Foreword, Digital Libraries economics: an introduction, 2009, xx.

61 Rydén, Are digital, 2016, 1. The threat is highlighted in Art. 3 UNESCO Charter on the Preservation of Digital Heritage, accessible at <http://portal.unesco.org/en/ev.php-URL_ID=17721&URL_DO=DO_TOPIC&URL_SECTION=201.html>, last accessed 29 June 2017.

62 Michael W. Carroll, 'Creative Commons and the New Intermediaries', 2006, Michigan State Law Review, 45–65, 51; Klass and Rupp, EUROPEANA... 2014, 970.

63 Rydén, Are digital, 2016, 2.

64 Derek Law, 'Digital library economics: aspects and prospects' in David Baker and Wendy Evans (eds), *Digital library economics: an academic perspective* (Chandos, 2009) 77.

will continue to be useable.[65] Digital preservation refers to activities to maintain access to digital works, either works that are born digital[66] or works that have been digitised.[67] Thus digital preservation includes digital reproduction.[68] Promoting access to works in the analogue world meant lending hard-copies to users, whereas in the digital environment it can either refer to e-lending or to making works available online on a website, both of which fall under the communication to the public right. Furthermore, in order to enable access in the digital world analogue works need to be digitised.[69]

15. Some attempts have been made at defining the term digital libraries. The Digital Library Federation (DLF) established a working definition in 1998 in an attempt to regulate the use of the term:

> Digital libraries are organizations that provide the resources, including the specialized staff, to select, structure, offer intellectual access to, interpret, distribute, preserve the integrity of, and ensure the persistence over time of collections of digital works so that they are readily and economically available for use by a defined community or set of communities.[70]

This definition covers in some detail the functions of digital libraries in their role as an extension of traditional libraries. However, the much simpler definition put forward in connection with the "EU i2010: Digital library initiative" should be sufficient for the purpose of this book:

> Digital libraries are organised collections of digital content made available to the public. They can consist of material that has been digitised, such as digital copies of books and other 'physical' material from libraries and archives. Alternatively, they can be based on information originally produced in digital format.[71]

Although the definition refers to making digital works available to the public it does not determine whether this means through remote digital access or only on site. Technically a library can be a digital library without providing for remote digital access, although providing remote access in one way or another or aspiring to do so seems to be inherent in the notion digital library.[72] At this point it is worth highlighting that most libraries today are still so-called "hybrid

---

65 Crews, 2008 Study, 2008, 51; Congress and others, International Study on the Impact of Copyright Law on Digital Preservation, 2008, 4.

66 An example of that could be the preservation of websites, cf. Crews, 2008 Study, 2008, 53.

67 Congress and others, International Study on the Impact of Copyright Law on Digital Preservation, 2008, 5.

68 Boulanger and others, Assessing, 2014, 12.

69 Jean-Paul Triaille and others, *Study on the Application of Directive 2001/29/EC on Copyright and Related Rights in the Information Society (The "InfoSoc Directive")*, (October 2013) 258–262.

70 DLF, 'A working definition of digital library' (1998) <http://old.diglib.org/about/dldefinition.htm > accessed 9 December 2015.

71 COM(2009) 440 final, Europeana, 2009, 3.

72 Besek, Digital libraries, 2010, 188.

libraries"[73], i.e. libraries combining traditional formats (i.e. printed matter) with electronic media[74] and it seems likely that most libraries will carry on being hybrid libraries for the foreseeable future. Furthermore, the "utopian goal of universally accessible digital libraries" is still far from being reached.[75]

2.2. COPYRIGHT

16. Copyright gives rightholders[76] the exclusive right to authorise or prohibit use of their works while they are under protection. The Berne Convention[77] stipulates that exclusive rights afforded by copyright protection should last for the lifetime of the author and fifty years after his or her death.[78] In Europe the protection lasts for 70 years after the death of the author.[79]

17. Exclusive rights are based on national copyright law but are also enshrined in international Conventions and Treaties. The most relevant ones for this study are the Berne Convention[80], the TRIPs Agreement[81] and the WIPO Internet Treaties.[82] These conventions and treaties set out the minimum framework for their signatory states for the protection of exclusive rights, as well as limitations and exceptions[83] to those exclusive rights.[84] In addition, in Europe there are several directives that harmonise copyright. The InfoSoc Directive[85], the

---

73 Law, Digital library economics, 2009, 72.

74 Jean Sykes, 'Hybrid library management' in David Baker and Wendy Evans (eds), *Digital library economics: an academic perspective* (Chandos, 2009) 105.

75 Besek, Digital libraries, 2010, 188. However, some belief this is within reach or "only one click away", cf. Klass and Rupp, EUROPEANA… 2014, 948.

76 See fn. 21 in Ch. 1.1 on the use of the term.

77 *Op.cit.*

78 Art. 7 BC.

79 Art. 1 of Directive 2006/116/EC of the European Parliament and of the Council of 12 December 2006 on the term of protection of copyright and certain related rights (codified version), hereafter the Term Directive.

80 In June 2017 Contracting Parties to the BC were 174. In comparison the United Nations had 193 Member States and two permanent observers, the Holy See and the State of Palestine.

81 The Agreement on the Trade-Related Aspects of Intellectual Property Rights of 15 April 1994 (TRIPs) was adopted under the auspices of the World Trade Organisation (WTO). In July 2016 there were 164 Member States to the WTO.

82 The WIPO Copyright Treaty (WCT) and the WIPO Performances and Phonograms Treaty (WPPT) adopted in Geneva on 20 December 1996 under the auspices of the World Intellectual Property Organisation (WIPO). The Treaties were approved on behalf of the European Community by Council Decision 2000/278/EC of 16 March 2000 (OJ 2000 L 89, p. 6).

83 The terms "exception" and "limitation" will be used in this thesis without any distinction, either together or on their own, unless otherwise specified, see discussion on the terms in Ch. 4.1.1.

84 Jane Ginsburg and Edouard Treppoz, *International Copyright Law: U.S. and EU Perspectives; Text and Cases* (Edward Elgar, 2015), 436.

85 *Op.cit.*, fn. 31 in Ch. 1.

Rental and Lending Directive[86], the Orphan Works Directive[87] and the CMO Directive[88] are the most relevant for the subject of this thesis, i.e. online use of works by libraries, the ECL system and the territoriality of copyright.[89]

18. Theories on the nature of copyright[90] and justifications for copyright protection are plentiful and diverse.[91] Without going into detail it is worth mentioning that in the continental European civil law tradition emphasis has been put on the property aspects of copyright derived from natural law theories[92], although in recent times more importance has been put on copyright's role in encouraging economic growth, employment and investment.[93] The Anglo-

---

86 Directive 2006/115/EC of 12 December 2006 of the European Parliament and of the Council on rental right and lending right and on certain rights related to copyright in the field of intellectual property (Rental and Lending Directive) (codified version, when referring to the Directive it will be to this version unless otherwise mentioned).

87 *Op.cit.*, fn. 29 in Ch. 1.

88 *Op.cit.*, fn. 21 in Ch.1.

89 Other directives on copyright are less relevant for the purpose of the study but will be referred to when appropriate. Those are: Council Directive 93/83/EEC of 27 September 1993 on the coordination of certain rules concerning copyright and rights related to copyright applicable to satellite broadcasting and cable retransmission (Satellite and Cable Directive); Term Directive, op. cit., fn. 50 in Ch. 2.2; Directive 2011/77/EU of the European Parliament and of the Council of 27 September 2011 amending Directive 2006/116/EC on the term of protection of copyright and certain related rights; Directive 96/9/EC of the European Parliament and of the Council of 11 March 1996 on the legal protection of databases (Database Directive); Directive 2001/84/EC of the European Parliament and of the Council of 27 September 2001 on resale right for the benefit of the author of an original work of art (Resale Right Directive); Directive 2009/24/EC of the European Parliament and of the Council on the legal protection for computer programs (Software Directive)(codified version).

90 The term copyright will be used here and throughout the research in its broadest sense as "... all that area of law or the right dealing with the protection of authors' works and of productions of modern technology incoprorating such works", cf. J.A.L. Sterling, *World Copyright Law* (2nd edn, Thomson Sweet and Maxwell, 2003), 995. If it becomes neccessary to distinguish between the common law copyright system and the author's right system in civil law countries that will be specifically mentioned.

91 See e.g. Samuel Ricketson and Jane Ginsburg, 'The Berne Convention: Historical and institutional aspects' in Daniel Gervais (ed), *International Intellectual Property: A Handbook of Contemporary Research* (2015) 6–8, 17; J.A.L. Sterling, *World Copyright Law* (2nd edn, Thomson Sweet and Maxwell, 2003), Ch. 2; WIPO, *Guide to the Berne Convention, WIPO publication No. 615(E)* (WIPO, 1978), 11.

92 Recital (9) i.f. InfoSoc Directive; Martin R.F. Senftleben, 'The International Three-Step Test: A Model Provision for EC Fair Use Legislation', 2010, JIPITEC, 67–82, 68; Alain Strowel, 'Droit d'auteur and Copyright: Between History and Nature' in Brad Sherman and Alain Strowel (eds), *Of Authors and Origins* (Clarendon Press, 1994) 236–237; Walter and von Lewinski (eds) European Copyright Law, A Commentary, 2010, 77. This is reflected in the term "intellectual property" of which the Charter of Fundamental Rights of the European Union, Official Journal of the European Communities 2000/C 364/01 (the EU Charter) stipulates the protection under the heading "Right to property", cf. Art. 17(2), see also C-277/10 – Luksan *Martin Luksan v Petrus van der Let* ECLI:EU:C:2012:65, CJEU, 9 February 2012 par. 66–70.

93 Marie-Christine Janssens, 'The Issue of Exceptions: Reshaping the Keys to the Gates in the Territory of Literary, Musical and Artistic Creation' in Estelle Derclaye (ed), *Research Handbook On The Future Of EU Copyright* (Edward Elgar Publishing, 2009) 324; COM(2015)

American copyright tradition on the other hand has placed more significance on copyright as a means to provide sufficient supply of knowledge and information "to promote the progress of science and useful arts".[94, 95] Thus the United States Court of Appeals for the Second District in the Google Book case stated that

> ...while authors are undoubtedly important intended beneficiaries of copyright, the ultimate, primary intended beneficiary is the public, whose access to knowledge copyright seeks to advance by providing rewards for authorship.[96]

However, it has been pointed out that the traditional sources for these differences, from the times of the French Copyright Decree of 1791 and the drafting of the United States Constitution in 1787, show that the arguments on both sides took note of both theories, even though developments since have led to a divergence.[97] Furthermore, the traditional differences between civil law countries and common law countries has become less evident with international harmonisation and a growing importance of the international economy. Nevertheless, an important vestige of this difference can be seen in the different approaches to use of in-copyright works without authorisation from the copyright holders. Thus such use that is deemed socially and culturally valuable but not disproportionally harmful to the market of in-copyrighted works in the United States is allowed under the doctrine of fair use whereas in most civil law countries such use is only allowed under clearly defined exceptions, often interpreted strictly.[98]

19. Copyright is also considered to have a base in human rights[99] although "the predominant forces that have shaped copyright law are economic."[100] The freedom of expression, which includes the freedom to receive and impart information, is recognised as one of the fundamental human rights[101] and thus

---

192 final, *Communication from the Commission to the European Parliament, the Council, the European Economic and Social Committee and the Committee of the Regions; A Digital Single Market Strategy for Europe*, (6.5.2015) 6; SWD(2015) 100 final, A Digital Single Market Strategy, 2015, 25.

94 Article I Section 8. Clause 8 of the US Constitution.

95 Senftleben, The International, 2010, 68; Strowel, Droit d'auteur, 1994, 235 (241–249); Christofe Geiger and others, 'The Information Society Directive' in Irini Stamatoudi and Paul Torremans (eds), *EU Copyright Law; A Commentary* (2014) 451.

96 *Authors Guild, Inc. v. Google Inc.* 13–4829-cv, US Court of Appeals for the Second Circuit, October 16, 2015 13.

97 Christophe Geiger, 'Copyright and Free Access to Information: For a Fair Balance of Interests in a Globalised World', 2006, (7), EIPR, 366–373, 367; Jane Ginsburg, 'A Tale of Two Copyrights: Literary Property in Revolutionary France and America' in Brad Sherman and Alain Strowel (eds), *Of Authors and Origins* (Clarendon Press, 1994) 158.

98 Goldstein and Hugenholtz, 3rd ed., 2013, 6–7; Senftleben, The International, 2010, 68; Strowel, Droit d'auteur, 1994, 249–250. See further discussion in Ch. 4.1.2.

99 Art. 27(2), Universal Declaration of Human Rights; Ricketson and Ginsburg, The Berne Convention, 2015, 3, 6.

100 Goldstein and Hugenholtz, 3rd ed., 2013, 8.

101 Art. 11, EU Charter and Art. 19, Universal Declaration of Human Rights.

exceptions should be made in copyright to honour this right.[102] Furthermore it is stipulated in the EU Charter of Fundamental Rights that arts and scientific research shall be free of constraints.[103]

20. The tension between these fundamental rights, right to property versus freedom of expression including access to information, was foregrounded with the advent of digital technology[104] and is at the core of the copyright discussion today. Thus the CJEU has on several occasions stated that Member States must rely on an interpretation of EU legislation on copyright that ensures a fair balance between fundamental rights.[105]

21. Copyright law has come in for considerable criticism in recent years, among other things for allegedly hindering access to knowledge, conserving monopoly control and sustaining outdated business models, as well as constituting barriers to the exercise of fundamental rights and the rights of consumers.[106] While, the copyright system in itself does not hinder technological change[107], rapid changes in technology call for revision of copyright laws in many respects. Technology is typically ahead of legislation but in order to preserve social legitimacy the time lag may not become too long.[108] Furthermore, it is worth mentioning that freedom of contract governs copyright transactions around the world[109] and contract practices affect many of the issues that are criticised with regard to copyright.

---

102 Alison Firth and Berverley Preira, 'Exceptions for Libraries and Archives' in Irini A. Stamatoudi (ed), *New Developments in EU and International Copyright Law* (Wolters Kluwer, 2016) 52.

103 Art. 13, EU Charter.

104 See e.g. Marie-Christine Janssens, 'The notion of the work and its place in the massive flow of information', 2001, (1), NIR, 87–108, 87–88, 103.

105 C-201/13 *Johan Deckmyn and Vrijheidsfonds VZW v Helena Vandersteen and Others.* ECLI:EU:C:2014:2132, CJEU, 3 September 2014 par. 27; C-314/12 *UPC Telekabel Wien GmbH v Constantin Film Verleih GmbH and Wega Filmproduktionsgesellschaft mbH* ECLI:EU:C:2014:192, CJEU, 27 March 2014 par. 46; C-461/10 *Bonnier Audio AB and Others v Perfect Communication Sweden AB* ECLI:EU:C:2012:219, CJEU, 19 April 2012 par. 56; C-360/10 *Belgische Vereniging van Auteurs, Componisten en Uitgevers CVBA (SABAM) v Netlog NV* ECLI:EU:C:2012:85, CJEU, 16 February 2012 par. 44; C-145/10 *Eva-Maria Painer v Standard VerlagsGmbH and Others* ECLI:EU:C:2013:138, CJEU, 7 March 2013 par. 134; C-70/10 *Scarlet Extended SA v Société belge des auteurs, compositeurs et éditeurs SCRL (SABAM)* ECLI:EU:C:2011:771, CJEU, 24 November 2011 par. 46; C-557/07 *LSG-Gesellschaft zur Wahrnehmung von Leistungsschutzrechten GmbH v Tele2 Telecommunication GmbH* ECLI:EU:C:2009:107, CJEU, 19 February 2009 par. 29; C-275/06 *Productores de Música de España (Promusicae) v Telefónica de España SAU* ECLI:EU:C:2008:54, CJEU, 29 January 2008 par. 68. See also discussion on this issue in Geiger and others, InfoSoc, 2014, 451–454.

106 See e.g., Ricketson and Ginsburg, The Berne Convention, 2015, 30–31; Geiger, Copyright and Free Access to Information: For a Fair Balance of Interests in a Globalised World, 2006, 366 ff.; Guido Westkamp, 'Copyright Reform and Necessary Flexibilities', 2014, IIC, 497–499; Bernt Hugenholtz, 'The Dutch case for flexibility' in Bernt Hugenholtz and Ian Hargeaves (eds), *Intellectual Property and Innovation* (2012) 53; European Commission, Report on the responses, 2014, 30.

107 IPO, *@the way ahead; A Strategy for Copyright in the Digital Age*, (October 2009) 22.

108 Hugenholtz, The Dutch, 2012, 54.

109 Goldstein and Hugenholtz, 3rd ed., 2013, 5.

2.2.1. COPYRIGHT AND LIBRARIES

22. Copyright affects the functioning of libraries as the majority of works in the collection of a library are works that fall under copyright.[110] However, in the analogue world the traditional role of libraries to preserve and provide access to works were less affected by copyright.[111] Exceptions and limitations for libraries aimed at facilitating their work and purpose in the analogue world were introduced in the wake of the advent of photocopying and other analogue reproduction methods.[112] Commercial rental and lending of works were not seen as a threat to the economic interest of copyright holders until the late twentieth century.[113] Thus the Commission concluded in its Green Paper in 1988 that there was no urgent need to find solutions at a Community level for the rental or lending of books.[114] Most European countries did not have explicit rental or lending rights as exclusive rights under copyright legislation and where such rights existed they did not cover all types of works.[115] The situation changed in the early nineties and by the end of 1992 the Rental and Lending Directive had been adopted, providing for an exclusive rental and lending right. The exclusive lending right could, however, be derogated from "provided that at least authors obtain a remuneration for such lending." Such remuneration can take into account "the cultural promotion objectives"[116] and furthermore Member States can exempt certain categories of establishments from such remuneration.[117] This derogation was to enable Member States to pursue their cultural policies, in particular to secure public access to works in libraries.[118] Although not explicitly stated in the Directive, it was assumed the derogation only applied to tangible copies, i.e. not to digital lending.[119] This has now changed with the decision in the VOB case.[120]

110 2011/711/EU, Recommendation, 2011, Recital (11).
111 Ringnalda, Orphan Works, 2011, 4.
112 See discussion on exceptions for libraries in the InfoSoc Directive in Ch. 4.2.2.
113 Sterling, World Copyright Law, 2003, 371–372.
114 COM (88) 172 final, *Green Paper on Copyright and the Challenge of Technology - Copyright Issues Requiring Immediate Action*, (7 June 1988) 153; Silke von Lewinski, 'Rental and Lending Rights Directive' in Michel M. Walter and Silke von Lewinski (eds), *European Copyright Law, A Commentary* (Oxford University Press, 2010) 253–254.
115 Sylvie Nérisson, 'The Rental and Lending Rights Directive' in Irini Stamatoudi and Paul Torremans (eds), *EU Copyright Law; A Commentary* (2014) 156.
116 However, this does not give Member States complete freedom to determine remuneration and there still has to have some association with the elements that cause harm to authors, i.e. how many borrowers and how many works lent, cf. C-271/10 *Vereniging van Educatieve en Wetenschappelijke Auteurs (VEWA) v Belgische Staat* ECLI:EU:C:2011:442, CJEU, 30 June 2011 par. 36–43.
117 Art. 1(1) and Art. 6 Rental and Lending Directive.
118 Von Lewinski, Rental and Lending Rights Directive, 2010, 260; Nérisson, The Rental and Lending Rights Directive, 2014, 178–179.
119 Von Lewinski, Rental and Lending Rights Directive, 2010, 266–267; Nérisson, The Rental and Lending Rights Directive, 2014, 169.
120 C-174/15 *Vereniging Openbare Bibliotheken v Stichting Leenrecht* ECLI:EU:C:2016:856, CJEU, 10 November 2016, see discussion on the case in Ch. 4.2.4.1.1.2.

23. Digital technology has not changed the role of libraries. Nevertheless, their role of preservation and providing access to works is now more dependent on technological methods, such as digital preservation and digital access, which touch upon the exclusive rights afforded to rightholders under copyright. Putting in-copyright works from their collection online involves the making available right, which requires authorisation from rightholders or an exception or limitation applicable for libraries. In order to make in-copyright works available online there needs to be a digital copy. Although an increasing proportion of works in libraries is in digital format, the bulk is still analogue. Making a digital copy from an analogue work entails reproduction. The making available of works online can include the possibility for end-users to download those works, which of course is also reproduction. Furthermore, the act of making available online results in temporary copies, i.e. involves reproduction, as well as the storing of works in digital form on a computer. Thus, the main exclusive rights involved in online use are the reproduction right[121] and the making available right, which falls under the right of communication to the public[122], as will be discussed in next chapter.[123] To fulfil their role of giving access to and preserving the cultural heritage still under copyright, libraries either need a licence, i.e. some form of express authorisation for the use, from the rightholders for each work they reproduce or make available, or specific exceptions from the exclusive rights in legislation. As will be discussed below[124], adequate exceptions and limitations facilitating the transition of libraries to the digital world do not yet exist.

24. Obtaining individual licences for the use of in-copyright works held by libraries can be complicated, time-consuming and costly.[125] Aside from potential remuneration for the use, the transaction costs of reaching agreement can be prohibitive. The transaction cost can be divided into four categories: search cost, bargaining or contracting cost, monitoring cost and enforcement cost.[126] Three factors affect the cost overall. First, the degree of uncertainty, either legal or business, the more uncertainty the more likely it is to increase transaction cost; second, the frequency of a given transaction affects the cost, thus repeated interactions may

---

121 Cf. Art. 2 InfoSoc Directive.

122 Cf. Art. 3 InfoSoc Directive.

123 See Ch. 3.2.

124 See Ch. 4.2.4.

125 Guibault, Cultural, 2015, 173; Boulanger and others, Assessing, 2014, 13–14, 17, 20; Axhamn and Guibault, Cross-border ECL, 2011, 70; COM(2007) 836 final, Creative Content Online, 2008, 23; Ringnalda, Orphan Works, 2011, 7; Raquel Xalabarder, 'Digital Libraries in the current legal and educational environment: Towards a remunerated compulsory license or limitation?' in Lionel Bently, U. Suthersanen and Paul Torremans (eds), *Global Copyright – Three Hundred Years since the Statute of Anne: From 1710 to Cyberspace* (Edward Elgar Publishing, 2010) 243.

126 Christian Handke, 'Collective Administration' in Richard Watt (ed), *Handbook on the Economics of Copyright: A Guide for Students and Teachers* (Edward Elgar, 2014) 183–184: Christian Handke and Ruth Towse, 'Economics of Copyright Collecting Societies', 2007, (8), IIC, 937–957, 938–939; Borghi, Erickson and Favale, With Enough, 2016, 150.

reduce cost and so may the presence of bodies that aggregate rights of rightholders, such as CMOs; third, the specificity of the transaction cost, e.g. if it is very specific to a given transaction it is more likely to incur higher transaction costs.[127]

25. There are several reasons why transaction costs are high for libraries. First, there is the sheer volume of in-copyright works. A study made by the British Library in 2011 claimed that rights clearance of works on an individual, item by item basis is unworkable in the context of mass digitisation as "it would take one researcher over 1,000 years to clear the rights in just 500,000 books".[128] Experts estimate that 100 times as much information has been created and stored since 1945 as in the whole of human history up to that point.[129] There are no reliable figures for either the number of published books[130] or the extent of what is in the public domain[131] although it is estimated that only around 20% of published books are in the public domain.[132] This means that a large part of the works in libraries is under copyright protection[133], i.e. most of the collections of the 20th century.[134] Works

---

127 Langus, Neven and Poukens, Economic, 2014, 88–90.

128 Stratton, Seeking New Landscapes, 2011, 5. See also Victoria Stobo, Ronan Deazley and Ian G. Anderson, *Copyright & Risk: Scoping the Wellcome Digital Library Project*, (December 2013), which found i.a. that on average it took institutions 2.58 hours and £31 GBP per work to search for rightholders in books; Borghi, Erickson and Favale, With Enough, 2016, 149.

129 SEC(2006) 1075, Impact Assessment, 2006, 13.

130 The Google book project based their original calculation in 2004 on digitizing around 30 million published books in research libraries, while raising the estimated number of books in existence to around 130 million in 2010, see Jonathan Band, 'The Long and Winding Road to the Google Books Settlement', 2009, Review of Intellectual Property Law, 227, 228–229; Marie-Christine Janssens, "If your books are not online, they are invisible' Gütenberg versus Google, Kritische kijk op de 'Google Books Settlement", 2010, TORB, 206, 206; Nick Poole, *The Cost of Digitising Europe's Cultural Heritage: A Report for the Comité des Sages of the European Commission*, (November 2010) 28–29. In the EU it was estimated in 2001 that more than 2.5 billion books and bound periodicals existed (25 Member States at the time), cf. SEC(2011) 615 final, Impact Assessment, 2011, 11.

131 The important debate on the public domain is outside the scope of this study apart from a mention of the traditional (but not undisputed) definitions of the term for clarification, i.e. it is defined as "encompassing intellectual elements that are not protected by copyright or whose protection has lapsed", cf. Séverine Dusollier, *Scoping Study on Copyright and Related Rights and the Public Domain, WIPO*, (30 April 2010) 6, and "an ever-growing corpus of material over which no author or successor in title may exercise a private right", cf. Jane Ginsburg, "Une chose publique'? The author's domain and the public domain in early British, French and US copyright law' in Paul Torremans (ed), *Copyright Law: A Handbook of Contemporary Research* (Edward Elgar, 2007) 134.

132 Band, The Long, 2009, 228. In Europe it is estimated to be between 10–20%, Rightscom, *The Economic and Social Impact of the Public Domain: Executive Summary Report*, (26th February 2010) 4–5.

133 2011/711/EU, Recommendation, 2011, Recital (11).

134 In October 2010 the oldest work in copyright in the British Library dated from 1859, see Comité des Sages, *Summary Record of the Public Hearing of the Comité des Sages on: "Bringing Europe's cultural heritage online"*, (28th October 2010) 13; Anna Vuopala, *Assessment of the Orphan works issue and Costs for Rights Clearance*, (May 2010) 5; Ringnalda, Orphan Works, 2011, 7.

created in 2018 in Europe will begin emerging into the public domain from about the year 2088 to 2138, depending on the longevity of the authors. Nevertheless, it has been suggested that waiting for works to fall into the public domain might be more efficient and possibly quicker than seeking individual licences.[135]

Second, a large proportion of in-copyright books are "orphan works"[136], i.e. works whose rightholders can either not be identified or located, making it impossible for libraries to obtain a licence from them.[137] This situation arises, for example, when the author is not indicated on the work itself, or if indicated his or her whereabouts are unknown. A publisher of a book can have ceased to exist leaving no information on where the publisher's right resides. Or an author may have transferred his or her right to a third party at some point whose identity is unknown when the question of use of the work by a digital library arises. Digital rights of older works normally do not belong to publishers and if the author is deceased, finding the author's heirs can be time-consuming and difficult.[138] This creates problems for libraries as in order to observe their legal obligations under copyright legislation they cannot make in-copyright works available without the prior consent of the rightholders.[139] The precise number of orphan works is unknown.[140] Estimates vary considerably[141] from one category to another as well as within each category. The fluctuation seems to be biggest for orphan works in the category of printed material or from the conservative estimate of 5% to the much larger amount of 50%, orphaned films are estimated to be around 12% and as much as 90% of photographs might be orphan works, whereas the problem is minimal for musical works.[142] A conservative estimate of orphan works in books in Europe in 2010 was around 13% of all in-copyrighted books.[143]

135 Ringnalda, Orphan Works, 2011, 7.

136 The term "orphan works" is attributed to Fay Kanin, Chair of the Library of Congress National Film Preservation Board, cf. Argyri Panezi, 'Legal challenges for online digital libraries', Internet, Law & Politics; A Decade of Transformations, Barcelona, 2014 150.

137 Vuopala, Assessment, 2010, 11; Jean-François Canat, Lucie Guibault and Elisabeth Logeais, Study, 2015, 28; Firth and Preira, Exceptions for Libraries, 2016, 23; Ringnalda, Orphan Works, 2011, 3; US Copyright Office, *Legal Issues in Mass Digitization: A Preliminary Analysis and Dicussion Document*, 29.

138 Vuopala, Extended, 2013, 30, 32; Klass and Rupp, EUROPEANA… 2014, 971; Ringnalda, Orphan Works, 2011, 4–5.

139 SEC(2011) 615 final, Impact Assessment, 2011, 9.

140 Janssens and Tryggvadóttir, Facilitating, 2015, 30; Katharina de la Durantaye, 'Orphan works: A comparative and international perspective' in Daniel J. Gervais (ed), *International Intellectual Property; A Handbook of Contemporary Research* (Edward Elgar, 2015) 191; Marie-Christine Janssens and Rán Tryggvadóttir, 'Orphan works, out-of-commerce works and making the European cultural heritage available: 'are we nearly there yet'?' in Irini Stamatoudi (ed), *New Developments in EU and International Copyright Law* (Wolters Kluwer, 2016) 2.

141 Ringnalda, Orphan Works, 2011, 4.

142 SEC(2011) 615 final, Impact Assessment, 2011, 11 to 12.

143 Vuopala, Extended, 2013, 33. However, a study conducted by the British Library in 2011 found that 43% of the works in the sample (140 books published between 1870 and 2010) were orphan, cf. Stratton, Seeking New Landscapes, 2011, 5, 51.

Third, licensing practices are not always adapted to digital distribution, especially cross-border online use because of the territorial aspect of copyright.[144] The territoriality principle may oblige libraries to obtain licences from rightholders for making it a work available in every country where it could be viewed.[145] Alternatively, in order to avoid the issue of territoriality and the increased cost it may confer, libraries may use geo-blocking in order to hinder access to their websites from users in other countries. An example of this is the Norwegian National Library Bokhylla project, an online service which gives users with Norwegian IP addresses access to every book published in Norway up until 2000.[146] The term geo-blocking is usually used to refer to commercial practices, i.e. when online sellers either deny consumers access to a website based on their location, or re-route them to a local store with different prices.[147] However, such geo-blocking is often based on copyright considerations.[148]

26. The challenges of direct licensing vary considerably depending on the type of content and affect the various stakeholders differently because of their divergent interests.[149] In a 2009 reflection document on creative content in the digital single market it was noted that consumers wanted easy access, regardless of borders and platforms, and clear indications of what is allowed in regard to user-created content and interactive services. Commercial users are mainly challenged by territorial restrictions in licensing, which are often based on contractual practices of derived rightholders, like publishers. Rightholders want to retain their contractual freedom and to be able to maximise their financial return, for which territorial restrictions can be useful.[150] Similar differences between stakeholders are apparent with regard to off-premises access of in-copyright works in library collections.[151]

27. Next I will briefly discuss the term "mass digitisation", the Google Book Project and European developments with regard to digital libraries.

---

144 See Ch. 8.2.

145 Eechoud and others, Harmonizing, 2009, 309; Jean-François Canat, Lucie Guibault and Elisabeth Logeais, Study, 2015, 28.

146 See description of the Bokhylla project in Ch. 5.3.1.4.

147 See e.g. the European Commission's DG Connect Glossary available at <https://ec.europa.eu/digital-single-market/en/glossary/#geoblocking>, last viewed 29 June 2017; Australian Government Productivity Commission, Intellectual Property Arrangements; Draft Report, 2016, 126–128.

148 COM(2015) 192 final, Communication, 2015, 7.

149 EU Commission, *Creative Content in a European Digital Single Market: Challenges for the Future, Reflection Document of DG INFSO and DG MARKT,* (22.10.2009) 4, 9; European Commission, Report on the responses, 2014, 43–45.

150 EU Commission, Creative Content, 2009, 10, 13.

151 European Commission, Report on the responses, 2014, 43–45.

2.2.2. MASS DIGITISATION

28. The term "mass digitisation" is commonly used for digital library projects, i.e. where digital copies are made of whole collections for preservation and access purposes.[152] Furthermore, the term "Mass-scale digitisation" has been used to denote reproduction on a mass-scale without a specific object other than a "need or wish" to enjoy the possibilities spurred by digital technology.[153] The term "mass digitisation" is generally understood "as conversion of copyright works in digital format on an industrial scale"[154] or "large-scale scanning" in the context of books[155] where works are not selected as such but "whole collections or significant and determined part thereof" are digitised.[156] It is not a scientific term nor does it lend itself to precise definition, in particular with regard to how many works a project must cover to qualify as a mass digitisation project.[157] In the digital area there is an overlap between the two exclusive rights inherent in online use of in-copyright works[158], i.e. the reproduction right and the communication to the public right, which is reflected in the fact that the term "mass digitisation" is often used to refer to activities that cover both reproduction and making available.[159] I will use the term mass digitisation to refer to "projects in which the scale of digital copying is so extensive as to make the individual clearance of rights a practical impossibility."[160] The term will not be used to indicate any form of access to digitised works unless specifically mentioned.

29. A large part of the discussion on digital libraries has revolved around mass digitisation and the challenges copyright poses to libraries wishing to engage in mass digitisation. However, it should not be forgotten that it is not only copyright that brings challenges to mass digitisation projects; the cost of the technical side of mass digitisation is in many cases prohibitive and hence also a

152 US Copyright Office, *Orphan Works and Mass Digitization*, (June 2015) 72; Boulanger and others, Assessing, 2014, 13; IA 2016, p. 59.

153 Triaille and others, Study, 2013, 260.

154 Borghi and Karapapa, Copyright and Mass Digitization, 2013, 1.

155 US Copyright Office, Mass Digitization Report 2011, 2011, 9.

156 Triaille and others, Study, 2013, 260.

157 US Copyright Office, Mass Digitization Report 2011, 2011, 8; US Copyright Office, Mass Digitization, 2015, 72.

158 Ansgar Ohly, 'Economic rights' in Estelle Derclaye (ed), *Research Handbook on the Future of EU Copyright* (Edward Elgar Publishing, 2009) 217; Triaille and others, Study, 2013, 111, 118; C-170/12 *Opinion of Advocate General Jääskinen in Peter Pinckney v KDG Mediatech AG* ECLI:EU:C:2013:635, CJEU, par. 27–30; Lucie Guibault and João Pedro Quintais, 'Copyright, technology and the exploitation of audiovisual works in the EU' in *The Influence of New Technologies on Copyright, IRIS plus 2014-4* (2014) 9, 22.

159 See e.g. DG Internal Market and Services, Public Consultation on the review of the EU copyright rules (2013), 22; Borghi and Karapapa, Copyright and Mass Digitization, 2013, 1; US Copyright Office, Mass Digitization, 2015, 73.

160 US Copyright Office, Mass Digitization, 2015, 73.

significant obstacle.[161] Nevertheless, the rights clearance may still be the greater cost.[162] Most initiatives rely on public funding[163] which in recent years has been difficult to attract. Hence in the foreseeable future mass digitisation of entire library collections is unlikely[164] and most libraries will engage in digitisation on a smaller scale, for specific purposes.[165]

30. Mass digitisation of books cannot be discussed without mentioning Google's Book Search Project which brought the discussion of libraries and their role in the digital age into the limelight. Thus I will discuss the project and the litigation around it next.

2.3. THE GOOGLE BOOK SEARCH PROJECT

31. In December 2004 Google announced[166] that as "... part of its effort to make offline information searchable online" it was working with several major libraries[167] "to digitally scan books from their collections so that users worldwide can search them in Google."[168] Google made partnership agreements with the libraries which allowed Google to digitise print books in the libraries' collections, to index their contents electronically and to display a maximum of three "snippets"[169] from the digitised books in Google's search results. The agreements obliged Google to provide the partner libraries with digital copies of their print books.[170] This partnership formed the Google Library Project. That project as well as the Google Partner Program, a program that allows authors

161 Besek, Digital libraries, 2010, 189–190; Samuelson, Google, 2010, 1311; Band, The Long, 2009, 228; SWD(2016) 301 final, IA Part I, 2016, 66.

162 Klass and Rupp, EUROPEANA… 2014, 956; Vuopala, Assessment, 2010, 44.

163 European Commission, *Cultural heritage: Digitisation, online accessibility and digital preservation. Report on the Implementation of Commission Recommendation 2011/711/EU, 2011–2013*, (September 2014) 6.

164 Jerker Rydén, *Comments in response to the June 9, 2015, Notice of Inquiry regarding Mass Digitization*, 2; Rydén, Are digital, 2016, 2.

165 Besek, Digital libraries, 2010, 195. As an example the National Library of Sweden will concentrate its digitisation efforts on user demanded areas for research and educational purposes, see further in Ch. 5.3.1.5.

166 Kate M. Manuel, *The Google Library Project: Is Digitization for Purposes of Online Indexing Fair Use Under Copyright Law?*, (November 27, 2009) 1; Alain Strowel, 'Google books: quel futur pour l'accès aux livres? Une bibliothèque universelle en devenir ou une future galerie commerciale? ', 2010, (1), Auteurs & Media, 1–7, 1.

167 The libraries of Harvard, Stanford, the University of Michigan, and the University of Oxford as well as the New York Public Library.

168 Google, 'Google Checks Out Library Books' (*Google*, 14.12.2004) <www.google.com/press/pressrel/print_library.html> accessed 30 June 2017.

169 Usually around 4 lines of the work, cf. Besek, Digital libraries, 2010, 202.

170 Authors Guild v. Google (USCA SC 2015), 5–10; Manuel, The Google, 2009, 1; Borghi, Erickson and Favale, With Enough, 2016, 137.

and publishers to submit their books for digitising and indexing, constitutes the digital corpus that Google uses for the Google Book Search Project.[171] Thus the Google Library Project is distinct from, although part of, the Google Books Search Project.[172]

32. Google highlighted the benefits for users and rightholders under the Google Books Search Project; users could search across library collections including out-of-print books and titles that were not previously available anywhere but on a library shelf. For rightholders, the program would increase the visibility of in- and out-of-print books, and generate book sales.[173] However, Google neither sought nor intended to seek rightholders' permission for the digitisation, indexing and making "snippets" available.[174]

33. Authors and publishers objected to the proposed program from the beginning on the grounds it infringed their copyright. In an attempt to respond to that criticism Google declared in August 2005 that rightholders could opt-out of the Library project by providing Google with a list of titles that they did not want Google to scan.[175] The rightholders, however, noted that by relying on opt-out Google was turning "copyright on its head"[176] and sued Google. The first to take action was the Authors Guild on behalf of "all persons or entities that hold the copyright to a literary work that is contained in the library of the University of Michigan".[177] Subsequently, five publishing companies followed with another lawsuit.[178] The cases were later consolidated. Google's main defence was that their uses constituted fair use.[179] The parties attempted for several years to settle the claims in the lawsuit with settlement agreements.

---

171 Manuel, The Google, 2009, 2; Samuelson, Google, 2010, 1308–1309.

172 Band, The Long, 2009, 231; US Copyright Office, Mass Digitization Report 2011, 2011, 9–10 and fn. 25.

173 Google, Google Checks Out Library Books, 14.12.2004.

174 Jane C. Ginsburg and Pierre Sirinelli, 'Google Book Search: Les enjeux internationaux pour le droit d'auteur', 2010, La Semaine Juridique Edition Générale, 486, par 1; Manuel, The Google, 2009, 1.

175 Band, The Long, 2009, 233; Manuel, The Google, 2009, 2–4; Ginsburg and Sirinelli, Google, 2010, par 2; Krista L. Cox, *Association of Research Libraries Issue Brief: Second Circuit Court of Appeals Affirms Fair Use in Google Books Case*, 1.

176 Manuel, The Google, 2009, 3; Band, The Long, 2009, 236. See also Alexander Peukert, 'Individual, Multiple and Collective Ownership of Intellectual Property Rights – Which Impact on Exclusivity?' in Annette Kur and Vytautas Mizaras (eds), *The Structure of Intellectual Property Law: Can One Size Fit All?* (Edward Elgar, 2011) 207.

177 Google began digitising their collection in the in the library of the University of Michigan, see *Authors Guild v. Google, Inc.* Class Action Complaint, No 05 CV 8136, USDC SDNY, Sept. 20, 2005 par. 20 and 31.

178 *McGraw Hill Cos. v. Google Inc.* Complaint, No 05 CV 8881, SDNY, Oct. 19, 2005. Samuelson points out that, interestingly, all the participating publishers were members of the Google Partnership Program, cf. Samuelson, Google, 2010, 1315.

179 Manuel, The Google, 2009, 3–4; Ginsburg and Sirinelli, Google, 2010, par 2; Cox, ARL Issue Brief in Google Books Case, 2015, 2. The "fair use" exception to copyright is a US doctrine developed by the courts and adopted in the US Copyright Act as Section 107 in 1976, see brief discussion on fair use in Ch. 4.1.2.

2.3.1. THE PROPOSED SETTLEMENT AGREEMENTS

34. The First Settlement Agreement (FSA) announced in October 2008[180] was heavily criticised, not least because it allowed Google to display far more of the works than envisaged by the snippet view of the original Library Project and in many cases the whole work.[181] It was further criticised that the FSA might give Google a potential monopoly with regard to digitised books and making them available[182], that orphan works could in future only be used with the agreement of Google[183], that the agreement would be the equivalent of legislation with regard to orphan works and that privacy protection was not sufficient and that restrictions against Google sharing user data were non-existent. There were also concerns regarding rights of foreign authors.[184] Hence it was opposed by many more stakeholders than the original project, including rightholders, privacy advocates, libraries, technology companies, and the governments of the United States, Germany and France.[185]

Those in favour of the FSA underlined the usefulness of the project. They claimed that the agreement in fact made competition easier in the book search market as it resolved many intellectual property issues. They argued that it did not give Google monopoly over orphan works, as all the works could still be found in the shelves of the libraries. Furthermore, they proposed that the agreement might resolve access issues to knowledge for print disabled people.[186] However, the criticism and amount of opposition led the parties to propose a revised agreement which was filed in November 2008.[187]

35. The Amended Settlement Agreement (ASA) covered significantly fewer foreign books.[188] It provided for the establishment of an independent fiduciary in order to represent rightholders who had not claimed their works and which would be authorised to spend part of the revenue from unclaimed works to

180 *Authors Guild, Inc. v. Google Inc., Settlement Agreement* Case No 05 CV 8136-JES, USDC SDNY, Oct. 28, 2008; Besek, Digital libraries, 2010, 202.

181 Band, The Long, 2009, 260–261, 266–267.

182 Manuel, The Google, 2009, 10–11; Samuelson, Google, 2010, 1318; Besek, Digital libraries, 2010, 205–206.

183 Samuelson, Google, 2010, 1317; Besek, Digital libraries, 2010, 205.

184 Manuel, The Google, 2009, 9–12. The FSA covered not only books published in the USA and registered with the U.S. Copyright office but also all other books published before the 5th of January 2009 regardless of where in the world the publication took place, cf. Marybeth Peters, 'The amended Google Book Settlement: Judge Chin's decision', 2011, (June, No. 3), WIPO Magazine, 9–11, 10.

185 Peters, The amended, 2011, 9; Samuelson, Google, 2010, 1317; Band, The Long, 2009, 260.

186 Manuel, The Google, 2009, 13; Samuelson, Google, 2010, 1320 and 1358.

187 *Authors Guild, Inc. v. Google Inc., Amended Settlement Agreement* Case No 05 CV 8136-JES, USDC SDNY, Nov. 13, 2008; Samuelson, Google, 2010, 1318.

188 The ASA was limited to books registered with the U.S. Copyright Office or published in the UK, Canada and Australia before the 5th of January 2009, cf. Amended Settlement Agreement, 1.19; Samuelson, Google, 2010, 1319; Peters, The amended, 2011, 11; Band, The Long, 2009, 321–322.

search for rightholders.[189] It abolished the clause giving Google the right to any more favourable terms the Registry negotiated with third parties, which had been part of the concern for the potential monopoly position of Google.[190] The ASA distinguished between in and out-of-commerce books.[191] Google would not under the ASA be allowed to display in-commerce works without the prior consent of rightholders but would have be granted some non-display uses. Google would be allowed, however, to display out-of-commerce books without the prior consent of the owner although that right would lapse if the rightholder opted out.[192] The ASA extended the opt-out period in which removal from the program could be requested[193] and revised the removal options.[194] After the deadline the rightsholder could only request exclusion from particular display uses but not removal.[195] The ASA allowed rightholders to specify that the books would be made available under the project at no charge under a standard licence like Creative Commons or specify the price at as low as $ 0.00.[196] It also allowed the Registry[197] at its own discretion to authorise more than one free terminal per public library.[198] In response to criticism of privacy issues the ASA contained the following provision: "In no event will Google provide personally identifiable information about end users to the Registry other than as required by law or valid legal process."[199]

36. Despite the amendments the settlement remained hotly disputed.[200] Samuelson summed up the objections, underlining that of main concern was the risk of excessive pricing by Google, the lack of a backup plan if Google decided to discontinue the Google Book Search Project and inadequate privacy protections. Furthermore, she mentioned the risk of reduced competition in the

---

189 Amended Settlement Agreement, 6.2(b)(iii) and (iv); Peters, The amended, 2011, 10; Samuelson, Google, 2010, 1319.

190 Manuel, The Google, 2009, 10; Peters, The amended, 2011, 10; Band, The Long, 2009, 324.

191 The determination was set out in Art. 3(2)(d) ASA, and obliged Google to confer to third-party databases that were available on fair and commercially reasonable terms as well as publicly accessable information on the internet, cf. *Amended Settlement Agreement, Authors Guild v. Google* Case No 05 CV 8136-DC, USDC SDNY, 13 Nov. 2009; Jane C. Ginsburg and June M. Besek, *Comments Pursuant to Notice of Inquiry on Mass Digitzation Piolt Program, 80 Fed. Reg. 32614 (June 9, 2015)*, (October 8, 2015) 4.

192 *Authors Guild, Inc. v. Google Inc., Opinion on ASA* Case No 05 CV 8136-JES, USDC SDNY, March 22, 2011 p. 10; Ginsburg and Besek, Comments, 2015, 3.

193 The final date for removal request was the 5th of April 2011, cf. Amended Settlement Agreement, 1.126(a).

194 Band, The Long, 2009, 323–324.

195 Amended Settlement Agreement, 3.5(a)(iii).

196 Ibid, 4.2(a)(i) and 4.2(b)(i)(1); Band, The Long, 2009, 328.

197 The ASA provided for the establishment of a Registry with the role to act on behalf of rightholders, manage a rights information database, locate rightholders, assist in dispute resolution and monitor pricing for foreign rightholders, cf. Amended Settlement Agreement, 6.1. The FSA also provided for a Registry with similar functions, cf. Besek, Digital libraries, 2010, 203, 212.

198 Amended Settlement Agreement, 4.8(a)(i)(3); Band, The Long, 2009, 326.

199 Amended Settlement Agreement, 6.6(f); Band, The Long, 2009, 327.

200 Samuelson, Google, 2010, 1326–1358; Peters, The amended, 2011, 10; Manuel, The Google, 2009, 15.

book market, the "broad reconstruction of rights and remedies" for rightholders and that the agreement would replace legislative action.[201] Thus many feared that Google would achieve *de facto* monopoly for digitising books and their use through the project and the settlement agreements.[202]

37. It is interesting to note that the ASA was in many ways similar to an ECL agreement.[203] However, it did not fulfil one of the main criteria for the ECL system which is that it must be negotiated by representative CMOs.[204] The US Copyright Office later proposed an ECL system as a solution for mass digitisation, referring i.a. to the Google Book settlement as an example.[205] It is worth noting that the Google agreement and the amended Google agreement both contained territorial limitations to the effect that works made available under them were only accessible for use by US libraries and their users within the USA[206]

2.3.2. LITIGATIONS IN THE USA

38. In March 2011, a final approval of the Google Book Search Settlement was denied[207] as it was "not fair, adequate, and reasonable". The judge summarised that

> [w]hile the digitization of books and the creation of a universal digital library would benefit many, the ASA would simply go too far. It would permit this class action ... to implement a forward-looking business arrangement that would grant Google significant rights to exploit entire books, without permission of the copyright owners. Indeed, the ASA would give Google a significant advantage over competitors, rewarding it for engaging in wholesale copying of copyrighted works without permission, while releasing claims well beyond those presented in the case.

The judge further stated that establishing a mechanism for exploiting orphan works was more suited for Congress than the Court. Furthermore, he observed that "it is incongruous with the purpose of the copyright laws to place the onus on copyright owners to come forward to protect their rights

201 Samuelson, Google, 2010, 1359.
202 Manuel, The Google, 2009, 10–11; Samuelson, Google, 2010, 1335.
203 See e.g. US Copyright Office, Mass Digitization, 2015, 85, fn. 350; Samuelson, Legislative, 2011, 706; Trumpke, Exklusivität, 2015, 107. In fact it has been suggested that the idea for the Agreements came from the Nordic ECL system, cf. Rydén, Are digital, 2016, 2.
204 Samuelson, Google, 2010, 1374; Samuelson, Legislative, 2011, 707; Ringnalda, Orphan Works, 2011, 9. See discussion in Ch. 5.2.1 on the representation requirement of CMOs.
205 US Copyright Office, Mass Digitization, 2015, 6, 83, 90–92. The proposal was, however, withdrawn in September 2017, see brief description in Ch. 7.5.2.
206 Strowel, Google books: quel futur pour l'accès aux livres? Une bibliothèque universelle en devenir ou une future galerie commerciale?, 2010, 3, 4 and 6.
207 Authors Guild v. Google, ASA, SDNY 2011, 1–2.

when Google copied their works without first seeking their permission" noting that "many of the concerns raised in the objections would be ameliorated if the ASA were converted from an "opt-out" settlement to an "opt-in" settlement."[208]

39. After the rejection of the ASA unsuccessful attempts were made between the parties to reach an "opt-in" settlement as proposed by Judge Chin. Consequently the Authors Guild refiled their complaint against Google in October 2011.[209] Both the District Court, in November 2013[210], and the Court of Appeals, in October 2015, ruled in favour of Google. The Court of appeals concluded that:

> (1) Google's unauthorized digitizing of copyright-protected works, creation of a search functionality, and display of snippets from those works are non-infringing fair uses. The purpose of the copying is highly transformative, the public display of text is limited, and the revelations do not provide a significant market substitute for the protected aspects of the originals. Google's commercial nature and profit motivation do not justify denial of fair use. (2) Google's provision of digitized copies to the libraries that supplied the books, on the understanding that the libraries will use the copies in a manner consistent with the copyright law, also does not constitute infringement. Nor, on this record, is Google a contributory infringer.[211]

40. The Author's Guild appealed the case to the Supreme Court but in April 2016 the Court declined to take up the appeal.[212]

41. Concurrently with its litigation against Google the Authors Guild instigated a lawsuit against HathiTrust's[213] use of scanned works under copyright protection, obtained from Google, for preservation purposes, for providing access to the works for people with print disabilities and for full-text searches.

---

208 Ibid, 1–2, 22, 35, 45.

209 The publishers, however, settled their case with Google in October 2012 where the Association of American Publishers agreed to the opt-out policy of Google on behalf of their members in a secret settlement. See <www.publishersweekly.com/pw/by-topic/digital/copyright/article/54220-google-publishers-settle-lawsuit-over-book-scanning.html>, accessed 30 June 2017. In France, on the other hand, the French Publishers Association and Google reached settlement in June 2012 based on opt-in policy, see e.g. Borghi and Karapapa, Copyright and Mass Digitization, 2013, 5.

210 *The Authors Guild, Inc. et al v. Google Inc.* 05 Civ 8136, USDC SDNY, November 14, 2013; Cox, ARL Issue Brief in Google Books Case, 2015, 2.

211 Authors Guild v. Google (USCA SC 2015), 46.

212 See <https://www.authorsguild.org/industry-advocacy/supreme-court-declines-review-fair-use-finding-decade-long-book-copying-case-google/>, accessed 30 June 2017, and <https://www.publishersweekly.com/pw/by-topic/digital/copyright/article/70002-supreme-court-rejects-google-books-appeal.html>, accessed 30 June 2017.

213 The HathiTrust is a collaborative partnership of major research institutions and libraries with the aim to ensure the preservation and accessibility of the cultural record, cf. <www.hathitrust.org/about#>, accessed 24 April 2018.

In October 2012 the New York District Court decided in a summary judgement that HathiTrust's use was fair use.[214] This was confirmed by the Second Circuit Court in New York in June 2014.[215]

2.3.3. EVALUATION

42. The Google Book Search Project revolutionised the scanning of books and brought the analogue written text squarely into the digital world. However, it is worth noting that Google is not a library and the aim behind the digitisation project was market-driven to create searchable and computable objects to feed algorithms, rather than to enable universal access to the cultural heritage to the public at large.[216] By 2015 Google had scanned more than 20 million books[217], most of them still under copyright protection.[218] Their target was 130 million books by 2020.[219] This ambitious target has been lowered, both with regard to the speed of scanning and the aim of the project. By spring 2017 Google had scanned 25–30 million books and has slowed down its activities in relation to the Book Search Books considerably.[220] Nevertheless, the Google Book Search Project brought worldwide attention to the digitisation of books and injected urgency into the discussion of mass digitisation of books and related copyright issues. The legal solution has still not been found for enabling mass online availability, although many attempts are underway, as will be discussed further below.

---

214 *The Authors Guild v Hathitrust* 11 CV 6351 (HB), USDC SDNY, 10 October 2012.

215 *Authors Guild v. HathiTrust* 12–4547-cv, USCA for the Second Circuit, June 10, 2014 2–3. This decision settled that the Hathitrust was allowed to create a full-text searchable database of copyrighted works and to provide those works in formats accessible to those with disabilities". However, the issue of preservation was referred back to the District Court. The parties settled the issue in January 2015, cf. *The Authors Guild v. HathiTrust (Settlement)* 11 Civ 6351 (NRB), USDC SDNY, January 6, 2015.

216 Besek, Digital libraries, 2010, 205; Pamela Samuelson, 'Google Books is not a library' *Huffington Post* (18 March 2010) <www.huffingtonpost.com/pamela-samuelson/google-books-is-not-a-lib_b_317518.html> accessed 29 June 2017; Borghi, Erickson and Favale, With Enough, 2016, 137–138.

217 Authors Guild v. Google (USCA SC 2015), 6; Cox, ARL Issue Brief in Google Books Case, 2015, 1.

218 Peters, The amended, 2011, 9; Samuelson, Google, 2010, 1309.

219 SEC(2011) 1274, *Commission staff working paper accompanying the document Commission Recommendation on the digitisation and online accessibility of cultural material and digital preservation, SEC(2011) 1274*, (27.10.2011) 12.

220 Scott Rosenberg, 'How Google book search got lost' <https://www.wired.com/2017/04/how-google-book-search-got-lost/> accessed 30 June 2017; James Somers, 'Torching the Modern-Day Library of Alexandria' The Atlantic <https://www.theatlantic.com/technology/archive/2017/04/the-tragedy-of-google-books/523320/> accessed 30 June 2017; Tim Wu, 'What Ever Happened to Google Books?' The New Yorker <www.newyorker.com/business/currency/what-ever-happened-to-google-books> accessed 30 June 2017.

2.4. EUROPEAN DEVELOPMENTS WITH REGARD TO DIGITAL LIBRARIES

2.4.1. THE DIGITAL LIBRARY INITIATIVE

43. There is a strong political commitment by the European Union (EU) to facilitating the preservation and dissemination of the European cultural heritage in the digital age.[221] This aim has been at the centre of the EU's policies since the beginning of this century.[222] The start of the Google Book Search Project further influenced the development encouraging i.a. the launch of the Digital Library Initiative in Europe in 2005, which was aimed at "making European information resources easier and more interesting to use in an online environment."[223]

44. The Commission established expert groups to help address challenges relating to the implementation of the initiative, first the High Level Expert Group on Digital Libraries (HLG) in 2006[224] followed by the "Comité des Sages" in April 2010. Their reports[225] have been the basis of further developments, such as the Orphan Works Directive[226] of 2012 and the MoU on out-of-commerce works in 2011.[227]

45. Europeana[228], a multi-media online library, launched[229] on November 2008, has been named the most visible achievement of the Digital Library Initiative.[230] The aim was to create a multilingual common access point to Europe's distributed cultural heritage which would "promote inter-cultural dialogue, increase mutual awareness amongst Europe's cultures and enrich

---

221 Triaille and others, Study, 2013, 284 ff.

222 The Council and the European Commission, *eEurope 2002 – An Information Society For All, Action Plan*, (14.6.2000); COM(2011) 287 final, IPR Strategy, 2011, 13; European Copyright Society, *Answer to the EC Consultation on the review of the EU copyright rules*, (March 2014) 13.

223 COM(2005) 465, i2010: Digital Libraries, 2005,; Iglesias, Digital, 2008,; SEC(2011) 615 final, Impact Assessment, 2011, 6–7.

224 Commission Decision of 27 February 2006 setting up a High Level Expert Group on Digital Libraries OJ L 63/25.

225 HLG, *Final Report: "Digital Libraries: Challenges and Recommendations for the Future"*, (December 2009); Comité des Sages, *The New Renaissance*, (January 2011).

226 See discussion in Ch. 4.2.3.

227 See discussion in Ch. 7.1.

228 The name Euorpeana is of Graeco-Latin origin meaning "European colletion", see Klass and Rupp, EUROPEANA… 2014, fn. 62.

229 The inception of Europeana can be traced back to the letter of April 2005 from six Heads of State and Government to the Presidency of the Council and to the Commission, advocating the creation of a virtual European library, cf. COM(2005) 465, i2010: Digital Libraries, 2005, 3.

230 HLG, Final report, 2009, 10; SEC(2011) 615 final, Impact Assessment, 2011, 6–8; Borghi and Karapapa, Copyright and Mass Digitization, 2013, 6, 11.

European identity with cross-cultural shared references" by "linking together resources dispersed over the largest possible number of European cultural heritage institutions" which would yield "a higher European value than the mere sums of the values of isolated collections."[231] Europeana is a digital website offering worldwide direct access to Europe's cultural heritage.[232] It provides a single access point but does not bring together content into a single database. In June 2017 Europeana provided access to over 54 million digitised objects[233] from 2500 institutions in over 30 European countries[234], which was well above its target for that year.[235] This remains, however, only a small percentage of digital works in Europe.[236] Furthermore, the bulk of works available are out-of-copyright because of the many unsolved problems in connection with online availability to in-copyright works.[237] Hence the goal of having Europe's entire cultural heritage digitised seems still some way off; a goal that has been given a target date of 2025.[238]

46. ARROW[239] was developed with EU funding to help identify rightholders and copyright statuses of works, but it does not provide licences or other rights clearance.[240] The aim of ARROW was to prevent the emergence of orphan works in the future and make one search in the ARROW database sufficient to establish the copyright status of a cultural good in Europe.[241] Hence ARROW was meant to help to facilitate the licensing process; however, it only covered text based works and embedded images and was only operational in a few European

231 SEC(2006) 1075, Impact Assessment, 2006, 17.

232 COM(2009) 440 final, Europeana, 2009, 2. Europeana was not designed as a content provider but nevertheless it has started projects based on end-users contributions, which it then hosts, cf. Klass and Rupp, EUROPEANA… 2014, 959–960.

233 See <http://pro.europeana.eu/about-us/europeana-statistics/2017-q1>, accessed 30.06.2017.

234 Europeana, *We transform the world with culture: Europeana Strategy 2015–2020*, 12, 15.

235 2011/711/EU, Recommendation, 2011, item 7(a). However, the target of making all public domain masterpieces available by 2015 was not reached and progress in introducing more sound and audiovisual material has progressed more slowly, cf. European Commission, Digitisation report 2014, 2014, 37–38; European Commission, *Cultural heritage: Digitisation, online accessibility and digital preservation. Report on the Implementation of Commission Recommendation 2011/711/EU, 2013–2015*, (June 2016) 43–53.

236 Only 10% of the European cultural heritage is digitised. That 10% is comprised of 300 million objects, cf. Europeana, Europeana Strategy 2015–2020, 2014, 9. See also Boulanger and others, Assessing, 2014, 14–15 and European Commission, Digitisation report 2014, 2014, 6.

237 Boulanger and others, Assessing, 2014, 13–16; Borghi and Karapapa, Copyright and Mass Digitization, 2013, 6–7; European Commission, Digitisation report 2014, 2014, 65; Ringnalda, Orphan Works, 2011, 3; SWD(2016) 301 final, IA Part I, 2016, 66; Borghi, Erickson and Favale, With Enough, 2016, 138.

238 2011/711/EU, Recommendation, 2011, Recital (15).

239 ARROW (Accessible Registries of Rights Information and Orphan Works).

240 SWD(2016) 301 final, IA Part I, 2016, 66–67, fn. 188.

241 Uma Suthersanen and Maria Mercedes Frabboni, 'The Orphan Works Directive' in Irini Stamatoudi and Paul Torremans (eds), *EU Copyright Law A Commentary* (Edward Elgar, 2014) 675–676; Ringnalda, Orphan Works, 2011, 4.

countries.[242] In 2015 the French National Library was the only active user of ARROW in initiatives to make cultural heritage available.[243] Since 2013, an EU-funded project FORWARD is working on an EU wide, standardized system to assess and register the rights status of audiovisual works with a focus on orphans.[244]

47. The CMO Directive[245] is not specifically aimed at digital libraries or other cultural heritage institutions. However, one of its major aims is to provide and coordinate rules on transparency and good governance for collective management of copyright and related works[246] in order to develop "solutions for the licensing of the aggregate repertoire of works administered by all European societies."[247] Thus the CMO Directive benefits and supports collective licensing, which can enable online use for cultural heritage institutions such as libraries.

48. Currently, the Orphan Works Directive and the MoU on out-of-commerce works are the main instruments available to digital libraries and other cultural heritage institutions in Europe for making in-copyright works available on-line. Neither of them provides an adequate solution for large-scale digitisation or online use of in-copyright works contained in digital libraries or other cultural institutions.[248] What is more, current exceptions in EU copyright legislation do not provide for adequate solutions either.[249] However, further reform efforts are ongoing, most notably in the newly proposed DSM Directive.[250]

2.4.2. CURRENT REFORM EFFORTS

49. The Commission has highlighted that the legal complexities around digitising and making the cultural heritage accessible online could provoke a "knowledge gap", if not addressed, calling for innovative licensing solutions as well as reviewing the need for updating exceptions and limitations under the

---

242 Janssens and Tryggvadóttir, Facilitating, 2015, 61–62; European Commission, Report on the responses, 2014, 43; Oostveen and Guibault, IPR issues, 2013, 4–5; Guibault, Report, 2015, 1; Boulanger and others, Assessing, 2014, 20–21, 23.

243 Cf. <www.ifrro.org/sites/default/files/ifrro_board_report_2015.pdf>, last viewed 2 July 2017. In fact when updating information on ARROW in April 2018 no information were to be found so the project may have been discontinued.

244 Cf. <http://project-forward.eu/forward-new/> last viewed 24 April 2018. However, the website does not seem to have been updated since May 2017.

245 See brief discussion on the CMO Directive in Ch. 6.3.4 and 9.4.

246 Recitals (8) and (9) CMO Directive.

247 Lucie Guibault, 'Collective Rights Management Directive' in Irini Stamatoudi and Paul Torremans (eds), *EU Copyright Law; A Commentary* (2014) 698.

248 See Ch. 4.2.3, 4.2.4.2 and 7.1.

249 See discussion in Ch. 4.2.4.

250 *Op.cit.* Ch. 1.1, fn. 38.

InfoSoc Directive.[251] Thus one of the key aims of the Digital Agenda for Europe as part of the Europe 2020 strategy was to facilitate the digitisation and cross-border online use of the cultural heritage.[252] A public consultation was launched end of 2013 where it was i.a. asked whether the current framework for access to content in libraries and archives "...continues to achieve the objectives envisaged or whether it needs to be clarified or updated to cover use in digital networks."[253] With the exception of publishers, stakeholders mostly responded that the current framework did not enable enough access. However, suggested solutions varied within each group of stakeholders as well as between different stakeholder groups. Some preferred wider access through exceptions and limitations, whereas many mentioned improved licences and licensing practice, in particular through collective management, i.a. under extended collective licences.[254]

50. The Digital Single Market Strategy of May 2015 advocated strongly better access to digital content and for preventing "unjustified geo-blocking" by online sellers. Legislative proposals were announced that would include greater legal certainty for the cross-border use of content for specific purposes (e.g. research, education, text and data mining) through harmonised exceptions.[255] Furthermore, the "work of the institutions in charge of promoting access to knowledge should be facilitated" in order to provide such institutions "a clearer framework and a level playing field regardless of the Member State in which they are based."[256]

The European Council meeting of June 2015 concluded that in order to "benefit fully" from the digital technological "revolution" market fragmentation must be tackled. The Council agreed that action must be taken i.a. to deal with unjustified discrimination on the grounds of geographic location and to ensure the portability and cross-border access to online material protected by copyright. Thus it is clear that both the Commission and Council are cautious when discussing geo-blocking, on the one hand to underline the undesirability of the effect of such practices on the Digital Single Market, but on the other hand refraining from deeming such use unjustified in connection with the dissemination of works protected by copyright.

51. The European Parliament adopted a resolution in July 2015 calling i.a. for the strengthening of exceptions for "institutions of public interest, such as libraries, museums and archives, in order to promote wide-ranging access to

251 COM(2011) 287 final, IPR Strategy, 2011, 6, 13.
252 2011/711/EU, Recommendation, 2011, Recitals (1)-(8), which i.a. highlight earlier reports and recommendations in the area.
253 Public Consultation on the review of the EU copyright rules (2013), 19.
254 European Commission, Report on the responses, 2014, 43–46.
255 COM(2015) 192 final, Communication, 2015, 6–8.
256 SWD(2015) 100 final, A Digital Single Market Strategy, 2015, 30.

cultural heritage, including through online platforms" and for an assessment of adopting "an exception allowing libraries to digitalise content for the purposes of consultation, cataloguing and archiving".[257] The Resolution further called on the Commission to address the issues of geo-blocking and portability of content.[258]

52. In December 2015, the Commission announced[259] that options and legislative proposals were being assessed and considered in order to allow for wider online access to works by users across the EU. Those options and proposals included enhancing cross-border distribution of television and radio programmes online in connection with a review of the Satellite and Cable Directive; supporting agreements between rightholders and distributors on licences for cross-border access to audio-visual works; and facilitating the digitisation and making available across the EU of out-of-commerce works.[260]

53. In September 2016 the Commission put forward several proposals to implement the Single Digital Market strategy.[261] The DSM proposal with its solution for the use of out-of-commerce works for cultural heritage institutions is of much

257 European Parliament, *Resolution of 9 July 2015 on the implementation of Directive 2001/29/EC of the European Parliament and of the Council of 22 May 2001 on the harmonisation of certain aspects of copyright and related rights in the information society (2014/2256(INI))*, item 39. The Parliament also called for assessment of exceptions for e-lending by libraries, cf. item 53 of the Resolution.

258 European Parliament, Resolution, 2015, item 9, 10, 14 and 15; Christophe Geiger and others, *Reaction of CEIPI to the Resolution on the Implementation of Directive 2001/29/EC on the Harmonisation of Copyright in the Information Society adopted by the European Parliament on the 9th July 2015*, 10.

259 As well as tabling this proposal: COM(2015) 627, *Proposal for a Regulation of the European Parliament and of the Council on ensuring the cross-border portability of online content services in the internal market*, (9 Dec 2015).

260 COM(2015) 626 final, *Communication from the Commission to the European Parliament, the Council, the European Economic and Social Committee and the Committee of the Regions; Towards a modern, more European copyright framework*, (9 December 2015) 6.

261 COM(2016) 593 final, Proposal, 2016, *op.cit.*; COM(2016) 594 final, *Proposal for a Regulation of the European Parliament and of the Council laying down rules on the exercise of copyright and related rights applicable to certain online transmissions of broadcasting organisations and retransmissions of television and radio programmes*, (14 September 2016); COM(2016) 596 final, *Proposal for a Directive of the European Parliament and of the Councilon on certain permitted uses of works and other subject-matter protected by copyright and related rights for the benefit of persons who are blind, visually impaired or otherwise print disabled and amending Directive 2001/29/EC on the harmonisation of certain aspects of copyright and related rights in the information society*, (14 September 2016); COM(2016) 595 final, *Proposal for a Regulation of the European Parliament and of the Council on the cross-border exchange between the Union and third countries of accessible format copies of certain works and other subject-matter protected by copyright and related rights for the benefit of persons who are blind, visually impaired or otherwise print disabled*, (14 September 2016); COM(2016) 289 final, *Proposal for a Regulation of the European Parliament and of the Council on addressing geo-blocking and other forms of discrimination based on customers' nationality, place of residence or place of establishment within the internal market and amending Regulation (EC) No 2006/2004 and Directive 2009/22/EC*, (25 May 2016).

interest for the subject of this book and is, consequently, referred to at various points as well as being discussed in more detail below.[262] The other proposals submitted are briefly discussed below in connection with the issue of territoriality.[263]

2.5. CONCLUSION

54. The terms "library" and "digital library" have been discussed in this chapter as well as how the role of libraries is affected by digital technology. It seems clear that the fundamental role of libraries remains unchanged in the digital world although the digitalisation of this role brings many of their activities into conflict with the exclusive rights under copyright protection. Many of the issues affecting libraries in the digital age were brought to light through the Google Book Project and the subsequent litigations, although the purpose of the market-driven digitisation project was fundamentally different from the aim of European legislators; their aim with regard to mass digitisation projects is based on the public mission of cultural institutions to disseminate content to the general public.[264] The Google saga has now been concluded in US courts, which have declared scanning of books under the project as fair use and hence not a breach of copyright. Furthermore US courts have affirmed that certain uses of those scanned books for text and datamining, for access for print-disabled persons and for preservation also constitute fair use. Nevertheless, the issue of making works available online by libraries, whether orphan or out-of-commerce, has not been solved in the USA. Neither has the issue been solved in Europe, as can be seen from the overview of European developments in this chapter, although the proposed DSM Directive may be helpful, if adopted.

55. Increasingly, national legislators are looking to the system of ECLs as a possible answer to the licensing needs of cultural heritage institutions. The question is whether national ECL agreements can provide for cross-border online use, at least within Europe. To decide on the issue the ECL system will be examined in the context of international treaties and European legislation and with regard to the principle of territoriality. However, before turning to that I will look at which exclusive rights are concerned by online use of in-copyright works, and what tools, i.e. exceptions and limitations, libraries currently have for using in-copyright works online.

262 The proposal contains several other provisions, many of which are outside the scope of this thesis. However, some of them, such as the preservation exception in Art. 5, will affect libraries, see discussion in Ch. 4.2.4.1.1.1, and Ch. 10.2.4. The proposed controversial new right for publishers in Art. 11, cf. e.g. European Copyright Society, *General Opinion on the EU Copyright Reform Package*, (24 January 2017) 6, will not be specifically addressed.

263 See Ch. 8.3.3.

264 Borghi, Erickson and Favale, With Enough, 2016, 137–138.

CHAPTER 3
EXCLUSIVE RIGHTS IN ONLINE USE

Increasingly if library content is not found on the Web, it effectively does not exist for many potential users.[265]

56. When libraries make in-copyright works available online the act falls under the exclusive right of communication to the public. However, in order to make works available online there needs to be a digital copy. Making a digital copy from an analogue work entails reproduction. The making available of works online can include the possibility for end-users to download those works, which of course is also reproduction. Furthermore, as will be discussed below, the very act of making a work available online results in temporary copies, i.e. involves reproduction, as well as the storing of works in digital form in a computer.[266] Thus, the main exclusive rights involved in online use are the communication to the public right, especially the making available right[267], and the reproduction right.[268] In the digital area there is an overlap between these two rights[269] which leads to a somewhat blurred distinction "between access provision and access-supportive activities" and a "legal uncertainty as to the boundaries of permissible uses."[270]

57. The following discussion will, nevertheless, attempt to consider these two applicable exclusive rights separately. The examination is based on a European perspective and the exclusive rights are looked at to the extent relevant for digital libraries and the making works available with cross-border effect. I will begin to look at the reproduction right and then move on to the communication to the public right with particular emphasis on the making available right.

265 Brindley, Phoenixes in the internet era – the changing role of libraries, 2010, 178.

266 See e.g. Jörg Reinbothe and Silke Von Lewinski, *The WIPO Treaties on Copyright* (2 edn, Oxford University Press, 2015), 136.

267 Art. 3 InfoSoc Directive, *op.cit.* See e.g. Triaille and others, Study, 2013, 109–111, 118; Lucie Guibault and others, *Study on the Implementation and Effect in Member States' Laws of Directive 2001/29/EC on the Harmonisation of Certain Aspects of Copyright and Related Rights in The Information Society. Part I; The Impact of Directive 2001/29/EC on Online Business Models*, (Februar 2007) 22; European Copyright Society, Answer to the EC Consulation 2014, 4.

268 Art. 2 InfoSoc Directive.

269 Ohly, Economic rights, 2009, 217; Triaille and others, Study, 2013, 111, 118; C-170/12 – AG opinion in Pinckney, par. 27–30; Guibault and Quintais, Copyright, 2014, 9, 22.

270 Borghi and Karapapa, Copyright and Mass Digitization, 2013, 13.

3.1. REPRODUCTION RIGHTS IN ONLINE USE

3.1.1. DEFINITION AND DEVELOPMENT

58. The reproduction right is one of the "classical" exclusive rights and has been considered the core of copyright as it gives the rightholder control over subsequent exploitation acts.[271] Even so, a provision for a general right of reproduction was not introduced into the Berne Convention until 1967.[272] Art. 9(1) of the Berne Convention provides that authors of literary and artistic works shall have the exclusive right of authorising the reproduction of their works. The provision is intended to cover all forms of reproduction as can be seen from the wording "in any manner and form". This was deemed also to include digital reproduction, even if not "perceptible to the human eye".[273] Hence no new definition with regard to the reproduction right was adopted in the WCT.[274]

59. Within Europe no general harmonised reproduction right existed prior to the adoption of the InfoSoc Directive.[275] In order to ensure the smooth functioning of the internal market, also in the "new electronic environment", it was felt necessary to define in clearer terms the scope of the reproduction right in the digital age[276], and in particular that it extends to temporary acts and that digitisation of a work constitutes reproduction.[277] Thus Art. 2 of the InfoSoc Directive specifies that the reproduction right also applies in the

---

271 Ginsburg and Treppoz, International, 2015, 311; Geiger and others, InfoSoc, 2014, 401; Sari Depreeuw and Jean-Benoît Hubin, *Study on the making available right and its relationship with the reproduction right in cross-border digital transmissions*, 40; von Lewinski and Walter, Information Society Directive, 2010, 963; Ohly, Economic rights, 2009, 213; COM(95) 382 final, *Green Paper: Copyright and Related Rights in the Information Society*, 49; COM(96) 568 final, *Communication from the Commission; Follow-up to the Green Paper on Copyright and Related Rights in the Information Society*, (20.11.1996) 10; COM(97)628 final, *Proposal for a European Parliament and Council Directive on the harmonization of certain aspects of copyright and related rights in the Information Society*, (10.12.1997) 12.

272 Art. 9(1) adopted at the Stockholm Revision Conference. In the Brussels Act of 1948 there had been provisions dealing with some aspects of the reproduction right but no general provision, cf. WIPO, *Berne Convention Centenary 1886–1986* (the International Bureau of Intellectual Property, 1986), 196; Ginsburg and Treppoz, International, 2015, 311.

273 COM(97)628 final, InfoSoc Proposal, 1997, 14.

274 Cf. Agreed statements concerning Art. 1(4) WCT, *op.cit.* However, the basic negotiation text for the WCT treaty had contained an article with a broad definition of the reproduction right, including temporary reproduction, cf. von Lewinski and Walter, Information Society Directive, 2010, 1023 but no agreement could be reached for the definition of the right, cf. Guibault and others, InfoSoc Study, Part I, 2007, 22.

275 COM(97)628 final, InfoSoc Proposal, 1997, 12; Guibault and others, InfoSoc Study, Part I, 2007, 22; Thomas Dreier and P. Bernt Hugenholtz (eds), *Concise European Copyright Law* (1 edn, Kluwer Law International, 2006) 357.

276 COM(97)628 final, InfoSoc Proposal, 1997, 12–16. See also Recital (6) and (21) InfoSoc Directive.

277 Von Lewinski and Walter, Information Society Directive, 2010, 964, 969, 1024.

digital environment.[278] The article states that Member States must "provide for the exclusive right to authorise or prohibit direct or indirect, temporary or permanent reproduction by any means and in any form, in whole or in part". There is, however, no further definition of what reproduction entails.[279] Recital (21) underlines that acts covered by the reproduction right should be defined broadly[280] with regard to the different beneficiaries, to ensure legal certainty within the internal market.

Nevertheless, the lack of a clear definition means that the reproduction right is not harmonised in the Member States, which diminishes legal certainty. There remain several important issues regarding the right that can be and are interpreted differently within Europe, such as the question of the localisation of the reproduction in an online environment or the question of who is actually making the copy when there is more than one person concerned with different roles, in particular when technical intermediaries are involved. National legislations seem to take different approaches as to whether it is the up-loader of a work who makes the reproduction or the end-user who has requested the digital transmission of the copy.[281] Until we either have an interpretation by the CJEU on these as yet non-harmonised issues or EU legislation clarifying them, there remains a risk to the smooth functioning of the Digital Single Market which could undermine attempts to reduce the complications of the territorial effect of copyright in online services.[282]

60. The CJEU has interpreted the reproduction right from a technical rather than a functional standpoint[283], deeming that reproduction is the result of every instance when a work is fixed in a tangible medium, regardless of how ephemeral.[284] The term "reproduction" in the InfoSoc Directive "must be given an autonomous and uniform interpretation throughout the European Union".[285] Thus, the act of storing extracts of works in a data capture process falls under the exclusive reproduction

---

278 COM(97)628 final, InfoSoc Proposal, 1997, 24–25.

279 C-5/08 *Infopaq International A/S v Danske Dagblades Forening* ECLI:EU:C:2009:465, CJEU, 16 July 2009 par. 31; Ohly, Economic rights, 2009, 216.

280 C-301/15 *Marc Soulier, Sara Doke v Ministre de la Culture et de la Communication, Premier ministre* ECLI:EU:C:2016:878, CJEU, 16 November 2016 par. 30–31; C-301/15 *Opinion of Advocate General Wathelet in C-301/15 Marc Soulier, Sara Doke v Ministre de la Culture et de la Communication, Premier ministre* ECLI:EU:C:2016:536, CJEU, 7 July 2016 fn. 23; C-5/08 – Infopaq I, par. 43; Geiger and others, InfoSoc, 2014, 450–451; Recitals (9) and (11) InfoSoc Directive also underline "high", "rigorous" and "effective" protection.

281 Triaille and others, Study, 2013, 111–113; Depreeuw and Hubin, Study 2014, 2014, 43–44.

282 Depreeuw and Hubin, Study 2014, 2014, 45.

283 Von Lewinski and Walter, Information Society Directive, 2010, 968.

284 Triaille and others, Study, 2013, 49, 111, 120.

285 C-5/08 – Infopaq I, par. 27–29, see also Joined cases C-403/08 and C-429/08 *Football Association Premier League Ltd and Others v QC Leisure and Others; Karen Murphy v Media Protection Services Ltd* ECLI:EU:C:2011:631, CJEU, 4 October 2011 par. 154. See e.g. Geiger and others, InfoSoc, 2014, 454–456.

right, given that the extract is considered an expression of the intellectual creation of the author.[286] Furthermore, the reproduction right extends to:

> ... transient fragments of the works within the memory of a satellite decoder and on a television screen, provided that those fragments contain elements which are the expression of the authors' own intellectual creation, and the unit composed of the fragments reproduced simultaneously must be examined in order to determine whether it contains such elements.[287]

61. In this manner the provision in Art. 2 of the InfoSoc Directive and its interpretation has led to the broadening of the reproduction right. It has been pointed out that acts that were permitted in the analogue world, i.e. mere uses of work such as reading a book, receiving a television signal or searching for information in analogue sources such as "yellow pages" of phone books, can constitute a copyright infringement in the digital world because online use encompasses technical reproduction as well as the making available right.[288] An instance of this is evident in the Infopaq case, where it was accepted that consent was not required from rightholders to:

> ...engage in press monitoring activity and the writing of summaries consisting in manual reading of each publication, selection of the relevant articles on the basis of predetermined search words, and production of a manually prepared cover sheet for the summary writers, giving an identified search word in an article and its position in the newspaper. Similarly, the parties in the main proceedings do not dispute that genuinely independent summary writing per se is lawful and does not require consent from the rightholders.[289]

However, undertaking the same activity with the help of a data capture process constituted reproduction in part that required consent from rightholders, i.e. was not a "genuinely independent summary writing".[290]

This accumulation of rights in the digital environment may require double or multiple authorisations for online use of works[291], i.e. both for the reproduction right and the communication to the public right. This complicates rights clearance as the rights are not always held by the same persons or administered by the same entities.[292] Some rights, such as the reproduction right, tend to be

---

286 C-5/08 – Infopaq I, par. 51.

287 Joined cases C-403/08 and C-429/08 – Premier League, par. 159.

288 Bernt Hugenholtz and others, *The Recasting of Copyright & Related Rights for the Knowledge Economy; final report (IVIR 2006 study)*, (November 2006) 54; Guibault and others, InfoSoc Study, Part I, 2007, 23–24; Ohly, Economic rights, 2009, 217; Guibault and Quintais, Copyright, 2014, 9; Dreier and Hugenholtz (eds) Concise, 2006, 359, 371.

289 C-5/08 – Infopaq I, par. 23.

290 Ibid, par. 30–51, 73–74.

291 Guibault and Quintais, Copyright, 2014, 9; Guibault and others, InfoSoc Study, Part I, 2007, 24–24.

292 Triaille and others, Study, 2013, 119–120; Jean-Paul Triaille and others, 'Preliminary studies to the future EU Copyright review: about (some) exclusive rights and (some) exceptions', 2015, (2), Auteurs & Média, 147–157, 148–149.

managed by CMOs, which deal less with the making available right.[293] Thus the 2006 IVIR study concludes that "a broad reproduction right and a broad communication to the public right, including a right of making available online, cannot co-exist."[294]

62. It has been suggested that of the two exclusive rights inherent in online use, the making available right[295] is of more economic significance while the acts of reproduction in the context of online use of works have little or no independent economic significance. Hence in those circumstances the clearance of the making available right should also cover necessary reproduction.[296] This seems to be the conclusion of the CJEU in the TU Darmstadt case. In that case the Court came to the conclusion that Art. 5(3)(n) of the InfoSoc Directive, read in conjunction with Art. 5(2)(c), should be interpreted as allowing national legislation to confer on the relevant institutions the right to digitise works that they can make available under the former provision "...if such act of reproduction is necessary for the purpose of making those works available to users, by means of dedicated terminals, within those establishments."[297]

63. There are some limitations of the reproduction right which are meant to mitigate the effect of this broad technical reproduction right provided for in Art. 2 of the InfoSoc Directive, which I will discuss next.

3.1.2. LIMITATIONS TO THE REPRODUCTION RIGHT IN ONLINE USE

64. The scope of protection afforded under Art. 2 of the InfoSoc Directive is limited by the mandatory exception in Art. 5(1) in order to prevent "an undesirable overextension of protection".[298] It has been implemented literally

---

293 Hugenholtz and others, Recasting, 2006, 54–55; Ohly, Economic rights, 2009, 217.

294 Hugenholtz and others, Recasting, 2006, 55.

295 Although the making available right is a sub-category of the communication to the public right I will be using the former term more frequently here as that is the central exclusive right for digital libraries wishing to make works available online, cf. e.g. European Copyright Society, Answer to the EC Consulation 2014, 6.

296 Ibid, 5–6.

297 *Case C-117/13, Technische Universität Darmstadt v. Eugen Ulmer KG* ECLI:EU:C:2014:2196, CJEU, 11 September 2014 par. 17 and 49.

298 Von Lewinski and Walter, Information Society Directive, 2010, 968; Dreier and Hugenholtz (eds) Concise, 2006, 359. The exception in Art. 5(1) was partly modelled on a proposed provision on an exception to the reproduction right in the basic negotiation text for the WCT, which was never adopted, cf. von Lewinski and Walter, Information Society Directive, 2010, 1023; Hugenholtz and others, Recasting, 2006, 68.

in most Member States.[299] The exception has important implications for the making available right, although it is not exclusively linked to that right.[300] The aim is to enable the lawful use of works in the digital environment, such as browsing and caching.[301] The exception has five cumulative[302] conditions, i.e. the reproduction act must be, first, temporary; second, either transient or incidental; third, an integral and essential part of the process; fourth, for the sole purpose of enabling "a transmission in a network between third parties by an intermediary" or "a lawful use" and fifth, without any "independent economic significance".[303] The interpretation of the conditions is, however, not straightforward.[304] The CJEU has underlined that they need to be interpreted strictly.[305] At the same time the Court has stated that, in accordance with the objective of the exception, it must

> ...allow and ensure the development and operation of new technologies and safeguard a fair balance between the rights and interests of right holders, on the one hand, and of users of protected works who wish to avail themselves of those new technologies, on the other.[306]

65. The Infopaq I case was the first case to consider the conditions of temporary and transient acts of reproduction under the exception in Art. 5(1) of the InfoSoc Directive. The Court came to the conclusion that

> ...a temporary and transient act of reproduction is intended to enable the completion of a technological process of which it forms an integral and essential part. In those circumstances ... those acts of reproduction must not exceed what is necessary for the proper completion of that technological process.[307]

---

299 In the Netherlands it was not implemented as a limitation but as a "carve-out" of the scope of the exclusive reproduction right, cf. Guido Westkamp, *Study on the Implementation and Effect in Member States' Laws of Directive 2001/29/EC on the Harmonisation of Certain Aspects of Copyright and Related Rights in The Information Society. Part II; The Implementation of Directive 2001/29/EC in the Member States*, (Februar 2007) 12; Geiger and others, InfoSoc, 2014, 447.

300 Triaille and others, Study, 2013, 113.

301 Recital (33) Infosoc Directive; von Lewinski and Walter, Information Society Directive, 2010, 1024; Hugenholtz and others, Recasting, 2006, 68; Geiger and others, InfoSoc, 2014, 447.

302 C-5/08 – Infopaq I, par. 55; Geiger and others, InfoSoc, 2014, 448; Dreier and Hugenholtz (eds) Concise, 2006, 371–372.

303 C-5/08 – Infopaq I, par. 54–55; Joined cases C-403/08 and C-429/08 – Premier League, par. 161; C-302/10 *Infopaq International A/S v Danske Dagblades Forening* ECLI:EU:C:2012:16, CJEU, 17 January 2012 par. 25–26; C-360/13 *Public Relations Consultants Association Ltd (PRCA) v Newspaper Licensing Agency Ltd and Others* ECLI:EU:C:2014:1195, 5 June 2014 par. 22.

304 Triaille and others, Study, 2013, 111; Sari Depreeuw, Publication: The variable scope of the exclusive economic rights in copyright, Kluwer Copyright Blog, June 29, 2015; 1 July 2017.

305 C-5/08 – Infopaq I, par. 56–57; C-302/10 – Infopaq II, par. 27; Joined cases C-403/08 and C-429/08 – Premier League, par. 162; C-360/13 – PRCA par. 23.

306 Joined cases C-403/08 and C-429/08 – Premier League, par. 164 and 179; C-360/13 – PRCA par. 24; Geiger and others, InfoSoc, 2014, 448.

307 C-5/08 – Infopaq I, par. 61.

The Court further elaborated that legal certainty for rightholders requires that the storage and deletion of the temporary and transient reproduction may not be dependent on the discretion of a human intervention, in particular not on the user of the protected works. Furthermore, the duration of the act must not exceed the period necessary for the proper completion of the technological process in question.[308]

66. The first two conditions, i.e. that an act should be temporary and transient or incidental, should be assessed together. A temporary act need not necessarily be of short duration. However, in order to fulfil the condition of Art. 5(1) it must either be transient, which is normally considered to be an act of particularly short duration, or incidental.[309] This was put to the test in the PRCA case in which the Court asserted that acts of reproduction are temporary when copies are deleted or automatically replaced within a certain time.[310] The Court underlined that the second criterion comprises alternative requirements, i.e. that the act must be transient or incidental.[311] It recalled from the Infopaq I case that an act will be held to be transient in the light of the technological process used:

> ...if its duration is limited to what is necessary for that process to work properly, it being understood that that process must be automated inasmuch as it deletes such an act automatically, without human intervention, once its function of enabling the completion of such a process has come to an end.[312]

However, the Court explains that the requirement of automatic deletion does not preclude human intervention activating the process of deletion[313], i.e. when an on-screen copy is automatically deleted when the user moves away from the website in question.[314] The Court then proposed that "an act of reproduction can be regarded as 'incidental' if it neither exists independently of, nor has a purpose independent of, the technological process of which it forms part."[315] The Court observes that cached copies fulfil this criterion with regard to the technological process at hand in the main proceedings and must therefore be considered incidental, although they might not be defined as transient as they are not deleted automatically when an internet user terminates the technological process used for viewing the website concerned.[316] Thus it is clear that a copy can fulfil the first two requirements if it is either temporary and transient <u>or</u> temporary

308 Ibid, par. 62 & 64.
309 Von Lewinski and Walter, Information Society Directive, 2010, 1024–1025; Dreier and Hugenholtz (eds) Concise, 2006, 371–372.
310 C-360/13 – PRCA par. 26.
311 Ibid, par. 39.
312 Ibid, par. 40; C-5/08 – Infopaq I, par. 64.
313 C-302/10 – Infopaq II, par. 32.
314 C-360/13 – PRCA par. 32, 41–42, 44–46.
315 Ibid, par. 43.
316 Ibid, par. 47–51.

and incidental. Even so, inevitably there is some overlap in the definition of when an act is temporary and transient or incidental.[317]

67. The third condition for the exception, that the temporary and transient or incidental reproduction acts should be an integral and essential part of the process, describes the automatic and technological nature of the process, which is inevitable and cannot be "directly achieved" by humans[318] and applies to reproductions that exist due to technical necessities.[319] This requirement was discussed in the Infopaq I & II cases and the PRCA case. Infopaq I highlighted that the temporary and transient reproduction acts should be intended to enable the completion of the technological process of which they form an integral and essential part.[320] The questions referred to the CJEU in the Infopaq II case related to the acts of reproduction that passed the test of being transient in the Infopaq I case and concerned whether those acts fulfilled the condition of being an integral and essential part of the process. In particular, the question was posed whether it mattered at which stage of the process such acts took place and if it was of consequence that an act involved human intervention.[321] The Court clarified that

> [t]he concept of the 'integral and essential part of a technological process' requires the temporary acts of reproduction to be carried out entirely in the context of the implementation of the technological process and, therefore, not to be carried out, fully or partially, outside of such a process. This concept also assumes that the completion of the temporary act of reproduction is necessary, in that the technological process concerned could not function correctly and efficiently without that act.[322]

The Court then further observed that nothing in the provision specified at which stage the temporary reproduction acts took place in the technological process nor was there any indication that the process must be free of any human intervention.[323] The Court thus came to the conclusion that the acts in question were an integral and essential part of the process, regardless of the fact that they initiated and terminated the process in question and involved human intervention. It was undisputed that they were completed inside the technological process, it was irrelevant that they were activated manually and terminated by an act of temporary reproduction and, finally, it was asserted that the technological process could not function without the temporary

317 See C-302/10 – Infopaq II, e.g. par. 36, 38 & 39 where the acts that were defined as transient in Infopaq I are called temporary, rather than temporary and transient.
318 Von Lewinski and Walter, Information Society Directive, 2010, 1025.
319 Dreier and Hugenholtz (eds) Concise, 2006, 372.
320 C-5/08 – Infopaq I, par. 61.
321 C-302/10 – Infopaq II, par. 23 & 29.
322 Ibid, par. 30.
323 Ibid, par. 31–32.

reproduction acts in question. The fact that the subsequent summaries could be drafted without any reproduction was irrelevant.[324]

The same criteria as used in the Infopaq cases outlined above were then applied by the CJEU in the PRCA case to establish that the temporary, transient or incidental on-screen and cached copies were created by acts of reproduction that were integral and essential parts of the technological process in question.[325]

68. The fourth condition of the exception in Art. 5(1) is that the sole purpose of the process should be to enable "a transmission in a network between third parties by an intermediary" or "a lawful use". Recital (33) of the Directive sets out that the first prong of this condition should include:

> ...acts which enable browsing as well as acts of caching to take place, including those which enable transmission systems to function efficiently, provided that the intermediary does not modify the information and does not interfere with the lawful use of technology, widely recognised and used by industry, to obtain data on the use of the information.

This element of the fourth condition seems not to have raised difficulties.[326] However, the "lawful use" part has raised questions that have been referred to the CJEU. Recital (33) explains that a "use should be considered lawful where it is authorised by the rightholder or not restricted by law." An authorisation by the rightholder could be explicit or implicit.[327]

In the Premier League case it was undisputed that the reproductions concerned, i.e. transient fragments of works within the memory of a satellite decoder and on a television screen, fulfilled the first three conditions of the exception in Art. 5(1).[328] With regard to the fourth requirement it was clear that the acts of reproduction were not intended to enable transmission in a network between third parties by an intermediary, so the Court had to determine whether the acts concerned a "lawful use". As the acts were not authorised by the rightholders the Court had to decide whether the acts were restricted by law.[329] It was acknowledged that the "ephemeral acts of reproduction" enabled the satellite decoder and the television screen to operate properly and allowed the viewers to receive the works. The Court concluded that the "mere reception of those broadcasts" in private circles did not constitute an act restricted by EU legislation or the legislation of the Member State in question and was hence lawful.[330] However, the Court did not deliberate on the fact that the broadcasts in the case were actually received in a public space.[331]

---

324 Ibid, par. 33–39.
325 C-360/13 – PRCA par. 28–33.
326 Triaille and others, Study, 2013, 115.
327 Dreier and Hugenholtz (eds) Concise, 2006.
328 Joined cases C-403/08 and C-429/08 – Premier League, par. 165.
329 Ibid, par. 167–169.
330 Ibid, par. 170–171.
331 Triaille and others, Study, 2013, 115.

In the Infopaq II case the Court came to the conclusion that the temporary and transient copies resulting from the data capturing process fulfilled the condition of lawful use. This was because the sole purpose of the process was to enable the summarising of articles in a more efficient manner, which was neither restricted by EU nor Danish legislation.[332, 333] Hence it can be concluded that lawful use is intended use[334] authorised by rightholders, allowed under an exception[335] or not restricted by legislation.[336]

69. Finally, the fifth condition is that the temporary act must not have any "independent economic significance". This has been seen as an application of the three-step test in Art. 5(5) and underlines that the exception concerns exclusively reproductions that exist solely due to technical necessities.[337] In the Premier League case the Court asserted that all acts enabling access to protected works have economic significance.[338] However, the Court underlined that the exception in Art. 5(1) would be rendered redundant unless the economic significance of the temporary acts had an independent significance, i.e. went beyond the economic significance generated by the use that the temporary act was enabling. In the case at hand it was the reception of a broadcast containing protected works. The temporary acts enabling the reception of the broadcast formed "an inseparable and non-autonomous part" of the process and hence were not "capable of generating an additional economic advantage".[339]

In the Infopaq II case the Court explained that temporary acts falling under Art. 5(1) are intended to facilitate the use of works or make the use more efficient. This purpose inherently aims at increasing profits or reducing production costs, i.e. the goal of the temporary acts is to have an economic significance. However, that in itself is not of independent economic significance. In order to have an independent economic significance the temporary act must either be distinct or separable from the economic advantage derived from the lawful use of the work concerned and it must "generate an additional economic advantage going beyond that derived from that use of the protected work." Such an additional economic advantage would arise if the user of the temporary act were to make a profit with the aid of the temporary reproductions themselves or if the temporary act led to a change in the subject matter reproduced. That was not the

332 The right of adaptation is not harmonised in the EU, Ohly, Economic rights, 2009, 233; von Lewinski and Walter, Information Society Directive, 2010, 970; Triaille and others, Study, 2013, 115, fn. 315.

333 C-302/10 – Infopaq II, par. 42–45.

334 It is noteworthy that the intended use (sole purpose) of the process does not have to be a part of it, cf. Triaille and others, Study, 2013, 115.

335 Von Lewinski and Walter, Information Society Directive, 2010, 1026.

336 Triaille and others, Study, 2013, 115.

337 Dreier and Hugenholtz (eds) Concise, 2006, 373.

338 C-302/10 – Infopaq II, par. 48.

339 Joined cases C-403/08 and C-429/08 – Premier League, par. 174–178.

situation with regard to the temporary reproduction carried out with the data capturing process at hand in the dispute concerned.[340]

70. It is interesting to note that the Advocate General in his opinion in the VOB case argued that the reproduction made by a user on his computer or other electronic reading devices when downloading a book from a library would be covered by the exception in Art. 5(1) of the InfoSoc Directive.[341]

3.1.3. DIGITAL REPRODUCTION AND LIBRARIES

71. Digital libraries need to make digital copies, which constitutes reproduction. Digitizing analogue works is reproduction whether it is for preservation purposes, for e-lending purposes or for making works available online for viewing or downloading. Preservation of digitally born material also requires reproduction. Furthermore, best practices in digital preservation can require access which would fall under the making available right.[342] Making works available online involves making copies, whether temporary or permanent, as mentioned above. Hence, it is important to clarify who is responsible for the reproductions that occur in the process of making available.

72. The copying involved in the process of making works available can be distinguished as "upstream" or "downstream" reproduction. The "upstream" reproduction involves the copies "kept on the hosting server from which the work is available for transmission at the individual demand of the users." These are usually either permanent copies or temporary copies not exempt under the limitation in Art. 5(1) of the InfoSoc Directive. The "downstream" reproduction involves the copies that are at the point of the end-user who has requested the transmission. Such copies can either be permanent, i.e. files that the end-user downloads and keeps, or a copy of a work that has been sent to an end-user with an e-mail, as is common practice for libraries in many countries, or temporary such as on-screen copies and cache copies created by the viewing of websites. Permanent "downstream" copies will require the rightholder's authorisation, unless they fall under an exception in national legislation, whereas the situation with temporary copies is less clear. They may or may not fall under the exemption in Art. 5(1) of the InfoSoc Directive.[343]

---

340 C-302/10 – Infopaq II, par. 47–54.
341 C-174/15 – VOB, AG opinion, par. 58.
342 Congress and others, International Study on the Impact of Copyright Law on Digital Preservation, 2008, 6.
343 Triaille and others, Study, 2013, 119.

73. In the PRCA case the CJEU clarified that on-screen copies and cache copies created by the viewing of websites fall under the limitation in Art. 5(1) of the InfoSoc Directive. The Court pointed out that

> ...the viewing of websites by means of the technological process at issue represents a normal exploitation of the works which makes it possible for internet users to avail themselves of the communication to the public made by the publisher of the website concerned.

and concluded that

> ...the on-screen copies and the cached copies made by an end-user in the course of viewing a website satisfy the conditions that those copies must be temporary, that they must be transient or incidental in nature and that they must constitute an integral and essential part of a technological process

Hence no licence was required from the end-users for the viewing of the website in this case.[344]

If this approach is applied to online use by libraries it can be concluded that if libraries use in-copyright works online under either a licence or under an exception, i.e. legally, they are not liable for reproduction that occurs when those works are viewed online, as it falls under the exception in Art. 5(1) of the InfoSoc Directive. Neither are the viewers liable for the same reason, as long as their use is limited to viewing.

For other reproductions that either happen in or around the making available process, i.e. copies down-loaded by end-users or copies made in order to make works available the question of who is liable can vary under different national legislations in Europe.[345] Digital copies of in-copyright works from the collections of libraries, made by libraries themselves or at their request, will presumably be under the liability of the libraries. Thus they need to acquire authorisation for such reproduction unless there is an applicable exception, as was found to be the case in the TU Darmstadt case.[346]

74. As can be seen from this account it can be hard to distinguish between the exclusive right of reproduction and the exclusive right of making available under the communication to the public right. In the next sub-chapter I will, nevertheless, attempt to describe and analyse the communication to the public right with regard to how the making available right affects online uses of in-copyright works by libraries, separately from the reproduction right.

---

[344] C-360/13 – PRCA par. 61–63.

[345] Triaille and others, Study, 2013, 119.

[346] See C-117/13 – TU Darmstadt, par. 17, 49. See further discussion in Ch. 4.2.2.2.

3.2. THE RIGHT OF COMMUNICATION TO THE PUBLIC AND THE MAKING AVAILABLE RIGHT

75. The author's right to communicate his or her work to the public has traditionally included a wide spectrum of acts, ranging from giving performances of the work in the presence of the public to the transmission by wire or wireless of the works to the public not present at the performance. However, in many instances, both in national and international legislation, there exist distinct provisions regarding different forms of communication.[347] Thus the Berne Convention sets out provisions, sometimes confusing and contradictory, on different forms of communication[348], i.e. public performance, broadcasting, transmission by wire to the public, satellite broadcasting, retransmission by cable etc. which do not, however, cover all forms of communication to the public.[349] Even more importantly, the Convention does not afford the same scope of rights to all works; musical and dramatic works are afforded the broadest protection and images the narrowest, while literary works receive a level of protection somewhere in-between.[350] Furthermore, the Convention differentiates between communication with regard to whether the public is present at the performance (public performance) or not, whereas in the legislation of many European countries public performance falls under a general right of communication to the public.[351] Thus there was no "general" right of communication to the public at international level.[352]

76. The advent of the digital environment created several challenges for copyright and related rights. Consensus soon emerged that the act of making protected works available on the internet should require the rightholder's consent but there was disagreement on under which of the exclusive rights the activity should fall. Some, notably the USA, argued that digital transmission was a form of distribution when it resulted in copies being made and that, if no copies were made, it was public performance, and thus should be classified accordingly,

347 Sterling, World Copyright Law, 2003, 372–374; Ohly, Economic rights, 2009, 224–225; von Lewinski and Walter, Information Society Directive, 2010, 976–977; ALAI, *Report and Opinion on the making available and communication to the public in the internet environment – focus on linking techniques on the Internet*, 4–5; Hugenholtz and others, Recasting, 2006, 44.

348 Ginsburg and Treppoz, International, 2015, 314.

349 Cf. Art. 11, 11*bis*, 11*ter* and 14 Berne Convention.

350 Sterling, World Copyright Law, 2003, 620; Jane Ginsburg, 'The (New?) Right of Making Available to the Public', 2004, Columbia Law and Economics Working Paper No 481, 2; von Lewinski and Walter, Information Society Directive, 2010, 976–977; Ginsburg and Treppoz, International, 2015, 314.

351 Ohly, Economic rights, 2009, 224–225; von Lewinski and Walter, Information Society Directive, 2010, 976–977; ALAI, Report, 2013, 4–5.

352 Hugenholtz and others, Recasting, 2006, 44; Guibault and others, InfoSoc Study, Part I, 2007, 25.

whereas others preferred the activity to be included under the communication to the public right.[353]

Within WIPO it was decided in 1996 to include digital transmissions under the exclusive right of communication to the public as a new specific right, the making available right.[354] Additionally, the WCT provides for a general right of communication to the public which covers all types of communications, except for public performance, and for all types of works that are covered by copyright but not for related rights.[355] This is progress from the piecemeal approach in the Berne Convention. The InfoSoc Directive transposed Art. 8 of the WCT into EU law, and thus also provides for a general right of communication to the public of protected works for authors (but not for related rightholders) for all transmissions or retransmissions by wire or wireless means, excluding public performance.[356]

77. The specific right of making works available to the public "in such a way that members of the public may access these works from a place and at a time individually chosen by them"[357] is designed to make clear that on-demand online services are communications to the public.[358] That was not clear before the adoption of the WIPO Internet Treaties. Neither the Berne Convention nor national legislations were clear with regard to whether the "public" was limited to persons receiving the communication at the same time.[359] Hence it was important to clarify that the making available right covers the situation where in-copyright works are offered to the public at large, i.e. the stage preceding the one-to-one transmission that can result from making works available, as is the case when works are posted online on the web.[360]

This was done by underlining that the right of communication to the public included acts of making available to the public from a place and at a time individually chosen by the members of the public which otherwise might have been considered private use, like telephone communications. Accordingly

---

353 Von Lewinski and Walter, Information Society Directive, 2010, 974–975. See also Ohly, Economic rights, 2009, 225; M. Schlesinger, 'Legal issues in peer-to-peer file sharing, focusing on the making available right' in Alain Strowel (ed), *Peer-to-peer file sharing and secondary liability in copyright law* (Edward Elgar, 2009) 47; Reinbothe and Von Lewinski, The WIPO Treaties, 2015, 135.

354 Ginsburg and Treppoz, International, 2015, 314; von Lewinski and Walter, Information Society Directive, 2010, 978; Guibault and others, InfoSoc Study, Part I, 2007, 25.

355 Art. 8 WCT; von Lewinski and Walter, Information Society Directive, 2010, 975–979; ALAI, Report, 2013, 2–3; Ginsburg and Treppoz, International, 2015, 314.

356 Recital (23) InfoSoc Directive; Ohly, Economic rights, 2009, 224–225; von Lewinski and Walter, Information Society Directive, 2010, 980–981; ALAI, Report, 2013, 3, 5; Geiger and others, InfoSoc, 2014, 407; Guibault and others, InfoSoc Study, Part I, 2007, 25.

357 Art. 8 WCT.

358 COM(97)628 final, InfoSoc Proposal, 1997, 25; Guibault and others, InfoSoc Study, Part I, 2007, 25.

359 Ginsburg and Treppoz, International, 2015, 314–315; von Lewinski and Walter, Information Society Directive, 2010, 973–974; Goldstein and Hugenholtz, 3rd ed., 2013, 335.

360 Triaille and others, Study, 2013, 32; Guibault and others, InfoSoc Study, Part I, 2007, 25–26.

the making available right "neither requires a simultaneous addressing of the public nor that the public is gathered at a place, or that a pre-established 'programme' is provided."[361] This is also reflected in the wording of Art. 3(1) and (2) of the InfoSoc Directive and reiterated in Recital (25). Hence it is clear that the communication to the public right, in particular the making available right, is the fundamental exclusive right in any online use for libraries and other users.

78. The making available right has a broad scope. It is not limited to any specific sector of works or use.[362] The term 'making available' is supposed to be technologically neutral in the sense that it applies regardless of how a work is uploaded to a network or how an end-user accesses it. It covers both making material available to the public to view, i.e. by viewing from an open website on screen, and to access by downloading. However, the work must be available for the user to access by a time individually chosen by him or her, i.e. when the user demands, and not by the sender or uploader. In the latter case, such as in broadcasting, simulcasting and webcasting, it is the general communication to the public right that applies rather than the making available right.[363]

As things stand, it is not clear which exclusive rights the making available right covers and which not.[364] However, it is important that the making available right is interpreted in a manner compatible with the characteristics of the right of communication to the public[365] as well as the reproduction right.[366] Yet, neither of these exclusive rights is clearly defined in the digital age. As discussed above the scope of the reproduction right has been blurred with the advent of the making available right. Similarly, the scope of the communication to the public right has been difficult to define, especially with regard to what constitutes the public and where the communication takes place in case of transmission to a public not present at the performance. The advent of the internet did not simplify matters. No clear definition exists of the communication to the public right in international treaties; in particular, they are silent on where the relevant acts in internet transmissions take place.[367]

361 Von Lewinski and Walter, Information Society Directive, 2010, 978, 983.

362 Triaille and others, Study, 2013, 26.

363 C-279/13 *C More Entertainment AB v Linus Sandberg*, CJEU, 26 March 2015 par. 25–28; C-135/10 *SCF Consorzio Fonografici v Marco Del Corso* ECLI:EU:C:2012:140, 15 March 2012 par. 59–60; Geiger and others, InfoSoc, 2014, 412–413; von Lewinski and Walter, Information Society Directive, 2010, 983; Triaille and others, Study, 2013, 27, 44, 110; Stefan Bechtold, 'Directive 2001/29/EC – Information Society Directive' in Thomas Dreier and P. Berndt Hugenholtz (eds), *Concise European Copyright Law* (2 edn, Wolters Kluwer, 2016) 444.

364 Triaille and others, Study, 2013, 21, 25, 44, 109; Public Consultation on the review of the EU copyright rules (2013), 10–11.

365 Geiger and others, InfoSoc, 2014, 411.

366 Triaille and others, Study, 2013, 124.

367 Sterling, World Copyright Law, 2003, 136, 372; Triaille and others, Preliminary studies, 2015, 148.

3.2.1. COMMUNICATION TO THE PUBLIC IN THE EU

79. Rightholders are granted the exclusive right to "any" communication to the public in Art. 3(1) of the InfoSoc Directive. Recital (23) highlights that the communication to the public right should cover any transmission or retransmission of a work to the public not present at the place where the communication originates, by wire or wireless means, including broadcasting. Art. 3(3) of the InfoSoc Directive, furthermore, states that this exclusive right shall not be exhausted by any act of communication to the public.[368]

The InfoSoc Directive does not further define the term communication to the public[369], nor the making available right[370] despite intentions of the Commission to the contrary.[371] Before the inclusion of the right in the Directive it was left to national courts to interpret the content of the right. The InfoSoc provision has in fact harmonised the application of the right within Europe as the CJEU has on several occasions interpreted the content of the right.[372] Nevertheless, the growing number of referrals of specific instances in recent years has resulted in complicated and difficult to navigate case-law, which has cast doubt as to whether the Court's attempts have actually clarified the content of the right.[373]

80. The Court has underlined that the communication to the public right should be interpreted broadly as set out in the InfoSoc Directive[374], yet in a balanced way, taking into account the various facts and circumstances of the cases.[375] Thus the Court established that Member States cannot give rightholders wider protection "by laying down that the concept of communication to the

368 C-607/11 *ITV Broadcasting Ltd and Others v TVCatchup Ltd.* ECLI:EU:C:2013:147, CJEU, 7 March 2013 par. 23; Bechtold, Directive 2001/29/EC, 2016, 445.

369 C-306/05 *Sociedad General de Autores y Editores de España (SGAE) v Rafael Hoteles SA.* ECR 2006 Page I-11519, 7 December 2006 par. 33; Joined cases C-403/08 and C-429/08 – Premier League, par. 184; C-607/11 – ITV Broadcasting and Others, par. 22.

370 Triaille and others, Study, 2013, 176; Triaille and others, Preliminary studies, 2015, 148; Bechtold, Directive 2001/29/EC, 2016, 441–444.

371 COM(95) 382 final, Green Paper, 1995, 54. The Commission is currently examining whether a definition is needed, cf. COM(2015) 626 final, Towards, 2015, 9–10.

372 Ohly, Economic rights, 2009, 227.

373 Patricia Mariscal, The Ten Commandments of Communication to the Public: A Brief Review of CJEU Case-law, Kluwer Copyright Blog, 29 May 2017; Stavroula Karapapa, 'The requirement for a "new public" in EU copyright law', 2017, (1), European Law Review, 63–81; Eleonora Rosati, 'GS Media and Its Implications for the Construction of the Right of Communication to the Public within EU Copyright Architecture', 2017, (4), Common Market Law Review, 1221–1242.

374 Recital (23) InfoSoc Directive; C-301/15 – Soulier, par. 30–31; C-306/05, SGAE, par. 36; Joined cases C-403/08 and C-429/08 – Premier League, par. 186; C-117/15 *Reha Training Gesellschaft für Sport- und Unfallrehabilitation mbH v Gesellschaft für musikalische Aufführungs- und mechanische Vervielfältigungsrechte (GEMA)* ECLI:EU:C:2016:379, CJEU, 31 May 2016 par. 36; Bechtold, Directive 2001/29/EC, 2016, 442.

375 Marcella Favale, Martin Kretschmer and Paul Torremans, 'Is there a EU copyright jurisprudence? An empirical analysis of the workings of the European Court of Justice ', 2016, (1), Modern Law Review, 31–75, 59–60.

public includes a wider range of activities" than those referred to in Art. 3(1) of the InfoSoc Directive, claiming that another conclusion would create legal uncertainty and adversely affect the internal market.[376]

Furthermore, the Court has emphasised that Community law and its concepts must be given an autonomous and uniform interpretation throughout the Community[377] unless there exists a "different intention expressed by the European Union legislature in the specific context" of a given directive.[378] Moreover, the Court has also stated that EU legislation must be interpreted as far as possible in line with international laws. This is especially relevant with regard to provisions intended to implement international agreements to which the EU is party.[379] As the origin of the making available right lies in the WIPO Internet Treaties[380] the preparatory documents for these WIPO treaties can be used for determining the content of the right in the InfoSoc Directive.[381] The fact that it was the EU and its Member States that made the proposal for the provision on the communication to the public that became the adopted Art. 8 of the WCT makes this even more pertinent.[382]

---

376 C-466/12 *Nils Svensson, Sten Sjögren, Madelaine Sahlman, Pia Gadd v Retriever Sverige AB* ECLI:EU:C:2014:76, CJEU, 13 February 2014 par. 33–41; Bechtold, Directive 2001/29/EC, 2016, 444–445. See also discussion on the issue, prior to the Svensson case in European Copyright Society, *Opinion on the Reference to the CJEU in Case C-466/12 Svensson*, (27 January 2015) 15–16. Member States can provide more protection to related rightsholders than afforded under Art. 3(2) InfoSoc Directive as the Directive did not harmonise the related rights referred to there "provided such an extension does not undermine the protection of copyright." cf. C-279/13, C More Entertainment, par. 28–37; Bechtold, Directive 2001/29/EC, 2016, 445.

377 C-245/00 *Stichting ter Exploitatie van Naburige Rechten (SENA) v Nederlandse Omroep Stichting (NOS)* ECLI:EU:C:2003:68, CJEU, 6 February 2003 par. 23; C-306/05, SGAE, par. 31; C-5/08 – Infopaq I, par. 27; Joined cases C-403/08 and C-429/08 – Premier League, par. 188; C-510/10 *DR and TV2 Danmark A/S v NCB – Nordisk Copyright Bureau* ECLI:EU:C:2012:244, CJEU, 26 April 2012 par. 33–35; C-5/11 *Criminal proceedings against Titus Alexander Jochen Donner* ECLI:EU:C:2012:370, CJEU, 21 June 2012 par. 25; C-173/11 *Football Dataco Ltd, The Scottish Premier League Ltd, The Scottish Football League, PA Sport UK Ltd v Sportradar GmbH and Sportradar AG* ECLI:EU:C:2012:642, CJEU, 18 October 2012 par. 33; C-201/13 – Deckmyn and Vrijheidsfonds, par. 14; C-117/15 Reha Training, par. 28–34. See also discussion in Geiger and others, InfoSoc, 2014, 454–456.

378 C-128/11, *UsedSoft GmbH v Oracle International Corp.* ECLI:EU:C:2012:407, CJEU, 3 July 2012 par. 60.

379 C-306/05, SGAE, par. 35; C-456/06 *Peek & Cloppenburg KG v Cassina SpA* ECLI:EU:C:2008:232, 17 April 2008 par. 30; Joined cases C-403/08 and C-429/08 – Premier League, par. 189; C-135/10, SCF, par. 51–55; C-5/11, Donner, par. 23; C-419/13 *Art & Allposters International BV v Stichting Pictoright* ECLI:EU:C:2015:27, CJEU, 22 January 2015 par. 38; Bechtold, Directive 2001/29/EC, 2016, 441; Ana Ramalho, 'Conceptualising the European Union's Competence in Copyright – What Can the EU Do?', 2014, (2), IIC, 178–200, 186.

380 Recital (15) InfoSoc Directive; Triaille and others, Study, 2013, 26, 44; COM(97)628 final, InfoSoc Proposal, 1997, 25; C-135/10, SCF, par. 72; Ginsburg and Treppoz, International, 2015, 314.

381 European Copyright Society, Opinion on C-466/12, 2013, 4–5; Triaille and others, Study, 2013, 26.

382 WIPO CRNR/DC/4, *Basic Proposal for the Substantive Provisions of the Treaty on Certain Questions Concerning the Protection of Literary and Artistic Works to be Considered by the*

81. In its deliberation on the communication to the public right the CJEU has come to the conclusion that the exclusive right of communication to the public consists of "two cumulative criteria", firstly, the act of communication of a work and, secondly, the communication of that work to the public.[383] I will look at these elements as far as they are pertinent to digital libraries, in particular with regard to the localisation of the communication to the public right, as that may affect the issue of cross-border licensing relevant for libraries.

3.2.2. THE ACT OF COMMUNICATION

82. The CJEU has underlined that the "act of communication" should be interpreted broadly[384] to achieve a high level of protection as set out in Recitals (4) and (9) of the InfoSoc Directive.[385] The Court has noted that the term is not defined exhaustively in the Directive and thus must be interpreted "in the light of the context in which it occurs and also in the light of the objective" of the Directive as stated above.[386]

3.2.2.1. Communication versus transmission

83. In the preparatory documents for the WCT treaty it is stated that "communication always involves transmission" and hence the term "transmission" could have been used instead in the proposal for the provision on the exclusive right of communication to the public. However, in order to cover the different terminology in national legislation it was decided to keep the word "communication". That term, the preparatory document explains, has a slightly broader denotation as it refers to the fact that a work is communicated, in addition to the technical transfer that the term "transmission" involves.[387]

84. The CJEU has held that an "act of communication" refers to any transmission of a protected work, irrespective of the technical means or process used and must as a rule be authorised by the author.[388] So it was assumed that

Diplomatic Conference, (August 30, 1996) 42, 44, notes 10.07 and 10.08.

383 C-607/11 – ITV Broadcasting and Others, par. 21 and 31; C-466/12 – Svensson, par. 16; C-325/14 *SBS Belgium NV v Belgische Vereniging van Auteurs, Componisten en Uitgevers (SABAM)* ECLI:EU:C:2015:764, CJEU, 19 November 2015 par. 15; C-117/15 Reha Training, par. 37.

384 See to that effect Joined cases C-403/08 and C-429/08 – Premier League, par. 193; C-325/14 – SBS Belgium, par. 14.

385 C-466/12 – Svensson, par. 17.

386 C-607/11 – ITV Broadcasting and Others, par. 21.

387 WIPO CRNR/DC/4, Basic Proposal, 1996, 5.

388 C-325/14 – SBS Belgium, par. 16–17; Joined cases C-403/08 and C-429/08 – Premier League, par. 193; C-607/11 – ITV Broadcasting and Others, par. 24; C-117/15 Reha Training, par. 38–39.

some sort of transmission was necessary in order for "communication to the public" to take place.[389] Nevertheless, the CJEU came to the conclusion that the making available right does not have to include transmission, only the possibility of transmission. Thus in the Svensson case the CJEU stated that "it is sufficient ...that a work is made available to a public in such a way that the persons forming the public may access it, irrespective of whether they avail themselves of that opportunity" and hence "the provision of clickable links to protected works must be considered to be 'making available' and, therefore, an 'act of communication'".[390]

85. Hence it is clear that the starting point for the act of making available is the stage before transmission. It is the act of making available that is protected not the act of receiving, at least not in private.[391] It is irrelevant whether the work made available is in fact looked at or downloaded by anyone. The fact that it has been made available, making it possible for the public to consult it or download it, suffices.[392] However, it has to be possible for the public in practice to access the works, i.e. the public has to have some means of knowing where the works are accessible.[393] Thus it is clear that if a library uploads works from its collection onto its website so that the public can view it, it falls under the communication to the public right, regardless of whether anyone views the works or not. It is assumed that the act of uploading by a library to its website would normally happen in the country where the library was situated.

In this connection it is interesting to reflect on the fact that the USA, although a member of the WCT and the WPPT, has not implemented a specific "making available right". The making of work available through an electronic network for downloading is considered to fall under the distribution right.[394] Questions have been raised as to whether the distribution right will also cover the act of making the work available without proof of an actual receipt of the works.[395]

---

389 Geiger and others, InfoSoc, 2014, 408.

390 C-466/12 – Svensson, par. 19–20. It is noteworthy that the Court does not mention transmission in its definition, cf. Guibault and Quintais, Copyright, 2014, 16.

391 Joined cases C-403/08 and C-429/08 – Premier League, par. 171. In the case the viewing was in fact not in private but in a public space, i.e. a pub, but the Court did not deliberate on that issue.

392 Triaille and others, Study, 2013, 32–33, 39; WIPO CRNR/DC/4, Basic Proposal, 1996, 44; von Lewinski and Walter, Information Society Directive, 2010, 983; Dreier and Hugenholtz (eds) Concise, 2006, 361; Geiger and others, InfoSoc, 2014, 411–412 C-466/12 – Svensson, par. 19; C-117/13 – TU Darmstadt, par. 41; Bechtold, Directive 2001/29/EC, 2016, 442, 444.

393 Triaille and others, Study, 2013, 35, 44.

394 Besek, Digital libraries, 2010, 190.

395 Robert A. Gorman, Jane C. Ginsburg and R. Anthony Reese, *Copyright; Cases and Materials* (8 edn, Foundation Press, 2011), 706–715. See also discussion on the subject in Reinbothe and Von Lewinski, The WIPO Treaties, 2015, 135.

86. The "mere provision of physical facilities for enabling or making a communication" is not enough to infringe the making available right.[396] This would not apply to libraries making their collections available online with cross-border effect, which clearly entails more than the mere provision of physical facilities. The role of the user, such as a library that gives online access to works in full knowledge of the consequences of its action, in the communication to the public right is indispensable as otherwise the end-user would not have access.[397]

87. Another issue which may affect whether a communication is deemed to fall under the exclusive right of communication to the public or not is the profit-making nature of the communication. The CJEU has discussed this in several cases.[398] The discussion revolves around whether certain rebroadcasting, retransmission and hyperlinks are considered communication to the public or not. This research, on the other hand, looks at how libraries can upload works legally on the web. The act of uploading works onto the internet falls without doubt under the act of communication. The fact that public libraries are generally non-profit institutions does not change that. However, as discussed later, the profit-making nature of the communication to the public is relevant as it has a bearing on the remuneration due for such use.[399] I will next discuss where the end-point of the act of communication lies, as that may affect the requirements for cross-border use under licensing.

---

396 Recital (27) InfoSoc Directiv; C-306/05, SGAE, par. 45–47; Joined cases C-431/09 and C-432/09 *Airfield NV and Canal Digitaal BV v Belgische Vereniging van Auteurs, Componisten en Uitgevers CVBA (Sabam) (C-431/09) and Airfield NV v Agicoa Belgium BVBA (C-432/09)* ECLI:EU:C:2011:648, 13 October 2011 par. 74; See also WIPO CRNR/DC/4, Basic Proposal, 1996, 44, note 10.10; von Lewinski and Walter, Information Society Directive, 2010, 979; Geiger and others, InfoSoc, 2014, 409–410; Bechtold, Directive 2001/29/EC, 2016, 442.

397 C-162/10 *Phonographic Performance (Ireland) Limited v Ireland and Attorney General* ECLI:EU:C:2012:141, CJEU, 15 March 2012 par. 33; C-135/10, SCF, par. 82; C-117/15 Reha Training, par. 46; C-160/15 *GS Media BV v Sanoma Media Netherlands BV, Playboy Enterprises International Inc., Britt Geertruida Dekker* ECLI:EU:C:2016:644, CJEU, 8 September 2016 par. 35; C-527/15 *Stichting Brein v Jack Frederik Wullems* ECLI:EU:C:2017:300, CJEU, 26 April 2017 par. 31; C-610/15 *Stichting Brein v Ziggo BV and XS4All Internet BV* ECLI:EU:C:2017:456, CJEU, 14 June 2017 par. 26.

398 C-306/05, SGAE, par. 44; Joined cases C-403/08 and C-429/08 – Premier League, par. 204; Joined cases C-403/08 and C-429/08 *Opinion of Advocate General Kokott in: Football Association Premier League Ltd and Others v QC Leisure and Others; Karen Murphy v Media Protection Services Ltd* ECLI:EU:C:2011:43, 3 February 2011 par. 118–119; Joined cases C-431/09 and C-432/09 – Airfield and Canal Digitaal, par. 80, 82–83; C-135/10, SCF, 90–91, 97–100; C-162/10, Phonographic Performance, par. 42; C-607/11 – ITV Broadcasting and Others, par. 44; C-117/15 Reha Training, par. 49–52, 63–64; C-160/15 – GS Media, par. 51.

399 C-117/15 Reha Training, par. 49 and discussion in Ch. 10.3.2.

3.2.2.2. *The end-point of communication*

88. It is unclear where the communication to the public right ends, i.e. whether it extends to the following transmission and/or the reception of the transmission by a person.[400] Art. 3 of the InfoSoc Directive leaves the issue open. There is no scholarly agreement on the issue[401] nor has the question been assessed by national courts or directly by the CJEU. Some argue that the transmission is not covered by the making available right[402] whereas others state the upload, the entire transmission and eventual download is entailed in the right.[403]

89. The CJEU has indirectly dealt with the question of the endpoint of the communication right through its deliberations on what acts fall under the concept "re-utilisation" of the *sui generis* data base protection in the Football Dataco II case. Re-utilisation is defined in Art. 7 (2) (b) of the Database Directive where it is provided that

> 're-utilization' shall mean any form of making available to the public all or a substantial part of the contents of a database by the distribution of copies, by renting, by on-line or other forms of transmission.

The questions referred to the court in the case were, firstly, whether the sending of data from a webserver in Member State A to a user, at his or her request, in Member State B constituted "extraction" or "re-utilisation" by that party and, secondly, where such an act occurred.[404] The Advocate General asserted that the act of sending in "the situation under consideration" was clearly "an act forming a necessary constituent part of a process of making available to the public".[405]

The Court came to the conclusion that the sending was in fact re-utilisation in the meaning of the Database Directive and that it was the person sending that made the relevant data available to the public. However, that in itself was not enough to conclude that the act of re-utilisation by the sender had taken place in the receiving country.[406] In order to establish this it had to be shown that the

400 Triaille and others, Study, 2013, 37–39, 44–45; European Commission, Report on the responses, 2014, 10.

401 Triaille and others, Study, 2013, 37; Ohly, Economic rights, 2009, 225; Geiger and others, InfoSoc, 2014, 412–413.

402 Von Lewinski and Walter, Information Society Directive, 2010, 983; Triaille and others, Study, 2013, 37.

403 Peukert, Territoriality, 2011, 17, cited page-numbers refer to the version available at <http://papers.ssrn.com/sol3/papers.cfm?abstract_id=1592263>, last viewed 23 January 2017; Reinbothe and Von Lewinski, The WIPO Treaties, 2015, 136–138.

404 C-173/11, Football Dataco II, par. 17.

405 *Opinion of Advocate General Cruz Villalón on Case C-173/11, Football Dataco Ltd, The Scottish Premier League Ltd, The Scottish Football League, PA Sport UK Ltd v Sportradar GmbH and Sportradar AG* ECLI:EU:C:2012:377, CJEU, 21 June 2012 par. 41.

406 C-173/11, Football Dataco II, par. 20–21, 38, 47.

sender had intentionally targeted the public in the receiving country.[407] If such intentional targeting were established the infringing act would be deemed to have taken place "at least" in the country where the sending was received. Any other conclusion would diminish the effect of protection of the right within the receiving country.[408] The fact that the act was deemed to take place in "at least" the Member State where the public was targeted consequently made it unnecessary to define the endpoint of the act of re-utilisation.[409]

90. This definition of the localisation of the re-utilisation right could be seen to be applicable to the localisation of the making available right, as the definition of concepts under EU legal acts must be given an interpretation independent of the legislation applicable to the particular incident, as mentioned above.[410] This would mean that in cases where it was manifest that a website was targeted at an audience in a different Member State, the act of making available would be deemed to have taken place there. The CJEU has since rejected the targeting approach with regard to jurisdiction in copyright infringement cases and established that, within the EU, national courts can have jurisdiction with regard to in-copyright work that has been made available online on a website, in every country where it can be accessed or received.[411] From the point of view of libraries wishing to make works from their collections available online with cross-border effect, the targeting approach could be relevant in cases where there are only works in a specific language. However, if the online use had the objective of participating in a European effort to make European culture more easily available, regardless of national origin of works, the targeting approach would have little relevance, as all European countries would be "targeted".

91. Next I will look at the second constituent of the exclusive right of communication to the public, namely the public.

3.2.3. THE PUBLIC

92. Placing the making available right under the communication to the public signifies that the making available right is only applicable when it is aimed at

---

407 Ibid, par. 39; See also C-324/09 *L'Oréal SA and Others v eBay International AG and Others* ECLI:EU:C:2011:474, CJEU, 12 July 2011 par. 65; Joined Cases C-585/08 and C-144/09 *Peter Pammer v Reederei Karl Schlüter GmbH & Co KG (C-585/08), and Hotel Alpenhof GesmbH v Oliver Heller (C-144/09)* ECLI:EU:C:2010:740, 7 December 2010 par. 75; C-5/11, Donner, par. 27–28.

408 C-173/11, Football Dataco II, par. 45–47.

409 Triaille and others, Study, 2013, 39.

410 See e.g. discussion in Ch. 3.2.1.

411 C-170/12 *Peter Pinckney v KDG Mediatech AG* ECLI:EU:C:2013:635, CJEU, 3 October 2013 par. 39–44; C-441/13 *Pez Hejduk v EnergieAgentur.NRW GmbH.* ECLI:EU:C:2015:28, CJEU, 22 January 2015 par. 22–34. See also Ch. 8.2.2.1 and 8.3.1.

the public.[412] The "public" is not defined in any of the international treaties or the InfoSoc Directive.[413] In fact it is stated in the preparatory documents for the Directive that it is "a matter for the national law to define "public"."[414] However, the CJEU has since ruled that "for the uniform application for Community law and the principle of equality" provisions of Community law must "normally be given an autonomous and uniform interpretation throughout the Community". Thus, the court concluded, it cannot be reasonably maintained that it is for the Member States to establish the definition of "public".[415]

93. The CJEU has defined the term "public" as an indeterminate number of potential listeners or viewers.[416] This indicates "a fairly large" group of people[417] which in turn implies a certain *de minimis* threshold, excluding from the definition small or insignificant groups that have access.[418]

In the SCF case the CJEU explained the term "indeterminate" by referring to a WIPO Glossary definition of communication to the public: "making a work ... perceptible in any appropriate manner to persons in general, that is, not restricted to specific individuals belonging to a private group."[419] The Court concluded that patients of a dentist did not constitute "persons in general" and that conclusion led cumulatively to the decision that the broadcasting by the dentist of phonograms in his dental practice was not communication to the public.[420] The Court did not state which WIPO glossary it referred to. The claim has been made that the Court used an outdated version[421] and it has been suggested that, had it used a newer version[422] the outcome might have been different.[423] It might, however, be that the court deliberately chose the narrower

412 Triaille and others, Study, 2013, 39.

413 Bechtold, Directive 2001/29/EC, 2016, 442.

414 COM(97)628 final, InfoSoc Proposal, 1997, 25.

415 C-306/05, SGAE, par. 31. See also Geiger and others, InfoSoc, 2014, 416.

416 C-89/04 *Mediakabel BV v Commissariaat voor de Media* ECLI:EU:C:2005:348, CJEU, 2 June 2005 par. 30; C-192/04 *Lagardère Active Broadcast v. SPRE & GVL* ECR 2007 p I-07199, CJEU, 14 July 2005 par. 31; C-306/05, SGAE, par. 36; C-466/12 – Svensson, par. 21; C-607/11 – ITV Broadcasting and Others, par. 32; C-117/15 Reha Training, par. 41.

417 C-135/10, SCF, par. 84; C-306/05, SGAE, par. 38; C-466/12 – Svensson, par. 21; C-607/11 – ITV Broadcasting and Others, par. 32; C-325/14 – SBS Belgium, par. 22; C-117/15 Reha Training, par. 41; Guibault and Quintais, Copyright, 2014, 10.

418 C-135/10, SCF, 86; C-162/10, Phonographic Performance, par. 35; C-117/15 Reha Training, par. 43.

419 C-135/10, SCF, par. 85; C-117/15 Reha Training, 42.

420 C-135/10, SCF, par. 85–102.

421 Cf. WIPO, *WIPO Glossary of Terms of the Law of Copyright and Neighboring Rights* (WIPO, 1980), 42.

422 Cf. Mihály Ficsor, *Guide to the copyright and related rights treaties administered by WIPO and glossary of copyright and related rights terms* (WIPO, 2003), 306.

423 Mihály Ficsor, Svensson: honest attempt at establishing due balance concerning the use of hyperlinks – spoiled by the erroneous "new public" theory, Copyright See-Saw, 5 May 2014; 2 July 2017.

definition on this occasion, in which case an explanation would have been helpful.

In the SBS Belgium case the CJEU came to the conclusion that the transmission by a broadcasting organisation by a "direct inject" method was not communication to the public as the transmission of signals was to specified individual distributors, without potential viewers being able to access them.[424] This interpretation by the Court in these two cases, the SCF and the SBS Belgium case, seems at odds with the usual practices in Member States.[425]

94. In order to determine the number of potential listeners or viewers, account must be taken of the cumulative number, that is, simultaneously and in succession.[426] It is irrelevant whether the communication to the public takes place in a private or public place.[427] However, the term "public" under Art. 3 of the InfoSoc Directive only applies with a regard to a public not present at the place where the communication originates.[428] Furthermore, the Court concluded in the SCF case that the public must be "both targeted by the user and receptive, in one way or another" with the communication in question.[429]

It may be deduced from the above account that the definition of the public "tends to shrink or expand depending on the nature of the right at stake" and that the CJEU has not yet alighted on the final definition of the term.[430] However, there is no doubt that libraries wishing to make in-copyright works from their collections available online would be making them available to the public, although one might raise the question whether making, for example, Icelandic books available online with cross-border effect would fulfil the criterion for being made available to the public in countries outside Iceland. Given the small size of Icelandic speakers outside of Iceland this might be a borderline case, whereas most other languages would presumably fulfil the criterion, at least under the cumulative approach. Thus the definition of the public is mainly interesting for the purpose of online use by libraries with regard to how it affects the issue of remuneration.[431]

---

424 C-325/14 – SBS Belgium, par. 22–23, 34. It has been pointed out that the "direct injection" technique replaces retransmission by cable for which authors had an un-waivable right of remuneration. Thus authors seem to get short changed with the technological change in this respect, cf. Guibault and Quintais, Copyright, 2014, 22.

425 Geiger and others, InfoSoc, 2014, 416; Jan Bernd Nordemann, Communication to the public in copyright law – the German struggle with the CJEU concept, Kluwer Copyright Blog, 28 April 2016; accessed 23 January 2017.

426 C-135/10, SCF, 87; C-306/05, SGAE, par. 39; C-607/11 – ITV Broadcasting and Others, par. 33; C-162/10, Phonographic Performance, par. 35.

427 C-306/05, SGAE, par. 50–51.

428 Recital (23) InfoSoc Directive; Joined cases C-403/08 and C-429/08 – Premier League, par. 200–203; Guibault and Quintais, Copyright, 2014, 10–11.

429 C-135/10, SCF, par. 91; Guibault and Quintais, Copyright, 2014, 11.

430 ALAI, Report, 2013, 7.

431 C-117/15 Reha Training, par. 49–51 and Ch. 10.3.2.

95. In this book I am mainly concerned with the question of how to enable libraries to put in-copyright works online with cross-border effect. Uploading such works and making them available clearly involves the communication to the public right. The communication to the public right will not be exhausted.[432] Thus, an interesting side question is whether linking to websites is communication to the public or not. This is in particular interesting for European institutions such as Europeana[433] but also for any national library that would like to facilitate legal access to the European cultural heritage for its customers.

3.2.4. HYPERLINKING AND COMMUNICATION TO THE PUBLIC

96. In order to discuss the issue of hyperlinking and the exclusive right of communication to the public within Europe it is necessary to identify what constitutes a new communication, and this in turn involves the controversial concepts "new public" and the sub-categories thereof, "specific technical means" and "restricted access".

3.2.4.1. "New public"

97. The term "new public" appeared for the first time in the SGAE case. In this case the CJEU found, citing a WIPO Guide[434] to the Berne Convention as an explanation, that a transmission of broadcast works using television sets in hotel rooms, if done by a different party than the original broadcaster, was a communication to a new public and "not just a technical means to ensure or improve reception of the original catchment area." Such a "new public" is distinct from the public targeted by the original broadcast; the "new public" would not be able to enjoy the broadcast without the intervention, even though they were physically within the catchment area of the original broadcast.[435]

---

432 Art. 3(3) InfoSoc Directive; C-607/11 – ITV Broadcasting and Others, par. 23; Bechtold, Directive 2001/29/EC, 2016, 445.

433 See brief discussion on Europeana in Ch. 2.4.1, par. 68.

434 It is not divulged which WIPO Guide to the Berne Convention the Court is citing but according to Ficsor, the author of the 2003 WIPO Guide, it is presumably the 1978 Guide, see WIPO, Guide to the Berne Convention, WIPO publication No. 615(E), 1978, 68–69, cf. Ficsor, Svensson, Copyright See-Saw; Mihály Ficsor, 'The Right of Communication (and Making Available) to the Public in the Light of the Case Law of the Court of Justice of the E.U.' in Irini Stamatoudi (ed), *Copyright and the Digital Agenda for Europe: Current Challenges for the Future* (Sakkoulas Publications, 2015) 100; ALAI, *Opinion on the on the criterion "New Public", developed by the Court of Justice of the European Union (CJEU), put in the context of making available and communication to the public*, (17 September 2014) 10, 16; Ginsburg and Treppoz, International, 2015, 344.

435 C-306/05, SGAE, par. 40–42; Joined cases C-403/08 and C-429/08 – Premier League, par. 194.

98. In the Premier League case the Court states that in order for there to be a "communication to the public" within the meaning of Art. 3(1) of the InfoSoc Directive in circumstances such as those of the main proceedings, "it is also necessary for the work broadcast to be transmitted to a new public".[436] This seems to be a stronger emphasis on the role of the "new public" than in the SGAE case, where the Court seemed to underline that execution of the communication to the public by a different entity than the original broadcaster was instrumental in making the communication to a "new public".[437] The Court has then used this approach in the Svensson case[438] and the Reha Training case.[439] Thus it seems that the "new public" has evolved from being "a consideration to a condition."[440]

99. The "new public" solution soon faced challenges in a subsequent case where the potential viewers or listeners were the same as those in the first (original) communication to the public. This the Court attempted to solve by the concept of "specific technical means".

3.2.4.1.1. "Specific technical means"

100. The term "specific technical means" was introduced in the ITV Broadcasting case, where the CJEU concluded that the EU legislator intended that each transmission or retransmission of a work which uses a "specific technical means" required individual authorisation by the author of the work in question.[441] Thus the transmission of works by the defendant in the case over the internet to the public, albeit an identical public as the original public, required authorisation by the rightholders because it was made under "specific technical conditions, using a different means of transmission". Therefore, the Court concluded, it was no longer necessary to examine whether or not there was a "new public".[442]

101. However, apparent loopholes remained in the approach of "new public" and "specific technical means" to when retransmissions constitute communication to the public in the area of internet transmissions. Next the CJEU had to determine whether a retransmission by the same technical means and to potentially the same public could be considered a communication to the

---

436 Joined cases C-403/08 and C-429/08 – Premier League, par. 195–199. In the Airfield case the CJEU came to the conclusion that authorisation is also required when an intervention in a communication makes the protected works accessible to a new public not taken into account when the rightholders authorised the original instigator of the communication, cf. Joined cases C-431/09 and C-432/09 – Airfield and Canal Digitaal, par. 72–73.

437 C-306/05, SGAE, par. 40, see also ALAI, "New Public", 2014, 11, where it is disputed that the fact that a communication is made by a different actor leads to a "new public".

438 C-466/12 – Svensson, par. 24.

439 C-117/15 Reha Training, par. 45–47, 60–62.

440 Ginsburg and Treppoz, International, 2015, 331.

441 C-607/11 – ITV Broadcasting and Others, par. 24–26.

442 Ibid, par. 39.

public. In the light of the foregoing development the answer was unsurprisingly in the negative except for situations where there was "restricted access".

3.2.4.1.2. "Restricted access"

102. The concept of "restricted access" as a condition for a re-transmission falling under the exclusive right of communication to the public was introduced by the CJEU in the Svensson case, where hyperlinking was at issue. The Court observed that under Art. 3(1) of the InfoSoc Directive it suffices that a work is made available to the public by providing access to it and concluded that, therefore, clickable links to protected works must be considered to be "making available" and an "act of communication" under that provision. Furthermore, the Court deduced that the list of clickable links on the website was aimed at all potential users of the website and hence an act of communication to the public. Nevertheless, as the communication was not to a new public and as the means for the communication were the same as the initial communication, the Court, citing "settled case-law", concluded that there was no need for authorisation by the rightholders for the latter communication.[443]

Thus, the Court came to the conclusion that placing clickable links to works freely available on another website was not an act of communication to the public in the meaning of Art. 3(1) of the InfoSoc Directive. On the other hand, if the clickable links led to a website where the access to the protected works was restricted and the clickable links made it possible to access such works, then these would be deemed to make the works available to a new public and would, consequently, fall under the exclusive right of communication to the public in Art. 3(1) of the InfoSoc Directive.[444] Given the factual circumstances that the articles on the newspaper website were normally only accessible for three weeks after being put there[445], it is not surprising that the Court specifically underlined that this is in particular the case "where the work is no longer available to the public on the site on which it was initially communicated or where it is henceforth available on that site only to a restricted public, while being accessible on another Internet site without the copyright holders' authorisation."[446]

103. The decision in the Svensson case has, it seems, laid to rest the discussion on whether hyperlinking falls under the communication right or not, an issue which has been discussed since the advent of the linking technique and

443 C-466/12 – Svensson, par. 19–28.

444 Ibid, par. 24–32.

445 Jan Rosén, What happened to Svensson and his friends after the CJEU decision?, The IPKat Weblog, 7 December 2014; 2 July 2017 (last access date).

446 C-466/12 – Svensson, par. 31.

which has led national European courts to different conclusions.[447] Unless the legislator intervenes, hyperlinking will be considered an act of making available to the public, though with no requirement for authorisation unless the hyperlink is deemed to be to the widely criticised notion[448], the "new public".[449]

3.2.4.1.3. Unauthorised content

104. However, the Svensson decision left some unanswered lacunas. One concerns the implications of the decision for works that are initially made "freely" available without the consent of the author or rightholder. This has since been discussed in the GS Media case, the Filmspeler case and the Ziggo case, the CJEU concluding that hyperlinks to unauthorised content are to be considered communication to the public if the person providing the hyperlink was aware of the unauthorised content and to a varying extent the profit making aspect of the activity.[450] This is a simplified summary of the conclusion of these cases but will have to suffice here, mainly as there is not a direct question of libraries making works available without authorisation. Libraries that make works available on the basis of an ECL agreement have a legal basis for using them. However, the question is whether it is a legally certain enough basis in other countries where the works would be available. This is relevant both with regard to the legal implications of the works being accessible in other countries and also for other institutions that link to the website.

3.3. CONCLUSION

105. In this chapter I have looked at which exclusive rights are entailed in making works available online in general. The account has highlighted that the interplay between the two applicable exclusive rights, i.e. the reproduction right and the communication to the public right, more exactly the making available

447 See e.g. Ohly, Economic rights, 2009, 228; von Lewinski and Walter, Information Society Directive, 2010, 970–971; European Copyright Society, Opinion on C-466/12, 2013, 9–11; ALAI, Report, 2013, 1, see further 8–10; Geiger and others, InfoSoc, 2014, 414.

448 ALAI, "New Public", 2014, 2, 13–16; Ficsor, The Right of Communication, 2015, 97 ff.; Guibault and Quintais, Copyright, 2014, 11–12; Jan Rosén, 'How Much Communication to the Publis is "Communication to the Public?"' in Irini A. Stamatoudi (ed), *New Developments in EU and International Copyright Law* (Wolters Kluwer, 2016); P. Berndt Hugenholtz and van Velze, 'Communication to a new public? Three reasons why EU copyright law can do without a "new public"', 2016, (7), IIC, 797–815; Rosati, GS Media, 2017, 16–17.

449 This is also true for "embedded linking", cf. C-466/12 – Svensson, par. 13, 29–30; C-348/13 *BestWater International GmbH v Michael Mebes and Stefan Potsch* ECLI:EU:C:2014:2315, 21 October 2014.

450 C-610/15 – Ziggo, par. 45–46; C-527/15 – Filmspeler, par. 50–51; C-160/15 – GS Media, par. 47–55; Christina Angelopoulos, CJEU Decision on Ziggo: The Pirate Bay Communicates Works to the Public, Kluwer Copyright Blog, June 30 2017; 1 July 2017.

right, is unclear. Neither of them is clearly defined either by international treaties or national legislation. The lack of a harmonised definition of the rights and their cumulative application in online use of works creates legal uncertainties and complications for licensing processes.[451] Particularly unclear is where to localise the endpoint of the making available right, which in turn makes it difficult to assess the cross-border implication of online use of in-copyright works by libraries. However, it seems clear that within the EU the accessibility of a website in a given country gives rise to jurisdiction of a national court in that country.

106. If libraries make in-copyright works from their collections available online this is a clear act of communication to the public which requires authorisation or an exception or limitation applicable for libraries. The public interest mission or non-profit status of libraries does not alter this, although it may affect the applicability of exceptions. However, the above account demonstrates that if national libraries and other national cultural heritage institutions put in-copyright material legally on their websites, first, that neither the libraries nor the end-users are liable for the reproduction inherent in the online viewing of such works, as demonstrated in the PRCA[452] case, and second, that linking to such material, by Europeana or other cultural heritage institutions, does not require authorisation, as demonstrated in the Svensson case.[453]

107. The next chapter will examine whether there are applicable exceptions and limitations in the exclusive reproduction right and the communication to the public right in EU legislation for such use.

---

451 Triaille and others, Study, 2013, 120–122, 124.

452 C-360/13 – PRCA *supra*.

453 C-466/12 – Svensson, *supra*.

CHAPTER 4

EXCEPTIONS AND LIMITATIONS FOR CROSS-BORDER ONLINE USE OF IN-COPYRIGHT WORKS BY LIBRARIES

The interests of the public are ... a reason for granting protection but also a reason for limiting it.[454]

4.1. GENERAL

108. Restrictions in the form of exceptions or limitations[455] on copyright are as old as the copyright system itself[456] and an integral part of the system.[457] They enable uses of in-copyright works without the consent of the rightholder either with or without remuneration.[458] The purpose of exceptions or limitations is to create a balance between the rights and interests of rightholders and users of in-copyright works.[459] They are traditionally justified by considerations of public

454 Geiger, Copyright and Free Access to Information: For a Fair Balance of Interests in a Globalised World, 2006, 167. See also Bernt Hugenholtz and Ruth L. Okediji, *Conceiving an international instrument on limitations and exceptions to copyright* (March 2008) 6.

455 Here I will only be discussing limitations or exceptions on the exclusive right of the rightholder, not limitations such as the term of protection or "subject matter limitations", i.e. where certain categories of works are excluded from copyright protection, cf. Samuel Ricketson and Jane C. Ginsburg, *International Copyright and Neighbouring Rights – the Berne Convention and Beyond* (2 edn, Oxford, 2006), 756–757; Annette Kur, 'Of Oceans, Islands, and Inland Water – How Much Room for Exceptions and Limitations Under the Three-Step Test?', 2008, (3), Richmond Journal of Global Law & Business, 287–350, 289; Guibault, Evaluating Directive 2001/29/EC, 2008, 63; Lucie Guibault, 'Copyright Limitations and Contracts. An Analysis of the Contractual Overridability of Limitations on Copyright', (PhD, 2002) 15–16.

456 Sterling, World Copyright Law, 2003, 434; Samuel Ricketson, *WIPO Study on Limitations and Exceptions of Copyright and Related Rights in the Digital Environment*, 3; Janssens, The Issue of Exceptions, 2009, 319–320; Guibault, The Nature, 2003, 2; Jean-François Canat, Lucie Guibault and Elisabeth Logeais, Study, 2015, 11.

457 Xalabarder, Digital Libraries, 2010, 245; Lucie Guibault, 'Contracts and Copyright Exemptions' in P. Bernt Hugenholtz (ed), *Copyright and Electronic Commerce, Legal Aspect of Electronic Copyright Management* (2000) 127, 131.

458 Hugenholtz and others, Recasting, 2006, 59–60; Public Consultation on the review of the EU copyright rules (2013), 16; Ricketson and Ginsburg, International, 2006, 757, 775–777.

459 Triaille and others, Study, 2013, 249; C-145/10 – Painer, par. 132; Guibault, Evaluating Directive 2001/29/EC, 2008, 63; COM(2016) 593 final, Proposal, 2016, 2.

interest as is reflected in the preamble to the WCT, which recognises "the need to maintain a balance between the rights of authors and the larger public interest, particularly education, research and access to information".[460]

109. In order to fulfil their role of giving access to and preserving cultural heritage still under copyright, libraries need either a licence from the rightholders for each work they reproduce or make available, or specific exceptions from the exclusive rights in legislation. Traditionally, exceptions and limitations have been considered the main tool for enhancing access to information.[461] Specific exceptions for libraries are thus justified with reference to the importance of securing access to information and transfer of knowledge.[462]

110. Exceptions are likewise justified as protecting fundamental rights such as freedom of expression (e.g. quotation, criticism and parody) and the freedom of the press.[463] They are seen by many as stimulating the creation of new works, which often are built to some extent upon older works.[464] Sometimes exceptions and limitations are introduced as a response to a market failure, such as the inability of the licensing markets to come up with contractual solutions or when transaction cost in acquiring authorisation outweighs the economic benefit of doing so.[465] In fact certain exceptions may be based on more than one ground[466] or the justification may have changed over time.[467]

---

[460] Reinbothe and Von Lewinski, The WIPO Treaties, 2015, 151–153. The preamble to the WCT (and the WPPT) was the first express justification in an international treaty of exception and limitations, cf. Janssens, The Issue of Exceptions, 2009, 322–323.

[461] Johan Axhamn, 'Exceptions, limitations and collective management of rights as vehicles for access to information' in Dana Beldiman (ed), *Access to Information and Knowledge 21st Century Challenges in Intellectual Property and Knowledge Governance: 21st Century Challenges in Intellectual Property and Knowledge Governance* (Edward Elgar, 2013) 169–171, 176; Christophe Geiger and others, 'Declaration: A Balanced Interpretation of the "Three-Step Test" in Copyright Law', 2010, (2), JIPITEC, 119–122, 119; Hugenholtz and Okediji, Conceiving, 2008, 8.

[462] Triaille and others, Study, 2013, 245; Crews, 2008 Study, 2008, 14. See also with regard to museums, Jean-François Canat, Lucie Guibault and Elisabeth Logeais, Study, 2015, 13.

[463] Hugenholtz and others, Recasting, 2006, 59; European Commission, Report on the responses, 2014, 30; European Parliament, Resolution 2015 on the InfoSoc Directive, 2015, item 40 and 47; Guibault, Evaluating Directive 2001/29/EC, 2008, 64.

[464] Geiger and others, InfoSoc, 2014, 437; European Copyright Society, 'Opinion on the Judgment of the CJEU in Case C-201/13 Deckmyn', par. 1, <http://papers.ssrn.com/sol3/papers.cfm?abstract_id=2564772> accessed 1 October 2015; Fred Von Lohmann, 'Google on what is driving creativity and innovation in the digital economy', 2016, (2), WIPO Magazine, 26–28.

[465] SWD(2015) 100 final, A Digital Single Market Strategy, 2015, 29; Triaille and others, Study, 2013, 256; Guibault, Evaluating Directive 2001/29/EC, 2008, 64; SWD(2016) 301 final, IA Part I, 2016, 80.

[466] Janssens, The Issue of Exceptions, 2009, 342–343.

[467] Guibault, Evaluating Directive 2001/29/EC, 2008, 64.

111. Some commentators see exceptions and limitations as the "users' right"[468] and the CJEU has on some occasions referred to the rights of users.[469, 470] However, the traditional exceptions for libraries, related to research and preservation, are generally not set out as a positive right in statutes.[471] Furthermore, what is considered the "legitimate interest" of the user or "public interest" is mainly a matter of national policy, as each legislator makes its own assessment of the balance of interest between the user, the rightholders and society at large.[472]

4.1.1. TERMINOLOGY AND DEFINITIONS

112. The terms "exception" and "limitation" are commonly used together in international copyright treaties and European legislation since they were first coupled together in the TRIPS Agreement.[473] A fair amount of scholarly discussion exists on the potential difference between the two terms. Thus some have explained the parallel use of the terms as a compromise between the terminologies in different legal traditions.[474] It has also been argued that the word "limitation" encompasses better all types of restrictions on the rightholder's copyright.[475] Still, there are no definitions in either international treaties or EU

468 Geiger and others, InfoSoc, 2014, 437; Crews, 2008 Study, 2008, 27; European Copyright Society, Opinion on C-201/13 Deckmyn, 2014, par. 22; Firth and Preira, Exceptions for Libraries, 2016, 52; Bechtold, Directive 2001/29/EC, 2016, 454; IFLA, *Treaty Proposal on Limitations and Exceptions for Libraries and Archives*, (December 6, 2013) 5; Dreier and Hugenholtz (eds) Concise, 2006, 369; Guibault, Contracts, 2000, 125. An Australian Government Draft Report proposes to introduce "users right" by adopting a "US-style fair use exception", cf. Australian Government Productivity Commission, Intellectual Property Arrangements; Draft Report, 2016, 121, 159.

469 See e.g. C-201/13 – Deckmyn and Vrijheidsfonds, par. 26; C-314/12 – UPC Telekabel Wien, par. 57; C-117/13 – TU Darmstadt, par. 43, on the right of communication of works under exceptions for publicly accessible libraries.

470 The European Parliament uses the term "consumer rights" in their Resolution of July 2015, cf. European Parliament, Resolution, 2015, item 59 and 67, which is a novelty in the copyright context and has been criticised, cf. Geiger and others, Reaction of CEIPI, 2015, 6.

471 Crews, 2008 Study, 2008, 27.

472 Hugenholtz and others, Recasting, 2006, 59; Ricketson and Ginsburg, International, 2006, 756, 773; Janssens, The Issue of Exceptions, 2009, 339.

473 Art. 13 TRIPs. Martin R.F. Senftleben, *Copyright, Limitations and the Three-Step-Test* (Kluwer Law International, 2004), 22, 115 ff.; Trumpke, Exklusivität, 2015, 426; SWD(2016) 301 final, IA Part I, 2016, 80.

474 Christophe Geiger, 'Promoting Creativity through Copyright Limitations: Reflections on the Concept of Exclusivity in Copyright Law', 2010, (3), Vanderbilt Journal of Entertainment and Technology Law 515, 518–519, esp. fn. 517; see also use of terms in Hugenholtz and others, Recasting, 2006, 59 and Geiger and others, InfoSoc, 2014, 438–439; Axhamn, Exceptions, 2013, 172–173; Reinbothe and Von Lewinski, The WIPO Treaties, 2015, 158.

475 Guibault, Copyright, 2002, 16.

legislation of what the terms actually mean[476], or on the difference between them.[477] Neither is there scholarly agreement on the difference. Thus, for want of a better alternative, in this thesis the terms "exception" and "limitation" will be used interchangeably, either together or separately, unless otherwise specified.

113. It has been suggested that the terms apply "to statutory limitations that curtail the rights of right holders in specific circumstances to cater for the interest of certain user groups or the public at large"[478] or simply "forms of use that are permitted by law on the basis of an exemption."[479] In a recent Commission document exceptions are defined as "a 'legal authorisation' to beneficiaries to use protected material without needing to seek authorisation from the rightholders."[480] However, this broad approach does not always help in ascertaining whether a legal restriction on a rightholders's right constitutes a limitation or exception, which is important when discussing compatibility of such restrictions with international principles.[481] Nevertheless, it can be assumed that the less restrictions encroach upon the exclusive right of rightholders the more likely it is that they are compatible with international norms. Furthermore, some restrictions may be considered not to be limitations or exceptions in the understanding of international treaties on copyright. Thus attempts have been made to classify restrictions with regard to how much they restrict the exclusive right.

114. Exceptions and limitations, as restrictions on the exclusive right of rightholders set out in legislation[482], can be grouped into five categories, ranked here in order of their level of restriction. Under the first category are free uses[483] or exemptions, for uses without authorisation or remuneration. These restrict the exclusive right the most. Free uses are justified by public interest, such as

---

476 Axhamn, Exceptions, 2013, 172; Hugenholtz and Okediji, Conceiving, 2008, 19; Guibault, Copyright, 2002, 16; Trumpke, Exklusivität, 2015, 176, 426–427; Martin Senftleben, 'WIPO Copyright Treaty (WCT)' in Thomas Dreier and P. Berndt Hugenholtz (eds), *Concise European Copyright Law* (2 edn, Wolters Kluwer, 2016) 123–124; Pierre Sirinelli, *Exceptions and Limitations on Copyright and Neighboring Rights*, (3 December 1999) 2.

477 Sterling, World Copyright Law, 2003, 434; Axhamn and Guibault, Cross-border ECL, 2011, 47, esp. fn. 240; Annette Kur, 'Limitations and Exceptions Under the Three-Step-Test – How Much Room to Walk the Middle Ground?' in Annette Kur (ed), *Intellectual Property Rights In A Fair World Trade System; Proposals for Reform of TRIPS* (Edward Elgar Publishing, 2011) 210 ff.; Kur, Of Oceans 2008, 290–292.

478 Hugenholtz and Okediji, Conceiving, 2008, 19.

479 Senftleben, WCT, 2016, 124.

480 SWD(2016) 301 final, IA Part I, 2016, 6.

481 Trumpke, Exklusivität, 2015, 169–175; Andrew F. Christie, 'Maximising Permissible Exceptions to Intellectual Property Rights' in Annette Kur and Vytautas Mizaras (eds), *The Structure of Intellectual Property Law: Can One Size Fit All?* (Edward Elgar, 2011) 122 ff.; Hugenholtz and Okediji, Conceiving, 2008, 19.

482 Excluding the inherent limits on copyright such as length of protection, cf. fn. 456.

483 Sterling, World Copyright Law, 2003, 434.

the freedom of expression.[484] The second category constitutes the "statutory licence", a legal licence, under which the level of remuneration is decided by the legislator. Category three is another legal licence, the "compulsory licence"[485], where remuneration is negotiated by the rightholders. The compulsory licence can be described as an obligation on the rightholder to contract with the user and thus can be seen as a less limiting restriction than the "statutory licence" as it only restricts the rightholder's freedom to choose the contracting partner, not the scope of the exclusive right as such.[486] These two terms in category two and three are, however, often used interchangeably. The fourth and fifth categories concern restrictions provided for in the form of legislative support for collective management which gives CMOs a legal mandate to negotiate collective agreements that will bind outsiders or where collective agreements are extended to outsiders by a legal provision. Category four would be mandatory collective management.[487] The difference between mandatory collective licensing and compulsory licences is not great, at least not from an economic point of view.[488] Finally, the fifth category of restriction on the exclusive right of rightholders is collective management with legislative support which extends collective agreements to outsiders, either through legally presumed mandate or by extension through a legal provision (ECL system).[489] The main difference between this group and mandatory collective management is that, at least in theory, the rightholders can individually licence their rights in the absence of a collective management agreement or in some cases by opting-out of such an agreement.

115. This attempt to categorise restrictions shows that there is a gradation in the severity of restrictions. In this chapter I will only discuss restrictions which are undisputedly in the category of exceptions and limitations that need to fulfil international norms, such as the three-step test discussed below. In part II of the book I will discuss restrictions in the form of legislative support for collective management, especially extended collective licences and their nature with regard to international norms and EU legislation.[490]

---

484 Guibault, Copyright, 2002, 21–22.

485 Tarja Koskinen-Olsson, *Collective management in reprography* (April 2005) 20–21; Trumpke, The Extended, 2012, 270–271.

486 Guibault, Copyright, 2002, 22–26.

487 See Ch. 9.3.

488 Anke Schierholz, 'Collective Management in Europe – Practice and Legal Framework' in Michel M. Walter and Silke von Lewinski (eds), *European Copyright Law, A Commentary* (Oxford University Press 2010) 1152; Annette Kur and Jens Schovsbo, 'Expropriation or fair game for all? The gradual dismantling of the IP exclusivity paradigm' in *Max Planck Institute for Intellectual Property, Competition & Tax Law Research Paper Series No 09-14* (2009) 14; Guibault, Copyright, 2002, 26.

489 See Ch. 5, 6 and 7 for ECLs and Ch. 9.2 on presumed mandate.

490 See Ch. 6.1.

4.1.2. COMMON LAW AND CIVIL LAW APPROACHES

116. There have been diverging approaches to provision for exceptions and limitations in civil law countries, mainly continental European countries, and common law countries.[491] The former tend to see such provision in the light of natural rights of authors, which implies the ownership by authors of their works; consequently, the balance of interest should be interpreted in favour of authors in case of doubt. Hence exceptions and limitations are defined narrowly and interpreted strictly.[492] National copyright legislation in civil law countries thus traditionally provides for exhaustive lists of limitations and exceptions[493] such as for private use and copying, quotations, use by libraries, uses for research and education, use by disabled people as well as some use for media.[494] Many of these uses require the payment of "equitable remuneration" or "fair compensation"[495], based on the notions of natural law theories that authors have "a right to remuneration for each and every act of usage of their copyrighted works."[496] This is i.a. reflected in the InfoSoc Directive.[497]

117. In common law countries exceptions and limitations have been regulated more flexibly with open-ended provisions providing for broader interpretation.[498] Thus in the USA, in addition to several non-remunerated statutory limitations or exceptions[499] and compulsory licences[500], there is

---

491 In fact the USA diverges with respect to exceptions from Canada, Australia and New Zealand, as well as Europe, cf. Ginsburg, Fair Use, 2014, 1414.

492 Janssens, The Issue of Exceptions, 2009, 323; Crews, 2008 Study, 2008, 27; Geiger and others, InfoSoc, 2014, 449–451; Senftleben, The International, 2010, 68; Jonathan Griffiths, 'Unsticking the centre-piece–The liberation of European copyright law?', 2010, (2), JIPITEC, 87–95, 88; P. Bernt Hugenholtz and Martin R.F. Senftleben, *Fair Use in Europe. In Search of Flexibilities*, (November 2011) 7.

493 Geiger and others, InfoSoc, 2014, 440; Hugenholtz and Senftleben, Fair Use, 2011, 2; Senftleben, The International, 2010, 68.

494 Sterling, World Copyright Law, 2003, 435–439, 447–448; COM(2008) 466, Green paper, 2008, 4; Hugenholtz, The Dutch, 2012, 54.

495 The concept of fair compensation was a novel term when it was introduced in the InfoSoc Directive. There was initially some concern about possible friction between the concept of fair compensation and equitable remuneration; however, in practice there seems to be little difference between them, cf. Bechtold, Directive 2001/29/EC, 2016, 459; Geiger and others, InfoSoc, 2014, 470–471; Hugenholtz and others, Recasting, 2006, 70–71. Thus no specific distinction will be made between these two terms in this research.

496 Bechtold, Directive 2001/29/EC, 2016, 459.

497 See Recitals (4), (9)-(12) and (21)-(23) InfoSoc Directive.

498 Janssens, The Issue of Exceptions, 2009, 323; Crews, 2008 Study, 2008, 27; Geiger and others, InfoSoc, 2014, 449; Senftleben, The International, 2010, 68; Griffiths, Unsticking the centre-piece, 2010, 88; Hugenholtz and Senftleben, Fair Use, 2011, 7; G. Dworkin, 'Exceptions to copyright exclusivity: Article 9(2) (Berne) and Article 13 (TRIPS): what is fair use in the new international order' in Hugh C. Hansen (ed), *International Intellectual Property Law and Policy*, vol 4 (2000) 7–9 (66).

499 Ginsburg, Fair Use, 2014, 1386.

500 Kur, Of Oceans 2008, 299.

the fair use exception which provides for "an unremunerated exception of overarching general application".[501, 502]

> The "fair use" doctrine was developed by the courts and finally adopted in the US Copyright Act as Section 107 in 1976.[503] There are four considerations put forward in the statute that have to be included when "determining whether the use made of work in any particular case is fair use". Those considerations are (1) the purpose and character of the use; (2) the nature of the copyrighted work; (3) the amount and substantiality of the portion used in relation to the copyrighted work as a whole and (4) the effect of the use upon the potential market for or value of the copyrighted work. These considerations are supposed to offer some guidelines to users for determining when the principles of the doctrine apply[504] but do "not furnish standards for recognition of fair use".[505] Furthermore, they are not to "be treated in isolation, one from another. All are to be explored, and the results weighed together, in light of the purposes of copyright."[506] Section 107 further provides that fair use can apply to unpublished works if other factors apply. If a particular use is found to constitute fair use it is allowed without payment.[507]

118. Comparison is frequently made of the advantages and disadvantages of the exhaustive list of exceptions, prevailing in civil law systems versus the fair use doctrine. The fair use clause offers more flexibility[508], which seems desirable in times of swift technological change, whereas the exhaustive list is presumed to offer more legal certainty and predictability.[509] Scholars have suggested combining the two approaches discussed above by complementing the exhaustive lists in Europe with a fair use type provision allowing for application

---

501 Ginsburg and Treppoz, International, 2015, 473; Gorman, Ginsburg and Reese, Copyright, 2011, 746–805.

502 In Commonwealth countries e.g. Australia and New Zealand, there is a 'fair dealing' exception. The main difference between the 'fair dealing' approach in Australia and 'fair use' as in the USA is the closed list of included matter of what can constitute fair dealing by the legislator, whereas in the USA the courts are only restricted by the fair use factors, cf. Australian Government Productivity Commission, Intellectual Property Arrangements; Draft Report, 2016, 140–143.

503 Gorman, Ginsburg and Reese, Copyright, 2011, 805; Authors Guild v. Google (USCA SC 2015), 13; Hugenholtz and Senftleben, Fair Use, 2011, 6.

504 H.R. Rep. No. 94–1476, 94th Cong., 2d Sess. 65–66 (1976) as reproduced in Gorman, Ginsburg and Reese, Copyright, 2011, 806–807.

505 Authors Guild v. Google (USCA SC 2015), 14–15.

506 *Campbell v. Acuff-Rose Music, Inc.* 510 US 569 (1994), Supreme Court of the United States, March 7, 1994 8–9; Authors Guild v. Google (USCA SC 2015), 14–15.

507 Ginsburg, Fair Use, 2014, 1385–1386; Kur, Of Oceans 2008, 299; Dworkin, Exceptions, 2000, 12 (66); Tomas A. Lipinski, 'Toward a Functional Understanding of Fair Use in U.S. Copyright Law', 2011, (1), Annual Review of Information Science and Technology, 523–621.

508 However, it has been pointed out that it offers less flexibility than the three-step test in the sense that if fair use is established it automatically means that the use is cost free, whereas under the three-step test there can be use under limitations that are remunerated, cf. Dworkin, Exceptions, 2000, 12, 20 (66).

509 Senftleben, The International, 2010, 68–69.

of an exception in similar cases to those the exhaustive lists apply to.[510] This seems to be a practical approach in today's digital environment where the scope of copyright has grown extensively, both with regard to subject matter as well as scope of protection[511], and thus covers a wide spectrum of everyday acts by many users.

Global harmonisation of copyright has focused on securing rightholders' ability to benefit from new modes of exploitation and business models.[512] This trend has possibly left too little flexibility for the balancing of interest between stakeholders in the fast changing digital environment. Perhaps there should instead be more emphasis on a level playing field for all stakeholders.[513] This could be achieved by allowing more flexibility in copyright exceptions and limitations and their interpretation.[514] However, as one commentator states "interpretations of limitations must neither be narrow nor broad – it must quite simply be "correct"."[515] The balance of the "correct" interpretation is, nevertheless, not easy to find.

4.1.3. THE THREE-STEP TEST

119. One of the main reference points when attempting to find the right balance of interest between stakeholders in copyright legislation and policy making is a test developed in international treaties and known, with "a faint allusion to ballroom dancing"[516], as the three-step test.[517] The first three-step provision was introduced

---

510 Hugenholtz and Senftleben, Fair Use, 2011, 2, 9; Kur, Of Oceans 2008, 297–298, see fn. 33 listing those who have come forward with such suggestions; The Wittem Project, *European Copyright Code* (deLex, 2010), Art. 5(5).

511 Guibault, The Nature, 2003, 1; Janssens, The Issue of Exceptions, 2009, 318–319; Geiger, Promoting Creativity through Copyright Limitations, 2010, 516–517; Xalabarder, Digital Libraries, 2010, 250–251.

512 Dworkin, Exceptions, 2000, 1(66).

513 Ohly, Economic rights, 2009, 238–239.

514 Geiger and others, Declaration, 2010, 1; Christophe Geiger, 'The Role of the Three-step Test in the Adaption of Copyright law to the Information Society', 2007, (January – March 2007), UNESCO e-Copyright Bulletin, 17; Hugenholtz, The Dutch, 2012, 54; European Parliament, *Draft Report on the implementation of Directive 2001/29/EC of the European Parliament and of the Council of 22 May 2001 on the harmonisation of certain aspects of copyright and related rights in the information society (2014/2256(INI))* Par. 13; European Parliament, Resolution, 2015, par. 43; Christophe Geiger and others, *Reaction of the CEIPI to the Resolution on the Implementation of Directive 2001/29/EC on the Harmonisation of Copyright in the Information Society adopted by the European Parliament on the 9th July 2015*, 17.

515 Kur, Of Oceans 2008, 295.

516 Ricketson and Ginsburg, International, 2006, 763.

517 Christophe Geiger, Daniel Gervais and Martin R.F. Senftleben, 'Understanding the "three-step test" ' in Daniel Gervais (ed), *International Intellectual Property: A Handbook of Contemporary Research* (2015) 173, 182; Senftleben, The International, 2010, 67, 75; Geiger, The Role, 2007, 4; Hugenholtz and others, Recasting, 2006, 60, 69.

in 1967 at the Stockholm Revision Conference of the Berne Convention.[518] It is contained in Art. 9(2) of the Convention, which stipulates that exceptions[519] can be made to the reproduction right if they fulfil three conditions, namely that they, first, be for certain special cases, second, do not conflict with a normal exploitation of the work, and third, do not unreasonably prejudice the legitimate interests of the author. Its "open-ended" wording was due to a compromise at the international level between the different traditions with regard to exceptions in civil law countries and common law countries.[520] Despite being extensively debated there was at the onset a lack of clear agreement as to its exact meaning when adopted, and there is still uncertainty as to its precise scope.[521] Nevertheless, the test has assumed "a life of its own"[522] and found its way into various legal instruments[523] with some variations on its wording[524] as well as broadening of its scope. Of particular importance is the fact that the TRIPs Agreement made its use obligatory for all exclusive rights.[525] In fact, the inclusion of the three-step test in TRIPS made it the "general yardstick" for limitations and exceptions for all areas of intellectual property, i.e. not only copyright but also patents, trademarks and design.[526]

The WIPO Internet treaties also have three-step test provisions.[527] Additionally, in the Agreed Statements accompanying the treaties, a general declaration was incorporated which underlines that Contracting Parties are permitted "to carry forward and appropriately extend into the digital environment limitations and exceptions in their national laws" and "to devise new exceptions and limitations and exceptions that are appropriate in the digital network environment".[528] Hence, as the making available right is a new right, i.e.

518 Ricketson and Ginsburg, International, 2006, 759; Sterling, World Copyright Law, 2003, 435; Geiger, The Role, 2007, 3; Kur, Of Oceans 2008, 307.

519 The word "exception" is not found in the provision itself, only in the heading of Art. 9 BC.

520 Geiger, Gervais and Senftleben, Understanding... 2015, 173.

521 Samuel Ricketson, *The Berne Convention for the protection of Literary and Artistic Works: 1886–1986* (Kluwer Law International, 1987), 455–476; Ricketson and Ginsburg, International, 2006, 759–763; Dworkin, Exceptions, 2000, 5(66); COM(95) 382 final, Green Paper, 1995, 50–51.

522 Janssens, The Issue of Exceptions, 2009, 321.

523 Art. 9(2) BC, Art. 13 TRIPS, Art. 10(1) WCT, Art. 16(2) WPPT, Art. 5(5) Infosoc Directive and Art. 11 Marrakesh VIP Treaty (Marrakesh Treaty to Facilitate Access to Published Works for Persons Who Are Blind, Visually Impaired, or Otherwise Print Disabled adopted by the Diplomatic Conference to Conclude a Treaty to Facilitate Access to Published Works by Visually Impaired Persons and Persons with Print Disabilities in Marrakesh, on June 27, 2013).

524 Geiger, Gervais and Senftleben, Understanding... 2015, 170; Kur, Of Oceans 2008, 310–311; Geiger, The Role, 2007, 3.

525 Art. 13 TRIPS, cf. Ricketson and Ginsburg, International, 2006, 765; Thomas Dreier and P. Bernt Hugenholtz, 'Agreement on Trade-Related Aspects of Intellectual Property Rights (TRIPS)' in Thomas Dreier and P. Berndt Hugenholtz (eds), *Concise European Copyright Law* (2 edn, Wolters Kluwer, 2016) 231; Crews, 2008 Study, 2008, 21.

526 Kur, Of Oceans 2008, 305–306; Reinbothe and Von Lewinski, The WIPO Treaties, 2015, 150.

527 Art. 10 WCT and Art. 16(2) WPPT. The three-step-test is not an obligatory criterion for exceptions regarding related rights under either the Rome Convention or the TRIPS.

528 Agreed Statements to Art. 10 WCT and Art. 16(2) WPPT. COM(97)628 final, InfoSoc Proposal, 1997, 15.

a more extensive right than provided for in the Berne Convention, exceptions can be made to that right within the scope of the three-step test. However, the last paragraph of the statement provides that Art. 10(2) WCT "neither reduces nor extends the scope of applicability of the limitations and exceptions permitted by the Berne Convention". This seems to limit the scope of the agreed statements and consequently the potential contribution of the treaties to the discussion on exceptions and limitations for digital uses.[529] Unsurprisingly, it has been suggested that it would be helpful if WCT members agreed to remove this last paragraph.[530]

120. The importance of the three-step-test was highlighted by the WTO panel decision in June 2000[531], which found that the US had breached its TRIPS obligations by adopting an exception that violated the three-step-test in Art. 13 of TRIPS.[532] Since then the test has been the "benchmark for all copyright limitations"[533]

121. The three-step test has generally been seen as guidance for national lawmakers although it can also have relevance to national courts.[534] Next I will discuss the interpretation of the three-step test mainly with regard to law-making, i.e. the question of when an exception in national legislation is deemed to pass the three-step test and thus to be a viable basis for a limitation on the exclusive right of authors or other rightholders, with or without compensation.

4.1.3.1. Interpretation

122. There is considerable debate about the "correct" interpretation of the three-step test and "no clear common understanding of its significance."[535] At least two different schools of thought can be identified, the first advocating

529 Janssens, The Issue of Exceptions, 2009, 323; Jean-François Canat, Lucie Guibault and Elisabeth Logeais, Study, 2015, 14; Dworkin, Exceptions, 2000, 15 (66).

530 Sam Ricketson, 'WIPO Study on Limitations and Exceptions of Copyright and Related Rights in the Digital Environment' (WIPO Information Session on Limitations and Exceptions, 2008); Geiger and others, InfoSoc, 2014, 443.

531 WT/DS160/R, *Panel Report, United States – Section 110(5) of the US Copyright Act*, (June 15, 2000).

532 Geiger, Gervais and Senftleben, Understanding... 2015, 173, 182; Geiger, The Role, 2007, 4; Hugenholtz and others, Recasting, 2006, 60, 69.

533 COM(2008) 466, Green paper, 2008, 5; Firth and Preira, Exceptions for Libraries, 2016, 7; Dreier and Hugenholtz, TRIPS, 2016, 231.

534 Walter and von Lewinski (eds) European Copyright Law, A Commentary, 2010, 1060; C-462/09 *Opinion of Advocate General Jääskinen in Stichting de Thuiskopie v Opus Supplies Deutschland GmbH and Others* ECLI:EU:C:2011:397, CJEU, 10 March 2011 par. 41; Geiger, Gervais and Senftleben, Understanding... 2015, 169; Richard Arnold and Eleonora Rosati, 'Are National Courts the Addressees of the InfoSoc Three-Step Test?', 2015, (10), Journal of Intellectual Property Law & Practice, 741–749. Many national legislation have incorporated the three-step test in library exceptions, cf. Crews, 2008 Study, 2008, 21–22. See further discussion in Ch. 4.2.1.2.

535 Janssens, The Issue of Exceptions, 2009, 323; Ricketson and Ginsburg, International, 2006, 763; Firth and Preira, Exceptions for Libraries, 2016, 7; Dreier, Berne, 2016, 45.

narrow and schematic interpretation based on the WTO panel's decision[536], whereas the second school promotes a broader and more overall approach.[537] The latter approach is encapsulated in a Declaration by several European copyright scholars in 2008[538] which i.a. stated:

> The Three-Step Test has already established an effective means of preventing the excessive application of limitations and exceptions. However, there is no complementary mechanism prohibiting an unduly narrow or restrictive approach. For this reason, the Three-Step Test should be interpreted so as to ensure a proper and balanced application of limitations and exceptions. This is essential if an effective balance of interests is to be achieved.

123. Traditionally the three conditions of the three-step test have been considered to apply cumulatively[539] based on the drafting history of its origin.[540] Thus the WTO panel[541] stated that failure to comply with any one of the steps means that an exception will not pass the test. However, not everybody agrees with this cumulative interpretation and claim it to be too restrictive and narrow. They have suggested that the three-step test should be read in the same way as the factors judges bear in mind when deciding on the fair use doctrine in the US entailing a comprehensive overall assessment.[542] In this manner the 2008 Declaration states that the three-step test constitutes an indivisible entirety.[543]

124. The fact remains, there are three steps in the test, which have to be interpreted and assessed, either cumulatively or as a whole. The WTO panel decision is the only international analysis so far on the three-step-test. We will thus look at this interpretation and then at some of the reactions to it in the following sub-chapters. However, when evaluating the decision it must be borne in mind that it is only binding on the parties to those particular legal

---

536 WT/DS160/R, Panel Report USA, 2000, *Op.cit.*

537 Riis and Schovsbo, ECLs, 2010, 486.

538 Geiger and others, Declaration, 2010, 1. The Declaration was first published on September 1, 2008 at the ATRIP (International Association for the Advancement of Teaching and Research in Intellectual Property) Conference in Munich, and will hereafter be referred to as the "2008 Declaration".

539 COM(97)628 final, InfoSoc Proposal, 1997, 15; Ricketson and Ginsburg, International, 2006, 763; Dreier, Berne, 2016, 46; Senftleben, WCT, 2016, 123; Dreier and Hugenholtz, TRIPS, 2016, 231.

540 See report of the Stockholm Revision Conference, par. 85, reproduced in WIPO, Berne Convention Centenary, 1986, 197; Geiger, Gervais and Senftleben, Understanding... 2015, 168.

541 Both parties to the dispute agreed on the cumulative nature of the three-step test, cf. WT/DS160/R, Panel Report USA, 2000, par. 6.97.

542 Geiger, Gervais and Senftleben, Understanding... 2015, 162, 168–169; Xalabarder, Digital Libraries, 2010, 247–248; Kur, Of Oceans 2008, 306, 317, 340–341; Geiger and others, Declaration, 2010, 2; Dreier, Berne, 2016, 46; Senftleben, WCT, 2016, 123.

543 Geiger and others, Declaration, 2010, 4.

proceedings. Neither other Member States nor even a later panel are legally bound by the decision.[544]

4.1.3.1.1. The first step

...certain special cases...

125. The first step sets out the limits for the scope and the precision of the limitation.[545] The WTO panel came to the conclusion that the term "certain" in the first step means that "an exception or limitation in national legislation must be clearly defined." However, the panel added, it does not follow that there is a "need to identify explicitly each and every possible situation to which the exception could apply, provided that the scope of the exception is known and particularised" to guarantee "a sufficient degree of legal certainty."[546]

126. Ricketson and Ginsburg maintain that this first step involves "consideration of all aspects of a proposed exception, including such matters as the right(s) and works covered, the person who may take advantage of it, and the purpose of the exception."[547]

127. Some commentators have questioned whether the US fair-use exception fulfils the three-step test, in particular whether it is "certain" enough.[548] Other commentators are of the opinion that it does[549], advancing two main arguments: firstly, that the binding power of precedents in common law ensures a certain degree of legal certainty, combined with the four considerations to be included when analysing whether a particular use is fair use[550]; secondly, that the signatories of the TRIPS agreement were aware of the legal approach taken in the US Copyright Act[551] and the draft in TRIPS was hence a deliberate attempt to find a compromise between the two approaches.[552] In this manner, the 2008 Declaration suggests that step one should not prevent legislatures

544 Firth and Preira, Exceptions for Libraries, 2016, 8–9; Kur, Of Oceans 2008, 328–330.
545 Ricketson and Ginsburg, International, 2006, 764; Rydning, Extended, 2010, 46.
546 WT/DS160/R, Panel Report USA, 2000, par. 6.108.
547 Ricketson and Ginsburg, International, 2006, 764.
548 See e.g. Sam Ricketson, *The three-step test, deemed quantities, libraries, and closed exceptions*, 150–154; Ricketson, WIPO Study, 2003, 67–69; Reinbothe and Von Lewinski, The WIPO Treaties, 2015, 152.
549 Kur, Of Oceans 2008, 296; Senftleben, Copyright, Limitations and the Three-Step-Test, 2004, 162; Senftleben, The International, 2010, 76; Dreier, Berne, 2016, 46; Senftleben, WCT, 2016, 126; Dreier and Hugenholtz, TRIPS, 2016, 231: Geiger, Gervais and Senftleben, Understanding... 2015, 188.
550 Kur, Of Oceans 2008, 296–297.
551 As well as those who drafted Art. 9(2) BC in 1967.
552 Kur, Of Oceans 2008, 314–315; Geiger, The Role, 2007, 3, 6–7. See also Geiger, Gervais and Senftleben, Understanding... 2015, 188.

from introducing open-ended limitations and exceptions, as long as they are reasonably predictable. Nor should it prevent courts from applying existing limitations and exceptions to similar factual circumstances or from creating further limitations or exceptions where possible within the legal system of which they form a part.[553] This is in fact what has been proposed in the Wittem Copyright Code.[554]

128. With regard to the term "special" the panel concluded that in addition to being clearly defined "an exception or limitation must be limited in its field of application or exceptional in its scope." They further explained this by stating:

> ...an exception or limitation should be narrow in a quantitative as well as a qualitative sense. This suggests a narrow scope as well as an exceptional or distinctive objective. To put this aspect of the first condition into the context of the second condition ("no conflict with a normal exploitation"), an exception or limitation should be the opposite of a non-special, i.e., a normal case.[555]

This fits in with the panel's general assertion regarding the three step-test that it cannot "have more than a narrow or limited operation".[556] This is, however, opposed by many.[557]

129. The panel rejected the condition that in order to fulfil the first step the exception must serve a public policy purpose[558] but added that, "[h]owever, public policy purposes stated by law-makers when enacting a limitation or exception may be useful from a factual perspective for making inferences about the scope of a limitation or exception or the clarity of its definition."[559] Thus the panel avoided having to analyse "the legitimacy of the public policy purpose" of the exception at hand in the dispute.[560]

Ricketson and Ginsburg sustained this approach for the three-step test both under the TRIPS Agreement and the Berne Convention and concluded

---

553 Geiger and others, Declaration, 2010, point 3; Geiger and others, InfoSoc, 2014, 445.

554 Wittem Project, European Copyright Code, 2010, Art. 5.5. The Wittem Project was established in 2002 and is based on the collaboration of several EU copyright scholars, cf. Ibid, 9. Many of the participants in the Wittem project and group were also contributors to the 2008 Declaration. See e.g. Geiger, Gervais and Senftleben, Understanding... 2015, 187–188.

555 WT/DS160/R, Panel Report USA, 2000, par. 6.109.

556 Ibid, par. 6.97.

557 Geiger, Gervais and Senftleben, Understanding... 2015, 162, 168–169; Xalabarder, Digital Libraries, 2010, 247–248; Kur, Of Oceans 2008, 306, 317, 340–341; Geiger and others, Declaration, 2010, 2; Dreier, Berne, 2016, 46; Senftleben, WCT, 2016, 123.

558 WT/DS160/R, Panel Report USA, 2000, par. 6.111. See also Ricketson and Ginsburg, International, 2006, 765–767.

559 WT/DS160/R, Panel Report USA, 2000, par. 6.112.

560 Jane Ginsburg, 'Toward Supranational Copyright Law? The WTO Panel Decision and the "Three-step-Test" for Copyright Exceptions', 2001, The Center for Law and Economic Studies, Working Paper No 181, Columbia University Public Law & Legal Theory, Research Paper Series, 5; Geiger, Gervais and Senftleben, Understanding... 2015, 174; Kur, Of Oceans 2008, 316.

that the normative evaluation of exceptions should be considered under steps two and three.[561] However, others maintain that there is room for a normative evaluation under the first step and, indeed, that it should be carried out already there. The reference to "special cases" could lend itself to normative analysis. The interpretation of the first step should not be based on a "purely quantitative assessment" but rather based on assessment of "whether the exception is limited enough in view of its purpose and potential impact." This is particularly so if the cumulative approach of the three-step test is applied. Thus an exception that might allow for a relatively "large" amount of use might fail the first step under a "purely quantitative assessment" but might still be considered limited enough if assessed with regard to its purpose and potential impact.[562] This can indeed be said to be true with regard to the US court fair use decisions in the Google Books case[563] and the HathiTrust case.[564, 565]

130. In this context it is worth mentioning the Tunis Model Copyright Law of 1976, sponsored by WIPO and UNESCO[566], which contains a library exception for reproduction provided that "such reproduction and the number of copies made are limited to the needs of their activities, do not conflict with the normal exploitation of the work and do not unreasonably prejudice the legitimate interests of the author …", i.e if step two and three of the three-step test are fulfilled. In the commentary to the provision it is stated that it "seemed preferable to deal with this question only in very general terms and by reference to Article 9(2) of the Berne Convention". The commentary then goes on to explain that the first step requiring that an exception be only for "certain special cases" was seen as fulfilled by limiting the uses to "public libraries, non-commercial documentation centres, scientific institutions and educational establishments".[567]

4.1.3.1.2. The second step

…do not conflict with a normal exploitation of the work…

131. The WTO panel defined "exploitation" as using the works in order to "extract economic value" from the exclusive rights conferred on rightholders.[568] Ricketson and Ginsburg suggest that a consequence of this definition may be that certain acts would not be considered "exploitation" by third parties

561 Ricketson and Ginsburg, International, 2006, 766–767; Ginsburg, Toward, 2001, 11–12.
562 Kur, Of Oceans 2008, 316–317; Senftleben, WCT, 2016, 126.
563 Authors Guild v. Google (USCA SC 2015), *supra*.
564 HathiTrust 2nd Cir 2014, *supra*.
565 See Ch. 2.3.2.
566 United Nations Educational, Scientific, and Cultural Organization.
567 Section 7(v) Model Law and commentary (par. 51). See also Crews, 2008 Study, 2008, 26.
568 WT/DS160/R, Panel Report USA, 2000, par. 6.165.

"because they are not done for commercial end." They also underline that the term "exploitation" refers to activities by the rightholder rather than the user.[569]

"Normal", in the view of the panel, has both an "empirical" and a "normative" meaning.[570] The empirical approach looks at how the rightholder would ordinarily expect to be able to exploit the work[571], whereas the normative approach would include "those forms of exploitation which, with a certain degree of likelihood and plausibility, could acquire considerable economic or practical importance."[572]

132. Ginsburg and Treppoz point out that the panel focused mainly on the "empirical" aspect of "normal exploitation" by concentrating on what market the rightholder was in fact exploiting or would be likely to exploit. The "normative" aspect on the other hand was not clearly carved out, probably because of the matter at hand in the panel decision i.e. public performance of radio or television transmissions in commercial settings. Ginsburg and Treppoz underline that the normative valuation is important in deciding what "normal exploitation" is, especially if the three-step test is to be applied cumulatively. In their view the normative valuation should centre around what "market" the rightholder should be entitled to cover.[573]

This understanding of normative interpretation is explained in greater detail by Ricketson and Ginsburg, who suggest that such an inquiry would involve "non-economic as well as economic considerations, and inevitably" include "some kind of balancing process". Such a balancing process is left to national legislators who have to pass the necessary value judgements. Those would, however, always need "a clear public-interest balance that goes beyond the purely individual interests of copyright users." This kind of normative interpretation is also supported, in their view, by the fact that, otherwise, step three of the test would most often be redundant.[574]

Kur agrees with this approach by Ricketson and Ginsburg and highlights that it is compatible with the three-step formulation for patent rights, cf. Art. 30 TRIPS, which states that exceptions should not "unreasonably conflict with a normal exploitation". She questions at the same time the approach taken by the WTO panel that interpretation of "normal exploitation" must take as its starting point full exploitation of "what actual or potential markets may yield." Rather the measurement should be a relative or "gradual measurement to be undertaken in light of the strength and urgency of the legal motives underlying the rule at stake."[575]

569 Ricketson and Ginsburg, International, 2006, 768.
570 WT/DS160/R, Panel Report USA, 2000, 6.166.
571 Ibid, 6.177–176.178.
572 Ibid, 6.180.
573 Ginsburg and Treppoz, International, 2015, 471–472.
574 Ricketson and Ginsburg, International, 2006, 771–773.
575 Kur, Of Oceans 2008, 320–321.

133. The 2013 InfoSoc study argues that an exception would only conflict with the normal exploitation of works if its systematic use deprived authors of "major sources of revenues". Otherwise there would not be room for exceptions justified by public interest.[576] Likewise, Geiger, Gervais and Senftleben warn that the second step has considerable potential to limit the scope of policy making by national legislators. They maintain that the WTO panel's interpretation of the step could, in particular, hinder exceptions in the digital environment, given the possibilities rightholders have to control the uses of their works through technical measures.[577] Thus, the 2008 Declaration holds that the conditions of step two should be considered fulfilled if limitations or exceptions are based on important competing considerations or if they help counter anti-competitive practices or effects, in particular if adequate compensation is ensured.[578]

4.1.3.1.3. The third step

...do not unreasonably prejudice the legitimate interests of the rightholder...

134. The WTO panel noted that there were various terms included in the third step that required interpretation.[579] First, they discussed the term "interest" which they found to refer to "a legal right or title to a property or to use or benefit a property" and also "actual or potential economic advantage or detriment." However, the interest might be of non-economic consideration.[580] Then, they asserted that the term "legitimate" had both a "legal positivist perspective" and a "normative perspective".[581] As both parties agreed that the rightholders had a legitimate interest in exercising their right for economic gain[582] the panel did not further dwell on the normative side of rightholders' legitimate interest.[583] Next the panel noted that the ordinary meaning of "prejudice" implies "damage, harm or injury" and observed that the term "not unreasonably" hints at a "slightly higher threshold" than "reasonable"[584], i.e. that it allows for "exceptions that may cause prejudice of a significant or substantial kind to the author's legitimate interests" provided that it fulfils the first two steps and the proportionality test of not being unreasonable.[585]

---

576 Triaille and others, Study, 2013, 255–256. See also Senftleben, WCT, 2016, 127.
577 Geiger, Gervais and Senftleben, Understanding... 2015, 175; see also Geiger, The Role, 2007, 6–9.
578 Geiger and others, Declaration, 2010, point 4; Geiger and others, InfoSoc, 2014, 445.
579 WT/DS160/R, Panel Report USA, 2000, 6.222.
580 Ibid, par. 6.223; Ginsburg, Toward, 2001, 8–9.
581 WT/DS160/R, Panel Report USA, 2000, par. 6.224.
582 Ibid, 6.226.
583 Ginsburg, Toward, 2001, 9.
584 WT/DS160/R, Panel Report USA, 2000, par. 6.225.
585 Ricketson and Ginsburg, International, 2006, 776.

The above analysis led the panel to determine that "prejudice to the legitimate interests of right holders reaches an unreasonable level if an exception or limitation causes or has the potential to cause an unreasonable loss of income to the copyright owner."[586] The panel indicated, nonetheless, that unreasonable prejudice to "the legitimate interests" of a rightholder could be alleviated if there remuneration were granted for use that falls under an exception.[587] Thus the 2008 Declaration focuses in particular on adequate compensation for limitations and exceptions, which should provide for "sufficient incentives for the continued creation and dissemination of works."[588] However, public policy objectives could justify a limitation passing the third step without remuneration.[589]

135. This step should call for the evaluation of balance of interests of the rightholder on the one hand and of the user benefitting from the limitation on the other hand.[590] Kur has criticised the panel for not going into policy issues at all in their argumentation and concentrating only on the financial side. In her view there would have been an opportunity to discuss the possible legislative motives behind the exceptions at hand.[591]

136. Geiger proposes that the third step is by far the most important one. He suggests that as it allows for normative interpretation this invites a judiciary to carry out a proportionality test, "permitting an adjustment of the application of limitations not only in function of the economic interest of the right holder, but also of the diverging interests of users or even of authors when these differ from those of right-holding owners."[592] Hence, he and other scholars have suggested that a more holistic and liberal interpretation of the three-step test should begin by applying the third step first, thus starting to balance the different interests involved.[593]

---

586 WT/DS160/R, Panel Report USA, 2000, par. 6.229.

587 Ibid, par. 6.229, fn. 205; WIPO, *Records of the intellectual property conference of Stockholm (1967)*, 1145–1146; Paul Goldstein and Bernt Hugenholtz, *International Copyright; Principles, Law, and Practice* (2 edn, Oxford University Press, 2010), 366; Rydning, Extended, 2010, 67–68; Ginsburg, Toward, 2001, 9; Ricketson and Ginsburg, International, 2006, 775; Ginsburg and Treppoz, International, 2015, 439, 470; Geiger, Gervais and Senftleben, Understanding... 2015, 168–169; Kur, Of Oceans 2008, 300; Guibault, The Nature, 2003, 3; Axhamn, Exceptions, 2013, 175.

588 Geiger and others, InfoSoc, 2014, 445; Geiger and others, Declaration, 2010, point 4 and considerations.

589 Rydning, Extended, 2010, 67; Jane Ginsburg, 'Berne-Forbidden Formalities and Mass Digitization', 2016, Boston University Law Review, 745–775, 762, 774.

590 Axhamn and Guibault, Cross-border ECL, 2011, 51.

591 Kur, Of Oceans 2008, 324.

592 Geiger, The Role, 2007, 18. See also Dreier, Berne, 2016, 46–47.

593 Geiger, Gervais and Senftleben, Understanding... 2015, 181–182.

4.1.3.2. Evaluation

137. There seem to be convincing arguments that the three-step test should not be interpreted exclusively in the light of economic interest of rightholders. In my view, such a narrow interpretation fails to take into account the public interest justifications for many exceptions and limitations. In particular, it seems that applying the three-step test cumulatively can be too restrictive, particularly with regard to digital use, such as mass digitisation for preservation and other public interest purposes for digital libraries. Thus, it seems important that when applying the three-step test the interest of third parties can be taken into account, as is underlined in the three-step test provisions for other intellectual property rights in the TRIPS agreement.[594]

138. It has been suggested that the lack of mention of third party interest in the three-step test for copyright was an omission. Hence the 2008 Declaration proposes that the three-step test should be interpreted "in a manner that respects the legitimate interests of third parties" such as interests deriving from human rights and fundamental freedoms, interests in competition and other public interest, e.g. cultural development.[595] In order for libraries to fulfil their role of preserving and disseminating the cultural heritage in the digital age a more enabling approach to the three-step test which underlines its role as a "flexible framework" and its function to enable "tailor-made solutions at the national level" seems a desirable development.[596]

4.1.4. INTERNATIONAL DEVELOPMENTS REGARDING EXCEPTIONS AND LIMITATIONS FOR LIBRARIES

139. Copyright limitations and exceptions have not been harmonised at the international level. Relatively few exceptions or limitations on copyright are to be found in international instruments and where they exist they are mainly optional.[597] There are no provisions for exceptions for libraries in the Berne Convention or other international treaties.[598] In the discussion that led to the adoption of the WIPO Internet treaties, a proposal for library and archive exceptions with regard to the reproduction right, i.e. for replacement copies and copies for third persons, was submitted but did not gain sufficient support.[599]

---

594 Art. 17, 26(2) and 30 of TRIPS. See e.g. Kur, Of Oceans 2008, 340–341.

595 Geiger and others, Declaration, 2010, 2, 5. See also Art. 5(5) i.f., Wittem Copyright Code.

596 Geiger, Gervais and Senftleben, Understanding... 2015, 183–189.

597 Jean-François Canat, Lucie Guibault and Elisabeth Logeais, Study, 2015, 14.

598 Crews, 2008 Study, 2008, 19; Ricketson, WIPO Study, 2003, 10–65; Xalabarder, Digital Libraries, 2010, 232.

599 WIPO, *Prepatory Document for the Second Session of the Committee of Expert on a Possible Protocol to the Berne Convention for the Protection of Literary and Artistic Works*, (February 10–17, 1992) par. 76–92; Reinbothe and Von Lewinski, The WIPO Treaties, 2015, 148.

Hence exceptions in national legislation for libraries are based on the three-step test.[600]

140. Exceptions for libraries are a relatively recent development in copyright. New technology enabling reproduction, such as photography and photocopying, spurred adoption of specific exceptions in national legislation in the 1950s[601] for libraries for preservation purposes as well as to allow such institutions to secure replacement copies of out-of-print works.[602] Today, most countries have specific library exceptions focusing on issues such as reproduction of copyrighted works for preservation and replacement of materials, document supply and inter-library lending as well as for private research and study.[603] The 2008 WIPO study observed that the complexity and diversity of copyright exceptions in legislation around the world is "remarkable".[604] However, this "variety of different solutions" impedes the progress of online use of in-copyright works by digital libraries.[605] Furthermore, despite the fact that most national exceptions allow libraries specific uses of in-copyright works without payment of compensation to rightholders[606], the exceptions are not widely used either because of their complex nature or because they fail to address the actual needs of libraries in the digital age.[607] In particular, national solutions tend not to extend to digital uses, which is a further impediment to the advancement of digital libraries.[608]

4.1.4.1. IFLA Treaty Proposal

141. The International Federation of Library Associations and Institutions (IFLA) has been working on a Treaty proposal for an international instrument for limitations and exceptions for libraries and archives since 2009, for both digital and non-digital works.[609] It covers the key issues for libraries and archives, including cross-border uses of works and materials reproduced under

600 Crews, 2008 Study, 2008, 19–21; Senftleben, The International, 2010, 75; Xalabarder, Digital Libraries, 2010, 238; Geiger, Gervais and Senftleben, Understanding… 2015, 184; with regard to museums see Jean-François Canat, Lucie Guibault and Elisabeth Logeais, Study, 2015, 15; Firth and Preira, Exceptions for Libraries, 2016, 10–11.

601 The first was enacted into British copyright law in 1956, cf. Crews, 2008 Study, 2008, 14 and 68; Firth and Preira, Exceptions for Libraries, 2016, 10.

602 Folketingstidende 1959–60 Tillæg A, *Forslag til Lov om ophavsretten til litterære og kunstneriske værker*, (15.01.1960) 2706–2709.

603 Cf. Kenneth Crews, *Study on Copyright Limitations and Exceptions for Libraries and Archives*, (December 2014) 4. The study establishes that 153 of the then 186 Member States of WIPO had specific library exceptions.

604 Crews, 2008 Study, 2008, 68–71.

605 Xalabarder, Digital Libraries, 2010, 231.

606 Crews, 2008 Study, 2008, 38.

607 Ibid, 68–71.

608 Xalabarder, Digital Libraries, 2010, 231.

609 The latest version of the proposal dates from December 6, 2013, cf. Version 4.4, at <www.ifla.org/files/assets/hq/topics/exceptions-limitations/tlib_v4_4.pdf>, last viewed 3 July 2017.

a limitation and exception, which IFLA proposes should be permitted to "the extent that it is necessary for the exercise of a limitation or exception provided for in this Treaty".[610] In the explanatory note to the article IFLA states that this is not a "carte blanche provision" since each exception in the draft Treaty has a set of conditions which have to be applied. IFLA is of the opinion that licensing will not solve the digital issues for libraries as they "may prohibit reproduction for sharing across borders, prevent the exercise of rights enshrined in copyright law through exceptions and limitations, or allow publishers to withhold the sale of digital content to libraries entirely."[611] The IFLA draft Treaty proposal has been criticised by some as being a wish-list.[612] However, it was incorporated into the proposed draft WIPO Treaty on Exceptions and Limitations.[613]

4.1.4.2. Draft WIPO Treaty on Exceptions and Limitations

142. In 2011 a proposal for a WIPO Treaty on Exceptions and Limitations for Persons with Disabilities, Educational and Research Institutions, Libraries and Archives was tabled[614], which incorporated, as mentioned above, the IFLA draft Treaty provisions. One of the topics covered is the cross-border use of copies of works made under a limitation or exception. It is proposed that such a copy "may be distributed, lent or made available by a library or archive to another library or archive in another Member State."[615]

Not much progress has been made in the negotiations since 2011 and commentators are pessimistic as to when or whether a Treaty will be adopted.[616]

4.2. EUROPEAN DEVELOPMENTS

143. In this sub-chapter I will explore exceptions and limitations for digital libraries within the EU relevant to online use of in-copyright works. Thus the central focus will be on the InfoSoc Directive and the Orphan Works Directive. The co-existing exceptions[617] provided for in the Software Directive, the Rental

---

610 Art. 13 of Version 4.4.

611 Cf. <www.ifla.org/node/10057?og=29>, last visited 3 July 2017.

612 Firth and Preira, Exceptions for Libraries, 2016, 49–50.

613 WIPO SCCR/22/12, *Draft WIPO Treaty on Exceptions and Limitations for the Persons with Disabilities, Educational and Research Institutions, Libraries and Archives: Proposal by the African Group*; IFLA, Treaty Proposal, 2013, 2; Firth and Preira, Exceptions for Libraries, 2016, 49.

614 WIPO SCCR/22/12, Draft WIPO Treaty, 2011, *Op.cit.*

615 WIPO SCCR/29/4, *Consolidation of proposed texts contained in document SCCR/26/3*, (8 December 2014) Topic 6.

616 Firth and Preira, Exceptions for Libraries, 2016, 51.

617 Art. 1(2) of the InfoSoc Directive; Hugenholtz and others, Recasting, 2006, 62; Janssens, The Issue of Exceptions, 2009, 325–326; Triaille and others, Study, 2013, 246–247.

and Lending Directive and the Database Directive will only be mentioned if and when applicable. I will start by looking at some general issues relating to the exceptions and limitations in the InfoSoc Directive before discussing specifically libraries and exceptions under the Directive. I will then discuss the Orphan Works Directive and, finally, evaluate the current exceptions applicable to libraries with regard to online use.

4.2.1. THE INFOSOC DIRECTIVE AND EXCEPTIONS AND LIMITATIONS

144. The goals of the InfoSoc Directive were to harmonise copyright legislation in the EU Member States, to respond to technological changes, to foster the development of the information society in Europe and to implement international obligations under the then recently adopted WIPO Internet Treaties.[618] Harmonisation based on a high level of protection was supposed to create legal certainty benefitting rightholders as well as the public at large.[619] In fact the CJEU has described the provision of a high level of protection as "the principal purpose" of the Directive.[620]

145. This harmonisation included limitations and exceptions[621], which at the time varied considerably between the Member States.[622] Thus the Directive should also "seek to promote learning and culture by protecting works and other subject-matter while permitting exceptions or limitations in the public interest for the purpose of education and teaching."[623] However, it was also stated that "proper support for the dissemination of culture must not be achieved by sacrificing strict protection of rights".[624] In Recital (31) of the InfoSoc Directive the harmonisation objectives of exceptions and limitations are explained in the following manner[625]:

> A fair balance of rights and interests between the different categories of rightholders, as well as between the different categories of rightholders and users of protected subject-

618 Recitals (1)-(7) and (15) InfoSoc Directive; Janssens, The Issue of Exceptions, 2009, 327; Geiger and others, InfoSoc, 2014, 397–399; Bechtold, Directive 2001/29/EC, 2016, 421; Guibault, Contracts, 2000, 142; SWD(2016) 301 final, IA Part I, 2016, 6.

619 Recital (4) and (9) InfoSoc Directive.

620 C-145/10 – Painer, par. 107; Arnold and Rosati, Are National Courts... 2015, 741.

621 Recital (31) InfoSoc Directive.

622 Geiger and others, InfoSoc, 2014, 437.

623 Recital (14) InfoSoc Directive.

624 Recital (22) InfoSoc Directive.

625 Recitals set out "concise terms for the chief provisions of the enacting terms", cf. European Union, *Joint Practical Guide of the European Parliament, the Council and the Commission for persons involved in the drafting of European Union legislation*, point 10. See further discussion on the role of recitals in Ch. 6.3.1.

matter must be safeguarded. The existing exceptions and limitations to the rights as set out by the Member States have to be reassessed in the light of the new electronic environment. Existing differences in the exceptions and limitations to certain restricted acts have direct negative effects on the functioning of the internal market of copyright and related rights. Such differences could well become more pronounced in view of the further development of transborder exploitation of works and cross-border activities. In order to ensure the proper functioning of the internal market, such exceptions and limitations should be defined more harmoniously. The degree of their harmonisation should be based on their impact on the smooth functioning of the internal market.

146. The provisions on exceptions and limitations were among the most controversial issues in the legislative process of the Directive.[626] The InfoSoc Directive provides for an exhaustive[627], but mainly optional, list of 20 exceptions and limitations in Art. 5. Only one is mandatory[628], the exception in Art. 5(1) for temporary acts of reproduction.[629] Art. 5(2) sets out optional exceptions and limitations regarding the reproduction right and 5(3) regarding both the reproduction and communication to the public right. Art. 5(4) provides that where Member States may provide for an exception or limitation to the reproduction right they can also provide for an exception or limitation to the right of distribution. Finally Art. 5(5) stipulates that the three-step test shall be applied to exceptions and limitations provided for in Art. 5. Recitals (31)-(40) set out the general functions of Art. 5.[630]

147. Some exceptions under the InfoSoc Directive, if implemented, must provide for "fair compensation".[631] In other instances the national legislator is free to provide for fair compensation when and if implementing exceptions. In fact fair compensation may be necessary in some of those instances under the three-step test.[632] However, if a rightholder has already received payment, e.g. as a part of a licence fee, no specific or seperate payment may be due.[633] Fair compensation under the exceptions in the InfoSoc Directive is an autonomous concept of EU

---

626 Bechtold, Directive 2001/29/EC, 2016, 421.

627 Recital (32) InfoSoc Directive; C-301/15 – Soulier, par. 26. See, however, Art. 5(3)(o) which allows for some uses of minor importance under already existing limitations or exceptions in national legislation.

628 Art. 6 OWD also provides for a mandatory exception to be added to the list in Art. 5 of the InfoSoc Directive, cf. Recital (20) OWD, see discussion on the Directive in Ch. 4.2.3.

629 See discussion on the exception in Ch. 3.1.2.

630 Geiger and others, InfoSoc, 2014, 449; Bechtold, Directive 2001/29/EC, 2016, 453–454; von Lewinski and Walter, Information Society Directive, 2010, 1020.

631 Art. 5(2)(a) for reprographic reproduction, Art. 5(2)(b) for private copying and Art. 5(2)(e) for reproduction of braodcast programs by social institutions. See also discussion in Bechtold, Directive 2001/29/EC, 2016, 458–460; Geiger and others, InfoSoc, 2014, 470–473.

632 Recital (36) InfoSoc Directive; Bechtold, Directive 2001/29/EC, 2016, 458; Geiger and others, InfoSoc, 2014, 470–471; Hugenholtz and others, Recasting, 2006, 70.

633 Recital (35) InfoSoc Directive.

law.[634] If implemented into national legislation the exceptions and limitations shall not "prevent the definition of contractual relations designed to ensure fair compensation for the rightholders insofar as permitted by national law."[635]

The provisions on exceptions in Art. 5 do not specify whether they can be applied to unpublished works or works that have not been legally made available in any other way.[636] The author of an unpublished work may have decided that the work should not be made public or may not have had the opportunity to exploit it. Thus some scholars have maintained that exceptions that pertain to uses of works which have not been disclosed to the public in any manner will be less likely to pass the three-step test.[637] Yet, many undisclosed works form an important part of the cultural heritage and can be essential for research and study.[638] There is no consensus on how this issue should be handled in Europe.[639]

148. The exhaustive list of exceptions in the InfoSoc Directive has been criticised as lacking flexibility, especially with regard to future technological developments and the expanding market for online content.[640] It is worth mentioning in this connection that it was decided at the 1967 Stockholm Conference for the revision of the Berne Convention that it would be unwise to adopt an exhaustive list of exceptions as lists tend to "be arbitrary and can never be comprehensive" and risk omitting "present and future" circumstances worthy of exception to the exclusive right.[641]

The InfoSoc Directive has also been criticised for the "asymmetry" between the wide-ranging and flexible non-exhaustive provisions granting exclusive rights and the exhaustive list of more narrowly described exception provisions.[642] At the same time, the imprecise wording and the optional nature of exceptions and limitations in Art. 5 of the InfoSoc Directive only provides for a "fragmentary legislative *acquis*" and thus not for sufficient harmonisation.[643] However, some find that the imprecision may be a blessing in disguise as it opens

---

634 C-572/13 *Hewlett-Packard Belgium SPRL v Reprobel SCRL* ECLI:EU:C:2015:750, CJEU, 12 November 2015 par. 35–39; C-467/08 *Padawan SL v Sociedad General de Autores y Editores de España (SGAE)* ECLI:EU:C:2010:620, CJEU, 21 October 2010 par. 33–37.

635 Recital (45) InfoSoc Directive.

636 Triaille and others, Study, 2013, 253–255.

637 Ricketson and Ginsburg, International, 2006, 778; Triaille and others, Study, 2013, 253–254.

638 Crews, 2008 Study, 2008, 46; Triaille and others, Study, 2013, 258, 269, 296, 319.

639 Triaille and others, Study, 2013, 255. See further discussion on the issue in Ch. 10.2.2.

640 Hugenholtz and others, Recasting, 2006, 66, 75.

641 Ricketson and Ginsburg, International, 2006, 779.

642 Ohly, Economic rights, 2009, 236; Senftleben, The International, 2010, 69.

643 Hugenholtz and others, Recasting, 2006, 66; Janssens, The Issue of Exceptions, 2009, 327–329; Lucie Guibault, 'Why cherry-picking never leads to harmonisation: The case of limitations on copyright under Directive 2001/29/EC', 2010, JIPITEC, 55–66, 57–58; Frank Gotzen, 'Copyright in Europe: quo vadis?', 2007, (211), Revue Internationale du Droit d'Auteur, 2–89, 15; European Copyright Society, Opinion on C-201/13 Deckmyn, 2014, par. 6; Arnold and Rosati, Are National Courts... 2015, ssnr 3; Geiger and others, InfoSoc, 2014, 445–446; COM(2015) 626 final, Towards, 2015, 6; Bechtold, Directive 2001/29/EC, 2016, 454.

up the possibility for more flexibility to legislate exceptions at the national level than a first glance of the InfoSoc Directive would suggest.[644]

149. In recent years the CJEU has had ample opportunity to interpret the exception and limitation provisions, which in turn has advanced harmonisation[645], although some commentators maintain that the Court has failed to "develop coherent, copyright specific reasoning under a teleological interpretation of European Law".[646] In its interpretation efforts the Court has applied a "strongly harmonising approach", i.a. referring to Recital (32) of the Directive, which calls for a "coherent application" of exceptions and limitations.[647] Furthermore, the Court has stressed that it has the sole responsibility for interpreting the scope of Arts. 5(2) and (3).[648] Some commentators welcome this development, asserting that the Court is able to resolve much more quickly sensitive legal issues on which there is a lack of political unity in the formal legislative process. Others are more critical, observing that law reform is not the role of the Court.[649]

4.2.1.1. CJEU decisions

150. The CJEU has repeatedly emphasised that limitations and exceptions should be interpreted strictly[650] and in accordance with the three-step test. This is in line with Recital (44), which seems to assert a narrow interpretation of exceptions and limitations, in particular with regard to the "new electronic environment". However, the Court has also simultaneously stated that an exception should be interpreted in such a way as to enable its effectiveness and purpose.[651] In fact, in a recent analysis of copyright jurisprudence by the Court it

---

644 Geiger and others, InfoSoc, 2014, 440, 457; Hugenholtz, The Dutch, 2012, 55; Hugenholtz and Senftleben, Fair Use, 2011, 13–14.

645 Geiger and others, InfoSoc, 2014, 449, 456.

646 Favale, Kretschmer and Torremans, EU copyright jurisprudence?, 2016, 31–34, 36–37.

647 Triaille and others, Study, 2013, 251; Padawan, par. 35; European Copyright Society, Opinion on C-201/13 Deckmyn, 2014, 2.

648 C-510/10 – DR and TV2 Danmark, par. 34–36.

649 Lionel Bently, 'Harmonization by Stealth: The Role of the ECJ', CRID/Ivir Conference, Ten Years after the EU Directive on Copyright in the Information Society: Locking Back and Looking Forward, European Parliament, Brussels, 2012 13 January 2012; Geiger and others, InfoSoc, 2014, 456; Rán Tryggvadóttir, 'Balancing of interests and cross-border use: Room for Nordic co-operation?', 2015, (6), NIR, 652–665, 655; European Copyright Society, Opinion on C-201/13 Deckmyn, 2014, 2–3; Favale, Kretschmer and Torremans, EU copyright jurisprudence?, 2016, 31–32.

650 See, e.g., *C-5/08 – Infopaq I, par. 56–57*; Joined cases C-403/08 and C-429/08 – Premier League, par. 162; C-145/10 – Painer, par. 109; C-302/10 – Infopaq II, par. 27; C-435/12 *ACI Adam BV and Others v Stichting de Thuiskopie and Stichting Onderhandelingen Thuiskopie vergoeding* ECLI:EU:C:2014:254, CJEU, par. 22–23; C-201/13 – Deckmyn and Vrijheidsfonds, par. 22.

651 Joined cases C-403/08 and C-429/08 – Premier League, par. 163; C-145/10 – Painer, par. 133; C-117/13 – TU Darmstadt, par. 43; C-201/13 – Deckmyn and Vrijheidsfonds, par. 23; Geiger

was found that exceptions and limitations were only construed narrowly in half of the relevant cases.[652] In the other half, the Court has i.a referred to the need to preserve a "fair balance" between stakeholders as set out in Recital (31)[653] as well as a "fair balance … between the applicable fundamental rights".[654]

151. The Court has stated that strict interpretation may be inappropriate in some instances as it may be incompatible with the aim of the relevant provision. Thus the Court explained in the TU Darmstadt case that a strict interpretation advocated by the rightholder would be:

> …hard to reconcile with the aim pursued by Article 5(3)(n) of Directive 2001/29 which is to maintain a fair balance between the rights and interests of rightholders, on the one hand, and, on the other hand, users of protected works who wish to communicate them to the public for the purpose of research or private study undertaken by individual members of the public.[655]

Furthermore, the Court has pointed out that strict interpretation may result in making normal exploitation of the work, which the exception is meant to facilitate, impossible. Accordingly the Court stated in the PRCA case,

> …that the viewing of websites by means of the technological process at issue represents a normal exploitation of the works which makes it possible for internet users to avail themselves of the communication to the public made by the publisher of the website concerned. Given that the creation of the copies in question forms part of such viewing, it cannot operate to the detriment of such an exploitation of the works."[656]

Moreover, where the aim of the exceptions is to strike a fair balance between a fundamental right of expression and the exclusive right of the author, no additional requirements for the use of the exception should be imposed on the application than are prescribed in the relevant provision of the Directive.[657] In addition, the Court has come to the conclusion that even though exceptions from the exclusive right should be interpreted strictly, this does not mean that concepts in such exceptions related to fundamental principles of law, such

---

and others, InfoSoc, 2014, 454; Christian Berger, 'Aktuelle Entwicklungen im Urheberrechts – Der EuGH bestimmt die Richtung', 2012, (5), ZUM, 353–432, 358.

652 Favale, Kretschmer and Torremans, EU copyright jurisprudence?, 2016, 58–59. The analysis covered all copyright and database right cases decided from the year 1992 to February 2014, cf. Ibid, 37–38.

653 Joined cases C-403/08 and C-429/08 – Premier League, par. 163; C-145/10 – Painer, par. 132; C-117/13 – TU Darmstadt, par. 31; C-201/13 – Deckmyn and Vrijheidsfonds, par. 26; C-360/13 – PRCA par. 24. See also Bechtold, Directive 2001/29/EC, 2016, 455.

654 C-314/12 – UPC Telekabel Wien, par. 46; C-461/10, Bonnier Audio AB, par. 56; C-360/10 – SABAM, par. 44; C-70/10 – Scarlet Extended, par. 46; C-557/07 – Tele2, par. 29; C-275/06 – Promusicae, par. 68.

655 C-117/13 – TU Darmstadt, par. 31.

656 C-360/13 – PRCA Par. 61.

657 C-145/10 – Painer, par. 134–136; Triaille and others, Study, 2013, 252.

as freedom of expression and the public interest, should be interpreted in a restrictive manner.[658]

152. The Court has stressed that Member States must exercise their discretion afforded under Art. 5 of the InfoSoc Directive, within the limits imposed by EU Law. This should i.a. take into account the principles of proportionality, high level of protection of copyright as the principal purpose of the InfoSoc Directive, and the need for legal certainty.[659] However, although Member States are free to introduce the optional exceptions and limitations under Art. 5, they may not define the limits of these in an un-harmonised manner.[660] The Court has also emphasised that the discretion of Member States when introducing exceptions is limited by the three-step test.[661]

4.2.1.2. The three-step test

153. Art. 5(5) of the InfoSoc Directive stipulates that the exceptions provided for in Art. 5 must comply with the three-step test, i.e. be interpreted and applied in accordance with its criteria.[662] How and by whom it must be done is, however, not clear. Although the CJEU has considered the three-step test in quite a number of judgements, it has not given a definitive ruling on the question as to how the test should be applied or by whom and, indeed, some of its rulings have been contradictory.[663]

154. The CJEU has stated that in introducing exceptions, Member States are limited by the three-step test.[664] The Court has furthermore asserted that the provision in Art. 5(5) is not intended to extend the scope of exceptions and limitations under Art. 5.[665] However, this does not seem to affect whether the Court interprets them narrowly or broadly. In the Infopaq I case the Court underlined that Art. 5(5) further supported strict interpretation of exceptions as

---

658 C-201/13 – Deckmyn and Vrijheidsfonds, par. 22–28.

659 C-145/10 – Painer, par. 104–108; Triaille and others, Study, 2013, 251.

660 C-510/10 – DR and TV2 Danmark, par. 36; C-435/12 – ACI Adam and Others, par. 34; Bechtold, Directive 2001/29/EC, 2016, 455; Geiger and others, InfoSoc, 2014, 455–456.

661 C-145/10 – Painer, par. 110.

662 C-5/08 – Infopaq I, par. 58; C-351/12 *Ochranný svaz autorský pro práva k dílům hudebním, o.s. (OSA) v Léčebné lázně Mariánské Lázně a. s.* ECLI:EU:C:2014:110, CJEU, 27 February 2014 par. 40; C-117/13 – TU Darmstadt, par. 47; Axhamn and Guibault, Cross-border ECL, 2011, 13; Geiger and others, InfoSoc, 2014, 442.

663 Arnold and Rosati, Are National Courts… 2015, 744–745.

664 C-145/10 – Painer, par. 110. See also C-301/15 – Soulier, AG opinion, par. 29.

665 C-117/13 – TU Darmstadt, par. 47; C-5/08 – Infopaq I, 58; C-435/12 – ACI Adam and Others, par. 26; C-463/12 *Copydan Båndkopi v Nokia Danmark A/S* ECLI:EU:C:2015:144, CJEU, 5 March 2015 par. 90; Arnold and Rosati, Are National Courts… 2015, 745; Jean-François Canat, Lucie Guibault and Elisabeth Logeais, Study, 2015, 17; C-301/15 – Soulier, AG opinion, fn. 17.

established by "settled case-law"[666] whereas in the TU Darmstadt case the Court rejected strict interpretation of the exception in the case at hand.[667]

In the ACI Adam case the Court was asked directly whether the three-step test can "form the basis for the expansion of the scope of the exception of Article 5(2), or [whether] ... its application [can] only lead to the reduction of the scope of the limitation." The Court answered that the test in Art. 5(5) of the Directive was "not intended either to affect the substantive content of provisions falling within the scope of Article 5(2) of that Directive or, inter alia, to extend the scope of the different exceptions and limitations provided for therein."[668] The Court came to the conclusion that the wording of the provision in case, Art. 5(2)(b), was to be interpreted strictly. Hence, although not specified in the provision, the interpretation precluded allowing reproduction for private use from unlawful sources, as the alternative interpretation would i.a. be incompatible with the exclusive right of reproduction and distort the functioning of the internal market. The Court then added that,

> ...national legislation, ..., which does not draw a distinction according to whether the source from which a reproduction for private use is made is lawful or unlawful, may infringe certain conditions laid down by Article 5(5) of Directive 2001/29.[669]

In the Copydan case the Court again stated that the provision in Art. 5(5) was not intended either to affect the substantive content or to extend the scope of the various exceptions and limitations in Art. 5(2). Hence the provision in Art. 5(2)(b) should not be read in the light of Art. 5(5).[670] The Court concluded that the fact that the EU legislator omitted to mention the characteristics of the devices used for private copying signified that the legislator did not consider that issue relevant.[671] Thus the Court seems to interpret the exceptions in Art. 5 independently of Art. 5(5).

155. The three-step test has generally been seen as addressed to national lawmakers.[672] However, there has been some controversy as to whether the three-step test in the InfoSoc Directive is aimed at the national courts as well as the national legislators.[673] The dispute has been fuelled by the fact that some

---

666 C-5/08 – Infopaq I, 57–58; Senftleben, WCT, 2016, 124.

667 C-117/13 – TU Darmstadt, par. 25–31; Senftleben, WCT, 2016, 125.

668 C-435/12 – ACI Adam and Others, par. 26.

669 Ibid, par. 29–41.

670 C-463/12 – Copydan Båndkopi, par. 90.

671 Ibid, par. 86–88.

672 Walter and von Lewinski (eds) European Copyright Law, A Commentary, 2010, 1060; C-462/09 – AG opinion in Stichting de Thuiskopie, par. 41; Geiger, Gervais and Senftleben, Understanding... 2015, 169; Arnold and Rosati, Are National Courts... 2015, 743.

673 Bechtold, Directive 2001/29/EC, 2016, 469; Hugenholtz and others, Recasting, 2006, 70; Janssens, The Issue of Exceptions, 2009, 328–329; Arnold and Rosati, Are National Courts... 2015, 741, 743–744; Geiger, The Role, 2007, 13; Torremans, Archiving exceptions, 2010, 118–119.

Member States have included the provision in their national legislation when implementing the Directive.[674]

Some of the case law of the CJEU has referred to the role of the three-step test in Art. 5(5) of the Directive at the implementation stage.[675] However, those cases do not exclude application of the test by national courts although the wording in the ACI Adams case stating that the provision "takes effect only at the time when they are applied by the Member States" may be seen to come close to such an implication.[676]

In the Stichting de Thuiskopie case the Advocate General explained that the three-step test is in general aimed at national legislatures but when interpreting national provisions "national judges will have to do so in light of that test, to the extent that national laws are ambiguous or leave room for different results."[677] Furthermore, in some cases the CJEU has held that the acts that fall under a specific exception must also fulfil the conditions of Art. 5(5)[678], thereby indicating that the three-step test is also aimed to national courts when deciding whether exceptions or limitations are applicable in specific cases.[679] Yet, in the Infopaq II case the CJEU explained that if an act of reproduction fulfilled all the criteria in Art. 5(1) of the InfoSoc Directive it would consequently fulfil the conditions of Art. 5(5).[680] In the Premier League case the Court stated that an act must both fulfil the condition of the specific exception as well as the three-step test. However, in its assessment of whether the acts in the case fulfilled the latter it referred to previous arguments as to why the acts fulfilled the specific exception, thereby implying that, if the acts could be considered as falling under the specific exception, they also fulfilled the three-step test.[681]

156. From the above I deduce that the three-step test in Art. 5(5) of the InfoSoc Directive is also addressed to the national courts[682] regardless of whether it has been implemented into national legislation. This "radically transforms [the three-step test's] purpose and meaning"[683] and assigns it a "*supra*-legal" quality.[684]

674 Von Lewinski and Walter, Information Society Directive, 2010, 1061; Senftleben, The International, 2010, 69–71.

675 C-462/09 *Stichting de Thuiskopie v Opus Supplies Deutschland GmbH and Others* ECLI:EU:C:2011:397, CJEU, 16 June 2011 par. 21–22, 33; C-145/10 – Painer, par. 110; C-435/12 – ACI Adam and Others, par. 25.

676 C-435/12 – ACI Adam and Others, par. 25; Arnold and Rosati, Are National Courts… 2015, 746.

677 C-462/09 – AG opinion in Stichting de Thuiskopie, par. 42.

678 Joined cases C-403/08 and C-429/08 – Premier League, par. 181; C-117/13 – TU Darmstadt, par. 56; C-360/13 – PRCA par. 54–63.

679 Arnold and Rosati, Are National Courts… 2015, 747.

680 C-302/10 – Infopaq II, par. 55–57; Arnold and Rosati, Are National Courts… 2015, 745–746; Geiger and others, InfoSoc, 2014, 448.

681 Joined cases C-403/08 and C-429/08 – Premier League, par. 181; Triaille and others, Study, 2013, 252.

682 Arnold and Rosati, Are National Courts… 2015, 747.

683 Geiger, Gervais and Senftleben, Understanding… 2015, 169.

684 Kur, Of Oceans 2008, 34; Crews, 2008 Study, 2008, 21–22.

Many have voiced concern that this will have a further restrictive effect on limitations and exceptions.[685] However, some commentators have suggested that the inclusion of the three-step test in the Directive could be seen as an enabling clause rather than an additional restriction to the scope of exceptions and limitations in Art. 5. Thus the three-step test could be seen as defining the outer limits of the system of exceptions as set out in the 2008 Declaration.[686]

4.2.2. THE INFOSOC DIRECTIVE AND LIBRARIES

157. There were wide differences in national exceptions for libraries in Europe before the adoption of the InfoSoc Directive in 2001, ranging from none to fairly liberal exceptions for reproduction purposes. There were, however, no general exceptions to the communication to the public right for libraries. Nevertheless, because of the wide divergences in the concept of what constituted communication to the public right, on-demand online transmission could potentially be considered to be outside of the exclusive right in some Member States.[687]

There are two optional exceptions in the InfoSoc Directive for "publicly accessible" libraries and other cultural heritage institutions: one fairly broadly worded provision providing for an exception to the reproduction right and another, much more specifically worded, regarding an exception to the communication to the public or making available right. The following sub-chapters will look at the relevance of these exceptions for enabling libraries to make in-copyright works available online.

4.2.2.1. The reproduction exception for libraries

158. The exception in Art. 5(2)(c) of the InfoSoc Directive is for "specific acts of reproduction" as repeated in Recital (40). This wording refers directly to the first prong of the three-step test.[688] The provision does not, however, stipulate

685 Torremans, Archiving exceptions, 2010, 119; Martin R.F. Senftleben, 'Overprotection and Protection Overlaps in Intellectual Property Law – the Need for Horizontal Fair Use Defences' in Annette Kur and Vytautas Mizaras (eds), *The Structure of Intellectual Property Law; Can One Size Fit All?* (Edward Elgar, 2011) 152; Senftleben, The International, 2010, 69.

686 European Copyright Society, Opinion on C-201/13 Deckmyn, 2014, par. 11; Geiger and others, Declaration, 2010, 119 et seq.; Geiger, Gervais and Senftleben, Understanding… 2015, 183–189. Geiger suggested already in 2007 that judges could use the three-step test to "open" the system of exceptions and limitations and extend their scope to circumstances unforeseen by the law, cf. Geiger, The Role, 2007, 17.

687 COM(97)628 final, InfoSoc Proposal, 1997, 12–13, 16–17.

688 SEC(2007) 1556, *Commission staff working document: Report to the Council, the European Parliament and the Economic and Social Committee on the application of Directive 2001/29/EC on the harmonisation of certain aspects of copyright and related rights in the information society*, 5; COM(2008) 466, Green paper, 2008, 7–8; Dreier and Hugenholtz (eds) Concise, 2006, 376; Bechtold, Directive 2001/29/EC, 2016, 462.

for which purposes such specific acts of reproduction should or could be.[689] It is generally accepted that the underlying purpose is for preservation and archiving[690] activities although further purposes are not excluded, as can be deduced from the legislative history of the provision.[691]

159. The list of beneficiary institutions is exhaustive[692] i.e. publicly accessible libraries, educational establishments, museums and archives. There has been some discussion, based on the different language versions of the provision, as to whether only libraries must be publicly accessible or also the other institutions. Recital (40) seems to favour the understanding of the English version, i.e. that all institutions, except archives, must be publicly accessible. There is, furthermore, no definition of what publicly accessible means, although the common understanding is that an institution fulfils the requirement if it is equally accessible to everybody on a non-discriminatory basis. This does not exclude user fees or even variable user fees for different groups of the public.[693]

160. The last part of the provision in Art. 5(2)(c) i.e. "which are not for direct or indirect economic or commercial advantage"[694], can be understood differently in the various language versions. Thus in the English, German and Swedish versions the relevant part can be understood to refer to the permitted reproduction rather than the beneficiary institutions, whereas the French and the Dutch versions refer to the beneficiary institutions.[695] The Commission seems to support the former understanding[696] while some scholars support the latter.[697] However, in the light of the fact that Recital (40) states that beneficiary institutions must be "non-profit" and the fact that the exception must pass the three-step test[698], the discussion does not have much practical importance. If the institutions are meant to be "not for direct or indirect economic or commercial

---

689 Hugenholtz and Senftleben, Fair Use, 2011, 14.

690 The terms preserving and archiving are used here in a broad and general sense as maintaining and keeping safe. Thus archiving is understood i.a. to make a copy to place in a collection or archive, cf. Triaille and others, Study, 2013, 265.

691 Ibid, 265–266; von Lewinski and Walter, Information Society Directive, 2010, 1038; European Copyright Society, Answer to the EC Consulation 2014, 14; Xalabarder, Digital Libraries, 2010, 239–241; Guibault, Evaluating Directive 2001/29/EC, 2008, 69.

692 Triaille and others, Study, 2013, 265, 267.

693 Von Lewinski and Walter, Information Society Directive, 2010, 1035–1036; Axhamn and Guibault, Cross-border ECL, 2011, 14; Dreier and Hugenholtz (eds) Concise, 2006, 376–377; Bechtold, Directive 2001/29/EC, 2016, 463; Triaille and others, Study, 2013, 267–268, 308.

694 Same wording as in Recital (11) Rental and Lending Directive; Triaille and others, Study, 2013, 271, 298–299; Dreier and Hugenholtz (eds) Concise, 2006, 377.

695 Axhamn and Guibault, Cross-border ECL, 2011, 15, fn. 58.

696 COM(2008) 466, Green paper, 2008, 8; COM(2009) 532 final, *Communication from the Commission: Copyright in the Knowledge Economy* (19.10.2009) 4.

697 Von Lewinski and Walter, Information Society Directive, 2010, 1036–1037; Dreier and Hugenholtz (eds) Concise, 2006, 377; Bechtold, Directive 2001/29/EC, 2016, 463.

698 Axhamn and Guibault, Cross-border ECL, 2011, 11, 15, fn. 58.

advantage" it excludes company libraries and archives, even though they may be open to the public without charge, not to mention private initiatives such as the Google Book project.[699] Even so, there is no stipulation that such institutions are publicly funded as long as they fulfil other requirements of the provision. Neither does the requirement exclude membership fees and other fees to cover the cost of running the institution in question, such as administration or operation costs.[700] This description would seem to be equally applicable to "non-profit" institutions.[701] On the other hand what constitutes non-commercial use does have practical implications but can be difficult to define, e.g. in private-public cooperation projects.[702] However, preservation acts per se are unlikely to confer great commercial advantages.[703]

161. All Member States have provisions which fall within the scope of Art. 5(2)(c), although not all have implemented the provision from the Directive as such.[704] For that reason and the unspecific wording of the provision in Art. 5(2)(c) national provisions vary considerably, both with regard to which institutions they cover and for what purposes reproduction is authorised.[705] Importantly, national provisions tend to be more restrictive than is required by the provision in the InfoSoc Directive.[706] There are several other issues not specified in this provision. One is the issue of compensation, which is not obligatory; hence Member States are free to provide for compensation or not.[707] The 2007 Study on the implementation of the InfoSoc Directive observes that some Member States have imposed on institutions a compensation scheme for use under this exception, whereas other Member States have not.[708] Another important issue is the question of format shifting. As it is not specified how reproduction under

---

699 Torremans, Archiving exceptions, 2010, 117; Klass and Rupp, EUROPEANA... 2014, 967–968.

700 Von Lewinski and Walter, Information Society Directive, 2010, 1036–1037; Dreier and Hugenholtz (eds) Concise, 2006, 377; Bechtold, Directive 2001/29/EC, 2016, 463; Triaille and others, Study, 2013, 268.

701 Axhamn and Guibault, Cross-border ECL, 2011, 14; Triaille and others, Study, 2013, 271.

702 European Commission, Report on the responses, 2014, 41.

703 Triaille and others, Study, 2013, 271, 299; Boulanger and others, Assessing, 2014, 37; Torremans, Archiving exceptions, 2010, 117.

704 Some Member States kept their exceptions for libraries unchanged from before the adaptation of the InfoSoc Directive, cf. Westkamp, Study, 2007, 22–25.

705 Guibault, Cultural, 2015, 186; Westkamp, Study, 2007, 22–27; SEC(2007) 1556, Infosoc Report 2007, 2007, 5; Axhamn and Guibault, Cross-border ECL, 2011, 17; Borghi and Karapapa, Copyright and Mass Digitization, 2013, 12; Boulanger and others, Assessing, 2014, 13; Guibault, Evaluating Directive 2001/29/EC, 2008, 69; Jean-François Canat, Lucie Guibault and Elisabeth Logeais, Study, 2015, 23; SWD(2016) 301 final, IA Part I, 2016, 120–122.

706 Xalabarder, Digital Libraries, 2010, 247; Boulanger and others, Assessing, 2014, 33; Triaille and others, Study, 2013, 272–278, 281–282; COM(2015) 626 final, Towards, 2015, 6; SWD(2016) 301 final, IA Part I, 2016, 120–122.

707 Bechtold, Directive 2001/29/EC, 2016, 458; Triaille and others, Study, 2013, 271; von Lewinski and Walter, Information Society Directive, 2010, 1027 and Recital (36).

708 E.g. Italy, Ireland and the UK, cf. Westkamp, Study, 2007, 27.

the exception should be executed it can cover digital reproduction, regardless of whether the original copy is analogue or digital.[709] This is confirmed in the Commission's Infosoc Report 2007, which states that it is possible for national legislators to enable format shifting.[710] However, in 2014 only 14 Member States had explicit provisions allowing for format shifting for preservation purposes.[711]

There is no limitation in Art. 5(2)(c) on which works it covers. It seems to be safe to assume that even unpublished works and works not made available could be reproduced under the exception, in particular for preservation purposes, as such reproduction will normally not affect the divulgation issue.[712]

162. Although there is general agreement that acts for preservation fall under the exception in Art. 5(2)(c) there is no clear consensus on the definition of such acts. Mass digitisation for preservation purposes is one of the disputed areas. At the time of the adoption of the Directive in 2001 mass digitisation was not envisaged.[713] In the wake of mass digitisation projects, such as the Google Book Search Project[714], discussion on whether the exception in Art. 5(2)(c) would allow digital libraries to make digital copies of their entire collections for preservation purposes became relevant. Commission reports from 2007 and 2008, which mention the exception, simply say that the provision would cover acts "necessary for the preservation of works contained in the libraries' catalogues."[715] However, in 2009 the Commission specifically stated that the provision does not give libraries and other beneficiary institutions a "blanket exception to digitise their entire collections".[716] This seemed also to be the conclusion of most scholars, based on the explicit reference in the provision to "specific acts". Yet, some maintain that it remains the prerogative of Member States to determine the precise scope of the exception in conformity with the three-step test.[717] In fact, libraries and other cultural heritage institutions seem to have relied on this exception to engage in mass digitisation, despite the lack of legal certainty.[718]

---

709 Guibault, The Nature, 2003, 25; Dreier and others, Museen, Bibliotheken, 2012, 279.

710 SEC(2007) 1556, Infosoc Report 2007, 2007, 5; 2006/585/EC, *Commission Recommendation on the digitisation and online accessibility of cultural material and digital preservation*, (24 August 2006) item 9.

711 European Commission, Digitisation report 2014, 2014, 51, 55; COM(2015) 626 final, Towards, 2015, 7. See also discussion in COM(2008) 466, Green paper, 2008, 8; SWD(2016) 301 final, IA Part I, 2016, 127.

712 Triaille and others, Study, 2013, 268–269, 296.

713 Ibid, 265–267, 285.

714 See discussion in Ch. 2.3.

715 SEC(2007) 1556, Infosoc Report 2007, 2007, 5; COM(2008) 466, Green paper, 2008, 8.

716 COM(2008) 466, Green paper, 2008, 7 COM(2009) 532 final, Communication on Copyright, 2009, 4.

717 Mihály Ficsor, *The Law of Copyright and the Internet; The 1996 WIPO Treaties, their Interpretation and Implementation* (Oxford University Press, 2002), 527.

718 Triaille and others, Study, 2013, 281. In Norway the National Library can digitise all its collection for preservation purposes, cf. Norwegian National Library, *Response to the Public Consultation on the review of the EU copyright rules*, 20; St.meld. nr. 24, *Nasjonal strategi*

In my view interpretation of this exception depends on whether digital preservation is deemed to be necessary or not. Digital preservation might be seen as the optimal solution, and thus necessary, for preserving our cultural heritage for the future, and preferable to a piecemeal replacing of copies that are in immediate danger of becoming obsolete.[719] If digital preservation were to be regarded as "necessary" then it should qualify as being "specific" enough[720] and could be the basis for digitising the whole collection. Such an understanding of the provision would, of course, in no way authorise the beneficiary institutions to make the digitised works available. However, in order to create more legal certainty for this interpretation it would be preferable to amend the provision accordingly. The proposed preservation provision in the DSM proposal August 2016 would make this clear.[721] However, it is not clear in the proposed provision whether such copies could be used for any other legal purposes.[722] Some scholars have argued that copies made under the current exception in Art. 5(2)(c) cannot be used for online dissemination.[723] However, it is hard to see a justification for preventing librararies from using a legally created copy for another legal use[724], i.e. under a licence or if an exception or limitation allows making available, such as under Art. 5(3)(n) of the InfoSoc Directive. This is the understanding in Denmark, Finland and Norway where ECL agreements on online availability of in-copyright works exclude the necessary digitisation act from the agreement as they fall under the preservation exceptions.[725]

4.2.2.2. The exception for making available by dedicated terminals

163. The exception in Art. 5(3)(n) is a narrowly formulated[726] provision and limited in several aspects.[727] It only applies to consultation on "dedicated terminals on the premises" of the relevant beneficiaries for the purpose of research and private study, and it excludes use of works and other subject matter which are "subject to purchase or licensing terms".[728]

---

for digital bevaring og formidling av kulturarv (2008–2009), (17 April 2009) 106; Vigdis Moe Skarstein, 'The Bookshelf: digitisation and access to copyright items in Norway', 2010, (1), Program, 48–58, 52.

719 Triaille and others, Study, 2013, 293.

720 Iglesias, Digital, 2008, 350.

721 Art. 5 of the DSM proposal.

722 See Ch. 4.2.4.1.1.1.

723 Axhamn and Guibault, Cross-border ECL, 2011, 17.

724 European Copyright Society, Answer to the EC Consulation 2014, 17.

725 See discussion in Ch. 5.3.1.2, 5.3.1.4, 5.3.2.1 and 10.2.4.

726 COM(2008) 466, Green paper, 2008, 9; Torremans, Archiving exceptions, 2010, 117.

727 Guibault, Cultural, 2015, 186 Triaille and others, Study, 2013, 307; Jean-François Canat, Lucie Guibault and Elisabeth Logeais, Study, 2015, 27–28; European Copyright Society, Answer to the EC Consulation 2014, 14–15.

728 Bechtold, Directive 2001/29/EC, 2016, 468; Dreier and others, Museen, Bibliotheken, 2012, 278–279.

164. There is no indication in the preparatory acts or elsewhere of the rationale for the provision. However, the aim of the provision seems to be to create similar conditions for the consultation of digitised material as for browsing of a book in the library.[729] The provision stipulates that the communication or the making available should be to individual members of the public, i.e. not to the general public or a gathered audience. Currently the twofold limitation on the permitted communication to the public under Art. 5(3)(n), i.e. that it has to happen through dedicated terminals and on the premises of the relevant establishment, excludes any remote access for consultation.[730] Recital (40) of the InfoSoc Directive underlines that exceptions or limitations for the benefit of non-profit establishments, such as publicly accessible libraries, should not "cover uses made in the context of on-line delivery of protected works" and this is restated in the 2008 Green Paper.[731] Instead online dissemination should be "promoted" with "specific contracts or licences" favouring cultural heritage institutions.[732]

However, using the CJEU approach of interpreting provisions in the light of their purpose[733], the provision could be interpreted more broadly, so as to include the use of personal computers on site and also possibly to allow for consultation on the general site of e.g. educational institutions.[734] Today's technological possibilities to remotely consult material supports demands to widen or clarify the notion of "on-site" consultation.[735] The decision in the VOB case[736], discussed below[737], may influence the scope of exception in Art. 5(3)(n).

165. The beneficiary institutions are the same as under Art. 5(2)(c).[738] As with that provision there is no requirement in Art. 5(3)(n) that compensation be paid to rightholders, although Member States are still free to require such compensation in their national legislation.[739] In contrast to Art. 5(2)(c) there is no stipulation that acts under the provision should not be "for direct or indirect

---

729 Von Lewinski and Walter, Information Society Directive, 2010, 1056; Axhamn and Guibault, Cross-border ECL, 2011, 17.

730 Triaille and others, Study, 2013, 310–312; Dreier and Hugenholtz (eds) Concise, 2006, 381; Bechtold, Directive 2001/29/EC, 2016, 468; von Lewinski and Walter, Information Society Directive, 2010, 1056; Axhamn and Guibault, Cross-border ECL, 2011, 18.

731 COM(2008) 466, Green paper, 2008, 10.

732 Recital (40) InfoSoc Directive.

733 See discussion in Ch. 4.2.1.1.

734 Triaille and others, Study, 2013, 311–312; Guibault, The Nature, 2003, 23.

735 Triaille and others, Study, 2013, 307; 316; EBLIDA, Response to the European Commission's Green Paper on the online distribution of audiovisual works in the European Union: opportunities and challenges towards a digital single market, 2011, 3.

736 C-174/15 - VOB, *op.cit.*

737 Ch. 4.2.4.1.1.2.

738 Bechtold, Directive 2001/29/EC, 2016, 468; Dreier and Hugenholtz (eds) Concise, 2006, 381; von Lewinski and Walter, Information Society Directive, 2010, 1056; Triaille and others, Study, 2013, 308.

739 Bechtold, Directive 2001/29/EC, 2016, 458; Triaille and others, Study, 2013, 271, 313; von Lewinski and Walter, Information Society Directive, 2010, 1027 and Recital (36).

economic or commercial advantage".[740] There is no definition of what constitutes "research or private study". Commentators have pointed out that private study is narrower than private use and that, although research does not need to be "scientific", it presumably should not include commercial research.[741]

166. Member States have generally implemented[742] the exception in Art. 5(3)(n) literally.[743] Thus, national implementations are no more restrictive than the provision itself and there are hardly any differences in implementation between Member States.[744]

167. The exception in Art. 5(3)(n) is not limited to particular categories of works other than that they have to be "contained" in the collection of the relevant institution. Furthermore, there is seemingly no limit as to how many copies could be installed for consultation or the number of instances of simultaneous access.[745] Nevertheless, it is unlikely that the number of copies and/or simultaneous access could be unlimited as that would probably be incompatible with the three-step test in Art. 5(5).[746]

168. However, the exception in Art. 5(3)(n) was seen as being of limited value for libraries because it excluded use of works and other subject matter "subject to purchase or licensing terms". The interpretation of this condition by scholars varied from excluding works that were commercially available[747] to excluding only works that were actually purchased under licensing terms forbidding on-site consultations.[748] Now the TU Darmstadt case has provided some clarification. One of the questions referred in the case was whether a work was "subject to purchase or licensing terms" in the meaning of Art. 5(3)(n) when a rightholder offers the use of that work to the relevant institution under a licensing agreement on appropriate terms. The Court's conclusion was that the term referred to a licensing agreement that had actually been concluded and that set out the conditions for the use of the work in question. They maintained that a different

740 Axhamn and Guibault, Cross-border ECL, 2011, 18.
741 Triaille and others, Study, 2013, 308; von Lewinski and Walter, Information Society Directive, 2010, 1056.
742 Not all Member States have implemented this exception. In the 2013 InfoSoc Study it is stated that nine Member States had not implemented the provision, cf. Triaille and others, Study, 2013, 313.
743 Westkamp, Study, 2007, 45–48; Guibault, Evaluating Directive 2001/29/EC, 2008, 70; Iglesias, Digital, 2008, 350; Triaille and others, Study, 2013, 313; Guibault, Cultural, 2015, 186.
744 Triaille and others, Study, 2013, 317.
745 Ibid, 313.
746 See in this respect C-117/13 – TU Darmstadt, par. 56.
747 Von Lewinski and Walter, Information Society Directive, 2010, 1056; Dreier and Hugenholtz (eds) Concise, 2006, 381.
748 Triaille and others, Study, 2013, 309–310; Axhamn and Guibault, Cross-border ECL, 2011, 18.

conclusion would be difficult to reconcile with the balancing aim pursued by the exception.[749]

The TU Darmstadt case also clarified whether the exception under Art. 5(3)(n) covered any form of reproduction. One of the questions posed in the case was whether the provision should be interpreted as allowing national legislation to confer on the relevant institutions the right to digitise works that they can make available under that provision. The CJEU conclusion was in the affirmative, stating that Art. 5(3)(n), read in conjunction with Art. 5(2)(c),

> ...must be interpreted to mean that it does not preclude Member States from granting to publicly accessible libraries covered by those provisions the right to digitise the works contained in their collections, if such act of reproduction is necessary for the purpose of making those works available to users, by means of dedicated terminals, within those establishments.[750]

The CJEU stated that libraries cannot digitise the entire library under the exception in 5(3)(n).[751] However, there is no obvious limiting principle in the Court's opinion.[752] Ginsburg and Treppoz claim that in the TU Darmstadt case the CJEU goes further than the US Court in the Hathi Trust case.[753] However, in the Google Book case the second circuit court states expressly that if "the library had created its own digital copy to enable its provision of fair-use digital searches, the making of the digital copy would not have been an infringement."[754]

4.2.3. THE ORPHAN WORKS DIRECTIVE AND LIBRARIES

169. The above account makes it clear that neither of the two exceptions provided for in the InfoSoc Directive facilitate the making of in-copyright works available online by libraries. Given that Recital (40) of the Directive expressly states that online dissemination by libraries and similar institutions should be facilitated by specific contracts or licences rather than exceptions or limitations, this is not surprising. Nevertheless, the Orphan Works Directive has since introduced a mandatory exception[755] for the reproduction and making

749 C-117/13 – TU Darmstadt, par. 22–35.

750 Ibid, par. 2, 10–13, 17, 49. The German Federal Court has since ruled in favour of TU Darmstadt on both accounts, see BGH 16. April 2015 – I ZR 69/11 – Elektronische Leseplätze II.

751 Ibid, par. 45; Guibault, Cultural, 2015, 186; Jean-François Canat, Lucie Guibault and Elisabeth Logeais, Study, 2015, 23.

752 Ginsburg and Treppoz, International, 2015, 502.

753 Ibid, 502–503.

754 Authors Guild v. Google (USCA SC 2015), 44. See Ch. 2.3.2.

755 Art. 6 and Recital (20) OWD; Bechtold, Directive 2001/29/EC, 2016, 463; Lucie Guibault, 'Orphan Works Directive' in Thomas Dreier and P. Berndt Hugenholtz (eds), *Concise European Copyright Law* (2 edn, Wolters Kluwer, 2016) 534; Janssens and Tryggvadóttir, Orphan, 2016, 195.

available of orphan works in order to "promote learning and the dissemination of culture."[756]

4.2.3.1. Background

The issue of orphan works and the importance of finding a solution to allow libraries to use orphan works, in particular online[757], was one of the copyright challenges identified in the Digital Library Initiative.[758] Thus the 2006 Recommendation encouraged Member States to create mechanisms and rights information lists to facilitate the use of orphan works.[759] In subsequent years the various expert groups[760] on the issue recommended national and non-mandatory solutions:

> The High Level Expert Group on Digital Libraries (HLG) recommended solutions based on diligent prior search and mutual recognition.[761] The "Comité des Sages" recommended an "8-step-test" for the use of orphan works, mostly in line with the previous HLG recommendations except prior diligent search was not prescribed.[762]

170. Despite these recommendations, only a few Member States implemented solutions[763] and those were limited to their national territories.[764] The Commission concluded that the voluntary approach was not working and that "… the coexistence of uncoordinated national approaches governing orphan works in online libraries makes it difficult for a library to make orphan works available across EU Member States."[765] The Commission asserted that EU action was necessary, as otherwise Member States could not recognize orphan work status from other Member States or implement exceptions that were outside the InfoSoc Directive. Furthermore, because of the territoriality of copyright, national legislation could not allow for online access to orphan works across national borders. Moreover, the Commission found it doubtful that in the absence of EU action the Member States would recognise and give effect to

---

756 Recital (20) OWD.

757 SEC(2011) 615 final, Impact Assessment, 2011, 6.

758 COM(2005) 465, i2010: Digital Libraries, 2005, 6 to 7. See Ch. 2.4.1.

759 2006/585/EC, Recommendation, 2006, Item 6 and Recital (11).

760 See Ch. 2.4.1.

761 HLG, Final report, 2009, 4.

762 Cf. Comité des Sages, The New Renaissance, 2011, 17 to 18.

763 SEC(2011) 615 final, Impact Assessment, 2011, 12 and 48; KEA European Affairs, *Audiovisual Orphan Works in Europe – national survey; Report prepared for the British Film Institute (BFI)*, 4; Suthersanen and Frabboni, The Orphan, 2014, 655; Eleonora Rosati, 'The Orphan Works Directive, or throwing a stone and hiding the hand', 2013, Journal of Intellectual Property Law & Practice, 303–310, 304.

764 COM(2011) 289 final, Proposal 2011, 1; SEC(2011) 615 final, Impact Assessment, 2011, 12; Suthersanen and Frabboni, The Orphan, 2014, 655–656.

765 COM(2011) 289 final, Proposal 2011, 3 and 4.

searches carried out in other jurisdictions, which would lead to duplication of work.[766] Hence a legislative proposal in the form of a Directive was deemed to be necessary[767], as otherwise Europe might be left behind in the quest to fill the "knowledge gap" compared to the Google initiative.[768] The Orphan Works Directive was adopted in October 2012, after a relatively short adoption process.[769, 770]

4.2.3.2. *Beneficiary institutions*

171. The Directive allows specified institutions, not individuals[771], certain uses of orphan works to enable them to achieve aims related to their public-interest missions. The institutions can be divided into four categories[772]: first, publicly accessible libraries, educational establishments and museums; second, archives, which need not be publicly accessible[773]; third, film or audio heritage institutions; and fourth, public-service broadcasting organisations. All must be established in a Member State.[774] The list of beneficiary organisations is exhaustive.[775] However, it is not clear whether Member States are obliged to implement the Directive in such a way that all these institutions would be beneficiaries and able to use orphan works. Member States seem to have interpreted it as giving them a choice. Recital (20) of the OWD underlines that the first two categories cover the same institutions as in Art. 5(2)(c) of the InfoSoc Directive, whereas the remaining two are additional to that list. The Recital seems to indicate that some official recognition is required for the institutions in categories three and four.[776]

172. Neither the OWD nor the InfoSoc Directive provides a definition of what constitutes a "publicly accessible" institute.[777] The OWD does not specify whether the institutions must be public or whether the directive also applies to private institutions with a "public-interest mission". The omission seems to

---

766 SEC(2011) 615 final, Impact Assessment, 2011, 14; Janssens and Tryggvadóttir, Facilitating, 2015, 48; Rosati, Orphan Works, 2013, 307.

767 COM(2011) 289 final, Proposal 2011, 3 and 4.

768 SEC(2011) 615 final, Impact Assessment, 2011, 7; Rosati, Orphan Works, 2013, 304.

769 Guibault, Orphan, 2016, 511.

770 See discussion in Ch. 5.2.1.1 and 6.3.2 on ECLs as a solution for the orphan works issue.

771 Suthersanen and Frabboni, The Orphan, 2014, 657; Janssens and Tryggvadóttir, Facilitating, 2015, 39; Janssens and Tryggvadóttir, Orphan, 2016, 192.

772 Janssens and Tryggvadóttir, Facilitating, 2015, 39; Janssens and Tryggvadóttir, Orphan, 2016, 192–193.

773 In this respect the OWD provision is clearer than the provision in Art. 5(2) (c) InfoSoc Directive, cf. Janssens and Tryggvadóttir, Facilitating, 2015, 40. See discussion in Ch. 4.2.2.1.

774 Art. 1(1) OWD. Janssens and Tryggvadóttir, Orphan, 2016, 192; Guibault, Orphan, 2016, 521.

775 Cf. OHIM presentation for the Copyright Contact Committee 5 June 2013, *Setting up of single EU Orphan Works database* (05.06.2013); Janssens and Tryggvadóttir, Facilitating, 2015, 39.

776 Janssens and Tryggvadóttir, Facilitating, 2015, 41; Janssens and Tryggvadóttir, Orphan, 2016, fn. 25; Guibault, Orphan, 2016, 520–521.

777 See discussion in Ch. 4.2.2.1.

indicate that it applies to both.[778] Thus, unlike under the exception in Art. 5(2)(c) of the InfoSoc Directive, the beneficiaries under the OWD are not restricted by their non-profit purpose.[779] However, the directive is not applicable to purely commercial undertakings even if they should be publicly accessible, as applicable institutions have to have a public-interest mission.[780]

4.2.3.3. Orphan works: scope and definition

173. The Directive is applicable to many categories of works[781] but not all.[782] Works that can obtain orphan work status are literary works[783], cinematographic or audio-visual works and phonograms[784] contained in collections or archives of the applicable institutions[785], which have been first published or broadcast in a Member State and that are still protected by copyright or related rights.[786] This excludes works first published or broadcasted elsewhere in the world.[787] This was decided for reasons of international comity. No definition of when works are first published in a Member State is provided, but the provisions in Art. 3(3) of the Berne Convention must be taken into account.[788] There are no guidelines regarding works for which it is impossible to locate the place of first publication or broadcast.[789]

Unpublished works that have been made publicly accessible by a beneficiary institution with the consent of the rightholders can also fall under the Directive "provided that it is reasonable to assume that the rightholders would not oppose the uses ..."[790] No further information is found in the Directive or preparatory documents on how this requirement should be accessed. The criteria by which it can be assumed that an author would not be opposed to a particular use will be very hard to determine.[791] The Directive also includes works embedded in the literary, cinematographic or audio-visual works and phonograms.[792]

---

778 Suthersanen and Frabboni, The Orphan, 2014, 657; Janssens and Tryggvadóttir, Facilitating, 2015, 40.

779 Guibault, Orphan, 2016, 521.

780 Rosati, Orphan Works, 2013, 308.

781 The Directive applies to related rights as well, cf. Art. 1(2) i.f. and Recital (3) OWD.

782 Janssens and Tryggvadóttir, Orphan, 2016, 193.

783 Art. 1(2)(a) refers to printed matter, including electronic versions thereof, cf. Guibault, Orphan, 2016, 522; Suthersanen and Frabboni, The Orphan, 2014, 658–659.

784 Here the term work will be used to cover both works and phonograms.

785 Art. 1(2) (a)-(c) OWD.

786 Art 1(2) and Recital (12) OWD.

787 Recital (12) OWD.

788 Janssens and Tryggvadóttir, Facilitating, 2015, 43; Guibault, Orphan, 2016, 523. See also discussion in Ch. 10.2.2.

789 Janssens and Tryggvadóttir, Orphan, 2016, 193.

790 Art. 1(3) OWD.

791 Janssens and Tryggvadóttir, Facilitating, 2015, 43; Triaille and others, Study, 2013, 254; Suthersanen and Frabboni, The Orphan, 2014, 661–662; Guibault, Orphan, 2016, 523; Rosati, Orphan Works, 2013, 308.

792 Art. 1(4) OWD.

An important category of works not covered by the Directive is stand-alone photographs and other images[793], which are commonly orphan.[794] Furthermore, the Directive only applies to works contained in the archives of public service broadcasting organisations if they are produced before or on 31 December 2002. The cut off date is said to be necessary in order to take "into account the special position of broadcasters as producers of audio and audio-visual material and the need to adopt measures to limit the phenomena of orphan works in the future".[795] Although the cut-off date is clearly intended to reduce the occurrence of orphan works in the future[796] there is no further elucidation of the special position of broadcasters or why the proposed cut-off date was chosen.[797]

174. The definition of an orphan work is set out in Art. 2 of the Directive where it is stated that a work "shall be considered an orphan work if none of the rightholders in that work or phonogram is identified or, even if one or more of them is identified, none is located despite a diligent search for the rightholders having been carried out and recorded ..."

In the event that one or more of a number of rightholders has been identified and located, the organisations entitled to use orphan works may still use such works provided that the rightholders already identified and located authorise them to do so in relation to the rights they hold in the work.[798] Originally it was suggested that if one rightholder had been identified and located then that work could not be considered orphan.[799] However, this interpretation was abandoned as it would have rendered the Directive inapplicable to the majority of works, in particular in the audiovisual field. Nevertheless, the situation under the current wording remains that if only one of many rightholders is identified and located, he or she can hinder the use of the work. This can prove problematic in e.g. the audiovisual field.[800]

4.2.3.4. Diligent search and orphan work status

175. Diligent search is a prerequisite for awarding an orphan work status. The conduct of a diligent search is described in Art. 3 of the Directive, where it is

793 Art. 10(1) OWD; Guibault, Orphan, 2016, 524; Suthersanen and Frabboni, The Orphan, 2014, 660–661.

794 SEC(2011) 615 final, Impact Assessment, 2011, 11; Jean-François Canat, Lucie Guibault and Elisabeth Logeais, Study, 2015, 29.

795 Recital (10) OWD.

796 Guibault, Orphan, 2016, 522; Suthersanen and Frabboni, The Orphan, 2014, 660.

797 The special position referred to may be that broadcasters should be able to identify rightholders to material they have produced themselves; however, this still does not explain the cut-off date, cf. Janssens and Tryggvadóttir, Facilitating, 2015, 44. The European Broadcasting Union (EBU) was against a specific cut-off date and argued it should be left to Member States to decide on the issue according to the situation in each country, cf. EBU's position on the proposal for the OWD, 27 March 2012.

798 Art. 2(2) and Recital (17) OWD.

799 COM(2011) 289 final, Proposal 2011, Art. 2(2).

800 Guibault, Orphan, 2016, 525–526.

stated that the beneficiary institutions shall be responsible for ensuring that a diligent search in good faith is carried out prior to the use of each work.[801] The diligent search can either be carried out by the institution wishing to use the work or by another organisation, which may charge for the service.[802] Each Member State shall determine the sources to be consulted in collaboration with stakeholders. Included must be sources listed in the Annex to the Directive.[803] The approach taken in the OWD offers flexibility.[804] However, most Member States have chosen to specify only the mandatory list of sources[805], which is already quite extensive.[806]

176. Diligent search need only be carried out in the Member State where the work was first published or broadcast, in order to avoid duplication of search efforts[807], unless there is evidence to suggest that there is relevant information to be found in another country.[808] It is not specified whether 'countries' in this instance refers only to Member States of the EU or the whole world, but the latter seems to be the logical conclusion.[809] In the case of cinematographic or audio-visual works the producer of which has his or her headquarters or habitual residence in a Member State, the diligent search shall be carried out in that Member State. In the case of works that have neither been published nor broadcast but have been made publicly accessible by a beneficiary organisation, the diligent search shall be carried out where that organisation is established.[810]

177. Search records should be kept on file by the organisation concerned in order to verify that the search was diligent.[811] This is important because if a work has been wrongly found to be an orphan work due to a non-diligent search the use must be compensated according to national provisions on copyright infringement.[812] It is not stipulated for how long the search records should be kept.

---

801 Art. 3(1) OWD; Suthersanen and Frabboni, The Orphan, 2014, 671–672; Janssens and Tryggvadóttir, Orphan, 2016, 194; Guibault, Orphan, 2016, 525, 528.

802 Recital (13) OWD.

803 Art. 3(2) OWD. See also Recital (14).

804 Janssens and Tryggvadóttir, Facilitating, 2015, 52; HLG – Copyright Subgroup, *Final Report on Digital Preservation, Orphan Works and Out-of-Print Works*, (04.06.2008) 15.

805 Janssens and Tryggvadóttir, Orphan, 2016, 197.

806 Janssens and Tryggvadóttir, Facilitating, 2015, 52; Suthersanen and Frabboni, The Orphan, 2014, 672.

807 Klass and Rupp, EUROPEANA… 2014, 973.

808 Article 3(4) OWD.

809 Janssens and Tryggvadóttir, Orphan, 2016, 194; Guibault, Orphan, 2016, 530; Suthersanen and Frabboni, The Orphan, 2014, 673.

810 Art. 3(3) and 3(4) and Recital (15) OWD.

811 Art. 3(5) and Recital (15) OWD.

812 Art. 6(5) and Recital (19) OWD.

Member States must provide for a competent national authority (CNA) to which the beneficiary organisations are to forward the results of the diligent search as well as information on the use made of an orphan work, any change in the orphan work status of works and the relevant contact information of the organisation concerned.[813] There is no further provision on the CNA and what its role should be. It varies considerably from one Member State to another which institutions have been appointed as the CNA.[814]

178. The information provided to the CNA must also be recorded in a single publicly accessible online database.[815] The Database became operational at the end of October 2014 and is managed by the European Union Intellectual Property Office (EUIPO).[816] It is not stipulated who should be responsible for forwarding information to the EUIPO Orphan Works Database, only that the Member States should forward it without delay after receiving the information from the relevant organisation. In practice it will probably be the task of the CNAs.[817]

179. There is lack of clarity on several points regarding how the orphan work status of a work is established. In particular, the Directive does not establish at what point a work receives legal orphan work status and whose responsibility this is.[818] Presumably this will not be clarified unless a case is referred to the CJEU.

---

813 Art. 3(5) OWD.

814 From the list of participants at a meeting on the Orphan Works Database and the Orphan Works Directive, held on 14 April 2015 at OHIM in Alicante ('the 2015 CNA OHIM meeting') it can be seen that the Ministry of Culture is most often the designated CNA, followed by national IP offices and national libraries. In the preparatory stages the Member States were concerned that the role of the CNA should not be too burdensome, cf. discussion at the EU Copyright Contact Committee on the 5 June 2013. See Janssens and Tryggvadóttir, Facilitating, 2015, 56–57; Janssens and Tryggvadóttir, Orphan, 2016, 197; Guibault, Orphan, 2016, 531.

815 Art. 3(6) OWD. This requirement has raised several questions with regard to the issue of a ban on formalities under Art. 5(2) BC, cf. Suthersanen and Frabboni, The Orphan, 2014, 674; Janssens and Tryggvadóttir, Facilitating, 2015, 57; Vuopala, Extended, 2013, 37, but will not be further investigated here.

816 The EUIPO is the successor of the Office for Harmonization in the Internal Market (OHIM), cf. Art. 2 of Regulation (EU) 2015/2424 of the European Parliament and of the Council of 16 December 2015 amending Council Regulation (EC) No 207/2009 on the Community trade mark and Commission Regulation (EC) No 2868/95 implementing Council Regulation (EC) No 40/94 on the Community trade mark, and repealing Commission Regulation (EC) No 2869/95 on the fees payable to the Office for Harmonization in the Internal Market (Trade Marks and Designs).

817 OHIM Orphan Works User Interfaces, *Prototype Version 2.0*, (April 1, 2014); Janssens and Tryggvadóttir, Orphan, 2016, 195; Guibault, Orphan, 2016, 531. This was an issue of concern for Member States at the EU Copyright Contact Committee meeting on 5 June 2013. Many wondered how the validation would be performed and how much involvement that would mean for the relevant CNA.

818 Janssens and Tryggvadóttir, Orphan, 2016, 200.

4.2.3.5. Cross-border applicability

180. Cross-border use of orphan works is facilitated by a provision on mutual recognition which enables relevant institutions to make the orphan work available to the public in other Member States.[819] Mutual recognition was a novelty in copyright law. It includes two aspects. First, the recognition of orphan work status in all Member States once recognised in one, and second, if a work is made available as an orphan in one Member State, such use is recognised as legal in all the other Member States.[820] The mutual recognition only operates within the territory of the EEA.[821] It makes it possible for beneficiaries that have a copy of the orphan work in their collection to make use of the work as permitted by the Directive in all the Member States, until the moment the rightholder puts an end to the orphan status.[822]

181. The aim of the provision was to avoid the need for "multiple diligent searches and duplication of task" and to ensure a high level of "legal certainty for the library community while respecting different legal and cultural traditions".[823] However, the Directive does not stipulate how precisely the mutual recognition should be established, leaving a lot of margin for manoeuvre, which can lead to differences in national implementation and therefore weakens legal certainty.[824]

4.2.3.6. The end of orphan work status

182. Member States must ensure that if a rightholder to a work that has been granted an orphan work status comes forward, he or she has an opportunity at any time to put an end to the orphan status as far as his or hers rights are concerned.[825] The Directive again does not establish how this should be done, i.e. to whom the rightholder should turn and who should then be responsible for communicating to users of the work the changed status or at what precise stage the orphan work status comes to an end.[826] These issues are also

819 Art. 4 and Recital (23) OWD.
820 Ringnalda, Orphan Works, 2011, 6.
821 Guibault, Orphan, 2016, 521.
822 Janssens and Tryggvadóttir, Facilitating, 2015, 49.
823 SEC(2011) 615 final, Impact Assessment, 2011, 33–34; Suthersanen and Frabboni, The Orphan, 2014, 679.
824 Reto M. Hilty and others, *Stellungsname des Max-Planck-Institut für Immaterialgüter- und Wettbewerbsrecht zur Anfrage des Bundesministeriums der Justiz vom 6. Juli 2011; Zum Richtlinienvorschlag der Europäischen Kommission über bestimmte zulässige Formen der Nutzung verwaister Werke, KOM(2011)289* (10 August 2011) 7; Janssens and Tryggvadóttir, Facilitating, 2015, 49; Guibault, Orphan, 2016, 531–532.
825 Art. 5 OWD.
826 Janssens and Tryggvadóttir, Facilitating, 2015, 49–50; Guibault, Orphan, 2016, 532–533.

relevant with regard to when an orphan work enters the public domain and at what point beneficiaries can start using the work simply because it is out of protection.

Furthermore, there is no provision in the Directive on mutual recognition of the termination of the orphan work status. However, it seems likely that termination of the orphan status would follow the process for its establishment, i.e. that once it is terminated in one Member State it is considered terminated in the others, as otherwise there would be an imbalance between the interest of the rightholders and the cultural heritage institutions able to use the orphan work.[827] While it seems clear that the beneficiaries, i.e. the users of orphan works, bear responsibility for establishing the orphan status of a work, it is not as clear who should be responsible for alerting them to the end of the orphan work status. This is an important issue as continued lawful use of such a work is contingent on authorisation by the newly "found" rightholder.[828] Member States have taken different approaches, thus in Finland the orphan work status does not end until a notice to that effect is introduced into the EUIPO Orphan Works Database, whereas in Austria and Germany[829] the beneficiary institution must stop using an orphan work as soon as it becomes aware of the identity and location of a rightholder.[830]

A rightholder that has terminated the orphan work status shall receive fair compensation.[831] The compensation should ensure that re-appearing rightholders are not significantly negatively affected by the use of their works by the beneficiary institutions.[832] This can be seen as an attempt to put re-appearing rightholders of orphan works on a same or similar level as recognised rightholders of comparable works. The work of the latter would not be used without their consent and probably would command a certain remuneration.[833] However, some commentators during the proposal stage were of the opinion that if the use of orphan works under the Directive complied with the three-step test, then no compensation was needed.[834]

---

827 Oostveen and Guibault, IPR issues, 2013, 20; Janssens and Tryggvadóttir, Facilitating, 2015, 49–50; Guibault, Orphan, 2016, 533.

828 Recital (17) OWD.

829 Art. 61b, German Copyright Act (GCA), see also Trumpke, Exklusivität, 2015, 657, fn. 2419.

830 Information from the 2015 CNA OHIM meeting. See also Janssens and Tryggvadóttir, Orphan, 2016, 8; Janssens and Tryggvadóttir, Facilitating, 2015, 50, fn. 72.

831 Art. 6(5) and Recital (18) OWD. In the original proposal there was no obligation for compensation for uses for the "public mission interest" of the beneficiary institutions, cf. COM(2011) 289 final, Proposal 2011, 11.

832 Boulanger and others, Assessing, 2014, 23.

833 Janssens and Tryggvadóttir, Facilitating, 2015, 70–71; Janssens and Tryggvadóttir, Orphan, 2016, 196.

834 ALAI, Orphan works – compatibility of the draft Directive with the international norms, (January 14, 2012); Janssens and Tryggvadóttir, Facilitating, 2015, 70, fn. 152.

It can be assumed that the organisation that has used the work in question is liable for the payment of the compensation. However, it is left up to Member States to decide how to organise compensation, taking due account i.a. of cultural promotion objectives, the non-commercial nature of the use and of the possible harm to rightholders.[835] Hence the actual compensation could be modest and under some circumstances none. However, one would assume that account should also be taken of remuneration to other rightholders of similiar non-orphan works.[836]

An important question here is how the compensation is to be determined in case of use in other Member States and who will be responsible for such payment.[837] One solution could be for national legislators to link the definition of notional "fair compensation" to the number of downloads of the work/ phonogram in question.[838] Such a solution could, however, create some friction with privacy issues, and in any case would still not answer the question of who should pay. Another question left unanswered by the Directive is when or if the right to compensation should expire. Again this leaves room for differences in implementation.[839]

4.2.3.7. Permitted uses

183. Member States must provide for an exception[840] to ensure that beneficiary organisations are permitted to use orphan works contained in their collections. Beneficiaries will then be allowed to make orphan works available to the public and to reproduce them for the purposes of digitisation, making available, indexing, cataloguing, preservation or restoration.[841] Permitted uses may only be "... in order to achieve aims related to their public interest missions, in particular the preservation of, the restoration of and the provision of cultural and educational access to, works and phonograms contained in their collections."[842] There are no further guidelines as what public interest mission entails.[843] However, the use is not restricted to non-commercial purposes.[844]

835 Janssens and Tryggvadóttir, Facilitating, 2015, 72; Suthersanen and Frabboni, The Orphan, 2014, 686; Guibault, Orphan, 2016, 536.

836 Janssens and Tryggvadóttir, Facilitating, 2015, 71.

837 Hilty and others, Nutzung verwaister Werke, 2011, 8.

838 Lucie Guibault, Are European orphans about to be freed?, Kluwer Copyright Blog, 21 September 2012; Last accessed 4 July 2017.

839 Rosati, Orphan Works, 2013, 309. For example, in Austria the right to compensation expires 10 years after the work has been first used, whereas such a limitation does not exist in the Finnish Act, cf. Janssens and Tryggvadóttir, Orphan, 2016, 197.

840 This mandatory exception must be added to the exhaustive list provided for in Art. 5 InfoSoc Directive, cf. recital (20) OWD.

841 Art. 6(1) OWD.

842 Art. 6(2) OWD and Recital (20).

843 Suthersanen and Frabboni, The Orphan, 2014, 658.

844 Guibault, Orphan, 2016, 535.

Recital (20) states that the exception can only be applied in conformity with the three-step test.[845]

184. When orphan works are used, the identity, where known, of authors and other rightholders must be indicated.[846] This requirement may be based on respect for the moral rights of authors although hitherto this aspect has not been harmonised at EU level.[847] However, in light of the importance that the Directive places on tracing rightholders, it is more likely that this obligation is to help locate rightholders who have been identified, in order to terminate the orphan work status if they reappear.[848]

Although the exception is mandatory there is no provision in the OWD securing that the permitted use under the exception is not over-ridden by contract. The wording of Art. 7 OWD even seems to point to the opposite, i.e. where it says 'This Directive shall be without prejudice to ... the law of contract ...'[849]

185. Institutions that are permitted to use orphan works may charge for their use but only in order to recover costs of digitising orphan works and making them available; however, no mention is made of the cost of recovering costs of establishing a work as an orphan work.[850] This provision to enable the institutions to recover their costs is meant to incentivise digitisation. Furthermore the beneficiary institutions are free to conclude contracts with commercial partners in pursuit of their public interest mission. This allows financial contributions from commercial partners. Nevertheless, it does not allow any restriction to be made to the use of the beneficiary institutions nor any right to such commercial partners to use or control the use of orphan works.[851] The requirement of public-interest mission is clearly aimed at preventing commercial entities from controlling access to the cultural heritage, as was feared might happen with the Google Book project. Thus it is regrettable that the requirement is not more clearly defined.[852]

---

845 Suthersanen and Frabboni, The Orphan, 2014, 688.

846 Art. 6(4) OWD.

847 Guibault, Orphan, 2016, 535.

848 Janssens and Tryggvadóttir, Facilitating, 2015, 67; Janssens and Tryggvadóttir, Orphan, 2016, 7.

849 Janssens and Tryggvadóttir, Orphan, 2016, fn. 48; Suthersanen and Frabboni, The Orphan, 2014, 688–689.

850 Guibault proposes that this provision should be read in conjunction with Art. 6(2)(c) of Directive 2003/98/EC of the European Parliament and of the Council of 17 November 2003 on the re-use of public sector information (the Public Sector Information Directive) which exempts e.g. libraries from limiting charges to marginal costs, cf. Guibault, Orphan, 2016, 535.

851 Art. 6(2) i.f., 6(4), Recital (21) and (22) OWD; Suthersanen and Frabboni, The Orphan, 2014, 685.

852 Janssens and Tryggvadóttir, Orphan, 2016, 196; Suthersanen and Frabboni, The Orphan, 2014, 658, 684–685.

4.2.3.8. Implementation

186. The Directive was to be implemented by Member States by 29 October 2014.[853] Most have opted for fairly literal implementation. Nevertheless, because of the flexibility allowed for in the Dirctive there are considerable differences in national implementation, such as in relation to the diligent search, end of the orphan works status and regulation of compensation.[854]

187. The Commission is to constantly review the development of sources with rights information and submit a report on the inclusion of works and other subject matter not currently included in the scope of the Directive, as well as a report on the application of the Directive in the light of the development of digital libraries.[855] Furthermore it is stipulated that if a Member State has valid reason to believe that the Directive is hampering national arrangements for management of rights[856], the Commission must react with a report on the situation and assess the need for a proposal amending the Directive. This applies to i.a. extended collective licenses for e.g. mass digitisation.[857] However, from a practical point of view it is unlikely that an amending proposal will come forward in the very near future as it will take the Commission a fair amount of time to assess the impact of the Directive as adopted and implemented.[858] Furthermore, in the light of the proposed provisions on the use of out-of-commerce works in the DSM proposal, it is unlikely that the OWD will be amended as its importance will be greatly diminished by the new Directive, if it is adopted.[859]

188. Next I will evaluate the current EU exceptions relevant for online use of works by libraries, beginning with the library exceptions in the InfoSoc Directive before moving on to evaluating the Orphan Works Directive.

---

853 Art. 9 OWD. The last EU Member State to officially transpose the Directive did so in November 2016, cf. Report from the Joint Meeting of the EFTA Working Group on Intellectual Property Rights with the EU Commission, 20 December 2016. The EFTA-EEA Member States have also implemented it.

854 Janssens and Tryggvadóttir, Orphan, 2016, 197; Rosati, Orphan Works, 2013, 309.

855 Art. 10 OWD. No such reports seem to have been issued, although the EUIPO is currently conducting a survey on orphan works, cf. <https://euipo.europa.eu/ohimportal/en/web/observatory/orphan-works-database>, access date 4 July 2017.

856 Cf. Art. 1(5) OWD.

857 Recital (24) OWD.

858 Information from the 2015 CNA OHIM meeting; Janssens and Tryggvadóttir, Orphan, 2016, 200.

859 See discussion on the DSMP in Ch. 11.3.

4.2.4. EVALUATION OF CURRENT EU EXCEPTIONS FOR DIGITAL LIBRARIES

4.2.4.1. *The InfoSoc Directive*

189. It has been stated that the provisions in both Art. 5(2)(c) and Art. 5(3)(n) show "a blatant discrimination of digital libraries."[860] Whether this is an exaggeration or not, it is clear that these provisions are not sufficient to enable libraries to fulfil their role properly in the digital age[861], even apart from the issue of making in-copyright works available online.

There are four main problems with the current provisions. The first is that both exceptions are too narrow to accommodate the needs of libraries in the current technological environment. The second, which mainly affects the optional provision in Art. 5(2)(c), is the lack of harmonisation in national implementation. The third is common to all other exceptions in the Directive and is the fact that exceptions can be overridden by contracts. The fourth, which will be discussed at a later stage[862], is the effect of the territoriality of copyright on cross-border use of exceptions in the online environment.[863]

4.2.4.1.1. The narrow scope

190. When the InfoSoc Directive was being prepared there were concerns that traditional exceptions to the exclusive right of rightholders might have too disruptive an impact on balance of rights in the digital world.[864] Thus the starting premises became that exceptions under the Directive should be narrow. However, the narrow scope of the exceptions for libraries has more or less deprived them of their ability to ensure the preservation and dissemination of the cultural heritage in the modern information age.[865]

4.2.4.1.1.1. Art. 5(2)(c)

191. Mass digitisation of books had not yet become a practical reality when the InfoSoc Directive was conceived and thus the legislators did not reflect on the digitising needs of libraries when adopting the exception. Hence current needs for digital preservation are not met in Art. 5(2)(c), both because of the

860 Xalabarder, Digital Libraries, 2010, 239; Firth and Preira, Exceptions for Libraries, 2016, 18.

861 Dreier and others, Museen, Bibliotheken, 2012, 278, 281; Kerremans, Janssen and Valcke, Collective solutions, 2011, 639.

862 See discussion in Ch. 8.2.

863 See e.g. SWD(2016) 301 final, IA Part I, 2016, 81.

864 Triaille and others, Study, 2013, 248; COM(97)628 final, InfoSoc Proposal, 1997, 18.

865 COM(2009) 532 final, Communication on Copyright, 2009, 4; Dreier and others, Museen, Bibliotheken, 2012, 281; Triaille and others, Study, 2013, 248; European Parliament, Resolution, 2015, item 39; SWD(2016) 301 final, IA Part I, 2016, 84.

unforeseen developments in digitisation and the uncertainty around the scope of the exception.[866] This discourages cross-border co-operation between libraries in digitisation projects.[867] Despite a recommendation from the Commission to Member States to make use of the scope of the exception, the implementation of the exception has in many cases been narrower than the provision allows. This fact, plus the political emphasis by the EU on the importance of preserving European culture in the digital age, is a valid argument for amending the exception to clarify that libraries are permitted to make digital reproductions of their whole collections.[868]

192. Fear, particularly among publishers, that digitisation by libraries might negatively impact nascent online business models are reflected in Recital (40), which underlines that exceptions or limitations for libraries and equivalent institutions should be limited to "certain special cases" covered by the reproduction right and should not cover uses made in the context of on-line delivery of protected works.[869] However, a recent study on the economic impact of adapting certain limitations and exceptions to copyright has found that an exception for preservation purposes for libraries would not affect rightholders substantially, as sales of replacement copies do not constitute a significant part of their revenue. Hence the study, in line with a previous one, recommended a mass digitisation provision for preservation purposes.[870] These recommendations were taken up by the Commission[871] and, in the DSM proposal, a mandatory exception was proposed to permit cultural heritage institutions "to make copies of any works or other subject-matter that are permanently in their collections, in any format or medium, for the sole purpose and to the extent necessary for the preservation of such works or other subject matter."[872] This would be in addition to the optional exception in Art. 5(2)(c)[873], but for a different group of beneficiaries, i.e. cultural heritage institutions. These are defined as "a publicly accessible library or museum, an archive or a film or audio heritage institution".[874]

The proposed exception for preservation purposes in the DSM proposal makes clear that cultural heritage institutions can make copies in any format or

[866] Triaille and others, Study, 2013, 284–285. See discussion in Ch. 4.2.2.1.

[867] Guibault, Cultural, 2015, 186; Recital (19) DSMP.

[868] Triaille and others, Study, 2013, 289. Both the 2006 and 2011 Commission Recommendations on the digitisation and online accessibility of cultural material and digital preservations called on Member States to adopt clear and explicit provisions on digital reproduction, see 2006/585/EC, Recommendation, 2006, item 9, item 9, and 2011/711/EU, Recommendation, 2011, item 9, item 9.

[869] Triaille and others, Study, 2013, 286.

[870] Boulanger and others, Assessing, 2014, 37–40; Triaille and others, Study, 2013, 293, 299.

[871] COM(2015) 626 final, Towards, 2015, 8.

[872] COM(2016) 593 final, Proposal, 2016, Art. 5.

[873] Cf. Art. 17(2)(a) DSMP.

[874] Cf. Art. 2(3) DSMP.

medium of any work permanently in their collection. The exception is intended to be without fair compensation or remuneration to rightholders. This is not spelled out in the provision itself but referred to in the Impact Assessment. This will help to limit the transaction costs for the relevant institutions and, as highlighted above, lost revenues for replacement copies of works in libraries do not constitute a substantial part of rightholders' revenue.[875]

The proposed preservation exception would not authorise the beneficiary institutions to make the digitised works available.[876] Nevertheless, an important question is whether the copies made under such a preservation exception might be used if libraries obtained licences to make digitised works available, or if they were authorised in some other way to make digital works available. This would depend on the interpretation of the words "for the sole purpose and to the extent necessary for preservation" if the proposed provision were adopted verbatim. In my view the wording should be interpreted in a "dynamic" or "evolving" manner.[877] Otherwise it would mean duplications of efforts for libraries if they had to digitise copies separately for other uses.[878] This wider understanding seems also to be indicated in the Impact Assessment of the proposal, which states that the provisions will not "as such (my underlining) ... permit further distribution or uses of the content, for example its making available."[879] This would also be in line with the ruling in the TU Darmstadt case.[880]

In considering the DSM proposal, one European Parliament Committee proposed that the purpose for the mandatory reproduction exception would be to allow beneficiaries[881] "to make copies of any works or other subject-matter that are permanently in their collections, in any format or medium, to the extent necessary for such reproduction, for the purpose of, individually or collaboratively with others, carrying out their public interest mission in preservation, research, culture, education and teaching."[882] In the ongoing consideration of the DSM proposal in the Council this wording has not been taken up. Nevertheless, in the "consolidated presidency compromise proposal" of March 2018 the proposed provision in Art. 5 has been slightly altered. The wording has been modified by removing the word "sole" so the exception is "for

875 Art. 5 DSM proposal; SWD(2016) 301 final, IA Part I, 2016, 128–130.

876 Ibid, 124.

877 C-174/15 – VOB, AG opinion, par. 28.

878 See e.g. criticism of such minimalist approach in European Copyright Society, General Opinion on the EU Copyright Reform Package, 2017, 3.

879 SWD(2016) 301 final, IA Part I, 2016, 124.

880 C-117/13 – TU Darmstadt, *op.cit.*, see discussion in Ch. 4.2.2.2.

881 Which they want to expand to include educational institutions.

882 EP IMCO, *Opinion of the Committee on the Internal Market and Consumer Protection for the Committee on Legal Affairs on the proposal for a directive of the European Parliament and of the Council on copyright in the Digital Single Market (COM(2016)0593 – C8-0383/2016 – 2016/0280(COD))*, (14 June 2017) 34–35.

the purpose of the preservation".[883] However, in the relevant recital a sentence has been added that:

> Acts of reproduction undertaken by cultural heritage institutions for purposes other than the preservation of works and other subject-matter in their permanent collections should remain subject to the authorisation of rightholders, unless permitted by other exceptions or limitations provided for by Union law.[884]

It remains to be seen whether this proposal will be integrated into the proposed legislation.

193. In my view a mandatory exception, as proposed in Art. 5 of the DSM proposal, is the best course of action. Simply revising Art. 5(2)(c), for example by replacing the words "of specific acts" with "acts of reproduction necessary to their purpose"[885], without making the exception mandatory would not have the same harmonising effect. Furthermore, not taking any action and depending on the CJEU to pave the way to clarify the limits under the current provisions with a flexible approach would be risky and not in line with the strong political emphasis on the importance of libraries in the digital age.[886]

My conclusion is thus that a mandatory preservation exception, allowing for mass digitisation by libraries and other cultural heritage institutions, would be of great importance for digital libraries to enable them to carry out their public interest missions of preserving the cultural heritage in the digital age. The benefits of allowing such "mass" digital reproduction for (future) preservation purposes would be manifold: first, it would secure future online availability to the cultural heritage when it comes into the public domain and, second, it would enable libraries to achieve economies of scale when digitising[887], i.a. via cross-border

883 2016/0280 (COD) 13842/17, *Proposal for a Directive of the European Parliament and of the Council on copyright in the Digital Single Market – Consolidated Presidency compromise proposal*, (30 October 2017) Art. 5; 2016/0280 (COD) 7450/18, *Proposal for a Directive of the European Parliament and of the Council on copyright in the Digital Single Market – Consolidated Presidency compromise proposal*, (23 March 2018) Art. 5.

884 2016/0280 (COD) 7450/18, Compromise proposal, 2018, recital (20). This recital is also in Council of the European Union agreed negotiating mandate on the proposal, cf. 2016/0280 (COD) 9134/18, *Proposal for a Directive of the European Parliament and of the Council on copyright in the Digital Single Market – Agreed negotiation mandate*, (25 May 2018).

885 Triaille and others, Study, 2013, 298. Similarly it has been suggested that the scope of the exception should allow for "All acts of reproduction of the works and other subject matter in the collections of beneficiary institutions for all non-commercial purposes related to their public-interest missions", cf. Discussion Paper from the 4th Europeana Licensing Workshop, Luxembourg, 26–27 November 2015.

886 European Commission, Report, 2016, 9, 54–73; SWD(2016) 301 final, IA Part I, 2016, 123–131; Triaille and others, Study, 2013, 286–288.

887 Boulanger and others, Assessing, 2014, 30–31; Council of the European Union, 'Council conclusions on the digitisation and online accessibility of cultural material and digital preservation', 3164th Education, Youth, Culture and Sport Council meeting 10 and 11 May 2012, Brussels, 2012 5. The 2011 Recommendation also highlighted the economies of scale of mass digitisation, cf. 2011/711/EU, Recommendation, 2011, recital (10), recital (10).

co-operation.[888] In my view, such a provision would be compatible with the three-step test. The first step should be fulfilled by the fact that it is limited to institutions with a public interest mission. However, it might be advisable to set out in clearer terms that it was for acts related to such mission.[889] With regard to step two, I maintain that allowing for mass digitisation for preservation purposes would not conflict with the normal exploitation of the works as libraries would still buy or license copies for their collections. Finally, as outlined above, the economic interest of the rightholders would not be unreasonably prejudiced, which should enable the broadened exception to be considered to comply with step three. This would also put European libraries on an equal footing with libraries in the US, where it was established in the Google Book Search litigations that the digitisation of their collections for use consistent with the copyright law was fair use.

4.2.4.1.1.2. Art. 5(3)(n)

194. The exception in Art. 5(3)(n) with regard to making available is very limited. It has been claimed that the "restriction to dedicated terminals is outdated and too narrow and does not grant enough leeway to libraries in providing services to their patrons."[890] However, as the wording of the provision is specific and clear[891] it can be said that it provides legal certainty.

195. Many have proposed that the provision be amended to facilitate consultation by users on their own laptops and also off-site through secure networks.[892] Some have further suggested extending the beneficiaries to include film or audio heritage institutions and broadcasting archives.[893] Still others have suggested that it should cover non-commercial use for other purposes than research and private study.[894] Not all commentators, however, agree on the need for expansion of the provision.[895] To me an obvious amendment in light of technological developments is to allow users remote consultation for research and study purposes. Such an extension would make libraries' public mission role of securing transfer of

---

888 Recital (19) DSMP.

889 See Art. 6(2) OWD.

890 European Copyright Society, Answer to the EC Consulation 2014, 15.

891 Triaille and others, Study, 2013, 318.

892 European Copyright Society, Answer to the EC Consulation 2014, 15; Triaille and others, Study, 2013, 318–322; Xalabarder, Digital Libraries, 2010, 245–251; Torremans, Archiving exceptions, 2010, 118; Paul Keller, Lucie Guibault and Patrick Pfeiffer, 'Discussion Paper', 4th Europeana Licensing Workshop, Luxembourg, 2015 1. The Norwegian National Library proposes making an exception for online use for scientific and educational purposes without restricting it to onsite consultation or alternatively introduce EU ECL system, cf. Norwegian National Library, Response, 2013, 21.

893 Keller, Guibault and Pfeiffer, Discussion Paper, 2015, 1.

894 Institutional users, see European Commission, Report on the responses, 2014, 44.

895 Notably the CRA report recommended against it as in their view it would decrease rightholders "incentives for content creation", cf. Boulanger and others, Assessing, 2014, 29.

knowledge and access to information easier while technological development can provide measures for secure networks for such on- and off-site consultations.

196–198. The Commission announced in 2015 that legislative proposals were being considered to "support remote consultation, in closed electronic networks … for research and private study."[896] However, no provision for such an expansion of Art. 5(3)(n) was in the DSM proposal as the Commission maintained that the issue needed to be considered in the light of the outcome of the then pending VOB case.[897]

The VOB case, which was lodged with the CJEU in April 2015, deals with the question of whether the lending of electronic books falls under the scope of the exception of Art. 6 in the Rental and Lending Directive.

In June 2016, Advocate General Szpunar delivered his forceful opinion in the case. His conclusion was that e-lending should fall under the exception. He asserted that "it is imperative to give legal acts an interpretation which takes into account developments in technology, markets and behaviour and not to fix such acts in the past by adopting too rigid an interpretation." He stated that it is vital that the interpretation of the Directive meets "…the needs of contemporary society and make[s] it possible to reconcile the various interests at stake" while being consistent with the EU's international obligations and principles underlying EU law in the field of copyright. He pointed out that the intention of the EU legislator was to adapt to new technological and economic developments and concluded that this could only be achieved by giving the acts in question adequate interpretation. Thus he used "dynamic" or "evolving" interpretation to come to the conclusion that electronic books should fall under the Directive. He argued that this kind of interpretation was "necessary, particularly in fields where technological progress has a profound effect, such as copyright."[898]

The Advocate General argued, first, that as e-lending is the modern day equivalent of the lending of printed books, an adequate interpretation of the Rental and Lending Directive must take that reality into account; second, that the main purpose of copyright is to protect the interest of authors and an interpretation of the derogation for public lending in a manner allowing e-books would benefit authors; third, the "importance of books for the preservation of, and access to culture and scientific knowledge has always taken precedence over considerations of a purely economic nature" and "in the digital age, libraries must be able to continue to fulfil the task of cultural preservation and dissemination that they performed when books existed only in paper format" which may not be possible in an environment that is solely governed by the laws of the market.[899]

---

896 COM(2015) 626 final, Towards, 2015, 8.

897 C-174/15 – VOB,; SWD(2016) 301 final, IA Part I, 2016, 9, 81.

898 C-174/15 – VOB, AG opinion, par. 23–29.

899 Ibid, 27–39.

The CJEU, in its decision in November 2016, concluded that e-lending came within the scope of the exception in Art. 6 of the Rental and Lending Directive. The Court argued, first, that the concepts "objects" and "copies" with regard to lending are not limited to fixed copies or hard copies, despite such limitation with regard to the rental right, as those two rights do not necessarily concern the same subject matter.[900] Second, the Court saw no indication in the preparatory works or the final wording of the Directive that digital lending should be excluded in all cases. Finally, the aim of the Directive to adapt to new economic development, such as new forms of exploitation, and the general principle of high protection for authors, led the Court to conclude that the meaning of lending under the Rental and Lending Directive covers digital lending, such as in the specific case before them.[901] That is an important departure from what was assumed to be the case before the judgement and shows that the court is willing to use a "dynamic" or "evolving" interpretation necessary where technological progress has a profound effect.[902]

199. The conclusion that e-books and digital lending fall under the exception in Art. 6 of the Rental and Lending Directive will affect the question of online availability in general. There has been no official response from the Commission on the outcome of the case. In my view, in order to create legal certainty around the issue, the provision in Art. 5(3)(n) still needs to be explicitly expanded to facilitate consultation on users' own laptops as well as off-site through secure networks. The Committee on Legal Affairs, responsible for the file on the DSM proposal in the European Parliament, proposed the introduction of a mandatory exception, which rightholders could opt-out of, for use of out-of-commerce works in the secure electronic networks of cultural heritage institutions; Member States could make these dependent on whether there were non-exclusive collective licences available.[903] The European Parliament Committee on Culture and Education in their draft opinion to the Legal Affairs Committee, similarly proposed that Member States could on a voluntary basis extend the consultation exception to uses in secure electronic networks in lieu of dedicated terminals.[904] In my view, the extension of the consultation exception should be mandatory, as proposed by the Legal Affairs Committee. Hopefully this will be included in the current revision of the digital copyright.

---

900 C-174/15 – VOB, par. 28–39.

901 Ibid, par. 40–54.

902 C-174/15 – VOB, AG opinion, par. 28.

903 EP JURI, *Draft Report on the proposal for a directive of the European Parliament and of the Council on copyright in the Digital Single Market (COM(2016)0593 – C8-0383/2016 – 2016/0280(COD))*, (10.3.2017) 31–33.

904 EP CULT, *Draft Opinion of the Committee on Culture and Education for the Committee on Legal Affairs on the proposal for a directive of the European Parliament and of the Council on copyright in the Digital Single Market (COM(2016)0593 – C8-0383/2016 – 2016/0280(COD))*, (6 February 2017) 16.

200. However, the question of remote access does not directly deal with cross-border online access as such. It is likely, not least now that the Portability Regulation[905] is adopted, that digital lending will also include cross-border lending, at least for registered customers of the library. This is nevertheless distinct from open online cross-border access inherent in the quest for libraries to use materials from their collections online. Digital lending can be said to be generated more by demand by end-user, whereas general online use would mainly be generated by libraries but with end-users in mind.

4.2.4.1.2. Lack of harmonisation

201. Lack of harmonisation of exceptions and limitations in the EU creates fragmentation and legal uncertainty.[906] Legal uncertainty discourages cross-border co-operation between libraries[907], especially if they rely on limitations or exceptions for their activities.[908] Cross-border co-operation should result in economies of scale.[909]

202. Cross-border co-operation has been recommended by the Commission "in order to prevent duplication of efforts and promote collaboration and synergies at European level"[910] and in particular to "avoid overlap in digitisation".[911] Despite the recommendation by the Commission, co-operation still occurs mainly within national borders.[912] This may partly be explained by lack of harmonisation.[913] If libraries in different Member States have to operate under different legal frameworks they will not be on an equal footing in trans-European projects. In particular, the diverse implementation of the reproduction exception for libraries under Art. 5(2)(c) "creates a fragmented scene for a European agenda of digitization of cultural heritage".[914] This situation should

905 Regulation (EU) 2017/1128 of the European Parliament and of the Council of 14 June 2017 on cross-border portability of online content services in the internal market. See a brief discussion on its content in Ch. 8.3.3.

906 Janssens, The Issue of Exceptions, 2009, 327–333; SWD(2015) 100 final, A Digital Single Market Strategy, 2015, 29.

907 Axhamn and Guibault, Cross-border ECL, 2011, 17; European Commission, Report on the responses, 2014, 40; Xalabarder, Digital Libraries, 2010, 231; Guibault, Evaluating Directive 2001/29/EC, 2008, 77; Triaille and others, Study, 2013, 283–284.

908 European Copyright Society, Answer to the EC Consulation 2014, 8, 12–13; SWD(2015) 100 final, A Digital Single Market Strategy, 2015, 29–30; European Parliament, Reda Draft Report 2015, 6; European Parliament, Resolution 2015 on the InfoSoc Directive, 2015, item 37; Guibault, Evaluating Directive 2001/29/EC, 2008, 68, 77; Geiger and others, InfoSoc, 2014, 445.

909 Triaille and others, Study, 2013, 283; Guibault, Cultural, 2015, 15.

910 2006/585/EC, Recommendation, 2006, Recital (6).

911 2011/711/EU, Recommendation, 2011, recital (8) and point 4.

912 European Commission, Digitisation report 2014, 2014, 8, 19–21; European Commission, Report, 2016, 19–21.

913 See e.g. Recital (20) DSMP.

914 Triaille and others, Study, 2013, 284.

be improved when and if the proposed new preservation provision in the DSM proposal[915] is adopted.

203. The optional nature of the provisions in Art. 5 of the InfoSoc Directive is often cited as the cause of the lack of harmonisation.[916] Yet, this is not the only problem; even when national legislation in different Member States has implemented the same exceptions there are still differences in how they are enacted and interpreted at the national level.[917] The lack of autonomous terminology thus affects the harmonisation. The Court has affirmed that the principle of "an autonomous and uniform interpretation" also applies to exceptions under the InfoSoc Directive, despite their optional nature.[918] However, not all terms have been referred to the Court.

204. Many are of the opinion that at least some of the exceptions and limitations in the InfoSoc Directive should be made mandatory.[919] It has been suggested that exceptions and limitations that affect the single market and those that concern fundamental rights should be made mandatory. Other exceptions and limitations could be left to the competence of the national legislator, such as reproduction carried out by social institutions (e.g. hospitals, prisons) or use of works in religious ceremonies.[920] A recent European Parliament draft report suggested "to make mandatory all the exceptions and limitations referred to in Directive 2001/29/EC, to allow equal access to cultural diversity across borders within the internal market and to improve legal certainty."[921] However, the resolution finally adopted by the Parliament simply noted that "more common rules" for some exceptions and limitations were needed and called on the Commission to examine "the application of minimum standards across the exceptions and limitations, and further to ensure the proper implementation of the exceptions and limitations".[922]

---

915 Art. 5 DSMP.

916 Janssens, The Issue of Exceptions, 2009, 329, 332–333; Triaille and others, Study, 2013, 248; SWD(2015) 100 final, A Digital Single Market Strategy, 2015, 29; Hugenholtz and others, Recasting, 2006, 66.

917 Triaille and others, Study, 2013, 248; Hugenholtz and others, Recasting, 2006, 66–67; Guibault, Evaluating Directive 2001/29/EC, 2008, 68.

918 C-201/13 – Deckmyn and Vrijheidsfonds, par. 16; C-510/10 – DR and TV2 Danmark, par. 35–36. See also Geiger and others, InfoSoc, 2014, 454–456.

919 Hugenholtz and others, Recasting, 2006, 75; European Copyright Society, Answer to the EC Consulation 2014, 9; Geiger and others, InfoSoc, 2014, 462; Wittem Project, European Copyright Code, 2010, Art. 5 (1)-(4); COM(2011) 427/4, *GREEN PAPER on the online distribution of audiovisual works in the European Union: opportunities and challenges towards a digital single market*, (13.07.2011) 18.

920 Janssens, The Issue of Exceptions, 2009, 343.

921 European Parliament, Reda Draft Report 2015, 6.

922 European Parliament, Resolution, 2015, item 37 and 38; Geiger and others, Reaction of CEIPI, 2015, 14; Tryggvadóttir, Balancing of interests, 2015, 654.

205. One of the reasons for making exceptions and limitations optional is the perceived need to allow national legislators flexibility in maintaining European cultural diversity.[923] This may have been the reason for the watered down approach to the call by the Parliament for mandatory exceptions.[924] However, Janssens has put forward a convincing case that "if one supports the ultimate goal of achieving a coherent European copyright system, it will be necessary to (gradually) abandon the long cherished belief that the notion of what constitutes a legitimate or public interest should always accommodate national particularities." She concludes by arguing that the "notions and values that justify the exceptions" should gradually "be considered from a more 'community-oriented' angle."[925]

206. I would submit that in the interests of the dissemination of the European cultural heritage, the exceptions for libraries should be made mandatory.[926] Exceptions for libraries and archives are crucial because of their key role in the transfer of knowledge and providing access to information.[927] This justifies making them mandatory. However, it is also possible that a very precisely worded exception could bring about the necessary harmonisation, even though it was optional. This has been suggested with regard to the on-site consultation exception in Art. 5(3)(n), at least while it is confined to on-site consultation which precludes cross-border effect.[928] Nevertheless, I maintain that both provisions should be made mandatory to guarantee equal access to the cultural heritage for all users within the EU. A mandatory provision could either be precisely defined or simply provide the basic and most important conditions. The question of how specific they should be is a question of flexibility versus legal certainty.[929] It is, however, important that the main conditions of use be outlined in line with the purpose of the exception.

The approach of making the exception for libraries mandatory seems to be favoured by the Commission, at least with regard to the preservation exception, as can be seen from the DSM proposal.[930] However, it remains to be seen how the EU legislator will react to the conclusion of the CJEU in the VOB case

---

923 European Commission, Report on the responses, 2014, 30–31; Ringnalda, Orphan Works, 2011, 6.

924 European Parliament, Resolution, 2015, item 37, which refers to the importance of European cultural diversity.

925 Janssens, The Issue of Exceptions, 2009, 339–340; Triaille and others, Study, 2013, 301.

926 COM(2011) 427/4, Audiovisual works, 2011, 18.

927 Triaille and others, Study, 2013, 245; Janssens, The Issue of Exceptions, 2009, 343; Crews, 2008 Study, 2008, 14. See also with regard to museums, Jean-François Canat, Lucie Guibault and Elisabeth Logeais, Study, 2015, 13.

928 Triaille and others, Study, 2013, 300–303, 317.

929 Dreier and others, Museen, Bibliotheken, 2012, 281; Triaille and others, Study, 2013, 301–302; Tryggvadóttir, Balancing of interests, 2015, 656–657.

930 See Art. 5 DSMP.

and whether that will lead to changes to the on-site consultation exception in Art. 5(3)(n).

4.2.4.1.3. Exceptions and contracts

207. The exceptions available to libraries under the InfoSoc Directive can be overridden by contracts.[931] While this is not expressly stated in the Directive neither is it prohibited, as e.g. in the Software Directive and the Database Directive[932], and so Member States may, if they wish, legislate to that effect.[933] This situation has been criticised as seriously undermining the balance that the exceptions are meant to bring between rightholders and users as well as creating legal uncertainty.[934]

208. Contracts offered to libraries often override available exceptions for libraries.[935] Many consider this justifiable based on the argument that although library exceptions have a public interest rationale[936] they are not based on more fundamental rights, such as right to privacy or right to expression and free flow of information.[937] Others maintain that the override-ability of the exception in Art. 5(3)(n) should not be modified as it protects the development of adapted offers by publishers.[938] This is, however, not a universal opinion. In Australia it has been proposed that "... any term of an agreement that restricts or prevents the doing of an act, which would otherwise be permitted by specific libraries and archives exceptions ..." should be unenforceable.[939]

---

931 Guibault and others, InfoSoc Study, Part I, 2007, 148, 153, 157, 167; IPO, @the way ahead, 2009, 25–26, 48; Janssens, The Issue of Exceptions, 2009, 341; von Lewinski and Walter, Information Society Directive, 2010, 1022–1023; Crews, 2008 Study, 2008, 27; Iglesias, Digital, 2008, 351.

932 Art. 8(2) Software Directive and Art. 16 Database Directive prohibit contractual overriding of certain exceptions, cf. Bechtold, Directive 2001/29/EC, 2016, 455; Marie-Christine Janssens, 'The Software Directive' in Irini Stamatoudi and Paul Torremans (eds), *EU Copyright Law; A Commentary* (2014) 144; Estelle Derclaye, 'The Database Directive' in Irini Stamatoudi and Paul Torremans (eds), *EU Copyright Law; A Commentary* (2014) 352; Guibault, Contracts, 2000, 152.

933 Triaille and others, Study, 2013, 255; Hugenholtz and others, Recasting, 2006, 67; Xalabarder, Digital Libraries, 2010, 246. Recital (45) and Art. 9 InfoSoc Directive also seem to support that interpretation, cf. Dreier and Hugenholtz (eds) Concise, 2006, 371; Bechtold, Directive 2001/29/EC, 2016, 455.

934 Guibault and others, InfoSoc Study, Part I, 2007, 167; Hargreaves, Digital Opportunity, 2011, 51; WIPO SCCR/29/4, Consolidation of proposed texts contained in document SCCR/26/3, 2014,; European Parliament, Resolution, 2015, item 61; Firth and Preira, Exceptions for Libraries, 2016, 47.

935 Hargreaves, Digital Opportunity, 2011, 51; Ben White, 'Guaranteeing Access to Knowledge: The Role of Libraries', 2012, (4), WIPO Magazine, 15–18, 18.

936 Triaille and others, Study, 2013, 245; Crews, 2008 Study, 2008, 14. See also with regard to museums, Jean-François Canat, Lucie Guibault and Elisabeth Logeais, Study, 2015, 13.

937 Guibault, Contracts, 2000, 156–157; Xalabarder, Digital Libraries, 2010, 246.

938 European Copyright Society, Answer to the EC Consulation 2014, 15.

939 Recommendation 20–1, see ALRC, *Copyright and the Digital Economy (ALRC Report 122)*, (November 2013) 18.

209. In my view, given their public interest rationale, exceptions for libraries should not be subject to override by contracts. Exceptions enable libraries to preserve the cultural heritage and provide further and equal access to it by the public. The fact that it is end users that benefit from them, either directly or in the long-term, further supports that view.[940] Case studies suggest it is unlikely that rightholders would refuse to authorise reproduction for preservation or even seek remuneration for such reproduction.[941] This may lessen the need for explicitly excluding the possibility of an override option with regard to preservation. Nevertheless, in the Council Agreed negotiating mandate of May 2018 for the DSM proposal, it is expressly stipulated that the preservation exception cannot be overridden by contract, which if adopted, will provide clarity in the matter and strengthen the position of the beneficiaries of the exception.[942]

210. No proposal has been put forward to amend the consultation exception in Art. 5(3)(n) of the InfoSoc Directive, either with regard to expanding it or with regard to whether or not contracts can override the exception. However, the interpretation by the CJEU in the TU Darmstadt case with regard to when a work is subject to purchase or licensing terms under Art. 5(3)(n) leaves a fair amount of flexibility for libraries. The Court's conclusion was that, in order for such contractual restrictions to apply, the library would actually have to have concluded a licensing agreement. Thus the contractual override-ability of the consultation exception has less of an impact after the CJEU decision[943] Nevertheless, for legal clarity it would be good if the consultation exception were to be amended to reflect this interpretation of the CJEU as well as the interpretation in the VOB case.[944]

4.2.4.2. The Orphan Works Directive

211. Even though it was designed to be a useful tool with regard to mass digitisation and dissemination of works by cultural institutions[945] the Orphan Work Directive will not solve any of the main issues of mass digitisation or mass use[946] as its procedures are time consuming and hence costly.[947]

---

940 Ibid, 288, 454.

941 Cf. SWD(2016) 301 final, IA Part I, 2016, 122–123.

942 2016/0280 (COD) 9134/18, Agreed negotiation mandate, 2018, Art. 6(1).

943 C-117/13 – TU Darmstadt, par. 23–35.

944 See discussion in Ch. 4.2.4.1.1.2.

945 Recital (1)-(8) OWD; SEC(2011) 615 final, Impact Assessment, 2011, 6–8.

946 Janssens and Tryggvadóttir, Orphan, 2016, 201; Rydén, Are digital, 2016, 15–16; White, Guaranteeing Access, 2012, 17; Ringnalda, Orphan Works, 2011, 11.

947 Guibault, Cultural, 2015, 174; Boulanger and others, Assessing, 2014, 18; Ginsburg, Fair Use, 2014, 1409; SEC(2011) 615 final, Impact Assessment, 2011, 25, 56–57. In his report for the National Library of Luxemburg, Klimpel maintains that the requirement for diligent search is in general too cumbersome for cultural heritage institutions, not only with regard to mass digitisation purposes, cf. Paul Klimpel, *Copyright Law, Practice and Fiction: Rights clearance for cultural heritage in the digital age with examples from the audiovisual sector*, (Mai 2013) 16, 22.

Firstly, there is the cost of prior diligent search.[948] Thus during the legislative process of the Directive, libraries and other cultural heritage institutions objected to the requirement for diligent search, in particular that it had to be done for each and every work.[949] The mandatory list in the annex to the Directive alone is daunting, in particular as not all of the sources listed are easily accessible.[950] Additionally, a separate diligent search must be conducted for embedded works, which will be particularly burdensome for newspapers and magazines. Further, the search must often be conducted abroad, both in cases where the first publication of a work is not in the same country as the seat of the beneficiary institution and also if "there is evidence to suggest that relevant information on rightholders is to be found in other countries".[951] Projects like ARROW and FORWARD can make the process faster and less costly; however, they are not yet fully operational and may never be.[952] A recent report concluded that in three Member States investigated, between 30–46% of mandatory sources for the diligent search were not easily accessible, i.e. in the form of free online information without the need to establish direct contact with someone responsible for the source.[953] Furthermore, information from CMO databases, which are one of the obligatory sources[954], is only available to rightholders, other CMOs and users in the understanding of Art. 3(k) of the CMO Directive, i.e. not to consumers. Thus there is no obligation to provide information to institutions such as digital libraries.[955] Unsurprisingly, in light of all of this, it has been suggested that it may be faster and much cheaper simply to wait for the works to come out of copyright.[956]

Secondly, the process of reporting and recording the diligent search is also time consuming and costly.[957] According to guidelines, the relevant institution

948 Art. 3(1) OWD. See Guibault, Are European orphans about to be freed?, Kluwer Copyright Blog; IPO, *Factsheet – Orphan Works Licensing Scheme and Extented Collective Licensing* (2014), 1; Ringnalda, Orphan Works, 2011, 7.

949 Guibault, Orphan, 2016, 528.

950 Marcella Favale, Simone Schroff and Aura Bertoni, *Requirements for Diligent Search in the United Kingdom, the Netherlands, and Italy*, (April 2016) 38.

951 Art. 3(4) OWD. See Janssens and Tryggvadóttir, Orphan, 2016, 198; Guibault, Orphan, 2016, 529–530; Suthersanen and Frabboni, The Orphan, 2014, 673.

952 SEC(2011) 615 final, Impact Assessment, 2011, 25–26; SWD(2016) 301 final, IA Part I, 2016, 66–67, fn. 188; Boulanger and others, Assessing, 2014, 20–21, 23; Janssens and Tryggvadóttir, Orphan, 2016, 198–199. See brief discussion on ARROW and FORWARD in Ch. 2.4.1.

953 In the UK 30% of the mandatory sources were not easily accessible, 46% of mandatory sources in the Netherlands and 44% in Italy, cf. Favale, Schroff and Bertoni, Requirements, 2016, 38.

954 Guibault, Collective, 2014, 761–762; COMMUNIA, 'Policy paper on proposed Directive on collective management of copyright' (2013) 2–4 <www.communia-association.org/2013/01/07/communia-policy-paper-on-proposed-directive-on-collective-management-of-copyright/> accessed 16 July 2017.

955 Guibault, Orphan, 2016, 529.

956 Ringnalda, Orphan Works, 2011, 7–8.

957 Janssens and Tryggvadóttir, Orphan, 2016, 199; Guibault, Orphan, 2016, 530–531.

must manually fill in an application for each work that they consider orphan and then forward it to a competent national authority which validates the application.[958] This is not feasible for any mass use of works.

212. Furthermore, it is doubtful how much legal certainty the Directive will confer[959], despite that being one of its main aims.[960] First, it does not cover all works.[961] Second, it is unclear when the orphan work status begins and, in particular, when it ends.[962] Third, the Directive is to be without prejudice to several arrangements and provisions, such as solutions in the Member States to address mass digitisation issues and contract law.[963] There is also need for clarification with regard to potential overlap between the OWD and the exceptions in Art. 5 of the InfoSoc Directive.[964] Moreover, the financial implications for the beneficiary institutions may outweigh the legal certainty that is achieved. Although, as discussed above, compensation for reappearing rightholders could be very modest, the possibility still creates financial risk for cultural heritage institutions. Additionally, the rightholder has the right to forbid further use of the work, which the beneficiary institution may have invested considerably in by digitising it.[965]

213. Another weakness is the fact that the Directive does not allow commercial uses and leaves commercial entities unable to use orphan works.[966] The original proposal for the Orphan Works Directive included a provision enabling beneficiary institutions to use orphan works for purposes other than their public interest mission.[967] It was dropped in the course of the legislative process.[968] The provision did not define commercial use and was criticised as potentially in conflict with the three-step test.[969]

214. The cost of the diligent search and its reporting and registration may make it financially impractical for the beneficiary institutions to make use of the Directive, despite the fact that they can generate revenues in order to cover

958 OHIM Orphan Works User Interfaces, Prototype Version 2.0, 7–14.

959 Guibault, Are European orphans about to be freed?, Kluwer Copyright Blog; Rosati, Orphan Works, 2013, 309; Janssens and Tryggvadóttir, Orphan, 2016, 9–11.

960 Recital (25) OWD.

961 See Ch. 4.2.3.3.

962 See Ch. 4.2.3.4. and 4.2.3.6.

963 See Recital (4), Art. 1(5) and Recital (25), Art. 2(5) and Art. 8(2) OWD.

964 Janssens and Tryggvadóttir, Orphan, 2016, 6, 10.

965 Klimpel, Copyright Law, Practice and Fiction, 2013, 22.

966 Ibid, 14–16; Boulanger and others, Assessing, 2014, 20; Rosati, Orphan Works, 2013, 309–310.

967 Art. 7 of the original proposal, cf. COM(2011) 289 final, Proposal 2011, 11; Suthersanen and Frabboni, The Orphan, 2014, 686. See also recommendation in HLG, Final report, 2009, 4.

968 Council, *Proposal for a Directive of the European Parliament and of the Council on certain permitted uses of orphan works – Presidency compromise proposal*, (06.10.2011) 10.

969 ALAI, Orphan Works, 2012, 2–5, 7.

their cost.[970] Most of the funding for digitisation projects by libraries and other cultural heritage institutions comes from public purse, despite the emphasis in the EU on the importance of Private Public Partnership for the purpose of financing.[971] Given this and the potential lack of legal certainty it seems likely that beneficiary institutions will only use the Directive for a very limited part of their collections, such as easily identified orphan works or categories with a limited number of items.[972] This seems to be confirmed by the slow start in use of the EUIPO Orphan Works Database; nearly three years after it became operational it only contains 11,000 works.[973] The Database may become "the authoritative and comprehensive one-stop search" for certain works[974] and thus limit the diligent search cost. However, currently this seems very much a future music.[975] It therefore has to be concluded that it is unlikely that mass use in any understanding of that term will be facilitated by the Directive.

215. In fact, the Directive itself intimates that it is only a solution for small scale projects. Thus Recital (4) underlines that the Directive is without prejudice to specific solutions by Member States to address "larger mass digitisation issues". For those issues Member States are encouraged to pursue voluntary agreements based on the Memorandum of Understanding of 2011 on out-of-commerce works.[976]

4.3. CONCLUSIONS

216. In this chapter I first looked at exceptions and limitations in general and from an international level. The discussion on the international three-step test illustrated that there is no general consensus on how to apply the test. In my view the test should be applied holistically rather than cumulatively, and should not be interpreted solely in the light of the economic interest of rightholders but also of the public interest, such as the public interest to have (digital) access to the cultural

---

970 Art. 6(2) *in fine* and Recital (21) OWD.

971 In 2011 private funding was less than 10% of costs, see 1274, SEC(2011) 1274, 2011, 14; Durantaye, Orphan works, 2015, 205–206. This has not changed sufficiently, cf. European Commission, Digitisation report 2014, 2014, 6, 16–19; European Commission, Report, 2016, 7, 16–19.

972 White, Guaranteeing Access, 2012, 17; Janssens and Tryggvadóttir, Orphan, 2016, 11; Vuopala, Extended, 2013, 35.

973 The data on how many works are registered in the EUIPO database is not publicly available. In July 2017 there were just over 11,000 works registered in the Database according to information from EUIPO in June 2016; 5,186 main works and 5,833 embedded works, cf. e-mail from Mr. Jonathan Kuperman, dated 5 July 2017.

974 Suthersanen and Frabboni, The Orphan, 2014, 674.

975 There are discussions within the community of libraries on how to make the database more effective and harmonised, cf. cf. Report from the EFTA-EEA Working Group on Intellectual Property Rights with the Commission on 28 November 2016, Ref. 16-6636, 20 December 2016, par. 93.

976 Suthersanen and Frabboni, The Orphan, 2014, 662–663. See discussion on the MoU in Ch. 7.1.

heritage in libraries. I then looked at exceptions in the EU legislative framework, mainly under the InfoSoc Directive and the Orphan Works Directive. The InfoSoc Directive's aim is to encourage creativity and innovation through high protection for rightholders while at the same time maintaining a balance between rightholders and users, as well as safeguarding some public interest missions and fundamental rights. However, the conclusion is that the exhaustive and optional list of exceptions does not create the necessary legal certainty necessary to maintain that balance in the digital age, in particular with regard to cultural heritage institutions such as libraries. The exceptions provided for libraries in the InfoSoc Directive are too narrow and, what is more, their optional nature has resulted in a lack of harmonisation within the EU. Thus the exceptions fail to provide a basis for smooth cross-border use necessary for proper online use. The same applies for the Orphan Works Directive. The process provided for under the Directive is too cumbersome to be useful except for very small and defined projects.

217. Already in 2008 the Commission indicated that there was a need to assess whether exceptions and limitations enabling public dissemination of knowledge were adequate for the digital environment.[977] However, stakeholders' views on such a revision diverge. Institutional users, such as libraries and other cultural heritage institutions and end-users, have favoured review whereas rightholders have tended to dismiss the need.[978] These conflicting interests and views have meant that, despite the discussion since 2008, none of the exceptions in the InfoSoc Directive have been revised.

218. This situation seems, however, to be evolving; in September 2016 the Commission put forward the DSM proposal, which contains some important exceptions for libraries. The exception most relevant for this research is the proposed mandatory exception for preservation, which would enable the digitisation of the entire collections of libraries.[979] This would mean that libraries could make digital copies of their entire collections, which then could potentially be made available, either under an exception or a licence. Even so, the wording of the proposed exception is fairly restrictive, in the sense that it could be understood to exclude any other use, even under a licence. That is unfortunate and should be clarified. Furthermore, no provision was proposed for extension of the consultation exception in Art. 5(3)(n) of the InfoSoc Directive as it was deemed necessary to wait for the outcome of the VOB case[980] The CJEU confirmed that e-books and digital lending do fall under the exception in Art. 6 of the Rental and Lending Directive. This conclusion should affect the question of online availability in general.

---

977 COM(2008) 466, Green paper, 2008, 7–11; Triaille and others, Study, 2013, 245.

978 European Commission, Report on the responses, 2014, 30–33; SWD(2016) 301 final, IA Part I, 2016, 123–125.

979 Art. 5 DSMP.

980 C-174/05, *op.cit.*; SWD(2016) 301 final, IA Part I, 2016, 9, 81.

Nevertheless, in my view, to establish legal certainty the provision in Art. 5(3)(n) should be explicitly expanded to facilitate consultation by users on their own laptops and also off-site through secure networks under a mandatory exception. It remains to be seen whether this will come about in this round of revisions.[981]

Clearly, mandatory and fully harmonised exceptions allowing for online cross-border use by libraries would offer the greatest level of certainty for all parties involved.[982] However, it is unclear how far reaching exceptions can be without tipping the balance that the three-step test safeguards. A study on the economic impact of exceptions maintained that a broad exception for remote access might harm revenues for rightholders and thereby weaken the incentive for rightholders to produce new works.[983] At the same time it is clear that libraries need additional resources for copyright clearance to be able to fulfil their role in their digital age. This is especially true with the making available right.[984]

As reflected in Recital 40 of the InfoSoc Directive, the prevailing opinion has been that promoting specific contracts or licences is the best way to enable online use by cultural heritage institutions. Libraries have advocated for specific licences that would take into account their role in providing access to information and to the transfer of knowledge.[985] At the same time, library representatives have criticised current licensing mechanisms, referring to unbalanced, unfavourable bargaining positions and expressing concerns about the balance between libraries' financial capacities and the licensing conditions set by rightholders. Thus many favour exceptions for mass digitisation and making available to the public, at least for out-of-commerce works. Alternatively, members of the library community suggest solutions based on collective management, such as extended collective licences.[986] Publishers, however, generally see licensing as a more flexible tool than exceptions to foster remote access to works contained in libraries and thus prefer the former. Thus many of them argue that the Memorandum of Understanding on Out-of-Commerce Works is a sufficient solution for ensuring access to digitised works and that no further legislation would be needed if it were effectively implemented in all Member States.[987]

219. Collective administration is commonly seen, especially in Europe, "as a solution to the transaction costs that so often arise at the intersection of copyright

---

[981] See suggestion for amendments to the DSM Proposal regarding the issue: EP JURI, Draft, 2017, Amendments 14 and 40.

[982] Guibault, Cultural, 2015, 187.

[983] Boulanger and others, Assessing, 2014, 2.

[984] Triaille and others, Study, 2013, 303.

[985] Guibault, Cultural, 2015, 186; Guibault, Evaluating Directive 2001/29/EC, 2008, 71.

[986] European Commission, Report on the responses, 2014, 43, 50.

[987] Ibid, 38, 44–45, 52. Newspaper publishers on the other hand "consider that providing mechanisms to facilitate the mass digitisation of newspaper content would threaten publishers' business models and their ability to respond to digital challenges", cf. Ibid, 52.

and new technologies."[988] CMOs "play an essential role in enabling the mass dissemination of content that is protected by copyright ... especially when such dissemination takes place over the internet."[989] Thus many have suggested that collective licences would be the answer for digital cultural heritage institutions.[990] Collective licences may indeed be better than exceptions as a way of maintaining the right balance with regard to the making available right. Nevertheless, – there is the problem of outsiders[991], which may affect the transaction costs of even collective licensing negatively.[992] The issue of outsiders requires some legal support, such as extended effect of collective licences or presumed mandate.

220. In my view, given the impact of online use, licensing is a more appropriate tool than exceptions for online use with cross-border effect of in-copyright works. However, individual licensing in the context of digital libraries would lead to prohibitive transactions costs. At the same time, due to the issue of outsiders, even collective licensing would not confer the legal certainty libraries require in order to fulfil their role of disseminating the cultural heritage. Hence some form of legislative support to collective licensing with regard to outsiders is essential. I argue that for libraries the system of extended collective licensing is a flexible solution which supports the necessary balance between rightholders and users of in-copyright works and which can offer legal certainty for cross-border online use. This view seems to be shared by the Commission. In August 2016 the Commission tabled the DSM proposal where they propose measures to improve licensing practices and to ensure wider access to content. There it is proposed that Member States adopt a system of extended collective licences or the similar system of presumed mandate to enable cultural heritage institutions to use out-of-commerce works with cross-border effect.[993]

221. The next part of this thesis will concentrate on analysing the system of extended collective licences and how it is suited to achieve the needs of libraries to fulfil their role in the digital age. I will describe and analyse the ECL system as it has developed in the Nordic countries in Ch. 5; in Ch. 6 I will analyse the system's compatibility with international and EU legal norms; and in Ch. 7 I will describe collective licensing with legislative support for making the cultural heritage available outside the Nordic countries.

---

988 Goldstein and Hugenholtz, 3rd ed., 2013, 5.

989 Guibault, Collective, 2014, 697.

990 Lucky Belder, 'Friends or foes? Two ways of thinking on the relation between the tasks of cultural heritage institutions and the protection of copyright' in Estelle Derclaye (ed), *Copyright and Cultural Heritage; Preservation and Access to Works in a Digital World* (Edward Elgar Publishing, 2010); Kerremans, Janssen and Valcke, Collective solutions, 2011, 639.

991 See the term in e.g. Ch. 1.2 and Ch. 5.1.

992 Tryggvadóttir, Balancing of interests, 2015, 7.

993 See discussion in Ch. 11.3.

PART II

COLLECTIVE LICENCES WITH LEGISLATIVE SUPPORT FOR CROSS-BORDER ONLINE USE BY LIBRARIES

CHAPTER 5

THE NORDIC SYSTEM OF EXTENDED COLLECTIVE LICENCES

Apart from making mass licensing more effective than individual or traditional collective licensing, part of the allure of the ECL model is its ideological advantage, in the form of a subtle mixture of autonomy and state intervention. ECLs have the effectiveness of compulsory licenses but at the same time leave right holders in control of the use of their works.[995]

5.1. INTRODUCTION

222. The system of extended collective licences (ECL) was developed in the Nordic countries in the early sixties and has since been used extensively there.[996] An ECL is a license for a specific use of in-copyright works in a specified field based on a freely negotiated agreement that a collective management organisation (CMO) makes with a user and which is extended to righthowlders that are not members of the CMO, commonly termed outsiders.[997] The legal effect of the extension is made possible by a provision in a copyright act.[998]

995 Riis and Schovsbo, ECLs, 2010, 472.

996 Ds 2003:35, Upphovsrätten, 2003, 277; Riis and Schovsbo, ECLs, 2010, 472, 496 to 497; Rognstad, Avtalelisens, 2012, 621; Tryggvadóttir, Digital libraries, 2014, 315–316; Mendis and Stobo, Extended, 2016, 208; Tarja Koskinen-Olsson, 'Collective Management in the Nordic Countries' in Daniel Gervais (ed), *Collective Management of Copyright and Related Rights* (2 edn, Kluwer Law International, 2010) 290; Trumpke, The Extended, 2012, 264; Axhamn and Guibault, Cross-border ECL, 2011, 25; Guibault, Cultural, 2015, 174; SWD(2016) 301 final, *Commission staff working document: Impact Assessment on the modernisation of EU copyright rules, Part III*, (14 September 2016) 130. Although Iceland participated in the Nordic co-operation no ECL provision were adopted in the Icelandic Copyright Act until 1992.

997 See e.g. Trumpke, The Extended, 2012, 273; Riis and Schovsbo, ECLs, 2010, 472; Kyst, Aftalelicens, 2009,.

998 See e.g. Tryggvadóttir, Digital libraries, 2014, 315; Guibault, Cultural, 2015, 176; Koskinen-Olsson, Collective Management, 2010, 290; Strowel, The European, 2011, 666; Rydning, Extended, 2010, 11; Thomas Riis, Ole-Andreas Rognstad and Jens Hemmingsen Schovsbo, 'Collective Agreements for the Clearance of Copyrights: The Case of Collective Management and Extended Collective Licenses' in Thomas Riis (ed), *User Generated Law: Re-Constructing Intellectual Property Law in a Knowledge Society* (Edward Elgar Publishing, 2016) 58.

This extension effect can only be made effective by legislation.[999] The scope and applicability of the ECL is based on the agreement. The primary objective of ECLs, as with collective licensing in general, is to provide a practical and efficient method of clearing rights when individual rights-clearance is impracticable, mainly in situations of mass use.[1000] However, the difference is that ECLs apply to mass use where it is deemed important to obtain the license for a use of the whole repertoire of works in a given field, not only the works of those who belong to a particular CMO.[1001]

223. The function of an ECL provision can be represented diagrammatically as below:

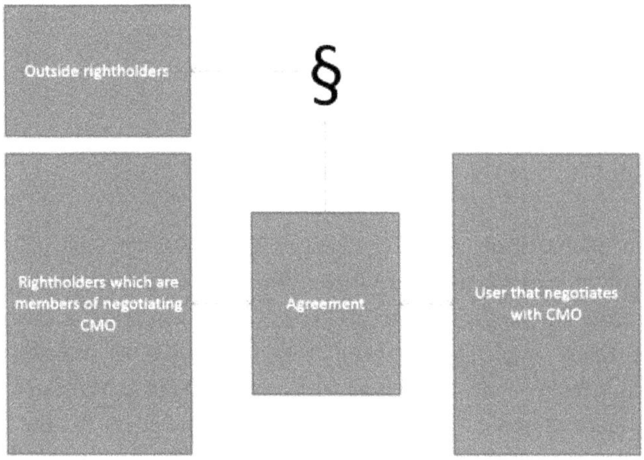

224. Although the ECL system is commonly referred to as the "Nordic ECLs system", there are considerable differences in the ECL provisions of the five Nordic countries, both in scope of use as well as with regard to central issues

---

999 In Belgium the CMO for photographers (SOFAM) attempted to install an ECL for orphan works in their field without legislation but had to abandon it as they could not guarantee legal enforceability of the licence to users, cf. Kerremans, Janssen and Valcke, Collective solutions, 2011, 641.

1000 Peter Schønning, *Ophavsretsloven med kommentarer* (5th edn, Thomson Reuters, 2011), 459; Rydning, Extended, 2010, 69; RP 181/2014 rd, *Regeringens proposition med förslag till ändring av upphovsrättslagen*, (2014) 12; Ringnalda, Orphan Works, 2011, 9, 11; Trumpke, The Extended, 2012, 281–282, fn. 124; Prop. 2004/05:110, *Regeringens proposition: Upphovsrätten i informationssamhället – genomförande av direktiv 2001/29/EG m.m.*, 254; Axhamn and Guibault, Cross-border ECL, 2011, 41; Trumpke, Exklusivität, 2015, 265, 538.

1001 Tryggvadóttir, Digital libraries, 2014, 351; 2007/2 LSF 58, *Forslag til Lov om ændring af ophavsretsloven (Overdragelse af ophavsret og digitalisering af kulturarven m.v.)*, (30.01.2008) 9, 11; Schønning, Ophavsretsloven, 5th ed., 2011, 459–461; Trumpke, The Extended, 2012, 274.

of the system[1002], as well as between individual ECL provisions in national legislation. There are, however, three main elements of the Nordic ECLs which justify the joint grouping. First, ECLs are based on negotiations between CMOs that are representative of "a substantial number of authors of a certain type of works which are used"[1003] in each respective country, and the prospective user. Second, the application of the agreement is extended by a provision in copyright law to rightholders that are not represented by the CMO.[1004] The field and scope of application for ECLs is determined by the individual ECL provision in the copyright acts.[1005] The third element concerns measures to secure the rights of the outsiders of the CMOs who are bound by the agreement due to the ECL provision in law.

225. In this chapter I will describe the features, development and use of the ECL system in the Nordic countries, where it originated. I will begin with a short discussion on collective licensing and a brief historical account, followed by a general description of the ECL system, while highlighting the differences in ECL provisions of the five Nordic countries. I will in particular concentrate on the common features of the Nordic ECL systems, first, the representativeness of the CMOs and negotiations of ECL agreements; second, the extension effect and how it is facilitated for libraries; third, safeguard measures for outsiders as well as transparency requirements.

5.1.1. COLLECTIVE LICENSING

226. Copyright protection is based on exclusivity[1006] and it has been maintained that the exclusive right is enjoyed to the fullest if it is exercised

---

1002 Tryggvadóttir, Digital libraries, 2014, 316–317; Rognstad, Avtalelisens, 2012, 621; Axhamn and Guibault, Cross-border ECL, 2011, 42; Riis, Rognstad and Schovsbo, Collective Agreements, 2016, 59; Riis and Schovsbo, ECLs in Action, 2012, 930–931.

1003 This is the wording of the English translation of Art. 50(1) of the of the Danish Copyright Act No. 395 of 14.6.1995 as subsequently amended, hereafter DCA.

1004 Vuopala, Extended, 2013, 9. In 2015 the wording of Art. 26 of the Finnish Copyright Act No. 404/1961 as subsequently amended, hereafter FCA, the ECL provision which stipulates the framework of ECLs in Finland was changed with Act No. 607/2015. Now Art. 26(1) FCA stipulates that authorised CMOs are deemed to represent outsiders with regard to ECL agreements. This change was stated to be only of a semantic nature and was adopted to align the system more towards discussion within Europe to prepare for cross-border use, cf. RP 181/2014 rd, Regeringens proposition, 2014, 25, 49, see also discussion in Ch. 5.3 and 9.2.

1005 Ole-Andreas Rognstad, *Opphavsrett* (Universitetsforlaget, 2009), 276.

1006 It has been pointed out that to a large extent the "ideal world" of exclusivity and property rules is a mirage and that in reality international copyright law is based on liability rules, cf. Jens Schovsbo, 'The necessity to collectivize copyright – and the dangers thereof' in Jan Rosén (ed), *Individualism and Collectiveness in Intellectual Property Law* (2012) 174, see further references to this discussion in Trumpke, The Extended, 2012, 291–293, where it is

individually.[1007] However, some uses which fall under the exclusive right, especially secondary uses like broadcasting and photocopying, are such that remuneration for the use of each work would not justify individual management[1008], at least in the pre-digital age.[1009] Collective management thus was developed to cope with mass use of in-copyright works.[1010] Hence, large portions of copyright are managed collectively[1011], i.e. CMOs license the work of their members on the basis of mandates from them or by legislative mandate.[1012] The mandates form the pool of works that the CMO can license, or the repertoire[1013] of the relevant CMO. Thus collective management makes use of economies of scale by reducing transaction costs[1014] for the negotiation, monitoring and enforcing of agreements on the use of works that otherwise might not be possible[1015], at least not legally. Furthermore, one of the main justifications for collective management is the stronger bargaining power of the

---

argued that copyright has never been based on "irrevocable" exclusivity and that the aim of copyright to foster creativity and protect the author can only be reached by viewing exclusivity together with limitations and exceptions.

1007 Mihály Ficsor, 'Collective Management of Copyright and Related Rights from the Viewpoint of International Norms and the Acquis Communautaire' in Daniel Gervais (ed), *Collective management of Copyright and Related Rights* (2 edn, Kluwer Law International, 2010) 40.

1008 Svante Bergström, '"Program för upphovsrätten", originally published in Rättsvetenskapliga studier ägnade minnet av Phillips Hult, Acta Universitatis Upsaliensis, Studia Iuridica Upsaliensia 2, Uppsala 1960, 58–83', (1960) 2011, (2), NIR 143, 153.

1009 Marco Ricolfi, 'Individual and collective management of copyright in a digital environment' in Paul Torremans (ed), *Copyright Law A Handbook of Contemporary Research* (Edward Elgar Publishing, 2008) 283–286.

1010 Gervais, Collective Mangement, 2010, 3 and 27; Ficsor, Collective Management, 2010, 32; COM(2012) 372/2, *Proposal for a Directive of the European Parliament and of the Council on collective management of copyright and related rights and multi-territorial licensing of rights in musical works for online uses in the internal market,* (11.07.2012) 2; Handke and Towse, Economics, 2007,; Josef Drexl and others, *Comments of the Max Planck Institute for Intellectual Property and Competition Law on the Proposal for a Directive of the European Parliament and of the Council on collective management of copyright and related rights and multi-territorial licensing of rights in musical works for online uses in the internal market, 11.7.2012, COM(2012) 372/2,* (February 2013) 4; Riis, Rognstad and Schovsbo, Collective Agreements, 2016, 55–56; Vappu Verronen, 'Extended Collective Licence in Finland: A Legal Instrument for Balancing the Rights of the Author with the Interests of the User', 2002, Journal of the Copright Society of the USA, 1143–1160, 1144–1145; Axhamn, Exceptions, 2013, 177.

1011 Schovsbo, The necessity to collectivize, 2012, 168.

1012 Gervais, Collective Management, 2001, 27–28. The definition of a CMO in the CMO Directive leaves open whether the CMO has been mandated by law or by rightholders directly, cf. Guibault and van Gompel, Collective, 2016, 143.

1013 Art. 3(j) COM Directive and 2005/737/EC, *Commission recommendation of 18 May 2005 on collective cross-border management of copyright and related rights for legitimate online music services*, Art. 1(c).

1014 See discussion on transaction cost in Ch. 2.2.1.

1015 See e.g. Handke, Collective, 2014, 183–184; Gervais, Collective Management, 2001, 80–81; Australian Government Productivity Commission, Intellectual Property Arrangements; Draft Report, 2016, 132.

CMO compared to individual licensing.[1016] Today CMOs play an essential role in the dissemination of in-copyright works on the internet.[1017]

227. CMOs traditionally only issue licenses for use in their own country[1018], despite normally having a mandate from their members for worldwide exploitation.[1019] The system for dealing with the use of foreign works has been that once national CMOs have obtained the right to license from a substantial number of rightholders in the relevant field in their territory they can enter into "reciprocal representation agreements"[1020] with similar CMOs in other countries. Such agreements make it possible for a CMO in one territory to license the repertoire of a CMO in another territory.[1021] This practice has been rationalised with reference to the territoriality of copyright[1022] and the consequent difference in national legislation, which makes negotiating licenses, monitoring use and enforcing rights across borders complicated.[1023] Hence the territorial restriction, i.e. that CMOs only license use in their national territories, has been deemed necessary as it would be prohibitively expensive for CMOs

---

1016 Handke, Collective, 2014, 180–181; Peter Schønning, *Ophavsretsloven med kommentarer* (6th edn, Karnov Group, 2016), 495; Axhamn and Guibault, Cross-border ECL, 2011, 51; Koskinen-Olsson, Collective Management, 2010, 291; Geiger, The Role, 2007, 11–12; Silke von Lewinski, 'Mandatory Collective Administration of Exclusive Rights – a Case Study on its Compatibility with International and EC Copyright Law', 2004, (January – March 2004), UNESCO e-Copyright Bulletin, 8–9; Silke von Lewinski, 'Collectivism and its Role in the Frame of Individual Contracts' in Jan Rosén (ed), *Individualism and Collectiveness in Intellectual Property Law* (2012) 124; Verronen, Extended, 2002, 1148; Axhamn, Exceptions, 2013, 178; Schovsbo, The necessity to collectivize, 2012, 177; Terese Foged, 'Danish Licences for Europe', 2015, (1), EIPR, 15–21, 17; US Copyright Office, Mass Digitization, 2015, 82, 103; Drexl and others, Comments, 2013, 19.

1017 Guibault, Collective, 2014, 697; Tarja Koskinen-Olsson and Nicholas Lowe, *Educational Material on Collective Management of Copyright and Related Rights; Module 4: Management of rights in print and publishing* (August 31, 2012) 8, 32, 38–39, 43–44, 55–56, 63.

1018 Handke and Towse, Economics, 2007, 940.

1019 Schierholz, Collective Management in Europe, 2010, 1154.

1020 2005/737/EC, Recommendation 2005, 2005, Art. 1(i); Adriana Moscoso, 'Cross-Border Issues in Collective Management', 2011, (4), Columbia Journal of Law & the Arts, 651–656; Kerremans, Janssen and Valcke, Collective solutions, 2011, 641; Daniel Gervais, 'Collective Management of Copyright: Theory and Practice in the Digital Age' in Daniel Gervais (ed), *Collective Management of Copyright and Related Rights* (3 edn, Wolters Kluwer, 2016) 9. There are two types of reciprocal representation agreements between CMOs, often called A-type and B-type Agreements. The A-type is based on the distribution of royalties across borders whereas the B-type provides that collected royalties stay in the territory where they are collected, cf. IFRRO, 'Principles for Bilateral Agreements' (2006) Recommendation 1 <www.ifrro.org/node/1115> accessed 6 January 2017 and IFRRO, 'Sample Bilateral Agreement – Type A' <www.ifrro.org/node/1116> accessed 6 January 2017; IFRRO, 'Sample Bilateral Agreement – Type B' <www.ifrro.org/node/1118> accessed 6 January 2017. See also Gervais, Collective, 2016, 11.

1021 Gervais, Collective Mangement, 2010, 7; Gervais, Collective, 2016, 9; Tryggvadóttir, Digital libraries, 2014, 317; Riis, Rognstad and Schovsbo, Collective Agreements, 2016, 57; Guibault and van Gompel, Collective, 2016, 158.

1022 See discussion on territoriality in Ch. 8.

1023 Schierholz, Collective Management in Europe, 2010, 1154.

to establish control systems outside their national territories, at least with regard to analogue works.[1024] However, with the advent of the digital network environment this may change, as monitoring may be done from a distance.[1025]

228. Collective licensing is almost always in the form of blanket licensing, i.e. bundling the whole repertoire into a single blanket license, where the user will have a license to use a whole repertoire of works in the same field, e.g. music for radio stations, for the same price and on the same conditions, regardless of whether the music is well known or not, and then charged by some calculated estimate of use.[1026] This way collective management enables mass use as the copyright "exclusivity becomes manageable".[1027] Even so, CMOs normally cannot make agreements that are binding on outsiders.[1028]

Collective licensing may be a better solution than exceptions for maintaining the right balance with regard to online use, e.g. for cultural heritage institutions.[1029] However, in order to be a practicable solution for libraries the issue of outsiders has to be solved. A collective licence that does not include outsiders would neither confer enough legal certainty for libraries nor sufficiently deal with the potentially prohibitive transaction costs of finding and negotiating with outsiders in mass use situations.[1030] The outsider problem is not only a problem for users; it can also be a problem for rightholders that are members of a CMO, as if the issue is not solved it can mean that an agreement is not reached and thus potential remuneration lost for all rightholders.[1031] Thus many countries have adopted legislative support in order to allow collective licences to apply to works of outsiders.[1032] This support is typically in the form of

---

1024 Josef Drexl, 'Competition in the field of collective management: preferring "creative competition" to allocative efficiency in European copyright law' in Paul Torremans (ed), *Copyright Law A Handbook of Contemporary Research* (Edward Elgar Publishing, 2008) 261; Mihály Ficsor, 'Collective Management and Multi-territorial Licensing: Key Issues of the Transposition of Directive 2014/26/EU' in Irini Stamatoudi (ed), *New Developments in EU and International Copyright Law* (Wolters Kluwer, 2016) 228–233.

1025 Guibault and van Gompel, Collective, 2016, 159.

1026 Handke and Towse, Economics, 2007, 942; Riis and Schovsbo, ECLs in Action, 2012, 933; Drexl and others, Comments, 2013, 20; Riis, Rognstad and Schovsbo, Collective Agreements, 2016, 63–64.

1027 Schovsbo, The necessity to collectivize, 2012, 174.

1028 Axhamn, Exceptions, 2013, 178.

1029 Belder, Friends or foes? Two ways of thinking on the relation between the tasks of cultural heritage institutions and the protection of copyright, 2010, 231; Kerremans, Janssen and Valcke, Collective solutions, 2011, 639. See also brief discussion in Ch. 1.1. i.f.

1030 SWD(2016) 301 final, IA Part I, 2016, 67–68; Mihály Ficsor, 'Collective Rights Management from the Viewpoint of International Treaties, with Special Attention to the EU 'Acquis'' in Daniel Gervais (ed), *Collective Management of Copyright and Related Rights* (3 edn, Wolters Kluwer, 2016) 66–67.

1031 Schønning, Ophavsretsloven, 6th ed., 2016, 494.

1032 SWD(2016) 301 final, IA Part III, 2016, 130; Gunnar Karnell, 'Outsiders' Rights: A Dilemma for Collective Administration of Authors' Rights in a Present and Enlarged European

extended collective licences[1033], presumption of representation[1034] or mandatory collective management.[1035, 1036]

5.1.2. GENERAL DEVELOPMENT OF THE NORDIC SYSTEM

229. The honour of conceiving the idea for the ECL system is attributed to a Swedish professor of law, Dr. Svante Bergström[1037], who was a specialist in both labour law and copyright law. The ECL system is thus based on collective agreements in the labour market and their extension to non-union members.[1038] The Nordic countries have long-standing and close co-operation in legal matters including copyright and for that reason they have a very similar structure and harmonised copyright legislation. There is also a high degree of organisation and cooperation among rightholders in the various fields of copyright.[1039] Hence the system of ECLs in the Nordic countries is based on the existence of well-functioning representative CMOs with good governance and transparency.[1040] The system was established to enable users to use the works of outsiders by protecting them from legal action[1041] but it benefits outside rightholders, as well as rightholders who are members of the relevant CMO, as they receive remuneration for use that they might otherwise not receive.[1042]

Community', 1991, EIPR, 430–435; Riis, Rognstad and Schovsbo, Collective Agreements, 2016, 57–58.

1033 Caterina Sganga, 'The eloquent silence of Soulier and Doke and its critical implications for EU copyright law', 2017, (4), Journal of Intellectual Property Law & Practice, 321–330, 330; Ringnalda, Orphan Works, 2011, 10; Boulanger and others, Assessing, 2014, 19.

1034 See Ch. 9.2.

1035 See Ch. 9.3.

1036 European Commission, Digitisation report 2014, 2014, 33; European Commission, Report, 2016, 37; Axhamn, Exceptions, 2013, 178.

1037 Bergström, Program för upphovsrätten, (1960) 2011, 160; Riis and Schovsbo, ECLs, 2010, 473; Trumpke, The Extended, 2012, 274; Rognstad, Opphavsrett, 2009, 276.

1038 Riis and Schovsbo, ECLs, 2010, fn. 4; Trumpke, The Extended, 2012, fn. 72; Verronen, Extended, 2002, 1154; Thomas Nyh, 'Rättighetsklarering vid film- och TV-utnyttjanden; TV- och sat/cab direktivens genomslag i praktiken', 1996, NIR, 191–195, 194–195. It has been pointed out that the purpose of the system was mainly to protect the user, not the authors, cf. H. Lund Christiansen, 'The Nordic licensing systems – extended collective agreement licensing', 1991, (9), EIPR, 346–349, 348; Verronen, Extended, 2002, 1149, 1151; and Trumpke, The Extended, 2012, fn. 177.

1039 Koskinen-Olsson, Collective Management, 2010, 283; Tarja Koskinen-Olsson and Vigdís Sigurðardóttir, 'Collective Management in the Nordic Countries' in Daniel Gervais (ed), *Collective Management of Copyright and Related Rights* (3 edn, Wolters Kluwer, 2016) 243.

1040 Axhamn and Guibault, Cross-border ECL, 2011, 41.

1041 Christiansen, The Nordic, 1991, 348; Verronen, Extended, 2002, 1149, 1151; and Trumpke, The Extended, 2012, fn. 177.

1042 Ysolde Gendreau, 'What's in a Name? Extended Collective Licences in Canada' in Gunnar Karnell (ed), *Liber Amicorum Jan Rosén* (eddy.se ab, 2016) 283; Jan Rosén, 'Copyright Contracts – EU Solutions or National Concern? A Swedish Proposal to Amend the Copyright Act on Individual and Collective Contracts' in Hans Hendrik Lidgard (ed), *National*

230. The system of ECL was first introduced as a compromise in order to solve insufficient rights clearance in broadcasting.[1043] At the time broadcasting stations had agreements with the major CMOs for blanket use of their repertoire but found it too complicated and cumbersome to clear rights with outsiders before broadcasting and, therefore, only paid those outsiders who made a claim. The solution proposed in order to regularise and legalise the situation was to introduce a compulsory licence, a solution that the rightholders opposed. The ECL solution thus was a compromise which ensured remuneration to outsiders.[1044]

Once ECLs had been introduced for broadcasting the concept spread into other areas. Thus specific ECLs for reprography in institutions were introduced in the seventies for photocopying; for secondary use of audio-visual works in the eighties and for certain digital uses in education in the nineties. Specific ECLs for further digital uses were introduced with the implementation of the Infosoc Directive.[1045] In 2008 a general, i.e. non-specific ECL provision, was adopted in Denmark[1046] and similar general ECL provisions have since been adopted in Sweden[1047], Norway[1048] and Iceland.[1049] A general ECL provision allows eligible CMOs in a relevant field to conclude licence agreements for a specific use, to be specified in the agreement, and subsequently to apply for that agreement to be extended to outside rightholders. Unlike the specific ECL provisions, a general ECL provision does not delimit or specify for which use or which field of works it can be applied and is thus general.[1050]

231. Thus the main rationale for ECLs is practical[1051], as can be seen from the account above. The specific rationale for individual ECL provisions varies. Sometimes there is a correlation between the subject matter of ECL provisions,

---

Developments in the Intersection of IPR and Competition Law: From Maglite to Pirate Bay (2011) 169–170; Schønning, Ophavsretsloven, 6th ed., 2016, 494.

1043 Ds 2003:35, Upphovsrätten, 2003, 277; Ot. prp. nr. 15, *Om lov om endringer i åndsverkloven m m*, 18; Koskinen-Olsson, Collective Management, 2010, 284; Trumpke, The Extended, 2012, 274.

1044 Ole-Andreas Rognstad, 'Avtalelisenser', 2004, (2), Nordiskt Immateriellt Rättsskydd (NIR), 151–159, 152; Rydning, Extended, 2010, 13; Riis, Rognstad and Schovsbo, Collective Agreements, 2016, 60; Koskinen-Olsson and Sigurðardóttir, Collective, 2016, 244–245; Verronen, Extended, 2002, 1149. The CMOs also initially criticised the ECL solution as a limitation on the outsider righolders rights, cf. Bergström, Program för upphovsrätten, (1960) 2011, 157.

1045 Tillæg A Folketingstidende 1994–1995, Lovforslag nr. L 119, 1344; Koskinen-Olsson, Collective Management, 2010, 286–287; Koskinen-Olsson and Sigurðardóttir, Collective, 2016, 244.

1046 Art. 50(2) DCA.

1047 See Art. 42h of the Swedish Copyright Act No. 160:729, of December 30, 1960, as subsequently amended, hereafter SCA, which was adopted with Act SFS 2013:691 on 27 June 2013 and came into force 1 November 2013.

1048 Art. 36(2) of the Norwegian Copyright Act No. 1961–05–12–2 as subsequetly amended, hereafter NCA.

1049 Art. 26.a(2) of the Icelandic Copyright Act No. 73, of 29 May 1972, as subsequently amended, hereafter ICA.

1050 See discussion in Ch. 5.3.2.

1051 Verronen, Extended, 2002, 1149, 1151.

i.e. which works and subject-matter ECL agreements can cover, and exceptions and limitations. Thus ECL legislation can be a useful additional tool to exceptions, e.g. to facilitate use of in-copyright works for general information purposes or critical or scientific presentation for commercial purposes. Such commercial use would be outside the relevant Nordic exceptions.[1052] In this context it is worth noting that none of the Nordic ECL provisions are limited to non-commercial use.[1053] To sum up: the underlying justification for ECL legislation is the need for legislative support for collective licences in order to include outsiders, for whom transaction costs on an individual basis would be prohibitive.[1054] There is a public interest in enabling use, which would otherwise not be legally enabled, where exceptions, even those that are compensated, might be deemed too detrimental for rightholders.[1055] The outsiders benefit as they would not be able to achieve better results by acting on their own.[1056]

232. In next sub-chapter I will discuss the representativeness of the CMOs that negotiate ECL agreements, governmental authorisations and dispute settlements.

5.2. REPRESENTATIVE CMOS AND DISPUTE SETTLEMENT

233. An ECL agreement will only come into being if stakeholders, i.e. a relevant CMO and a prospective user, negotiate and conclude a collective agreement. The rationale behind the system is that if a CMO on behalf of its members has negotiated and accepted the terms of a collective agreement in the area where there are ECL provisions, such an agreement must *prima facie* be acceptable for unrepresented rightholders in the same area of works or uses.[1057]

5.2.1. REPRESENTATIVE ORGANISATIONS

234. It is central to the justification of the ECL system that the relevant CMO is presumed to be representative for the interest of the non-member rightholder as

1052 See Vuopala, Extended, 2013, 9 and fn. 16 for Finnish examples where ECLs are used instead of limitations. The Danish provision on ECL for use of visual art is intended to supplement exceptions that allow free use for non-commercial purposes, cf. Schønning, Ophavsretsloven, 5th ed., 2011, 355.

1053 Vuopala, Extended, 2013, 12.

1054 Riis and Schovsbo, ECLs, 2010, 478; Axhamn and Guibault, Cross-border ECL, 2011, 54.

1055 Axhamn, Exceptions, 2013, 182; Vuopala, Extended, 2013, 12.

1056 Liedes, Memorandum, 2010, 6.

1057 Foged, Danish licences, 2015, 17–18.

well as for its members.[1058] Hence eligibility requirements for CMOs to conduct negotiations on ECLs are of paramount interest. These are laid down in specific provisions dealing with the common requirements of ECLs in each country. It is then for the negotiating parties, i.e. the CMO and the user, to assess the representativeness of the CMO to license a specific use in a specific sector. If there is a requirement for governmental authorisation of the CMO, the relevant authority will examine if the requirement is fulfilled.[1059]

235. The key eligibility requirement for a CMO is that it represents: "a substantial number of authors of a certain type of works which are used" in the country concerned.[1060] The representativeness requirement is always with regard to a certain territory.[1061] Formerly, the reference was to a "substantial number of national authors" but this was changed after the Commission criticised the provision as not being compatible with EU rules banning discrimination based on nationality.[1062] Deleting the reference to national authors in the requirement for representativeness makes it possible for foreign CMOs to fulfil the criterion, at least in theory[1063], and gives more legitimacy to ECLs *vis-à-vis* foreign outsiders.[1064]

236. A non-explicit but important prerequisite for the representativeness requirement is that the relevant CMO has the mandate from its members to negotiate the uses of works that an ECL provision covers.[1065] There is, however, no provisions on how such mandates should look like. Thus they take different forms.[1066] It is interesting, however, to note that the original understanding of

---

1058 Rydning, Extended, 2010, 77; Tryggvadóttir, Digital libraries, 2014, 317; Guibault, Cultural, 2015, 177.

1059 ALAI, *Opinion on the cross-border effect of licences granted for digitization and communication of out-of-commerce works by cultural heritage institutions under a regime of Extended Collective Licences (ECL)*, (14 September 2016) 5. See further Ch. 5.2.1.3.

1060 See the English translation of Art. 50(1) DCA; Art. 26(1) FCA, uses the word "numerous" rather than "substantial" in the English translation; Art. 26.a(4) ICA; Art. 38a(1) NCA, uses the word "substantial" as well as Art. 42 a. SCA.

1061 Trumpke, Exklusivität, 2015, 661.

1062 Rognstad, Avtalelisenser, 2004, 157; Rognstad, Avtalelisens, 2012, 625; SOU 2010:24, *Avtalad upphovsrätt: Delbetänkande af Upphovsrättsutredningen*, 20 and 198; Axhamn and Guibault, Cross-border ECL, 2011, 30–31; Schønning, Ophavsretsloven, 5th ed., 2011, 463; Rosén, Copyright Contracts, 2011, 161, 170–171. Norway and Iceland are not members of the EU but Art. 4 of the Agreement on the European Economic Area prohibits any discrimination on grounds of nationality within the scope of the Agreement.

1063 Riis and Schovsbo, ECLs, 2010, 490; Riis, Rognstad and Schovsbo, Collective Agreements, 2016, 66. No foreign CMOs have attempted to gain authorisation to issue ECLs in Denmark, Finland or Norway, cf. Axhamn and Guibault, Cross-border ECL, 2011, 31.

1064 Rognstad, Avtalelisens, 2012, 625.

1065 Guibault, Cultural, 2015, 179; RP 181/2014 rd, Regeringens proposition, 2014, 11–12; Koskinen-Olsson and Sigurðardóttir, Collective, 2016, 250; Vuopala, Extended, 2013, 13–14; Rognstad, Avtalelisens, 2012, 622.

1066 Liedes, Memorandum, 2010, 7.

the CMO's capacity to bind its member was not only based on mandates but on how well the obligations fitted with the express goals of the CMO, such as in their statues.[1067] This would presumably not be possible any longer after the implementation of the CMO Directive.[1068]

237. It has been suggested that ECL provisions could also be used to supplement collective agreements in cases where the CMO's mandate from its members does not fully cover the use falling under an ECL provision.[1069] Such use of ECL provisions would imply a limitation on the rights of the members of the relevant CMO, i.e. for the uses that fall outside of the mandate that they have given. This type of management of rights seems to have been deemed incompatible with the InfoSoc Directive in the Soulier case.[1070]

238. The question of mandates with regard to the representativeness requirement was an issue in a Norwegian case submitted to the Norwegian Cable Dispute Tribunal in 2011.[1071]

> The circumstances of the case were that Norwaco, an umbrella CMO that deals with secondary use of audiovisual works, had not reapplied for authorisation for concluding ECL agreements following a substantial change in the legislation on representation for ECLs. The Tribunal decided that the changes were of such nature that Norwaco should have reapplied for authorisation. This they had not done until after the dispute had arisen.

After evaluating contracts submitted by the relevant CMO to prove that it represented foreign rightholders, the tribunal concluded that most of those were not representation mandates but rather collection mandates and hence could not be taken as giving the CMO the necessary mandate to fulfil the representation requirement.[1072]

239. Finally, a fundamental requirement for representativeness is that the relevant CMO has the capacity to manage the rights of outsiders properly. This is not only determined by the number of members the CMO has but also other factors, i.e. how well the CMO is run and whether it fulfils requirements of good management and governance, as well as its financial capacity to manage the relevant affairs.[1073]

1067 Bet. 1981/912, *Licenskonstruktioner og fotokopiering*, 51–52.

1068 Art. 5(6) COM Directive. See also brief discussion in Ch. 6.3.3.

1069 See discussion in Rognstad, Opphavsrett, 2009, 276.

1070 C-301/15 – Soulier, *op.cit.*, see discussion in Ch. 11.2.

1071 Kabeltvistnemnda, cases no. 1/2010 og 4/2010, Norwaco v. RiksTV AS and Canal Digital Kabel TV AS.

1072 Rognstad, Avtalelisens, 2012, 627; Riis and Schovsbo, ECLs in Action, 2012, 938.

1073 Schønning, Ophavsretsloven, 6th ed., 2016, 502–503; ALAI, Opinion ECL, 2016, 3; L 141, *Forslag til lov om ændring af ophavsretsloven (Digital eksemplarfremstilling til personlig brug, aftalelicens m.v.)*, (10 January 2001) Comments on item 4(3); Prop. 69 L, *Proposisjon til Stortinget (forslag til lovvedtak): Endringer i åndsverkloven (gjennomføring av EUs hitteverkdirektiv og innføring av generell avtalelisens mv.)*, (20 Mars 2015) 28–29; Johan

240. Next I will discuss further the criterion of representativeness, in particular the interpretation of what constitutes a "substantial number of authors".

5.2.1.1. "Substantial number of authors"

241. The definition of the term "substantial number of authors" is not clear-cut. In the countries which require governmental authorisation for CMOs eligible to conclude ECL agreements, it is the relevant authority[1074] which decides in the first instance whether the criterion is fulfilled.[1075] The term should be understood in the context of the type of works that are used in the country concerned.[1076] This already delimits the notion to some extent as it implies that, although it is not sufficient to represent only national authors, it is not required that the CMO be representative of all authors in the world, working in the particular field – only those whose works are actually being used in the country. This can mean that although only a small proportion of authors worldwide are represented by a particular CMO, it may still be deemed to represent a substantial number of authors of works used in a particular country.[1077] The definition of "substantial" can be contextual; thus it has been claimed that the threshold should be different and potentially lower in new areas of licensing but accompanied by a higher degree of requirement of proof as to good management and capacity to running an ECL scheme successfully.[1078]

242. One of the main reasons for the introduction of the general ECL provision[1079] in Denmark was to enable the digitisation of the cultural heritage and its digital distribution, including online distribution of the collections of libraries and for the use of orphan works.[1080] It is interesting to note that in the Swedish preparatory documents for the Swedish general ECL provision[1081] it is stated that, as one prerequisite for ECL agreements is that the CMO party to an ECL agreement is representative of the relevant rightholders, an ECL agreement

---

Axhamn and Lucie Guibault, 'Solving Europeana's mass-digitization issues through Extended Collective Licensing?', 2011, (6), NIR, 509, 516; Verronen, Extended, 2002, 1148; and explicitly stated in Art. 26(1) and (2) FCA.

1074 See Ch. 5.2.1.3.

1075 ALAI, Opinion ECL, 2016, 5.

1076 Schønning, Ophavsretsloven, 6th ed., 2016, 494–496; Rognstad, Opphavsrett, 2009, 277; Parliamentary document 400, docket 333, 145th session of Althingi, 2015–2016, 26.

1077 Rydning, Extended, 2010, 49–50, 71.

1078 Daniel Gervais, 'Extended Collective Licensing: A Significant Contribution to International Copyright Law and Policy' in Gunnar Karnell (ed), *Liber Amicorum Jan Rosén* (2016) 318.

1079 See Ch. 5.3.2.

1080 2007/2 LSF 58, Forslag, 2008, 11–12; SOU 2010:24, Avtalad upphovsrätt, 2010, 276–282; Riis, Rognstad and Schovsbo, Collective Agreements, 2016, 62; Riis and Schovsbo, ECLs, 2010, 476–477; Kyst, Aftalelicens, 2009, 47 and 50; Schønning, Ophavsretsloven, 5th ed., 2011, 465–466. See Ch. 5.3.2.1.

1081 See Ch. 5.3.2.4.

can never just cover use of orphan works.[1082] However, it can also be argued that a CMO representative for the type of works that the collection consists of would fulfil the underlying criterion of representativeness, i.e. to be trusted to take care of the interest of the rightholders in the field. In reality this is a theoretical discussion as few library collections would consist solely of orphan works, although it may be the case of some archives. In the case of small specific collections of works that are known to be orphan the Orphan Works Directive would of course offer the appropriate solution for use for cultural heritage institutions.[1083] Allowing for an ECL agreement just for the use of orphan works was probably not the intention in Denmark and so far no ECL agreement has been concluded that specifically deals with orphan works. Indeed, ECL licences are blanket licences and hence include all the works that are of the "same nature"[1084] as works represented by the CMO and fall under the ECL agreement regardless of whether they are orphan or not.[1085] Hence the issue of orphan works under an ECL licence ceases to be an issue for the user and becomes the responsibility of the relevant CMO, which must find all relevant rightholders for remuneration, at least if there is an individual remuneration.

243. The interpretation of what is a "substantial number of authors" is not set in stone as the following account of the practice in the Nordic countries shows:

244. In Denmark, where only one CMO in each field can negotiate ECLs, the evaluation is based on an overall estimate. If more than one CMO is operating in the field it is not necessarily simply the number of members that is the deciding factor but also the number of members whose works are in fact mainly used.[1086] Hence the term is not interpreted to mean majority.[1087] The evaluation would be based on all rightholders, e.g. publishers or heirs, as well as the original authors. This can be deduced from the wording in preparatory documents where the terms authors and rightholders are used simultaneously.[1088]

245. In Finland the requirement for representativeness is that the CMO represents, in the field of the ECL agreement, numerous[1089] authors of works

1082 Prop. 2012/13:141, Regeringens proposition, 2013, 57. See also IPO, Government, 2014, 41.

1083 See discussion in Ch. 4.2.4.2.

1084 See discussion in Ch. 5.3.

1085 See e.g. St.meld. nr. 24, Nasjonal strategi, 2009, 107.

1086 Schønning, Ophavsretsloven, 5th ed., 2011, 463–464.

1087 Riis and Schovsbo, ECLs in Action, 2012, 937; Schønning, Ophavsretsloven, 6th ed., 2016, 496.

1088 Bet. nr. 1197/1990, *Revision af ophavsretslovgivningen; Slutbetænkning fra udvalget vedrørende revision af ophavsretslovgivningen*, 189; Schønning, Ophavsretsloven, 5th ed., 2011, 464, 468.

1089 In the Swedish language version of Art. 26(1) FCA the term used was "en betydende del" which can also mean significant, substantial, considerable or major part. However, with the amendment Act 607/2015 the wording of the Finnish provision was changed to "ett flertal", which is the same as is used in the Swedish legislation.

used in Finland, and is authorised by the Ministry of Education and Culture. Despite the term author in the relevant provision it is clear from discussion by commentators and in legal preparatory documents that the term "author" and "rightholder" with regard to the representativeness requirement is used interchangeably and covers derivative rightholders as well.[1090]

246. In Norway, where more than one CMO in each field can negotiate ECLs, it is explicitly stated in the preparatory work that "substantial"[1091] does not necessarily mean majority but that a CMO with the plurality of authors in the relevant field could be eligible.[1092] The evaluation is limited only to authors.[1093] This has been questioned as possibly not securing sufficient representation of all rightholders.[1094] However, publishers are *de facto* represented in the relevant Norwegian CMOs.[1095]

The issue of what qualifies as "substantial" was evaluated by the Norwegian Cable Dispute Tribunal in 2011 regarding the retransmission of audio-visual works where it was submitted that over 90% of the rightholders under the relevant ECL agreements were foreigners.[1096] The Tribunal's conclusion was that the requirement of "substantial" representation meant that a CMO, in order to be eligible, had to represent around 50% of relevant authors and the majority of authors whose works were being used in Norway. Furthermore the Tribunal rejected the underlying assumption in the preparatory legislative work that a CMO representing a substantial proportion of Norwegian authors in the relevant area would fulfil the representation requirement for negotiating ECLs in the area. The Tribunal came to the conclusion that the CMO in question did not fulfil the requirement of being representative of a "substantial number of authors" as they did not have representation mandates from enough foreign CMOs.[1097]

> The CMO in question, Norwaco (N) reapplied for an authorisation[1098] and obtained it in 2013. The authorisation authority underlined that the term "substantial" did not mean majority, referring to the preparatory work to the relevant provision on representation. It was furthermore observed that N had agreements with all the other Nordic CMOs in the area and from many other countries, as well as international rights organisations in relevant areas of rights. This, concluded the Ministry, proved that N fulfilled the criterion for substantial representation.[1099]

1090 Vuopala, Extended, 2013, 14; Liedes, Memorandum, 2010, 7; RP 181/2014 rd, Regeringens proposition, 2014, 39, 64.

1091 The Norwegian term is "en vesentlig del", cf. Art. 38a NCA.

1092 Ot. prp. nr. 46, *Om lov om endringer i åndsverkloven m.m.*, 55; Rognstad, Opphavsrett, 2009, 277. This was restated in the 2015 revision NCA, cf. Prop. 69 L, Proposisjon, 2015, 28.

1093 Ot. prp. nr. 46, Endringer, 2005, 55; Rydning, Extended, 2010, 21.

1094 Rognstad, Avtalelisenser, 2004, 157; Trumpke, Exklusivität, 2015, 476–477.

1095 Rydning, Extended, 2010, 74; Ot. prp. nr. 46, Endringer, 2005, 55; Ot. prp. nr. 15, Om lov, 1994, 146–147.

1096 Kabeltvistnemnda, cases no. 1/2010 og 4/2010, *op.cit.*

1097 See discussion in Ch. 5.2.1.

1098 Cf. Art 34 NCA.

1099 Cf. the Ministry's authorisation letter of 18.10.2013.

247. In the recent revision of the Norwegian Copyright legislation it was underlined that the representativeness requirement did not necessitate a majority or something close to majority. It was a flexible requirement which could be influenced by several factors. The number of rightholders would be an important factor but not necessarily a deciding one. Other factors such as the ability of the CMO to represent and safeguard the interests of the rightholder are important. In order to determine those issues the CMO's structure with regard to collecting and distributing remuneration might be assessed as well as its ability to conclude representation agreements with foreign CMOs.[1100]

248. In Sweden the provision on representation uses the term "ett flertal" which in English translates into "substantial" or "several". Again this is not a requirement of majority[1101] of rightholders.[1102] That can i.a. be seen from the fact that in Sweden more than one CMO can be authorised to be representative CMOs to negotiate ECL agreements as discussed next. The provision uses the term author but it is clear from preparatory documents that it also covers derivative rightholders.[1103]

5.2.1.2. More than one CMO in a given field

249. Whether more than one CMO in a given field is eligible to negotiate ECL agreements or whether more than one can be deemed representative varies between the Nordic countries. The question has been raised whether limiting authorisation to negotiate ECL agreements to only one CMO is compatible with the provisions of the Services Directive.[1104] However, the CJEU has come to the conclusion that neither the Services Directive nor the TFEU[1105] prevents legislation stipulating that the exercise of collective management of copyright be limited to one CMO in a certain area.[1106]

1100 Prop. 69 L, Proposisjon, 2015, 28–29; Riis, Rognstad and Schovsbo, Collective Agreements, 2016, 65–66.

1101 There can be room for confusion between the Swedish term "ett flertal" and the word "flertal" used on its own, the latter being a synonym for majority, see e.g. Riis, Rognstad and Schovsbo, Collective Agreements, 2016, 66.

1102 Henry Olsson, *Upphovsrättslagstiftningen: En kommentar* (2 edn, Norstedts Gula Bibliotek, 2006), 307; Henry Olsson, *Copyright: Svensk och internationell upphovsratt* (7 edn, Norstedts Juridik, 2006), 263.

1103 Proposition 1985/86:146, *Om vidaresändning av radio- och TV-program*, 28; Olsson, Upphovsrättslagstiftningen, 2006, 306; SOU 2010:24, Avtalad upphovsrätt, 2010, 74.

1104 Directive 2006/123/EC of the European Parliament and of the Council of 12 December 2006 on services in the internal market, *Official Journal L 376, 27/12/2006 P. 0036 – 0068 (hereafter the Services Directive).*

1105 Treaty on the Functioning of the European Union.

1106 C-351/12, OSA, par. 91. See also *Opinion of Advocate General Sharpston in C-351/12, Ochranný svaz autorský pro práva k dílům hudebním, o.s. (OSA) v Léčebné lázně Mariánské Lázně a. s.* ECLI:EU:C:2013:749, CJEU, 14 November 2013 par. 54–82. The case is further discussed in Ch. 6.3.4.

250. Two possible scenarios can be envisaged with regard to this issue. One is when there is more than one CMO in the same field of works or uses. The other relates to when CMOs in different fields need to negotiate together a particular use under an ECL agreement.

251. In the latter scenario there is a need to make sure that all relevant rights can be licensed in one-stop.[1107] An example of this is the licensing of the use of a book containing embedded images, such as photos or drawings. The CMO for literary works usually would not have mandates from the artists who created the embedded images. In Europe specific CMOs for reproduction rights in the print and publishing sector have sprung up, called reproduction rights organisations (RROs), which manage rights of both authors and publishers in text and image based works.[1108] They usually have mandates from visual artists, either through individual mandates or via membership of their CMOs in the relevant RRO. RROs have increasingly started licensing digital use, not limited to reproduction.[1109] However, if there is no RRO available or if an RRO does not have a mandate to license all the relevant rights, several CMOs may need to cooperate on negotiating and managing specific ECL agreements. A specific provision to address this issue is to be found in all those Nordic countries that have an authorisation system for representative CMOs.[1110]

252. As mentioned above, it varies from one Nordic country to another whether more than one CMO in the same field of works or rights[1111] can negotiate ECL agreements for the same use. However, in practice only one CMO operates in each field in the traditional areas of ECLs.[1112] This is partly for practical reasons as administrative costs increase if there is more than one organisation managing the same field of works.[1113]

253. In Denmark the premise is that the nature of ECLs requires that only one CMO in each field be eligible to negotiate contracts with ECL effect[1114] and hence this is not even specified in the law.[1115]

1107 Schønning, Ophavsretsloven, 6th ed., 2016, 503.

1108 According to IFRRO, the international non-governmental organisation representing RROs, there were RROs in 25 EU Member States in 2017. The EU Member States that do not have RROs are Cyprus, Estonia and Malta. The EFTA-EEA Member States also have RROs although Lichtenstein's rightholders' rights are managed by Swiss RROs.

1109 Koskinen-Olsson, Collective, 2005,; Tarja Koskinen-Olsson and Lowe, Educational Material, 2012, 8, 32, 38–39, 43–44, 55–56, 63.

1110 Art. 50(4) DCA; Art. 26(2) FCA; Art. 26.a (4) ICA; Art. 38a (1) NCA.

1111 E.g. CMOs for non-fiction books, or CMOs for particular use like reproduction, cf. Rydning, Extended, 2010, 20–21.

1112 Thomas Riis, 'Collecting societies, competition and the Services Directive', 2011, (7), Journal of Intellectual Property Law & Practice, 482–493, 492; Rosén, Copyright Contracts, 2011, 171–175.

1113 Prop. 2012/13:141, Regeringens proposition, 2013, 26.

1114 Bet. nr. 1197/1990, Revision, 1990, 189.

1115 It was specified in an older version of the DCA but deemed to be unnecessary in the 2008 revision of the Act, cf. 2007/2 LSF 58, Forslag, 2008, comments on no. 13 (Art. 50); Schønning,

254. In Finland it is clear that more than one organisation can be authorised to negotiate ECL licences as long as they represent numerous authors of works used in a given field in Finland. In the event that more than one organisation is authorised the related decision shall ensure that the licences are granted simultaneously and on compatible terms.[1116]

255. In Iceland there is a recent provision regulating the authorisation of CMOs capable of negotiating ECLs. However, there is no express mention of the issue of authorising more than one CMO in the same field beyond a clause mandating the minister responsible for the authorisation to decide that an authorisation shall be shared by two or more CMOs in the relevant field.[1117] This provision is designed to address the situation where no one CMO covers the use mandated in the ECL agreement. Currently there is only one CMO in each field under the specific ECL provisions.

256. In Norway the wording of the relevant provision is neutral and appears to leave the door open for one or more CMOs.[1118] From preparatory documents it is clear that it is possible to authorise more than one organisation in a given field, although this is expected to be an exception rather than the rule given the requirements for being representative. It is also highlighted that CMOs must adhere to competition rules.[1119] If more than one CMO should be authorised in the same field their cooperation with regard to the ECL would have to be ensured.[1120]

257. In Sweden the Supreme Court has concluded that more than one CMO could be eligible to claim remuneration for the re-sale right[1121] if they fulfil certain requirements regarding structure and stability.[1122] As the wording of the relevant provision is the same as for the eligibility of CMOs to conclude ECL agreements, it would seem likely that the same would be deemed to apply in those instances. However, in practice there have never been competing CMOs in any given area in Sweden.[1123]

Ophavsretsloven, 5th ed., 2011, 469; Riis, Collecting, 2011, 492.

1116 Art. 26 (2) FCA.

1117 Art. 26.a.(4) ICA.

1118 Art. 38a (1) NCA.

1119 Prop. 69 L, Proposisjon, 2015, 18–19.

1120 Ot. prp. nr. 46, Endringer, 2005, 55. According to Professor Rognstad there are two CMOs authorised in Norway to negotiate ECL agreements under Art. 34 NCA for retransmission of broadcasts, cf. private e-mail dated 4 February 2014.

1121 See now Art. 26 p SCA, cf. Art. 6(2) Resale Right Directive.

1122 *Bildkonst Upphovsrätt i Sverige (BUS) v. Konstnärernas Intresseförening för droit de suite upphovsrätt í Sverige, DUR* NJA 2000 s 445, Högsta Domstolen, 10.6.2000; Olsson, Upphovsrättslagstiftningen, 2006, 307; Rosén, The Nordic ECL Model, 2012, 76; SOU 2010:24, Avtalad upphovsrätt, 2010, 191–193; Rosén, Copyright Contracts, 2011, 171.

1123 Rosén, The Nordic ECL Model, 2012, 78; Olsson, Copyright, 2006, 263; Rosén, Copyright Contracts, 2011, 173.

258. During the revision process of the Swedish Copyright Act (SCA) in 2010–2011 it was proposed that only one CMO in each area should be eligible for negotiating an ECL, i.e. "the most representative one and which best represents authors of works in a given field in Sweden".[1124] The special commissioner appointed to revise the SCA and in particular the ECL system[1125], came to the conclusion that providing for only one organisation at a time in any given field to be competent to negotiate ECL licences would provide clarity and prevent competition between CMOs. The view was that competition tends to create downward pressure on authors' revenues.[1126] Nevertheless, this provision was not included in the final proposal adopted in June 2013 and the possibility is left open for more than one CMO in each field to negotiate and issue ECL licences.[1127] The main argument against the proposed change was that it would not have provided for more clarity for outside rightholders or users as it was difficult to decide which CMO was the most representative and represented authors best. Furthermore, it was claimed that such a change might affect competition negatively.[1128]

259. The proposed Swedish criterion of "the most representative one" might have solved the problem of no CMO being able to fulfil the criteria of being representative of a substantial number of authors of a type of works used in Sweden in cases where the majority of the work is foreign. This, however, would not have solved the issue of representation of foreign rightholders and might have affected the applicability of ECLs with regard to international norms. Nevertheless, the requirement of "the most representative" CMO is clearer than the requirement that CMOs have to represent "a substantial number of authors of a certain type of works which are used" in its area. If it was combined with a certain minimum requirement for foreign representation it might also solve the legitimacy issue with regard to use of foreign works.[1129]

5.2.1.3. Governmental authorisation

260. In all the Nordic countries, except for Sweden[1130], there is a requirement that CMOs be authorised to negotiate ECL agreements[1131] by the relevant

1124 SOU 2011:32, *En ny upphovsrättslag; Slutbetänkande af Upphovsrättsutredningen*, 46; SOU 2010:24, Avtalad upphovsrätt, 2010, 33–34, 46–47 and 189–205; Rosén, Copyright Contracts, 2011, 160.

1125 Rosén, The Nordic ECL Model, 2012, 71.

1126 Ibid, 80; Rosén, Copyright Contracts, 2011, 171–175.

1127 Act SFS 2013:691.

1128 Prop. 2012/13:141, Regeringens proposition, 2013, 32–34.

1129 Rognstad, Avtalelisens, 2012, 628–629.

1130 The reason partly being a different administrative structure in Sweden, cf. SOU 2010:24, Avtalad upphovsrätt, 2010, 199.

1131 Koskinen-Olsson, Collective Management, 2010, 296; Koskinen-Olsson and Sigurðardóttir, Collective, 2016, 255.

Ministry.[1132] If the CMO is not authorised the ECL provision does not take effect and the agreement in question will only be binding for the members of the CMO.[1133] In Sweden the limits of the CMOs conduct are provided by the competition legislation.[1134]

261. It is the CMO that is authorised to negotiate ECL agreements; not the ECL agreements *per se* that are authorised.[1135] This is the case with regard to the specific ECL provisions. The situation is different with regard to ECL agreements under the general ECL provision, at least in Denmark.[1136] The authorisation is not only determined by the representativeness of the CMO but also other factors, i.e. how well the CMO is run and how capable it is deemed to be to collect and distribute remuneration.[1137] Thus the Finnish Act stipulates that the "organisation to be approved must have the financial and operational prerequisites and capacity to manage the affairs in accordance with the approval decision" and, furthermore, report annually to the Ministry.[1138] This requirement of good governance of authorised CMOs now will also have to be judged in accordance with the relevant rules set out in the CMO Directive.

262. The Finnish provision on the authorisation explicitly states that the authorisation must be for a fixed period of maximum five years.[1139] This is not expressly stated in the Danish, Icelandic and Norwegian Acts. However, in practice, authorisations in Denmark are limited in time, from 2–5 years, and thus must be renewed regularly.[1140] In Norway authorisations for CMOs to negotiate ECL agreements under the specific ECL provisions are not limited in time, although time-limited authorisations may be issued for ECL agreements under the new general ECL provision.[1141] In Iceland such authorisations are not limited in time.[1142]

1132 The Ministry of Culture in Denmark, cf. Art. 50(4) DCA; the Ministry of Education in Finland, cf. Art. 26(1) FCA; the Minister of Education, Science ad Culture in Iceland, cf. Art. 26.a(4) ICA and the Ministry of Culture in Norway, cf. Art. 38a(1) NCA.

1133 Riis and Schovsbo, ECLs, 2010, 493.

1134 Axhamn and Guibault, Cross-border ECL, 2011, 32.

1135 Prop. 69 L, Proposisjon, 2015, 26.

1136 See discussion in Ch. 5.3.2.1 and Ch. 5.3.2.3.

1137 Schønning, Ophavsretsloven, 6th ed., 2016, 502–503; L 141, Forslag, 2001, Comments on item 4(3); Prop. 69 L, Proposisjon, 2015, 28–29; Axhamn and Guibault, Solving Europeana's mass-digitization issues through Extended Collective Licensing?, 2011, 516.

1138 Art. 26(2) FCA.

1139 Art. 26(2) FCA.

1140 See current authorisations at <http://kum.dk/kulturpolitik/ophavsret/godkendelser/>, (in Danish) last accessed 6 July 2017.

1141 Prop. 69 L, Proposisjon, 2015, 27.

1142 The Icelandic ECL provisions have all recently been updated and a general provision adopted that sets out common rules applicable to all adopted, cf. Art. 26.a-c ICA. There it is stipulated

263. Foreign CMOs can in theory be authorised to issue ECLs in all of the Nordic countries, since the requirement that CMOs represent a substantial number of national authors has been abolished[1143], but none have attempted to gain authorisation.[1144]

264. The requirement for authorisation of CMOs had been a bone of contention within the EU. Thus the Commission was of the opinion[1145] that public authorisation is incompatible with the Services Directive, which prohibits Member States from imposing obligations on a service provider to obtain an authorisation[1146], whereas the Nordic authorities and some Nordic scholars, as well as the Max Planck Institute and IFRRO, disagreed and claimed that the requirement for authorisation for eligible CMOs falls under the exception provided for in the Directive for copyright and other IP rights.[1147, 1148] Other scholars, however, maintained that the rationale behind the authorisation scheme was to ensure efficiency rather than for "reasons of public policy, public security, public health or the protection of the environment" as is the Directive's requirement for national measures that might restrict services and thus it was unlikely that it was compatible with the Services Directive.[1149] The issue seems to have been indirectly settled following the OSA case in which the CJEU came to the conclusion that Art. 16 does not apply to CMOs due to the exception in Art. 17(11) of the Services Directive.[1150] Hence, public authorisation should not be incompatible with EU legislation.[1151]

265. Next I will discuss dispute settlement in ECL negotiations.

---

that the responsible Minister shall set a regulation on authorisation, i.a. on their revisions, cf. Art. 26.a(4).

1143 See discussion in Ch. 5.2.1.

1144 Axhamn and Guibault, Cross-border ECL, 2011, 30–31.

1145 Directorate-General for Internal Market and Services, *Handbook on implementation of the Services Directive*, 42; SWD(2012) 204 final, *Impact Assessment accompanying the document Proposal for a Directive of the European Parliament and of the Council on collective management of copyright and related rights and multi-territorial licensing of rights in musical works for online uses in the internal market*, (11.7.2013) 11, fn. 43.

1146 Art. 16(2) (b) Services Directive.

1147 Art. 17(11) Services Directive.

1148 Rognstad, Avtalelisens, 2012, 629; Rosén, Copyright Contracts, 2011, 170–171; Riis and Schovsbo, ECLs, 2010, 494; Axhamn and Guibault, Cross-border ECL, 2011, 56; Kyst, Aftalelicens, 2009, 54; Drexl and others, Comments, 2013, 17; IFRRO, *IFRRO position paper on the proposal for a Directive on Collective Management of copyright and related rights and multi-territorial licensing of rights in musical works for online uses in the internal market* (November 2012) point 1.

1149 Riis and Schovsbo, ECLs, 2010, 494; Riis, Collecting, 2011, 492.

1150 C-351/12, OSA, par. 64–65.

1151 See further discussion in Ch. 6.3.4. and 10.1.3.

5.2.2. DISPUTE SETTLEMENT

266. It should be emphasised that an ECL provision is simply enabling legislation, which in itself will not assure that an ECL agreement is negotiated.[1152] However, the fact that an ECL provision is enacted implies the expectation of the legislator that ECL agreements will be concluded.[1153] Nevertheless, it is up to the stakeholders, i.e. the CMOs that are entitled to negotiate licences and the potential user, to decide and conclude negotiations on an ECL agreement.[1154] Arrangements for obligatory conflict resolution would make the system more akin to exceptions.[1155] This situation was highlighted in a dispute that arose in Denmark in 2007 regarding reproduction within educational institutions where the parties could not agree on the issue of digital copying. The authorities intervened when the educational institutions complained to the Ministry of Education and the conflict became an issue of debate in the Parliament and the media. In meetings on the dispute organised by the Ministry of Culture, responsible for copyright in Denmark, the authorities underlined that ECL negotiations were based on a free bargaining process but also emphasised that as the issue was of significant public interest, it was important to reach an agreement.[1156]

267. In order to facilitate the conclusion of ECL agreements all the Nordic countries have provisions on mediation or arbitration, or both to support parties in reaching agreements.[1157] The rationale for this is the public interest with regard to the use that ECLs make possible.[1158] However, the provisions for mediation and arbitration have not been used extensively.[1159]

268. In Denmark a provision on mediation[1160] was introduced in 1995, but was hardly used, as it did not entail powers to make decisions binding on the parties.[1161] In order to rectify this a "Copyright Licence Tribunal" was

1152 Koskinen-Olsson, Collective Management, 2010, 300; Verronen, Extended, 2002, 1148; Ringnalda, Orphan Works, 2011, 10.

1153 Trumpke, The Extended, 2012, 276.

1154 Koskinen-Olsson, Collective Management, 2010, 291 and 300.

1155 Rydning, Extended, 2010, 103.

1156 Riis and Schovsbo, ECLs in Action, 2012, 941.

1157 Koskinen-Olsson, Collective Management, 2010, 295; Koskinen-Olsson and Sigurðardóttir, Collective, 2016, 255.

1158 Axhamn and Guibault, Cross-border ECL, 2011, 39; Prop. 1979/80:132, Regeringens proposition 1979/80:132 om ändring i uppbovsrättslagen (1960:729), m. m., 14–15.

1159 Gunnar Karnell, 'Extended Collective License Systems, Provisions, Agreements and Clauses – A Nordic Copyright Invention with an International Future? ' in *Essays in honour of George Koumantos* (2004) 7 (page number from author's copy).

1160 Art. 52 DCA.

1161 Kyst, Aftalelicens, 2009, 49; Riis and Schovsbo, ECLs in Action, 2012, 942; Koskinen-Olsson and Sigurðardóttir, Collective, 2016, 255.

introduced in 2008, which was given power to decide on most issues regarding ECLs, including remuneration.[1162] Still, the Tribunal cannot issue a licence[1163] except in certain limited cases.[1164] Its decision cannot be brought before another administrative authority[1165] but can be tried by courts. The use of the Tribunal is voluntary and either party can ask for the Tribunal's decision if negotiations do not succeed.[1166]

The Tribunal has not yet received any requests to resolve ECL issues and it is doubtful whether, if it had to decide on an ECL issue, it would lead to an outcome different from a mediation proposal as it does not have the power to actually grant a licence, only to determine the terms of a licence. If one of the parties does not agree with the terms and rejects the Tribunal's decision the parties would be free to re-negotiate and hence the Tribunal's decision cannot be seen as binding. This fact, i.e. the non-binding nature of the Tribunal's decisions is perhaps the main reason why no ECL agreements have been referred to the Tribunal. Another reason may be that the Tribunal may not necessarily have a better knowledge of the commercial value of the licence than the parties and hence referring the issue of remuneration to the Tribunal could be risky. The same applies to the courts, which also have no power to issue a licence, as that would amount to a compulsory licence, which needs a legal basis.[1167]

269. In Finland disputes about ECL agreements on photocoping, reproduction for educational purposes, and for the simultaneous and unaltered retransmission of a radio or television broadcast, are to be settled by an arbitration procedure.[1168] If one party refuses to follow the arbitration procedure the dispute can be referred to the courts, which can issue an authorisation for an ECL licence and the terms for such a licence.[1169] Thus there seems to be more coercion in the Finnish ECL system with regard to these three areas than in the other Nordic

---

1162 Art. 47 DCA.

1163 Riis and Schovsbo, ECLs in Action, 2012, 942.

1164 For certain rights of broadcasting organisations in connection with retransmission or use by educational institutions and for handicapped individuals, cf. Art. 48 DCA.

1165 Art. 47(2) DCA.

1166 Art. 13(5), 14(2), 16b (2), 24a (2) and 30(6) DCA. The Tribunal cannot be used by parties with regard to ECLs on the use of works in archives of broadcasting stations, cf. Art. 30a DCA, or for certain reproductions for handicapped people, cf. Art. 17(4) DCA, unless an ECL agreement with an authors' CMO has already been adopted on the basis of Art. 17(4). In such a case the Tribunal can actually issue a licence with regard to the rights of broadcasting stations under the DCA and determine the conditions for such a license, if one of the parties so request, cf. Art. 48(2) and (3).

1167 Riis and Schovsbo, ECLs in Action, 2012, 944; Bet. 1981/912, Licenskonstruktioner, 1981, 41, 67; Verronen, Extended, 2002, 1148. See similar discussion in Rydning, Extended, 2010, 103.

1168 Art. 54 FCA, cf. Art.13, Art. 14(1) and Art. 25h(1). Parties can also agree to submit the matter under the Finnish Arbitration Act No. 967/1992, cf. Art. 54(3) FCA.

1169 Cf. Art. 54(4) FCA.

countries. There are no express provisions on mediation or arbitration with regard to other ECL provisions in the Finnish Copyright Act.[1170]

270. In Iceland general rules on mediation have recently been adopted.[1171] In case of disagreement in negotiations on ECL agreements either party may send a request to the Minister of Education, Culture and Science who will nominate a special mediator whose role is limited to recommendations, i.a. to propose that the case be put to arbitration.[1172] Prior to this there was a process for disputes limited to remuneration issues, which were decided by a specially appointed committee. That process was only used once.

271. In Norway either party can demand a mediation procedure if negotiations for ECL agreements are not successful.[1173] If the parties agree, the matter can be concluded in a binding manner, as well as any dispute concerning the interpretation of the agreement.[1174]

272. In Sweden, where there has traditionally been a strong resistance to any compulsory measures to ensure that an ECL agreement is reached[1175], there is a specific Act on mediation in certain copyright disputes that covers the ECL provisions.[1176] The Act offers voluntary a mediation process for disputes regarding all the specific ECL provisions[1177] except for the ECL provision for cable retransmission, which establishes an obligation to participate in mediation.[1178] If mediation under the Act fails the mediator shall notify the government[1179], which implies that if the government believes it is in the public interest to have an ECL agreement in the area it might consider some action.[1180]

273. None of the Nordic provisions on arbitration and mediation extend to ECL agreements under the general ECL provisions.[1181] In preparatory documents for the general ECL provision it is highlighted that the difference between the specific

---

1170 Axhamn and Guibault, Cross-border ECL, 2011, 40.

1171 Cf. Amendment Act No. 9/2016.

1172 Art. 26.c. ICA.

1173 Cf. Art. 38(1) NCA.

1174 Cf. Art. 38(2) and Art. 35(1) NCA; Prop. 69 L, Proposisjon, 2015, 30, 61–62.

1175 Koskinen-Olsson, Collective Management, 2010, 295; Axhamn and Guibault, Cross-border ECL, 2011, 39.

1176 Act 1980:612 as last amended by Act 2013:690; Koskinen-Olsson and Sigurðardóttir, Collective, 2016, 255.

1177 Art. 1 of Act 1980:612 as last amended. Act 2013:690 added the ECL provision in Art. 42e SCA on primary broadcasting to the list in Art. 1 of Act 1980:612 as it was also seen as an area where it was necessary to have this option, cf. Prop. 2012/13:141, Regeringens proposition, 2013, 52.

1178 Art. 52a SCA.

1179 Art. 6 of Act 1980:612.

1180 Axhamn and Guibault, Cross-border ECL, 2011, 39.

1181 See discussion on the general ECL provisions in Ch. 5.3.2.

ECL and general ECL provisions is that in the former the legislator has decided that ECL agreements would be useful in a given field, or for certain works or uses, but not in the latter. Thus there is a stronger expectation that the parties agree in ECL agreements under the general ECL provision. Therefore it is not obvious that it should be obligatory for a dissenting stakeholder to participate in arbitration or mediation for those ECL agreements.[1182] Any mandatory resolution process might also decrease the likelihood of ECL agreements being concluded in new areas, which the general ECL provisions are supposed to encourage, as rightholders would be less willing to enter into such negotiations.[1183]

274. In this respect it is worth mentioning Art. 16 and Recital (31) of the CMO Directive, which requires that licensing negotiations be carried out in good faith.[1184] The Max Planck Institute for Intellectual Property and Competition Law recommended that the Directive should provide for an obligation to negotiate, a requirement that exists in some Member States.[1185] This recommendation was not taken on board although the Directive went some way towards it by stipulating in Art. 16(3) that CMOs shall answer requests for licences without delay and upon receipt of "all relevant information" either by offering a licence or a reasoned statement of why a licence is declined. This, of course, does not guarantee smooth negotiations or a satisfactory outcome in all instances, especially when there is an imbalance in negotiating power of parties, which may be true with regard to libraries versus established CMOs.[1186] The Directive provides that Member States shall ensure that there is a dispute resolution mechanism in place between CMOs and users, cf. Art. 35, concerning i.a. disputes about proposed licensing conditions.

5.2.3. EVALUATION

275. There are differences in the requirements for representativeness between the Nordic countries. Nevertheless, the term is interpreted in a similar manner. Importantly, an underlying requirement is that representativeness is based on express mandates. Furthermore, the term "substantial number of authors" is understood: first, to cover all relevant rightholders, including derivative rightholders, except in Norway where the CMOs are, however, also representative of other relevant rightholders; second, to be substantial in regard to the specific type of works used in the country as a whole, rather than to mean substantial

1182 Prop. 69 L, Proposisjon, 2015, 29; Prop. 2012/13:141, Regeringens proposition, 2013, 59.
1183 Axhamn and Guibault, Cross-border ECL, 2011, 40.
1184 Guibault, Collective, 2014, 749–750.
1185 Drexl and others, Comments, 2013, 8.
1186 Guibault, Collective, 2014, 752; Kerremans, Janssen and Valcke, Collective solutions, 2011, 645.

number of rightholders of works used by an individual licensee.[1187] Furthermore, preparatory documents clarify that "substantial" does not mean a majority of rightholders or works but, rather, substantial representation of the works or rights most commonly used in the specific field. However, the Norwegian Cable Dispute Tribunal case[1188] highlights the problem of the representation requirement with regard to foreign rightholders and their representation when foreign works are being used[1189], and underlines the necessity to find a solution to the problem.

276. There are several arguments for limiting eligibility to negotiate ECLs in a given field to just one CMO. First, having more than one may create confusion on the part of outside rightholders as to where to claim remuneration; second, it might also create confusion for users as to which organisation administers which works; third, remuneration might vary between the different ECLs for the same use; and fourth, CMOs might not have the incentive to guarantee the rights of outsiders, who cannot in any case influence the decisions of the CMO. The last of these arguments seems, however, to be applicable regardless of whether there is one or more CMO eligible to negotiate ELCs. The others are not particularly compelling reasons against authorising more than one CMO[1190] and the effects could be mitigated by obliging the CMO to co-ordinate, as is stipulated in Finland and Norway. Another possibility would be to put in place rules to secure the rights of outsiders at the same level as members. However, it has been suggested that this might undercut the whole existence of the CMOs, as there would be no incentive for rightholders to become members and pay membership fees.[1191]

Technically it is possible to have more than one eligible CMO if certain rules are adopted to further secure the rights of outsiders as well as guidelines with regard to eliminating the possibility of overlapping agreements. Nevertheless, having only one CMO eligible for negotiating ECLs in each field together with an authorisation system would eliminate confusion. It would also increase the bargaining power of the relevant CMOs, which could be in the interest of rightholders, although it could also create situations where it would be difficult or impossible for a user to obtain an ECL agreement.

277. Governmental supervision is often justified by referring to the *de facto* monopoly CMOs often hold and the public mission they perform of facilitating access to creative works. This is even more applicable to collective management with legislative support, which involves the use of

[1187] The latter being a requirement under the UK ECL system, see Ch. 7.3.3.
[1188] Kabeltvistnemnda, cases no. 1/2010 og 4/2010, *op.cit.*
[1189] Rognstad, Avtalelisens, 2012, 627–628.
[1190] Riis and Schovsbo, ECLs, 2010, 493.
[1191] Riis, Collecting, 2011, 492.

works by outsiders.[1192] There are arguments for and against a system of government authorisation for CMOs to negotiate ECLs. Clearly, without an authorisation system initiation and conclusion of negotiations could be more flexible, faster and simpler, e.g. for foreign CMOs.[1193] On the other hand an authorisation system will reduce the danger of conflicts and disputes by making it clear which CMOs are entitled to negotiate ECLs; authorisation also allows for more effective control of whether CMOs fulfil the requirements to be eligible to negotiate ECLs. An authorisation system confers more legal certainty[1194] as well as being a safety valve for ensuring that CMOs fulfil the representativeness requirements. However, the system in Sweden seems to function just as well as in the other four countries. With the implementation of the CMO Directive there should be even firmer guarantees for the well-functioning of the collective licensing system, both in general and also in particular for the ECL system.

Having an efficient copyright clearance system may be part of public policy in copyright matters.[1195] Lack thereof can lead to either illegal use of protected works or to a situation where protected works are not used or made available[1196], which limits access to the cultural heritage. Having an authorisation requirement may make the system more efficient. Thus there can be valid public policy reasons that could justify an authorisation system. Furthermore, authorisation coupled together with clear procedures that are adapted for foreign CMOs could further the legitimacy of ECLs in the international context.[1197] Thus I support a coherent system of authorisations for CMOs eligible to negotiate ECL agreements which should fulfil the necessary governmental supervision of the activities of CMOs without going "beyond what is needed for guaranteeing that their activities are in accordance with the relevant legal norms".[1198] However, it is worth noting that the discussion of how much regulation of CMOs there should be, including the question of governmental authorisation, is usually conducted from a point of view of principle, and a preliminary empirical study on the subject was inconclusive in its finding on the impact of regulation on the effiency of CMOs.[1199]

1192 Oleksandr Bulayenko, 'Permissibility of Non-Voluntary Collective Management of Copyright under EU Law – The Case of the French Law on Out-of-Commerce Books', 2016, JIPITEC, 51–68, 59.

1193 Rognstad, Avtalelisens, 2012, 629; Kulturdepartementet, *Høringsnotat, Endringer i åndverkloven*, (1 July 2014) 16; Prop. 69 L, Proposisjon, 2015, 25–27.

1194 Kulturdepartementet, Høringsnotat, 2014, 16; Prop. 69 L, Proposisjon, 2015, 24–26.

1195 C-351/12, OSA, AG opinion, par. 68.

1196 Rydning, Extended, 2010, 89.

1197 Rognstad, Avtalelisens, 2012, 630.

1198 Ficsor, Collective Management, 2010, 69; Drexl and others, Comments, 2013, 34.

1199 Handke and Towse, Economics, 2007, 950 to 951.

278. An important rationale behind the ECL system is that it is a better arrangement for rightholders than compulsory licences.[1200] Thus it is essential that ECL agreements do not become compulsory and in fact is an important element of the system's legitimacy.[1201] This means that there is an inbuilt risk that an ECL agreement may not be reached.[1202] In cases where it is necessary to secure access to a use that is deemed essential in the public interest, compulsory licences may sometimes be more appropriate than ECL provisions.[1203] However, at the same time providing for this voluntary system is in itself a policy instrument, i.e. enabling the extended effect of free negotiations. Although, in principle, there is little room to use ECLs to impose public interest, such as access to cultural heritage[1204], the fact that there is a system which lowers transaction costs and offers flexibility is a policy instrument in itself, which benefits users as well as rightholders and can thus enable public policy. Furthermore, CMOs rarely refuse to conclude a licence, in part because of competition concerns.[1205]

279. Next I will discuss the field and scope of the extension effect of the ECLs, in particular how it facilitates use for libraries.

5.3. THE EXTENSION EFFECT OF ECLS: FIELD AND SCOPE OF APPLICATION

280. The key, defining feature of extended collective licences, which differentiates them from general collective licences, is that they extend the effect of an agreement between a CMO and a user to rightholders who are not members of the CMO, otherwise known as outsiders. This extension effect is achieved with a provision in a copyright act, an ECL provision[1206], and thus makes a collective licence valid for the user, such as a library, in relation to outsiders. In other words the legislation is the basis for the extension possibility.[1207]

281. The ECL system is a collective management system with legislative support. The legislative support is to be found in the ECL provision extending the effect of an ECL agreement to outsiders. The wording of these provisions used to be almost identical in the five Nordic countries. As an example we can look at the wording of Art. 50(3) of the DCA: "The extended collective licence

---

1200 Axhamn, Exceptions, 2013, 182.
1201 Karnell, Extended, 2004, 1 (page number from author's copy).
1202 Riis and Schovsbo, ECLs in Action, 2012, 950; Verronen, Extended, 2002, 1148.
1203 Rognstad, Avtalelisenser, 2004, 158; Trumpke, Exklusivität, 2015, 525–526.
1204 Ringnalda, Orphan Works, 2011, 10.
1205 Ficsor, Collective, 2016, 62.
1206 Art. 42 a(1) SCA; Art. 50(3) DCA; Art. 36(1) NCA; 26(1) FCA; Art. 26. gr. a. ICA.
1207 Rosén, Copyright Contracts, 2011, 169.

gives the user right to exploit other works of the same nature even though the authors of those works are not represented by the organisation." This explains the practical outcome of the extension effect but is not clear with regard to the legal means to reach it. The wording of the Finnish provision was changed in 2015, as explained in the preparatory documents, to better reflect the content of the system and align it to discussions within Europe and the potential adoption of similar systems in other European countries. Thus the provision now stipulates that the relevant CMO is deemed, with regard to the specific ECL agreement, to represent authors of other works in the same field, rather than simply specifying that the users can use works of unrepresented authors under the agreement.[1208] This change seems to indicate that the legislative support for the collective management in the ECL system is afforded by a legally presumed mandate to the relevant CMOs whereas the former co-ordinated wording, which is still in use in the other four Nordic countries, might be understood as a legal licence[1209] with regard to the outsider. The distinction between these two possible understandings of the legal nature of the extension provision is of importance as will be discussed further in Ch. 6.1 below.

282. The field and scope of application of ECLs is determined by the individual ECL provision in the copyright acts.[1210] These provide the outer limits of the subject matter for ECL agreements. ECL provisions are very flexible, but it is important to remember that they do not have an automatic effect. They only come into force if an agreement is reached between a relevant CMO and a user and the actual scope of the licence is determined in that agreement, i.e. what use, by whom and for which works.[1211] This can be seen from e.g. Art. 50(3) of the DCA:

> The extended collective licence gives the user right to exploit other works of the same nature even though the authors of those works are not represented by the organisation. The extended collective licence gives the user right only to exploit the works of the unrepresented authors in the manner and on the terms that follow from the licence agreement made with the organisation.

The equivalent provisions in Iceland, Norway and Sweden have a similar wording and highlight specifically that the exploitation of outsiders works can only be in the same field as the agreement.[1212] That refers to the different fields of application stipulated in the individual ECL provisions, i.e. in education,

---

1208 Art. 26(1) FCA as changed by Act No 607/2015, cf. RP 181/2014 rd, Regeringens proposition, 2014, 25, 39.

1209 See discussion in Ch. 4.1.1.

1210 Rognstad, Opphavsrett, 2009, 276.

1211 Tryggvadóttir, Digital libraries, 2014, 317; Rydning, Extended, 2010, 20, 73; Bet. 1981/912, Licenskonstruktioner, 1981, 40; Trumpke, Exklusivität, 2015, 327.

1212 Art. 26.a.(1) ICA; Art. 36(1) NCA; Art. 42a(1) SCA.

broadcasting etc.[1213] In other words the impact of the extension, which is provided by a legal provision, only comes into effect through conclusion of a contract (i.e. an ECL agreement).[1214] The agreement in turn is dependent on the mandate that the CMO has from its members, i.e. what capacity it has to grant licences with respect to the rights it administers.[1215]

283. An ECL agreement cannot allow wider use or apply to works other than those specified by the ECL provision but can, and mostly does, stipulate a narrower use, narrower scope of works[1216] or limits the categories of beneficiaries (users) or rightholders to which it applies, e.g. only authors and not publishers.[1217] If the agreement allows use outside the delimitations in the ECL provision it cannot apply for the use of works of outsiders.[1218]

284. It can be difficult to determine when works are of the "same nature". When such a question arises a decision has to be made with reference to the underlying agreement and the type of works the negotiating CMO represents.[1219] In Denmark, the tendency has been to interpret the term "same nature" broadly.[1220] However, the vagueness of the term does not seem to have been a persistent problem in the use of the ECL system.

285. The number of specific ECL provisions varies between the Nordic countries as does the extent of subject matter that can be covered by ECL agreements. Specific ECL provisions exist in all of the countries for broadcasting[1221] and for the retransmission of broadcasts[1222]; for the use of archived broadcasts by broadcasting stations[1223]; for the making of ephemeral recordings (only in Finland); for institutional reproduction in all[1224]; for use by

---

1213 Rydning, Extended, 2010, 19.

1214 Gendreau, What's in a Name? Extended Collective Licences in Canada, 2016, 283.

1215 Sterling, World Copyright Law, 2015, 629–630; Guibault, Cultural, 2015, 179; Tarja Koskinen-Olsson and Nicholas Lowe, *Educational Material on Collective Management of Copyright and Related Rights; Module 1: General aspects of collective management*, (August 31, 2012) 28; Gervais, Collective Management, 2001, 27–28.

1216 Axhamn and Guibault, Cross-border ECL, 2011, 33; Rydning, Extended, 2010, 16, 17, 50.

1217 Kyst, Aftalelicens, 2009, 48; Trumpke, Exklusivität, 2015, 461, 463.

1218 Schønning, Ophavsretsloven, 5th ed., 2011, 467.

1219 Rognstad, Opphavsrett, 2009, 278; Rydning, Extended, 2010, 19.

1220 Schønning, Ophavsretsloven, 5th ed., 2011, 466.

1221 Art. 30(1) DCA, Art. 25f FCA, Art. 23(1) ICA, Art. 30(1) NCA and Art. 42e SCA.

1222 Art. 35 DCA, Art. 25h FCA, Art. 23a and 45a ICA, Art. 34 NCA and Art. 42f SCA.

1223 Art. 30a DCA, Art. 25g FCA, Art. 23.b ICA; Art. 26Art. 32 NCA and Art. 42g SCA.

1224 The ECL provisions for institutional reproductions are split between educational institutions on the one hand and other institutions on the other, such as public authorities and institutions, private enterprises and organisations other than those established for educational purposes, except in Iceland, cf. Art. 13 and 14 DCA, Art. 13, 13a and 14 FCA, Art. 18 ICA, Art. 13b and 14 NCA and Art. 42b and 42c SCA.

libraries (and in some cases by other heritage institutions)[1225]; and for certain use of works by handicapped persons in Denmark, Iceland and Norway.[1226] In Denmark and Finland there are, furthermore, specific ECL provisions for certain uses of works of visual fine art[1227] which can be used for cultural heritage institutions. In addition to the specific ECL provision enumerated above there are general ECL provisions in all the Nordic countries, except Finland, that are not limited to specific types of works, users or uses. These general ECL provisions were introduced in part to respond to the needs of libraries in the digital age.[1228]

In the following I will describe the specific ECL provisions for libraries as well as the general ECLs.

5.3.1. SPECIFIC ECL PROVISIONS FOR LIBRARIES

286. All the Nordic countries have specific ECL provisions for libraries and archives. In Finland, Iceland, Norway and Sweden these provisions are also applicable to museums. The provisions, however, vary considerably in scope. In fact, this ECL provision is the one that differs most in scope between the Nordic countries, the Danish and Swedish version being more restrictive than the Finnish, Icelandic and Norwegian counterparts, both with regard to types and quantity of work that the ECL can cover and also with regard how to communicate the digital copies. As with other ECL provisions, none of the specific ECL provisions for libraries are limited to non-commercial use.

5.3.1.1. Denmark

287. Denmark has the narrowest formulated provision.[1229] It is only applicable to public libraries and libraries wholly or partly publicly financed. Coverage is limited to articles from newspapers, magazines and composite works, brief excerpts of books and other published literary works, and illustrations and music reproduced in connection with the text. The provision does not expressly stipulate that the works must be in the collection of the libraries but it can be presumed that this is a requirement. An ECL agreement can allow for acts of reproduction, both digital and analogue, as well as uses of the reproduced copies.

1225 Art. 16b DCA, Art. 16d FCA, Art. 12. b ICA, Art. 16a NCA and Art. 42d SCA.

1226 Art. 17(4) DCA; Art. 17b NCA; Art. 19(4) ICA.

1227 This is in addition to the ECL provision for broadcasting in these countries, which also covers works of fine art.

1228 Guibault, Cultural, 2015, 176; Riis and Schovsbo, ECLs, 2010, 477; 2007/2 LSF 58, Forslag, 2008, 3.3.1.; ibid, general comments, section 3.2; Kyst, Aftalelicens, 2009, 47 and 50; Schønning, Ophavsretsloven, 5th ed., 2011, 465–466.

1229 Art. 16b DCA.

However, uses by broadcasting and uses involving making works available online are expressly excluded. There is no requirement for an opt-out clause in an ECL agreement negotiated under this provision.

288. The background for the provision, which was adopted in 2002, is that according to the Danish Copyright Act individuals may not engage outside help to make digital copies.[1230] This ban hampered libraries from distributing works digitally to end-users, whether directly or via other libraries, as that would be seen as outside help in making digital copies for individuals.[1231] Since 2004, a framework ECL agreement has been in place between the national board of libraries and the relevant CMO[1232] for literary works, giving participating libraries the possibility of making digital copies from printed scientific journals in response to a direct order and communicating them, either via interlibrary loan or directly to the end-user. They may not, however, make them available on-demand online. The agreement does not cover articles from newspapers, trade journals, composite works or excerpts from books. The digital copy can be kept in a database but access to the database must be restricted to library staff.[1233] The use under the agreement must respect other agreements that the libraries may have or will conclude with rightholders.[1234] Stipulating that use under an ECL agreement may be limited by future agreements seems to go further than the general rule that older agreements have precedence over ECL agreements.[1235] The preparatory documents accompanying the proposal for the library ECL provision only mentioned that ECL agreements under the provision should respect older agreements, e.g. subscriptions to journals or a database that could restrict the uses available to libraries.[1236] However, this can perhaps be explained by the fact that there is no opt-out provision in the agreement, so allowing future agreements to take precedence may be a form of opt-out. Another issue with older agreements or even newer agreements is the risk that libraries might risk paying twice for the same use.[1237]

1230 Cf. Art. 12(2) (v) DCA and Schønning, Ophavsretsloven, 5th ed., 2011, 297; Rán Tryggvadóttir, 'Heimildir (bóka)safna til eintakagerðar og dreifingar á efni sem lýtur höfundarétti (e. What permission do libraries and museums have to make copies of and distribute works that fall under copyright protection)' in *Ragnarsbók* (Hið íslenska bókmenntafélag, 2009) 403; Trumpke, Exklusivität, 2015, 124.

1231 Lovforslag nr. L 19, *Lov til ændring af ophavsretsloven: Gennemførelse af infosoc-direktivet og nye aftalelicenser m.v.*, (2 October 2002) 8–9, 21.

1232 Copydan, Tekst&Node (e. Copydan Writing).

1233 See Art. 1 and 2 of the Copydan's Library Agreement (CLA), accessable (in Danish) at Copydans web, <http://tekstognode.dk/sites/default/files/pictures/Interurbanaftale%2C%20statslige%20biblioteker.pdf>, last viewed 9 January 2017.

1234 Art. 3 CLA.

1235 Ot. prp. nr. 46, Endringer, 2005, 51–52; Kyst, Aftalelicens, 2009, 47; 2007/2 LSF 58, Forslag, 2008, comment to par. 4 of Art. 50; Rydning, Extended, 2010, 11; Rognstad, Avtalelisenser, 2004, 159; Schønning, Ophavsretsloven, 5th ed., 2011, 464.

1236 Lovforslag nr. L 19, Infosoc, 2002, 22.

1237 Rognstad, Avtalelisenser, 2004, 159.

289. As mentioned above, the Danish ECL provision for libraries is narrower than in the other Nordic countries. However, when evaluating the provision it is worth remembering that Denmark has a general ECL provision, introduced in 2008, that supplements other specific ECL provisions[1238] and which was in particular expected to be needed for the digitising and digital use of the cultural heritage in libraries and other cultural heritage institutions.[1239]

5.3.1.2. Finland

290. The Finnish library ECL provision[1240] can also apply to archives and museums and may cover all works in the collection of the relevant institution, regardless of whether they are published, have been made public in another way or not.[1241] All reproduction of such works can be licensed under an ECL and used for all types of communication to the public, i.e. which are not already authorised under other provisions granting exceptions for libraries.[1242] The provision requires an opt-out possibility.[1243]

291. This ECL provision was used for the first time[1244] in September 2014 when the Ministry of Education and Culture, the CMO for visual artists[1245], the CMO for reproduction rights and photographic artists[1246] and the Finnish National Gallery signed an agreement[1247] that enables the worldwide online display of visual artworks by Finnish artists[1248], excluding audio-visual works and works that are subject to other agreements.[1249] The agreement covers the making available right, whereas the necessary digitisation of works falls under the reproduction exception for libraries.[1250] The agreement is extended to non-members of the relevant CMOs, who can opt-out.[1251] The CMOs undertake,

---

1238 Cf. Art. 50(2) DCA, discussed in Ch. 5.3.2.1.

1239 2007/2 LSF 58, Forslag, 2008, 3.3.1.

1240 Art. 16d FCA, was implemented with the legislation of 14.10.2005/821.

1241 See discussion in Ch. 5.3.3 and 10.2.2.

1242 Art. 16 and 16a-c FCA are specifically dealing with exceptions for libraries.

1243 Art. 16d (2) FCA.

1244 Vuopala, Extended, 2013, 20.

1245 Kuvasto.

1246 Kopiosto.

1247 Tryggvadóttir, Balancing of interests, 2015, 662; Koskinen-Olsson and Sigurðardóttir, Collective, 2016, 260–261; Press release of 20 November 2014 by the Finnish Ministry of Education and Culture (no longer available online). The Finnish National Gallery Agreement (FNGA) is in Finnish and not publicly accessible.

1248 Point 6 FNGA.

1249 Point 12 FNGA; e-mail of 2 March 2015 from Anna Vuopala, Government Counsellor at Ministry of Education and Culture, Finland.

1250 Arts. 16, 16a and 16b FCA, cf. e-mail from Vuopala, *op.cit.*

1251 Under certain circumstances authors who are members of the CMOs can opt-out, cf. e-mail from Vuopala, *op.cit.*

however, to work actively with the artists and subsequent rightholders to minimise the use of opt-outs.[1252] In October 2016 no opt-outs had been received.[1253]

292. The agreed remuneration is paid in a lump sum to the CMOs[1254] who then distribute it to all relevant rightholders based on a system agreed by the general assembly of the CMO. The National Gallery is responsible for acquiring a further licence and for providing remuneration if the Gallery wishes to add works of new or additional authors.[1255] The remuneration for rightholders who cannot be identified will be distributed collectively as grants.[1256] The agreement provides the National Gallery with a permanent licence which can only be terminated in case of breach of the agreement by the Gallery.[1257]

293. The agreement covers the works of around 930 Finnish artists[1258], amounting in March 2015 to just over 37,000 works of which around 33,500 were accessible on the internet worldwide.[1259]

5.3.1.3. Iceland

294. An ECL provision for libraries was adopted in 2016.[1260] The new ECL provision allows public archives, public libraries, university libraries and any other libraries enjoying support from public funds, as well as public collections and museums, to reproduce and make available works in their collections that have been made public[1261], if they have entered into an ECL agreement with the relevant CMO. Thus the provision is not limited as to which type of works it applies to and there is no requirement that the work has been published, only that it has been made available publicly.[1262] The preparatory document with the proposal explains that it was thought right that the stakeholders had the freedom to negotiate the relevant uses and which works in their collections the agreement should apply to.[1263] With regard to works never made available publicly, it was stated in the preparatory document that such works in the relevant institutions were normally donations under a contract that often stipulated how the documents or works

1252 Points 9 and 10 FNGA.
1253 Cf. e-mail of 5 October 2016 from from Tommi Nilson, the executive director of Kuvasto.
1254 Cf. point 22 FNGA.
1255 Cf. e-mail from Nilson, *op.cit.*
1256 Cf. e-mail from Vuopala, *op.cit.*
1257 Point 32 and 36 FNGA; e-mail from Nilson, *op.cit.*
1258 Cf. e-mail of 5 October 2016 from Nilson, *op.cit.*
1259 Cf. e-mail of 14 April 2015 from Vuopala. The works can be viewed on <http://kokoelmat.fng.fi/app>, last viewed 9.7.2017. Works by foreign authors are shown in search results but with no images.
1260 Cf. Art. 5 of Act. 9/2016 which added a new Art. 12.b to the ICA.
1261 See discussion in Ch. 5.3.3 and 10.2.2.
1262 Art. 3(1) ICA stipulates that a work has been made public when it has legally been made available to the public, i.e. with the consent of the rightholder.
1263 Cf. Parliamentary document 400, docket 333, 145th session of Althingi, 2015–2016, p. 17–18.

could be used. Furthermore, reference was made to the general ECL provision proposed and adopted in the same Act, which could facilitate the negotiation of an ECL agreement covering works never made publicly available.[1264] There is no requirement for an opt-out clause in an ECL agreement under this provision.

295. No ECL agreement has been concluded yet based on the library ECL provision.

5.3.1.4. Norway

296. In Norway the specific library ECL provision[1265], adopted in 2005, applies to archives, libraries and museums, as well as educational and research institutions. An ECL agreement under the provision can cover all published works in the collection of the relevant institutions. In 2015 its use was extended to works of visual art and photographs that have been made public.[1266] This addition was adopted in order to promote ECL agreements in museums.[1267] Works that are in the collections due to legal deposit are, however, not included[1268] and use of films under an ECL agreement and the distribution and use of films reproduced under an ECL agreement is more limited than for other types of works.[1269] These restrictions to the Norwegian ECL provision are found in the preparatory legal documents for the provision and not in the provision itself. The resulting lack of transparency has been criticised.[1270]

ECL agreements under the provision may permit all reproduction and communication to the public. The provision was intentionally left open and flexible in order to take account of new technological developments.[1271] There is no requirement for an opt-out possibility in the provision. As with other Nordic ECL provisions, there is no express mention that uses should be non-commercial.

297. One of the main intentions behind the adoption of the specific library ECL provision was to facilitate the delivery of digital copies of works to end-users.[1272] Currently an agreement[1273] between the Norwegian National Library

1264 Cf. ibid, p. 18.
1265 Art. 16a NCA.
1266 Changes made to Art. 16a NCA with Act. No 73 of 11 June 2015. See discussion in Ch. 5.3.3.
1267 Prop. 69 L, Proposisjon, 2015, 58; Kulturdepartementet, Høringsnotat, 2014, 48.
1268 Ot. prp. nr. 46, Endringer, 2005, 84; St.meld. nr. 24, Nasjonal strategi, 2009, 106.
1269 Ot. prp. nr. 46, Endringer, 2005, 85.
1270 Rognstad, Opphavsrett, 2009, 286.
1271 Ot. prp. nr. 46, Endringer, 2005, 75; Tryggvadóttir, Heimildir, 2009, 423.
1272 Tryggvadóttir, Heimildir, 2009, 404, 422.
1273 Avtale om digitial kopiering og formidling i bibliotek, avialable (hereafter the NNLA) at <www.kopinor.no/avtaletekster/avtale-om-digitial-kopiering-og-formidling-i-bibliotek> (in Norwegian), last viewed 7 July 2017.

(NNL) and Kopinor[1274] provides that all libraries eligible under the provision may make digital copies and distribute them to individuals that have directly requested such copies and where such copies are to be used for their research or individual study purposes. The agreement does not cover uses that are allowed in legislation, e.g. under exceptions, or through individual licences with rightholders. Furthermore, it is expressly stipulated that the agreement yields to other licence agreements and purchase terms that the libraries are bound by. Works that may be used under the agreement are single articles from printed publications and short excerpts from longer works, such as books. The agreement does not cover works that are published and provided to the libraries in digital format, nor articles from newspapers or sheet music.[1275] In further instructions on how to use the agreement it is stated that the intended use neither covers putting the works on the intranet of the institutions that the agreement covers, nor does it extend to sending digital copies to foreign libraries. However, copies may be sent to users of Norwegian libraries even if they happen to be residing abroad. Furthermore, the agreement does not entitle libraries to keep scanned works for later distribution.[1276] The agreement stipulates that libraries and the CMO may make the agreement public.[1277] There is no opt-out provision provided for in the Agreement. The agreement will be automatically renewed for a year unless it is terminated with three months' notice.[1278]

298. Another ECL agreement between the Norwegian National Library and Kopinor[1279] based on the library ECL provision is the internationally known Bokhylla project.[1280] Before the conclusion of the current Bokhylla agreement a pilot project[1281] was launched in May 2009, making Norway among the first countries in the world to digitise the cultural heritage.[1282]

1274 The Norwegian CMO for reproduction rights. Kopinor represents copyright holders of published works through 22 member organisations, 5 publishers' associations and 17 authors' associations and is empowered by its member organisations to negotiate and conclude collective agreements on copying and digital use of copyright protected works in all areas of society, cf. <www.kopinor.no/en/about-kopinor>, last viewed 6 Oct. 2016.

1275 Art. 1-5 NNLA.

1276 See Guide to the use of the agreement, <www.kopinor.no/artikler/veiledning-til-digital-formidling-for-bibliotek#ref1> (in Norwegian), last viewed 17 September 2016.

1277 Art. 12 NNLA.

1278 Art. 16 NNLA.

1279 The Bokhylla Agreement (BA) can be accessed in English translation on < https://www.nb.no/pressebilder/Contract_NationalLibraryandKopinor.pdf >, last viewed 2 May 2018.

1280 Koskinen-Olsson and Sigurðardóttir, Collective, 2016, 258; Trumpke, Exklusivität, 2015, 126–127, 461; Vuopala, Assessment, 2010, 37; Alain Strowel, Bokhylla.no, the Norwegian bookshelf: a model?, IPdigIT, 3 October 2010; last accessed 7 July 2017.

1281 The pilot project aimed to make 50,000 Norwegian works available in the following three years, cf. Skarstein, The Bookshelf, 2010, 48–50; Vuopala, Assessment, 2010, 37.

1282 Trumpke, Exklusivität, 2015, 125–126.

299. The current Bokhylla agreement allows the NNL to make books published in Norway before the year 2001 available on their webpage. Thus the agreement only applies to national publications, including translations. The NNL can make use of digital copies made under the preservation exception.[1283] The Bokhylla project is limited to Norwegian IP numbers, which restricts viewing availability to Norway, although the NNL may upon specific request give other users access, i.e. those without Norwegian IP numbers, for specific purposes, such as research and education.[1284] This limitation is secured by technological protection measures, i.e. geo-blocking. Some have voiced doubts whether the limitation in the Bokhylla agreement to Norwegian IP numbers is practically effective and legally viable.[1285] However, that question has not been tested before the courts.

The works that the agreement covers are only to be made available for viewing on a computer screen in the format used by the NNL web-page and no arrangements are to be made for downloading or printing the material while it is still under copyright.[1286] This limitation is interesting in the light of the Norwegian exception for making private copies.[1287] However, the Norwegian provisions on technological measures do not oblige users of such measures to ensure that individuals can use the private use exception for reproduction.[1288] The collection of works made available can be searched by author, title, words, text or quotation.[1289]

The agreement contains an opt-out possibility for all rightholders, members and non-members, although the relevant ECL provision does not impose such an obligation. However, it is worth noting that less than 2% of the number of works made available under the Norwegian Bokhylla agreement have been opted-out.[1290]

Remuneration is calculated per page per year[1291], i.e. it is not based on how often the work is viewed. The NNL is obliged, if requested, to make arrangements, as far as possible, for Kopinor to have access to statistics for the material made available under the agreement.[1292] The current statistics do not identify each and every work contained in the books, such as embedded illustrations. This fact as well as a pragmatic cost-driven approach means that

1283 Cf. Art. 2 BA and Art. 3 BA, cf. Art. 16 NCA and Art. 1–3(3) of FOR 21.12.2001 no. 1563, see also par. Ch. 10.2.4.

1284 Cf. Art. 4 BA. As of September 2016, 55 individuals without a Norwegian IP number have had access to the service, cf. information from Kopinor 31 October 2016.

1285 Riis, Rognstad and Schovsbo, Collective Agreements, 2016, 72.

1286 Art. 5 BA.

1287 Cf. Art. 12 NCA.

1288 Cf. Art. 53b.(1) NCA. The InfoSoc Directive does not oblige Member States to ensure such use under the exception in Art. 5(2)b), cf. Art. 6(4)(2).

1289 Skarstein, The Bookshelf, 2010, 48.

1290 According to information from Kopinor in September 2016, 211,454 book titles were available in the Bookhylla project and approx. 3,700 titles had been withdrawn. See also SWD(2016) 301 final, IA Part I, 2016, 75.

1291 Art. 8–10 BA. From 2015 and onwards it is NOK 0,33 (ca. 0,04 €) index linked.

1292 Art. 18 BA.

the distribution of remuneration is based on a combination of individual and collective remuneration.[1293]

The current contract entered into force in September 2012 and with termination first being possible in January 2016 and thereafter in January of each year. If not terminated with six months' notice the contract will be renewed automatically for a year.[1294]

300. The Bokhylla Agreement is a clear example of how ECL agreements tend to be more limited than what is allowed under an ECL provision.[1295]

5.3.1.5. Sweden

301. In Sweden the library ECL provision[1296] was revised in 2013.[1297] While it applies only to public libraries and archives, it can be extended to other libraries and archives by Government decree. An ECL agreement may cover all works in the collections of the library or archive for reproduction and such copies may be communicated to the public if they have lawfully been made public[1298] and there is no particular reason to assume that the author would oppose such use. Communication to the public would include the right to make works available online.[1299] The provision stipulates an opt-out possibility as a requirement. According to the legal preparatory documents, the Government is of the view that allowing works which have not lawfully been made public, to be communicated to the public under an ECL licence would have too wide ramifications, even with an opt-out possibility. The main reason for this is that once works have been communicated to the public this allows for further use of the work under some exceptions and limitations in the Copyright Act, which are only applicable to works that have been made public.[1300] It is further explained in the preparatory work that copies of films and stage works made under an ECL agreement can only be viewed at the premises of the relevant institution.[1301] This limitation is, however, not in the provision itself and hence not very transparent.

302. Since the revision of the library ECL provision two ECL agreements have been concluded under the provision, one with regard to the digitisation

---

1293 According to information from Kopinor in October 2016.

1294 Art. 21 BA.

1295 Trumpke, Exklusivität, 2015, 461–462.

1296 Art. 42d SCA.

1297 Changes made to the SCA by Act SFS 2013:691; Rosén, Copyright Contracts, 2011, 160. The older ECL provision for libraries, which was very narrow, was never used, cf. *SOU 2010:24, Avtalad upphovsrätt, 2010, 252*; Trumpke, Exklusivität, 2015, 122–123.

1298 See discussion in Ch. 5.3.3 and 10.2.2.

1299 Rosén, The Nordic ECL Model, 2012, 80–81; Rosén, Copyright Contracts, 2011, 176.

1300 Prop. 2012/13:141, Regeringens proposition, 2013, 41–42.

1301 In line with Art. 21 SCA, cf. Ibid, 35 and 45.

of newspapers and another with regard to photographs.[1302] Furthermore, a very interesting pilot project has been launched under the revised library ECL provision by the Swedish National Library (SNL)[1303], which aims to make published audio-visual recordings from the broadcasting station, Sveriges Radio AB, which were broadcast during the 1960s available for on-demand streaming with cross-border effect, in order to replace interlibrary loan.[1304] As a first step in this project a Memorandum of Understanding was signed by SNL in November 2015 regarding the principles which will form the basis for an extended collective licence agreement with the collective management organisations Copyswede (Sweden) and Kopiosto (Finland) in order to make cross-border remote access possible. An interesting aspect of the SNL initiative is the idea that the digitisation of analogue works would be based on end-user demand.[1305] This might be one way to deal with the cost-side of digitisation, i.e. instead of aiming to digitise every single work the approach would be user-led, at least up to a point.[1306]

303. Next I will discuss the general ECL provisions.

5.3.2. GENERAL ECL PROVISION

304. Ongoing innovation in digital technology provides for new ways to use protected works not envisaged in copyright acts. In the Nordic countries this has resulted in a growing demand for new ECL provisions for new uses based on the justification that, in the absence of such provisions, such uses might not be legally possible and would not provide remuneration for rightholders.[1307] All the Nordic countries, except Finland[1308], have, as a response to these new uses, introduced open or general ECL provisions. Such general ECL provisions enable

---

1302 Cf. e-mail of 25 October 2016 from Jerker Rydén, Chief Legal Adviser of the Swedish National Library.

1303 One of NLS's ancillaries is the Swedish Media Database (SMDB), a partly digitized database consisting of the audiovisual and audio media delivered to NLS as the legal depository for audio visual works. SMDB is available to researchers at NLS's premises and through interlibrary loans, cf. Rydén, NLS Comments 2015, 2015, 6.

1304 Ibid, 6–11.

1305 National Library of Sweden, 'Remote access across borders' (2015) <www.kb.se/english/about/news/Making-the-material-available-through-streaming-via-the-Internet-/> accessed 7 July 2017; Rydén, Are digital, 2016, 16.

1306 Works of great cultural importance would presumably also be priortised. Then it is always a question what inspires user demand, surley digital accessibility would be one factor to increase user-demand.

1307 Prop. 2012/13:141, Regeringens proposition, 2013, 53.

1308 There is no intention to introduce a general ECL provision in Finland according to information from Anna Vuopala, government counsellor at the Finnish Ministry of Education and culture, in an e-mail of 30 September 2016, although for a while there were discussions to that effect, cf. Rognstad, Avtalelisens, 2012, 631.

ECL agreements in new areas without having to introduce specific legislation each time.[1309] Denmark was first in line in 2008[1310] followed by Sweden in 2013[1311], Norway in 2015[1312] and Iceland in 2016.[1313] General ECL provisions are not limited to specific types or fields of works, users or uses, although agreements based on a general provision must be specific with regard to what they cover. Neither is there any stipulation that uses should be non-commercial or not for direct or indirect economic or commercial advantage.

305. It was suggested in Sweden to use the term "special" ECL rather the term "general" as the latter might be understood to cover general areas for ECL effect rather than the intended specific and well-defined area.[1314] However, this was criticised by some academics, who maintained that such an open ECL provision is general as the area for which it can be used is not predetermined, notwithstanding the fact that the agreement that releases the ECL effect of the general ECL provision must be specific.[1315] This was also the conclusion in the final legislative preparatory work in Sweden and the adopted provision is under the heading: "General ECL". The other Nordic countries also use the term "general".

5.3.2.1. Denmark

306. The Danish general ECL provision has the following wording:

> Extended collective licenses may also be invoked by users who, within a specified field, have made an agreement on the exploitation of works with an organisation comprising a substantial number of authors of a certain type of works which are used in Denmark within the specified field. However, this does not apply if the author has issued a prohibition against use of his work in relation to any of the contracting parties.[1316]

The general ECL provision is intended to be supplementary to the specific ECL provisions in the Copyright Act and can either be negotiated for new areas of use or as an addition to areas that are already partly covered by specific provisions.[1317] The driving force behind the provision was the need to find

1309 Prop. 2012/13:141, Regeringens proposition, 2013, 53; Prop. 69 L, Proposisjon, 2015, 13.

1310 Art. 50(2) DCA, introduced with Act No. 231 of 8.4.2008; Koskinen-Olsson and Sigurðardóttir, Collective, 2016, 249.

1311 See Art. 42h SCA adopted with Act SFS 2013:691 on 27 June 2013.

1312 Cf. Art. 36(2) NCA as changed by Act No 73 of 19 of June 2015.

1313 Art. 26.a(2) ICA, as introduced by Art. 14 of Act No 9/2016.

1314 SOU 2010:24, Avtalad upphovsrätt, 2010, 283; Rosén, Copyright Contracts, 2011, 160, 177–178.

1315 Rognstad, Avtalelisens, 2012, 631.

1316 Art. 50(2) DCA.

1317 2007/2 LSF 58, Forslag, 2008, comment to par. 2 of Art. 50; Schønning, Ophavsretsloven, 5th ed., 2011, 466.

a solution with regard to the orphan works issue and a framework for the digitisation of the cultural heritage.[1318] The Danish provision is neither limited to certain types of works nor to published works nor to works that have made publicly available in another way. Neither is it limited to certain groups of users or certain types of uses. However, each ECL agreement made under the general ECL provision must be between a user within a specified field and a CMO representative for that particular field.[1319] What "specified field" in this context actually means is not defined, either in the provision itself or in the preparatory documents. CMOs that negotiate ECL agreements under the general provision must be authorised to do so.[1320] The only guideline in the preparatory documents for what can fall under a general ECL agreement is that care should be taken not to authorise ECL agreements under this provision in areas where individual licensing is possible.[1321] This gives the authorisation authority a wide margin to determine what can fall under such an agreement.[1322]

307. The Ministry of Culture in Denmark is the authorising authority for ECL agreements under both the specific and the general provisions. The Ministry publishes a list of all the currently valid authorisations on its webpage.[1323] One of the differences between specific and general ECL provisions in Denmark is the authorisation process. Under the specific provisions eligible CMOs are authorised beforehand to negotiate and conclude ECL agreements, which then come into force as soon as they have been agreed upon. Under the general ECL provision the relevant CMOs apply for an authorisation for the extension effect after the conclusion of an agreement with a user. This can lead to a period of uncertainty until the authorisation is issued.[1324]

308. In May 2018 there were 27 authorisations in force, issued under the general ECL provision, thereof four authorisations allowing libraries to make works available online. The authorisations for online use are all issued for the CMO Copydan Tekst & Node (e. Copydan Writing). One is for an agreement with the Danish State and University Library to deliver a digital copy of a periodical on

---

1318 2007/2 LSF 58, Forslag, 2008, 11–12; SOU 2010:24, Avtalad upphovsrätt, 2010, 276–282; Riis, Rognstad and Schovsbo, Collective Agreements, 2016, 62; Riis and Schovsbo, ECLs, 2010, 476–477; Kyst, Aftalelicens, 2009, 47 and 50; Schønning, Ophavsretsloven, 5th ed., 2011, 465–466.

1319 2007/2 LSF 58, Forslag, 2008, comment to par 2 of Art. 50; Schønning, Ophavsretsloven, 5th ed., 2011, 464; Kyst, Aftalelicens, 2009, 47.

1320 Art. 50(4) DCA.

1321 2007/2 LSF 58, Forslag, 2008, general comments, section 3.3.1 and comment to Par. 4 of Art. 50; Schønning, Ophavsretsloven, 5th ed., 2011, 469; Rydning, Extended, 2010, 51.

1322 It has been suggested that the authority should define the field very narrowly, cf. Rydning, Extended, 2010, 51.

1323 See <http://kum.dk/kulturpolitik/ophavsret/godkendelser/>, (in Danish), last viewed 2 May 2018.

1324 Foged, Danish licences, 2015, 18.

women's issues published in the period 1921–1953 to some institutions in order for them to make it available online in connection with the centenary of women's voting rights.[1325] Another is for an agreement with the Royal Library, allowing the library to make available 913 books, 180 maps and 863 pamphlets from the First World War on their website.[1326] It is interesting to note that these two authorisations expressly state that the digitisation is not covered by the licence but rather under the preservation exception in Art. 16 of the DCA. The other two authorisations relate to the use of book covers on library websites and on social media.[1327]

309. Like all the other authorisations, the authorisations are issued with application to Danish territory. However, online accessibility to the relevant works seems to vary. Thus the works digitised from the First World War are accessible worldwide, both through the Danish Royal Library and Europeana[1328] whereas the women's issues periodicals are only accessible with an access code.[1329] None of the relevant authorisations are limited to Danish rightholders, although in all four cases the likelihood is that the majority of rightholders would be Danish.

310. The Danish general ECL provision provides that the ECL agreement does not apply if the author has issued a prohibition against the use of his or her works. The authorisation for the digital use of the women's issues periodicals states that the ECL agreement it authorises must expressly mention that both outsiders and CMO members can opt out.[1330] The other authorisations under discussion here do not expressly mention the opt-out possibility, only that the authorisation is conditional on the activities of the relevant CMO being within

---

[1325] Issued 30 January 2015 for three years, so the authorisation should have lapsed end of January 2018 but the periodical seems still to be accessible online, albeit under member access code. The authorisation has not been removed from the ministry's website cf. <http://tekstognode.dk/sites/default/files/pictures/Godkendelse%20af%20Kvinden%20og%20Samfundet.pdf>, last viewed 3 May 2018.

[1326] Issued 27 June 2014 for a renewable period of three years, cf. <http://kum.dk/fileadmin/KUM/Documents/Kulturpolitik/Ophavsret/Aftalelicensgodkendelser/Generelle_aftalelicenser/Copydan_TekstNode_1_verdenskrig.pdf>, in Danish, last viewed 3 May 2018. The authorisation seems not to have been renewed but is still on the ministry's website.

[1327] One is for children's books, valid from 29 October 2014 until end of 2019 with an option of renewal, cf. <https://kum.dk/fileadmin/KUM/Documents/Kulturpolitik/Ophavsret/Aftalelicensgodkendelser/Generelle_aftalelicenser/Copydan_TekstNode_Palles_Gavebod.pdf>, and the other for book covers in general, valid from October 2017 to end of 2020, cf. https://kum.dk/fileadmin/KUM/Documents/Kulturpolitik/Ophavsret/Aftalelicensgodkendelser/Generelle_aftalelicenser/Aftale_mellem_DDB__VISDA_og_Copydan_Tekst___Node_om_digital_brug_af_bogomslag.pdf, last viewed 3 May 2018.

[1328] See <www.kb.dk/da/nb/tema/historie/wwl/om_samling.html>, last accessed 3 May 2018.

[1329] See <www.statsbiblioteket.dk/nationalbibliotek/nyheder/kvinden-og-samfundet>, last viewed 3 May 2018.

[1330] Ibid. It is also stated in the authorisation that the ECL agreement has to expressly mention the ECL effect.

the confines of relevant legislation, such as the copyright act. Currently there are no registered opt-outs for any of the digitisation projects that the relevant CMO (Copydan Writing) is party to.[1331]

311. Most of the authorisations under the general ECL provisions are issued for three to five years. Some can be extended simply at the request of rightholders, i.a. the authorisation for the CMO Copydan Writing regarding the ECL agreement for the online use by the Royal Library of First World War material, whereas others have to be reapplied for. Many of the authorisations for "general" ECL agreements have been renewed. Most authorisations are for ECL agreements that are fairly narrow in scope. Interestingly at least one authorisation concerns an ECL agreement without a remuneration obligation; this is for the reproduction of music CD's and film DVD's and storage and use from media centres when the reproduction is done by assistants of handicapped individuals who are not able to do so themselves.[1332] There are standard provisions in all of the authorisations with the following stipulations: first, that the authorisation is dependent on the CMO representing a substantial number of the rightholders[1333] of the works covered by the authorisation and the works are used in Denmark during the whole period of authorisation; second, that the CMO is obliged upon request to inform the Ministry about all its affairs; third, that the CMO operates within the framework of applicable legislation, i.a. the Copyright Act and relevant international obligations; finally, that the CMO, in line with the Services Directive, specifies publicly on its website that it has the Ministry's authorisation. The authorisations contain a concluding paragraph announcing that in issuing the authorisation the Ministry took particular account of the following factors: first, the representativeness of the CMO and whether the CMO has previously been authorised to negotiate an ECL agreement in the relevant area; second, the fact that the relevant rights are held by a disparate group of rightsholders that is difficult to identify and localize; and finally, the large number of rightsholders making it difficult to license the rights individually.

5.3.2.2. Iceland

312. In March 2016 a general ECL provision was adopted in Iceland.[1334] The provision stipulates that users may negotiate uses under an ECL agreement with

1331 Cf. <http://tekstognode.dk/node/253>, in Danish, last viewed 3 May 2018.

1332 Cf. <http://kum.dk/fileadmin/KUM/Documents/Kulturpolitik/Ophavsret/Aftalelicensgodkendelser/Generelle_aftalelicenser/Copydan_AVU-medier_Danske_Handicaporganisationer.pdf>, last viewed 3 May 2018. Such reproduction and use would fall under the private use exception of Art. 12 DCA if the individuals were able to do it themselves. See also Riis, Rognstad and Schovsbo, Collective Agreements, 2016, 63.

1333 The term used is rightholders, rather than authors.

1334 Cf. Art. 14.a(2) of Act. 9/2016 which added a new Art. 26.a(2) to the ICA.

authorised CMOs if the agreement applies to a clearly defined area of uses and works, if such use can only be achieved via an ECL agreement and if the agreement is in a written form, clearly stating that it is an ECL agreement. In the preparatory document with the proposal it is explained that the provision was considered necessary to enable simple and quick negotiations for mass use enabled by new communication technology, such as for libraries and other cultural heritage institutions, in order to preserve and disseminate the cultural heritage, without having to resort to legislation each time new technology emerged. The provision applies to published and unpublished works and to works that have not been made public in any way. In the preparatory documents it is observed that sometimes there are works in collections of cultural heritage institutions where it is difficult to ascertain whether they have been published or made publicly available in another way, such as stand-alone photos. However, it was also underlined that contracts regarding the use of, for example, private archives in the collection of relevant institutions, had priority over any potential ECL agreement. As for the requirement that the use requested had to be of such nature that it was impracticable to negotiate use without an ECL agreement, it is stated that it is not necessary to prove that individual licensing had been tried and failed. It should suffice that it is obvious that individual licensing would be difficult due to cost and volume of the works.[1335] An opt-out possibility must be available at least for outsiders.[1336] No ECL agreements have yet been concluded under this general provision.[1337]

5.3.2.3. Norway

313. In 2015 a general ECL provision was adopted in Norway.[1338] The provision stipulates that an ECL agreement can also be used in situations that do not fall under the specific ECL provisions if a user for a specifically defined area has entered into an agreement for the use with a CMO which represents a significant part of the authors of the relevant works that are used in Norway and this is authorised by the Ministry of Culture.

314. The provision covers all types of uses, both reproduction and communication to the public, including the making available right, and all types of works made publicly available.[1339] It is up to the negotiating parties to reach an agreement on these issues. However, it is clear that an ECL agreement under the provision must be for specific uses or a specific field and can thus

1335 Cf. Parliamentary document 400, docket 333, 145th session of Althingi, 2015–2016, p. 25–26.
1336 Cf. Art. 26.a(3)ICA and discussion in the Parliamentary document, p. 19 and 26.
1337 At the time of writing in May 2018.
1338 Cf. Art. 36(2) NCA as changed by Act No 73 of 19 of June 2015. The same Act implemented the Orphan Works Directive.
1339 The other Nordic general ECL provisons and the Finnish ECL provision for libraries do not require that works have been made publicly available.

not allow all uses for all works. This has to be clearly defined in the agreement. Furthermore, as with all ECL agreements, a prerequisite is that individual licensing is impracticable, such as when there is a need for mass-use of works and where it is impossible to decide which works will be called for at any given time. The provision does not limit who can be a beneficiary of an ECL agreement.[1340]

315. In the lead up to the adoption of the general ECL provision there was discussion on whether authorisation of the relevant CMO was necessary or not.[1341] As most commenting stakeholders supported authorisation and because it was in line with the requirements for ECL agreements under the specific ECL provision, the final outcome was that a requirement for authorisation was proposed and adopted. However, it is not specified whether such authorisation should be issued before an agreement is negotiated, as is the case with authorisation for the specific ECL provisions in Norway and elsewhere in the Nordic countries[1342], or after the agreement is reached, as is the practice in Denmark with regard to ECL agreements under the general ECL provision. The preparatory documents state that the CMO must prove that the conditions for an ECL agreement under the provision are fulfilled and must provide the necessary information. Furthermore, it was also decided not to specify whether authorisations for ECL agreements under the general provision should be time limited or not.[1343]

316. The provision provides for an opt-out possibility for outsiders. Although not stipulated in the provision, such an opt-out can be addressed either to a user under an ECL agreement under the provision or to the CMO that has negotiated it. There are no specific requirements for how an opt-out should be expressed other than it must be clear as to which works and uses it applies.[1344] Furthermore, there is a general ban on letting works fall under an ECL agreement under the general provision if there is reason to think the rightholder would oppose such use.[1345] In October 2016 only one authorisation had been issued under the general ECL provision in Norway.[1346]

5.3.2.4. Sweden

317. The Swedish general ECL provision was adopted in 2013.[1347] As with the general ECL provisions in the other Nordic countries there is no specification as

1340 Prop. 69 L, Proposisjon, 2015, 18–20.
1341 Kulturdepartementet, Høringsnotat, 2014, 16–17.
1342 Except for Sweden that has no authorisation system.
1343 Prop. 69 L, Proposisjon, 2015, 26–27.
1344 Ibid, 24.
1345 Ibid, 24, 61. See also discussion in Ch. 5.4.3.3.
1346 Information from the Department of Media and Copyright of the Norwegian Ministry of Culture on 10 October 2016. The authorisation was for the clearance of certain use of visual art for on-demand television.
1347 See Art. 42h SCA adopted with Act SFS 2013:691 on 27 June 2013 and which came into force 1 November 2013.

to which works, uses or users this provision can be applied. Such specification is left to the negotiating parties. The only prerequisite for an ECL agreement under this provision is that individual licensing is impracticable, which is commonly in mass-use situations where it is difficult to predict which works will be needed. According to the preparatory documents the prerequisite means that it is not possible to obtain an ECL agreement just because individual negotiations have failed or because the user believes it would be easier to have an ECL agreement. The negotiating parties must be able to specify the use, with regard to activity or purpose, and what type of works the ECL agreement covers, so as not to have the agreement too wide. Although not stipulated in the provision, it has to be clear from the agreement that it is intended to have ECL effect.[1348] It is suggested in the preparatory document that an ECL agreement under this general provision could be used for digitisation by cultural heritage institutions in collaboration with private institutions. Outsiders can opt out of the agreement if they do not want their work used under an ECL agreement. The provision simply talks about "author" but it is clear from the preparatory document that the opt-out possibility applies to the outsider author or other outsider rightholder. The opt-out must be well defined and clear. Furthermore, as in Norway, there is a general ban on allowing works to fall under an ECL agreement covered by the provision if there is reason to believe the rightholder would oppose such use.[1349] As with the other Nordic general ECL licence provisions, there is no obligation on the parties to participate in an arbitration process if they cannot agree to adopt an agreement.[1350]

318. As with other ECL provisions in Sweden, no authorisation is required for an ECL agreement to take effect under this provision. If a question arises as to the competence of a CMO to negotiate an ECL agreement the courts will decide on that issue.

319. In October 2016 at least four ECL agreements had been concluded on the basis of the general ECL provision.[1351]

5.3.3. EVALUATION

320. The extension effect is the core of the ECL system. By extending collective agreements to rightholders of works of the same nature it enables users to use all works in the same field without raising the transaction cost to unacceptable

1348 It was suggested to be included in the provision but not adopted, cf. Rosén, Copyright Contracts, 2011, 177.

1349 See also discussion in Ch. 5.4.3.3.

1350 Prop. 2012/13:141, Regeringens proposition, 2013, 54–59.

1351 Cf. e-mail of 25 October 2016 from Jerker Rydén, Chief Legal Adviser of the Swedish National Library.

levels. For this reason the ECL system is generally well accepted in all the Nordic countries and has functioned well since its introduction.[1352] However, there are some issues with regard to the extension effect in ECL provisions that are important, either with regard to the ECL system in general or from the point of view of ECL agreements for libraries, or both. First is the legal nature of the extension effect which will be discussed in Ch. 6.1 below. Second, the question of whether works need to be published or made publicly available in another way in order to be covered by an ECL agreement, and, third, criticism of the general ECL provisions.

321. In the Nordic countries a work shall be considered published if, with the consent of the author, copies of the work have been put on the market or otherwise distributed to the public.[1353] A work shall be considered to have been made public if it has lawfully been made available to the public.[1354] It is worth noting that the term "made available" in the Nordic copyright acts refers to all modes of communication to the public, i.e. distribution, exhibition, performance in public and the making available right.[1355] This means that all published works are by default also legally made public.

Older ECLs used to be limited to published or broadcast works.[1356] This was partly based on the assumption that as the author had thus released the work for distribution he or she would not oppose use of the work under an ECL agreement.[1357] However, this is changing as more ECL provisions apply to works that have legally been made public. One reason for this development is the fact that it can be difficult to know if works made legally available on the internet are published or not, and in many cases works are no longer published in the legal sense.[1358]

This is a difficult area that has to be handled with care. Obviously, if an agreement has been made or instructions issued by rightholders on how unpublished works, or works that have not been made public, may be used in libraries and archives, such instructions would override provisions in the copyright legislation.[1359] However, such information is not always available, e.g. when the donor is not the rightholder of the work and does not have the right to

---

[1352] Riis and Schovsbo, ECLs, 2010, 496 to 497; Rognstad, Avtalelisens, 2012, 621; Tryggvadóttir, Digital libraries, 2014, 316; Mendis and Stobo, Extended, 2016, 208.
[1353] Art. 8 (2) DCA, Art. 8(2) FCA, Art. 3(2) ICA, Art. 8(2) NCA and Art. 8(2) SCA.
[1354] Art. 8(1) DCA, Art. 8(1) FCA, Art. 3(1) ICA, Art. 8(1) NCA and Art. 8(1) SCA.
[1355] Art. 2(3)-(4) DCA, Art. 2(3)-(4) ICA; Art. 2(3)-(4) FCA, Art. 2(3)-(4) NCA, Art. 2(3) SCA.
[1356] Karnell, Outsiders, 1991, 433.
[1357] Bergström, Program för upphovsrätten, (1960) 2011, 156. See also discussion in USA where it is advised against letting ECL apply to unpublished works because of administrative burdens that would create as well as authors right to determine when their work is first released, cf. US Copyright Office, Mass Digitization, 2015, 84–85.
[1358] Olsson, Upphovsrättslagstiftningen, 2006, 315.
[1359] Prop. 2012/13:141, Regeringens proposition, 2013, 41.

issue instructions on the use of the work. This situation may arise, for example, when private letters to and from a donor are given to archives; the letters to the donor are not under his or her copyright. It might not be unreasonable to allow works that have neither been published nor been legally made public rest until the protection period has expired, as then there would be no hindrance under copyright legislation to making them public in whichever form. On the other hand the cultural information contained in such works may be of great importance and in such cases it might seem to be justifiable to enable libraries and archives to make use of them and communicate them to the public. In my view it seems reasonable, given there is an opt-out possibility, to allow libraries to determine whether the unpublished work is of such cultural value that it merits being digitised and made available. In this context it is interesting to note that the opt-out provisions in Sweden and Norway stipulate that works will not be used under an ECL agreement under the general provision if there is a specific reason to believe that the author would oppose such use.[1360] In my view this is a sensible and practical provision and provides a safeguard when issuing ECLs for works that have not been published or made legally available in another way.[1361]

322. The general ECLs have been described as problematic because of their open-ended nature.[1362] However, the fact remains that the main merit of the general ECL provision is its flexibility. The provision can be used for agreements for any use in any area of work that the stakeholders agree on and which is impracticable to license individually, without having to await legislative initiatives for ECLs in that particular field.[1363] It can be used for new areas of work or new uses that go beyond the scope of existing specific ECL provisions, as long as the relevant CMO has a mandate for such uses. Thus it can be an important tool for enabling the use of in-copyright works in areas of fast growing technologies.

323. General ECL provisions can be seen as more intrusive on the exclusive right than the specific ECL provisions, especially for foreign rightholders, as the field of use of general provisions is less predictable than the specific provisions which are limited to certain fields. ECLs are most appropriate in areas where individual management is difficult and leads to insufficient results because of outsiders, but might, at least theoretically, be possible.[1364] It may be that ECLs are not appropriate in areas of uses that have public interest objectives where individual management is impossible as if no agreement is reached the use will not be possible. In those instances pure exceptions or limitations might

---

1360 Art. 42h SCA and Art. 36(2) NCA, cf. Prop. 69 L, Proposisjon, 2015, 61.

1361 See discussion in Ch. 5.4.3.3.

1362 Riis, Rognstad and Schovsbo, Collective Agreements, 2016, 62; Riis and Schovsbo, ECLs, 2010, 476–477.

1363 Koskinen-Olsson and Sigurðardóttir, Collective, 2016, 250.

1364 Rognstad, Avtalelisens, 2012, 625, 630–632.

be more appropriate to secure the use. Thus it is almost inbuilt in the ECL system that individual management might be possible if there were no time or cost restraints. Hence some have criticised the development towards further collectivism of copyright which the general ECL provision represents. In their view it is a fundamental change from the principle of individual management of the exclusive right and should be discussed as a matter of principle rather than to be led by pragmatism.[1365]

324. There is a possibility that the general ECL provision will be overused to the detriment of the outsider's interest. However, the main justification for ECLs is that it enables use that would otherwise be impracticable.[1366] This is true also with regard to the general ECL provisions. Both the Swedish and Icelandic general ECL provisions expressly underline that in order for the provisions to extend an agreement the extension effect must be a prerequisite for the use the agreement covers.[1367] This is also the underlying requirement in Denmark and Norway.[1368] Furthermore, the opt-out possibility should diminish the danger of excessive use. If there are too many opt-outs then the benefit of the ECL will be lost, hence the negotiating parties will have to take the interest of outsiders into consideration. In the case of the Danish, Icelandic and Norwegian general ECL provisions the use will be regulated by the fact that CMOs wishing to have ECL effect in their agreement must be authorised. The authorisation defines in which fields an agreement can have an ECL effect. This gives the Ministry a fair amount of room to exercise control.[1369] Finally, the ECL process itself requires considerable effort[1370] which should minimise the risk that the system will be used for situations where individual licensing might be more appropriate. In my view the combination of these factors, in particular the opt-out possibility and the authorisation, where applicable, are sufficient safeguards against overuse in the light of the benefits achieved by the flexibility offered by the general ECL provision. It remains to be seen how the general ECL provisions in Sweden, Norway and Iceland will be used. If the Danish practice is to go by then the use can be expected to be prudent.

325. It has been claimed that due to the proportionally high membership in the Nordic CMOs and extensive reciprocal agreements with foreign CMOs that the extension effect has a relatively small application.[1371] However, it is questionable whether this is true with regard to foreign outsiders. Although

1365 Schovsbo, The necessity to collectivize, 2012, 188 to 190; Rognstad, Avtalelisens, 2012, 632.
1366 See Ch. 5.1.1, par. 256 and 5.1.2.
1367 Art. 42h SCA and Art. 26.a(2) ICA.
1368 See e.g. Prop. 69 L, Proposisjon, 2015, 60–61.
1369 Rydning, Extended, 2010, 22.
1370 Vuopala, Extended, 2013, 35; Rognstad, Avtalelisenser, 2004, 158.
1371 Koskinen-Olsson, Collective Management, 2010, 297.

one of the factors assessed when authorising CMOs to negotiate ECL agreements is the number of reciprocal agreements with foreign CMOs, it is not a prerequisite for the authorisation.[1372] It is true that the extension effect has not been widely opposed and the opt-out possibility, where it exists, has been relatively seldom used[1373] in the past. However, this may partly be due to the fact that most outsiders, the largest group being foreigners, are often unaware of the uses based on the extension effect of ECLs[1374] or do not have the means to pursue the issue.[1375] There must be transparent practicable safeguard measures to enable outsiders to opt-out when necessary. This and other safeguard measures for outsiders I will look at in further detail in the next sub-chapter.

5.4. MEASURES TO SECURE THE RIGHTS OF NON-REPRESENTED RIGHTHOLDERS

326. A fundamental requirement in any ECL agreement is that outsiders should be treated in the same way as members under the agreement. Securing the outsiders' interest is of utmost importance, obviously for the outsiders but also for the ECL system as a whole, as if not fulfilled the system might not comply with international norms.[1376] This requirement is most prominently reflected in the fact that outsiders are entitled to the same remuneration as members. However, as outsiders have not given the CMO the mandate to negotiate on their behalf and not had any opportunity to influence the negotiation of the agreement, there are additional safeguard measures in the Nordic ECL system for outsiders.

There are two main additional elements in the Nordic ECL provisions aimed at securing the right of outsiders. One is that outsiders are entitled to individual remuneration even under collective remuneration schemes, and the other, which is, however, not inherent in all ECL provisions, is the possibility of opting out. Below I will give an account of these two measures and discuss the issue of transparency, which is an underlying requirement of the system and important in regard to outsiders. However, first I will look at the identity of the outsiders or the non-represented rightholders, as their interest can vary depending on where they come from.

1372 Axhamn and Guibault, Cross-border ECL, 2011, 34; Liedes, Memorandum, 2010, 7.

1373 Schønning, Ophavsretsloven, 5th ed., 2011, 380; Tryggvadóttir, Digital libraries, 2014, 321; Olsson, Upphovsrättslagstiftningen, 2006, 316; Rydning, Extended, 2010, 86; Trumpke, The Extended, 2012, 280.

1374 Riis and Schovsbo, ECLs, 2010, 491.

1375 Karnell, Outsiders, 1991, 430 and 433.

1376 Trumpke, The Extended, 2012, 275.

5.4.1. CATEGORIES OF NON-REPRESENTED RIGHTHOLDERS

327. Outsiders can be divided into three main groups[1377], as well as a number of subgroups. The main groups identified are the following: first; national or resident non-members of a national CMO; second, foreigners, i.e. those who are neither members of the CMO nor residing in the country where the ECL is negotiated; and third, rightholders of orphan works.[1378]

328. The first main group is relatively small in the Nordic countries as national representation in CMOs is traditionally high.[1379] This group can be divided into three sub-groups; firstly, inheritors of rights that may not be eligible for membership of a CMO[1380]; secondly, new artists or amateur artists who have not yet had the occasion or the right to become members[1381] or those that have negligible income from their works[1382]; and thirdly, those who do not want to be members of a CMO for various reasons. This could include well-known and established authors who wish to manage their rights individually or those who for principle reasons do not want to be members[1383], for example those authors who prefer to license their work under the Creative Commons system. The first two sub-groups depend partly on the membership rules of CMOs. The more stringent the membership rules the higher the number of outsiders.[1384]

329. The second main group, i.e. foreigners who are neither members of the national CMO nor residing in the country where the ECL is negotiated, can be divided into foreigners residing within the EU/EEA and foreigners outside the EU/EEA[1385] because of the EU's harmonisation of copyright. The rightholders in this group, regardless of whether they are from outside or inside of EEA, can be members of a CMO that has a reciprocal agreement with the national CMO eligible to negotiate ECL agreements. In this instance those rightholders will receive information and remuneration for the use of their work, unless it is below the distribution minimum for sending abroad[1386]; these rightholders are thus not "proper" outsiders. Those who are "double" outsiders, i.e. neither members

1377 Strowel, The European, 2011, 665.
1378 Tryggvadóttir, Digital libraries, 2014, 318.
1379 Koskinen-Olsson, Collective Management, 2010, 297; Riis and Schovsbo, ECLs, 2010, 495; Lovforslag nr. L 119, 1344; Ot. prp. nr. 15, Om lov, 1994, 21.
1380 Bergström, Program för upphovsrätten, (1960) 2011, 158.
1381 Ibid, 159; Drexl and others, Comments, 2013, 15.
1382 Von Lewinski, Mandatory, 2004, 7; Drexl and others, Comments, 2013, 15.
1383 Bergström, Program för upphovsrätten, (1960) 2011, 159.
1384 Drexl and others, Comments, 2013, 22.
1385 Strowel, The European, 2011, 665.
1386 Riis and Schovsbo, ECLs, 2010, 491.

of the national CMO nor a CMO that has a reciprocal agreement with the ECL negotiating CMO are less likely to be informed about the potential use of their works and/or receive remuneration, especially when remuneration is distributed collectively rather than individually. The foreign outsiders, regardless of whether they are members of a CMO that has a reciprocal agreement or not with the national CMO will not have a possibility to influence the decision making process of the national CMO.

330. The third main group of outsiders consists of rightholders of orphan works. These rightholders may be nationals or residents or foreigners in relation to the country of establishment of the CMO. However, as the works are orphan it is inherent in most cases that the rightholder is unknown and thus often impossible to categorise in the other groups.[1387]

331. A forth group of outsiders can be identified in cases where an umbrella CMO administers the ECLs in a certain area and where not all CMOs that handle rights in that same area are members of the relevant umbrella CMO. This is discussed in a Swedish Governmental report from 2010 where a case is described where two CMOs[1388] complained to the Market Court[1389] that the Swedish reproduction rights organisation, an umbrella CMO[1390], was abusing its market dominant position by not granting them membership. They claimed that this made it impossible for their members to receive remuneration for use of their works under the ECL agreements for copying in educational institutions. The Court found that the umbrella CMO was not abusing its dominant position by refusing membership to organisations which were neither major organisations in their field nor had signed an ECL licence. The Swedish Competition Authority had ruled in the same dispute and had come to the conclusion with reference to the structure of the ECL system that this was not abuse of the umbrella CMO dominant position.[1391] In this book I concentrate mainly on the first three groups, i.e. individual outsiders.

332. This account demonstrates that the outsiders do not constitute one coherent group and thus their interests can differ, which can affect their relationship to the ECL system. Another consideration is whether CMOs look after the interest of non-members in general as well as of their members.[1392] The

1387 See discussion in Ch. 5.2.1.1 and 6.3.2 on orphan works and ECLs.

1388 Svenska Konstnärsförbundet (The Swedish Artist Society) and Föreningen Förlagsutgiven Fackpress (The Association of Trade Press Publishers).

1389 The Market Court (Marknadsdomstolen) is a specialized court that handles cases related to the Competition Act as well as cases involving the Marketing Act and other consumer and marketing legislation.

1390 Bonus Presskopia.

1391 SOU 2010:24, Avtalad upphovsrätt, 2010, 224.

1392 Riis and Schovsbo, ECLs in Action, 2012, 939.

safeguard measures for outsiders in the Nordic ECL system designed to protect the interest of non-members, are the right to individual remuneration and the-opt out possibility. However, how these duties are to be executed is not regulated, so it is up to each CMO to establish rules and routines for themselves.[1393] This I will look at in the following sub-chapters in order to evaluate the efficacy of the safeguard measures.

5.4.2. INDIVIDUAL REMUNERATION

333. Remuneration for uses of works under an ECL agreement is decided in the agreement.[1394] As with all collective agreements an ECL agreement is most often based on blanket licensing which means a uniform pricing structure for all works.[1395] It is assumed that the financial interest of rightholders, members as well as outsiders, is secured by the fact that remuneration for the use of their work under an ECL agreement is negotiated and accepted by a CMO that represents a substantial number of rightholders in the same field and thus has a stronger bargaining power than an individual rightholder.[1396] However, a remuneration model may constitute an abuse of a dominant position by a CMO. This, the CJEU found, may be the case if the model is based on "a percentage of a revenue deriving from television broadcasts directed at the general public and/or subscription sales" if

> ...another method exists which enables the use of those works and the audience to be identified and quantified more precisely and that method is capable of achieving the same legitimate aim, which is the protection of the interests of composers and music editors, without however leading to a disproportionate increase in the costs incurred for the management of the contracts and the supervision of the use of musical works protected by copyright.[1397]

334. The distribution of remuneration to rightholders, both members of the CMO in question and outsiders, is decided by the CMO.[1398] Outside rightholders

1393 SOU 2010:24, Avtalad upphovsrätt, 2010, 211 and 226.

1394 It is possible that negotiating parties will come to an agreement that there is no remuneration due for certain uses under an ECL agreement, as there is no stipulation obliging the parties to negotiate remuneration, cf. Trumpke, Exklusivität, 2015, 327, fn. 1246. As mentioned in Ch. 5.3.2.1 there is at least one agreement under the Danish General ECL provision that stipulates free use. However, that is unlikely to be the case other than in exceptional circumstances.

1395 Riis, Rognstad and Schovsbo, Collective Agreements, 2016, 63.

1396 See Ch. 5.1.1.

1397 C-52/07 *Kanal 5 Ltd, TV 4 AB v Föreningen Svenska Tonsättares Internationella Musikbyrå (STIM)* ECLI:EU:C:2008:703, CJEU, 11 December 2008 par. 10, 28–40; Rosén, Copyright Contracts, 2011, 174.

1398 Art. 51(1) DCA; Art. 26(4) FCA; Art. 37(1) NCA; Art. 42a (4) SCA. See also Art. 13 CMO Directive.

have the same right to remuneration as members[1399] and the CMOs that administer ECLs are considered to have a duty to actively search for those who have a right to remuneration under an ECL agreement.[1400] This obligation to search for rightholders is now stipulated in the CMO Directive.[1401]

335. Remuneration received for use of works under ECLs is, however, not always distributed in the form of direct individual remuneration but by ways of collective benefits such as pensions or grants. This practice is now indirectly accepted in the CMO Directive[1402] and has also been approved by the CJEU. In the Amazon.com case the Court concluded, with regard to Art. 5(2)(b) InfoSoc Directive, that "indirect payment to those entitled, through the intermediary of social and cultural establishments set up for their benefit" can constitute fair compensation for private copying.[1403]

336. How remuneration is to be distributed can be stipulated in the ECL agreement, or if not determined there, decided by the relevant CMO.[1404]

> In Sweden, for example, the umbrella CMO, Bonus Presskopia, negotiates and administers ECL agreements for reproduction in institutions. The remuneration is then distributed to its member associations which all have different methods of distributing to their members. Thus the association of educational publishers base their distribution on overall salesfigures in the field whereas the association of authors of educational works distribute the remuneration in the form of grants to members and non-members alike. The Swedish union of photographers uses the remuneration to finance legal counseling for its members as well as non-members whereas the newspaper publishers use the remuneration for educational purposes open to members and non-members.[1405]

337. It is usually up to the CMOs in question whether the distribution is individual or collective[1406] but in Norway the presumption of the legislator is that the distribution of remuneration for ECL licences is collective.[1407] The

1399 Art. 51(2) DCA; Art. 26 (4) FCA; Art. 26.b(1) ICA; Art. 37(1) NCA; Art. 42a(2) SCA.

1400 Schønning, Ophavsretsloven, 5th ed., 2011, 473.

1401 Art. 13(3) CMO Directive. Although this is not one of the provisions referred to in Art. 7 of the Directive regarding the rights of outsiders, it seems obvious that it should apply to outsiders bound by an ECL agreement.

1402 Art. 12(4) CMO Directive.

1403 *Amazon.com International Sales Inc. and Others v Austro-Mechana Gesellschaft zur Wahrnehmung mechanisch-musikalischer Urheberrechte Gesellschaft mbH* ECLI:EU:C:2013:515, CJEU, 11 July 2013 par. 46–55.

1404 See e.g. Art. 37(1) NCA.

1405 SOU 2010:24, Avtalad upphovsrätt, 2010, 214.

1406 Rydning, Extended, 2010, 77.

1407 Ot. prp. nr. 46, Endringer, 2005, 50. The Norwegian ECL provision for the broadcast of works is an exception as it requires individual remuneration, cf. Art. 30(1) NCA which has the phrase "on payment of remuneration" in it, cf. Rognstad, Avtalelisenser, 2004, 152; Rydning, Extended, 2010, 18.

main reason for collective distribution of remuneration is that in some cases it is virtually impossible to identify actual use of individual works in a cost-effective way.[1408] Hence, collective distribution of remuneration for ECLs is more efficient, both for users, who will not have to register and monitor the use of works under the licence, except occasionally for statistical purposes, and for the CMO, which will save on administration costs.[1409] In Norway it was discussed in connection with the implementation of the Infosoc Directive in 2005 whether the assumptions of collective distribution in connection with ECL licences should be reassessed in the light of wider ECL provisions and the three-step test. The conclusion was, however, that despite technological developments there was still a long way to go before technology could guarantee an easy and cost-effective method for securing individual remuneration in the area of ECL licences.[1410]

338. Collective distribution of remuneration is not always in the interest of outsiders, despite general guidelines that non-discrimination and common interest should guide collective contributions[1411], and sometimes it is difficult or even impossible for outsiders to receive remuneration under collective schemes.[1412] Hence, outside rightholders are entitled in these situations to claim individual remuneration, regardless of whether such a right is stipulated in the ECL agreement or in the CMO's rules of distribution. Claims for individual remuneration by outside rightholders can only be directed towards the CMO that negotiated the ECL agreement.[1413] However, this only applies to outsiders in the case where there is collective remuneration, not if there is individual remuneration.[1414] In case of individual remuneration all rightholders, members and outsiders alike, are individually remunerated by the CMO. Furthermore, the CMOs are not obliged to offer individual remuneration on their own initiative to outsiders in case of collective numeration but need to respond if a claim for such individual remuneration is made.[1415] The fact that CMOs take the responsibility for dealing with remuneration to outsiders is one of the main benefits of ECLs for users.[1416]

1408 SOU 2010:24, Avtalad upphovsrätt, 2010, 227–228.

1409 Rydning, Extended, 2010, 80.

1410 Ot. prp. nr. 46, Endringer, 2005, 50.

1411 In the Norwegian preparatory documents it is stated that when the remuneration is distributed collectively the purpose of it has to be of common interest to all rightholders and if the remuneration is in the form of individual grants the application criterion for such has to be non-discriminatory with regard to non-members, cf. Ot. prp. nr. 15, Om lov, 1994, 148 and Rydning, Extended, 2010, 77. See also Art. 12.(4) CMO Directive.

1412 Rydning, Extended, 2010, 78–80; Bet. 1981/912, Licenskonstruktioner, 1981, 44–49.

1413 Art. 51(2) DCA; Art. 26 (5) FCA; Art. 26.b(2) ICA; Art. 37(2) NCA; Art. 42a(2) SCA. See e.g. RP 181/2014 rd, Regeringens proposition, 2014, 11; Riis and Schovsbo, ECLs, 2010, 492.

1414 RP 181/2014 rd, Regeringens proposition, 2014, 39.

1415 Schønning, Ophavsretsloven, 5th ed., 2011, 473.

1416 Tryggvadóttir, Digital libraries, 2014, 320.

339. Outsiders must substantiate their claim for individual remuneration as is expressly stated in the Norwegian provision.[1417] This is not expressly specified in the other Nordic countries but is the underlying premise.[1418] It can be difficult for outsiders to prove the use of their work as ECLs are often in areas where it is difficult to determine the extent of use of individual works[1419], as is the case in photocopying in educational or other institutions. Thus it was claimed in a Norwegian government document, where ECL for photocopying was discussed, that the right of outsiders to claim individual remuneration had no practical importance and thus it was recommended not to implement such a provision.[1420] However, on occasion exact information is available such as when music is used in radio or TV broadcasts which then can be used to prove the use.[1421] In other instances the proof can be based on statistical samples that the CMOs carry out in order to determine how to distribute remuneration.[1422] The fact that there are no guidelines on how to compute individual remuneration for outsiders can result in under-compensation.[1423] Thus it has been suggested that collective remuneration should not be used except for non-commercial uses under ECLs.[1424]

340. Claims for individual remuneration usually have a short term of limitation[1425] with the reasoning that a longer period could create administrative burdens for the CMOs.[1426] However, some Swedish CMOs apply longer limitation periods, or even none at all, for individual remuneration for foreign rightholders; non-payment of remuneration due to expired limitation periods is an exception. Furthermore, Swedish CMOs actively seek out foreign rightholders and other outside rightholders to pay them their share of remuneration.[1427] In Finland it has also been established that the CMOs are diligent in identifying and locating non-represented rightholders.[1428] In light of the similarities of the

---

1417 Art. 37(2) NCA.

1418 Schønning, Ophavsretsloven, 5th ed., 2011, 473; Bet. 1981/912, Licenskonstruktioner, 1981, 49.

1419 Axhamn and Guibault, Cross-border ECL, 2011, 36.

1420 NOU 1988:22, *Endringer i åndverksloven m.v.*, 23–24.

1421 SOU 2010:24, Avtalad upphovsrätt, 2010, 210.

1422 Axhamn and Guibault, Cross-border ECL, 2011, 36; Ot. prp. nr. 15, Om lov, 1994, 148; Rydning, Extended, 2010, 79.

1423 Riis and Schovsbo, ECLs, 2010, 492.

1424 Rognstad, Avtalelisenser, 2004, 158.

1425 The term of limitation is three years, cf. Art. 49 DCA, cf. Schønning, Ophavsretsloven, 6th ed., 2016, 487; Art. 26(5) FCA; Art. 37(2) NCA and Art. 42a(2) SCA, except in Iceland where it is four years, cf. Art. 26.b(5) ICA.

1426 Peter Schønning, *Ophavsretsloven med kommentarer* (3rd edn, Forlaget Thomson, 2003), 437. The term of limitation used to be shorter than for other claims under civil law, cf. Karnell, Outsiders, 1991, 433; however, at least in Denmark the term is now in line with general statutes of limitation since 2007, cf. Schønning, Ophavsretsloven, 5th ed., 2011, 454.

1427 SOU 2010:24, Avtalad upphovsrätt, 2010, 217, 229; Axhamn and Guibault, Cross-border ECL, 2011, 35; Rosén, Copyright Contracts, 2011, 175.

1428 Liedes, Memorandum, 2010, 14; Vuopala, Extended, 2013, 34.

ECL systems and the infrastructure for collective management in the Nordic countries, the likelihood is that the same applies to the practice of other Nordic CMOs with regard to remuneration.

341. In Denmark and Norway there are procedures for resolving disputes around claims for individual remuneration by outsiders[1429] while in the other Nordic countries the outside rightholders must refer disputes to the general courts. Given the difficulty of proving which works have in fact been used[1430] and the financial cost of court proceedings the latter would in most cases not be an attractive option. Not surprisingly, claims for individual remuneration by outside rightholders are rare.[1431] This may also indicate that outside rightholders are either not sufficiently aware of the use of their work under ECL agreements or are not aware of the possibility of individual remuneration.[1432] In either case, such a situation calls for increased transparency of ECL agreements.[1433]

5.4.3. THE OPT-OUT

342. The "opt-out" possibility in ECLs, sometimes called "veto right"[1434], gives a rightholder who is not a member of the CMO the possibility to ban the use of his or her work under an ECL licence.[1435] The first ECL provisions for broadcasting contained an opt-out possibility in all the Nordic countries, as they still do.[1436] These were limited to published works and the ECL system was based on the presumption that as the author had thus released the work for distribution, he or she would not oppose its use if agreed to by a representative CMO. This presumption could then be overturned, either if it could be assumed that the author would be against the use (the broadcasting) of his work or if the outside author explicitly opposed (opted-out) the use.[1437]

343. Today there are several ECL provisions in each of the Nordic countries, but not all provide for a mandatory opt-out possibility.[1438] Denmark has

1429 In Denmark the issue can be referred to the Copyright License Tribunal, cf. Art. 51(2), and in Norway the dispute can be referred by either party to a committee according to the rules in Arts. 4(1)-(4) in Regulation 2001-12-21 nr 1563: Forskrift til åndsværksloven, cf. Art. 37(2) NCA.

1430 NOU 1988:22, Endringer i åndverksloven m.v., 1988, 39–40; Rydning, Extended, 2010, 79.

1431 SOU 2010:24, Avtalad upphovsrätt, 2010, 213, 217, 220 and 229; IPO, Government, 2014, 37.

1432 Riis and Schovsbo, ECLs, 2010, 492.

1433 Tryggvadóttir, Digital libraries, 2014, 320.

1434 Koskinen-Olsson, Collective Management, 2010, 291; Trumpke, The Extended, 2012, 278–281.

1435 Koskinen-Olsson, Collective Management, 2010, 292.

1436 Art. 30(2) DCA; Art. 25(1) FCA; Art. 23(1) ICA; Art. 30(3) NCA and Art. 42e (2) SCA.

1437 Bergström, Program för upphovsrätten, (1960) 2011, 156–158.

1438 Riis and Schovsbo, ECLs, 2010, 276; Trumpke, The Extended, 2012, 279–280; Koskinen-Olsson, Collective Management, 2010, 294.

nine ECL provisions[1439] but only four of them require provision for an opt-out[1440]; Finland, which has ten ECL provisions, requires an opt-out possibility in seven of them[1441]; Iceland has eight ECL provisions and requires opt-out in five of them[1442]; Norway has eight ECL provisions[1443] in the Norwegian Copyright Act but opt-out is only explicitly provided for in three of them[1444]; Sweden, which has seven ECL provisions[1445], has a mandatory opt-out possibility in all of them except for cable retransmission of broadcast works.[1446]

344. There are thus considerable differences between the Nordic countries in this matter, in particular between Sweden and Norway. In Sweden the opt-out possibility has been considered an important feature of the legality of the system[1447] whereas in Norway the main principle has been that outsiders do not have a right to opt-out.[1448] Thus Norwegian preparatory documents have on several occasions asserted that having an opt-out right would be impractical and difficult to enforce.[1449] The reason for not having an opt-out provision is mainly for the benefit of users of the ECL system to ensure legal certainty. Opting out diminishes legal certainty. Another reason for not allowing opt-outs is that they can reduce efficiency. In Norway concerns were expressed that "free-riders" might misuse the opt-out right to seek unwarranted better economic benefits and thus diminish the efficiency of the system.[1450] Furthermore, there were fears, at least in the beginning, that authors could deny access to works of central cultural importance.[1451]

1439 See Art. 50(1)-(2) DCA; Schønning, Ophavsretsloven, 6th ed., 2016, 494.

1440 Cf. Art. 24a (reproduction of art works), Art. 30 (primary broadcasting), Art. 30a (use of television programs stored in archives of broadcasting stations), Art. 50(2) (the general ECL provision) DCA.

1441 Cf. Arts. 13 (for photocopying, no opt-out), 13a, 14, 16d, 25a, 25f(1) and 25f(3) (for making a copy for internal use by broadcasting stations, no opt-out), 25g, 25h (retransmission, no opt-out) and 25l FCA.

1442 Art. 12.b (library ECL, no opt-out), 14(3), 18(1), 19(4) (for use by handicapped persons, no opt-out), 23(1), 23.a (retransmission, no opt-out), 23.b and 26.a(2) ICA.

1443 See Art. 36 NCA.

1444 Cf. Art. 30 (primary broadcasting), cf. Art.32 (use of television programs stored in archives of broadcasting stations), Art. 36(2) (the general ECL provision) NCA.

1445 Cf. Art. 42a SCA.

1446 Art. 42f SCA.

1447 Prop. 2010/2011:33, *Återanvändning av upphovsrättsligt skyddat material i radio och tv*, (4 November 2010) 29–30.

1448 Kulturdepartementet, Høringsnotat, 2014, 15.

1449 NOU 1988:22, Endringer i åndverksloven m.v., 1988, 40; Ot. prp. nr. 46, Endringer, 2005, 51; Rydning, Extended, 2010, 86.

1450 Rydning, Extended, 2010, 86–87; NOU 1988:22, Endringer i åndverksloven m.v., 1988, 40; Ot. prp. nr. 46, Endringer, 2005, 51. This concern was also raised in Danish government documents, cf. Bet. 1981/912, Licenskonstruktioner, 1981, 41.

1451 Rydning, Extended, 2010, 86, fn. 207.

345. It is worth noting that an ECL agreement can contain an opt-out possibility even when it is not mandatory in the ECL provision.[1452] Such an opt-out provision in the actual ECL agreement can be applicable to all authors or rightholders, both members of the CMO and outsiders.[1453] This is the case in the ECL agreement for the Norwegian Bokhylla project[1454], despite the fact that the ECL provision for libraries in the Norwegian Copyright Act does not require an opt-out.[1455] Furthermore, it is stated in the preparatory documents for the general ECL provision in Denmark that members of a CMO which was negotiating an ECL could choose to remain outside an ECL licence under the general provision and would, therefore, also have this opt-out possibility to prevent their works from being be used under the extension effect.[1456]

5.4.3.1. Entitlement and process

346. The Nordic legislation contains no specific rules on the procedure for opting-out. An opt-out possibility clearly exists only for outsiders[1457], unless otherwise specified in the ECL agreement, as members of the negotiating CMO are bound by an agreement if it falls under the mandate given by them to the CMO. But whether the right to opt out for outsiders only applies for the original author or also for other subsequent rightholders is not specified in any of the ECL provisions.

347. The opt-out possibility in the ECL provision on primary broadcasting[1458] in Norway used to apply only for the original author and not for successors of the rights of the work in question.[1459] This was changed in 1995 as it was deemed to be incompatible with Art. 3(2) of the Satellite and Cable Directive.[1460] There were similar issues with regard to the Danish ECL provision on primary broadcasting[1461] as, in the preparatory documents for the 1995 Danish Copyright Act, it was stated that for the opt-out clause to be effective and binding, the application for opt-out had to be made directly by the author or those clearly authorised to opt-out on his or her behalf.[1462] However, it was declared in the

1452 Ot. prp. nr. 15, Om lov, 1994, 29, Tillæg A Folketingstidende 1984–1985, Bind II, Lovforslag nr. L 113, 1994; Prop. 69 L, Proposisjon, 2015, 23.
1453 Schønning, Ophavsretsloven, 5th ed., 2011, 468; Trumpke, 2015, p. 264–265, 306.
1454 Discussed in Ch. 5.3.1.4.
1455 Art. 16a NCA.
1456 2007/2 LSF 58, Forslag, 2008, 3.3.1.
1457 Schønning, Ophavsretsloven, 5th ed., 2011, 379.
1458 Art. 30 NCA.
1459 Rognstad, Opphavsrett, 2009, 280.
1460 Ot. prp. nr. 15, Om lov, 1994, 74; Ot. prp. nr. 46, Endringer, 2005, 107. See also discussion on the issue in relation to the adoption of the general ECL provision in Norway, where it was stated in the preparatory documents that the term "author" could apply to subsequent rightholders, cf. Prop. 69 L, Proposisjon, 2015, 23.
1461 Art. 30 DCA.
1462 Lovforslag nr. L 119, 1364.

preparatory documents that this opt-out clause was considered to be in conformity with Art. 3(2) of the Satellite and Cable Directive. In the light of this declaration, the opt-out possibility in Denmark must be interpreted to apply to all rightholders that have rights to the work, either by assignment or by inheritance. In Sweden the prevailing view seems to be that all rightholders that are not members of the negotiating CMO may opt out. This can be deduced by the fact that literature on the subject uses the term author and rightholder interchangeably without specifying that different rules apply to the author vis-à-vis other rightholders.[1463]

348. In general there are no formal requirements that need to be fulfilled by outsiders wishing to opt out.

In Denmark a printed statement in published works or a general announcement on use of all of author's work sufficed as an opt-out.[1464] This practice has, however, changed and now the outsider must explicitly opt out, either with regard to a specific work or to all his or her works.[1465] Some Danish ECL provisions indicate that outsiders may direct the communication on the opt-out to any of the negotiating parties, i.e. either the CMO or the user[1466], whereas in others the opt-out must be communicated to the individual user.[1467] The former situation entitles the rightholder to lay down a general ban against the use of his or her works with the relevant CMO, whereas in the latter the rightholder can only ban each individual user from using his or her works. In case of a general opt-out the relevant CMO is obliged to inform the users of the opt-out.[1468] A general opt-out can be *a priori* although this is not expressly provided.[1469]

In the preparatory works for the Norwegian general ECL provision it is explained that an opt-out may be exercised either towards the user or the CMO; that the opt-out must be as clear as possible; and that it must indicate whether it is a general ban for all uses or just some.[1470]

In Swedish preparatory documents there was a discussion on whether there should be a requirement that an opt-out should be based on factual and objective reasons. This was rejected with the argument that the opt-out possibility was an important element for the legality of the ECL system, which had so far worked well, and hence it should not be limited by obliging the outside rightholder to justify the opt-out.[1471]

1463 Olsson, Upphovsrättslagstiftningen, 2006, 321; Prop. 2010/2011:33, Återanvändning av upphovsrättsligt skyddat material i radio och tv, 2010, 30.

1464 Tillæg A, Forslag til Lov om ophavsretten til litterære og kunstneriske værker, 1960, 2723.

1465 Lovforslag nr. L 119, 1365; Schønning, Ophavsretsloven, 5th ed., 2011, 356, 380.

1466 E.g. Art. 24a and 50(2) DCA.

1467 E.g. Art. 30(2) DCA.

1468 Schønning, Ophavsretsloven, 5th ed., 2011, 356, 379–380, 466.

1469 Prop. 2012/13:141, Regeringens proposition, 2013, 58. See a different understanding in Bulayenko, Permissibility, 2016, 65.

1470 Prop. 69 L, Proposisjon, 2015, 61.

1471 Prop. 2010/2011:33, Återanvändning av upphovsrättsligt skyddat material i radio och tv, 2010, 29–30, Trumpke, 2015, 307.

349. None of the ECL opt-out provisions state explicitly how information about an opt-out should be communicated or recorded.[1472] This may be because opt-outs were relatively seldom used in the past.[1473]

5.1.3.2. The effect of opt-out

350. The main effect of the opt-out is that, once an outsider has initiated it, the user cannot legally make use of the works in question.[1474] One of the criticisms of the opt-out is that practically speaking it does not stop the use of individual works used under an ECL agreement. However, in response to this criticism it has been observed that once a ban has been issued and communicated to the relevant party, the rightholder is then in the same position as other rightholders with regard to unauthorised use of his or her works.[1475]

351. There is also the question of the effect of the opt-out on the position of the outsider once he or she has opted out. It is clear that the user cannot thereafter use the work legally.[1476] However, not everybody agrees how or whether the outsider is entitled to make use of the work following an opt-out. It has been maintained that if an outsider opts out of an ECL, it has the effect that neither the user, i.e. the ECL agreement licensee, nor the outsider, can use the work in question, i.e. the outside rightholder of the opted-out work could not thereafter make individual agreements regarding the use of the work, at least not with the user that has concluded the ECL agreement in question.[1477] It is important here to distinguish between outsiders and rightholders that are members of the relevant CMO. Some ECL agreements allow members of the CMO also to opt-out.[1478] Nevertheless, if members have given the CMO their mandate to exclusively licence the use that falls under the ECL agreement they cannot, on their own account license such use after an opt-out, at least not without withdrawing the mandate to the CMO. Advocates of the view that outsider cannot individually licence the use of works that have been subject to their opt-out under an ECL agreement, argue that otherwise the system of ECLs would not serve its purpose, as rightholders with more bargaining power would withdraw from the relevant

[1472] Some comments on the Norwegian proposal for a general ECL provision suggested that an information obligation between the stakeholders should be introduced, cf. Prop. 69 L, Proposisjon, 2015, 23.

[1473] Schønning, Ophavsretsloven, 5th ed., 2011, 380; Olsson, Upphovsrättslagstiftningen, 2006, 316; Rydning, Extended, 2010, 86; Trumpke, The Extended, 2012, 280.

[1474] Schønning, Ophavsretsloven, 5th ed., 2011, 380.

[1475] Prop. 2012/13:141, Regeringens proposition, 2013, 28.

[1476] Schønning, Ophavsretsloven, 5th ed., 2011, 380; Prop. 2012/13:141, Regeringens proposition, 2013, 28.

[1477] This has e.g. been the opinion of some Icelandic CMOs.

[1478] E.g. the Bokhylla agreement, cf. Ch. 5.3.1.4.

CMO, or withdraw those particular rights[1479], and make individual agreements with users.

352. Little has been written about this precise point in Nordic literature, either because so far the opt-out possibility has not been used very frequently or because those who wrote about ECLs believed the effect was obvious, either way. Thus the Swedish scholar Bergström, commonly deemed to be the inventor of the Nordic ECL system, does not mention this at all in his article on ECLs.[1480] With the elevated interest in the ECL system from outside the Nordic countries an increasing amount has been written about the structure and rationale of the system. However, this rarely includes elaboration on this point. Those who mention it, directly or indirectly, are all of the opinion that the opt-out effect is that the rightholder then can manage his or her right individually.[1481] That view is also reflected in the Satellite and Cable Directive which allows for ECLs for the broadcasting of programmes by satellite, provided that "the unrepresented rightholder shall, at any time, have the possibility of excluding the extension of the collective agreement to his works and of exercising his rights either individually or collectively."[1482]

353. The conclusion must be that the accepted view of the effects of opt-out is that the rightholder will regain his or her exclusive right. The question, however, still remains whether the exclusive right can then be conditioned as to preventing individual agreements between a user (the licensee) of an ECL agreement and an opting-out rightholder. Although it seems unlikely that a user that already has an ECL agreement for a blanket use of works would be willing to enter into individual agreements with a rightholder that has opted out[1483], it is possible to envisage that a well-known author might have the required bargaining power to convince a user, for example a broadcasting station, to enter into individual agreements in addition to an ECL agreement. Such an eventuality could potentially weaken the bargaining power of the CMO negotiating an ECL and thus undermine the position of other rightholders. Nevertheless, in my view it would be necessary to explicitly stipulate in legislation that the opt-out was to

1479 Cf. Art. 5(4) CMO Directive.

1480 Bergström, Program för upphovsrätten, (1960) 2011, 158–160.

1481 Ficsor, Collective Management, 2010, 62; Gervais, Collective Mangement, 2010, 26–27; Olsson, Upphovsrättslagstiftningen, 2006, 316; Riis and Schovsbo, ECLs, 2010, 476; Schønning, Ophavsretsloven, 5th ed., 2011, 356, 380; Schønning, Ophavsretsloven, 6th ed., 2016, 406; Axhamn and Guibault, Cross-border ECL, 2011, 37, 43; Trumpke, The Extended, 2012, 278; Trumpke, Exklusivität, 2015, 1847; NOU 1988:22, Endringer i åndverksloven m.v., 1988, 40; Ot. prp. nr. 46, Endringer, 2005, 51; Rydning, Extended, 2010, 84–85; RP 181/2014 rd, Regeringens proposition, 2014, 64–65.

1482 Art. 3(2). See also discussion where the same is assumed in SWD(2012) 204 final, Impact Assessment, 2012, 46.

1483 Rydning, Extended, 2010, 84–85.

be accompanied by the constraint that the outsider could not after opting-out enter into individual agreements with the user of the ECL agreement. Such arrangement is more akin to mandatory collective management.[1484]

Furthermore, if individual agreements are in fact possible to the extent that rightholders would choose to be outside a collective management organisation in order to be able to opt-out of an ECL agreement with a particular user and then would negotiate an individual agreement with the same user, then it could be argued that perhaps one of the fundamental criteria for establishing an ECL is missing, i.e. that individual licensing should not be practically feasible. In my view it is clear that, if there is an opt-out right stipulated in an ECL provision or ECL agreement, then outsiders who opt out will regain their full exclusive rights, including the (theoretical) possibility to individually licence the use of their work to a user, even if that user already has an ECL agreement with the CMO. However, as discussed below, the opt-out right is not, on its own, an essential requirement for the compatibility of ECLs with international norms.[1485] Hence there can be situations where it is inadvisable to provide for opt-out as this would diminish the effectiveness of an ECL agreement but where the system of ECLs is still preferable to compulsory remunerated exceptions or mandatory collective licensing.

354. The question regarding the point of time at which an opt-out takes effect was discussed in Denmark in the nineties when a grace period of six months was proposed.[1486] That proposal was rejected and thus in Denmark the opt-out has immediate effect from the time when the user has knowledge of it.[1487] I have not found any reference to this issue with regard to the other Nordic countries. In the absence of an express stipulation to the contrary it is to be assumed that the opt-out also has immediate effect there.

5.4.3.3. Opt-out and moral right

355. The ECL system does not affect the general moral right granted to authors and thus the moral right in all works used under an ECL agreement must be respected.[1488] Furthermore, the opt-out possibility under the ECL system gives the author the possibility, not available in legal or compulsory licences, to exercise up to a point the non-economic right of deciding how or whether his or her work is used. This possibility does not alter the fact that, initially, the use of the works of outsiders under an ECL agreement is

[1484] See Ch. 9.3.
[1485] See Ch. 6.2.3.3.
[1486] Bet. nr. 1197/1990, Revision, 1990, 194 f.
[1487] Schønning, Ophavsretsloven, 5th ed., 2011, 380.
[1488] Ot. prp. nr. 46, Endringer, 2005, 51; Karnell, Outsiders, 1991, 433; Trumpke, Exklusivität, 2015, 484. This obligation is expressly set out in e.g. Art. 11 DCA and Art. 26 ICA.

allowed without the consent of the author.[1489] The first ECL provisions only concerned works that had already been published, disseminated or broadcast. This ensured that ECLs would not impinge on the author's right to first make his work public, which is guaranteed in some legislation.[1490] However, this is changing with newer ECL provisions, such as the general ECL provisions, which do not limit the use of the ECL effect to works that have been published.[1491]

356. The relevance of the opt-out possibility to the moral right of the author to be able to oppose changes in his or her work has been considered one of the main justifications for opt-out clauses.[1492] Thus in Norway when revising the ECL provision for photocopying in 1988 it was stated that the danger of inappropriate changes to works was limited in the area of photocopying and hence not necessary to provide for an opt-out possibility.[1493] Another instance of moral right could arise where the author would object to the re-use or rebroadcasting of his or her work for some reason, e.g. political or aesthetic.[1494] This moral right aspect is reflected in some ECL provisions. In the Swedish and Norwegian ECL provisions for primary broadcasting as well as in the ECL provision on the reuse of works in broadcasters' archives there is, in addition to an opt-out clause for authors, a restriction against allowing a licence agreement to apply to authors who could be assumed to be against the broadcasting of the work.[1495] Furthermore the same limitation exists in the ECL provision for libraries and archives in Sweden.[1496] Finally, the same reservation is taken up in the Swedish and Norwegian general ECL provisions.[1497] This moral right aspect is also to be found in the Orphan Works Directive.[1498]

357. The justification for including this reservation in the Norwegian general ECL provision rested mainly on the fact that such a reservation already existed in other Norwegian ECL provisions giving outsiders an opt-out right. It was, however, also submitted that the requirement was vague and could lead to uncertainty about the permitted use under an ECL agreement.[1499]

1489 Trumpke, The Extended, 2012, 280.
1490 The right to decide when, where and in what form the work will be divulged, cf. Sterling, World Copyright Law, 2003, 340–341.
1491 See discussion in Ch. 5.3.2.1, 5.3.2.2, 5.3.2.3 and 5.3.3.
1492 Prop. 2010/11:33, *Återanvänding av upphovsrättsligt skyddat material i radio og tv*, 30; Trumpke, The Extended, 2012, 281–282.
1493 NOU 1988:22, Endringer i åndverksloven m.v., 1988, 40; Ot. prp. nr. 46, Endringer, 2005, 51.
1494 Prop. 2010/11:33, Återanvänding, 30; Trumpke, The Extended, 2012, 281–282.
1495 Art. 30 and 32 NCA and Art. 42e and 42g SCA.
1496 Art. 42d SCA.
1497 Art. 36(2) i.f. NCA; Art. 42h SCA.
1498 See discussion and references in Ch. 4.2.3.3.
1499 Prop. 69 L, Proposisjon, 2015, 24.

358. There is limited literature about this requirement, which seems to indicate that it is not often used. It would be most likely to be used in situations where authors had radically changed their views with regard to art, politics or religion and might not want publicity for earlier works reflecting their previous views. Another instance might concern a work that had caused an author negative attention in the past and which he or she might not want to re-experience.[1500] These moral considerations would seem to be applicable to all authors, not just the outsiders. However, it is not clear from the literature whether the restriction only applies to works of outsiders or also members of the CMO, although the provision in the Norwegian general ECL provision seems to be aimed at outsiders only. The situation of insiders may depend on whether they have the opportunity to exempt some of their works from the mandate they give the CMO, as is now required as a right of rightholders under the CMO Directive.[1501]

5.4.4. TRANSPARENCY

359. No explicit provision were to be found in the Nordic countries, until a recent provision adopted in Iceland, regarding transparency of ECL agreements in the sense of requiring that they be publicly advertised or communicated in some other way to outsiders or others. However, some CMO are beginning to publish their ECL agreements online.[1502] Thus the Norwegian Bokhylla agreement is published online, both on the website of Kopinor, the relevant CMO, and the National Library.[1503]

360. During a review of ECL provisions in Sweden in 2010 it was proposed that a clause on transparency be included in the provision on the general requirements for ECL agreements have to fulfil. According to the proposal the relevant CMO should in an appropriate manner publicise that an ECL agreement on a certain use had been concluded and provide information about the agreement to enable outsiders to claim compensation.[1504] However, such a provision was not maintained in the final version as it was considered unnecessary, given that CMOs already actively searched out outsiders in order to compensate them. This consideration may have been influenced by the fact that in the meantime the proposal for the CMO Directive had been tabled and the government foresaw that changes might be needed to rules regarding the governance and transparency of CMOs once the Directive was adopted.[1505]

1500 Olsson, Upphovsrättslagstiftningen, 2006, 321–322.
1501 Art. 5(2) and Recital (19) CMO Directive.
1502 Trumpke, The Extended, 2012, 279.
1503 See discussion on the Bokhylla agreement in Ch. 5.3.1.4.
1504 SOU 2010:24, Avtalad upphovsrätt, 2010, 47 and 206.
1505 Prop. 2012/13:141, Regeringens proposition, 2013, 28.

361. Such a transparency provision was adopted in Iceland in 2016 when a general ECL provision was implemented in the Copyright Act. Accordingly CMOs that negotiate ECL agreements under the general ECL provision must publish information about the agreement in an "appropriate" manner so that outsiders can claim remuneration.[1506] In the comments with the proposal it is suggested that "appropriate" manner could consist of making such information available on the CMO's website.[1507]

362. Another requirement, proposed but not adopted, in the Swedish proposal of 2010 for the general ECL provision was that such ECL agreements should be in written form and include a statement that it was intended to have an ECL effect.[1508] The argument for not including such a requirement was that the general ECL provision was in reality not so different from the specific ECL provision, where there is no such requirement. It was, however, stated that in reality most ECL agreements were in written form and clear from the agreements that they were supposed to have ECL effect.[1509] This requirement was explicitly incorporated in the Icelandic Copyright Act when general ECLs were adopted in 2016.[1510] In Denmark it is understood that it must be clear from an ECL agreement that it is intended to have ECL effect, although it is not spelled out in any of the provisions.[1511]

5.4.5. EVALUATION

363. Different groups of outsiders can have diverse interests. Most of them, it can be presumed, are interested in having their works used and in receiving remuneration for the use.[1512] In general it is thought that, as collective management gives increased negotiating power to rightholders[1513], which also benefits outsiders under the ECL system, the extension is also in the outsiders' interest.[1514]

364. Even so, approaches to safeguarding the interest of outsiders can vary depending on which subgroup they belong to. Thus the most challenging group

1506 Art. 26.b(3) ICA, cf. Art. 14.b. of Act. 9/2016.

1507 Cf. Parliamentary document 400, docket 333, 145th session of Althingi, 2015–2016, p. 28.

1508 SOU 2010:24, Avtalad upphovsrätt, 2010, 47.

1509 Prop. 2012/13:141, Regeringens proposition, 2013, 56–57.

1510 Art. 26.b.(3) ICA, cf. Art. 14.b Act No. 9/2016.

1511 2007/2 LSF 58, Forslag, 2008, 74; Schønning, Ophavsretsloven, 5th ed., 2011, 467; Kyst, Aftalelicens, 2009, 48.

1512 Bergström, Program för upphovsrätten, (1960) 2011, 158 to 159. This research focuses on outsiders other than those who object to the exclusive right system under copyright or who prefer to license their work e.g. under the Creative Commons licences.

1513 See Ch. 5.1.1.

1514 See Ch. 5.1.2.

to safeguard are the "double" outsiders', i.e. those who are neither members of a national CMO, nor residents of the country where the national ECL agreement is negotiated, nor members of a foreign CMO with a reciprocity agreement, making it logistically difficult to reach those to inform them of an ECL agreement. This is true in general for outsiders residing abroad, even when they are members of CMOs that have a reciprocity agreement with the CMO that negotiates a national ECL agreement.[1515]

365. The fact that outsiders are guaranteed the same remuneration as members under an ECL agreement is of pivotal importance. However, it can be complicated for outsiders, especially those residing abroad, to receive the negotiated remuneration. There are several ways outsiders, who reside abroad, can be disadvantaged in this regard compared to outsiders resident in the country of origin of the ECL agreement. The former are less likely to know about the use of their work under ECL schemes abroad and hence are not able to claim their remuneration. Unclaimed remuneration is used for the benefit of members of the CMO and does not benefit foreign rightholders.[1516] Furthermore, some reciprocal agreements between CMOs prescribe that collected remuneration be kept in the country of collection and is then generally used for the benefit of national rightholders.[1517] Moreover, remuneration below a specified minimum amount is often not distributed among rightholders but used instead for collective purposes for members of the CMO. Finally, there is the generally accepted practice in collective management of deducting a certain percentage of collected remuneration for collective purposes[1518], which again is unlikely to benefit foreign outsides. Even so, it should not be forgotten that CMOs actually do their best to track down outsiders in order to pay them, whether national or foreign, as discussed above.[1519] Nevertheless, the difficulty for outsiders residing abroad of receiving remuneration is a consideration that needs to be taken into account when extending applicable fields for ECLs, especially for cross-border uses.[1520]

366. Another issue for outsiders with regard to remuneration is the fact that compensation for use under ECLs is often distributed collectively. In such instances outsiders have the right to individual remuneration. This is important as rules regarding distribution of remuneration cannot be influenced by

---

1515 Riis and Schovsbo, ECLs, 2010, 491; Trumpke, Exklusivität, 2015, 340–341.

1516 Riis and Schovsbo, ECLs, 2010, 491–492; Axhamn and Guibault, Cross-border ECL, 2011, 44–46.

1517 Under B-type of reciprocal agreements, see Ch. 5.1.1.

1518 Riis and Schovsbo, ECLs, 2010, 491–492; Axhamn and Guibault, Cross-border ECL, 2011, 44–46; Rita Matulionyte, 'Cross-Border Collective Management and Principle of Territoriality: Problems and Possible Solutions in the EU ', 2009, (5–6), The Journal of World Intellectual Property, 467–497, 481; IPO, Government, 36; Art. 12(4) CMO Directive.

1519 Ch. 5.4.2.

1520 Tryggvadóttir, Digital libraries, 2014, 322.

outsiders[1521] and are hence not always in their best interest.[1522] However, there are no guidelines as to how such individual payments should be calculated and the onus is on the outsider to prove the actual use. If users do not provide statistics for the works used it can indeed be very difficult to demonstrate the use of individual works.[1523] Hence the right to individual remuneration may be more theoretical than real, especially for foreign outsiders residing abroad. This being said, there is an increasing number of technical solutions available to solve the issue of identifying and registering online uses of works used under an ECL agreement.[1524] Such solutions will make the administration of individual remuneration practically feasible. This is especially true in the world of libraries, which have always been based on the cataloguing of their collections.[1525]

367. The opt-out is an important safety valve for outsiders, both for moral and economic reasons, allowing them to reclaim their exclusive right, as well as imposing discipline on CMOs. ECLs are used in situations where individual licensing is difficult or not practically possible. There can be a fine line between cases where it is almost impossible to reach individual agreements and cases where it is possible, albeit difficult. If that line is judged wrongly the rate of opt-out will probably rise to an unacceptable level, indicating that individual licensing is in fact viable.[1526] Too many opt-out clauses can diminish the practical benefits of ECLs both with regard to efficiency and legal certainty.[1527] Thus there can be justifiable reasons for not providing for an opt-out in some ECL agreements and this can be achieved without the agreement automatically becoming unreasonable for outsiders. Opt-outs should be a practical solution in ECLs for libraries, as libraries traditionally register all their works and generally have systems in place to monitor and implement potential opt-outs.[1528] The representativeness of the CMO is also likely to affect the number of opt-outs[1529]; the more representative it is, the less likely it is that opt-outs will rise to unacceptable levels. Finally, an opt-out possibility may encourage the CMOs that negotiate ECL agreements to take account of all rightholders' interests in

1521 SOU 2010:24, Avtalad upphovsrätt, 2010, 225. The Max-Planck institute recommended that the CMO Directive should recognise some minimum rights of outsiders to participate in the decision making process of CMOs, cf. Drexl and others, Comments, 2013, 16. This recommendation was not acted upon.

1522 Riis and Schovsbo, ECLs, 2010, 491–492.

1523 Rydning, Extended, 2010, 79.

1524 Sterling, World Copyright Law, 2015, 629–630.

1525 Tryggvadóttir, Digital libraries, 2014, 325.

1526 Trumpke, The Extended, 2012, 282, fn.; Tryggvadóttir, Digital libraries, 2014, 321; Prop. 2012/13:141, Regeringens proposition, 2013, 57–58; Ficsor, Collective, 2016, 68.

1527 Ot. prp. nr. 46, Endringer, 2005, 51; Rydning, Extended, 2010, 83; IPO, Government, 18–19.

1528 Rydning, Extended, 2010, 86–87.

1529 Guibault, Cultural, 2015, 177.

order to mitigate the risk that an increased rate of opt-out could undermine the usefulness of the ECL agreement.[1530]

368. The opt-out possibility has in fact not been commonly used in the Nordic countries.[1531] Sweden, where there is an opt-out option in nearly all of the ECL provisions, has not seen a higher instance of opt-outs than the other Nordic countries, which provide for fewer mandatory opt-outs.[1532] This may change in new areas of use of in-copyright works made possible via ECLs. However, it is noteworthy that opt-outs in the Norwegian Bokhylla agreement are less than 2% of the works covered by the agreement.[1533]

369. In my view the opt-out possibility is an important safeguard measure and a key element with regard to the compatibility of the ECL system with EU legislation and international norms.[1534] Furthermore, if there should be an overwhelming number of opt-outs this might indicate that the area of use is not fit for ECLs. However, as the account above shows, there are some issues around the opt-out possibility that would benefit from clarification, such as who is entitled to opt-out, what the effect of an opt-out is for rightholders, how to secure a clear and simple procedure for opt-outs and how to make it easy for users of ECL licences to identify opt-outs.[1535] Some sort of a register for opt-outs could be an important feature for both users and rightholders, in particular opt-outs that were declared before an ECL agreement was concluded. A register system would confer more legal certainty for users and be a safety valve for rightholders in the sense that it would make it more likely that users would respect the opt-out if they were aware of it beforehand. Thus efficient safeguard measures rely on adequate transparency measures.[1536]

5.5. CONCLUSION

370. In this chapter I have looked at the Nordic ECL system. I began by discussing collective management in general and justification for its use. The main justification is that collective management makes possible uses of works that otherwise might not be feasible, for example where the cost of individual licensing would be prohibitively high. This is not only a major benefit for users

1530 Prop. 2012/13:141, Regeringens proposition, 2013, 57–58. See similiar discussion but different conclusion in SWD(2012) 204 final, Impact Assessment, 2012, 48, 173.

1531 Schønning, Ophavsretsloven, 5th ed., 2011, 380; Olsson, Upphovsrättslagstiftningen, 2006, 316; Rydning, Extended, 2010, 86; Trumpke, The Extended, 2012, 280.

1532 Rydning, Extended, 2010, 86.

1533 See discussion on the agreement in Ch. 5.3.1.4.

1534 See e.g. IPO, Government, 2014, 28.

1535 Ibid, 28–29.

1536 See discussion in Ch. 10.1.4. and 10.3.5.

but also for rightholders, as it provides a source of income that might otherwise not be realised. In addition, the stronger negotiating power of CMOs benefits rightholders who might not individually achieve the same result as a CMO which also benefits outsiders. The ECL system, albeit developed in close cooperation between the Nordic countries, is not identical in the five countries. Nevertheless, the main structure of the system is the same in all of them. Most importantly, as the system of ECL provides that collective management agreements are extended to non-members of the CMO, the so-called outsiders, there are several safeguards in place to guarantee their interests in the Nordic countries. I describe the main structure of the ECL system and how they are sometimes implemented in different ways in the five Nordic countries.

371. First, there is the requirement the CMOs eligible to negotiate ECL agreements be representative. Application of this requirement of representativeness is fairly uniform in all five countries although it varies, for example with regard to whether more than one CMOs can be considered representative. In practice, however, there is only one CMO considered as representative in each field, with some minor exceptions. However, although most ECL agreements allow for use of national and foreign works, establishing the representativeness of foreign rightholders is not always straightforward.

372. Second, I describe the scope of the extension effect of the ECL provisions, both in regard to the specific ECL provision for libraries and in regard to the general ECL provisions, which have been adopted in all the Nordic countries except Finland. Those general ECL provisions have i.a. been adopted in order to facilitate improved access to the cultural heritage. In my view, the combination of specific and general ECL provisions available to libraries provides them with a sufficiently wide spectrum of possible uses of all types of works from the collection of libraries, under ECL agreements, enabling them i.a. to make works available online, such as in the Bokhylla project.

373. Third, I describe the specific safeguard measures for outsiders. They consist, firstly, in that outsiders should be treated equally to members under any ECL agreement with regard to remuneration; secondly, the outsiders should always be entitled to individual remuneration for the use of their works; and thirdly, often outsiders have an opt-out possibility. It is established that Nordic CMOs generally do their best to seek out outsiders to pay them their due remuneration. However, it is clear that accepted distribution methods are often unfavourable to foreign outsiders residing abroad. Furthermore, the opt-out possibility, when available, is not frequently used. That may reflect a general acceptance of the system by outsiders, although it could indicate that transparency measures are not adequate. My conclusion is that sufficient transparency is vital for the safeguard measures to be effective.

374. My overall conclusion is that the Nordic system of ECL is a flexible and pragmatic system. It has kept pace with new technology and enabled solutions for mass uses at the national level, which have benefitted both users, such as libraries, and also rightholders, including outsiders. It enables the rightholders that are members of the relevant CMOs to benefit from their exclusive rights by mandating the CMO to manage them in situations where individual licensing would be impracticable. The same applies to the exclusive right of the outsiders, which is managed by the CMOs to their benefit. However, the CMO manages their right under a legal mandate rather than an explicit mandate. This limits the control outsiders have over their exclusive right. In the next chapter I will look at this issue specifically in an effort to determine the legal nature of the extension effect and how it conforms to the international and EU legal framework.

CHAPTER 6

THE COMPATIBILITY OF THE ECL SYSTEM WITH INTERNATIONAL NORMS AND EU LEGISLATION

...the fact that ECL regimes have existed in several Nordic countries for decades without ever being challenged on these grounds would seem to belie any suggestion that a properly crafted ECL system ... would conflict with international norms.[1537]

375. Increased international focus on the ECL system as a possible solution to the legal concerns thrown up by digitisation of the cultural heritage, following the Google Book Search Project dispute in the USA[1538] and the orphan works issue[1539, 1540] has highlighted the need for scrutiny of whether the system is compatible with international norms.[1541]

376. None of the international treaties in the area of copyright have provisions on collective management[1542], let alone extended collective licensing[1543], in the case of the latter presumably because until recently they only existed in the Nordic countries.[1544] The Berne Convention sets out minimum requirements for the protection of authors' works in countries other than the country of origin[1545] while the protection of nationals of a Member State is solely a matter for national legislation in that State. Thus national ECLs that only affect national works are

1537 US Copyright Office, Mass Digitization, 2015, 103.

1538 See Ch. 2. 3.

1539 See Ch. 2.2.1.

1540 Axhamn and Guibault, Cross-border ECL, 2011, 45, 49; US Copyright Office, Mass Digitization, 2015, 49, 82–104; ALRC, *Copyright and the Digital Economy: Discussion Paper*, (May 2013) 229–234; ALRC, Copyright and the Digital Economy, 2013, 274; US Copyright Office, Mass Digitization Report 2011, 2011, 34–37 Trumpke, The Extended, 2012, 265; Samuelson, Legislative, 2011, 705–715; van Gompel and Hugenholtz, The Orphan, 2010, 65 ff.; Hargreaves, Digital Opportunity, 2011, 37–38; COM(2011) 289 final, Proposal 2011, 3; Gervais, Collective Mangement, 2010, 21 ff.; Wang, Should China adopt, 2010,; von Lewinski, Certain Legal Problems Related to the Making Available of Literary and Artistic Works and other Protected Subject Matter through Digital Networks, 2005, 15.

1541 Axhamn and Guibault, Cross-border ECL, 2011, 45, 49; Rognstad, Avtalelisenser, 2004, 157; Riis and Schovsbo, ECLs, 2010, 481.

1542 Ficsor, Collective Management, 2016, 33.

1543 Ot.prp. nr. 46 (2004–2005), *Om lov om endringer i åndsverkloven m.m.*, 67.

1544 Bet. 1981/912, Licenskonstruktioner, 1981, 43.

1545 Art. 5 BC.

outside the scope of the Convention. However, ECL agreements that affect the rights of nationals of other countries as well as ECL agreements with cross-border effect must be in conformity with both the Berne Convention and other international conventions. Additionally, legislation in EEA Member States must fulfil conditions under EU legislation in the area of copyright.

377. In order to assess the compatibility of the ECL system with international norms in copyright I will look at the following areas: the principle of national treatment established under the Berne Convention, the Berne Convention ban on formalities for the "enjoyment and exercise" of copyright, and the international three-step test. Finally, I will look at the compatibility of the ECLs with specific EU legislation as well as EU's principle of non-discrimination and the principle of proportionality. With a view to preparing the ground for the above issues, I will begin this chapter with a discussion on the legal status or nature of the extension effect in the ECL system, as its status or nature will affect the system's compatibility with international norms.

6.1. THE LEGAL STATUS OF ECLS IN THE INTERNATIONAL CONTEXT

378. The discussion on the legal status or nature of the extension effect in the ECL system did not really become relevant until uses under the system emerged outside the expressly allowed areas for exceptions under international treaties. Until the early nineteen-nineties Nordic ECL provisions were established only in areas not problematic to international norms.[1546] However, once ECLs were adopted that were outside the expressly allowed areas of exception under the Berne Convention, the question arose whether the ECL system was to be considered an exception or limitation of the outsider's right or simply an arrangement for management of rights. In the latter case the problem of compliance with international norms does not arise at all.[1547] One challenge for the discussion is that there is no clear definition of the terms exception and limitation in international treaties or EU legislation[1548], which opens up to different interpretations and uses of the terms in different forums.[1549]

1546 Christiansen, The Nordic, 1991, 349; Karnell, Outsiders, 1991, 434; Trumpke, The Extended, 2012, fn. 142; Riis and Schovsbo, ECLs, 2010, 484–485; Verronen, Extended, 2002, 1151.

1547 Von Lewinski, Mandatory, 2004, 5; Schønning, Ophavsretsloven, 6th ed., 2016, 495; Séverine Dusollier and Caroline Colin, 'Peer-to-Peer File Sharing and Copyright: What Could Be the Role of Collective Management?', 2011, (4), Colum JL & Arts, 809–835, 826.

1548 See discussion on exceptions in Ch. 4.1.1.

1549 Trumpke, Exklusivität, 2015, 429.

379. There are important differences between the system of ECLs and exceptions or limitations in the common understanding of the terms. First, traditionally, exceptions are understood as uses authorized by legislation and which usually affect all relevant rightholders of works that the exception applies to. The ECL system, on the other hand, affects rightholders differently depending on whether they are members of the relevant CMO or not. For members the ECL agreement is a "normal" CMO agreement. The essential element of the ECL system is the voluntary membership of rightholders.[1550] Outsiders, for whom uses under an ECL agreement could be considered as exceptions to their exclusive rights, are a specific group, varying in size depending on how representative the CMO is.[1551] Second, the ECL system is based on a two tier system, i.e. the ECL provision and the actual ECL agreement. The provisions set out the conditions and parameters for ECL agreements and enable and activate their extension effect. However, it is the ECL agreement negotiated by a CMO on behalf of the relevant rightholders which determines which uses are allowed[1552], within the scope of the ECL provisions and their own mandates from rightholders. Third, although uses under exceptions are sometimes remunerated the amount of remuneration is commonly decided by governmental authorities not the stakeholders, whereas remuneration for uses under an ECL agreement is negotiated by the relevant CMO and the user.[1553]

380. In light of these differences many maintain that the ECL system does not fall under the normal system of exceptions or limitations but is simply a system for the management of rights.[1554] However, others maintain that the extension effect of ECLs constitutes an exception to the rights of outsiders, at least in practice.[1555] As the ECL system originates in the Nordic countries it is illuminating to look at legal documents and scholarly discussion on the matter and what they reveal about the legal nature of the system. As will become evident

1550 Triaille and others, Study, 2013, 305; Riis and Schovsbo, ECLs in Action, 2012, 930; Axhamn and Guibault, Cross-border ECL, 2011, 30 ff.

1551 Trumpke, Exklusivität, 2015, 687.

1552 Trumpke, The Extended, 2012, 278; Trumpke, Exklusivität, 2015, 334.

1553 Schønning, Ophavsretsloven, 5th ed., 2011, 462; Koskinen-Olsson, Collective Management, 2010, 293; Axhamn and Guibault, Cross-border ECL, 2011, 51; US Copyright Office, Mass Digitization, 2015, 82, 103; Foged, Danish licences, 2015, 17.

1554 See e.g. Vuopala, Extended, 2013, 12–13; Foged, Danish licences, 2015, 20; Schønning, Ophavsretsloven, 6th ed., 2016, 495; Axhamn, Exceptions, 2013, 184; Verronen, Extended, 2002, 1156, 1159.

1555 Strowel, The European, 2011, 668; Rognstad, Avtalelisenser, 2004, 154–155; Rognstad, Avtalelisens, 2012, 622, 631; Trumpke, The Extended, 2012, 281; Rydning, Extended, 2010, 24; Jane Ginsburg, '"With Untired Spirits and Formal Constancy": Berne-Compatibility of Formal Declaratory Measures to Enhance Title-Searching ', 2013, Berkeley Technology Law Journal, 1583–1622, 17; Ginsburg, Berne-Forbidden, 2016, 760–761; Axhamn and Guibault, Cross-border ECL, 2011, 48–49; Willi Egloff, 'Extended Collective Licenses – ein Modell auch für die Schweiz?', 2014, (11), sic! Zeitschrift für Immaterialgüter-, Informations- und Wettbewerbsrecht, 671–686, 677; Trumpke, Exklusivität, 2015, 340–342.

in the discussion below, the approach of the Nordic authorities has evolved since the adoption of the system in the sixties.

6.1.1. THE APPROACH OF THE NORDIC AUTHORITIES

381. The Danish position is that the ECL system is a rights management system and can as such be implemented even in areas where international acts prohibit restriction of the exclusive right of authors.[1556] This view is reflected in the title of the chapter containing ECL provisions in the Danish Copyright Act: "Limitations on Copyright and Management of Rights in the event of Extended Collective License".[1557] The chapter was previously named "Limitations on copyright"[1558] but was renamed in 2002 when the InfoSoc Directive was implemented.[1559] The Danish Government's position that the ECL system is not a real restriction on the outsider's exclusive rights was already evident in 1998 when the Database Directive was implemented.[1560] However, when the first ECLs were adopted in Denmark in the sixties the system was named "a modified compulsory licence"[1561] and in 1982 a Danish government report stated that ECLs, at least those that did not provide for an opt-out, could only be seen as compatible with international copyright conventions in areas where exceptions were allowed.[1562]

382. In Finland ECLs were also looked at as a restriction of copyright in the early years of the system. However, European developments in the nineteen-nineties, in particular the Satellite and Cable Directive, instigated the current view that the system is purely a system for the management of rights.[1563] The Constitutional Law Committee observed in 2004 that the ECL system is an important limitation of the outsider's freedom to contract. However, the Committee noted that the system was an accepted component of collective licensing with the aim i.a. of simplifying the procedure for users to obtain the necessary permission for use

---

1556 Schønning, Ophavsretsloven, 5th ed., 2011, 461–462; L 37, *Forslag til lov om ændring af ophavsretsloven. (Databaser, digital eksemplarfremstilling til undervisningsbrug m.v., gengivelse af kunstværker m.v.)*, (26 March 1998) Bilag 3; 2007/2 LSF 58, Forslag, 2008, chapter 3.1.

1557 In Danish: "Indskrænkninger i ophavsretten og forvaltning af rettigheder ved aftalelicens".

1558 Peter Schønning, *Ophavsretsloven med kommentarer* (2nd edn, GadJura, Thomson Information A/S, 1998), 31, 211.

1559 Cf. Act No. 1051 of 17.12.2002; Schønning, Ophavsretsloven, 6th ed., 2016, 495; Riis and Schovsbo, ECLs, 2010, fn. 44; Rydning, Extended, 2010, 22; Lovforslag nr. L 19, Infosoc, 2002, 16.

1560 L 37, Forslag, 1998, Bilag 3; Schønning, Ophavsretsloven, 2nd ed., 1998, 1998, 407.

1561 Tillæg A, Forslag til Lov om ophavsretten til litterære og kunstneriske værker, 1960, col. 273; Riis, Rognstad and Schovsbo, Collective Agreements, 2016, 59.

1562 Bet. 1981/912, Licenskonstruktioner, 1981, 43.

1563 Verronen, Extended, 2002, 1155, 1159.

of in-copyright works in mass-use situations. Thus the Committee's conclusion was that the ECL provisions were compatible with legal process and basic laws. This conclusion was reached in the light of the principle of proportionality, given the safeguard clauses involving the opt-out right and the right to individual remuneration, as well as the fact that the rightholders' title to enter into agreements regarding the use of his or her work is not affected by the ECL provisions.[1564] The Finnish Copyright Committee came to the same conclusion in 1992 stating that ECLs were more in compliance with the constitutional right to property than compulsory licences.[1565] As in Denmark, when the InfoSoc Directive was implemented in Finland the heading of the chapter which contains the ECL provision was amended[1566] to emphasize the nature of contractual licences as a means for collective administration of rights.[1567] Furthermore, in 2015 the Finnish legislator changed the wording of the ECL extension provision to underline that the CMO is presumed to represent outsiders.[1568]

383. Norway also renamed the chapter which contains exceptions and limitations as well as ECL provisions when implementing the InfoSoc Directive in 2005 in order to better explain the difference between the two.[1569] The proposal observes that none of the international conventions regulate management of rights through the system of ECLs.[1570] This understanding of ECLs as primarily management instruments seems to have emerged already in the early nineteen-nineties in Norway. Government documents refer to European legislation such as the Satellite and Cable Directive and the Rental and Lending Directive as accepting ECLs as primarily a system of management of rights, thereby obviating the need for ECLs to fulfil international rules for exceptions.[1571] Earlier government documents, however, considered the system to be an exception to outsiders' rights, e.g. the Norwegian

1564 RP 181/2014 rd, Regeringens proposition, 2014, 64–65; GrUU 7/2005 rd, *Grundlagsutskottets Utlåtande: Regeringens proposition med förslag till lagar om ändring av upphovsrättslagen och 49 kap. strafflagen (RP 28/2004 rd)*, 7.

1565 Verronen, Extended, 2002, 1153 quoting the Committee's Report No 4/1992, at 105.

1566 The title is "Limitations on copyright and provisions concerning extended collective licence" (the underlining is mine), cf. Act No. 14.10.2005/821.

1567 RP 28/2004 rd, *Regeringens proposition till Riksdagen med förslag till lagar om ändring av upphovsrättslagen och 49 kap. strafflagen*, (2004) 85; Olli Vilanka, 'Rough Justice or Zero Tolerance? – Reassessing the Nature of Copyright in Light of Collective Licensing (Part I)' in *In Search of New IP Regime* (2010) 145.

1568 See Ch. 5.3.

1569 Ot.prp. nr. 46 (2004–2005), Om lov, 2005, 29; Rydning, Extended, 2010, 22. Chapter II NCA is now titled "Delimitation of copyright and the management of rights with extended collective licensing" (my translation) but was simply "Delimitation of copyright" before, cf. Act 97/2005 which implemented the InfoSoc Directive. It is interesting to note that in the title the word delimitation (N. avgrensning) is used rather than restriction (N. begrensning) of copyright.

1570 Ot.prp. nr. 46 (2004–2005), Om lov, 2005, 66–67; Rydning, Extended, 2010, 23.

1571 Ot.prp.nr.15 (1994–1995), *Om lov om endringer i åndsverkloven m.m*, 69–70; Rydning, Extended, 2010, 23.

governmental report on ECLs for photocopying, but observed that it was closer to the exclusive right structure than exceptions and that the main emphasis should be on the role of the agreement in the system.[1572] Thus, the original ECL photocopying provision was limited to Norwegian works because collective remuneration, the prevailing distribution of remuneration under Norwegian ECL agreements, was not considered to be in line with the three-step test in the Berne Convention.[1573]

384. The same shift in views on the legal nature of ECLs also occurred in Sweden. Thus Swedish legal preparatory documents from 1993 expressly state that ECLs are exceptions to the exclusive right of the outsider. Even so, it is added that the ECL system is to be preferred to general exceptions as it affects only outsiders' rights, whereas the exclusive right of the members of the CMO negotiating the ECL agreement remains intact.[1574] Since the implementation of the InfoSoc Directive the Swedish government position has been that ECLs are a solution for simplifying agreements for use of protected works, referring to Recital (18) of the Directive, and hence not limitations or exceptions affected by the three-step test.[1575] Consequently the ECL provisions that used to be contained in a chapter together with provisions on exceptions and limitations under the heading "Restrictions on copyright"[1576] have now been transferred to a separate chapter in the Swedish Copyright Act under the heading "Extended Collective Licences".[1577, 1578] The Swedish Government has, however, underlined that the ECL provisions are a national solution that cannot support uses in other countries.[1579]

385. Thus it is clear that there has been a gradual shift in the Nordic perception[1580] of the nature of the ECL system with a pivotal point being the adoption of the InfoSoc Directive.[1581] The main motivation of the ECL system has always been pragmatic and practical.[1582] Thus it is not surprising that in order to maintain the possibility for further and future use of the system, which has

1572 NOU 1988:22, Endringer i åndverksloven m.v., 1988, 22–24, 34–35.

1573 Rognstad, Avtalelisenser, 2004, 155; NOU 1988:22, Endringer i åndverksloven m.v., 1988, 24.

1574 Prop. 1992/93:214, *Regeringens proposition om ändringar i upphovsrättslagen* 43–44; See also SOU 1990:30, *Översyn af upphovsrättslagstiftningen*, 166–168, where it is stated that ECLs can be introduced where exceptions are allowed under international copyright conventions.

1575 Prop. 2012/13:141, Regeringens proposition, 2013, 28–29; SOU 2010:24, Avtalad upphovsrätt, 2010, Prop. 2004/05:110, Regeringens, 2005, 246.

1576 S. Inskränkningar i upphovsrätten.

1577 S. Avtalslicenser.

1578 Prop. 2004/05:110, Regeringens, 2005, 244–246; SOU 2010:24, Avtalad upphovsrätt, 2010, 74.

1579 Prop. 2010/11:33, Återanvänding, 24; Prop. 2012/13:141, Regeringens proposition, 2013, 29.

1580 In Iceland the the official change did not happen until 2016 with Act No. 9/2016.

1581 Rydning, Extended, 2010, 22; Vilanka, Rough Justice or Zero Tolerance? – Reassessing the Nature of Copyright in Light of Collective Licensing (Part I), 2010, 145; Trumpke, Exklusivität, 2015, 336–338.

1582 Verronen, Extended, 2002, 1149; Koskinen-Olsson and Sigurðardóttir, Collective, 2016, 256; Trumpke, Exklusivität, 2015, 700.

functioned very well in the Nordic countries, the official view with regard to the legal nature of ECLs has evolved along with the system, in particular when the InfoSoc Directive was adopted with its exhaustive list of permitted exceptions.

6.1.2. DISCUSSION

386. The ECL system was developed as a practical compromise solution to a pressing problem and not based on a clear legal theory. The legal argument behind the system has evolved along with the development of the system as described above.[1583] It has worked well within the national boundaries of the Nordic countries where it originated, but as it is being extended to other countries and come to be used or considered to be used for cross-border activities, the importance of a clearer legal qualification becomes more pressing. However, that need does not mean that simple answers are available. The ECL system is based on collective management where the CMOs manage the rights of their members on the basis of their voluntary mandates. However, this does not hold for the rights of outsiders covered by an ECL agreement with binding effect on them due to an ECL provision in a copyright act.[1584] The outsiders have not in this case given the CMO a mandate to manage their rights. In practice the effect of the extension provision for the outsider is the same as a statutory licence.[1585] However, for the user the effect of the extension can be argued to be the same as under a presumption of a licence[1586], i.e. that the extension effect has the same result as legally presumed mandate. Thus it seems clear that the ECL system is a hybrid.[1587]

387. Most scholars agree that the ECL system entails some inherent limitations to the exclusive rights of the outside rightholder. However, views on whether or not the ECL system is restricted by international rules vary depending on whether the commentator considers the extension effect of the system to be one of exceptions or limitations on outsiders' rights on the one hand, or a system for the management of rights on the other.

Scholars who maintain that ECLs simply constitute a system of management of rights contend that the ECL system as such can bypass international restrictions on limitations, regardless of whether the system operates in areas where the Berne Convention allows for exceptions or not, with or without opt-out options.[1588]

1583 Ch. 6.1.1.

1584 Rognstad, Avtalelisens, 2012, 622.

1585 Riis, Rognstad and Schovsbo, Collective Agreements, 2016, 59; Riis and Schovsbo, ECLs, 2010, 482; Rognstad, Avtalelisenser, 2004, 154.

1586 Guibault, Copyright, 2002, 103.

1587 This is e.g. reflected in the title of the often quoted publication by Riis and Schovsbo: "Extended Collective Licenses and the Nordic Experience: It's a Hybrid but is it a VOLVO or a Lemon?", cf. Riis and Schovsbo, ECLs, 2010, *op.cit.*

1588 Schønning, Ophavsretsloven, 6th ed., 2016, 495.

Others submit that only ECLs with an opt-out possibility can be seen as an arrangement of management of rights of the outsider, as the opt-out possibility preserves "exclusivity and the ability of right holders to rely on their exclusivity" In their view ECLs without an opt-out possibility are limitations and exceptions that should be viewed in the light of the three-step test in areas which do not allow for exceptions and limitations.[1589] Some are, however, of the opinion that without opt-out, the system would stand little chance of complying with international norms.[1590] This view seems to be related to the approach that the opt-out possibility can be used to broaden the space for the introduction of exceptions under the three-step test.[1591]

Finally, some scholars are of the opinion that the ECL system constitutes an exception to the right of outsiders, regardless of whether there is an opt-out possibility or not. They claim that ECL provisions are clearly interventions in the exclusive right of the outside rightholder and, as such, must be viewed in the light of the three-step test and compatibility with international conventions. The fact that the restriction inherent in ECLs is normally limited to a specific group of rightholders, i.e. those not members of the CMO negotiating the ECL agreement, and that in many instances the system is beneficial for outsiders as well as the opt-out possibility clause only mitigates, but does not change the fact that ECLs are an intervention in the exclusive right, in their view. Any exception or limitation from which an author might opt-out must be compatible with the three-step test; the opt-out possibility as such will not make an impermissible exception Berne-compatible.[1592]

388. Thus there is no consensus amongst scholars as to whether the extended effect provided for by ECL provisions is an exception to the outsider's exclusive right to authorise the use of their works or whether the ECL system is to be considered simply management of rights. Even if most agree that ECLs constitute a restriction on the outsiders' rights there is no agreement on whether they are a limitation or exception that is governed by international norms, in particular the three-step test. EU legislation seems to have accepted that the ECL system is a system of management of rights with regard to outsiders.[1593] However, there is no mention in the Berne Convention and other international treaties of extended

---

1589 Riis and Schovsbo, ECLs, 2010, 485–486; Gervais, Collective Management, 2001, 42; Ficsor, Collective Management, 2010, 62; ALAI, Orphan Works, 2012, 1.

1590 Rosén, Copyright Contracts, 2011, 170; Ficsor, Collective, 2016, 66–68, 74–75.

1591 Martin Senftleben, 'How to Overcome the Normal Exploitation Obstacle: Opt-Out Formalities, Embargo Periods, and the International Three-Step Test', 2014, Berkeley Technology Law Journal Commentaries, 16; Axhamn and Guibault, Cross-border ECL, 2011, 71.

1592 Rognstad, Avtalelisenser, 2004, 154–155; Rognstad, Avtalelisens, 2012, 622, 631; Trumpke, The Extended, 2012, 281; Rydning, Extended, 2010, 24; Ginsburg, With Untired, 2013, 17; Ginsburg, Berne-Forbidden, 2016, 760–761; Axhamn and Guibault, Cross-border ECL, 2011, 48–49; Egloff, Extended, 2014, 677; Trumpke, Exklusivität, 2015, 340–342.

1593 See discussion in Ch. 6.3.1.

collective licences or collective management with legislative support of any kind. Hence no guidance either way can be deduced from these international treaties. There are several arguments for and against each position. Below, I will first list arguments for seeing the extension effect as management of rights and then follow with an account of arguments for seeing the extension effect as limitation or exception of the outsider's right.

389. There are a number of arguments for considering ECLs as a system for management of rights rather than exceptions or limitations on the outsider's right. First, technically the ECL system does not affect the exclusive right as such, but only restricts the way the author exercises the right when there is an ECL agreement adopted.[1594] The uses covered are not directly authorised by law but by a non-exclusive contract[1595] and thus the relevant rights are actually managed and their use negotiated.[1596] It has hence been argued that the ECL system does not affect the scope of the exclusive rights in question but only the presumption of who manages those rights.[1597] This approach seems to be established with regard to mandatory collective management[1598] in EU legislation[1599] and should be even more applicable to the ECL system where it is still possible to exercise the right individually, at least theoretically.[1600] However, Rognstad has argued that an important difference between mandatory collective management and ECLs is that the former is used in situations where it is impossible to license individually, whereas ECLs are used in areas where it is difficult and costly but theoretically possible to license individually.[1601] Second, although the "condition" or restriction on the exercise of the exclusive right of the outsiders might be considered to bring it under the wording of the Berne Convention on exceptions[1602], it has been argued that the historical background reveals that the relevant provision of the Convention deals with the relationship between users and authors, not authors and CMOs.[1603]

1594 RP 181/2014 rd, Regeringens proposition, 2014, 64–65.

1595 Guibault, Copyright, 2002, 26; von Lewinski, Mandatory, 2004, 5; Geiger, The Role, 2007, 9–10; Hugenholtz and Okediji, Conceiving, 2008, 19; Axhamn, Exceptions, 2013, 173–174; Kur and Schovsbo, Expropriation, 2009, 13.

1596 Rydning, Extended, 2010, 23, 98.

1597 ALAI, Opinion ECL, 2016, 6.

1598 See discussion on mandatory collective management in Ch. 9.3.

1599 Recital (28) Satellite and Cable Directive.

1600 Trumpke, The Extended, 2012, 285; Rydning, Extended, 2010, 23. However, it is worth remarking that Trumpke seems to be of the opinion that the extension effect of the ECL may be more restrictive than mandatory collective management, cf. Trumpke, The Extended, 2012, 278; Trumpke, Exklusivität, 2015, 334.

1601 Rognstad, Avtalelisens, 2012, 623–624. See also Ch. 9.3.

1602 Cf. Art. 11*bis*(2) BC.

1603 Von Lewinski, Mandatory, 2004, 5–6.

390. In line with the above arguments the extension provisions in the Nordic copyright acts could be seen as a legal presumption of transfer of right of management to the CMOs or a legal mandate and thus an arrangement of management of rights, rather than an exception or a limitation on the outsider's right.[1604] Such legal mandate is definitely implied in the wording adopted with regard to ECLs in Finland in 2015.[1605] This can be said to be further supported by the fact that in the Nordic countries, where CMOs are authorised for the purpose of ECL agreements, the authorisation is to the CMOs; in other words it is the CMOs that are authorised to negotiate and conclude ECL agreements. However, this reasoning is not clear-cut. In the case of general ECL agreements in Denmark authorisations are required for each and every ECL agreement that is concluded under the general ECL provision and the authorisation is for the ECL agreement itself, given after the collective agreement is made.[1606] This difference seems to weaken the argument that the extension effect gives the CMO a presumed mandate to negotiate on behalf of outsiders and can be seen to indicate that the extension effect, the binding obligation on outsiders, is based on the legal provision itself, in line with the coordinated wording of the ECL provision in the four Nordic countries and as it used to be in Finland.[1607]

391. It is clear that the intention of the Nordic legislator today is and has been in recent years that the system should be considered as an arrangement of management of rights, as outlined above. However, the intention alone cannot determine the nature of the arrangement. The decisive factor must be the actual effects of the ECL system and the ECL agreements.[1608] Thus the intention of the French legislator for the legislation on out-of-commerce books[1609] at issue in the Soulier case surely was to create a system that would be considered an arrangement of management of rights in line with the MoU of 2011 on out-of-commerce works.[1610] Nevertheless, the legislation, despite that intention of the legislator, was not acceptable from a legal point of view according to the CJEU.[1611] The French legislation and the system it created is fundamentally different from the Nordic ECL system, as discussed below.[1612] However, I mention it to illustrate that the intention of the legislator is not sufficient to determine the legal nature of restrictions on the exclusive rights of authors. Furthermore, the view of the Nordic legislator that the system is management

1604 See discussion in Ch. 9.2 on legal presumption of mandate.
1605 See Ch. 5.3.
1606 See Ch. 5.3.2.1 and Ch. 5.3.2.3.
1607 See Ch. 5.3.
1608 Riis and Schovsbo, ECLs, 2010, 485.
1609 See discussion of the legislation in Ch. 7.2.
1610 C-301/15 – Soulier, AG opinion, 54–61, see discussion in Ch. 11.2.1.
1611 C-301/15 – Soulier,, discussed in detail in Ch. 11.2.
1612 See discussion in Ch. 7.2 and in particular in Ch. 11.2.

of rights rather than an exception seems to stop at the national borders. If the ECL system was simply a management of rights, the ECL agreement should be seen as a contract that could have cross-border effect if the CMO had a mandate for the relevant territory.[1613] This is not the opinion of the Danish and Swedish authorities, and implicitly neither is it the opinion in Norway.[1614]

392. As mentioned above, many scholars hold that the opt-out possibility is a prerequisite for ECLs to be considered management of rights rather than exceptions. Thus the opt-out possibility can be perceived as an implied licence. However, in light of the Soulier case such implied licence based on opt-out is only possible if each outsider is "actually and individually" informed of the use.[1615] If this criterion is not fulfilled then the implied licence cannot be assumed.[1616] It is perhaps possible to qualify the decision in the Soulier case and limit its applicability to implied licence in the case of "commercial use" and/or situations where the system set up does not fulfil criteria for being an arrangement of management of rights. Thus it could be suggested that there might be less stringent requirements for opt-outs as implied licences if it was for non-commercial use.[1617] Alternatively, it could be argued that there would be more lenient requirements for opt-outs as implied licences within a system that could be considered mainly an arrangement of voluntary agreements[1618] such as the ECL system could be considered to be. However, neither of these alternatives would help the Nordic ECL system as a whole, with all its variations, to pass as a system of management of rights. None of the ECL provisions are limited to commercial uses[1619] and not all ECL provisions or agreements provide for an opt-out possibility for outsiders.[1620]

393. The primary argument for seeing the extension effect of the ECL system as an exception or limitation that needs to fulfil international norms is the fact that the licensing of authors' works by a CMO without the author mandating the CMO to licence those works is a significant restriction on the author's exclusive right. Practically speaking it resembles a legal licence. The inherent restriction, from the point of view of the outside author, is not ameliorated by the fact that it is only a restriction on non-members of a CMO. In fact it can be seen as aggravating the restriction, despite the right to remuneration, for

1613 See Ch. 8.4.2.1.
1614 See Ch. 9.1.1.
1615 C-301/15 – Soulier, par. 43–45.
1616 See discussion on this in Ch. 11.2.1.
1617 C-301/15 – Soulier, par. 44, i.f. where it is stated "in view of their commercial use in a digital format".
1618 C-301/15 – Soulier, AG opinion, par. 62–64.
1619 Ch. 5.1.2.
1620 Ch. 5.4.3.

example if the outsider is in principle against CMOs or if the outsider does not have the right to become a member and has no way to influence decisions.[1621] The inherent restriction is, furthermore, aggravated when there is not sufficient transparency with regard to concluded ECL agreements[1622], which is especially difficult to guarantee with regard to foreign outsiders. Lack of transparency makes it difficult for outsiders, especially foreign outsiders, to make use of the safeguard measures in the system, whether it is to opt-out or to demand individual remuneration. Furthermore, if the ECL agreement covers both national and foreign rights the number of outsiders can far outnumber the number of members of the relevant CMO, as can be seen from the account of the different categories of outsiders above.[1623] All foreign authors are outsiders as they cannot influence the ECL agreements as members of the ECL negotiating CMO. Thus, even if there are reciprocal agreements with foreign CMOs in force that actually give a mandate for ECLs the number of foreign authors will always outnumber national members of the relevant CMO. As discussed elsewhere, the representation of foreign authors and other rightholders by reciprocal agreements is not totally adequate and foreign outsiders are less likely to receive remuneration for use under an ECL agreement than nationals.[1624] Finally, although ECLs facilitate uses that are in the public interest, such as in order to encourage the communication and distribution of information[1625], such uses have traditionally not be seen as fundamental rights of users comparable to users' right to freedom of expression.[1626] Thus it could be argued that restrictions on the exclusive right of authors in such areas should be carefully scrutinised, and at least as well as exceptions based on fundamental rights. One way to secure such scrutiny of restrictions is to check their compatibility with international norms. However, in the digital environment this classification of justifications may have shifted with the public policy objective to disseminate information emerging as the central justification for copyright limitations.[1627]

394. From the account of the Nordic ECL library provisions and the general ECL provisions it is clear that they give room for potentially wide online use of all works in the collections of libraries.[1628] It is unlikely that unlimited online use for all works would be agreed upon by CMOs representing rightholders. Nevertheless, in my view there needs to be a safety check to ensure that the

---

1621 See discussion in Ch. 5.4.1 on the different categories of outsiders.
1622 Requirements for transparency have not been explicit in the Nordic ECL system, cf. Ch. 5.4.4.
1623 Ch. 5.4.1.
1624 See discussion in Ch. 6.2.1 and cross-references therein.
1625 See Ch. 5.1.2 and Ch. 5.3.
1626 See discussion in Guibault, Copyright, 2002, 105–107 on the influence of the justification on the limitation's nature.
1627 Senftleben, Copyright, Limitations and the Three-Step-Test, 2004, 30–32.
1628 See Ch. 5.3.

system is not employed for too wide a use of outsider's works. Thus I lean towards the opinion that the binding effect of an ECL agreement is a limitation or exception to the outsiders' exclusive rights that must fulfil international norms.[1629] Nevertheless, I simultaneously suggest that because of the hybrid nature of the ECL system it can also be seen as a system of management of rights, though only for uses that fulfil international norms. This view of the composite legal nature of the ECL system is based on how the system works in practise; it is a limitation on the outsider's exclusive right as it enables uses by others that the outsider has not authorised, but at the same time the exclusive right is being managed by a CMO. Whether the ECL system fulfils international norms with regards to outsiders will depend on individual ECL agreements as well as how the safeguard aspects of the system are applied in relation to the areas of use. Thus the area of use is of importance and the interplay of e.g. opt-out possibility, transparency requirements and the method of remuneration. Furthermore, as discussed below, I argue that Nordic ECLs, assessed on the basis of the actual agreements, generally fulfil international norms.[1630] Hence in the majority of cases the Nordic ECL system would be considered as an arrangement of management of rights with regard to outsiders. To me this seems to be the only way that the ECL system can be reconciled with the dichotomy between exception and management of right. From a theoretical point of view this may be less than satisfying, but for practical purposes it has worked, as discussed below with regard to conformity with the InfoSoc Directive.[1631] From a normative point of view such a hybrid solution should be supported, both because it preserves the possibility for a pragmatic solution that has worked well on a national level and, furthermore, it may have beneficial consequences with regard to the possibility of cross-border use of national ECL agreements, as discussed below.[1632]

395. In the light of this view I will next proceed to evaluate the compatibility of the ECL system with international norms. First I will look at the compatibility of the system with the national treatment principle, as well as the question of whether the opt-out possibility, when present, constitutes a prohibited formality under the Berne Convention. Then I will evaluate the ECL system with regard to the three step test, based mainly on the library applicable ECL provisions, before moving on the EU legislation and the compatibility of the system with the EU framework.

1629 Rognstad, Avtalelisens, 2012, 622–623; Rognstad, Avtalelisenser, 2004, 156; Trumpke, Exklusivität, 2015, 412–414, 689; Rydning, Extended, 2010, 24–25.

1630 Ch. 6.2.3.

1631 Ch. 6.3.1.

1632 Ch. 8.4.2.1.

6.2. THE COMPATIBILITY OF THE NORDIC ECLS WITH INTERNATIONAL NORMS

6.2.1. THE NATIONAL TREATMENT PRINCIPLE

396. The Berne Convention is based on the principle of national treatment.[1633] This principle is also the basis of collective management.[1634] Nevertheless, it has been claimed that the principle is not always observed in the regulations and operations of CMOs.[1635] In theory the national treatment principle is respected in all ECL provisions[1636] although this may not be the practice in all instances. In particular certain practices with regard to remuneration of foreign rightholders might not be in conformity with the principle. This is despite the fact that all the Nordic ECL provisions stipulate that equal remuneration shall be guaranteed to members and non-members alike, regardless of nationality.[1637] Practices such as distribution of unclaimed remuneration to members only, no pay-out of remuneration below a certain minimum and deduction for collective purposes, none of which benefit foreign rightholders, may not be compatible with the national treatment principle if used in connection with collection under ECL licences, while the ECL system is not universal.[1638]

397. The CMO Directive should improve the transparency and distribution of remuneration[1639] although it may not change significantly the specific issues mentioned above. Nordic CMOs do their best in any case to track down outside rightholders in order to pay them, though only where remuneration is distributed individually.[1640] For this reason as well as the fact that the representation of foreign rightholders is not always indicative of the number of foreign works used under an ECL agreement[1641], the notion that the ECL system passes the criterion of national treatment may be challenged. Nevertheless, it has been concluded that although it is hard for foreign rightholders to be remunerated under collective distribution, the fact that the aim of the system is not to exclude

---

1633 Art. 5(1) Berne Convention. Other international treaties have incorporated this provision, cf. TRIPS Art. 9(1) and WCT Art. 1(4).

1634 Tarja Koskinen-Olsson and Lowe, Module 1, 2012, 55.

1635 Ficsor, Collective Management, 2010, 73; Ficsor, Collective, 2016, 78–79; Bulayenko, Permissibility, 2016, 66.

1636 Axhamn and Guibault, Cross-border ECL, 2011, 46; Riis and Schovsbo, ECLs, 2010, 492.

1637 See discussion in Ch. 5.4.2 and 5.4.5.

1638 Riis and Schovsbo, ECLs, 2010, 490–492; Axhamn and Guibault, Cross-border ECL, 2011, 45, 55; Jonathan Band and Brandon Butler, 'Some Cautionary Tales About Collective Licensing', 2013, (3), Michigan State International Law Review, 687–728, 698.

1639 Chapters 2,3 and 5 of the CMO Directive.

1640 See discussion and references in Ch. 5.4.2 and 5.4.5.

1641 See discussion in Ch. 5.2.1.1 and 5.2.3.

foreigners and the practical problems with individual remuneration override the objections. Thus collective remuneration could be justifiable with regard to the national treatment principle.[1642] In my view this could be defensible for use that is limited to the country where the ECL agreement is issued, but the case could look different with regard to online use with cross-border effect. Hence as I deliberate on below, such use should be limited to national works, i.e. works first published in the country where the ECL agreement is negotiated between a national CMO and a national user.[1643]

6.2.2. FORMALITIES

398. The Berne Convention provides that the "enjoyment and exercise" of copyright shall not be subject to any formality.[1644] It has been maintained that in the framework of the Berne Convention "enjoyment" means the existence and scope of rights and "exercise" means their enforcement. Accordingly, if a work qualifies for protection under the Berne Convention no condition to "the enjoyment or exercise of domestic or conventional rights" may be introduced.[1645] The opt-out possibility requires some form of a declaration from the rightholders which has to be considered a formality requirement.[1646] The question is whether it is a prohibited formality or a Berne-compatible formality.

399. Most scholars are of the opinion that opt-out measures are a compatible formality as under the ECL system they relate to the administration of rights not the existence or scope of the right.[1647] The situation might be different if it were shown that remuneration for use based on an ECL agreement was much lower than under individual agreements.[1648] However, this is unlikely because of the increased negotiating power of the CMO.[1649] Furthermore, rightholders are in fact exercising their copyright even if they do not opt out of ECL agreements as their claims against the CMO are copyright claims. Opting-out is simply an act

---

1642 Cf. e.g. NOU 1988:22, Endringer i åndverksloven m.v., 1988, 24–25.

1643 See Ch. 10.2.1.

1644 Art. 5(2) BC. Other international treaties have incorporated this provision, cf. TRIPS Art. 9(1) and WCT Art. 1(4).

1645 Ginsburg, With Untired, 2013, 1587, 1589–1591; Ginsburg, Berne-Forbidden, 2016, 746, 750–751.

1646 See e.g. Senftleben, How to, 2014, 12–16; Ginsburg, Berne-Forbidden, 2016, 763.

1647 Riis and Schovsbo, ECLs, 2010, 483–484; Trumpke, The Extended, 2012, 280; Trumpke, Exklusivität, 2015, 691; Band, The Long, 2009, 314; Axhamn and Guibault, Cross-border ECL, 2011, 46; Gervais, Collective Mangement, 2010, 22–27; Gervais, Collective, 2016, 24–29; Ginsburg, Berne-Forbidden, 2016, 772–775; Gervais, Extended Collective Licensing: A Significant Contribution to International Copyright Law and Policy, 2016, 319; Ficsor, Collective, 2016, 75–77.

1648 Riis and Schovsbo, ECLs, 2010, 483–484.

1649 See Ch. 5.1.1.

of redirecting the claim to the user rather than the CMO in question.[1650] The history of Art. 5(2) of the Berne Convention shows that prohibited formalities are measures that would lead to no protection or the loss of protection, such as the requirement of registration with a governmental authority to establish copyright or the deposit of a copy, which is not the case under the ECL system.[1651] The Berne Convention generally does not address issues relating to ownership, transfer and licensing or author's right and thus it can also be concluded that the Convention does not prohibit opt-outs under the ECL system.[1652] However, a conditional opt-out that depends on proving that other persons are not holders of certain other rights in the work, is considered a formality inconsistent with Art. 5(2) of the Convention.[1653]

6.2.3. ECLS AND THE THREE-STEP TEST

400. If the ECL system is considered an exception or limitation on the outsider's right it must pass the international three-step test. As discussed above, this is a disputed area, not least because there is no agreed definition in international treaties of what an exception or limitation is.[1654] I have come to the conclusion[1655] that given that the outsider has not given his or her approval for the negotiated use, it is an exception which must pass the three-step. However, in my view ECLs should in general pass the three-step test. This is in particular the case for ECL provisions and agreements specifically for libraries and other cultural heritage institutions, as I will deliberate on here below.

401. Some observers have suggested that the compatibility of the ECL system with the three-step test has to be judged on the basis of the application of the provisions, i.e. the agreement itself.[1656] Others are, however, doubtful and point out that "what might be possible" under an ECL provision is of importance when evaluating the compatibility with international norms.[1657] In my view the contractual and collective basis of the ECL system is a key factor that makes the system different from other types of limitations and must be taken into

1650 Riis and Schovsbo, ECLs, 2010, 483–484; Trumpke, The Extended, 2012, 280. See also Band, The Long, 2009, 314.

1651 Gervais, Collective Mangement, 2010, 22–27. A similar argument was put forward with regard to the opt-out possibility in the Google Settlement Agreement, i.e. that the opt-out is only a procedure for rejecting one remedy in favour of another, cf. Band, The Long, 2009, 314.

1652 Ginsburg, Berne-Forbidden, 2016, 772–775.

1653 C-301/15 – Soulier, par. 50–51.

1654 See Ch. 4.1.1 and 6.1.

1655 Ch. 6.1.2.

1656 Riis and Schovsbo, ECLs, 2010, 485, 488; Rydning, Extended, 2010, 49–52; Axhamn and Guibault, Cross-border ECL, 2011, 49–50.

1657 Trumpke, The Extended, 2012, 286; Trumpke, Exklusivität, 2015, 430–431.

consideration when assessing the compatibility with the three-step test.[1658] Thus the compatibility of the system should be judged mainly by its application, i.e. the actual ECL agreements. However, that assessment will inevitably have to take into account the actual ECL provisions and the obligatory safeguard clauses.

402. Thus in order to assess the compatibility of the ECL system with the three-step test[1659], the following must be taken into account: first, the representativeness of the CMO negotiating the ECL agreement; second, the fact that the ECL provisions are only the outer parameters of scope of potential agreements. The actual agreements cannot be wider and are in fact often narrower in scope than the provisions allow. Third, only the rightholders that are non-members of the relevant CMO are affected by the limitation inherent in ECLs. Finally, the question of authorisation of the relevant CMO can affect the compatibility of ECLs with the three-step test. The assessment below is mainly based on the library relevant ECL provisions.

6.2.3.1. The first step

...certain special cases...

403. The Nordic ECL provisions applicable to libraries vary in scope. The specific library ECL provision in Denmark has the narrowest scope. This is also true of the other specific Danish ECL provisions. It is thus not surprising that some argue that all the Danish specific ECL provisions would pass the first step.[1660] The specific ECL library provisions in the other Nordic countries can, however, be very extensive in scope, both with respect to categories of works and uses covered.[1661]

404. The specific ECL library provisions are limited to certain beneficiaries or users, i.e. libraries and similar cultural heritage institutions. The WIPO sponsored Model Copyright Law suggests that limiting an exception for use by libraries and similar institutions makes an exception a "certain special case".[1662] That and the fact that no ECL provision takes effect unless there is an agreement specifying the use and works points to the conclusion that the specific library provisions should pass the first step. Furthermore, many maintain that normative considerations should be taken into account when assessing compatibility with the first step.[1663] Thus the public policy behind

1658 Rognstad, Avtalelisens, 2012, 623; Rydning, Extended, 2010, 69.
1659 See general discussion on the three-step test in Ch. 4.1.3.
1660 Riis and Schovsbo, ECLs, 2010, 487.
1661 See Ch. 5.3.1.
1662 See Ch. 4.1.4.1; see also C-174/15 – VOB, AG opinion, par. 67; US Copyright Office, Mass Digitization, 2015, 102–103.
1663 Cf. Ch. 4.1.3.1.1.

the specific library provisions, i.e. to enable public cultural heritage institutions to fulfil their purpose of preserving and disseminating the cultural heritage, must be taken into account when deciding whether the provisions are narrow enough.[1664]

405. The general ECL provisions are not limited to specific beneficiaries. Nevertheless, I propose they should also pass the first step. Although the general ECL provisions have seemingly unlimited scope of application they are in fact limited in line with their purpose. First, as already highlighted, agreements that are extended to outsiders under the general ECL provisions must be specific and, second, they can only be applied in situations where individual licensing is impracticable. This latter requirement is expressly stipulated in the Swedish and Icelandic general ECL provision and highlighted in the legal preparatory documents with regard to the Danish and Norwegian general ECL provisions.[1665] The purpose behind the general ECL provisions of enabling use of works in specific areas where legal use would not be possible without collective licensing with legislative support is both beneficial for rightholders and users and thus serves a public interest. Authorisation of ECL agreements under the general provisions is an important safety valve with regard to the compatibility of the agreements with that purpose, but these issues can also be left to the courts, as is the case with fair use. Hence, just as the fair use doctrine in the USA is accepted as passing the three-step test[1666] the general ECL provisions should also pass and be considered to be specific enough.

The experience from the use of the general ECL provision in Denmark has so far been that authorised agreements have been for very specific and limited areas.[1667] This does not preclude that larger projects with wider application could be deemed to be compatible with the requirement if considered a "special certain case", such as the digitisation and making available of out-of-commerce works or works published before a specific point in time, i.e. a cut-off date. Each specific cases would have to be evaluated.

406. My conclusion is thus that ECL agreements for libraries, both under the specific as well as the general ECL provisions, should be considered to fulfil the first step. This conclusion is dependent on the relevant legal framework being in place for ECL agreements, i.e. an extension provision in a copyright act, a representative CMO, safeguard clauses for the outsiders and a specified use of specific types of works, which falls under a public policy purpose, such as enabling access to the cultural heritage by libraries.

1664 See in this context C-174/15 – VOB, AG opinion, par. 67.
1665 See Ch. 5.3.2.1, 5.3.2.2, 5.3.2.3, and 5.3.2.4.
1666 Cf. Ch. 4.1.2 and 4.1.3.1.1.
1667 See discussion in Ch. 5.3.1.1.

6.2.3.2. *The second step*

...do not conflict with a normal exploitation of the work...

407. The aim of all ECL provisions is to enable use of works that under normal market conditions would be impracticable to enable.[1668] Hence, it seems implicit that use under an ECL agreement should not be in conflict with normal exploitation of the work. However, although the failure of the market to enable the specific use is in fact the background for most ECL agreements, none of the specific ECL provisions are expressly limited to such areas of use. The Swedish and the Icelandic general ECL provisions state that ECL agreements under them can only come into effect if the extension effect is an essential condition for the use in question. The same condition is highlighted in legal preparatory documents for the Danish and Norwegian general ECL provision.[1669] Thus, each specific ECL agreement has to be evaluated to establish whether it is limited to a use which would be impracticable.[1670]

408. Many ECL provisions are indeed very wide in scope.[1671] This is intentional in order to give stakeholders flexibility to negotiate agreements that best fit the needs of the parties.[1672] Nevertheless the contractual element of ECL provisions means that the actual scope of ECL agreements is usually more limited than the external limit provided by the provision itself. However, as such limitation is not guaranteed in the provisions[1673] the authorising authorities or the courts must judge whether the actual agreement goes beyond the second step, if disputed.

409. It has been claimed that ECL agreements make the exploitation under the agreement "normal" in the sense of the second step because they are based on negotiations between CMOs that represent a substantial number of authors in the relevant field of works.[1674] There is some truth in this. It has, however, been pointed out that the requirement of representativeness does not necessarily include derivative rightholders such as publishers.[1675] In Denmark the requirement of representativeness is based on all relevant rightholders, whereas in Norway it is

---

1668 Prop. 2004/05:110, Regeringens, 2005, 254; Axhamn and Guibault, Cross-border ECL, 2011, 41; Trumpke, Exklusivität, 2015, 265, 538. See also discussion and references in Ch. 5.1.1, 5.1.2 and 5.3.3.

1669 See Ch. 5.3.2.

1670 Trumpke, Exklusivität, 2015, 458; Rydning, Extended, 2010, 61.

1671 Trumpke, Exklusivität, 2015, 466.

1672 Rydning, Extended, 2010, 61; Axhamn and Guibault, Cross-border ECL, 2011, 50.

1673 Axhamn and Guibault, Cross-border ECL, 2011, 51; Rydning, Extended, 2010, 64; Trumpke, Exklusivität, 2015, 459–466.

1674 US Copyright Office, Mass Digitization, 2015, 103; Rydning, Extended, 2010, 61–63; Riis and Schovsbo, ECLs, 2010, 487.

1675 Trumpke, Exklusivität, 2015, 476–477.

limited to authors, but in practice the relevant CMO for e.g. reproduction rights is representative of publishers as well.[1676] It is presumed by IFRRO that the requirement of representativeness of CMOs for negotiating ECL agreements is based on a substantial number of authors and publishers of the relevant category of works.[1677] Obviously if derivative rightholders hold rights in a substantial part of the works used under an ECL agreement, it would be important for the compatibility of such an agreement with the three step test that the relevant CMO was in fact representative of a substantial part of those rightholders. If the representativeness requirement is thus fulfilled and coupled with the fact that ECL agreements are mostly in areas of use that are either impracticable to enforce[1678] or in areas of "untapped potential"[1679], ECLs should pass the second step.[1680]

410. There seems to be a general agreement that the term "normal exploitation" in the second step contains both an empirical and normative meaning.[1681] Thus the public interest in securing access to the cultural heritage should affect the assessment whether the ECL provisions applicable for libraries and other cultural heritage institutions pass the second step from a normative point of view. From an empirical point of view it must also be considered that if the collective licensing were not extended to outsiders then there would potentially not be any use at all, or at least no legal use, of the works and thus no remuneration for rightholders, whether members of the CMO or outsiders. Use that is impossible to licence because of transaction costs can hardly be considered normal exploitation.[1682]

411. Making works available as is possible under some of the Nordic specific library ECL provisions as well as the general ECL provisions, is a fairly wide-reaching use of in-copyright works and could be seen as conflicting with normal use. Nevertheless, my conclusion is that the ECL provisions, both specific and general, applicable for libraries should pass the second step. The main arguments for that conclusion are: first, use by public libraries normally does not have a commercial aim and, second, that it is up to the negotiating parties, i.e. the representative CMO and the library, to set out the inner limits of use in the actual ECL agreement, such as limiting the use to works before a certain date in order to reduce potential conflict with "normal exploitation". It must be

1676 See discussion in Ch. 5.2.1.1.

1677 IFRRO, *U.S. Public Consultation: "Mass Digitization Pilot Program"*, (10 August 2015) 4; see also Principle No. 2(1) of the MoU on out-of-commerce works; COM(2016) 593 final, Proposal, 2016, Art. 7(1)(a).

1678 As in the case of e.g. photocopying or other institutional reproduction.

1679 As is often the case with digitisation projects of works in the collection of libraries.

1680 Rydning, Extended, 2010, 59–64; Trumpke, Exklusivität, 2015, 466.

1681 See discussion in Ch. 4.1.3.1.2 and Axhamn and Guibault, Cross-border ECL, 2011, 50.

1682 Rydning, Extended, 2010, 59–61; Axhamn and Guibault, Cross-border ECL, 2011, 50.

assumed that if a CMO is indeed representative of rightholders in the relevant field this would make it highly unlikely that an ECL agreement would be reached that conflicted with normal exploitation in the field.[1683] Furthermore the public interest of giving access to the European heritage must be taken into account. Public interest arguments cannot be limited to areas untouched by economic activities.[1684] Even though the provisions themselves are wide, it should be acceptable to provide for the necessary flexibility to negotiate the optimal use that should be beneficial for both parties.

6.2.3.3. *The third step*

...do not unreasonably prejudice the legitimate interests of the rightholder.

412. It is asserted that limitations whose scope authors are able to influence, as is the case of ECLs, should be more likely to pass the third step.[1685] There are three important aspects of the inherent contractual element of the ECL system that are relevant for the third step: first the fact that it only affects outsiders, i.e. fewer authors than a general limitation[1686]; second, the stronger bargaining power of CMOs compared to the bargaining power of individual outsider versus a user[1687], and third, the effect of the delineation and approval of a representative number of authors in the same field on the actual limitation.[1688] Thus outsiders may be better off economically with having their work used under an ECL agreement, because they receive remuneration under the agreement, which they either might not receive at all or potentially at a lower level if individually negotiated.[1689] To these three factors can be added the opt-out possibility which, when present, may have an impact on the assessment of the conformity of the ECLs with the third step, as will be discussed below. Finally, the market failure[1690] reason behind the ECL system is also of relevance to the assessment of the system with regard to the third step, especially in the digital context.[1691] Progress in digital technology, although important for management of copyright,

---

1683 Trumpke, Exklusivität, 2015, 466.

1684 C-174/15 – VOB, AG opinion, par. 70.

1685 Axhamn and Guibault, Cross-border ECL, 2011, 51; Rydning, Extended, 2010, 68; US Copyright Office, Mass Digitization, 2015, 103.

1686 Rognstad, Avtalelisenser, 2004, 154; Rydning, Extended, 2010, 70; Triaille and others, Study, 2013, 305; Riis and Schovsbo, ECLs in Action, 2012, 930; Axhamn and Guibault, Cross-border ECL, 2011, 30 ff.

1687 See Ch. 5.1.1.

1688 Rydning, Extended, 2010, 73–76.

1689 C-174/15 – VOB, AG opinion, par. 74.

1690 Here the term market failure is used for situations where transaction costs make licensing undesirable, cf. Rydning, Extended, 2010, 12, 101. See also discussion on the term by Ginsburg, Fair Use, 2014, 1402; Axhamn and Guibault, Cross-border ECL, 2011, 50; Guibault, Contracts, 2000, 140.

1691 Rydning, Extended, 2010, 69–70.

will not supersede the need for collective management for some time, if ever[1692], whereas at the same time technology facilitates the administration of opt-outs and individual remuneration of outsiders.[1693]

113. The opt-out option applies to the administration of the exclusive right, not the extent or scope of the right.[1694] It has, however, been claimed that the opt-out possibility turns the premises of copyright upside-down[1695] in the sense that it is only the author who should be able to authorise the use of his or her work.[1696] Thus an opt-out possibility on its own cannot qualify a limitation to pass the three-step test.[1697] Still, if a limitation is deemed to pass the first and second step, perhaps for public policy reasons, such as providing access to the cultural heritage which might otherwise not be possible, an opt-out possibility would still significantly reduce the limitation in the ECL system and should thus help towards passing the third step.[1698] Moral right aspects can also be legitimate aspects and an opt-out possibility is a simpler way to stop use that an author deems as breaching his or her moral right than going to court.[1699] Thus, an opt-out possibility definitely helps to reduce a potential unreasonable prejudice of the legitimate interest of the rightholder and aligns the exception to the principle of proportionality[1700], despite requiring some effort on behalf of the rightholder.

Although the opt-out possibility may create costs and some level of uncertainty for users, it is far less burdensome for users than having to individually seek prior authorisation from each and every outsider of works that could be covered by ECL agreements.[1701] Libraries are better suited than many other users to deal with opt-outs, especially for digital uses, as they already use very precise cataloguing systems. Furthermore, new technology will make control of status of works, even analogue ones, easier. Moreover, experience has shown that there are not many opt-outs from digital library projects.[1702] Indeed, if opt-outs became prevalent it might indicate that the particular use was fit for individual licensing rather than collective licensing.[1703]

1692 Handke, Collective, 2014, 195–198.

1693 Rydning, Extended, 2010, 88–89.

1694 See discussion in Ch. 6.2.2.

1695 As was claimed with the Google Book Search Project, see Ch. 2.3.

1696 Rydning, Extended, 2010, 84; Trumpke, The Extended, 2012, 282.

1697 Trumpke, The Extended, 2012, 281; Ginsburg, With Untired, 2013, 1606.

1698 Rydning, Extended, 2010, 85; Rognstad, Avtalelisens, 2012, 623.

1699 Trumpke, Exklusivität, 2015, 484.

1700 See discussion in Ch. 6.3.6.and 11.4.3.2.

1701 This was also one of the arguments the Google book project case, i.e. that it was easier for rightholders to opt out than for Google to get a prior authorisation, cf. Band, The Long, 2009, 251–252. The opt-out possibility was, however, not one of the reasons that the project was deemed to fall under the US Fair Use doctrine, cf. Authors Guild v. Google (SDNY 2013); Authors Guild v. Google (USCA SC 2015), 2.

1702 SWD(2016) 301 final, IA Part III, 2016, 132; see also on the Bokhylla project in Ch. 5.3.1.4, and the German National Library project in Ch. 7.4.

1703 See discussion and references in Ch. 5.4.5.

Thus having an opt-out clause may make the ECL negotiating CMO more careful to consider the interests of outsiders in order to reduce the risk of excessive opt-outs.

Nevertheless, an ECL provision without an opt-out possibility could be deemed to pass the third step if opt-outs were considered to render the ECL agreement inefficient and thus preclude mass use of works in areas of public interest. It could be too cumbersome for users to have to check which works had been opted out and they might either use works illegally or not use them at all, thereby thwarting the aim of the ECL to release untapped potential. Each situation would need to be individually assessed as to whether it would merit passing the third step.[1704]

414. Assessing the economic harm to outsiders, which lies at the heart of the third step[1705], can be difficult, in particular in relation to out-of-commerce works[1706], which tend to make up a large part of library collections. It has been asserted that use of out-of-commerce works under an exception might not even need to be compensated for in order to pass the three-step test.[1707] At any rate, remuneration negotiated by a CMO representative of authors in the field would most likely be deemed to compensate for potential economic harm.[1708] Given that one of the main purposes and effects of the ECL system[1709] is to generate remuneration for rightholders, both for members of the CMO and outsiders, the system as a whole, individual ECL provisions and ECL agreements, should pass the third step.

A further question is whether collective distribution of remuneration would disqualify an ECL agreement from passing the third step. While outsiders have the right to individual remuneration even if the ECL agreement stipulates collective remuneration, the outsider must substantiate his or her claim for individual remuneration; this can be hard to demonstrate unless there is some registration or other forms of statistics provided by users.[1710] Nevertheless, it has been suggested that in some cases ECL agreements with collective remuneration schemes might pass the third step on the grounds of efficiency.[1711] All forms of registration and provision of statistics necessary for individual remuneration increase the transaction costs. Lower transaction costs are thus the main argument for collective distribution of remuneration.[1712] Yet, given modern technology and the tradition of registration within libraries, individual remuneration should be possible for their use of works under ECL

1704 Rydning, Extended, 2010, 87–88; Riis and Schovsbo, ECLs, 2010, 486.
1705 See Ch. 4.1.3.1.3.
1706 See discussion on definition on out-of-commerce works in Ch. 7.1 and Ch. 11.3.1.2.
1707 Ginsburg, Berne-Forbidden, 2016, 762, see fn.
1708 Riis and Schovsbo, ECLs, 2010, 488; Axhamn and Guibault, Cross-border ECL, 2011, 51; US Copyright Office, Mass Digitization, 2015, 103.
1709 Riis and Schovsbo, ECLs, 2010, 486.
1710 See Ch. 5.4.2 and 5.4.5.
1711 Rydning, Extended, 2010, 80–82.
1712 See Ch. 5.4.2.

agreements.[1713] Nevertheless, pragmatism also has to have room. Thus the mixed distribution method under the Bokhylla agreement[1714] reflects a combination of respect for the interest of rightholders to receive individual remuneration and a concession to efficiency and transaction costs. Thus it can be said to combine the necessary balance between the legitimate interests of the rightholder and the need for efficiency of the ECL agreement.

415. My conclusion is thus that ECL provisions and agreements for libraries which provide remuneration for outside rightholders should pass the third step. At the same time it is possible that in some specific cases ECL agreements without a remuneration might also be considered to be compatible. Furthermore, an opt-out will lessen the potential prejudice to outsider's interests both economic and moral, thus respecting the principle of proportionality, although providing for an opt-out may not be essential in all circumstances. However, in the case of making works available online by libraries, the opt-out possibility would seem appropriate as it would not be too burdensome for libraries and it would better safeguard the economic interest of the outsider. This would in particular be the case with online use with cross-border effect.[1715]

6.2.3.4. *Evaluation*

416. The answer to the question of the compatibility of the ECL system to international norms with regard to the limitation it confers on the outsiders' rights may vary depending on which right ECL provisions cover and may have to be assessed on the basis of actual agreements. The prerequisite for compatibility is that the general safeguard clauses for outsiders are guaranteed in the actual legislation, i.e. that negotiations are carried out by representative CMOs, that outsiders have the same right to remuneration as members, as well as a right to individual remuneration and in some instances, the right to opt-out. In my view the opt-out possibility is a safety valve, both for the individual outsider but also as a measure of the viability of the ECL agreement as such. If there are too many opt-outs the conclusion may be that the area of use or type of works that the agreement covers is not appropriate for an ECL agreement. If for some reason opt-outs are deemed impossible at a national level, the question is whether that area of use should not rather be facilitated under an exception or limitation.

417. My conclusion is thus that ECL provisions with regard to outsiders' rights, in particular ECL provisions applicable for libraries because of the inherent public interest such provisions serve, are able to pass the international three-step test if

---

[1713] Rydning, Extended, 2010, 81–83; Tryggvadóttir, Digital libraries, 2014, 325.
[1714] See Ch. 5.3.1.4.
[1715] See further discussion on the issue in Ch. 10.3.4.

the common traits of Nordic ECL provisions are present. If those are fulfilled it is most likely that individual ECL agreements will also pass the test in this regard. However, the next hurdle to look at is whether and to what extent ECLs, especially if seen as limitation or exception on outsiders' rights, are restricted by EU legislation.

6.3. ECLS AND EU LEGISLATION

418. Here I will look at the compatibility of the ECL system with EU legislation, beginning with the question of whether the system escapes the closed list of exceptions and limitations under Art. 5 of the InfoSoc Directive, if it is seen as a hybrid, i.e. a limitation on the outsider's exclusive right but which would be viewed as a presumed mandate for uses that pass international norms and therefore an arrangement of management of rights. I will look at other relevant directives, such as the Satellite and Cable Directive, the Orphan Works Directive, the CMO Directive and the Services Directive, as well as the compatibility of the ECL system with the principles of non-discrimination and proportionality.

6.3.1. THE INFOSOC DIRECTIVE AND THE SATELLITE AND CABLE DIRECTIVE

419. The closed list of exceptions in the InfoSoc Directive[1716] could be problematic for ECLs in areas that do not fall under that list if they are considered purely exceptions or limitations on the outsider's right. However, it seems that a pragmatic approach to the issue of the system of ECL was adopted during the legislative process with Recital (18)[1717] which states that the Directive is without prejudice to arrangements in Member States concerning the management of rights such as extended collective licences.[1718] But what effect does Recital (18) have?

420. Recitals in EU legislation are an aid to interpretation[1719] and have a clarifying function. Their purpose "...is to set out concise reasons for the chief provisions of the enacting terms, without reproducing or paraphrasing them. They shall not contain normative provisions or political exhortations".[1720]

1716 See discussion in Ch. 4.2.1.

1717 No mention of ECLs was in the original proposal cf. COM(97)628 final, InfoSoc Proposal, 1997, but the Recital was added at a later stage, cf. Common Position (EC) No 48/2000 adopted by the Council on 28 September 2000.

1718 Gunnar Karnell, 'The Swedish implementation of the European Infosoc-Directive', 2006, RIDA, 161–233, 209–211; Strowel, The European, 2011, 666; Bulayenko, Permissibility, 2016, 61; see also discussion and references in Ch. 6.1, par. 403–405.

1719 Favale, Kretschmer and Torremans, EU copyright jurisprudence?, 2016, 53–54.

1720 European Union, The Guide, 2014, point 10.

Nevertheless, it has been suggested that recitals can be used to broaden the interpretation of the closed list in Art. 5 of the InfoSoc Directive.[1721] However, the weight of recitals in interpreting legislation is not fully settled. It is clear that they cannot be used to contradict clear provisions in operative articles of EU legislation[1722], and indeed, the wording of the relevant provisions does not explicitly preclude the application of ECLs.[1723]

421. The negotiations concerning which exceptions would be allowed under the Directive were extremely complicated.[1724] Thus it must have seemed a good solution to simply place the issue outside of that discussion by adding a recital, even if, or maybe because, it was done without a clear definition of the nature of the ECL system. Thus the undermining of a well-functioning system in the Nordic countries seemed to have been avoided. This approach nevertheless raises several questions: first, whether the Recital applies to all forms of extended collective licences; second, whether this approach means that ECLs are exempted from having to conform to international norms, in particular the three-step test, and, third, what effect, if any, it has on cross-border use under national ECL agreements. The last question will be looked at in Chapter 9.1 while the first two questions will be discussed here.

422. The Nordic authorities pressed for the inclusion of Recital (18) in the InfoSoc Directive.[1725] Hence it is not surprising that the opinion of Nordic policy makers and some Nordic copyright specialists is that Recital (18) refers to all the Nordic ECLs, past and future.[1726] However, as shown above, the ECLs are not a homogeneous system, even within the Nordic countries.[1727] Thus, many

---

[1721] Firth and Preira, Exceptions for Libraries, 2016, 18; Geiger and others, InfoSoc, 2014, 450, referring to C-510/10 – DR and TV2 Danmark, par. 45, 55–56. An apparently opposing view seems to be taken by AG Wathelet in C-301/15 – Soulier, AG opinion, fn. 17.

[1722] See e.g. *C-134/08, Hauptzollamt Bremen v J. E. Tyson Parketthandel GmbH hanse j.* ECLI:EU:C:2009:229, 16 July 2009 par. 16; Rydning, Extended, 2010, 94; Geiger and others, InfoSoc, 2014, 449–450.

[1723] Rydning, Extended, 2010, 95.

[1724] See account of the process in von Lewinski and Walter, Information Society Directive, 2010, 937–951.

[1725] Cf. e.g. Riis, Rognstad and Schovsbo, Collective Agreements, 2016, 69; Axhamn and Guibault, Cross-border ECL, 2011, 53–55; Riis and Schovsbo, ECLs, 2010, 477–479; Rydning, Extended, 2010, 96; Ds 2003:35, Upphovsrätten, 2003, 278; Harald von Hielmcrone, 'Orphan works. The Danish solution: Extended collective licensing', 2008, EBLIDA News, 1–2, 1; Koskinen-Olsson and Sigurðardóttir, Collective, 2016, 251–252; Sganga, The eloquent, 2017, fn. 90.

[1726] Schønning, Ophavsretsloven, 6th ed., 2016, 495; Lovforslag nr. L 19, Infosoc, 2002, 9; Ds 2003:35, Upphovsrätten, 2003, 277–278; Prop. 2012/13:141, Regeringens proposition, 2013, 28–29; Koskinen-Olsson, Collective Management, 2010, 303; Prop. 204/05:110, *Upphovsrätten i informationssamhället – genomförande av direktiv 2001/29/EG, m.m.*, (10 March 2005) 245; Vuopala, Extended, 2013, 23–24; Koskinen-Olsson and Sigurðardóttir, Collective, 2016, 252; Verronen, Extended, 2002, 1156.

[1727] See discussion in Ch. 5.1.-5.4.

commentators doubt whether all ECLs fall under Recital (18) regardless of how they are formulated and executed.[1728]

423. The term "extended collective licences" in Recital (18) is not further defined in the InfoSoc Directive so there is no specific guidance to be found there.[1729] The Satellite and Cable Directive has played a pivotal role in the discussion as it is the only directive that has a concrete ECL provision.[1730, 1731] The ECL provision in the Satellite and Cable Directive requires an opt-out for outsiders. Thus many maintain that only ECLs with an opt-out possibility fall outside the closed list in Art. 5 of the InfoSoc Directive or at least that an opt-out would make it more likely that ECLs were considered compatible with the EU legislation.[1732]

424. EU law and its concepts must be given an autonomous and uniform interpretation throughout the Community unless there exists "different intention expressed by the European Union legislature in the specific context" of a given directive.[1733] Recital (18) of the InfoSoc Directive refers to arrangements in the Member States, which must be seen as a reference to national legislation for determining the meaning of such arrangements. Nevertheless, the ECL provision of the Satellite and Cable Directive is of relevance. The background of the provision was that the EU legislator did not want to allow a national compulsory licence to be the basis for use of the communication to the public right by satellite in the whole of the EU[1734] as reflected in Article 3(1) of the Directive.[1735] At the same time the Nordic countries wished to retain the possibility of having extended effect in the area of satellite broadcasting. Thus Article 3(2) was a compromise.[1736] Consequently it can be deduced that the EU legislator even at this stage saw ECLs as something different from compulsory

---

1728 Rydning, Extended, 2010, 94–104; Trumpke, The Extended, 2012, 283–284; Trumpke, Exklusivität, 2015, 371; Riis and Schovsbo, ECLs, 2010, 477–481; Rognstad, Avtalelisenser, 2004, 156–157; Rognstad, Avtalelisens, 2012, 622–623; Axhamn and Guibault, Cross-border ECL, 2011, 52–55; Kyst, Aftalelicens, 2009, 53; Ficsor, Collective Management, 2010, 63–64; Ficsor, Collective, 2016, 70.

1729 Rydning, Extended, 2010, 95; Rognstad, Avtalelisenser, 2004, 157.

1730 Art. 3(2) Satellite and Cable Directive.

1731 Ficsor, Collective, 2016, 69.

1732 Kyst, Aftalelicens, 2009, 53; Rydning, Extended, 2010, 103; Axhamn and Guibault, Cross-border ECL, 2011, 54; Sganga, The eloquent, 2017, 322.

1733 See discussion and references in Ch. 3.2.1.

1734 Which might have been a possibility given the country of origin principle adopted, cf. Art. 1(2)(b) Satellite and Cable Directive.

1735 COM(91) 276 final, *Proposal for a Council Directive on the coordination of certain rules concerning copyright and neighbouring rights applicable to satellite broadcasting and cable retransmission.*, (11 September 1991) 37; Rosén, The Nordic ECL Model, 2012, 67–68; Recital (21) Satellite and Cable Directive.

1736 Jan Rosén, 'The Satellite and Cable Directive' in Irini Stamatoudi and Paul Torremans (eds), *EU Copyright Law; A Commentary* (2014) 219–220. It is interesting to note that initially the extended effect in Art. 3(2) was to be limited in time, cf. COM(91) 276 final, Proposal, 1991, 56.

licences.[1737] There remains the question of whether this is limited to ECLs with an opt-out clause. The compatibility of ECLs with the InfoSoc Directive has not been tested by the CJEU. However, the Commission has accepted that the Infosoc Directive has been adequately implemented in all the Nordic countries and has not designated as incompatible with the Directive the ECL provisions that do not have mandatory opt-outs for outsiders. This can be seen to imply that Recital (18) would exclude the Nordic ECL model from the closed list in Art. 5 of the InfoSoc Directive, whether they include an opt-out clause or not.

425. It seems that the EU legislator intended to let the ECL system fall outside the closed list.[1738] However, this does not amount to a blanket licence to all ECL agreements.[1739] In my view it is more likely to be limited to ECLs that pass certain requirements, as otherwise it could be too much of a loophole for limitations. As discussed above[1740], the system of ECLs is a hybrid, and I suggest that the hybrid quality of the system could imply that for areas of uses that pass the three-step test the limitation aspect of the system recedes in favour of the presumed mandate aspect of the system. The fact that the three-step test is mentioned in Art. 5(5) as to how to be applied to exceptions allowed under Art. 5 of the InfoSoc Directive does not exclude that the three-step test is not applicable to other forms of restrictions that fall outside of Art. 5. This possible understanding of the effect of recital (18) could lead to the possibility that some ECL agreements might fall outside of the scope of the recital. However, as argued above my conclusion is that ECL agreements, based the common traits found in the Nordic legislation, in most cases fulfils international norms, including the three-step test.[1741] Thus I suggest that the ECL system in the majority of cases falls outside the closed list in Art. 5 of the InfoSoc Directive.

426. Interpretation of provisions of EU legislation has "to consider not only its wording, but also the context in which it occurs and the objectives pursued by the rules of which it is part".[1742] Recital (18) provides clues to the context and the objectives of the legislator. This further supports my view that the approach of "balancing" and "proportionality"[1743] should be used in the interpretation of the compatibility of the ECL system with the closed list of exceptions and limitations under the InfoSoc Directive. As mentioned earlier, the suggested leap over the dichotomy between exceptions and management of right inherent in the suggestion that use under ECL agreements that fulfil the three-step test would be

1737 Rydning, Extended, 2010, 98; Rosén, Copyright Contracts, 2011, 156–157.
1738 Bulayenko, Permissibility, 2016, 62–63.
1739 Rognstad, Avtalelisenser, 2004, 156–157.
1740 See discussion in Ch. 6.1.2.
1741 Ch. 6.2.
1742 C-306/05, SGAE, par. 34; Rydning, Extended, 2010, 94–95.
1743 Firth and Preira, Exceptions for Libraries, 2016, 21; Recital (31) InfoSoc Directive.

considered as use under management of rights, may be difficult to digest from a theoretical point of view and could be described as legal fiction. However, from a pragmatic point of view it seems to have worked and it offers a way past the closed list of exceptions in Art. 5 of the InfoSoc Directive.

427. Since the adoption of the InfoSoc Directive in 2001 there has been reference to extended collective licensing in the recitals of the Orphan Works Directive and the CMO Directive.

6.3.2. THE ORPHAN WORKS DIRECTIVE

428. In the search for a solution for the orphan works issue the suggestion was made to use the ECL system.[1744, 1745] In the proposal[1746] for the Directive[1747] the Commission rejected the use of the ECL system for orphan works as, in their view, the absence of a diligent search prevented an approach based on mutual recognition of the orphan work status and because an extended collective licence is normally only valid in the national territory in which the statutory presumption applies, and finally because it was deemed too costly[1748] for libraries.[1749]

429. Nevertheless, in Recital (24) of the Orphan Works Directive it is stated that the Directive is "without prejudice to the arrangements in the Member States concerning the management of rights such as extended collective licences, legal presumptions of representation or transfer, collective management or similar arrangements or a combination of them, including for mass digitisation." Again there is no further definition and no clarification of whether all ECLs fall under this recital or not. However, the Recital presumably echoes Art. 1(5) of the Directive, which states that the Directive does not interfere with any arrangements concerning the management of rights at national level. That provision read together with Recital (24) of the Directive seems to accept that

---

1744 European Commission, *Summary Minutes of the 1st meeting of the High Level Expert Group on Digital Libraries*, (26.03.2006) COM(2009) 532 final, Communication on Copyright, 2009, 5; EU Commission, Creative Content, 2009, 14, 20.

1745 See discussion on ECLs and orphan works in Ch. 5.2.1.1.

1746 At one stage in the proposal process there was an provision offering ECLs as an alternative solution, cf. Rosén, The Nordic ECL Model, 2012, 83–84.

1747 See description of the Directive in Ch. 4.2.3.

1748 The evaluation and conclusion of the cost was sharply criticised by the Nordic countries, in particular the EFTA-EEA countries, cf. discussion in Ch. 10.3.2.

1749 COM(2011) 289 final, Proposal 2011, 3; SEC(2011) 615 final, Impact Assessment, 2011, 27–29. IFFRO was of the opinion that orphan works should be administered through collective management and licensing, cf. James Boyd, 'IFRRO submits comments on proposed Orphan Works Directive' (*IFRRO*, 01.09.2011) <www.ifrro.org/content/ifrro-submits-comments-proposed-orphan-works-directive-0> accessed 8 May 2018.

ECLs can be used for orphan works, at least for national works at a national level.[1750] The fact that the Commission presumes that ECLs are "normally" only valid in the country where they are negotiated seems to indicate that the Commission does not, or did not at the time, see the system as pure management of rights.

6.3.3. THE CMO DIRECTIVE

430. Although the system of ECL was rejected as a solution for multi-territorial licences for online use of music works[1751] Recital (12) of the CMO Directive states that it does not interfere with arrangements concerning the management of rights, such as extended collective licensing. This again confirms that under EU legislation ECLs are viewed as arrangements for the management of rights rather than limitations. However, it does not define what ECLs are or whether all ECLs are to be considered arrangements concerning management of rights. Nevertheless, the Recital seems to underline that Member States can introduce new ECL provisions.[1752]

431. This Recital was not in the original proposal, which created concern at the time that the Directive would be detrimental to the ECL system as well as other collective management systems with legislative support.[1753] The concern was connected to a provision in the original proposal obliging Member States to provide that CMOs had the express consent of rightholders for each and every right they managed. The proposed provision had the following wording: "Member States shall ensure that the rightholder gives express consent specifically for each right or category of rights or type of works and other subject matter which that rightholder authorises the collecting society to manage and that any such consent is evidenced in documentary form."[1754] This would not be possible with regard to non-members such as outsiders under an ECL

[1750] Riis and Schovsbo, ECLs in Action, 2012, fn. 1. However, it is doubtful that the provision allows all types of national solutions cf. discussion in Eleonora Rosati, 'The Orphan Works Provisions of the ERR Act: Are They Compatible with UK and EU Laws?', 2013, (12), EIPR, 724–740; Ficsor, Collective, 2016, 70–71.

[1751] See discussion in Ch. 9.4.

[1752] Ficsor, Collective Management, 2016, 218.

[1753] E.g. Art. 9(1) Satellite and Cable Directive regarding mandatory management system for the cable retransmission right.

[1754] Cf. Art. 5(6) in COM(2012) 372/2, Proposal, 2012, 25. See criticism in i.a. Drexl and others, Comments, 2013, 23; IFRRO, Position Paper on CMO proposal, 2012, 1, 4; Standing Committee of the EFTA States, *Subcommittee I on the Free Movement of Goods: EEA EFTA Comment on the Commission proposal for a Directive of the European Parliament and of the Council on collective management of copyright and related rights and multi-territorial licensing of rights in musical works for online uses in the internal market, (COM (2012) 372)*, (21 February 2013) par. 6.

agreement.[1755] Eventually, these reservations were taken into account in the legislative process, with the inclusion of Recital (12)[1756] and by amending the relevant provision, which now reflects the fact that express consent relates to collective management on the basis of a mandate and does not affect situations where CMOs manage rights under legislation.[1757]

6.3.4. CMOS AND THE SERVICES DIRECTIVE

432. A further bone of contention with regard to the Nordic ECL model has been whether the requirement for an authorisation of representative CMOs as a prerequisite to negotiate ECL agreements is compatible with the Services Directive[1758] and whether such authorisation can be limited to a single CMO.[1759] CMOs clearly fall under the definition of service providers in the Services Directive[1760] as they provide services, first of all to rightholders, but also to users and other CMOs.[1761] The Services Directive guarantees the right of providers to provide services in a Member State other than that in which they are established and bans requirements that may hinder such rights[1762] i.a. an obligation to obtain an authorisation for providing services.[1763] Only authorising one single CMO would also affect this freedom.

433. The CJEU ruled in the OSA case that neither the Services Directive nor Art. 56 and 102 TFEU precludes legislation which reserves to a single CMO the exercise of collective management of copyright in respect of certain protected works in the territory of the Member State concerned.[1764] The Court arrived at this conclusion, first, by concluding that Art. 16 of the Services Directive does not apply to CMOs because of the exception set out in Art. 17(11) of the

1755 Guibault and van Gompel, Collective, 2016, 152.

1756 The Recital was introduced with the Irish Presidency compromise proposal, cf. Council, *Proposal for a Directive of the European Parliament and of the Council on collective management of copyright and related rights and multi-territorial licensing of rights in musical works for online uses in the internal market – Presidency compromise proposal*, (5 April 2013) Recital (7c).

1757 Cf. Art. 5(7) CMO Directive.

1758 See discussion in Ch. 5.2.1.3.

1759 See discussion in Ch. 5.2.1.2.

1760 Riis, Collecting, 2011, 490; COM(2012) 372/2, Proposal, 2012, 5; Riis and Schovsbo, ECLs, 2010, 493; Axhamn and Guibault, Cross-border ECL, 2011, 55; Guibault and van Gompel, Collective, 2016, 145–146.

1761 C-351/12, OSA, par. 57–63; C-351/12, OSA, AG opinion, para 58–60; SWD(2012) 204 final, Impact Assessment, 2012, 11; Drexl and others, Comments, 2013, 4.

1762 Art. 16 Services Directive.

1763 Art. 16(2)(b) Services Directive.

1764 C-351/12, OSA, par. 91. This had also been the opinion of the AG Sharpston in the case, cf. C-351/12, OSA, AG opinion, 54–82.

Directive, which excludes copyright from Art. 16[1765]; second, by establishing that it had not been shown that there was another method to secure the public interest policy of protecting territorial copyright, thus it did not contravene Art. 56 TFEU to reserve the right to a single CMO[1766], and third, Art. 102 TFEU does not prohibit monopoly as such, but only the abuse of monopoly. Thus, the Article does not preclude legislation that creates such a monopoly as long as the legislation does not lead to the abuse of a dominant position.[1767] The Court was not asked directly about the issue of authorisation[1768] but as it is Art. 16 of the Services Directive that bans authorisation as a requirement for the provision of a service and the conclusion of the Court was that Art. 16 is not applicable to CMOs, it is reasonable to deduce the authorisation of CMOs is not incompatible with EU legislation. In fact authorisation could be a safeguard against abuse of monopoly.[1769]

434. The original proposal for the CMO Directive contained recitals that referred to the applicability of the Services Directive.[1770] These were dropped in the final text as a result of the intervention of the European Parliament.[1771] Recital (50) of the CMO Directive expressly states that it is neutral on the issue of prior authorisation in Member States, in so far as such an authorisation is compatible with EU legislation and does not create an obstacle to the full application of the CMO Directive.[1772]

435. In the light of the OSA decision and the fact that the CMO Directive does not stipulate adherence of CMOs to the Services Directive, my conclusion is that a requirement of authorisation as a prerequisite to negotiate ECL agreements and the limitation of such an authorisation to one CMO in not incompatible with the Service Directive as its Art. 16 is not applicable to CMOs. The authorisation of CMOs, in particular for the negotiations of ECL agreements, can be a valuable tool and safeguard for the correct application of collective management.

1765 C-351/12, OSA, par. 64–65.
1766 Ibid, 67–79.
1767 Ibid, par. 80–84.
1768 Although Art. 98 of the Czech copyright legislation in question stipulated authorisation of CMOs, cf. Ibid, par. 10.
1769 Ficsor, Collective Management, 2016, 233.
1770 COM(2012) 372/2, Proposal, 2012, Recital (3), (8); Guibault and van Gompel, Collective, 2016, 145.
1771 Ficsor, Collective Management, 2016, 229.
1772 Guibault, Collective, 2014, 785, where she observes that the mention of compatibility with EU law may be referring to the Services Directive; Ficsor, Collective Management, 2016, 217–218.

6.3.5. ECLS AND THE EU'S PRINCIPLE OF NON-DISCRIMINATION

436. Within the EU and the EEA any discrimination on grounds of nationality is prohibited.[1773] This principle of non-discrimination has been interpreted strictly in copyright cases[1774] and has i.a. led to changes in the Nordic ECLs, abolishing references to national authors in provisions on the representativeness of CMOs negotiating ECL agreements.[1775]

437. As discussed above in relation to the national treatment principle[1776] the practice of some CMOs with regard to distribution of remuneration can be seen as incompatible with the principle of non-discrimination on grounds of nationality. The same conclusion applies here as there, i.e. the practices can be defensible when it is limited to use within the national territory of the ECL issuing country, but for online use with cross-border effect the issue might be different.

6.3.6. ECLS AND THE PRINCIPLE OF PROPORTIONALITY

438. According to Art. 52(1) of the EU Charter[1777]:

> Any limitation on the exercise of the rights and freedoms recognised by this Charter must be provided for by law and respect the essence of those rights and freedoms. Subject to the principle of proportionality, limitations may be made only if they are necessary and genuinely meet objectives of general interest recognised by the Union or the need to protect the rights and freedoms of others.

439. In my view all ECL agreements that meet the three-step test would be deemed to be respectful of the "essence" of copyright. The general interest behind all ECL provisions is to enable access to information and the cultural heritage. Thus they should be deemed to be necessary and they have proven to be a genuine way to meet that objective. The opt-out possibility would in particular enhance the likelihood that an ECL agreement would be deemed to adhere to the principle of proportionality.[1778]

1773 Art. 18 TFEU and Art. 4 EEA Agreement.

1774 See e.g. C-92/92 *Phil Collins v Imtrat Handelsgesellschaft mbH and Patricia Im- und Export Verwaltungsgesellschaft mbH and Leif Emanuel Kraul v EMI Electrola GmbH.* ECLI:EU:C:1993:847, CJEU, 20 October 1993 par. 29–35; C-28/04 *Tod's SpA and Tod's France SARL v Heyraud SA* ECLI:EU:C:2005:418, CJEU, 30 June 2005 par. 6–36; Riis and Schovsbo, ECLs, 2010, 492; Axhamn and Guibault, Cross-border ECL, 2011, 55.

1775 See discussion in Ch. 5.2.1.

1776 See Ch. 6.2.1.

1777 Charter of Fundamental Rights of the European Union, Official Journal of the European Communities 2000/C 364/01 (the EU Charter).

1778 See Ch. 11.4.3.2.

6.3.7. EVALUATION

440. It is clear from the above account that the EU legislator leaves room for ECL agreements. Although my conclusion is that in the first instance ECL provisions are exceptions on the outsider's right, I suggest that Recital (18) of the InfoSoc Directive implies that if ECLs fulfil the three-step test and other international norms they will be accepted within the EU as arrangements of management of rights. This may require an "inventive" and pragmatic interpretation of the relation between exceptions and exercise of rights. Such pragmatic approach is, however, in my view to be supported from a normative point of view.

441. If the ECL system is classified in EU legislation as management of rights if the system fulfils international norms it can have important implications. Thus the classification may affect rules regarding applicable laws in case of legal disputes in other countries for cross-border use of national ECL agreements within the EU. This will be further analysed below.[1779]

442. The conclusion that ECLs are compatible with EU law is now supported by the fact that the Commission has recently proposed that the use of out-of-commerce works within the EU could be facilitated by ECLs or the similar model of presumed mandate.[1780, 1781]

6.4. CONCLUSION

443. There is no general agreement as to whether the system of ECL constitutes a limitation or exception on the exclusive right of the outsider or is simply a system for the management of rights. The view of Nordic legislators in this regard seems to have shifted from considering the system an exception to the outsider's right to viewing it as an arrangement concerning the management of rights. However, that view has been limited to use of the system within national borders, except in Finland. Under EU legislation there seems to be a general acceptance of the ECL system as an arrangement concerning the management of rights and that, consequently, it does not fall under the exhaustive list of exceptions and limitations in the InfoSoc Directive. I maintain that this is only with regard to ECL system that fulfil international norms. In international treaties, however, there is no mention of collective management in general or the ECL system in particular. Thus it cannot be deduced from these treaties that ECLs are to

1779 See discussion in Ch. 8.4.2.1.

1780 See Ch. 9.2 on legal presumption.

1781 COM(2016) 593 final, Proposal, 2016, 26–27. See a description of the proposed solution for out-of-commerce works in Ch. 11.3.

be considered as an arrangement concerning the management of rights. The opposite cannot either be concluded from international treaties. Nevertheless, as argued above I suggest that, given that the works of outsiders will be used without their consent under an ECL agreement, such use constitutes an exception to their right in the broad understanding of that term and needs to fulfil international norms, such as the three-step test.[1782] This does not necessarily preclude, in my view, that the hybrid system of ECLs, when it fulfils international norms, could under EU legislation be seen as an arrangement concerning the management of rights, and thus fall outside of the closed list of exceptions under the InfoSoc Directive. As argued above[1783], most ECL agreements that fulfil the Nordic model provisions would pass the three-step test, in particular ECL agreements for libraries that have the aim to provide better access to the cultural heritage.

444. As to other international norms in copyright: there seems to be agreement that the ECL system is compatible with the principle of national treatment and the EU's principle of non-discrimination. Nevertheless, it may be doubtful whether the use of collective remuneration rather than individual remuneration for use of works under an ECL agreement is consistent with these principles, at least with regard to the use of foreign works for cross-border use.[1784] Finally, there seems to be an agreement that the opt-out option under the ECL system as such does not constitute a forbidden formality under the Berne Convention.

445. Some have expressed doubt that it would be possible to establish a viable ECL system outside of the Nordic countries, in particular in countries where there is less tradition of collective management and collective agreements.[1785] This is an important consideration and is one of the objections some commentators have regarding the US proposed ECL system.[1786, 1787] However, within Europe the CMO Directive should improve the governance and workings of CMOs in the region, which is a fundamental prerequisite for a functional ECL system. Indeed, an increasing number of EU countries have adopted ECL or similar systems, which is testimony to the interest in the system as a solution outside of the Nordic countries. The latest development in that vein is the proposed ECL type solution in the DSM proposal.[1788] The next chapter will discuss the various solutions already adopted in Europe.

1782 See Ch. 4.1.3 and 6.2.3.
1783 See Ch. 6.2.3.
1784 See further discussion on that in Ch. 10.2.1.
1785 Riis and Schovsbo, ECLs, 2010, 487–490.
1786 See a brief description of the US proposal in Ch. 7.5.2.
1787 See e.g. US Copyright Office, Mass Digitization, 2015, 6; Pamela Samuelson, *Comments in response to the June 9, 2015, Notice of Inquiry regarding Mass Digitization*, (6 October 2015) 5–7.
1788 COM(2016) 593 final, Proposal, 2016, Title III, Chapter 1, Art. 7–9. See Ch. 11.3.

CHAPTER 7

COLLECTIVE LICENCES WITH LEGISLATIVE SUPPORT OUTSIDE THE NORDIC COUNTRIES FOR MAKING THE CULTURAL HERITAGE AVAILABLE

... when ECLs have been implemented not only in the EU but also in the United States, a critical mass will arise which, in all likelihood, will lead to the rest of the world choosing the same solution – this will give the other libraries and their users a de facto opportunity to gain access to relevant collections.[1789]

446. Not everybody agrees that the Nordic ECLs are fit for export, nor would everybody be as optimistic about the spread of the system as is reflected in the above quotation. However, as indicated in the quotation, both the EU and the USA have recently considered ECL systems for the benefit of i.a. libraries.[1790] Furthermore, several European countries have adopted ECLs in one form or another and others are proposing to follow suit.

447. Legal policy in the EU with regard to online distribution of in-copyright works by publicly accessible libraries and other cultural heritage institutions has been that such use should be facilitated with specific contracts or licences.[1791] This policy, at least for "larger" mass digitisation projects is reflected in the 2011 Recommendation by the Commission on the digitisation and online accessibility of cultural material and digital preservation[1792] and in the facilitation by the Commission[1793] of the Memorandum of Understanding on Out-of-Commerce Works[1794] signed in September 2011 by stakeholders, i.e. organisations representing libraries on the one hand and publishers, authors and CMOs in the text and image based sector on the other.[1795]

1789 Rydén, Are digital, 2016, 17.

1790 US Copyright Office, Mass Digitization, 2015, 72 ff.; COM(2016) 593 final, Proposal, 2016, Art. 7–9.

1791 Recital (40) InfoSoc Directive.

1792 2011/711/EU, Recommendation, 2011, Item 6(b) and recital (12).

1793 1274, SEC(2011) 1274, 2011, 27; Triaille and others, Study, 2013, 278, 304; Janssens and Tryggvadóttir, Facilitating, 2015, 73–74; Janssens and Tryggvadóttir, Orphan, 2016, 203.

1794 See *op.cit.* fn. 30.

1795 The signatory stakeholders were the three European library associations, representing the national, public and scientific libraries; the relevant associations of writers and of book and

448. The MoU on out-of-commerce works is based on collective licensing with a presumption of management which has a similar effect to the ECL with regard to outsiders.[1796] The MoU has no binding effect on its signatories, let alone on Member States' obligation to legislate. Nevertheless, it has influenced legislation in some EU countries.[1797]

449. The 2011 Recommendation called for legal backing of licensing solutions for mass digitisation and cross-border use of out-of-commerce works.[1798] However, such solutions have been adopted in less than half of the EU Member States.[1799] Furthermore, mechanisms that have been implemented do not cover all types of works and in particular, do not provide for cross-border use. Thus the Commission felt obliged to propose a binding solution within a Directive.[1800] This solution, if adopted, will oblige EU Member States, to adopt ECL type or presumption of mandate type support for "non-exclusive licence for non-commercial purposes with a cultural heritage institution for the digitisation, distribution, communication to the public or making available of out-of-commerce works" from their collections.[1801] I will discuss the proposed solution in Ch. 11.3 below.

In this chapter I will discuss the MoU and national legislation in certain EU Member States which aims to enable libraries to digitise and make available in-copyright works from their collections. I will also briefly describe, the now abandoned, proposals for ECL systems in the USA and Australia.

7.1. THE MOU ON OUT-OF-COMMERCE WORKS

450. The MoU lays down principles for agreements between national CMOs and national "publicly accessible cultural institutions"[1802], authorising the

---

journal publishers; the European federation representing visual creators and their collectives; and IFRRO representing, in particular, reproduction rights organisations (RROs), the CMOs in print and publishing, cf. <http://ec.europa.eu/internal_market/copyright/docs/copyright-infso/20110920-mou_en.pdf>, accessed 11 July 2017.

1796 SWD(2016) 301 final, IA Part III, 2016, 130; Janssens and Tryggvadóttir, Facilitating, 2015, 78; Guibault, Cultural, 2015, 174; Talke, Verwaiste und vergriffene Werke, 2013, 133. See discussion on presumption of management in Ch. 9.2.

1797 SWD(2016) 301 final, IA Part I, 2016, 68; European Commission, Report, 2016, 37; Janssens and Tryggvadóttir, Orphan, 2016, 204.

1798 Art. 6(b) and Recital (12) 2011 Recommendation; Triaille and others, Study, 2013, 279.

1799 European Commission, Digitisation report 2014, 2014, 7; European Commission, Report, 2016, 37.

1800 SWD(2016) 301 final, IA Part I, 2016, 68–79; COM(2016) 593 final, Proposal, 2016, Art. 7–9.

1801 COM(2016) 593 final, Proposal, 2016, Art. 7(1).

1802 The same institutions as set out in Art. 5(2)(c) InfoSoc Directive, cf. Recital (1) MoU. However, in reality it is mainly applicable to libraries because of the limitation to books and journals, cf. e.g. Martin Kretschmer and et al., 'The European Commission's public consultation on the review of EU copyright rules: a response by the CREATe Centre', 2014, (9), EIPR, 547–553, 549.

latter to digitise and make available online, out-of-commerce books and journals, including embedded images[1803], first published in the country of the agreement.[1804] Thus the MoU applies to national publication and the agreements are to be negotiated in the country of origin of the works in the sense of Art. 5(4) of the Berne Convention. The primary assumption of the MoU is that rightholders should always have the first option to digitise and make their works available.[1805] It is specified that for the purpose of the MoU the term "rightholder" refers to authors of literary and artistic works and publishers.[1806] The MoU contains three main principles.

451. The first principle stipulates that agreements should be voluntary and involve all relevant parties. It is specified that this includes authors and publishers. Each agreement must set out exactly which works and uses it covers, the amount of remuneration and the author's moral rights. The determination of the commercial non-availability of a work must be agreed upon and follow the customary practices of the country of first publication. Each agreement should set out in detail how the process is to be executed. The MoU contains a basic definition of out-of-commerce works: "... a work is out of commerce when the whole work, in all its versions and manifestations is no longer commercially available in customary channels of commerce, regardless of the existence of tangible copies of the work in libraries and among the public (including through second hand bookshops or antiquarian bookshops)."[1807]

Many orphan works would fall under the category of out-of-commerce works but not all out-of-commerce works are orphan.[1808] Thus the MoU complements the Orphan Works Directive.[1809] It is interesting that the MoU presupposes that agreements can be both for commercial and non-commercial use.[1810]

452. The second principle of the MoU provides that licences shall only be granted by CMOs that represent substantial numbers of authors and publishers affected by the agreement.[1811] It contains guidelines on how to publicise in

1803 Recital (1) and (6) MoU.
1804 Recital (1) and (2) MoU; Triaille and others, Study, 2013, 278. If the agreement covers translated works the MoU requires special arrangements to ensure that not only the rights subsisting in the original language version but also the distinct rights in any translation of the original are respected and accounted for, cf. Principle No. 2(2) MoU.
1805 Recital (6) MoU; Janssens and Tryggvadóttir, Facilitating, 2015, 76.
1806 Recital (3) MoU.
1807 Definition and Principle No. 1(2) MoU.
1808 Talke, Verwaiste und vergriffene Werke, 2013, 133. He suggests that it is easier to determine when work is out-of-commerce than when it is orphan.
1809 Janssens and Tryggvadóttir, Orphan, 2016, 203. See discussion on the OWD in Ch. 4.2.3 and 4.2.4.2.
1810 Principle No. 1(3) MoU; Suthersanen and Frabboni, The Orphan, 2014, 663.
1811 In IFRROs submission to the US Copyright Office it is stated that the relevant CMO "undertakes to collect mandates from authors and publishers in the fields to be digitised;

advance each digital library project based on such agreements so that relevant rightholders can decide whether to participate.[1812] All rightholders, both members and outsiders, shall have the right to opt out.[1813]

The second principle further sets out a presumption rule regarding rightholders that have not transferred the management of their rights to a CMO. It provides that the relevant CMO will be presumed to manage the relevant rights with regard to the particular agreement. The presumption has a similar result with regard to outsiders' rights as the extension effect under the ECL system, i.e. the outsider will be bound by the agreement the CMO makes.[1814] In order for the presumption to apply the CMO in question must make its best efforts to alert rightholders in question. However, as indicated in the MoU[1815], the presumption rule will probably only have effect in countries where legislation exists confirming the presumption of representation in one way or another, such as where there is a system of ECL.[1816]

453. The third principle of the MoU deals with cross-border access to digital libraries and commercial use. The presumption of representation by the relevant CMO of outsiders shall apply for uses of the relevant work in other Member States.[1817] However, the CMO *may* limit the effects of such an agreement – i.e. the licence to use works – to the works of the rightholders it represents; thus excluding works of outsiders. Such a limitation is also possible with regard to commercial use of works of outsiders.[1818] Furthermore, "a specific procedure should be considered" to reach non-represented rightholders whose works are used frequently or intensively, either commercially or cross-border, where an agreement is concluded on the basis of the presumption. It is, however, up to the parties concerned to decide whether and when such procedures are necessary and how they should be organised.[1819]

454. The recitals of the MoU contain further deliberations on the principles and how they can be implemented. In particular, Recital (9) recognises that legislation might be needed to create legal certainty with regard to outsiders

this would normally be done in close cooperation with the associations of the authors and publishers", cf. IFRRO, U.S. Public Consultation: "Mass Digitization Pilot Program", 2015, 3.

1812 It is i.a. recommended that represented rightholders be notified individually, cf. Principle No. 2(2) and (3) MoU.

1813 This is confirmed in IFRRO's submission to the US Copyright Office, cf. IFRRO, U.S. Public Consultation: "Mass Digitization Pilot Program", 2015, 3. Some have, however, interpreted the provision more narrowly, cf. Oostveen and Guibault, IPR issues, 2013, 10.

1814 SWD(2016) 301 final, IA Part III, 2016, 130; Janssens and Tryggvadóttir, Facilitating, 2015, 78.

1815 Cf. Recital (9) MoU.

1816 Janssens and Tryggvadóttir, Facilitating, 2015, 79.

1817 Principle No. 3(3) MoU.

1818 Principle No. 3(1) MoU.

1819 Principle No. 3(2) MoU.

for the relevant institutions concerning use of work under a licence based on presumption of management of rights under the second principle.[1820] Furthermore, Recital (11) calls on the European Commission to consider legislation necessary to ensure legal certainty in a cross-border context. The Commission has now responded to this call with its proposal on a legal mechanism for collective licences for out-of-commerce works.[1821]

455. The strength of the MoU approach is that agreements based on it can be adapted to the needs of the negotiating parties, taking into account different categories of content, albeit currently only books and journals, as well as different users.[1822] It is thus flexible and not reliant on any particular legal system. Such agreements would also reduce transaction costs as they would be based on a commonly-agreed model, through collective management which provides for a single point of contact, both for the identification of rightholders and for clearing copyright.[1823] However, the MoU model also has significant deficiencies: first, its non-binding nature which means Member States do not need to take action[1824]; second, to be effective it needs legal backing both at national and EU level[1825]; and third, it only applies to restricted categories of works, i.e. books and journals.[1826] Hence it is of limited use as such, even for many libraries[1827], as it excludes for example newspapers[1828] and unpublished works, which can be a large part of the collection of libraries and, in particular, archives.[1829]

Another consideration is the fact that limiting agreements to out-of-commerce works may involve an extra search effort by users, i.e. to establish whether a given work is out of commerce or not.[1830] An alternative solution, which might be more efficient and less costly for libraries and archives, is to limit agreements to works published before a certain date, as stipulated for example in the Norwegian Bokhylla ECL agreement.[1831] Older works are more likely to be

---

1820 Sganga, The eloquent, 2017, 323; Trumpke, Exklusivität, 2015,; Janssens and Tryggvadóttir, Orphan, 2016, 207.

1821 COM(2016) 593 final, Proposal, 2016, Art. 7–9. See discussion in Ch. 11.3.

1822 Janssens and Tryggvadóttir, Orphan, 2016, 208.

1823 See e.g. Boulanger and others, Assessing, 2014, 19.

1824 C-301/15 – Soulier, AG opinion, par. 64; SWD(2016) 301 final, IA Part I, 2016, 68; Janssens and Tryggvadóttir, Orphan, 2016, 204, 207; Oostveen and Guibault, IPR issues, 2013, 6.

1825 Triaille and others, Study, 2013, 304–305; Janssens and Tryggvadóttir, Orphan, 2016, 207–208; Suthersanen and Frabboni, The Orphan, 2014, 662.

1826 Boulanger and others, Assessing, 2014, 23; Janssens and Tryggvadóttir, Orphan, 2016, 207; SWD(2016) 301 final, IA Part I, 2016, 68.

1827 Norwegian National Library, Response, 2013, 24.

1828 Cf. e.g. European Commission, Report on the responses, 2014, 52.

1829 Ronan Deazley and Victoria Stobo, *Archives and Copyright: Risk and Reform*, (10 April 2013) 48–49.

1830 Janssens and Tryggvadóttir, Orphan, 2016, 207.

1831 See discussion on the Bokhylla Agreement in Ch. 5.3.1.4.

out of commerce and hence of less economic importance for rightholders.[1832] At the same time the opt-out possibility should secure the position of rightholders of older works that are still economically viable.[1833]

The MoU was described as "pragmatic and realistic" at the time of signing.[1834] However, although it has influenced to some extent legislation in a number of Member States it has not been widely used.[1835] This is probably because it needs legal backing to create sufficient legal certainty for public institutions such as libraries.

456. The objectives of the MoU with regard to outsiders can be achieved through various methods of legislative support to collective management, such as ECL or mandatory collective management in addition to the presumption of management, as is exemplified in the following account of national legislation of some of the EU Member States.

7.2. FRANCE

457. The now defunct[1836] French legislation "on the Digital Exploitation of Unavailable Books[1837] of the Twentieth Century"[1838] was enacted in March 2012.[1839] It was intended to solve issues relating to digital rights for published books of the twentieth century and was presented as a response to the failed Google Books agreement. The legislation was prepared concurrently with the negotiation of the MoU on out-of-commerce works.[1840]

1832 See discussion and references in Ch. 10.2.3.

1833 Tryggvadóttir, Digital libraries, 2014, 324–325; Janssens and Tryggvadóttir, Facilitating, 2015, 92–93; Janssens and Tryggvadóttir, Orphan, 2016, 207; US Copyright Office, Mass Digitization, 2015, 86–87.

1834 James Boyd, Stakeholders sign groundbreaking MoU on Out of Commerce Works, IFRRO, 20 September 2011; accessed 11 July 2017.

1835 SWD(2016) 301 final, IA Part I, 2016, 68.

1836 See Ch. 7.2.3.

1837 The legislation is limited to books and does not cover any other type of works, cf. observation in C-301/15 – Soulier, AG opinion, fn. 7. However, the correct terminology would be "works published in books", cf. Bulayenko, Permissibility, 2016, 53.

1838 This is the literal translation. However, the term "out-of-commerce books" is more in line with the actual aim of the legislation, cf. Bulayenko, Permissibility, 2016, 52. Thus I will use that term for the legislation.

1839 Loi n° 2012-287 du 1er mars 2012 relative à l'exploitation numérique des livres indisponibles du XXe siècle. The Act introduced Art. 134-1 to 134-9 into the French Code of Intellectual Property (hereafter FCIP or the French legislation).

1840 C-301/15 – Soulier, AG opinion, par. 62; Lucie Guibault, France solves its XXe century book problem!, Kluwer Copyright Blog, 13 April 2012; accessed 11 July 2017; Sylvie Nérisson, Opinion of AG Wathelet in the Soulier and Doke case (C-301/15): Licensing exclusive rights requires express prior consent of the author; opt-out doesn't help, Kluwer Copyright Blog, accessed 11 July 2017.

7.2.1. THE LEGISLATION

458. The law imposed the obligation upon the French National Library to create a database of all books published in France[1841] before 2001, not available in print or digital form.[1842] The database was to be compiled by comparing the collection of the National Library with information from databases of commercially available books. In addition, anyone could enter relevant books into the database. The National Library was responsible for updating the database annually[1843] and managing the online platform operating the Registry of Out-of-Commerce Books in Electronic Publishing.[1844] It was estimated the project would eventually cover around 500,000 works.[1845]

459. The right to authorise the use of the books in the database was to be exercised by a CMO approved for that purpose by the Ministry of Culture and Communication. Approval of such a CMO was i.a. dependant on equal representation of authors and publishers, both as members and within the executive bodies.[1846] The CMO[1847] authorised by the Ministry[1848] fulfilled that requirement and claimed to represent 85% of French book sales.[1849] However, its mandate to digitize and make available the out-of-commerce books did not stem from its members but from the legislation.[1850]

460. There were two levels of opt-out possibilities from the scheme.[1851] Firstly, authors and publishers had a period of six months in which to opt

---

1841 The wording covered all books published in France, but in practice the system was not applied to translated works, cf. Bulayenko, Permissibility, 2016, 66–67.

1842 Art. 134-2 FCIP.

1843 Ginsburg, Fair Use, 2014, 1426; Janssens and Tryggvadóttir, Orphan, 2016, 205; Sganga, The eloquent, 2017, 323.

1844 The database ReLIRE (registre des livres indisponibles en réédition éléctronique) is avaible at <relire.bnf.fr>, last viewed 9 May 2018. However, since June 2017 the National Library only ensures the maintenance of the database.

1845 <www.senat.fr/dossier-legislatif/ppl11-054.html>, last viewed 23 June 2016; European Commission, Report, 2016, 39; Bulayenko, Permissibility, 2016, 54; Sganga, The eloquent, 2017, 323. In September 2016 the list covered 204,000 books. No books were added in 2017 in anticipation of the decision of the *conseil d'État* in the wake of the CJEU decision in the Soulier case, cf. <relire.bnf.fr>, last viewed 29 March 2017.

1846 Art. 134-3 FCIP; C-301/15 – Soulier, AG opinion, par. 10; C-301/15 – Soulier, par. 14; Sganga, The eloquent, 2017, 324.

1847 Société Française des Intérêts des Auteurs de l'Ecrit (SOFIA).

1848 Order by the Ministry of Culture and Communication of 21 March 2013.

1849 Bulayenko, Permissibility, 2016, 53–54, 65–66; Janssens and Tryggvadóttir, Orphan, 2016, 205; US Copyright Office, Mass Digitization, 2015, 26–27; C-301/15 – Soulier, AG opinion, par. 15; C-301/15 – Soulier, par. 22; Guibault, Cultural, 2015, 177–178.

1850 C-301/15 – Soulier, AG opinion, fn. 4, cf. par. 23 and fn. 31, 42; Ginsburg, Fair Use, 2014, 1428–1429; Sganga, The eloquent, 2017, 324, 327.

1851 Sganga, The eloquent, 2017, 324.

out following the entry of the work into the database; *a priori* opt-out.[1852] There were different rules for authors and publishers. The opt-out by authors was unconditional whereas publishers had to make the work commercially available within two years after they opted out.[1853] This conditional opt-out for publishers, i.e. that they had to exercise their right in order for the opt-out to be effective, was criticised.[1854] Secondly, there was an *a posteriori* opt-out which provided for different scenarios. First, authors could oppose the reproduction and communication to the public of their book at any time if they considered that it would adversely affect their reputation.[1855] Second, the author and publisher jointly, or authors on their own, if they provided evidence that they held the digital rights to the work alone[1856], could at any time "withdraw" the right of reproduction and communication to the public from the CMO.[1857] This condition on the opt-out by authors was criticised by scholars and by the CJEU.[1858]

461. If publishers and authors failed to opt-out *a priori* or if only publishers opted-out and then failed to make the work available, the CMO was entitled to offer licences to digitise and make available books that had been in the database for more than six months, subject to remuneration.[1859] There were no deliberations on how the level of remuneration should be established but it was stipulated that it should be equitably distributed between the author and the publisher.[1860] There was no requirement that use under such licences should be non-commercial. This was in line with the MoU, which does not explicitly stipulate that uses under agreements based on the MoU should be non-commercial. However, unlike the MoU, which is aimed at uses by publicly accessible cultural institutions[1861] that are usually not for commercial

---

1852 This period was criticised as being too short, cf. Bulayenko, Permissibility, 2016, 57.

1853 Ginsburg, Fair Use, 2014, 1426; US Copyright Office, Mass Digitization, 2015, 26; Sganga, The eloquent, 2017, 324.

1854 US Copyright Office, Mass Digitization, 2015, 27; Ginsburg, Fair Use, 2014, 1429.

1855 Art. 134-4 FCIP. In the Soulier case authors asserted that it was highly improbable that an adverse effect could be proven, whereas the French Government submitted that it would be enough for authors simply to plead such injury without further proof, cf. C-301/15 – Soulier, AG opinion, fn. 29.

1856 C-301/15 – Soulier, par. 46–51; Bulayenko, Permissibility, 2016, 58; Sganga, The eloquent, 2017, 324.

1857 Art. 134-6 FCIP; C-301/15 – Soulier, AG opinion, par. 18; Ginsburg, Fair Use, 2014, 1427. However, successors in title could not oppose the continuation of use that had commenced before the opposition, cf. Art. 134-6(5) FCIP.

1858 C-301/15 – Soulier, par. 50–51; Sganga, The eloquent, 2017, 324.

1859 Art. 134-3 I FCIP; Janssens and Tryggvadóttir, Orphan, 2016, 205.

1860 Art. 134-3 III 5 FCIP; Ginsburg, Fair Use, 2014, 1426. Royalty rates were approved by an ordinary General Assembly of SOFIA in June 2014 as 15–20% of sales or revenues, cf. Bulayenko, Permissibility, 2016, 55.

1861 See Ch. 7.1, par. 477.

purposes[1862], the French legislation was not limited to such beneficiaries but was in fact aimed at commercial licences.[1863]

462. The legislation provided different levels of licensing schemes.[1864] First, the CMO was required to offer the original print publisher a ten-year automatically renewable exclusive licence. If the publisher accepted they had three years to make the book available in digital form.[1865] The author could, however, oppose the granting of the exclusive licence to the publishers if they provided evidence "by any means" that the publisher did not have the right to publish the book in printed format.[1866] This procedure could be said to be in line with the MoU insistence that rightholders should always have the first option to digitise and make available an out-of-commerce work.[1867] However, the provision put publishers in a stronger position vis-à-vis authors as publishers could be offered an exclusive licence to digitise and make a digital copy available without the author's consent. Not surprisingly this was very controversial.[1868] Second, in the event the publisher declined the offer or failed to meet this deadline the CMO could offer any interested party five-year, non-exclusive renewable licences.[1869] Thus libraries and other parties potentially interested in digitising and making available out-of-commerce books were excluded, unless the original publisher declined or failed to make the books digitally available. Under both sets of licensing schemes the CMO had to take appropriate measures to identify and locate rightholders.[1870]

A third level of licencing was foreseen in the legislation. If no rightholder was identified for a particular work, despite diligent search, after it had been ten years in the database, the work was to be deemed orphan and libraries would have been able to use the work for non-commercial purposes, royalty free, for their subscribers.[1871] However, this scheme was revoked in February 2015 without having been applied in practice when the Orphan Works Directive was implemented into French legislation.[1872]

1862 See discussion on what constitutes institutions or uses "not for direct or indirect economic or commercial advantage" in Ch. 4.2.2.1, par. 182.

1863 This was i.a. highlighted by the CJEU, which concluded that the implicit consent of authors could not be presumed in the absence of opt-out for *commercial* (my emphasis) use in a digital format, see C-301/15 – Soulier, par. 44, 46. Furthermore, AG Wathelet underlined that, unlike the Orphan Works Directive, the legislation was concerned with the commercial exploitation of out-of-print books, cf. C-301/15 – Soulier, AG opinion, par. 53; Guibault, Cultural, 2015, 184; Sganga, The eloquent, 2017, 326.

1864 Bulayenko, Permissibility, 2016, 54–55.

1865 Art. 134–5 FCIP.

1866 Art. 134–5(5) FCIP.

1867 See Recital (6) MoU.

1868 Guibault, Cultural, 2015, 180; Ginsburg, Fair Use, 2014, 1427–1428; Sganga, The eloquent, 2017, 327.

1869 Art. 134–5(6) and Art. 134–3 I; US Copyright Office, Mass Digitization, 2015, 26.

1870 Art. 134–3 III 6 FCIP.

1871 Art. 134–8 FCIP; Ginsburg, Fair Use, 2014, 1427; US Copyright Office, Mass Digitization, 2015, 26.

1872 Art. 3, para II of the Loi n° 2015–195 du 20 février 2015 portant diverses dispositions d'adaptation au droit de l'Union européenne dans les domaines de la propriété littéraire

463. In October 2013 the database contained just over 63,000 works and 5,760 opt-outs were received, nearly 10% of the books in the database. In 2014 and 2015 the number of opt-outs diminished. The number of books in the database in 2015 was approximately 100,000 and the sum of opt outs just over 6,300 which makes around 6.3% of the books in the database at the time.[1873]

7.2.2. COURT CASES

464. The legislation was controversial from the start.[1874] In May 2013 two authors, Mr. Soulier and Ms. Doke[1875], sought an annulment from the French Council of State[1876] claiming that the legislation constituted misuse of state power and was inconsistent with the InfoSoc Directive. The French Constitutional Court came to the conclusion in February 2014 that the legislation neither entailed deprivation of property nor constituted a disproportionate interference with it, in the light of the public interest pursued by the legislature and was thus consistent with the Constitution.[1877] The Council of State then referred the question of the legislation's consistency with the InfoSoc Directive to the CJEU.[1878] In November 2016 the CJEU concluded that the legislation was inconsistent with Art. 2(a) and 3(1) of the InfoSoc Directive.[1879]

7.2.3. THE AFTERMATH

465. The ReLIRE database was put on hold following the CJEU decision, awaiting the decision of the Conseil d'État.[1880] In June 2017 the Council of State declared the decree implementing the relevant provisions[1881] in the French Code

et artistique et du patrimoine culturel (1), JORF n°0045, 22 February 2015, cf. Bulayenko, Permissibility, 2016, 54, 56; Sganga, The eloquent, 2017, 327.

1873 Bulayenko, Permissibility, 2016, 58, and the homepage of SOFIA, cf. <www.la-sofialivresindisponibles.org/2015/demandes_sortie_auteur.php?PHPSESSID=e3e162d1ec73c33ebb506d4706aa5bae>, last viewed 21 March 2017.

1874 Ibid, 51; Catherine Jasserand, Will out-of-commerce books soon be managed by a collective management society in France?, Kluwer Copyright Blog, 6 November 2011; accessed 11 July 2017.

1875 Later joined by authors' organisations and other authors in support of their claims. The CMO SOFIA also intervened seeking to have their claims dismissed, cf. C-301/15 – Soulier, par. 20–22.

1876 Conseil d'État.

1877 Decision No. 213-370 QPC of 28 February 2014; C-301/15 – Soulier, AG opinion, par. 16; Guibault, Cultural, 2015, 180; Bulayenko, Permissibility, 2016, 51–52.

1878 C-301/15 – Soulier, par. 1–2; C-301/15 – Soulier, AG opinion, par. 12–20.

1879 C-301/15 – Soulier, par. 52. See discussion of the case in Ch. 11.2.

1880 Cf. <relire.bnf.fr>, last viewed 9 May 2018. Since June 2017 the National Library only ensures the maintenance of the database.

1881 Art. 134-1 to 134-9 FCIP.

of Intellectual Property invalid due to misuse of power.[1882] The question remains whether the Soulier case will affect other national projects aiming to make the cultural heritage available based on collective management with legislative support, as many fear.[1883] I argue that it is only applicable to the particular French legislation in question and hence does not affect other projects unless they have the same flaws, see discussion in Ch. 11.2 below.

7.3. UNITED KINGDOM

466. The UK adopted an ECL system in 2014 after a long process.[1884] This was done through secondary legislation[1885] under the Enterprise and Regulatory Reform Act 2013 (ERR Act), which gave the Secretary of the State the power to authorise a licensing body to grant ECLs under regulation thereof.[1886] The UK ECL provision is similar to the general ECL provisions in the Nordic countries.[1887] According to the ERR Act each authorisation must specify to which types of works and what uses the authorisation applies[1888] and the regulations must ensure an opt-out possibility.[1889] Any licence under an authorisation must be non-exclusive.[1890] However, the ERR Act sets no limitations on whether an ECL scheme can apply to published or non-published works, or on which users can benefit from such a scheme, or on which types of uses can be authorised, commercial or non-commercial.[1891] After the adoption of the Act the UK Government conducted a consultation on the ECL schemes in 2013[1892] and published a report on the consultation[1893] before adopting the Regulation in 2014. Below is a short account of the system.

1882 Decision No. 368208 of 7 June 2017.

1883 See e.g. Sganga, The eloquent, 2017, 321, 330.

1884 Attempts to introduce an ECL system in the UK can be traced back to 2006, cf. Andrew Gowers, *Gowers Review of Intellectual Property*, (December 2006); IPO, @the way ahead, 2009, 5, 38–40; Hargreaves, Digital Opportunity, 2011, 8, 38–40; Mendis and Stobo, Extended, 2016, 209–211.

1885 The Copyright and Rights in Performances (Extended Collective Licensing) Regulations (SI 2014/2588) of 11th of September 2014. Hereafter "the Regulation" or "CRPR". The Regulation came into force on 1st October 2014, cf. Art. 1.

1886 Clause 77(3) ERR Act with the inclusion of Section 116B into the Copyright and Designs Patents Act (CDPA). The Secretary of the State was also given the authority to appoint a body or bodies to license orphan works through secondary legislation, cf. Clause 77(3) ERR Act by inclusion of Section 116A into the CDPA.

1887 Prop. 69 L, Proposisjon, 2015, 15; Riis, Rognstad and Schovsbo, Collective Agreements, 2016, 70.

1888 Section 116B(2) CDPA; Art. 4(2) CRPR.

1889 Section 116B(3) CDPA; Art. 4(4)(d) CRPR.

1890 Section 116B(4) CDPA; Art. 17(1) CRPR.

1891 US Copyright Office, Mass Digitization, 2015, 89.

1892 IPO, *Extending the benefits of collective licensing; Consultation on the UK's new extended collective licensing scheme*, (28 November 2013 – 28 January 2014).

1893 IPO, Government, 2014, *op.cit.* fn. 48.

7.3.1. RELEVANT LICENSING BODY

467. The Regulation defines the relevant terms applicable to the ECL system. The definition of a "relevant licensing body" restricts such a body to a traditional CMO.[1894] The CMO must fulfil several requirements to be granted authorisation.[1895] First, the relevant CMO must already be collectively licensing works of the type the proposed ECL will cover[1896]; second, the CMO must have "significant" representation in the type of work relevant for the proposed ECL[1897]; third, the code of practice of the CMO must be consistent with the specified criteria including the criteria concerning the protection of outsiders[1898]; fourth, there must be adequate opt-out arrangements to protect the interest of rightholders[1899]; fifth, there must be satisfactory arrangements for publicising the scheme, for contacting outsiders in order to distribute the net licence fees and for distributing any net licence fees which remain undistributed, which are appropriate for the proposed scheme, having regard to the interests of outsiders.[1900] Finally the CMO must obtain consent from its members for the proposed ECL.[1901] Any CMO that applies for an ECL scheme is required to supply the Secretary of State with evidence of the fulfilment of all these conditions in the application.[1902]

7.3.2. PRIOR COLLECTIVE LICENSING

468. The first condition requiring the CMO to already be collectively licensing the type of works that the extension effect applied to spurred a discussion of whether there should be a certain minimum time period for that collective licence to have been in force. In the end, such time limits were not made obligatory as it was felt that other safeguards, such as the requirement of significant representation and of informed consent were sufficient.[1903] Thus a CMO can enter into a collective agreement for a certain type of works and then immediately apply for an authorisation to have it extended to outsiders under an ECL scheme. As mentioned above there is no limitation in the legislation as

1894 Cf. Art 2 CRPR which refers to Art. 116(2) CDPA which provides that "a "licensing body" means a society or other organisation which has as its main object, or one of its main objects, the negotiation or granting, either as owner or prospective owner of copyright or as agent for him, of copyright licences, and whose objects include the granting of licences covering works of more than one author." See IPO, Extending, 2013, 7.

1895 Art. 4(4) CRPR; Guibault, Cultural, 2015, 179.

1896 Art. 4(4)(a) and 5(1)(l) CRPR.

1897 Art. 4(4)(b) and 5(1)(i) CRPR.

1898 Art. 4(4)(c) and 5(1)(l) CRPR.

1899 Art. 4(4)(d) and 5(1)(g) CRPR.

1900 Art. 4(4)(e) and 5(1)(r) CRPR.

1901 Art. 4(4)(f) and 5(1)(j-k) CRPR.

1902 Art. 5 CRPR.

1903 IPO, Government, 2014, 4.

to which types of works, published or un-published, or for which types of use, commercial or non-commercial, an ECL agreement could be used for.

7.3.3. REPRESENTATIVENESS

469. The second condition regarding the representativeness of the CMO is at the heart of the UK ECL scheme, as it is in the Nordic model from where the terminology "significant" is drawn. The CMO must thus demonstrate evidence of mandates from a "significant" number of rightholders.[1904] The preparatory document stated that the criteria for demonstrating representativeness should be flexible but that the relevant CMOs would have to show that they had made all reasonable efforts to determine the number of rightholders and works. While the existence of two CMOs in the same field would inevitably raise the question of representativeness, the fact that there was only one CMO operating in the field would not automatically prove that it was representative.[1905]

The effort necessary for providing evidence of significant representation will vary depending on whether the CMO manages a previous collective licensing scheme in the area or not. As an example the Guidance for CMOs applying for ECL schemes mentions:

> ...the case of a library wanting to digitise and display to the public an archive containing 1000 out of print works, the collective management organisation would need to demonstrate that it represented a significant number of the rights holders in the works. This might be a difficult threshold to reach unless each work was looked at to see who the rights holders were; thereafter, the collective management organisation would need to check whether or not it held the relevant rights of the identified rights holders, and if it did not it would have to secure these rights from a significantly representative number.[1906]

This seems to be an almost insurmountable task for any large collection, i.e. to have to determine for each and every work whether the rightholder is represented by the CMO or not before the conclusion of an ECL agreement. In fact this could face similar challenges as the diligent search requirement under the Orphan Works Directive, i.e. it would be too time consuming and costly to be practicable. One argument in the Nordic countries for the ECL system is the need for a licensing mechanism in situations where it is difficult or impossible to predict which works will be used.[1907] Having to determine beforehand which works will be used

---

1904 IPO, Extending, 2013, 7–8; IPO, Government, 2014, 1, 4–5, 7.

1905 IPO, Government, 2014, 5; Guibault, Cultural, 2015, 178;; Mendis and Stobo, Extended, 2016, 211.

1906 IPO, *Extended Collective Licensing (ECL): Guidance for relevant licensing bodies applying to run ECL schemes*, 2.

1907 See e.g. Prop. 69 L, Proposisjon, 2015, 19; Prop. 2012/13:141, Regeringens proposition, 2013, 54–55.

and who the rightholders are diminishes the usefulness of an ECL agreement considerably. Furthermore, assessing the representation only with regard to a small part of a library collection may make the requirement more difficult to fulfil than if it covers the whole collection. A CMO may represent a significant part of rightholders of print works as a whole but when looking at a certain part of a collection, in particular out-of-commerce works, it may be more difficult or even impossible to provide evidence of significant representation of that particular part. Thus in the Nordic countries the requirement of representativeness or a "substantial number" of authors is not interpreted to mean "substantial number" of rightholders of works used by an individual licensee but as representative of rightholders in regard to the specific type of works used in the country as a whole.

This interpretation of the representativeness requirement in the UK legislation may show in a nutshell how difficult the issue can be in countries where there may not be a culture of collective organisation of rightholders.[1908] It also highlights the problem of using ECLs in an area where there is unlikely to be any collective representation of rightholders, such as in archives consisting of private documents or unpublished material.

7.3.4. CODE OF PRACTICE

470. The third condition implies that the code of practice of the relevant CMO must "ensure clear governance, improve transparency and provide clear and concise information to users, members and non-members alike."[1909] As a matter of principle members and non-members should be treated alike. However, that does not need to be extended to the contractual benefits of membership.[1910] Furthermore, it is not excluded that deductions for non-members could be higher than for members, to meet the costs of the ECL scheme. However, such a difference would have to be explained and justified clearly in the distribution policy of the CMO. The deductions, albeit possibly higher, must still be reasonable and qualify as fair treatment of outsiders.[1911]

7.3.5. OPT-OUT ARRANGEMENTS

471. The fourth condition regarding the obligation to have adequate opt-out arrangements[1912] applies mainly to outsiders as the Regulation only guarantees

1908 Riis and Schovsbo, ECLs, 2010, 495.
1909 Dinusha Mendis and Victoria Stobo, UK: Extended Collective Licensing, Kluwer Copyright Blog, 3 December 2014; accessed 11 July 2017.
1910 IPO, Government, 2014, 11.
1911 Ibid, 36; IPO, ECL Guidance 2016, 2016, 13.
1912 Art. 4(4)(d) and 5(1)(g) CRPR.

them the right to opt-out. This is spelled out in a later provision which provides that members can only opt-out if their contract with the CMO or the collective licence agreement allows them to.[1913]

The CMO must draw up, maintain and make available to the public a list of rightholders that have opted-out and of the works that have been identified as opted-out, within 14 days of the receipt of the opt-out notice, as well as notifying any relevant user.[1914] In the preparatory documents it is suggested that the obvious place to make the list available to the public is the website of the CMO.[1915]

The Government has made a commitment that opting-out will be free, or at a minimum cost. Hence there is no requirement that rightholders list the specific works they wish to opt-out, as that would require some effort on the rightholders' part, their only obligation being to provide their name when opting-out. If rightholders do not identify or list the specific works they wish to opt-out of the agreement, it may mean that no list of specific works will be provided, as the CMOs are not obliged to research or compile such a list. Nevertheless, it is expected that one or other of these parties would compile such a list, as it would make it less likely that the relevant opted-out works would be used illegally. In the absence of such a list licensees would have to do the checking themselves.[1916]

The 2014 Government report underlines that if opt-outs become too numerous this may affect the question of representativeness.[1917]

7.3.6. TRANSPARENCY AND DISTRIBUTION OF LICENCE FEES

472. The fifth condition makes obligatory the publication of the scheme and arrangements for the distribution of fees to non-members and of undistributed fees with regard to the interest of outsiders.

473. The key principle with regard to the publicity will be proportionality, in particular with regard to publicising the schemes abroad, where there may be very few outsiders. The apparent place to publicise an ECL scheme is on websites of the relevant CMOs, their sister organisations and relevant international organisations such as WIPO, IFRRO and EUIPO.[1918]

Before an authorisation is issued to a CMO for an ECL scheme it must be publicised for at least 28 days in advance in a manner likely to gain the attention of those that may be affected by it and allow for comments from these parties.

1913 Art. 16(3)(c) CRPR; IPO, Government, 2014, 28–29.
1914 Art. 16(4) and (6) CRPR.
1915 IPO, Extending, 2013, 15.
1916 IPO, Government, 2014, 31–32.
1917 Ibid, 17–18. See also discussion in Ch. 5.4.5.
1918 Ibid, 17; IPO, ECL Guidance 2016, 2016, 14–16.

Furthermore, the decision to grant an authorisation must be published in an appropriate manner.[1919]

474. The CMO must contact non members who have been identified and located as soon as possible after the conclusion of the financial year for which a licence fee is collected, and no later than 9 months thereafter, in order to distribute to them their part of the licence fee. If they cannot be located the amount must be deposited in a designated account.[1920] The effort expended on finding outside rightholders should be proportionate to the amount the CMO holds for that rightholder.[1921] Furthermore, the CMO is required to make public information, for example on their website, about works that are licensed under the scheme but where the rightholders are either not known or not located, within three months after the end of the financial year in which the licence fee was collected.[1922] Thus it is expected that an ECL scheme could include orphan works, i.e. searches for an outsider could reveal that the work was in fact orphan. Nevertheless, the rule of significant representation entails that the majority of works in the scheme could not be orphans.[1923]

As under ordinary collective licensing schemes, part of the administrative fee collected by the CMO may be used for the collective benefits of members, such as for political advocacy and scholarships. In such cases the benefits of non-members and members alike should be considered.[1924]

475. In addition to being entitled to the same portion of the licence fee as members, an outsider can request an adjustment to such remuneration within three years after the end of the financial year for which the licence fee was collected. In making such a request the outsider must provide evidence of what a reasonable licence fee should be and/or evidence of the level of use of the works in question.[1925] This seems to go beyond provisions under the Nordic ECL system with regard to individual remuneration for outsiders, which are only applicable in case of collective distribution of licence fees.[1926] Not surprisingly many stakeholders, both CMOs and potential users, were critical of this possibility and maintained that it undermined the central principle of collective licensing. However, the Government maintained this option was necessary for compliance with international norms, while underlining that it would be difficult to overturn

1919 Art. 7 and 8(5) CRPR; Mendis and Stobo, Extended, 2016, 213.
1920 Art. 18(3) CRPR. There are further provisions about the handling of non-distributed licence fees in Art. 19 CRPR.
1921 IPO, Government, 2014, 38.
1922 Art. 18(5) CRPR; IPO, ECL Guidance 2016, 2016, 17. The wording of the provision is in line with the CMO Directive, cf. IPO, Government, 2014, 38.
1923 IPO, Government, 2014, 41.
1924 Art. 18(1) and (2) CRPR; ibid, 36.
1925 Art. 18(4) CRPR; ibid, 37.
1926 See Ch. 5.4.2, par. 363.

the collective rate.[1927] Nevertheless, in the event that an outsider succeeded in challenging the collective rate, the CMO would end up having to pay an outsider more than the user under the agreement was actually paying for the use.

7.3.7. INFORMED CONSENT

476. The sixth and final condition regards the consent required from members of the CMO in regard to the proposed ECL agreement. The argument for the requirement is that it further provides evidence of the rightholders' mandate to the CMO, in particular in cases where rightholders assign rights to the CMO by virtue of standard contracts. In such cases rightholders may not be fully aware of the rights they have assigned, especially in areas where the CMO is not actively licensing those rights.[1928] The requirement of the CMO Directive that a rightholder provides specific consent for each and every right or category of right which he authorises the CMO to manage[1929] seems likely to eliminate this situation and hence the need for such consent from members.

The requirement of consent in the Regulation is defined as an "informed consent of a substantial proportion of the members of the relevant licensing body who vote on the proposal".[1930] This demands, according to the Government's response, that more than 75% of those that vote should be in favour of the ECL scheme. Although not spelled out in the definition or elsewhere in the Regulation, the threshold for what is substantial is higher when the authorisation concerns a CMO that does not have pre-existing collective licensing in the relevant field.[1931] Acquiring informed consent is expected to be a costly process for the CMOs and, therefore, will only be required for the initial application. Even so, the Secretary of State retains the power at any time to ask for information relating to the ECL scheme[1932], including a renewed informed consent, if there is concern that members no longer support the scheme.[1933] The need for such recourse seems unlikely as if members become dissatisfied with an ECL scheme they can withdraw from it under the rules of the CMO Directive.[1934] An increasing or high rate of withdrawal should be sufficient evidence for lack of support.

477. In connection with the requirement of "informed consent" of members it is worth noting that members of foreign CMOs with which the relevant UK

1927 IPO, Government, 2014, 37.
1928 IPO, Extending, 2013, 7.
1929 Cf. Art. 5(7) CMO Directive.
1930 Art. 2 CRPR; IPO, ECL Guidance 2016, 2016, 6.
1931 IPO, Government, 2014, 6; IPO, ECL Guidance 2016, 2016, 7.
1932 Art. 20 CRPR.
1933 IPO, Government, 2014, 20.
1934 Cf. Art. 5(4) COM Directive.

CMO has a reciprocal agreement are neither members of the UK based CMO in the terms of voting rights nor are they non-members or outsiders as defined in the Regulation.[1935] Their works can, nevertheless, fall under an ECL scheme. The members of a foreign CMO that the scheme applies to will be remunerated in the same way as others under the scheme and they will be able to opt-out and have the same protection as other non-members. This, according to the preparatory documents, will put members of a foreign CMO in a better position than previously under UK collective licensing schemes.[1936]

7.3.8. AUTHORISATION PERIOD AND REVIEWS

478. An authorisation for operating an ECL scheme is awarded for five years unless it is revoked or cancelled and can be renewed, either for a fixed term or until it is revoked or cancelled.[1937] The renewed authorisation is then subject to a review every three years thereafter, while it is in force.[1938] Many potential users under the scheme criticised the five year authorisation period as too short to get digitisation projects off the ground.[1939] However, the Government felt that the initial authorisation period, akin to a pilot, should be short. The renewal process would be an opportunity to take stock and audit the scheme, and in the opinion of the Government that was better done sooner than later. Thus the initial authorisation period remains five years.[1940]

479. There does not seem to be any dispute resolution process for users and CMOs negotiating an ECL agreement in case of disagreement regarding licence terms and rates. Furthermore, there is no appeal other than judicial review with regard to the decision to authorise a CMO to manage an ECL agreement.[1941]

7.3.9. EVALUATION

480. The UK Intellectual Property Office had only received one ECL application by May 2018.[1942] This hesitant start may partly be due to the complexity of the system, which cultural heritage institutions think will hinder its use for any large

---

1935 Art. 2 CRPR.

1936 IPO, Extending, 2013, 9.

1937 Art. 4(6), 9, 14 and 15 CRPR.

1938 Art. 11 CRPR.

1939 E.g. the British Library and the Wellcome Trust, see consultation responses, available at <https://www.gov.uk/government/consultations/extending-the-benefits-of-collective-licensing>, accessed 10 July 2017.

1940 IPO, Government, 2014, 19–21.

1941 Ibid, 16.

1942 The Copyright Licensing Agency (CLA) applied in October 2017 for an ECL to licence the copying of extracts from books, journals, magazines and websites whether published in hard copy form or electronically in the education, business and public administration sectors.

scale digitisation.[1943] The requirements that CMO must fulfil to be authorised to manage an ECL scheme, in particular with regard to representativeness and informed consent of members, certainly seem to be more onerous than in the Nordic countries. Furthermore, although not expressly explicitly in the legislation, the UK ECL scheme is geographically limited to use of works within the UK.[1944] Some of the issues may though be resolved once the system is up and running.

7.4. GERMANY

481. The German Copyright Administration Act (GCAA)[1945] was amended in 2013[1946] to enable the digitisation and making available of out-of-commerce works on comparable principles as the MoU on out-of-commerce works.[1947] This Act was superseded in 2016 by the Act implementing the CMO Directive[1948] but the relevant provisions are unchanged. The provisions adopted are based on the legal presumption[1949], underlying legislative support for collective licences commonly used in Germany with regard to outsiders[1950], that unless otherwise proven a relevant CMO is presumed to administer the rights of all rightholders in the relevant area.[1951]

482. The provisions relate to works that have been published in 'books, journals, newspapers, magazines or other writings'[1952] before 1 January 1966[1953]

Available documents regarding the application can be accessed on <https://www.gov.uk/government/consultations/application-to-operate-an-ecl-scheme>, last viewed 9 May 2018.

1943 European Commission, Report, 2016, 39; Samuelson, Comments, 2015, 10.

1944 Mendis and Stobo, UK: ECL, Kluwer Copyright Blog; Sterling, World Copyright Law, 2015, 631; European Commission, Report, 2016, 39; IPO, Extending, 2013, 9.

1945 Das Urheberrechtswahrnehmungsgesetz vom 9. September 1965 as amended by Law of October 26, 2007 (hereafter 'GCAA').

1946 Act of 1 October 2013 'zur Nutzung verwaister und vergriffener Werke und einer weiteren Änderung des Urheberrechtsgesetzes' (BGBl. I 2013, S. 3728 (Nr. 59)), amending the GCAA.

1947 The adopted solution had, however, been elaborated on by stakeholders in Germany before the signing of the MoU, cf. Silke Von Lewinski, 'Recent Developments of German Author's Rights Law – Part I', 2015, (2), Auteurs & Média, 158–169, 159.

1948 Gesetz zur Umsetzung der Richtlinie 2014/26/EU über die kollektive Wahrnehmung von Urheber- und verwandten Schutzrechten und die Vergabe von Mehrgebietslizenzen für Rechte an Musikwerken für die Online-Nutzung im Binnenmarkt sowie zur Änderung des Verfahrens betreffend die Geräte- und Speichermedienvergütung (VG-Richtlinie-Umsetzungsgesetz), cf. Gesetzes vom 24.05.2016 (BGBl. I S. 1190) which came into force 01.06.2016 (VG-Richtlinie Act), see §51 and 52 of the new Act which are identical to §13d and 13e GCA.

1949 See discussion on legal presumption in Ch. 9.2.

1950 Jörg Reinbothe, 'Collective Management in Germany' in Daniel Gervais (ed), *Collective Management of Copyright and Related Rights* (2 edn, Kluwer Law International, 2010) 237.

1951 §13c(1) and (2) GCAA, see now §48 and 49 VG-Richtlinie Act.

1952 Cf. §51(1)(1) VG-Richtlinie Act. The Act does not specify that the works have to be published in Germany.

1953 Which is the date of the entry into force of the German Copyright Act of 9 September 1965 (GCA), currently in force, cf. Von Lewinski, Recent, 2015, 159.

and which are in a collection of a publicly accessible cultural heritage institution. If such works are entered into a registry of out-of-commerce works maintained by the German Patent and Trademark Office[1954], then it is presumed that the CMO in the relevant field also represents outside rightholders. The relevant CMO can, under the presumption of mandate, license non-commercial uses of such works to third parties, unless the rightholder has opted out within six weeks from a notice of the entry of the work into the registry (*a priori* opt-out).[1955]

483. The German Federal Government and the Federal States signed a Framework Agreement[1956] with the relevant CMO for text and images[1957] for the use of out-of-commerce works based on the 2013 amendment. The Agreement came into force on 1 January 2015 and the German National Library launched a licensing service for out-of-commerce works in autumn 2015.[1958]

The Framework Agreement explicitly provides that it only applies to unavailable works published before 1966 in Germany.[1959] Professional journals, newspapers and periodicals are excluded.[1960] Libraries and other cultural heritage institutions in Germany can apply to enter works from their collections into the register of out-of-commerce work if these works fulfil the criteria for being out-of-commerce. The German National Library operates a search service, free of charge, for the out-of-commerce status of works which the entitled institutions wish to license. The search is done by scanning for the works in "book trade lists" in an automatic search system. Once the out-of-commerce status has been confirmed by the National Library it forwards the application to the relevant CMO. The CMO enters the requested works into the register before issuing the licence. Once the licence is issued the relevant institutions can digitise the works and make them available.[1961] Uses are only allowed for non-commercial purposes[1962] which is a stricter requirement than under the MoU

[1954] §52 VG-Richtlinie Act.
[1955] Cf. §51(1) VG-Richtlinie Act.
[1956] The German title is "Rahmenvertrag zur Nutzung von vergriffenen Werken in Büchern", hereafter Framework Agreement or FA. The FA came into force on January 1, 2015, cf. Art. 12(1).
[1957] The relevant CMOs are VG Wort (for text) and VG Bild-Kunst (for images), cf. the Framework Agreement; European Commission, Report, 2016, 39; see also IFRRO, U.S. Public Consultation: "Mass Digitization Pilot Program", 2015, 5.
[1958] In September 2015, the first licences were issued, cf. the Press Release of the German National Library and VG Wort of 8 October 2015; Samuelson, Comments, 2015, 11.
[1959] Art. 1(1) FA.
[1960] Art. 1(3) FA. This is more limited than in the legislation, which allows for those to be included, cf. §51(1)(1) VG-Richtlinie Act. Another framework agreement is in the pipeline for professional journals, newspapers and periodicals, cf. European Commission, Report, 2016, 39.
[1961] Art. 2, 3 and 4 FA. See information about the service of the National Library at <www.dnb.de/EN/Service/DigitaleDienste/LizenzierungsserviceVW/lizenzierungsserviceVW_node.html>, accessed 11 July 2017.
[1962] §51(1)(3) VG-Richtlinie Act and Art. 2 FA; Guibault, Cultural, 2015, 184.

on out-of-commerce works.[1963] This may negatively affect the interest of private enterprises potentially interested in co-operating in a digitisation project.[1964] The question is whether the wording leaves room for generating revenues to cover costs of digitisation and making available.[1965]

484. There is no express requirement for representativeness of the relevant CMO. Nevertheless the legislation seems to be based on the premises that the relevant CMO already has a mandate from its members to reproduce and make available out-of-commerce works.[1966] Furthermore, CMOs that administer the exclusive rights of authors or other rightholders must be authorised.[1967] In order to be authorised the CMOs i.a. inform the Office of the number of persons that have entrusted them with the administration of their rights.[1968] The authorisation can only be rejected or withdrawn if the statutes of the CMO are not compatible with the law or the CMO is proven not to have the legal or financial capacities to manage the entrusted rights.[1969] As there is no specific requirement in the law for representativeness it is not clear whether there are any consequences of having too little representation.[1970] It might, however, be that a CMO which represented too few parties would be deemed to be financially unviable and thus refused an authorisation.

485. The outside rightholder, to which the legal presumption of mandate applies, enjoys the same rights and obligations as rightholders that have given their mandate to the CMO.[1971] In addition to the *a priori* opt-out possibility the outsider can at any time object to the presumption; *a posteriori* opt-out.[1972] Any opt-out has to be recorded in the registry of out-of-commerce works made public on the website of the Patent and Trademark Office.[1973] Only four opt-outs had been received in April 2017.[1974]

1963 Cf. Principle 1(3) MoU.

1964 Talke, Verwaiste und vergriffene Werke, 2013, 137.

1965 Cf. Art. 6(2) OWD.

1966 Cf. §51 VG-Richtlinie Act; Talke, Verwaiste und vergriffene Werke, 2013, 134.

1967 §77 VG-Richtlinie Act. CMOs established in other EU member states only have to be authorised in certain instances, i.a. for the licencing of out-of-commerce works under §51 VG-Richtlinie Act.

1968 §78 VG-Richtlinie Act.

1969 §79 and 80 VG-Richtlinie Act.

1970 Guibault, Cultural, 2015, 178; Hugenholtz and others, *Extended collective licensing: panacee voor massadigitalisering? Onderzoek in opdracht van het Ministerie van OCW*, (1 September 2014) 54.

1971 §51(4) VG-Richtlinie Act.

1972 §51(1)(5) and 51(2) VG-Richtlinie Act and Art. 2(6) and 5(1) FA.

1973 Cf. §52 VG-Richtlinie Act.

1974 Information from Dr. Katharina Schöneborn at the German National Library, in an e-mail dated 3 April 2017. See also SWD(2016) 301 final, IA Part I, 2016, 75.

486. No mention is made of cross-border use in the enacted provisions on the out-of-commerce works. However, it is clear from the Framework Agreement[1975] that the use intended is for Europeana[1976], as well as digital libraries in Germany, which implies cross-border use.[1977]

487. The relevant institutions are required to inform the CMO of the number of visits to the out-of-commerce works which they have made available.[1978] The remuneration, a one-time fee, varies depending on the age of the work, from 5 euros per work from before the 1920's to 15 euros for works published after 1940.[1979] In March 2017 licences had been granted for just over 12,500 works and licences for another 1,500 works were pending.[1980] Despite some initial doubts as to how the determination of the out-of-commerce status would be defined[1981], the fact that there are hardly any opt-outs seems to suggest that the German system is well received by rightholders. However, the number of licences issued so far is not very high, which may indicate some reluctance to use the system on behalf of the users.

7.5. OTHER INITIATIVES

7.5.1. EUROPE

488. The account above illustrates the range of different approaches used by national legislators within the EU. Other European countries have introduced legislation to enable large-scale digitisation and cross-border accessibility of out-of-commerce works, notably Croatia, Estonia, Hungary, Poland and the Slovak Republic.[1982, 1983] The Netherlands[1984] and the Czech Republic have proposed amendments to their copyright legislation in order to introduce ECL schemes

1975 See the Preamble and Art. 2(4) FA.
1976 See discussion on Europeana in Ch. 2.4.1.
1977 Cf. European Commission, Report, 2016, 39.
1978 Art. 6 FA.
1979 Art. 7(1) FA; Samuelson, Comments, 2015, 11; Guibault, Cultural, 2015, 184.
1980 Information from Dr. Katharina Schöneborn at the German National Library, in an e-mail dated 31 March 2017.
1981 Talke, Verwaiste und vergriffene Werke, 2013, 134.
1982 See an account and criticism of the new Slovakian ECL system, which seems to include a system similar to the general ECL provision in the Nordic countries, in Matej Gera, Extended, 2016, op.cit.*op.cit.*; Martin Husovec and Matej Gera, Slovakia adopts a new Copyright Act: It's a Mixed Bag – Part II, Kluwer Copyright Blog, 10 March 2016; last viewed 26 September 2016. However, there is no accessible translation of the Act into English (or other languages), which makes it difficult for non-Slovak speakers to do a meaningful comparison.
1983 European Commission, Report, 2016, 37–41.
1984 Riis, Rognstad and Schovsbo, Collective Agreements, 2016, 70.

for out-of-commerce works.[1985] It would be interesting to analyse and compare all these different initiatives. However, this lies outside the scope of this project.

7.5.2. OUTSIDE OF EUROPE

489. The ECL system is under consideration in several countries outside Europe.[1986] Although this research concentrates on the situation in Europe it is worth mentioning recent developments in Australia and the USA.

490. In Australia a form of ECLs for libraries for mass digitisation purposes and use of orphan works was considered by the Australian Law Reform Commission (ALRC).[1987] However, in the final report, the ALCR did not recommend the adoption of ECLs. Cultural heritage institutions opposed them, claiming that materials they would like to digitise had little or no economic value and that collective licensing would affect their relationships with creators and their descendants as ECLs would alter their ability to give direct licences.[1988] The ALRC concluded that the adoption of a fair use clause, a limitation on remedies for use of orphan works and the expansion of the preservation clause for cultural institutions would address the needs of cultural heritage institutions and provide an adequate framework for mass digitisation. If licensing solutions were additionally needed, blanket licences might be more efficient than ECLs, as they commonly provide "indemnity for content that are not expressly excluded, rather than requiring licensees to check the mandate in each case."[1989] This seems to be somewhat of a misconception of how at least the Nordic ECL system works, although this understanding of licensees having to check the mandate in each may be based on how the UK ECL system can be interpreted.[1990] However, so far these recommendations have not been incorporated into the Australian Copyright Act.[1991]

491. The US Copyright Office (USCO) proposed in 2015 the introduction of a limited pilot ECL scheme for mass digitisation purposes[1992] similar to the UK

1985 European Commission, Report, 2016, 37–41. The introduction of ECLs in Switzerland has also been discussed, cf. Egloff, Extended, 2014, *op.cit.*

1986 Gervais, Extended Collective Licensing: A Significant Contribution to International Copyright Law and Policy, 2016, 318; Gervais, Collective Mangement, 2010, 21; Wang, Should China adopt, 2010,; Riis, Rognstad and Schovsbo, Collective Agreements, 2016, 70; A positive study on the implementation of ECLs in Canada, cf. Daniel Gervais, *Application of an Extended Collective Licensing Regime in Canada: Principles and Issues Related to Implementation*, (June 2003), was ignored in favour of exceptions in 2012, cf. Gendreau, What's in a Name? Extended Collective Licences in Canada, 2016, 272, 278.

1987 ALRC, Copyright 2013, 2013, 229–234.

1988 ALRC, Copyright and the Digital Economy, 2013, 274.

1989 Ibid, 275. See also ALCRs Recommendations 12–1, 12–2, 13–1 and 13–2, cf. Ibid, 16.

1990 See Ch. 7.3.

1991 Cf. the Australian Copyright Act No. 63, 1968 as subsequently amended up to Act No. 4, 2016.

1992 US Copyright Office, Mass Digitization, 2015, 7–8, 104–105.

ECL scheme[1993], i.a. requiring the consent of the members to the scheme.[1994] However, the proposal was also based on the experience from the discussion and litigation of the Google Settlement Agreements.[1995] The USCO proposed that the ECL solution should, unlike the UK scheme, be limited to certain works, i.e. published[1996] literary works, embedded images[1997] and photographs. Furthermore, it was proposed that the use under an ECL agreement would only be for non-commercial purposes and limited to online use to certain end-users[1998], i.e. not general online use.[1999] Thus, the proposal seemed to have more in common with discussion on the revision of Art. 5(3)(n) of the InfoSoc Directive.[2000]

Similar to the Nordic ECL models, but unlike the UK ECL scheme, the USCO proposal included a non-binding dispute resolution process between negotiating parties on the terms and rates in the agreement.[2001] The licensee would furthermore have to demonstrate that an ECL agreement was necessary to clear rights for the digitisation project, a similar requirement as is found in the Nordic general ECL provisions, implicitly or explicitly. The USCO proposal did not limit which institutional users could benefit from an ECL scheme, thus they could be public and non-commercial entities as well as private and for-profit entities. However, all uses would have had to be for non-profit purposes.[2002] With regard to provisions on the distribution of royalties, the USCO referred to the UK ECL Scheme and the CMO Directive and suggested adoption of rules aligned to those instruments.[2003] USCO suggested that the ECL pilot scheme should contain a safeguard clause providing that nothing in the scheme was intended to affect the scope of fair use.[2004] Finally, USCO suggested that the pilot would run for five years to give Congress the opportunity to review the effectiveness of the ECL scheme.[2005]

492. Several public comments were received during the consultation from all over the world. Some were supportive whereas others were critical.[2006] End of

---

1993 Ibid, 83, fn. 343.
1994 Ibid, 90–91.
1995 See ibid, 85, fn. 350.
1996 Ibid, 84–85.
1997 As it would be too cumbersome to exclude those works and thus would diminish the efficiency of an ECL scheme, cf. Ibid, 87–88.
1998 Ibid, 89–90.
1999 Some obligatory security measures were proposed to secure that limitation, cf. Ibid, 98.
2000 See Ch. 4.2.4.1.1.2.
2001 US Copyright Office, Mass Digitization, 2015, 96–97.
2002 Ibid, 89.
2003 Ibid, 98–100.
2004 Ibid, 101.
2005 Ibid, 102.
2006 83 public comments were received from various organisations and individuals, i.a. from IFRRO and the Swedish National Library, supporting the adoption of an ECL

September 2017 the Register of the Copyrights of the United States of America withdrew the proposal for a limited ECL pilot project, mainly due to lack of interest among stakeholders.[2007]

7.6. CONCLUSION

493. The account above illustrates that those European countries that have implemented national legislation to enable digitisation and online use by libraries and other cultural heritage institutions have used a variety of methods and with different scopes.

494. The French legislation was very controversial and following the CJEU judgement in the Soulier case, has now been declared invalid. The British legislation is most similar to the Nordic ECL system. However, despite the fact that the scope of the legislation is very flexible with regard to users, uses and types of works, it seems that the additional safeguard measures adopted may have led to a reluctance on behalf of users to participate in the system. The German system, which is most limited in scope, seems to be fairly well accepted by rightholders, as indicated by the fact that two years after its adoption negligible opt-outs have been received. However, it is noteworthy that the number of licences issued is relatively low, which may signal some reluctance from users to use the system.

Furthermore, the above account seems to illustrate that there is still some way to go towards universality of a Nordic type ECL system, despite the optimism of the quotation at the beginning of the chapter. However, the recent Commission proposal for an EU solution for out-of-commerce works with cross-border effect, based on either ECL or presumed mandate[2008], may provide a boost for the use of ECLs.

495. None of the instruments described in this chapter reveal how to solve cross-border issues, although the German project is in fact used for cross-border purposes. The territoriality of copyright is one of the obstacles to making the European cultural heritage accessible online with cross-border effect, as will be discussed in detail in the following chapters in Part III, starting with a discussion of general issues of the territoriality of copyright and cross-border use.

---

system. Professor Samuelson was of the opinion that the system was not viable under US conditions, i.a. due to lack of one-stop representative CMOs cf. <www.copyright.gov/policy/massdigitization/comments/> last viewed 27 September 2016.

2007 Cf. <https://www.copyright.gov/policy/massdigitization/>, last viewed 10 May 2018.

2008 COM(2016) 593 final, Proposal, 2016, Art. 7–9. See discussion in Ch. 11.3.

PART III:

TERRITORIALITY OF COPYRIGHT AND CROSS-BORDER ONLINE USE BY LIBRARIES: IN SEARCH OF A SOLUTION

CHAPTER 8

TERRITORIALITY OF COPYRIGHT AND CROSS-BORDER ONLINE USE

...what we mean exactly when we say that intellectual property is territorial is often unclear, and consequently, so are the ramifications of the territorial view...[2009]

496. The principle of territoriality[2010] is one of the underlying principles of intellectual property law.[2011] In legal terms territoriality is generally understood to mean nationally defined territory, i.e. the geographical area that national legislation applies to.[2012] Still, the notion of the territoriality of a right does not necessarily need to be limited to national borders and could apply to regional borders.[2013] The roots of the territoriality principle with regard to intellectual property rights can be traced back to the medieval printing and manufacturing privileges granted by sovereign rulers on a case-by-case basis. Those privileges were replaced by national legislation in the area in the nineteenth and twentieth centuries.[2014] For copyright the effect of territoriality is that the exercise of the exclusive rights afforded by copyright in one country is geographically restricted to that country, unless the rights are specifically recognised in another country.[2015]

2009 Mireille van Eechoud, 'Alternatives to the Lex Protectionis as the Choice-of-Law Rule for Initial Ownership of Copyright' in Josef Drexl and Annette Kur (eds), *Intellectual Property and Private International Law, IIC Studies vol 24* (2005) 293. See also: Rita Matulionyte, 'Law Applicable To Copyright Infringements in the ALI and CLIP Proposals: A Rebalance of Interests Needed?', 2011, (1), JIPITEC, 26–36, 27.

2010 I use the term territoriality and principle of territoriality interchangeably unless otherwise specified.

2011 Mireille van Eechoud, *Choice of Law in Copyright and Related Rights, Alternatives to the Lex Protectionis* (2003), 97.

2012 Goldstein and Hugenholtz, 3rd ed., 2013, 97–98; Silke von Lewinski, *International Copyright Law and Policy,* (Oxford University Press, 2008), 6; Torremans, Copyright, 2012, 25, 27; Triaille and others, Study, 2013, 45; Ansgar Ohly, 'Choice of Law in the Digital Environment – Problems and Possible Solutions' in Josef Drexl and Annette Kur (eds), *Intellectual Property and Private International Law – Heading for the Future* (Hart, 2005) 241; EU Commission, Creative Content, 2009, 10; Marketa Trimble, 'Advancing national intellectual property policies in a transnational context', 2015, (2), Maryland Law Revue, 203–257, 213, 230; van Eechoud, Choice, 2003, 97.

2013 Geiger and others, Reaction of CEIPI, 2015, 7; Triaille and others, Study, 2013, 45; COM(2011) 287 final, IPR Strategy, 2011, 11.

2014 Toshiyuki Kono (ed), *Intellectual Property and Private International Law: Comparative Perspectives* (Hart, 2012) 15; von Lewinski, International, 2008, 6.

2015 Goldstein and Hugenholtz, 3rd ed., 2013, 95; Torremans, Copyright, 2012, 25; Matulionyte, Enforcing, 2015, 138; Peukert, Territoriality, 2011, 1–2, (cited page-numbers refer to the ssrn

497. The principle of territoriality is not unique to intellectual property rights (IPRs) but is a general feature of national legislations.[2016] Thus, as a fundamental principle of our legal order, territoriality is here to stay.[2017] One of the main justifications for the principle of territoriality is state sovereignty and, with regard to copyright in particular, the state's interest in regulating copyright protection of works on its territory.[2018] There are a number of benefits accruing from the territoriality principle in copyright. First, it can help States to pursue national cultural policy and thus preserve cultural diversity.[2019] Second, territoriality allows rightholders to divide the market by contracts. This can be necessary for cultural reasons, for example for the release of a film in a country with a different language or the translation of a book.[2020] Rightholders can also divide the market contractually if they deem this to be economically efficient or advantageous. Thus the short commercial lifespan of works has been put forward as an argument for price discrimination based on territoriality.[2021] Territoriality is hence the basis of many business models for distribution of content.[2022] Third, CMOs operate mostly on a national basis and thereby play an important role in fostering "cultural diversity", particularly within the EU.[2023] Finally, territoriality can provide legal certainty and secure business expectations in international commerce.[2024] Nevertheless, the reality is that the principle of territoriality complicates cross-border online use of in-copyright works for digital libraries as well as all online services.[2025] Furthermore, some of the benefits of the principle of territoriality, in particular for national cultural policies, can

---

version); Sterling, World Copyright Law, 2003, 116–117; BGH, case I ZR 24/92, 575.

2016 Torremans, Copyright, 2012, 25, 27; Goldstein and Hugenholtz, 3rd ed., 2013, 97–98; Triaille and others, Study, 2013, 46; Trumpke, Exklusivität, 2015, 616.

2017 Torremans, Copyright, 2012, 28.

2018 Goldstein and Hugenholtz, 3rd ed., 2013, 97; Axhamn and Guibault, Cross-border ECL, 2011, 19; von Lewinski, International, 2008, 6–7.

2019 Matulionyte, Enforcing, 2015, 138.

2020 Geiger and others, Reaction of CEIPI, 2015, 9; SWD(2016) 308 final, *Commission Staff Working Document: Evaluation of the Council Directive 93/83/EEC on the coordination of certain rules concerning copyright and rights related to copyright applicable to satellite broadcasting and cable retransmission*, 26; EU Commission, Creative Content, 2009, 13; Eechoud and others, Harmonizing, 2009, 310.

2021 COM(2010) 245 final/2, *Communication from the Commission to the European Parliament, the Council, the European Economic and Social Committee and the Committee of the Regions: A Digital Agenda for Europe* (19.05.2010) 8; COM(2015) 192 final, Communication, 2015, 7; Langus, Neven and Poukens, Economic, 2014, 64, 72, 86, 119.

2022 European Commission, Report on the responses, 2014, 91; Eechoud and others, Harmonizing, 2009, 309–310.

2023 EU Commission, Creative Content, 2009, 12, fn. 43; Eechoud and others, Harmonizing, 2009, 310.

2024 Goldstein and Hugenholtz, 3rd ed., 2013, 97; von Lewinski, International, 2008, 7.

2025 Matulionyte, Enforcing, 2015, 138; James Fawcett and Paul Torremans, *Intellectual Property and Private International Law* (Oxford University Press, 2011), 911; SEC(2007) 1710, Commission Staff Working Document, 2008, 24.

be obtained by other means, such as contract law, quotas on use of national cultural content for example in broadcasting, and statutory obligations on national collective management organisations.[2026]

498. Many claim that the extension effect of ECLs only applies on the national territory of the ECL agreement.[2027] Such views are based on the territoriality principle[2028] and the assumption that the extension effect is a limitation on the outsider's exclusive rights and that exceptions and limitations cannot have cross-border effect.[2029] In the following I will examine how the territoriality principle is reflected in international treaties and its effect on cross-border use of exceptions and ECLs, as well as discussing the different approaches for localising acts in online use of in-copyright works. I will then examine the issue of territoriality of copyright as reflected by the CJEU and EU legislation. Finally, I will briefly consider private international law and how the EU's legislation on jurisdiction and applicable laws has been interpreted with regard to copyright infringement cases.

8.1. TERRITORIALITY AND INTERNATIONAL TREATIES

499. The term territoriality as such does not appear in any international treaties on copyright.[2030] Nevertheless, the Berne Convention and other subsequent treaties are based on the principle of territoriality.[2031]

500. When the Berne Convention was established in the nineteenth century there were two competing views on how to deal with international protection

2026 Geiger and others, Reaction of CEIPI, 2015, 8.

2027 SEC(2011) 615 final, Impact Assessment, 2011, 27; Strowel, The European, 2011, 667, 669; Oostveen and Guibault, IPR issues, 2013, 11; Rosén, The Nordic ECL Model, 2012, 84; Prop. 2012/13:141, Regeringens proposition, 2013, 29.

2028 See e.g. SEC(2011) 615 final, Impact Assessment, 2011, 27.

2029 Vuopala, Extended, 2013, 24, 26.

2030 Torremans, Copyright, 2012, 25; European University Institute; Department of Law, Eleonora Rosati, 'Judge-made EU Copyright Harmonisation: The Case of Originality ', (The European University Institute 2012) 2; von Lewinski, International, 2008, 6.

2031 Ricketson and Ginsburg, International, 2006, 1301–1303; Kono (ed) Intellectual, 2012, 16; Triaille and others, Study, 2013, 21, 46; Axhamn and Guibault, Cross-border ECL, 2011, 19; von Lewinski, International, 2008, 6; Fawcett and Torremans, Intellectual Property, 2011, 675; COM(2003) 427 final, *Proposal for a Regulation of the European Parliament and of the Council on the law applicable to non-contractual obligations (Rome II)*, 20; Jane C. Ginsburg, 'Berne Without Borders: Geographic Indiscretion and Digital Communications (The Stephen Stewart Memorial Lecture 2001)', 2002, (2), IPQ 114; Graeme B. Dinwoodie, 'Conflicts and International Copyright Litigation: The Role of International Norms' in Jurgen Basedow and others (eds), *Intellectual Property in the Conflict of Laws* (2005) 195; Matulionyte, Cross-Border, 2009, 468.

for authors. One was to establish an international copyright code and the other, which prevailed, was the "national-sovereignty-sensitive" approach with various mechanisms to mitigate the effects of territoriality.[2032] Those mitigating mechanisms are in particular the national treatment principle, a cornerstone of the international copyright framework, and minimum standards of protection. Thus the Berne Convention provides in its Art. 5(1) that authors shall in other countries than the country of origin[2033] enjoy the same protection as authors in that country as well as "the rights specially granted by this Convention".[2034] In this manner the Convention assumes the existence of and relies on national borders[2035] and the territorial character of copyright is the practical outcome of this reliance on the national treatment principle rather than the cause or main rule underlying the system.[2036] In practice the national treatment principle means that an author has a bundle of national, independent rights, for which the conditions for protection, contents, and effects are governed by national legislation in each country.[2037]

501. Another cornerstone of the international copyright framework is the country of origin rule, which is also based on the principle of territoriality. It determines which rules are applicable to the enjoyment and exercise of the rights guaranteed, depending on whether the author is a national of the country of origin of the work for which protection is sought or not.[2038] The Berne Convention sets out specific criteria for determining the country of origin in Art. 5(4), the place of publication being the main criterion. If publication is simultaneous in many Berne Union member states then the country of origin is the country with the shortest term of protection.[2039] In the case of unpublished works or works solely published outside of the Berne

2032 Ginsburg, Berne Without Borders, 2002, 114.
2033 See Art. 5(4) BC and a brief discussion on the principle of country of origin in next paragraph.
2034 The minimum standards of protection relate to the works and rights to be protected and the duration of protection. Furthermore, there are some provisions for exceptions, and limitations to these minimum standards of protection See e.g. WIPO, *WIPO Intellectual Property Handbook: Policy, Law and Use* (2004), 263–265.
2035 Ginsburg, Berne Without Borders, 2002, 115.
2036 Torremans, Copyright, 2012, 26; Graeme B. Dinwoodie, 'Developing a Private International Intellectual Property Law: The Demise of Territoriality?', 2009, (2), William & Mary L Rev, 711–800, 716–717.
2037 Axhamn and Guibault, Cross-border ECL, 2011, 19; Fawcett and Torremans, Intellectual Property, 2011, 679; von Lewinski, International, 2008, 6; Public Consultation on the review of the EU copyright rules (2013), 7; Bernt Hugenholtz, 'Harmonization or Unification of EU Copyright Law' in Johan Axhamn (ed), *Copyright in a Borderless Online Environment* (Norstedts Juridik 2012) 195; Lucie Guibault and P. Bernt Hugenholtz, *Study on the conditions applicable to contracts relating to intellectual property in the European Union*, 134; Trumpke, Exklusivität, 2015, 616–617.
2038 Guibault, Cultural, 2015, 187.
2039 Cf. Art. 5(4)(a) BC.

Union, the country of origin is where the author is a national.[2040] What constitutes publication is defined in Art. 3(3) of the Convention as "works published with the consent of their authors, whatever may be the means of manufacture of the copies, provided that the availability of such copies has been such as to satisfy the reasonable requirements of the public, having regard to the nature of the work." However, increasingly works are not published as such but simply made available online. There is no general agreement on whether this counts as publication or not in the sense of the Berne Convention.[2041] If it were to be considered publication under the Convention it might create various problems with regard to the country of origin approach as potentially all Member States would have to be considered country of origin of such publication.[2042]

502. The Berne Convention sets clear national territorial restrictions to the exceptions on broadcasting and related rights and the right of recording of musical works.[2043] It has thus been assumed that the same territorial limitation applies to exceptions in other areas of copyright protection.[2044] However, it is interesting to note that the Berne Convention does not oblige member States to make liable to seizure copies of imported works that are lawfully made in the country of production, including copies made under an exception in the country of production. This can be inferred from the wording in Art. 16 of the Convention, which refers to "infringing" copies.[2045] This seems to imply that exceptions may have some cross-border effect. However, the principle of territoriality applies to exceptions and limitations under copyright in the same way as it does to the exclusive rights.[2046]

503. The question of the cross-border effect of exceptions with regard to the making available right is particularly pertinent when discussing the use of ECLs to enable libraries to use works from their collections online. When the

2040 Cf. Art. 5(4)(c) BC.

2041 Triaille and others, Study, 2013, 47, cf. fn. 89.

2042 Jane C. Ginsburg, *Internet publication and U.S. copyright imperialism (USA report)*, (28.06.2011) 3; Ginsburg, Berne Without Borders, 2002, 116–122.

2043 Cf. Art. 11*bis*(2) and Art. 13(1) BC; Ficsor, Collective Management, 2010, 52; Ricketson, Berne Convention, 1987, 523.

2044 Ginsburg, Berne Without Borders, 2002, 115–116; Ricketson and Ginsburg, International, 2006, 1323; von Lewinski and Walter, Information Society Directive, 2010, 977–978.

2045 Jane C. Ginsburg and June M. Besek, *Copyright Office Notice of Inquiry and Request for Comments on the Topic of Facilitating Access to Copyrighted Works for the Blind or Other Persons with Disabilities, 74 Fed. Reg. 52,507 (2009)*, (Nomvember 13, 2009) 3; Ricketson and Ginsburg, International, 2006, 661–662.

2046 Public Consultation on the review of the EU copyright rules (2013), 16–17; Reinbothe and Von Lewinski, The WIPO Treaties, 2015, 641; Marketa Trimble, 'The Marrakesh Puzzle', 2014, (7), IIC – International Review of Intellectual Property and Competition Law, 768–795, 780.

receiving country has the same exception as the country of origin of the online use there is usually no problem. The challenge arises when there is no equivalent exception. The same challenge arises with regard to online cross-border use under an ECL agreement if ECLs are seen as exceptions to the outsider's rights. Some scholars have maintained that exceptions can have cross-border effect in online use. Thus it has been argued that the exception for educational purposes in Art. 10(2) of the Berne Convention is intended to be technology neutral to enable teachers to use any kind of technology and hence it should also cover the use of the internet for online teaching for distance learning.[2047] Others claim that there is no basis for interpreting the exception to cover digital on-demand transmissions.[2048]

504. The making available right was created as a new right[2049] under the WCT.[2050] The Treaty allows exceptions[2051] from the rights it grants "that are appropriate in the digital network environment."[2052] This gives Contracting Parties to the WCT the freedom to introduce new exceptions as long as they are compatible with the three-step test.[2053] Digital networks, such as the internet, are based on universal access. Thus it makes sense that exceptions to the making available right could apply outside of national borders, with the proviso that they fulfil the three-step-test. However, it might be difficult to agree on which exceptions to the exclusive right of authorising the making available to the public would pass the three-step test.[2054]

505. The Marrakesh Treaty[2055] is the first international treaty to address specifically exceptions and cross-border access to copyrighted works.[2056] The Treaty creates a mandatory exception[2057] that allows authorised entities[2058] to produce, distribute and make available cross-border, accessible format copies

---

2047 Xalabarder, Digital Libraries, 2010, 233–234.

2048 Ricketson and Ginsburg, International, 2006, 794.

2049 Von Lewinski and Walter, Information Society Directive, 2010, 978; Ginsburg and Treppoz, International, 2015, 199.

2050 Cf. Art. 8 WCT.

2051 Cf. Art. 10(1) WCT.

2052 Cf. the agreed statements to Art. 10, which were adopted by consensus, cf. Ricketson and Ginsburg, International, 2006, 870.

2053 Senftleben, WCT, 2016, 125; Reinbothe and Von Lewinski, The WIPO Treaties, 2015, 163.

2054 Reinbothe and Von Lewinski, The WIPO Treaties, 2015, 156.

2055 The Marrakesh Treaty to Facilitate Access to Published Works for Persons Who Are Blind, Visually Impaired or Otherwise Print Disabled was adopted on June 27, 2013 and came into force 30 September 2016, hereafter the Marrakesh VIP Treaty, the Treaty or MT.

2056 Trimble, The Marrakesh, 2014, 771; Jonathan Band, *User Guide to the Marrakesh Treaty*, 1; Mihály Ficsor, Commentary on the Marrakesh Treaty on Accessible Format Copies for the Visually Impaired, Copyright See-Saw, 11 Octoeber 2013; accessed 12 July 2017.

2057 It is a matter for national legislation whether the exceptions are remunerated or not, cf. Art. 4(5) Marrakesh Treaty.

2058 Authorised entities are defined in Art. 2(c) MT, which can cover libraries.

of in-copyright works to visually impaired persons or an authorised entity in another Contracting Parties.[2059] To take account of the principle of territoriality there are provisions in the Treaty obliging the Contracting Parties to provide that accessible format copies, made under an exception, may be distributed or made available in another Contracting Party, as well as obliging them to allow the importation of an accessible format copy from another Contracting Party, without the authorisation of the rightholder.[2060] It is intriguing, however, that the provision obliging Contracting Parties to allow the reception of such copies only uses the term "importation". Importation is normally understood as only referring to the distribution of hard copies, whereas it is clear that the exception for the cross-border use applies both to the distribution of copies and to making them available. Presumably the word will be interpreted to include both.[2061] Nevertheless, the failure to specify that Contracting Parties must legalise the receiving of works online when they have been made available from another country without the authorisation of the rightholder, but made under an exception in legislation, is an interesting omission.

The key problem with the cross-border system under the Marrakesh Treaty remains that the system must operate in an environment where national legislations on the issues differ.[2062] This will create choice-of-law questions in disputes about the legality of cross-border use of accessible format copies, as Contracting Parties will need to decide which country's law applies. The Treaty does not mandate any choice-of-law rules, thus giving the Contracting Parties the freedom to choose which law or combination of laws they apply. There seem to be three main options for choice of law when implementing cross-border effect of the Treaty: first, applying the national law of the country concerned to all acts and issues; second, applying different national laws depending on where the issues arise and acts occur; third, a simultaneous use of the laws of both the country initiating the distribution or making available of the accessible format copy and of the receiving country. However, none of these approaches are problem free, resulting either in extraterritorial application of national law and so creating discord in international relations, or requiring national courts to rely on foreign legislation which can be difficult and lead to errors.[2063]

506. Thus none of the copyright treaties provide answers for how to deal with cross-border online use, in particular with regard to exceptions. I will now look in more detail at the issue of territoriality and online use.

2059 Art. 4, 5 and 6 MT; Public Consultation on the review of the EU copyright rules (2013), 26.

2060 Art. 5(1) and Art. 6 MT. Reinbothe and Von Lewinski, The WIPO Treaties, 2015, 641; Band, User Guide, 2013, 11; Trimble, The Marrakesh, 2014, 781–782.

2061 Reinbothe and Von Lewinski, The WIPO Treaties, 2015, 647.

2062 There are also some technical and financial issues that may hinder the free flow of accessible format copies, which the Treaty itself does not address, cf. Ibid, 623–625.

2063 Trimble, The Marrakesh, 2014, 782–789.

8.2. TERRITORIALITY AND ONLINE USE

507. Several issues arise when looking at the cross-border effects of online use of in-copyright works both with regard to territoriality and to potential infringement of the exclusive communication to the public right. If an ECL agreement provides for an online use with cross-border effect, there is always a possibility that an outsider would sue the user or the relevant CMO in a country other than where the agreement is concluded, for example if the outsider were a resident in such a country. The question would then be whether the ECL agreement would be considered a legal basis for such a use in a country other than where the ECL agreement was concluded, even if there were no equivalent ECL provisions in the receiving country. One key factor for answering such a question is the localisation of the acts which fall under the exclusive rights afforded by copyright protection, i.e. where such use would be deemed to take place.

508. Generally the reproduction right does not involve cross-border issues[2064] and localisation of the reproduction right should in principle be straight forward. Even so, making works available online, which falls under the exclusive communication to the public right, involves making copies which fall under the reproduction right. Such copies are usually made at different stages in the process and in cross-border online transmission this could occur in different countries. Where the act of reproduction inherent in digital transmission is deemed to happen can vary from country to country.[2065] There is no consensus on where the communication to the public right, including the making available right, should be deemed to take place.[2066] This situation, coupled with the principle of territoriality, leads to legal uncertainty with regard to the making available right and thus all online use of copyright.[2067] The legal uncertainty discourages libraries and other cultural heritage institutions from offering EU wide services and invites them to apply geolocation measures, such as is used by the Norwegian national library for its Bokhylla project.[2068] This is not compatible with EU's policies on the EU digital single market and creative content online.[2069]

2064 C-170/12 – AG opinion in Pinckney, par. 25 & 53; Triaille and others, Study, 2013, 49.

2065 Depreeuw and Hubin, Study 2014, 2014, 40; Triaille and others, Study, 2013, 111–112. See discussion in Ch. 3.1.

2066 See discussion in Ch. 3.2.

2067 Triaille and others, Study, 2013, 25, 63, 89, 95–96, 166, 176; Matulionyte, Law Applicable To Copyright, 2011, 27; European Copyright Society, Answer to the EC Consulation 2014, 12–13.

2068 See discussion on the Bokhylla project in Ch. 5.3.1.4. Martin Husovec, 'Comment on "Pinckney"', 2014, (3), IIC, 370–374, 373–374; Matulionyte, Enforcing, 2015, 134, 138; Jennifer Agate, 'Jurisdiction in the Context of internet Publication', 2012, (4), Journal of Intellectual Property Law & Practice, 241–243, 243.

2069 See e.g. COM(2016) 289 final, Proposal, 2016, 1; COM(2015) 626 final, Towards, 2015, 2–3; COM(2015) 192 final, Communication, 2015, 3–9.

509. This lack of consensus on the localisation in the making available right in online cross-border use creates questions with regard to jurisdiction and applicable laws in international disputes. Such questions fall under the sphere of private international law.[2070]

8.2.1. PRIVATE INTERNATIONAL LAW

510. Private international law[2071] is not international in the sense of containing rules universally or generally recognized in all legal systems but is rather a part of the private law of any one legal system which has to be invoked in a cross-border legal issue.[2072]

511. For many years private international law was not considered relevant for copyright because of the national treatment principle.[2073] However, satellite broadcasting and the internet have changed that.[2074] The fact that international copyright is a bundle of rights means that the question of jurisdiction and applicable law are of paramount importance in the age of the internet. The rapid evolution taking place in the area of copyright and internet distribution means that complex private international law questions frequently arise.[2075] At the same time it is worth bearing in mind that, as with the principle of territoriality, "private international law is a discipline in which it is often difficult to achieve certainty, and that is particularly true of the Internet, whose worldwide scope poses the traditional problem anew."[2076]

512. It has been asserted that the question of the localisation of an infringing act is not a private international law issue as such but rather an issue of

---

2070 As well as enforcements of foreign judgements, cf. i.a. Sterling, World Copyright Law, 2003, 122–123; David M. Walker, *The Oxford Companion to Law* (1980), 642. The question of enforcement of foreign judgements is not relevant for this research and will not be investigated.

2071 It should be underlined that the discussion on the issue of private international law is by no means exhaustive as it is only with regard to how copyright affects cross-border online use by libraries and the use of ECLs for such use.

2072 See discussion on terminology of how to best reflect this fact, cf. Walker, The Oxford Companion to Law, 1980, 642; von Lewinski, International, 2008, 4.

2073 Paul Torremans, 'Private International Law Issues on the Internet' in Irini A. Stamatoudi (ed), *New Developments in EU and International Copyright Law* (Wolters Kluwer, 2016) 379–380; Raquel Xalabarder, 'Jurisdiction and Applicable Law issues for the protection of moral rights online' in Fabienne Brison and others (eds), *Moral Rights Aspects in New Forms of Use* (2014) 188; Graeme B. Dinwoodie, Developing, 2009, 713.

2074 Torremans, Private, 2016, 379–380; Triaille and others, Study, 2013, 64; André Lucas, 'Applicable law in copyright infringement cases in the digital environment', 2005, (October-December), e-Copyright Bulletin, 1–14, 1–2, 9.

2075 Torremans, Private, 2016, 380.

2076 Lucas, Applicable law, 2005, 1.

substantive law.[2077] As the current basic rules on territoriality are likely to endure in the digital era, the strains on the copyright system produced by the internet should be alleviated by changes in substantive copyright law, for example by centralising liability for cross-border use of in-copyright works.[2078] Nevertheless, in the absence of clear substantive copyright provisions on the issue of localising online acts, the rules on jurisdiction and applicable laws will have an important impact on the outcome of infringement cases in connection with online use of in-copyright works, whether it is by libraries or other users. Thus I will look at a number of approaches, put forward by scholars and interested parties, to localising acts in online use in ubiquitous licensing and infringement cases for the purpose of choice of jurisdiction and applicable law.

8.2.2. APPROACHES TO LOCALISING ACTS IN ONLINE USE

There is no consensus on the best approach. With regard to private international law it has been maintained that the object of the choice of law should be "to identify the rule that will designate the country which is best placed to accord an effective international remedy" or settle defendants' lack of liability.[2079] Others maintain that "one of the more important" criteria against which a conflict-of-law rule should be measured is "the predictability that promotes certainty in copyright transactions."[2080] The three main approaches are, first, the country of reception approach; second, the targeting approach, and, finally, the country of origin approach. In the following sub-chapters I will look at these three approaches and assess how they fulfil the above-mentioned goals in relation to libraries wishing to put works from their collections online.

8.2.2.1. The country of reception

513. The principle of country of reception establishes that the act of making in-copyright works available online occurs not only in the country of transmission, but also in every country where it can be accessed or received.[2081]

514. The CJEU currently uses this approach for determining jurisdiction, notably in the Pinckney[2082] and the Hejduk[2083] cases. This has been criticised

2077 Cf. Fawcett and Torremans, Intellectual Property, 2011, 914; Goldstein and Hugenholtz, 3rd ed., 2013, 96.
2078 Fawcett and Torremans, Intellectual Property, 2011, 914; Goldstein and Hugenholtz, 3rd ed., 2013, 96; Lucas, Applicable law, 2005, 9.
2079 Ricketson and Ginsburg, International, 2006, 1303.
2080 Goldstein and Hugenholtz, 3rd ed., 2013, 135.
2081 Axhamn and Guibault, Cross-border ECL, 2011, 21; Lucas, Applicable law, 2005, 11.
2082 C-170/12 – Pinckney, par. 44.
2083 C-441/13 – Hejduk, par. 34.

as being detrimental to the balance of interest underlying copyright law, first, by giving advantages to rightholders, enabling them to sue for copyright infringement in every country where the work can be accessed, and second, by creating legal uncertainty and lack of predictability for users, especially online service providers that are only targeting specific countries and where access in others is merely an overspill.[2084] This is not only true with regard to service providers in the common sense of the term but also for cultural heritage institutions such as libraries that wish to put work from their collections online, for example under an ECL agreement.

515. If the country of reception approach were also used for determining applicable law in ubiquitous infringement cases, the copyright law of each EU Member State would have to be applied to achieve EU wide remedies, even if the forum had jurisdiction in respect of all the damage caused in all Member States.[2085] For non-contractual obligations, this situation combined with the *lex loci protectionis* principle would mean that users of in-copyright works online, such as libraries and other content provider, would have to comply with the national law of every Member State where their sites might be accessible[2086], thus making it very difficult to create legal certainty for such actors.[2087] However, for contractual obligations the determination of applicable laws is not based on territoriality, as will be discussed further below.[2088]

516. Some scholars have suggested that a compromise to the country of reception approach could be to disregard the law of those countries in question "if it cannot reasonably be foreseen by the operator."[2089] However, it could be difficult for an operator to prove that the law of a given Member State was not foreseeable in online cross-border use. Another compromise is the targeting approach.

8.2.2.2. The targeting approach

517. Under the targeting approach it is assumed that the making available right is only localised in countries where the public is actually targeted and not in countries where it is simply possible to access the uploaded work.[2090] Thus

---

2084 Matulionyte, Enforcing, 2015, 134.
2085 Ibid, 132, 138; Eechoud and others, Harmonizing, 2009, 309.
2086 See discussion in Ch. 8.4.2.2.
2087 Axhamn and Guibault, Cross-border ECL, 2011, 21; Lucas, Applicable law, 2005, 12; Triaille and others, Study, 2013, 89; Matulionyte, Law Applicable To Copyright, 2011, 27; Rognstad, Opphavsrett, 2009, 430.
2088 See Ch. 8.4.2.1.
2089 Lucas, Applicable law, 2005, 13.
2090 Triaille and others, Study, 2013, 22.

for an act to be deemed to have taken place in a given country for infringement purposes there must be evidence that the service provider intended to target the public in that country.[2091] The approach has been applied by the CJEU, both in order to determine jurisdiction and also with regard to substantive law, in order to localise acts in cross-border situations.[2092] However, in relatively recent online copyright cases the CJEU did not endorse the targeting approach.[2093]

518. The benefits of the targeting approach are that it could limit forum shopping, create more predictability for defendants and increase the connection between forum and action, thus leading "to sounder administration of court proceedings."[2094] However, there are several problems with the targeting approach, the main one being the difficulty of determining the criteria for what constitutes targeting for the purpose of jurisdiction and applicable laws. Furthermore, the approach might discourage online service providers from offering EU wide services, for example by the use of geo-location tools, which is detrimental for society at large and discouraged by the EU.[2095, 2096]

519. From the standpoint of this study the targeting approach would not be helpful. The making available of works by national libraries online for the purpose of enabling access to the cultural heritage in Europe would by definition have the aim to make the works available in all Member States.

8.2.2.3. Country of origin

520. The country of origin rule can refer to various places, such as the country of origin of the work, the origin of a certain activity or the location of the establishment responsible for the act.[2097] The *lex loci orginis* rule for applicable law is based on the country of origin as defined in Art. 5(4) of the Berne

---

2091 See e.g. Langus, Neven and Poukens, Economic, 2014, 4. The CLIP group has advocated for the targeting approach in online infringement cases, cf. European Max Planck Group on Conflict of Laws in Intellectual Property, *Conflict of Laws in Intellectual Property: The CLIP Principles and Commentary* (Oxford University Press, 2013), Art. 2:202.

2092 C-324/09 – L'Oréal and Others, (trademarks); C-5/11, Donner, (the exclusive distribution right); C-173/11, Football Dataco II, *supra*, (the *sui generis* database right); Joined Cases C-585/08 and C-144/09 – Pammer and Hotel Alpenhof, (jurisdiction over consumer contracts).

2093 C-170/12 – Pinckney, *op.cit.*; C-441/13 – Hejduk, *op.cit.*, see further in Ch. 8.4.1.

2094 Matulionyte, Enforcing, 2015, 136; Torremans, Private, 2016, 385–386.

2095 As mentioned at the beginning of Ch. 8.2.

2096 Matulionyte, Enforcing, 2015, 136–137; Husovec, Comment on "Pinckney", 2014, 373–374; Lucas, Applicable law, 2005, 14.

2097 Vuopala, Extended, 2013, 27; Trumpke, Exklusivität, 2015, 642, fn. 2372.

Convention, i.e. the country of origin of the work.[2098] The "country of origin" principle in connection with the communication to the public right can be used to refer to where the uploading of material takes place or where the institution or person is established that is responsible for the uploading act.[2099] An example is the Satellite and Cable Directive, according to which the country of origin is the country where the programme-carrying signals are introduced[2100], regardless of the origin of the works transmitted. Other examples of the application of the country of origin approach in EU substantive legislation are to be found in the E-Commerce Directive[2101] and the Services Directive.[2102] However, the fact that the country of origin principle contained in the E-Commerce Directive does not apply to copyright has been interpreted to mean that the country of origin approach should not be used with regard to internet transmissions.[2103]

521. Localising the communication to the public right to the country of origin would clarify that the applicable law in a ubiquitous infringement was the law of that country.[2104] Thus the main argument for the country of origin rule is the legal certainty it confers on the party making works available online.[2105] In addition, the country of origin approach simplifies licensing[2106] as well as the analysis of infringement in ubiquitous settings.[2107] Hence it has been maintained that the approach would lead to increased legal content online, which would benefit both rightholders through increased remuneration, and end-users by giving them access to more legal content online.[2108] It has even been suggested that the application of the country of origin principle might enable service providers to rely on the various exceptions in their home jurisdictions.[2109] Nevertheless, it has also been pointed out that until the interplay between the making available right

2098 Sterling, World Copyright Law, 2003, 328–330; 996; Guibault, Cultural, 2015, 187–190. See discussion in Ch. 8.1.

2099 Triaille and others, Study, 2013, 22, 139; Thomas Dreier, 'Satellite and Cable Directive' in Michel M. Walter and Silke von Lewinski (eds), *European Copyright Law, A Commentary* (Oxford University Press, 2010) 415; Langus, Neven and Poukens, Economic, 2014, 5.

2100 Art. 1(2)(b) Satellite and Cable Directive. See further discussion in Ch. 8.3.2.1.

2101 See Art. 3(3) and Annex of Directive 2000/31/EC of the European Parliament and of the Council of 8 June 2000 on certain legal aspects of information society services, in particular electronic commerce, in the Internal Market.

2102 *Op.cit.* (in Ch. 5.2.1.2). The country of origin principle is not expressly spelled out in the Directive, but can be derived from the freedom to provide services clause, albeit in more limited form than under the E-Commerce Directive, Art. 16; cf. Matulionyte, Cross-Border, 2009, 478.

2103 Ginsburg, Berne Without Borders, 2002, 116; von Lewinski and Walter, Information Society Directive, 2010, 946.

2104 Triaille and others, Study, 2013, 150; Lucas, Applicable law, 2005, 11.

2105 Lucas, Applicable law, 2005, 12; Matulionyte, Enforcing, 2015, 139.

2106 Axhamn and Guibault, Cross-border ECL, 2011, 66.

2107 Ricketson and Ginsburg, International, 2006, 1303.

2108 Axhamn and Guibault, Cross-border ECL, 2011, 66.

2109 Ohly, Choice of Law, 2005, 253.

and the reproduction right inherent in online transmissions has been clarified, localising the making available right in the country of origin would not entirely solve the complication of applicable laws or licensing issues.[2110]

522. The Commission has on several occasions raised the issue of the country of origin approach for digital cross-border transmissions.[2111] Even so, this has not been deemed a viable solution so far and the initiatives have been criticised by stakeholders.[2112] The main arguments against the country of origin approach with regard to clearing of rights for online use of in-copyright works and for identifying applicable law for infringement of copyright on the internet are thus the following:

Firstly, in the digital environment there are numerous points of origin, many of which may be irrelevant as well as difficult to establish[2113], such as hosting servers, centre of activities of the uploader or the geographical location of the material act of uploading. The conclusion seems to be that all of them raise some problems and none of them would be sufficient as a general reference point for the widely different users.[2114]

Secondly, the country of origin approach may cause forum shopping by service providers favouring countries affording the "lowest protection".[2115] This could even arise within the EU as a number of copyright issues are not harmonised, in particular exceptions and limitations to the exclusive right.[2116] Thus some maintain that the country of origin approach for the making available right in digital transactions would require full harmonisation of copyright.[2117] However, those in favour of the country of origin approach

2110 Depreeuw and Hubin, Study 2014, 2014, 80–82; European Copyright Society, *Response to the European Commission's Public Consultation on the Review of the EU Satellite and Cable Directive*, (15 March 2015) 18.

2111 E.g. COM(95) 382 final, Green Paper, 1995, 41 f.; SEC(2007) 1710, Commission Staff Working Document, 2008, 26; EU Commission, Creative Content, 2009, 12, 17 f.; COM(2015) 192 final, Communication, 2015, 7, 20.

2112 COM(96) 568 final, Follow-up to the Green Paper, 1996, 23.

2113 E.g. C-173/11, Football Dataco II, par. 44–46; Ricketson and Ginsburg, International, 2006, 1307; COM(97)628 final, InfoSoc Proposal, 1997, 9–10; Walter and von Lewinski (eds) European Copyright Law, A Commentary, 2010, 943, 946; Matulionyte, Enforcing, 2015, 140–141; SEC(2007) 1710, Commission Staff Working Document, 2008, 26; Axhamn and Guibault, Cross-border ECL, 2011, 65; Rognstad, Opphavsrett, 2009, 430.

2114 Triaille and others, Study, 2013, 134–139, 145–147.

2115 E.g. C-173/11, Football Dataco II, par. 44–46; Ricketson and Ginsburg, International, 2006, 1307, 1309; COM(97)628 final, InfoSoc Proposal, 1997, 9–10; Walter and von Lewinski (eds) European Copyright Law, A Commentary, 2010, 943, 946; Ginsburg, Berne Without Borders, 2002, 116; Lucas, Applicable law, 2005, 11, 14; SEC(2007) 1710, Commission Staff Working Document, 2008, 26; Triaille and others, Study, 2013, 89; Axhamn and Guibault, Cross-border ECL, 2011, 65.

2116 Matulionyte, Enforcing, 2015, 139; Triaille and others, Study, 2013, 134–139. Ohly notes that country or origin would enable service providers to rely on an exception in their country of origin as mentioned above, cf. Ohly, Choice of Law, 2005, 253.

2117 Matulionyte, Enforcing, 2015, 140; Dreier, Satellite and Cable Directive, 2010, 415–416; Trumpke, Exklusivität, 2015, 648.

argue that the level of harmonisation within the EU is sufficient to ensure that the application of the approach would not lead to a lower level of protection. Nevertheless, they also recommend full harmonisation of exceptions if the country of origin approach were to be adopted for online transmissions.[2118] Some have raised concerns that a single remuneration for a use in the entire internal market under a country of origin approach would risk devaluing copyright.[2119] Other commentators in favour of the approach underline that, as under the Satellite and Cable Directive[2120], due account would have to be taken of the actual audience, potential audience and the language version of the transmission.[2121]

Thirdly, the country of origin approach would result in a situation where works used in the same country might be subject to different rules of different countries depending on the origin of the works; this would not enhance legal certainty for users wanting to use a number of different works. It has also been claimed that the approach would deprive states of the possibility of "pursuing their territorial copyright policies in their own territories in respect of works originating abroad."[2122]

Fourthly, commentators have pointed out that there are differences in satellite broadcasting and making works available online that speak against using the country of origin approach for the latter. In particular it has been highlighted that the rights to satellite broadcasting are largely in the hands of a few stakeholders, which is not the case with the making available right online of in-copyright works.[2123] The making available right in online use can belong to numerous rightholders in different territories, which would make distribution of remuneration very burdensome.[2124]

Finally, there has been criticism that the country of origin approach would either mean that rightholders would have to go to a foreign court to adjudicate the dispute, or if jurisdiction rules allow for the defendant to be sued in the rightholder's home forum, then that court would have to apply foreign copyright law to establish EU-wide infringement and grant remedies.[2125] However, this criticism is also applicable of other approaches.

2118 European Copyright Society, Review of the EU Satellite and Cable Directive, 2015, 7, 20–21.

2119 SEC(2007) 1710, Commission Staff Working Document, 2008, 26; Walter and von Lewinski (eds) European Copyright Law, A Commentary, 2010, 946, see also 943. See similar concerns by public service broadcasters who, nevertheless, are in favour of the country of origin approach, cf. European Commission, Report on the responses, 2014, 91.

2120 Cf. Recital (17) Satellite and Cable Directive.

2121 European Copyright Society, Answer to the EC Consulation 2014, 4–5; Axhamn and Guibault, Cross-border ECL, 2011, 66.

2122 Matulionyte, Enforcing, 2015, 138–139.

2123 Dreier, Satellite and Cable Directive, 2010, 415.

2124 Axhamn and Guibault, Cross-border ECL, 2011, 66.

2125 Matulionyte, Enforcing, 2015, 139.

8.2.3. EVALUATION WITH REGARD TO ECLS FOR LIBRARIES

523. There may not be a single approach with regard to the localisation of acts and choice of law that is optimal for all ubiquitous situations where in-copyright works are used online. In particular, the country of origin approach, although offering legal certainty, might generate other problems if adopted as a general rule for online use of in-copyright works.

524. With regard to the question of establishing the best approach to the localisation of acts and choice of law for the specific case of online use of in-copyright works by digital libraries under national ECL agreements, the best approach seems to be the country of origin approach; the acts being located in the place where the agreement is concluded and where the parties are established, i.e. the library and the CMO negotiating the ECL agreement.[2126] However, I suggest that this should only apply to ECL agreements for national works, i.e. works that originate in the country concerned.[2127]

525. One of the main arguments against the country of origin approach is that in the digital environment there are many points of origin, many of which may be irrelevant. However, in the case of ECLs for online use by digital libraries of national works in their collection, there is a very clear and relevant point of origin, i.e. national libraries, and hardly any likelihood of forum shopping.[2128] With regard to the issue of the inherent reproductions in online transactions that can cause complications in the licensing of the making available right[2129], I maintain that this would not be so for use under ECL agreements for online use of national works by national libraries. First, the inherent reproduction in the receiving country would be exempted under Art. 5(1) of the InfoSoc Directive, according to the PRCA case.[2130] Second, it would be simple to define in the agreement that all reproduction inherent in the making available of the works should be covered by the agreement.[2131]

526. The answer to the question whether ECLs can have cross-border effect hinges mainly on whether the ECL system is seen as a system of management of rights or whether it is an exception to outsiders' rights. As discussed above, the system has a hybrid nature; in other words the ECL system is a mixture of

---

2126 Guibault, Cultural, 2015, 190–191.

2127 See further discussion on this point in Ch. 10.2.1.

2128 It is possible that in some cases there might be libraries with branches in other Member States, e.g. universities with operations abroad including library sections. However, this is relatively rare, so for the purposes of this study this possibility will not be further examined.

2129 Triaille and others, Study, 2013, 180; Depreeuw and Hubin, Study 2014, 2014, 80; European Copyright Society, Review of the EU Satellite and Cable Directive, 2015, 18.

2130 C-360/13 – PRCA par. 28–33. See Ch. 3.1.2, par. 89–90 and 3.3, par. 129.

2131 See e.g. suggestion for a solution in European Copyright Society, Review of the EU Satellite and Cable Directive, 2015, 18 and in Depreeuw and Hubin, Study 2014, 2014, 82–83.

management of rights and exception to the outsider's right. Depending on the area of use under ECL agreements and the deployment of safeguard measures, the characteristics of the system making it an exception recede in favour of a legal presumption of mandate from the outsider to the CMO once the three-step test is passed; thus the system can under these circumstances be seen as an arrangement of management of rights with regard to outsiders. This line of reasoning would be in conformity with Recital (18) of the InfoSoc Directive.[2132] Below I argue that the hybrid nature of the ECL system could enable an ECL agreement to have cross-border effect under certain circumstances.[2133] Adapting the country of origin approach to ECLs for libraries to make national work available online with cross-border effect would provide clarity and legal certainty and facilitate licensing that would provide for more access to the European cultural heritage.

527. As the research focuses principally on online use by libraries within Europe it is appropriate next to look at how the issue of territoriality, copyright and private international law is handled in the EU and the EEA.

8.3. TERRITORIALITY AND THE EU

528. It has been suggested that there would be no need for rules on territoriality if national copyright legislation were the same in all countries.[2134] While unification of law[2135] would achieve this end harmonisation on its own is not enough. Harmonisation creates legal certainty, which is a good thing in itself, but does not remove the inherent obstacles created by the rule of territoriality.[2136] Thus, harmonisation efforts within the EU have had little effect on the challenge of territoriality[2137] and territoriality of copyright is still the basis for the interaction between the different Member States, requiring them to protect the same work in parallel in the European Union.[2138]

2132 See Ch. 6.1.2 and Ch. 6.3.1.

2133 See Ch. 9.1.2.

2134 Goldstein and Hugenholtz, International Copyright, 2nd ed., 2010, 93.

2135 See Ch. 9.6.

2136 Eechoud and others, Harmonizing, 2009, 309; IIIID/1294/79-EN, *The Need for a European Trade Mark System. Competence of the European Community to Create One. Commission Working Paper*, 4.

2137 C-192/04, Lagardère, par. 46; Eechoud and others, Harmonizing, 2009, 313, 316; Triaille and others, Study, 2013, 62; Public Consultation on the review of the EU copyright rules (2013), 7; Axhamn and Guibault, Cross-border ECL, 2011, 20; Bernt Hugenholtz, 'Copyright without frontiers: the problem of territoriality in European copyright law ' in Estelle Derclaye (ed), *Research Handbook on the Future of EU Copyright* (Edward Elgar Publishing, 2009) 22; Hugenholtz and others, Recasting, 2006, 218.

2138 C-170/12 – AG opinion in Pinckney, par. 44; C-5/11 *Opinion of Mr Advocate General Jääskinen in case C-5/11, Criminal proceedings against Titus Donner* ECLI:EU:C:2012:195, CJEU, 29 March 2012 par. 24; Public Consultation on the review of the EU copyright rules (2013), 7; Rosati, Judge-made EU Copyright, 2012, 1–2.

529. An important factor with regard to territoriality is whether the right to a work is held by one rightholder or many and if those rightholders are the same throughout the EU/EEA area or not. Territoriality is not as problematic when the author holds the universal rights, which is normally the case unless they have transferred or licensed it. When rights have been transferred to, for example, different publishers, distributors or CMOs in different Member States then the issue becomes complex.[2139] Contracts play an important part in the use of copyright and affect the issue of territoriality substantially.[2140] Territoriality enables rightholders to split the market by contracts which can create economic efficiency or be deemed necessary for cultural reasons. Nevertheless, such contractual divisions seem to counteract the aim of achieving a "vibrant digital single market".[2141]

530. The principle of territoriality thus creates friction with the creation of a single market. It presents a structural obstacle to the free movement of goods and, in particular, of services that rely on in-copyright works within the EU/EEA area.[2142] Hence territoriality creates a competitive disadvantage for providers of content-related services across the European Union, including high transaction costs, as well as non-availability for end-users of digital content across the single market.[2143] The same applies for cultural heritage institutions such as libraries that wish to use modern digital technology to fulfil their role of giving access to the European cultural heritage.

8.3.1. TERRITORIALITY OF COPYRIGHT AND THE CJEU

531. The principle of territorial exploitation was confirmed by the CJEU in the early eighties[2144] and several times since. Thus in the Lagardère decision the Court submitted that:

2139 Eechoud and others, Harmonizing, 2009, 310–311.

2140 Public Consultation on the review of the EU copyright rules (2013), 8; COM(95) 382 final, Green Paper, 1995, 39; Sterling, World Copyright Law, 2003, 124.

2141 There seems to be some contradiction in the 2010 Digital Agenda communication as on the one hand it asserts that the free circulation of online content inside the EU and across its borders is fundamental, but then also states that solutions for cross-border and pan-European licensing should preserve the contractual freedom of rightholders, cf. COM(2010) 245 final/2, Digital Agenda, 2010, 7–8.

2142 Eechoud and others, Harmonizing, 2009, 308; Rosati, Judge-made EU Copyright, 2012, 2; Ohly, Economic rights, 2009, 222; Trumpke, Exklusivität, 2015, 667.

2143 COM(2011) 287 final, IPR Strategy, 2011, 6; Eechoud and others, Harmonizing, 2009, 313; Karl-Nikolaus Peifer, 'Das Territorialitatsprinzip im Europaischen Gemeinschaftsrecht vor dem Hintergrund der technischen Entwicklungen', 2006, (1), ZUM, 1–8, 4; Hugenholtz, Copyright without frontiers, 2009, 21–22; COM(2004) 261 final, *Communication from the Commission to the Council, the European Parliament and the European Economic and Social Committee on the Management of Copyright and Related Rights in the Internal Market*, (16.04.2004) 7–12.

2144 In C-62/79 *SA Compagnie générale pour la diffusion de la télévision, Coditel, and others v Ciné Vog Films and others*. ECR 1980 881, ECLI:EU:C:1980:84, CJEU, 18 March 1980, and C-262/81 *Coditel SA, Compagnie générale pour la diffusion de la télévision, and others v Ciné-Vog*

> ...it must be emphasised that it is clear from its wording and scheme that Directive 92/100 provides for minimal harmonisation regarding rights related to copyright. Thus, it does not purport to detract, in particular, from the principle of the territoriality of those rights, which is recognised in international law and also in the EC Treaty. Those rights are therefore of a territorial nature and, moreover, domestic law can only penalise conduct engaged in within national territory.[2145]

532. The Court stated in the Football Dataco II case that the effect of territoriality was that "...the person enjoying that protection can rely on it only against unauthorised acts of re-utilisation which take place in that territory."[2146] In the Pinckney and Hejduk cases the CJEU found that copyright must be automatically protected in each Member State, in particular in accordance with the InfoSoc Directive, and thus it could be infringed in each of the Member States under applicable substantive laws, because of the principle of territoriality. In both cases it was found that accessibility to an in-copyright work via a website could give rise to a damage in the country where the website was accessible.[2147]

533. The CJEU has placed limitations on the exercise of territoriality, but only in respect of the Community-wide exhaustion of the distribution right when it conflicts with the free movement of goods, and in respect of competition rules where it arises from restrictive agreements or concerted practices or an abuse of a dominant position. Thus the CJEU found already in 1971 that using the territoriality of copyright to prevent the marketing of a product legally put on the market in one Member State in another Member State would be against the essential purpose of the Treaty, which is to unite national markets into a single market, and that it was outside the "specific subject matter" of intellectual property rights to artificially divide markets.[2148]

534. The CJEU examined certain contractual practices with regard to territorial restrictions on satellite broadcasting in the Premier League case.[2149] One of the issues the Court evaluated was whether territorial restrictions constituted restrictions on the freedom to provide services under Art. 56 TFEU and whether such restrictions could be justified by an objective of protecting i.a. copyright.[2150] The Court's conclusion was that intellectual property protection

---

Films SA and others ECLI:EU:C:1982:334, CJEU, 6 October 1982, cf. COM(2004) 261 final, Communication, 2004, 7.

2145 C-192/04, Lagardère, para. 46.

2146 C-173/11, Football Dataco II, par. 27.

2147 C-170/12 – Pinckney, par. 39–44; C-441/13 – Hejduk, par. 22–34.

2148 C-78/70 *Deutsche Grammophon Gesellschaft mbH v Metro-SB-Großmärkte GmbH & Co. KG.* ECR 1971 p 487, CJEU, 8 June 1971 p. 500; Eechoud and others, Harmonizing, 2009, 310; COM(2004) 261 final, Communication, 2004, 7; Hugenholtz, Copyright, 2012, 196.

2149 Joined cases C-403/08 and C-429/08 – Premier League, par. 30–35.

2150 Ibid, par. 84–92.

could justify such restrictions[2151]; yet, these cannot go beyond what is necessary in order to attain the objective of protecting the intellectual property at issue. The Court underlined

> ...that the specific subject-matter of the intellectual property is intended in particular to ensure for the right holders concerned protection of the right to exploit commercially the marketing or the making available of the protected subject-matter, by the grant of licences in return for payment of remuneration.

However, the intention is not to guarantee the highest possible remuneration, but appropriate remuneration for each use of the protected subject matter. Such appropriate remuneration must be reasonable in relation to the economic value of the service provided and in particular "in relation to the actual or potential number of persons who enjoy or wish to enjoy the service" as well as the language version in relation to the audience.[2152]

Hence the Court does not preclude exclusive territorial licences if they have the aim of guaranteeing reasonable remuneration. Still, in the Premier League case the premium paid was i.a. to guarantee absolute territorial exclusivity, which resulted in partition and an artificial price difference which is "irreconcilable with the fundamental aims of the Treaty".[2153]

535. Thus territorial restrictions could be justifiable in certain cases, for example in the initial phase of distribution of a new work, but less so with regard to online exploitation of older works. Territorial restrictions could also be justifiable in some instances with regard to service providers' wish to control the amount of remuneration due, i.e. by thus restricting the potential public that could access the work.[2154] An example of such restrictions are the geo-blocking provisions in the Norwegian Bokhylla Agreement, which provide that access to in-copyright works is only for Norwegian IP numbers, except under certain circumstances.[2155] Thus the potential public is limited to residents in Norway.

8.3.2. TERRITORIALITY AND THE EU COPYRIGHT LEGISLATION

536. There are four binding EU legislative instruments that attempt to mitigate the effect of the territoriality principle: the Satellite and Cable Directive, which introduced the country of origin rule for satellite broadcast; the codification of the exhaustion of the distribution right; the CMO

2151 Ibid, par. 94.
2152 Ibid, par. 105–111.
2153 Ibid, par. 114–117.
2154 Triaille and others, Study, 2013, 156.
2155 See Ch. 5.3.1.4.

Directive, which sets out a system for multi-territorial licences of rights in musical works for online use in the internal market; and, finally, the Orphan Works Directive, which provides for cross-border use of orphan works within the EU and EEA territory. Additionally, in September 2016, the Commission submitted several proposals that expressly deal with online cross-border use in the digital single market. I will discuss these instruments briefly below, except for the Orphan Works Directive which was discussed at length above.[2156]

8.3.2.1. *The Satellite and Cable Directive*

537. The Satellite and Cable Directive, due to its technology specific provisions, does not deal with the making available right and is thus not applicable for online services.[2157] However, the country of origin approach taken in the Directive with regard to broadcasting by satellite has often been cited as a possible approach for online transactions in general.[2158]

538. Before the adoption of the Satellite and Cable Directive it was unclear in which country the communication to the public by satellite broadcast should be deemed to occur. In particular, it was unclear whether the consent of rightholders was required in every state where a satellite broadcast could be received.[2159] The issue was solved by Art. 1 (2)(b) which stipulates that:

> The act of communication to the public by satellite occurs solely in the Member State where, under the control and responsibility of the broadcasting organization the programme-carrying signals are introduced into an uninterrupted chain communication leading to the satellite and down towards the earth.

539. The impetus for this solution was to simplify rights-clearance for satellite transmitting[2160] and to hinder rightholders from dividing the communication to the public by a satellite broadcast into separate territorial parts.[2161] Still, this latter main goal has essentially failed[2162] as it has not led to a pan-European television market. This is mainly due to the use of

---

2156 See Ch. 4.2.3 and 4.2.4.2.

2157 SWD(2016) 308 final, Evaluation, 2016, 27; COM(2016) 594 final, Proposal, 2016, 2.

2158 Goldstein and Hugenholtz, 3rd ed., 2013, 141; EBU, *Modern copyright for digital media; E.B.U. Policy Paper*, (March 2010) pp. 3, 8–9; SEC(2007) 1710, Commission Staff Working Document, 2008, 26; Trumpke, Exklusivität, 2015, 642–644.

2159 Triaille and others, Study, 2013, 59; Dreier and Hugenholtz (eds) Concise, 2006, 263.

2160 Recitals (5)-(7), (13)-(15) Satellite and Cable Directive; Dreier and Hugenholtz (eds) Concise, 2006, 272; Ricketson and Ginsburg, International, 2006, 1307.

2161 Jan Rosén, The Satellite and Cable Directive, 2014, 210; Dreier and Hugenholtz (eds) Concise, 2006, 272.

2162 Eechoud and others, Harmonizing, 2009, 308; COM(2011) 427/4, Audiovisual works, 2011, 13; Hugenholtz, Copyright without frontiers, 2009, 22–23; Trumpke, Exklusivität, 2015, 654. The 2016 Evaluation of the Directive is slightly more positive stating that the Directive has

encryption technology and territorial licensing, which is not forbidden under the Directive.[2163]

Thus the effect of the country-of-emission principle in the Satellite and Cable Directive is undermined by territorial restrictions in contracts.[2164] However, in 2011 the CJEU found in the Premier League case that territorial restrictions in satellite broadcasting licences were restrictions on the freedom to provide services, cf. Art. 56 TFEU, as well as a restriction of competition within the internal market, cf. Art. 101 TFEU.[2165] Hence, such contractual restrictions could be deemed illegal if not necessary for the specific subject matter of copyright.[2166]

540. The provision in Art. 1(2)(b) is not a choice-of-law rule but a provision of substantive law.[2167] However, it is maintained that in practice it works as a choice-of-law rule.[2168] Thus every Member State that has implemented the Directive will apply the same criteria for where the communication to the public by satellite occurs. Hence even if a national conflict of laws rule in one Member State declared the copyright law of one or more of the receiving States applicable, that State's copyright law would not be infringed by the mere fact that reception of satellite signals took place in that State. This in turns means that a licence for broadcasting by satellite is only needed in the country of transmission and, furthermore, that legal remedies are determined by the law of the country of transmission.[2169] There are no decisions from the CJEU on the interpretation of Art. 1(2) of the Satellite and Cable Directive.[2170]

"contributed to improved access … to a limited but tangible extent", cf. SWD(2016) 308 final, Evaluation, 2016, 17.

2163 COM(2002) 430 Final, *Report from the European Commission on the application of Council Directive 93/83/EEC on the coordination of certain rules concerning copyright and rights related to copyright applicable to satellite broadcasting and cable retransmission*, (26.07.2002) 7; Eechoud and others, Harmonizing, 2009, 314; Triaille and others, Study, 2013, 60; Jan Rosén, The Satellite and Cable Directive, 2014, 210–211; Axhamn and Guibault, Cross-border ECL, 2011, 64–65.

2164 Triaille and others, Study, 2013, 60.

2165 Joined cases C-403/08 and C-429/08 – Premier League, Par. 85–89, 117 and 146, see Ch. 8.3.1.

2166 Triaille and others, Study, 2013, 61; Joined cases C-403/08 and C-429/08 – Premier League, par. 104–106.

2167 COM(95) 382 final, Green Paper, 1995, 40; Goldstein and Hugenholtz, 3rd ed., 2013, 135; Dreier, Satellite and Cable Directive, 2010, 410; Axhamn and Guibault, Cross-border ECL, 2011, 62; Dreier and Hugenholtz (eds) Concise, 2006, 272.

2168 Jan Rosén, The Satellite and Cable Directive, 2014, 209–210; Triaille and others, Study, 2013, 148; Paul Torremans, *Choice of law in EU copyright directives* (Estelle Derclaye ed, Edward Elgar Publishing, 2009), 457.

2169 Axhamn and Guibault, Cross-border ECL, 2011, 62; Dreier, Satellite and Cable Directive, 2010, 410–411.

2170 The Public Consultation on the Review of the EU Satellite and Cable Directive, Assessment, 1. It is no longer available online. However, a version of the Consultation

541. One of the initiatives of the 2015 Digital Single Market strategy[2171] was to review the Satellite and Cable Directive in order to assess whether its scope needed to be enlarged to cover broadcasters' online transmissions and whether further measures were needed to improve cross-border access to broadcasters' services in Europe.[2172] The review concluded that there was a need to extend the principles in the Satellite and Cable Directive to certain online transmissions of broadcasting organisations and retransmissions of television and radio programmes. Thus a proposal for a Regulation[2173] was tabled in September 2016 with the aim of promoting the cross-border provision of online services ancillary to broadcasts and to facilitate digital retransmissions over closed networks of TV and radio programmes originating in other Member States.[2174] Here the country of origin approach is extended to online ancillary services.[2175] It is further provided that when fixing the amount of payment for such use, all aspects of the ancillary online service, such as the audience and the language version must be taken into account.[2176] However, the proposal has been criticised as being too limited as it is restricted to ancillary online services.[2177]

8.3.2.2. The codified exhaustion rule

542. The Community-wide exhaustion rule as developed by the Court was codified in Art. 4(2) of the InfoSoc Directive.[2178] However, Art. 3(3) of the InfoSoc Directive stipulates that the exhaustion rule does not apply to the rights of communication to the public or making available to the public[2179], thus distinguishing between tangible versus intangible copies. This distinction has been criticised[2180] and recent case-law seems to indicate that it may be more

---

is to be found in e.g. European Copyright Society, Review of the EU Satellite and Cable Directive, 2015, 3.

2171 COM(2015) 192 final, Communication, 2015, 7, 20.

2172 COM(2016) 594 final, Proposal, 2016, 5.

2173 Proposal for a Regulation of the European Parliament and of the Council laying down rules on the exercise of copyright and related rights applicable to certain online transmissions of broadcasting organisations and retransmissions of television and radio programmes, cf. ibid, hereafter the Online Broadcasting Regulation Proposal or OBR.

2174 Ibid, 2, 9–15.

2175 Art. 2(1) OBR. Ancillary online services are defined in recital (8) OBR.

2176 Art. 2(2) OBR.

2177 European Copyright Society, General Opinion on the EU Copyright Reform Package, 2017, 3. It is also criticised for proposing to extend the rights clearance system for 'cable retransmission' to other kinds of 'retransmissions', without defining the concept of retransmission beyond the very circular definition of Art. 2(b) Satellite and Cable Directive.

2178 EU Commission, Creative Content, 2009, 11; Axhamn and Guibault, Cross-border ECL, 2011, 62.

2179 C-607/11 – ITV Broadcasting and Others, par. 23.

2180 Ohly, Economic rights, 2009, 237–238; Ole-Andreas Rognstad, 'Konsumpsjon og digitale overføringer; Et forslag til en alternativ løsningsmodell' in Mads Bryde Andersen, Caroline Heide-Jørgensen and Jens Schovsbo (eds), *Festskrift til Mogens Koktvedgaard* (Juris- og Økonomfobundets Forlag, 2003) 464, 470–471; von Lewinski and Walter, Information

difficult to maintain in the future.[2181] As the exhaustion of rights principle is based on distribution entailing transfer of ownership of a copy it will not be discussed further, as the online use of digital copies by digital libraries would not involve the question of transfer of ownership of such copies. However, the VOB case on digital lending is of considerable relevance for digital libraries as discussed above.[2182]

8.3.2.3. *The CMO Directive and multi-territorial licences of rights in musical works for online use*

543. The Commission also tried to mitigate the effect of territoriality with its 2005 Online Music Recommendation[2183], by inviting Member States to promote a regulatory environment for legal online music services as well as giving rightholders the right to mandate their online rights to a CMO of their choice. However, the Recommendation did not address or even raise the fundamental problem of territorially divided rights and was only concerned with music.[2184] The recommendation was superseded by the adoption of the CMO Directive in 2014, which sets out a system for multi-territorial licences of rights in musical works for online use in the internal market, as is further described below.[2185] However, although the Directive harmonises rules regarding the collective management of rights, it does not address the issue of territoriality. Thus the system for multi-territorial licences created by the CMO Directive will still only enable CMOs to "grant authorizations under 28 different national copyright titles with different scope."[2186]

8.3.3. RECENT DEVELOPMENTS

544. The Commission has in the past few years introduced several proposals to implement the Single Digital Market strategy[2187] which deal with the issue of territoriality.

545. In December 2015 a proposal for a Regulation to ensure the cross-border portability of online content services was submitted.[2188] The proposal

Society Directive, 2010, 987. The IVIR study from 2007 also noted that a tangible copy made from a work downloaded from the internet could fall under the exhaustion principle under certain circumstances, cf. Guibault and others, InfoSoc Study, Part I, 2007, 26.

2181 C-128/11, UsedSoft, *op.cit.*; C-174/15 – VOB, *op.cit.*

2182 Ch. 4.2.6.1.1.2.

2183 2005/737/EC, Recommendation 2005, 2005, recitals (7)-(8).

2184 Hugenholtz, Copyright without frontiers, 2009, 23–25; Matulionyte, Cross-Border, 2009, 484.

2185 See further in Ch. 9.4.

2186 Geiger and others, Reaction of CEIPI, 2015, 8; Matulionyte, Cross-Border, 2009, 483.

2187 COM(2015) 192 final, Communication, 2015, 6–8. See brief discussion in Ch. 2.4.2.

2188 COM(2015) 627, Proposal, 2015, *op.cit.* Hereafter the Portability Proposal or PP.

was adopted as a Regulation in June 2017.[2189] The Regulation addresses the restrictions on the access to online services purchased or subscribed to at home when EU residents are temporarily travelling in another Member State. It requires online content service providers to offer cross-border portability to their customers when they are temporarily present in other Member States[2190], and makes unenforceable all contrary contractual restrictions in the licences between rightsholders and service providers, as well as between the service provider and subscriber.[2191] The Regulation applies to a range of content services, such as audiovisual, music and e-book services, sporting events and other TV broadcasts – offered online by way of streaming, downloading or other technical means.[2192] The Regulation sets out a mechanism establishing the localisation of the service for purposes of portability based on the country of origin approach: the provision as well as the access to and use of the service by a subscriber who is temporarily present in another Member State is deemed to occur solely in the Member State of residence. This means that the relevant uses of copyright material, which occur when the service is provided to consumers on a basis of cross-border portability, are deemed to occur solely in the Member State of residence of the consumer, and thus, when licensing those uses, the licensing only has to take place in that Member State.[2193]

546. In September 2016 the Commission introduced the DSM proposal.[2194] As mentioned before the DSM proposal contains a solution for the use of out-of-commerce works for cultural heritage institutions which is of paramount importance for this study and is described in detail below.[2195] The DSM proposal also contains a provision for the use of works and other subject-matter in digital and cross-border teaching activities. It proposes a mandatory exception "to allow for the digital use of works and other subject-matter for the sole purpose of illustration for teaching" which takes place on the premises of an educational establishment or through a secure electronic network accessible only by the educational establishment's pupils or students and teaching staff. Use of works under the exception in electronic networks shall be deemed to occur solely in

---

2189 Regulation (EU) 2017/1128 of the European Parliament and of the Council of 14 June 2017 on cross-border portability of online content services in the internal market.

2190 Art. 3(1) Portability Regulation. In February 2017, negotiators from the European Parliament, the Council and Commission reached a compromise on the proposal which clarified i.a. that providers of free-of-charge online content services can also offer portability services to their subscribers, cf. Tambiama Madiega, *Cross-border portability of online content services; EPRS Briefing, EU Legislation in Progress*, (25 April 2017).

2191 Art. 5(1) PP which became Art. 7(1) in the adopted Regulation.

2192 Cf. <www.europarl.europa.eu/legislative-train/theme-connected-digital-single-market/file-portability-of-online-content>, last viewed 13 May 2018.

2193 Art. 4 PP and the adopted Regulation, cf. COM(2015) 627, Proposal, 2015, 8.

2194 *Op.cit.* fn. 38.

2195 Ch. 11.3.

the Member State where the educational establishment is established[2196], that is on the basis of the country of origin approach. Member States may, however, provide that the exception does not apply if adequate licences are in place.[2197] The Nordic CMOs for reproduction rights have voiced concern as to whether this mandatory exception might make the ECL system for use of work for educational purposes redundant. They claim it has functioned very well in the Nordic countries and adopting the mandatory exception would weaken the position of rightholders.[2198] However, it seems likely that the proposed "exception" to the mandatory exception is meant to cover such situations. At the same time others have criticised this possibility of contractual overridability.[2199]

547. Other proposals concerned with the issue of territoriality are the proposed EU Regulation for certain online transmissions of broadcasting organisations and retransmissions of television and radio programmes, mentioned above[2200], and the proposals for a Directive[2201] and a Regulation[2202] to amend the EU's legal framework in accordance with the Marrakesh Treaty.[2203] The latter two proposals were adopted as legislation in September 2017.[2204] The Marrakesh Directive ensures that authorised entities[2205] established in the territory of one Member State can make an accessible format copy and communicate, make available, distribute or lend an accessible format copy to a beneficiary person[2206] or authorised entity for the purpose of exclusive use by a beneficiary person[2207] in all Member States as well as ensuring that such authorised entities or beneficiary persons can obtain or have access to an accessible format copy from any Member State.[2208]

2196 Art. 4 DSM proposal, see SWD(2016) 301 final, IA Part I, 2016, 87–103.

2197 Art. 4(2) DSM proposal.

2198 Nordic position regarding the Commission Proposal for a New Copyright Directive, 21 April 2017.

2199 European Copyright Society, General Opinion on the EU Copyright Reform Package, 2017, 4.

2200 COM(2016) 594 final, Proposal, 2016, *op.cit.*

2201 COM(2016) 596 final, Proposal, 2016, *op.cit.*

2202 COM(2016) 595 final, Proposal for a Regulation, 2016, *op.cit.*

2203 See discussion on the Marrakesh Treaty in Ch. 8.1, par. 524. The EU signed the Marrakesh Treaty in April 2014, cf. Council Decision of 14 April 2014 on the signing, on behalf of the European Union, of the Marrakesh Treaty to Facilitate Access to Published Works for Persons who are Blind, Visually Impaired, or otherwise Print Disabled (2014/221/EU).

2204 Directive (EU) 2017/1564 of the European Parliament and of the Council of 13 September 2017 on certain permitted uses of certain works and other subject matter protected by copyright and related rights for the benefit of persons who are blind, visually impaired or otherwise print-disabled and amending Directive 2001/29/EC on the harmonisation of certain aspects of copyright and related rights in the information society and Regulation (EU) 2017/1563 of the European Parliament and of the Council of 13 September 2017 on the cross-border exchange between the Union and third countries of accessible format copies of certain works and other subject matter protected by copyright and related rights for the benefit of persons who are blind, visually impaired or otherwise print-disabled.

2205 Authorised entities are defined in Art. 2(4) Marrakesh Directive.

2206 Beneficiary persons are defined in Art. 2(2) Marrakesh Directive.

2207 Art. 3(1)(b) Marrakesh Directive.

2208 Art. 4 Marrakesh Directive.

548. Finally, a proposal for a Regulation addressing geo-blocking was adopted in February 2018.[2209] The geo-blocking Regulation is interesting with regard to the discussion on the territoriality principle although it only addresses "unjustified" geo-blocking, which means that geo-blocking based on the specific subject-matter of copyright is excluded.[2210] Nevertheless, the proposed regulation shows the emphasis within the EU that is put on the issue of an undivided digital single market.

549. It is obvious from this account on the issue of the territoriality of copyright within the EU that several initiatives have been taken to combat market fragmentation.[2211] However, it remains to be seen how effective these instruments will be and whether more efforts are needed in the area.

8.4. PRIVATE INTERNATIONAL LAW AND EU COPYRIGHT

550. The EU has not addressed issues of private international law in its copyright directives. However, EU rules on private international law can be applied to intellectual property and can form the starting point for addressing the cross-border aspects of intellectual property rights. Nevertheless, those rules are incomplete and inadequate on certain points.[2212] The lack of complete and adequate rules is particularly problematic with regard to online use of in-copyright works. It has been a challenge for national courts in the EU to determine which states have jurisdiction in such cases and what the applicable law is when a rightholder seeks EU wide remedies.[2213] This is highly relevant for digital libraries that want to put their works online, for example under an ECL agreement. As long as substantive legislation is not in force within Europe on where acts under the exclusive making available right are deemed to take place, it is the prerogative of each national court to decide whether it has jurisdiction and which laws are applicable. Potentially this means that in

2209 Regulation (EU) 2018/302 of the European Parliament and of the Council of 28 February 2018 on addressing unjustified geo-blocking and other forms of discrimination based on customers' nationality, place of residence or place of establishment within the internal market and amending Regulations (EC) No 2006/2004 and (EU) 2017/2394 and Directive 2009/22/EC (Text with EEA relevance.).

2210 COM(2016) 289 final, Proposal, 2016, 1 Art. 1(5) and 4(1)(b) of the Geo-blocking Directive. However, in an attached statement to the Regulation the Commission affirms that it intends to evaluate this exclusion of copyright-services.

2211 European Copyright Society, General Opinion on the EU Copyright Reform Package, 2017, 2.

2212 Paul Torremans, 'Intellectual property and the EU rules on private international law: match or mismatch?' in Irini Stamatoudi and Paul Torremans (eds), *EU Copyright Law; A Commentary* (2014) 1019–1029, 1060; Matulionyte, Cross-Border, 2009, 471–474.

2213 Matulionyte, Enforcing, 2015, 141.

order to establish legal certainty, libraries will need to negotiate licences in each and every country where the material could be accessed. In the following I will take a brief look at the question of jurisdiction and applicable law in the EU.

8.4.1. JURISDICTION

551. Jurisdiction in international law refers "to the power of a sovereign to affect the rights of persons by legislation, by executive degree or by the judgement of a court".[2214] Below I will focus on the competence of a national court within the EU area to deal with copyright issues in international situations and in particular with regard to cross-border online use. Judicial competence covers two distinct issues, personal jurisdiction, i.e. whether the court has competence to hear a case against the defendant, and subject-matter jurisdiction, i.e. whether the court has the competence to hear the subject matter of the claim, such as in case of alleged infringement of foreign copyright.[2215] It is the national court that will decide whether it has jurisdiction or not based on national legislation.[2216] There are no binding international treaties determining what principles should guide national legislation in this connection[2217] although there are regional instruments. The forum of a case is important for the outcome of the case, as the court that has jurisdiction decides, firstly, which laws are applicable i.e. the substantive law that will govern the dispute[2218], and secondly, the procedural framework of the whole litigation, cost and enforcement.[2219]

552. The issue of jurisdiction in the EU is regulated by the Brussels I Recast Regulation[2220] which aims to "unify the rules of conflict of jurisdiction in civil

2214 Walker, The Oxford Companion to Law, 1980, 677.

2215 Ricketson and Ginsburg, International, 2006, 1294.

2216 Ginsburg and Treppoz, International, 2015, 557; Goldstein and Hugenholtz, 3rd ed., 2013, 117.

2217 Triaille and others, Study, 2013, 64.

2218 Carmen Otero García-Castrillón, 'Choice of law in IP: rounding off territoriality' in Paul Torremans (ed), *Research Handbook on Cross-border Enforcement of Intellectual Property* (Edward Elgar, 2014) 421; Ricketson and Ginsburg, International, 2006, 1292; Rognstad, Opphavsrett, 2009, 427.

2219 Goldstein and Hugenholtz, 3rd ed., 2013, 117; Ricketson and Ginsburg, International, 2006, 1292; Lucas, Applicable law, 2005, 2.

2220 Regulation (EU) No 1215/2012 of the European Parliament and of the Council of 12 December 2012 on jurisdiction and the recognition and enforcement of judgments in civil and commercial matters (recast), hereafter the Regulation or Brussels I Recast. The Regulation repealed Council Regulation (EC) No 44/2001 of 22 December 2000 (Brussels I) Regulation. The Brussel I Recast applies from 10 January 2015 and references to the repealed Regulation shall be construed as references to the recast version, cf. Art. 81. The Lugano Convention on jurisdiction and the recognition and enforcement of judgments in civil and commercial matters of 30 October 2007, which replaced the Lugano Convention of 1988, (the

and commercial matters and to simplify the formalities with a view to rapid and simple recognition and enforcement of judgments from Member States"[2221] for the proper functioning of the internal market.[2222] The general principle of jurisdiction under the Regulation is the defendant's jurisdiction which provides that persons domiciled in a Member State shall, whatever their nationality, be sued in the courts of that Member State.[2223] However, special jurisdiction can be applicable in copyright infringement cases under Art. 7(2) of the Regulation[2224], which provides that in matters relating to tort, delict or quasi-delict, the plaintiff can opt for a jurisdiction where the "harmful event occurred or may occur."

553. Online cross-border use of in-copyright works poses a particular difficulty with regard to jurisdiction as one element of the act can be deemed to happen in one country and another in a different country or countries. Thus online cross-border use of in-copyright works can lead to infringement in more than one country; in fact there is a potential damage in every country where the material can be accessed via the internet.[2225]

554. The CJEU has concluded that Art. 7(2) of the Brussels I Recast Regulation is "intended to cover both the place where the damage occurred and the place of the event giving rise to it, so that the defendant may be sued, at the option of the applicant, in the courts for either of those places."[2226] However, the reach of the jurisdiction is different depending on the place of litigation. Thus, the place of the event giving rise to the damage: "... confers jurisdiction on the court before which proceedings are brought for all the damage sustained"[2227], whereas, the "extent of the jurisdiction of the courts of the place where the damage occurred is limited to damage that occurred on the territory of the Member State in question."[2228] The place where the damage is deemed to occur can vary

New Lugano Convention), unifies the rules on jurisdiction in civil and commercial matters and expands the applicability of the Brussels I Regulation to the relations between Member States of the EC, as well as Denmark, which opted out of the Brussels I Regulation, on the one hand, and Norway, Iceland and Switzerland on the other.

2221 Recital (4) "Brussels I Recast" [was Recital (2) "Brussels I"].

2222 C-441/13 – Hejduk, par. 3.

2223 Cf. Art. 4; Was Art. 2 "Brussels I".

2224 Was Art. 5(3) "Brussels I".

2225 Torremans, Private, 2016, 383; Ginsburg and Treppoz, International, 2015, 603; Fawcett and Torremans, Intellectual Property, 2011, Ch. 5.

2226 C-441/13 – Hejduk, par. 18; C-360/12 *Coty Germany GmbH v First Note Perfumes NV* ECLI:EU:C:2014:1318, CJEU, 5 June 2014 par. 46; C-170/12 – Pinckney, par. 26; C-68/93 *Fiona Shevill, Ixora Trading Inc., Chequepoint SARL and Chequepoint International Ltd v Presse Alliance SA* ECLI:EU:C:1995:61, CJEU, 7 March 1995 par. 20.

2227 C-170/12 – AG opinion in Pinckney, par. 57; C-523/10 *Wintersteiger AG v Products 4U Sondermaschinenbau GmbH* ECLI:EU:C:2012:220, CJEU, 19 April 2012 par. 30; C-68/93 – Shevill and Others v Presse Alliance, par. 25.

2228 C-170/12 – AG opinion in Pinckney, fn. 60; C-68/93 – Shevill and Others v Presse Alliance, par. 28 and 30.

depending on the right involved and whether that right is protected in a given country.[2229]

555. In the Football Dataco case concerning infringement of the *sui generis* right in databases, the CJEU justified localising the act of extraction and/or re-utilisation by underlining that it mattered with regard to jurisdiction where the harmful event occurred or may occur.[2230] The Court came to the conclusion that

> ...if the mere fact of being accessible were sufficient for it to be concluded that there was an act of re-utilisation, websites and data which, although obviously targeted at persons outside the territory of the Member State concerned, were nevertheless technically accessible in that State would wrongly be subject to the application of the relevant law of that State...[2231]

Thus the Court stated that in order for such an act to be located in a particular Member State there had to be evidence of an intention on the part of its performer to target persons in that territory.[2232] If such evidence of targeting persons in a Member State was present the relevant act was to be considered to have taken place "at least" in that Member State. Thus after the Football Dataco case it was assumed by many that the relevant criterion in the online environment for where the harm occurred or was likely to occur was the "targeting" of a certain Member State's public.[2233]

556. The "targeting" approach was, however, rejected in the Pinckney and Hejduk cases. There the CJEU found that it was not required under the Brussels I Regulation that the alleged infringing activity be directed at the country where the harm may occur.[2234] The sole condition laid down in Art. 5(3) of the Brussels I Regulation[2235] was that a harmful event had occurred or might occur.[2236] Hence it was irrelevant for the purpose of determining jurisdiction on the basis of where damage had occurred, whether the particular webpage which allegedly infringed copyright was directed at a Member State where the jurisdiction was claimed or not.[2237] Consequently a national court can have jurisdiction in any Member State where the website which allegedly infringes copyright protected in that State is accessible.[2238]

2229 C-170/12 – Pinckney, par. 32, 33 and 35; C-441/13 – Hejduk, par. 29; C-523/10 – Wintersteiger, par. 24.
2230 C-173/11, Football Dataco II, par. 17, 23 and 29.
2231 Ibid, par. 37.
2232 Ibid, par. 39.
2233 Matulionyte, Enforcing, 2015, 136; Husovec, Comment on "Pinckney", 2014; Public Consultation on the review of the EU copyright rules (2013), 10–11.
2234 C-170/12 – Pinckney, par. 42; C-441/13 – Hejduk, par. 32.
2235 Now Art. 7(2) of Brussels I Recast.
2236 C-170/12 – Pinckney, par. 41.
2237 C-441/13 – Hejduk, par. 33.
2238 Ibid, par. 38; C-170/12 – Pinckney, par. 43–44.

However, as mentioned above, the court has jurisdiction only to rule on the potential damage caused within that Member State.[2239] Courts in other Member States retain jurisdiction under Art. 5(3) with regard to damages caused in their respective Member State, as they are best placed to ascertain whether infringement has occurred in the State concerned and in case of infringement, the nature of the damage.[2240]

557. The accessibility criterion has drawn criticism. First, some have questioned whether the approach is compatible with the general aim of the Regulation to ensure that rules of jurisdiction are highly predictable for the defendant.[2241] In response, it can be said that the accessibility criterion is predictable, as it covers at least all countries within the EU/EEA. Second, the criterion has been criticised as facilitating "harassment" of defendants, especially those that cannot afford to defend themselves in multiple jurisdictions.[2242] Third, the approach could encourage forum shopping.[2243] Finally, the accessibility approach seems to stimulate a multiplication of courts having jurisdiction for the same incident and thus does not seem to serve "to minimise the possibility of concurrent proceedings and to ensure that irreconcilable judgments will not be given in different Member States."[2244, 2245]

558. The accessibility criterion implies that a library that puts in-copyright works online under a national ECL agreement could potentially face litigation in every jurisdiction where the work can be accessed. Even if they won the case or were directed to pay very low damages because of low use or potential low use[2246], for example in the case of Norwegian works being made available in other European countries where not many master the language, it would still be a time-consuming and expensive exercise. Stakeholders such as digital libraries need legal certainty above likelihood. Despite the fact that the limited scope of damages that the courts of countries of reception could award makes it unlikely that a rightholder would sue in such a country that on its own is still a weak protection against litigation in a country of mere accessibility.[2247] The circumstances vary with each case and there can be several reasons, both warranted and unwarranted,

---

2239 C-441/13 – Hejduk, par. 36, referring to C-170/12 – Pinckney, par. 45.

2240 C-170/12 - Pinckney, par. 46; C-441/13 – Hejduk, par. 37.

2241 Recitals (15) and (16) Brussels I Recast, cf. Matulionyte, Enforcing, 2015, 133.

2242 Torremans, Private, 2016, 384–385; Paul Torremans, 'Jurisdiction in Intellectual Property Cases' in Paul Torremans (ed), *Research Handbook on Cross-border Enforcement of Intellectual Property* (Edward Elgar, 2014) 385–389.

2243 Matulionyte, Enforcing, 2015, 134; Brad Spitz, Jurisdiction in EU copyright cases: accessibility of a website is a criterion, Kluwer Copyright Blog, 2 December 2013; accessed 13 July 2017.

2244 Recital (21) and Art. 45(1)(d) Brussels I Recast.

2245 C-360/12 *Opinion of Advocate General Jääskinen in Coty Germany GmbH v First Note Perfumes NV* ECLI:EU:C:2013:764, CJEU, 21 November 2013 par. 61.

2246 Matulionyte, Enforcing, 2015, 135.

2247 Husovec, Comment on "Pinckney", 2014, 373.

why rightholders might want to litigate in a country of reception, for example in the Hejdunk case, where the plaintiff sued in the country where she resided.[2248] Thus the country of reception approach to decide jurisdiction is not helpful for digital libraries wishing to make works from their collections available online.

559. The targeting approach might limit the choice of jurisdiction. Nevertheless, it would not be of much help for libraries that simply wish to make the works in their collections available online as part of giving access to the European culture. The purpose of such access is precisely to make it widely available, at least in Europe, so the targeting approach would not limit the choice of jurisdiction.

560. It has been suggested that jurisdiction in internet infringement cases could be based on where the alleged infringement originated.[2249] However, this approach has been criticised as leading to "unreasonable disadvantages to rightholders" and that it might "significantly weaken the enforcement of copyright online" as well as possibly encouraging forum shopping by online service providers.[2250] This seems convincing for online infringement cases in general. Still, the particular case of online use by libraries of in-copyright national works based on a national ECL agreement might be different. The country of origin would thus be that with the closest connection, i.e. where the library is based, where the works are first published and where the ECL agreement is concluded. Furthermore, if the use only concerned national works the outsider would also most likely be domiciled in that country. However, as the CJEU has determined that the country of reception or access is the criterion for jurisdiction in on-line infringement cases in the Pinckney and Hejduk decisions[2251] that will remain the prevailing approach for determining jurisdictions in online copyright cases.

561. Once the question of jurisdiction has been determined the question arises of what law is applicable to the claim.

8.4.2. APPLICABLE LAWS

562. There are two approaches with regard to applicable laws, a universal approach reflected in the country of origin, or *lex loci originis*, rule, and a

2248 C-441/13 – Hejduk, par. 2.

2249 See e.g. C-441/13 *Opinion of Advocate General P. Cruz Villalón in Pez Hejduk v EnergieAgentur.NRW GmbH.* ECLI:EU:C:2014:2212, CJEU, 11 September 2014 par. 41–45.

2250 Matulionyte, Enforcing, 2015, 137.

2251 C-170/12 – Pinckney, C-441/13 – Hejduk, and Depreeuw and Hubin, Study 2014, 2014, 30; Triaille and others, Study, 2013, 148; Torremans, Private, 2016, 383–384, referring to the decision in C-360/12 – Coty Germany, par. 61, where the CJEU declined the suggestion of the AG in the case to reconsider the jurisdiction approach.

territorial approach reflected in the *lex loci protectionis* rule. The territorial approach will submit "all works to the same level of protection within one country" whereas the universal approach will provide the rightholder with "the benefit of the same protection all over the world."[2252]

The *lex loci originis* rule refers to the law of the country of origin in the sense of Art. 5(4) of the Berne Convention.[2253] Many assume that the rule is incompatible with the national treatment principle[2254], which has been understood to "supply a choice of law rule directing application of the substantive law of the countries in which the author seeks to enforce her right"[2255] and is hence not used in many jurisdictions.[2256] Art. 5(2) of the Berne Convention has been interpreted to confirm that the law applicable to the act of exploitation of rights is the place of exploitation[2257] or where protection is claimed.[2258] Even so, some claim that it is possible to understand Art. 5(2) to mean the country from which the alleged infringement originated and still conform to the principle of territoriality.[2259] Thus there is no agreement on how to interpret the provision in Art. 5 of the Berne Convention with regard to applicable laws.[2260] The conclusion seems to be that the Convention fails to "create a general structure for identifying applicable law"[2261] and that the national treatment principle cannot provide for a complete choice-of-law rule.[2262]

Nevertheless, the applicable law is traditionally considered the law where protection is sought and the alleged infringement takes place, i.e. *lex loci protectionis,* either argued by referring to the principle of territoriality, private international law or a combination of both.[2263] However, in ubiquitous infringement cases, common in today's world linked by digital networks, the

---

2252 Ginsburg and Treppoz, International, 2015, 650; Matulionyte, Enforcing, 2015, 138; van Eechoud, Alternatives, 2005, 289.

2253 Triaille and others, Study, 2013, 82. See discussion on Art. 5(4) BC in Ch. 8.1.

2254 Art. 5(1) BC, see brief discussion in Ch. 8.2.1.

2255 Ricketson and Ginsburg, International, 2006, 1298; van Eechoud, Choice, 2003, 107.

2256 Matulionyte, Enforcing, 2015, 138.

2257 COM(2004) 261 final, Communication, 2004, 7.

2258 Kyst, Aftalelicens, 2009, 52; Triaille and others, Study, 2013, 87.

2259 Ricketson and Ginsburg, International, 2006, 1302–1303; Graeme B. Dinwoodie, Conflicts and International Copyright Litigation: The Role of International Norms, 2005, 203.

2260 Fawcett and Torremans, Intellectual Property, 2011, 671–685; Ricketson and Ginsburg, International, 2006, 1298; van Eechoud, Choice, 2003, 95–107.

2261 Ricketson and Ginsburg, International, 2006, 1297–1300; Triaille and others, Study, 2013, 47; van Eechoud, Alternatives, 2005, 293; van Eechoud, Choice, 2003, 95; C-28/04 – Tod's and Tod's France, par. 32.

2262 Goldstein and Hugenholtz, 3rd ed., 2013, 131–132.

2263 COM(95) 382 final, Green Paper, 1995, 38; Ricketson and Ginsburg, International, 2006, 1301; Axhamn and Guibault, Cross-border ECL, 2011, 20; von Lewinski, International, 2008, 6; Fawcett and Torremans, Intellectual Property, 2011, 678; COM(2003) 427 final, Proposal for the Rome II Regulation, 2003, 20; Matulionyte, Law Applicable To Copyright, 2011, 27; van Eechoud, Choice, 2003, 105; Goldstein and Hugenholtz, 3rd ed., 2013, 133, 140; Lucas, Applicable law, 2005, 2; Matulionyte, Enforcing, 2015, 138.

traditional choice-of-law of *lex loci protectionis* has been described as "unwieldy" or even "impracticable".[2264]

563. There are two European instruments that deal with choice of law relevant for copyright: the Rome I Regulation on the law applicable to contractual obligations[2265] and the Rome II Regulation on the applicable law for non-contractual obligations.[2266] Thus different laws may apply to the copyright as such and its infringement on the one hand and contractual transfer of copyright on the other hand.[2267]

8.4.2.1. Contractual obligations

564. The main rule under the Rome I Regulation, as in general with conflict of rules laws for contracts, is the freedom of choice.[2268] This means that the applicable law is the law agreed upon in the contract. In the absence of express or implied choice in the agreement the Rome I Regulation stipulates the applicable laws for different types of contracts.[2269] However, those provisions do not cover copyright contracts and hence, in the absence of choice, they will "be governed by the law of the country where the party required to effect the characteristic performance of the contract has his habitual residence" unless it is demonstrated that the contract is more closely connected to another country.[2270] Thus the applicable laws for contracts are not based on territoriality.[2271]

565. The question is whether ECL agreements can be treated as contracts that fall under the Rome I Regulation. Such a solution might be possible in my view. As I argue above[2272] the ECL system is a hybrid; a mixture of management of rights, based on voluntary mandates of members and the extension effect, which

---

[2264] Ricketson and Ginsburg, International, 2006, 1301–1302; Goldstein and Hugenholtz, 3rd ed., 2013, 134; van Eechoud, Choice, 2003, 229.

[2265] Regulation (EC) No 593/2008 of the European Parliament and of the Council of 17 June 2008 on the law applicable to contractual obligations (Rome I).

[2266] Regulation (EC) No 864/2007 of the European Parliament and of the Council of 17 June 2008 on the law applicable to non-contractual obligations (Rome II).

[2267] Torremans, Private, 2016, 392; Torremans, Intellectual property, 2014, 1057.

[2268] Art. 3 Rome I; Lucas, Applicable law, 2005, 6; Goldstein and Hugenholtz, 3rd ed., 2013, 144.

[2269] Art. 4(1) Rome I.

[2270] Art. 4(2)-(3) Rome I. Cf. C-533/07 *Falco Privatstiftung and Thomas Rabitsch v Gisela Weller-Lindhorst* ECLI:EU:C:2009:257, CJEU, 23 April 2009 par. 18–44; Triaille and others, Study, 2013, 85–86; Goldstein and Hugenholtz, 3rd ed., 2013, 144–147. The Rome I Regulation is not applicable to the EFTA-EEA countries. In Norway, if the contract does not provide for choice of law the law of the country closest to the contract will be applied, cf. Rognstad, Opphavsrett, 2009, 431.

[2271] Xalabarder, Jurisdiction, 2014, 187.

[2272] See Ch. 6.1.2, Ch. 6.3.1 and briefly in Ch. 8.2.3.

I suggest that in the first instance is an exception to the outsider's right. However, depending on the area of use under ECL agreements and the deployment of safeguard measures, the exception part of the system could be seen as subsiding in favour of legal assumption of mandate from the outsider to the CMO once the three-step test is passed. Thus in those circumstances I propose that the extension effect of the ECL system becomes a legal presumption or a legal mandate. Accordingly ECL agreements that fulfil the three-step test would be seen as based on an arrangement of management of rights.[2273] This reasoning would be one way to understand recital (18) of the InfoSoc Directive.[2274] In my view that could lead to the conclusion that ECL agreements which are seen as an arrangement of management of right, also with regard to outsiders, are contracts negotiated by CMOs based on the voluntary mandates from their members and presumed legal mandates from outsiders.

566. The choice-of-law question becomes relevant for ECL agreements for online use by libraries with cross-border effect where an outsider, residing abroad, brings a case in his or her country of residence, claiming that a use under an ECL agreement resulting in accessibility to his or her work in the country of residence, is a breach of his or her exclusive right as he or she has not authorised such use. If such a claim were brought before a court in a country where there were no compatible ECL provisions or any exception with regard to the making available right for the benefit of libraries, then the right of the outsider in that particular country might be deemed infringed. However, if the applicable law was the law of the country where the ECL agreement was concluded, the outcome might be different, as presumably the use under the agreement in the country of reception would be deemed authorised by the agreement in the country of origin.

567. If my argument is accepted that ECLs are, under certain conditions, ultimately considered arrangements concerning management of rights with regard to outsiders within the EU[2275], a logical conclusion seems to be that the Rome I Regulation should be used when determining applicable laws, as with collective licensing in general. This is true with regard to contractual issues, such as obligations between parties, formal validity, interpretation, and so on, whereas there is more doubt about copyright related issues, such as proprietary issues, the existence of a right, ownership, scope and duration.[2276] ECL agreements usually do not touch upon such copyright related issues as they are only concerned with the obligations of parties for a particular use of in-copyright works.

2273 See Ch. 9.1 and Ch. 10 for my discussion on which requirements ECL agreements for online cross-border use would have to fulfil in order to pass the three-step test.

2274 See Ch. 6.3.1.

2275 See discussion in Ch. 6.3.1.

2276 ALAI, Opinion ECL, 2016, 6; Matulionyte, Cross-Border, 2009, 469,473; Rognstad, Opphavsrett, 2009, 429; Goldstein and Hugenholtz, 3rd ed., 2013, 149–153.

568. If the Rome I Regulation were deemed to apply to the use of works of outsiders under an ECL agreement then the applicable laws would be the law explicitly or implicitly designated by the agreement.[2277] In the absence of explicit or implied provision to that effect, the applicable law would be of the country where the characteristic performer of the contract resides.[2278] That party is most commonly considered to be the rightholder or licensor, at least in non-exclusive contracts where the licensee has no obligations other than to pay remuneration.[2279] However, if it were clear from the circumstances that the contract was manifestly more closely connected to another country than where the characteristic performer resides the law of that country would apply.

An explicit provision on applicable law in a national ECL agreement would be most likely to stipulate the law of the country where the ECL agreement was negotiated. In such a case the foreign court would presumably come to the conclusion that the outsider's right had not been infringed in light of the ECL provision of the originating country of the ECL agreement, unless the agreement failed to fulfil the three-step test with regard to the outsider. That would be assessed on the basis of the law in the country where the ECL agreement was negotiated. However, if there were no explicit provision in the ECL agreement, the applicable law would be the law of the country where "the party required to effect the characteristic performance of the contract" resided. The "party" would presumably be deemed to be the CMO, which acts under a mandate from substantial numbers of rightholders as well as a legislative mandate for the extension effect with regard to outsiders. It is unlikely it would be considered to be the library as their only obligation is to pay remuneration, which is traditionally not considered characteristic performance.[2280] However, the foreign court, where the outsider resided, might also conclude that the party was the outside rightholder, in which case the applicable law would be the law of the country of the outsider's residence. Finally, there is also the possibility that the contract (ECL agreement) might be seen as more closely connected to another country than the country of residence of the outside rightholder.[2281] To me it seems likely that a national ECL agreement for the use of works from the collection of a national library, in particular if the works were limited to national works, i.e. published in that country, might be considered to be more closely connected to the country where it was concluded rather than the country of residence of the outside rightholder. Nevertheless, for legal certainty it would be advisable in ECL agreements to have an explicit choice-of-law provision.

2277 Art. 3 Rome I.
2278 Art. 4(2) Rome I.
2279 Goldstein and Hugenholtz, 3rd ed., 2013, 147; van Eechoud, Choice, 2003, 227–228, 199.
2280 Van Eechoud, Choice, 2003, 198.
2281 Art. 4(2)-(3) Rome I.

569. There remains the possibility that a court within the EU, or the CJEU, would not accept that the use of an outsider's right under an ECL agreement constituted use under a contract.[2282] In that case the court would need to consult the Regulation on non-contractual obligations.

8.4.2.2. Non-contractual obligations

570. The general rule of applicable law under the Rome II Regulation is *lex loci delicti* which is:

> ...the law of the country in which the damage occurs irrespective of the country in which the event giving rise to the damage occurred and irrespective of the country or countries in which the indirect consequences of that event occur.[2283]

However, for intellectual property rights "the universally acknowledged principle of the *lex loci protectionis*" is maintained[2284] as stipulated in Article 8 (1): "[t]he law applicable to a non-contractual obligation arising from an infringement of an intellectual property right shall be the law of the country for which protection is claimed."[2285] This is the rule with regard to the applicable law in case of infringement though not for other aspects of copyright, such as initial ownership or scope of the right.[2286] For those areas of copyright Member States are free to choose the applicable laws, for example the law of origin of the work.[2287]

571. The distinction between the *lex loci delicti* and the *lex loci protectionis* is not clear, either in doctrine or court practices.[2288] In many cases the applicable laws would be the same. Under both provisions the applicable law might not be that of the country where the proceedings are instituted.[2289] However, there are some differences, the main one being that the *lex loci delicti* doctrine can be derogated from in certain circumstances, cf. Art. 4(2) and (3), whereas Art. 8(3) forbids derogation from the principle of the *lex loci protectionis* in Art. 8(1) by contract.[2290] This absolute prohibition of agreement between litigants

---

2282 ALAI, Opinion ECL, 2016, 6.

2283 Art. 4(1) Rome II.

2284 Recital (26) Rome II.

2285 Treppoz observes that the connecting factor here is the same as under Art. 5(2) Berne Convention, cf. Edouard Treppoz, 'Commentary on Regulation No. 864/2007 (Rome II)' in T. Cottier and P. Veron (eds), *Concise International and European IP Law* (Wolters Kluwer, 2014) 431.

2286 Cf. Art. 15 Rome II; Torremans, Intellectual property, 2014, 1056.

2287 Ginsburg and Treppoz, International, 2015, 663; Treppoz, Rome II, 2014, 432. There is a controversy as to which laws are applicable to the question of original ownership, e.g. Triaille and others, Study, 2013, 95, 97, however, that discussion is outside the scope of this study.

2288 Rita Matulionyte, *Law Applicable To Copyright: A Comparison of the ALI and CLIP Proposals* (Edward Elgar Publishing 2011), 27.

2289 Lucas, Applicable law, 2005, 3.

2290 Treppoz, Rome II, 2014, 432–433.

on applicable law has its rationale in the link of IPRs with national economic policies.[2291] It has been criticised, in particular for cross-border infringement cases, and the observation made that the general public order exception in Art. 26 of the Regulation should be an adequate safeguard for national economic policies.[2292]

572. For the purpose of the subject of this book the most important aspect of the rule in Art. 8(1) is the fact that it does not stipulate how the localisation of the infringing act should be carried out in cases of ubiquitous infringement, such as in infringing online use of in-copyright works. In such situations the *lex loci protectionis* can be interpreted in various ways as to which laws are applicable.[2293] The WCT, which adopted the making available right as a specific right under the communication to the public right, does not designate which laws should be applicable in relation to that right.[2294] Scholars and interested parties have diverging opinions on how this issue should be resolved. However, as mentioned above, it has been submitted that the question of the localisation of the infringing act is not a private international law issue as such, but rather an issue of substantive law.[2295] To me, providing the answer to the localisation question in substantive law seems the most logical approach, at least with regard to the issue of online accessibility of works in the collection of libraries and other cultural heritage institutions, as there may not exist a universal "one-size fit all" solution.

8.5. CONCLUSION

573. In this chapter I have looked at the crucial issue of the principle of territoriality of copyright and its effect on cross-border online use, both on the exclusive rights of communication to the public right and reproduction. I also looked briefly at the issue of private international law, in particular with regard to the EU framework. Although EU Regulations on jurisdiction and applicable law are applied on copyright cases in an online context, they do not provide answers that simplify the situation. Clarifying the situation of territoriality and online use of in-copyright works would best be achieved by substantive legislation on copyright rather than through private international law regulations. In line with my previous argument that although the extension effect is an exception to the

2291 Torremans, Intellectual property, 2014, 1057.
2292 Carmen Otero García-Castrillón, Choice of law, 2014, 447.
2293 C-173/11, Football Dataco II, par. 32; Walter and von Lewinski (eds) European Copyright Law, A Commentary, 2010, 1513; Depreeuw and Hubin, Study 2014, 2014, 27–28; Triaille and others, Study, 2013, 88, 95–96; Axhamn and Guibault, Cross-border ECL, 2011, 20–21.
2294 Ricketson and Ginsburg, International, 2006, 1310.
2295 See Ch. 8.2.1.

outsider's exclusive right ECL agreements that fulfil the three-step test could be seen as based on an arrangement of management of rights[2296], it can be further argued that under certain circumstances ECL agreements can have cross-border effect in online use.[2297] In this chapter I demonstrate my view that for online use with cross-border effect of national in-copyright works by digital libraries under national ECL agreements, which fulfil international legal norms with regard to the limitation on outsiders[2298], the best approach for substantive legislation would be the country of origin approach: the place where the agreement is concluded and where the parties are established, i.e. the library and the CMO negotiating the ECL agreement.[2299] This is the approach that the Commission proposed in the DSM proposal with regard to the use of out-of-commerce works for cultural heritage institutions, as will be discussed below.[2300]

574. Application of the country of origin approach might be achieved with regard to ECL agreements within the EU on the basis of the Rome I Regulation on applicable laws for contractual obligations[2301] (or even internationally if ECL agreements, with regards to outsiders, were universally seen as arrangement concerning management of rights). However, that conclusion is by no mean undisputed and in order to obtain the necessary legal certainty it would be preferable to have EU legislation supporting the cross-border effect of such ECL agreements.

575. In the next chapter I will further discuss the cross-border applicability of ECL agreements and compare the ECL system to other legal solutions that might be applied to enabling cross-border online use for libraries.

2296 See Ch. 6.1.2, Ch. 6.3.1 and briefly in Ch. 8.2.3.
2297 See Ch. 9.1.
2298 See Ch. 6.2.3.4.
2299 Ch. 8.2.3.
2300 See Ch. 11.3.
2301 See Ch. 8.4.2.1.

CHAPTER 9

OPTIONS FOR LEGISLATIVE SOLUTIONS FOR ENABLING CROSS-BORDER ONLINE USE OF WORKS IN EUROPEAN LIBRARIES

...libraries currently exist in two worlds – the world of Gutenberg and the world of Gates.[2302]

576. An important element in equipping libraries with tools to bridge the two worlds of Gutenberg and Gates is to create a legal framework in which in-copyright works from library collections can be made available online with cross-border effect, at least within Europe. Enabling online cross-border use of in-copyright works from library collections is in line with their public-interest aim of giving access to the cultural heritage. Easier access to the cultural heritage can aid the development of creativity and harmonises well with the EU's aims for the digital single market as well as EU cultural policy.[2303]

577. The EU's stated policy with regard to online distribution of in-copyright works by publicly accessible libraries and similar institutions has been that such use should be facilitated with specific contracts or licences.[2304] However, this policy has already been deviated from with the mandatory exception for the making available to the public of orphan works.[2305, 2306] Thus exceptions might be deemed an appropriate channel for further enabling the public interest mission of libraries. Even so, the Orphan Works Directive underlines that solutions to address "larger" mass digitisation issues should be built "upon the consensus of the relevant stakeholders".[2307]

2302 Thomas W. Shaughnessy, 'Digital Information and the Library: Planning and Policy Issues' in S Lee (ed), *Economics of Digital Information: Collection, Storage and Delivery* (Haworth Press, 1997) 10.

2303 COM(2015) 192 final, Communication, 2015, 6–8; COM(2005) 465 final, *Communication from the Commission to the European Parliament, the Council, the European Economic and Social Committee and the Committee of the Regions – i2010: digital libraries*, (30.9.2005) 3ff.; Borghi, Erickson and Favale, With Enough, 2016, 138; Trumpke, Exklusivität, 2015, 557–558.

2304 Recital (40) InfoSoc Directive.

2305 Art. 6 OWD.

2306 See discussion on the OWD in Ch. 4.2.3.

2307 Recital (4) OWD.

578. Individual licensing is impractical or even impossible for mass digitisation and use[2308] in libraries and thus collective licensing would seem to be necessary. However, collective licensing on its own does not solve the whole problem because of the issue of outsiders. This is where collective management with legislative support could provide a way forward, specific models being the ECL system, presumption of representation or mandatory collective management.[2309] The Orphan Works Directive recommended the MoU for Out-of-Commerce Works[2310] as a framework for a solution.[2311] The MoU framework prescribes presumption of representation as a way to deal with the issue of outsiders. The system of ECL would also fit under this framework. The newly proposed legal solution in the DSM proposal[2312] for the use of out-of-commerce works by libraries and other cultural heritage institutions provides that collective licensing can be extended to outsiders by an extension effect, such as provided for under ECLs or by presumed mandate of outsiders.[2313]

579. However, the issue of outsiders becomes more complicated in relation to cross-border use of their works due to the territoriality principle.[2314] I argue that national ECL agreements can have cross-border effect under certain conditions, as will be discussed further both in this chapter and below.[2315] Furthermore, in this chapter I look at other collective management solutions with legislative support, i.e. legal presumption of mandates and mandatory collective management, and compare them to the system of ECL with regard to cross-border use. I also briefly discuss whether the solution for multi-territorial licences for online use of music could be a model for online use by libraries. Subsequently I look at a solution based on exception and finally, I briefly discuss the possibility of a unified single EU copyright and how this might affect the situation for libraries and online use.

9.1. ECLS AND CROSS-BORDER ONLINE USE

580. Traditionally the ECL system has operated for use of works within the national territory of the relevant CMO.[2316] With the advent of the internet, however, there has been increasing discussion on whether the ECL system can

2308 See discussion on "mass digitization" in Ch. 2.2.2.
2309 See discussion in Ch. 5.1.
2310 See discussion on the MoU in Ch. 7.1.
2311 Recital (4) OWD; 2011/711/EU, Recommendation, 2011, Recital (12); Talke, Verwaiste und vergriffene Werke, 2013, 133.
2312 COM(2016) 593 final, Proposal, 2016, Art. 7–9.
2313 See discussion on the proposal in Ch. 11.3.
2314 See discussion in Ch. 8.1–8.2.
2315 See Ch. 10.
2316 Tryggvadóttir, Balancing of interests, 2015, 661; Tryggvadóttir, Digital libraries, 2014, 323; Vuopala, Extended, 2013, 17, 38; Trumpke, Exklusivität, 2015, 640–641.

facilitate cross-border online use of works. No territorial limitation on the extension effect that binds outsiders is expressly stipulated in the ECL provisions in any of the Nordic countries[2317] nor in any of the other collective licensing systems with legislative support within Europe.[2318] However, it has been assumed by many that ECL agreements cannot be used for cross-border online use.[2319] Even so, within the Nordic countries there are diverging views on the issue.[2320]

9.1.1. THE SITUATION IN THE NORDIC COUNTRIES

581. In Denmark authorisations of ECL agreements for online use made under the general ECL provision[2321] are issued with regard to Danish territory. Nevertheless, works made available under these agreements are generally available worldwide online as no geo-blocking is used. This is the case with use under the four authorisations for online uses by libraries mentioned in Ch. 5.3.2.1 above, although in one instance use is limited by access code.[2322] Scholars have observed that the issue of cross-border effect in online use under the general ECL provision remains unresolved but have also underlined that in practical terms it would be of little consequence, as most digitisation projects would revolve around Danish works and be on Danish websites.[2323] Yet, none of the aforementioned authorisations are limited to Danish works.[2324] However, in the preparatory legal documents for the Danish implementation of the Orphan Works Directive in 2014, it was stated that ECLs could not have cross-border effect.[2325]

582. In Finland the general approach has been that ECLs can have cross-border effect. Thus a Finnish Copyright Society report in 2013 evaluating the use of the ECL system for Europeana came to the conclusion that the system was a "valid legislative construction" for cross-border use.[2326] More importantly, the Finnish Ministry of Education and Culture, the copyright organisations Kuvasto and Kopiosto and the Finnish National Gallery signed an agreement in September 2014 that expressly enables the worldwide display of works by Finnish artists online, both members of the CMOs and outsiders.[2327]

2317 Trumpke, Exklusivität, 2015, 624, 630–631.
2318 See Ch. 7.
2319 See brief discussion and references in Ch. 1.2.
2320 Tryggvadóttir, Digital libraries, 2014, 323; Tryggvadóttir, Balancing of interests, 2015, 661–662.
2321 Art. 50(2) DCA.
2322 See also Trumpke, Exklusivität, 2015, 629.
2323 Kyst, Aftalelicens, 2009, 52.
2324 See Ch. 5.3.2.1.
2325 Lovforslag nr. L 123 2014, Folketinget 2013–14. Forslag til Lov til ændring af ophavsretsloven (Visse tilladte anvendelser af forældreløse værker og ændring af aftalelicensbestemmelsen vedrørende kabelviderspredning)
2326 Vuopala, Extended, 2013, 28.
2327 See further in Ch. 5.3.1.2.

583. There is no mention of cross-border effect of ECL agreements in Icelandic legal preparatory documents nor are there any agreements with cross-border effect.

584. In Norway there is no explicit mention of cross-border effect in legal preparatory documents of ECLs, but the most relevant ECL agreement for the purpose of this study, the Bokhylla project[2328], is restricted to national IP numbers except in limited circumstances for educational purposes.[2329]

585. Swedish preparatory legal documents state that ECL agreements cannot enable cross-border use. There is, however, a slight difference in the use of expressions on the issue; thus in a document from 2010 it is stated that ECL licences are in the first instance (S: "i första hand" which can also be translated as "mainly" or "primarily") to be limited to Sweden[2330] whereas in a document from 2013, which refers to the earlier document, it is expressly stated that ECL licences are not intended for cross-border use (är ... inte avsedda).[2331] However, one of the main Swedish copyright experts states that, as the extended effect of ECLs is based on national legislation, this cannot be a valid basis for use of outsiders' work beyond the territory of the country where the ECL is issued.[2332] It is interesting, in the light of the clear statements in recent Swedish preparatory documents on the territorial limitations of ECLs[2333], that the radio broadcasts of the Swedish State Radio Station seem to be open to everyone on the internet, even for listeners outside Sweden[2334], given that use of in-copyright works by the radio is normally based on ECL agreements.[2335] The Swedish State Television Station, on the other hand, limits most of the programs available on its website to viewing within Sweden.[2336] The Swedish National Library is working on a pilot project to make audio-visual broadcasting available cross-border based on end-user demand. The pilot project is based on co-operation between the relevant Swedish and Finnish CMOs in a joint ECL agreement.[2337]

2328 See further Ch. 5.3.1.4.

2329 Art. 4 BA; Guibault, Cultural, 2015, 174.

2330 Prop. 2010/2011:33, Återanvändning av upphovsrättsligt skyddat material i radio och tv, 2010, 24.

2331 Prop. 2012/13:141, Regeringens proposition, 2013, 29.

2332 Rosén, The Nordic ECL Model, 2012, 84; Rosén, Copyright Contracts, 2011, 178.

2333 Prop. 2010/2011:33, Återanvändning av upphovsrättsligt skyddat material i radio och tv, 2010, 24, and Prop. 2012/13:141, Regeringens proposition, 2013, 29.

2334 See <http://sverigesradio.se>.

2335 Art. 42e (1) SCA as changed with Act 2013:691, cf. Prop. 2012/13:141, Regeringens proposition, 2013, 48–49.

2336 See <www.svtplay.se/>. See also Trumpke, Exklusivität, 2015, 629.

2337 See further Ch. 5.3.1.5.

9.1.2. EVALUATION

586. The crucial question is whether the extension effect of national ECL agreements can enable cross-border use of outsiders' works, at least within the EU/EEA area, without specific EU legislation. In a recent opinion on the issue ALAI concludes that "current ECL mechanisms operating at national level cannot, as such, permit or otherwise regulate uses of works that are carried out in other countries (i.e. on other territories) than the country which provides for the extended effect in its national legislation." Cross-border effect can thus, according to ALAI, only be achieved with a specific EU provision to that end or with joint licensing between two countries that have an ECL system, within the flexibility provided by international norms.[2338] However, at the same time ALAI concludes that an ECL system which fulfils certain requirements would not be in conflict with the three-step test, even if used in a cross-border situation, as the extension effect only concerns the transfer of the right to license exploitation and this does not affect the existence or the enforcement of the rights.[2339]

587. As argued above[2340], the extension effect of the ECL system is in the first instance a limitation on or exception to the outsider's right. However, I further argue that under certain conditions, notably for ECL agreements that fulfil the three-step test, the exception effect could be seen to give way in favour of legal presumption of mandate. Such ECL agreements could thus be perceived as based on an arrangement of management of rights with regard to the rights of outsiders. If this approach is taken then licensing of the outsiders' right under an ECL agreement could be seen as based on contract, i.e. the contract between the CMO and a user. As discussed above that could mean that under private international rules applicable laws would be deemed to be the law of the contract.[2341] Thus if the contract (the ECL agreement) stipulated that it enabled cross-border use and that was not in conflict with the national legislation of the contract and the CMO had the mandate to license cross-border use, the agreement could in my view enable cross-border use. However, such ECL agreements would also have to pass the three-step test and in my view there would be stricter requirements for them to do so than for ECL agreements that are only for national use. I briefly list such requirements here below. A more elaborated analysis will be provided in in Ch. 10:

I. The extension effect of the ECL agreements must be a pre-requisite for the use enabled under the agreement, i.e. that the use would otherwise be impracticable to facilitate[2342];
II. The relevant CMO must have a mandate from its members to license the intended geographical use;

[2338] ALAI, Opinion ECL, 2016, 2–3.
[2339] Ibid, 5–6.
[2340] See Ch. 6.1.2, Ch. 6.3.1, Ch. 8.2.3 and Ch. 8.4.2.1.
[2341] See discussion in Ch. 8.4.2.1.
[2342] See discussion in Ch. 5.1.1, 5.1.2, 5.3.3, and 6.2.3.2.

III. The CMO must be representative of the authors of works in the area that the ECL provision/agreement applies to;
IV. The negotiated remuneration must reflect the geographical use; and
V. The ECL agreement must contain certain safeguard measures to secure the rights of outsiders. Such safeguard measures would have to include the following minimum requirements:
   a. Equal treatment with regard to the terms of the agreement
   b. A possibility of individual remuneration for outsiders, independent of how remuneration was decided for members of the relevant CMO.
   c. An opt-out possibility which was transparent and easy to apply for outsiders.
   d. Comprehensive transparency rules so that outsiders have a realistic opportunity to make use of the safeguard measures.

Additional safeguard measures might include limiting the cross-border effect to out-of-commerce works or non-commercial uses, although such restrictions could be left to stakeholders to decide upon.[2343]

If appropriate safeguard measures are in place the interest of the outsider should be sufficiently protected. In addition, there must be a European public interest goal that is achieved by such an agreement. In my mind the public interest in enabling legal access to the cultural heritage in European library collections should fulfil that requirement. Last but not least an ECL agreement which only affects national outsiders, i.e. would be limited to works first published in, or with another sufficient connection to[2344], the country of the ECL agreement would be more likely to pass international norms with regard to cross-border use.

588. Nevertheless, in the absence of EU legislation, the key problem of legal uncertainty remains in regard to cross-border effect within Europe of national ECL agreements and outsiders' right. This is due to the application of EU rules on jurisdiction in online infringement cases and the uncertainty about applicable laws in case of litigation by an outsider whose work an ECL agreement with cross-border effect would cover in a country other than where the ECL agreement originates.[2345] This could support the view that the cross-border effect of ECL agreements without a specific EU provision is only possible between countries that have comparable ECL mechanisms and where the national CMO's have reciprocal agreements to that effect.[2346] In fact, there were at one point discussions between the Nordic countries on establishing a treaty committing

---

2343 See discussion in Ch. 10.2.3 and 10.2.5.
2344 See discussion in Ch. 10.2.1 and 10.2.2.
2345 Cf. Ch. 8.2.2, 8.3.1 and 8.4.
2346 ALAI, Opinion ECL, 2016, 2, 3.

the Nordic countries to mutually recognise each other's extended collective agreements on copyright.[2347] However, the discussion was abandoned because of uncertainty with regard to competence under the EU legal framework.[2348] The disadvantage of such an approach is that it would limit the cross-border effect to those countries that have an ECL mechanism in place[2349] and would thus not achieve EU or EEA wide applicability of ECL agreements. Hence, in the light of the uncertainties of the cross-border applicability and in order to guarantee EU or EEA wide applicability of ECL agreement, the most efficient and legally secure way would be to adopt an EU provision for that purpose.[2350] Such an EU provision may in fact be adopted in the near future for the benefit of cultural heritage institutions, at least for out-of-commerce works, if the DSM proposal[2351] is adopted.

589. I will discuss this approach of cross-border use of in-copyright works under national ECL agreements in more detail in the next chapter below[2352], as well as its compatibility with the EU's legal framework.[2353] In the remainder of this chapter I will discuss other options for legislative solutions for enabling online access with cross-border effect in European libraries and compare them to the ECL solution, starting with legal presumption, which is probably the solution that lies closest to the system of ECLs.

9.2. LEGAL PRESUMPTION

590. Legal presumption of mandate means that either statutory law or case law establishes that the relevant CMO is deemed to represent the interests and rights of non-members in a particular area. The main difference between legal presumption and the system of ECL is that the presumption does not apply to the licence or agreement itself, but to the CMO's mandate. Thus legal presumption gives the CMOs a general right of representation regardless of whether an agreement is made or not, whereas the extended effect of the ECL is only with regard to agreements that have been concluded.[2354] The legal presumption reverses the burden of proof for the user so that in case of

2347 Strowel, Bokhylla.no, the Norwegian bookshelf: a model?, IPdigIT; EFTA Secretariat, 'Vivid Discussions at EFTA's Copyright Seminar' (2010) <www.efta.int/eea/eea-news/2010-09-30-efta-copyright-seminar> accessed 7 July 2017.

2348 See discussion in Tryggvadóttir, Balancing of interests, 2015, 662–665, and in Ch. 11.4.

2349 See Ch. 7 for discussion on countries outside the Nordic countries that have adopted ECL systems.

2350 ALAI, Opinion ECL, 2016, 6.

2351 COM(2016) 593 final, Proposal, 2016, *op.cit.*

2352 See Ch. 10.

2353 See Ch. 11.

2354 Ficsor, Collective, 2016, 66; Koskinen-Olsson, Collective Management, 2010, 292–293.

disagreement the user does not need to prove that the CMO holds the right to license the outsiders' right. However, it has been suggested that if the presumption is not rebuttable, the system resembles a compulsory licence, especially if rightholders cannot opt out.[2355] Thus it seems that provisions stipulating presumed mandate, as with the extension effect of the ECL system, would have to pass the three-step test in order to be seen as an arrangement of management with regard to outsiders.[2356]

591. The effects of legal presumption are similar to the extended effect of the ECL system.[2357] The CMO is able to provide a licence which would cover works whose rights are owned by its members, as well as by non-members, in the areas of application, to the extent, and under the conditions allowed by national law. The main conditions for such presumed mandate are generally the same as for ECLs, i.e. sufficient representativeness by the CMO[2358], often an explicit possibility for outsiders to opt-out and manage their own rights[2359] and equal treatment between members and non-members with regard to remuneration.[2360] However, it is not clear whether legislation providing for legal presumption would necessarily provide for individual remuneration for outsiders in case of collective distribution of remuneration.

592. Finland has introduced presumption of representation in the ECLs, though only with regard to specific ECL agreements, as stipulated in Art. 26(1) of the FCA: "An approved organisation is with regard to this agreement deemed to represent authors of other works in the same field." Thus it is not a general presumed mandate. The reason for this change was to make the language of the provision more compatible with European traditions and thus make the system more comprehensible to those outside of the Nordic countries.[2361]

593. Given how small the difference between the two systems[2362] is it is not surprising that the Commission has opted to allow for both presumed mandate

---

2355 Gervais, Collective Management, 2001, 37; Ficsor, Collective, 2016, 66.

2356 See Ch. 6.1.2 for discussion.

2357 Tarja Koskinen-Olsson and Lowe, Educational Material, 2012, 24; Koskinen-Olsson, Collective Management, 2010, 292–293.

2358 This requirement, however, does not always seem to be explicit or to be based on mandates from rightholders, cf. Gervais, Collective Management, 2001, 41–42; Trumpke, Exklusivität, 2015, 106–107 although Trumpke does not seem to distinguish between legal presumption as such and mandatory collective management.

2359 However, that is not always the case, see e.g. Trumpke, Exklusivität, 2015, 107, (but see above footnote); Gervais, Collective Management, 2001, 37; Ficsor, Collective, 2016, 66.

2360 SWD(2016) 301 final, IA Part III, 2016, 130; IFRRO, U.S. Public Consultation: "Mass Digitization Pilot Program", 2015, 3; ALAI, Opinion ECL, 2016, 2.

2361 RP 181/2014 rd, Regeringens proposition, 2014, 25, 49. See also Ch. 5.3, par. 309.

2362 Koskinen-Olsson and Sigurðardóttir, Collective, 2016, 253.

and extended effect of collective agreements with regard to outsiders.[2363] This approach is in line with the 2011 MoU on out-of-commerce works.[2364] Mandatory collective management, which I will discuss next, differs somewhat more from the ECL system.

9.3. MANDATORY COLLECTIVE MANAGEMENT

594. Mandatory collective management means that rightholders are legally obliged to make claims with regard to their rights exclusively through a CMO. Thus users, i.e. those who have a licence to use works on the basis of a collective agreement, benefit from this system as outsiders cannot make claims against them, as is also the case under an ECL agreement.[2365] Several EU Directives provide either for the option of mandatory collective management or make it compulsory.[2366] The argument for the system has traditionally been that it serves the interest of both rightholders and users and ensures fair and efficient way to exercise rights.[2367]

595. There are certain similarities between mandatory collective management and the system of ECLs at least from the point of view of the user under a collective management agreement and, indeed, some commentators do not distinguish between the two.[2368] However, there is an important difference in that the ECL effect is only activated with regards to existing agreements and the outsiders can often opt-out. The opt-out possibility provides a critical difference between the two systems.[2369] If the outsider opts-out of an ECL agreement then he or she can theoretically negotiate the use individually with the user.[2370] In the case of mandatory collective management on the other hand, individual licensing is not possible, either

2363 COM(2016) 593 final, Proposal, 2016, Art. 7. See discussion of the proposal in Ch. 11.3.

2364 See discussion in Ch. 7.1.

2365 Tarja Koskinen-Olsson and Lowe, Educational Material, 2012, 25; Koskinen-Olsson, Collective, 2005, 20; Trumpke, The Extended, 2012, 277; Koskinen-Olsson, Collective Management, 2010, 293; Axhamn, Exceptions, 2013, 178–179; Trumpke, Exklusivität, 2015, 331; Karnell, Outsiders, 1991, 430 ff.

2366 Cf. Art. 6(2) Resale Right Directive, Art. 9(2) Satellite and Cable Directive, Art. 5(4) Rental and Lending Directive.

2367 Kur and Schovsbo, Expropriation, 2009, 14.

2368 Ficsor, Collective, 2016, 75; see an example of no distinction in Kerremans, Janssen and Valcke, Collective solutions, 2011, 644. Trumpke, on the other hand, does not seem to distinguish between mandatory collective management and presumed mandate, cf. Trumpke, Exklusivität, 2015, 106–107.

2369 Guibault, Report, 2015, 11; Guibault, Cultural, 2015, 180–181; ALAI, Orphan Works, 2012, 1; Axhamn and Guibault, Cross-border ECL, 2011, 48; Axhamn, Exceptions, 2013, 183; ALAI, Opinion ECL, 2016, 2; Ficsor, Collective, 2016, 75; Sganga, The eloquent, 2017, 321.

2370 See discussion on the issue in Ch. 5.4.3.2.

before or after an agreement is made.[2371] Thus although the management of the exclusive right is voluntary rightholders cannot negotiate individually.[2372] This is a key difference.

Another important difference between ECLs and mandatory collective management is that the representativeness requirement of the CMO is not essential in the same way as under the ECL system. Thus Art. 9(2) of the Satellite and Cable Directive only talks of a CMO that manages rights of the same category, without requiring that it is representative for a substantial number of rightholders.[2373] Under the French legislation for the digitisation of out-of-commerce books[2374], which established a system akin to mandatory collective management, the CMO was required to have equal representation of authors and publishers. However, there was no requirement for a mandate from a substantial number of rightholders for the particular use that the legislation enabled.[2375] Thus the mandate was statutory. This was a deciding factor in the Soulier case, which deemed the legislation to be incompatible with the exclusive rights guaranteed under the InfoSoc Directive.[2376]

596. It is disputed whether mandatory collective management constitutes an exception to the exclusive right. This is of importance when deciding whether the system can be used for the licensing of exclusive rights in areas outside of Art. 5 of the InfoSoc Directive and still be in conformity with EU legislation. Many claim that under such a regime the exclusivity remains intact and only the exercise of the exclusive right is affected.[2377] This seems to be confirmed in Recital (28) of the Satellite and Cable Directive which states: "whereas the authorization right as such remains intact and only the exercise of this right is regulated to some extent." However, mandatory collective management combined with an obligation on CMOs to grant licences[2378] can be said to be

[2371] Rydning, Extended, 2010, 11; Karnell, Outsiders, 1991, 434; Trumpke, The Extended, 2012, 278; Rognstad, Avtalelisens, 2012, 623; Koskinen-Olsson and Sigurðardóttir, Collective, 2016, 253.

[2372] Koskinen-Olsson, Collective Management, 2010, 293; Koskinen-Olsson, Collective, 2005, 20; Tarja Koskinen-Olsson and Lowe, Educational Material, 2012, 24–25; Rydning, Extended, 2010, 99–100.

[2373] Rognstad, Avtalelisens, 2012, 623–624; Trumpke, Exklusivität, 2015, 332–333. See discussion on the Nordic ECL representation requirement in Ch. 5.2.

[2374] See discussion on the legislation in Ch. 7.2.1.

[2375] Art. 134-3 FCIP; C-301/15 – Soulier, AG opinion, par. 10; C-301/15 – Soulier, par. 14. The relevant CMO, however, claimed to represent rightholders of over 85% of French books.

[2376] C-301/15 – Soulier, par. 52. See discussion on the case in Ch. 11.2.

[2377] Von Lewinski, Mandatory, 2004, 5, 12–14; Rydning, Extended, 2010, 23; Guibault, Copyright, 2002, 23; Geiger, The Role, 2007, 9–12; Trumpke, The Extended, 2012, 272; Ficsor, Collective Management, 2010, 54; Axhamn, Exceptions, 2013, 180–181; Trumpke, Exklusivität, 2015, 216–218, 412.

[2378] Be it by legislation or by the fact that refusing to grant a licence would constitute abuse of dominant market position. In Germany there is a legal obligation for CMOs to grant licences, cf. Geiger, The Role, 2007, 10; Ficsor, Collective, 2016, 62.

de facto a compulsory or legal licence.[2379] Thus a number of commentators argue that mandatory collective management is an exception or limitation to the outsiders' right in the sense of the Berne Convention.[2380] It seems clear that the rights of outsiders are more circumscribed under mandatory collective management than under an ECL system with an opt-out option.[2381] Nevertheless, it has been suggested that the outsiders' position is clearer under mandatory collective management as they know that their right can only be collectively managed, whereas under an ECL system the situation is more uncertain until an agreement is concluded.[2382]

597. There are somewhat different objectives behind a mandatory collective management and an ECL system. Mandatory collective management, such as that adopted under the Satellite and Cable Directive, aims to ensure smooth operation of contractual arrangements and to prevent hold-ups, whereas ECLs are mainly adopted to reduce transaction costs.[2383] It has been argued that an important difference between mandatory collective licences and ECL agreements is that the former are used in situations where it is impossible to licence individually, whereas ECL agreements are used mainly in areas which are difficult but not impossible to licence individually.[2384] For libraries the main obstacle to mass digitisation and use is the transaction cost of individual licensing of the outsiders' right. Thus ECLs are a sufficient licensing system for libraries with regard to outsiders. As mandatory collective management leaves no room for opt-out and subsequent individual licensing, they limit the outsider's right more than ECLs. Consequently it would be harder to argue that mandatory collective management for the online cross-border use by libraries would be compatible with the proportionality principle[2385] and it might have difficulties in passing the three-step test.[2386]

598. Finally, with regard to collective management of rights and cross-border use, it is worth looking at whether the new system of multi-territorial licences for online music could be used for the purpose of enabling cross-border online use by libraries.

2379 Schierholz, Collective Management in Europe, 2010, 1152; Kur and Schovsbo, Expropriation, 2009, 14.

2380 Ficsor, Collective Management, 2010, 43–45; Ficsor, Collective, 2016, 49–66; ALAI, Orphan Works, 2012, 1.

2381 Of different opinion: Trumpke, Exklusivität, 2015, 334; Trumpke, The Extended, 2012, 278.

2382 Trumpke, Exklusivität, 2015, 333.

2383 See discussion and references in Ch. 5.1.2.

2384 Rognstad, Avtalelisens, 2012, 623–624.

2385 See discussion in Ch. 11.4.3.2.

2386 See discussion in Ch. 4.1.3 and 6.2.3.

9.4. THE MULTI-TERRITORIAL LICENCES FOR ONLINE MUSIC UNDER THE CMO DIRECTIVE

599. Apart from establishing rules on transparency and good governance of CMOs the aim of the CMO Directive is to create a legal framework for multi-territorial licences for online music.[2387, 2388] The aim is to create legal certainty for rights clearance for legitimate online music services. It is limited to the area of music services as, according to the Commission, multi-territorial licensing had not given rise to any difficulties in other areas that needed to be addressed.[2389] Nevertheless, Recital (11) states that nothing in the Directive should preclude CMOs in other fields from concluding representation agreements with other CMOs, provided that competition rules were respected, and offering multi-territorial licences for other types of works in the same way as is set out in the Directive for music.[2390] Still, doubts have been voiced as to whether this will be feasible without legislative support, given the diversity of structure and composition of CMOs in different Member States.[2391] Furthermore, the system for multi-territorial licences created by the CMO Directive does not address the underlying issue of territoriality.[2392]

600. During the legislative process for the CMO Directive several policy options for multi-territorial licensing for online use of musical works were considered. One was ECLs combined with a country of origin principle.[2393] This option was rejected as it was presumed that ECLs would not simplify the multi-territorial licensing of rights because of the opt-out possibility, which could lead to the disaggregation of repertoire of the CMOs.[2394] Furthermore, it was claimed that ECLs would favour CMOs "without necessarily providing for efficiency gains to the advantage of both rightholders and service providers".[2395] However, no assessment seemed to be made as to whether the benefit of being able to license those that are outside CMOs would counteract the disadvantages of the opt-outs. In most cases, only non-members of CMOs can opt-out, hence the situation cannot be so much different from collective licensing without extension effect. If members of CMOs are not satisfied with a licensing agreement they can simply withdraw from membership, cf. Art. 5(4) of the CMO Directive, and

2387 Musical works have traditionally been licensed through collective management organisations, cf. e.g. Eechoud and others, Harmonizing, 2009, 314.
2388 Guibault and van Gompel, Collective, 2016, 139.
2389 COM(2012) 372/2, Proposal, 2012, 3; Guibault and van Gompel, Collective, 2016, 167.
2390 Guibault, Collective, 2014, 706.
2391 Guibault, Cultural, 2015, 187; Guibault, Report, 2015, 19.
2392 See Ch. 8.3.2.3.
2393 SWD(2012) 204 final, Impact Assessment, 2012, 45.
2394 COM(2012) 372/2, Proposal, 2012, 6–7; SWD(2012) 204 final, Impact Assessment, 2012, 45.
2395 SWD(2012) 204 final, Impact Assessment, 2012, 51.

thereby technically opt-out of all agreements the CMO has made, regardless of whether it is an ECL agreement or a regular CMO agreement.[2396]

601. In the end a "passport" system[2397] was adopted in the CMO Directive which enables a CMO, unwilling or unable to grant multi-territorial licences[2398] to request another CMO to represent it. The requesting CMO will then grant the representing CMO a non-exclusive mandate. Any CMO requested to represent another CMO is obliged to do so if it already represents the relevant rights for another CMO.[2399] The provisions in the CMO Directive for multi-territorial licences of online rights in musical works contain further safeguard clauses to protect the interest of rightholders of the mandating CMO. Additionally there are provisions to ensure that the mandating CMO delivers sufficient information about the works and rights they manage, to enable the mandated CMO to include them in their licences. However, there are some doubts as to how this will work in practice, i.a. whether the cost of providing the information in a usable form for the mandated CMO will in fact be less for the mandating CMO than to issue the multi-territorial licences themselves.[2400]

602. The main problem I see with using this approach for multi-territorial licensing for libraries is that the cross-border effect is based on voluntary licensing, i.e. that multi-territorial licences can only be issued with legal certainty for members of the relevant CMOs. Thus even if this approach were taken for works in libraries it would still lack legal certainty as to the cross-border use of works of outsiders.

603. Next I will look at exceptions and limitations as a means to enable cross-border online use by libraries.

9.5. EXCEPTIONS AND LIMITATIONS

604. Exceptions and limitations have traditionally been considered the main tool for creating the necessary balance of interest between rightsholders and

2396 See discussion on this provision and its potential destabilising effect on the current form of collective management in Drexl and others, Comments, 2013, 23. See also discussion of the interplay of opting-out and withdrawing rights from CMO in accordance with the CMO Directive in the UK: IPO, Government, 2014, 29; IPO, ECL Guidance 2016, 2016, 11–12.

2397 Art. 29 – 31 CMO Directive.

2398 Art. 24–28 CMO Directive set out requirements for CMOs to engage in multi-territorial licensing which i.a. demand considerable capacity to electronically process data necessary for the administration of multi-territorial licences.

2399 Recital (46) CMO Directive.

2400 Guibault and van Gompel, Collective, 2016, 167–172; Guibault, Collective, 2014, 763–764, 770, 774–776; Drexl and others, Comments, 2013, 31–32.

users. Mandatory and fully harmonised exceptions allowing for online use for libraries might offer the greatest level of certainty for all parties involved.[2401] However, current exceptions in the EU are not adequate to enable libraries to fulfil their purpose in the digital age.[2402] Thus, it is clear that libraries need additional options for copyright clearance. This is especially true with the making available right.[2403]

605. Many cultural heritage institutions have expressed a preference for an exception for mass digitisation of their collections and the digital use of works, including cross-border use. Accordingly some stakeholders, i.a. end-users and libraries, have called for further broadening of the exception in the InfoSoc Directive to include making available online of out-of-commerce works.[2404] Others have argued that at least the use of material in archives should be allowed under an exception "as the type of material held within archives typically does not fall within the repertoire of collecting societies" and thus cannot be licensed by them.[2405] However, other stakeholders, in particular publishers and CMOs, oppose the broadening of exceptions for libraries.[2406]

606. It is claimed that although library exceptions have a public interest rationale[2407] they are not based on more fundamental rights, such as right to privacy or freedom of expression and free flow of information.[2408] Thus it has been argued that although the exception for on-site consultation provision in Art. 5(3)(n) of the InfoSoc Directive[2409] aims to enable libraries to fulfil their public-interest mission of making their works available, that aim in itself is not a fundamental objective for the European Union. It is contended that the provision was designed to favour rightholders and was intended only to address market failure. Hence the exclusion of the exception for works subject to licensing conditions in Art. 5(3)(n) should not be modified as it protects

2401 Guibault, Cultural, 2015, 187.

2402 See Ch. 4.2.4.

2403 Triaille and others, Study, 2013, 303.

2404 European Commission, Report on the responses, 2014, 43–46, 50; Torremans, Archiving exceptions, 2010, 118; European Parliament, Resolution, 2015, item 51; Discussion Paper from the 4th Europeana Licensing Workshop in Luxembourg, 26th and 27th of November 2015 suggested an exception with an opt-out option. In Australia it was recommended in April 2016 that all uses of orphan works and out-of-commerce works should be allowed under a fair use clause, cf. Australian Government Productivity Commission, Intellectual Property Arrangements; Draft Report, 2016, 121–163.

2405 Firth and Preira, Exceptions for Libraries, 2016, 28; Kretschmer et al., The European, 2014, 549; Vuopala, Extended, 2013, 32; Deazley and Stobo, Archives, 2013, 48.

2406 European Commission, Report on the responses, 2014, 43–46; COM(2009) 532 final, Communication on Copyright, 2009, 4.

2407 Triaille and others, Study, 2013, 245; Crews, 2008 Study, 2008, 14. See also with regard to museums, Jean-François Canat, Lucie Guibault and Elisabeth Logeais, Study, 2015, 13.

2408 Guibault, Contracts, 2000, 156–157; Xalabarder, Digital Libraries, 2010, 246.

2409 See discussion on the provision in Ch. 4.2.2.2 and 4.2.4.1.1.2.

the development of adapted offers by publishers.[2410] Furthermore it is claimed that there is no need for specific copyright clearance facilitation for on-site consultation, as the provision already anticipates licensing agreements and, in any case, transaction costs for such individual clearance is not particularly high.[2411] For these reasons it is maintained by many that the exception should not enable online availability as it could prejudice normal exploitation of works.[2412] However, it is worth noting that it has been convincingly argued that access to information has become increasingly more important and will become a central justification for copyright limitations and exceptions in the digital environment.[2413]

607. The revision of the consultation provision[2414] of the InfoSoc Directive was excluded from the DSM proposal on the grounds that the issue might be dealt with by the CJEU in the VOB case.[2415] The CJEU has since concluded the case and determined that the Rental and Lending Directive covers digital lending, such as in the specific case before the court.[2416] Thus it seems clear that remote consultation of works in libraries has been enabled, although for legal clarity it would be advisable to amend the consultation clause in the InfoSoc Directive. However, the question of remote access does not directly deal with cross-border online access as such. It is likely, not least now that the Portability Regulation has been adopted[2417], that digital lending will also include cross-border lending, at least for registered customers of the library. This is nevertheless distinct from online cross-border access inherent in the quest for libraries to use materials from their collections online. Digital lending is a service for end-users who are normally registered members of the library, most commonly situated within the territorial boundaries of where the library is located, whereas online use on a website is open to all from wherever the website is accessible.

608. Compulsory licensing under the management of CMOs would in theory solve many or even most of the clearing of rights issues for libraries.[2418] However, it may be difficult to conceive an exception that is broad enough to fully serve the interest of libraries and still be narrow enough not to harm the interest of rightholders. There are practical problems with an exception that would allow libraries to make out-of-commerce works available online and there is also a

2410 European Copyright Society, Answer to the EC Consulation 2014, 15.
2411 Triaille and others, Study, 2013, 317.
2412 Ibid, 317–322. Similarly the European Copyright Society did not recommend further changes to the provision, cf. European Copyright Society, Answer to the EC Consulation 2014, 15.
2413 Senftleben, Copyright, Limitations and the Three-Step-Test, 2004, 30–31.
2414 Art. 5(3)(n) InfoSoc Directive.
2415 SWD(2016) 301 final, IA Part I, 2016, 9; C-174/15 – VOB,.
2416 C-174/15 – VOB, par. 40–54. See further discussion of the case in Ch. 4.2.4.1.1.2.
2417 See a brief discussion in Ch. 8.3.3.
2418 Guibault, Cultural, 2015, 187.

question whether such an exception would pass the three-step test.[2419] The practical problem relates to how the decision on what is out-of-commerce is made. This is particularly relevant in the light of the growing importance of print-on-demand publishing methods. The effort to determine when a work is out-of-commerce would presumably fall on the libraries, would demand resources and could result in a situation comparable to diligent search under the Orphan Works Directive.[2420]

609. Compulsory or legal licences reduce transaction costs, in the same way as collective licensing with legislative support, but such solutions are claimed to significantly reduce the negotiating power of rightholders.[2421] However, if compulsory licences provide for individual compensation[2422] it has been maintained they may be no worse for rightholders than an ECL agreement which provides for collective remuneration.[2423] This might be true with regard to outsiders who often are in a worse position to benefit from collective remuneration than members of the CMO.[2424]

However, there are practical concerns with compensation under an exception, such as how the amount would be calculated and distributed. This begs the question whether such a "legal licence" would be a "statutory licence", i.e. compensation decided by the legislator or a "compulsory licence" where the compensation is negotiable by the rightholders.[2425] Administration of compensated exceptions is usually provided by CMOs, which creates its own transaction cost. An obligation for compensation would need a secure basis in a detailed provision.[2426] If no compensation were required this might further reduce the compatibility of this solution with the three-step test.[2427]

610. An opt-out possibility might align an exception more closely to the proportionality principle.[2428] However, it might be of limited practical value to rightholders, unless implementation was supported by a centralised registry. In the absence of such a centralised registry it would be very difficult for rightholders to opt-out in practice.

2419 Ringnalda, Orphan Works, 2011, 8.

2420 See discussion on the diligent serach under the OWD in Ch. 4.2.3.5 and 4.2.4.2.

2421 Schønning, Ophavsretsloven, 5th ed., 2011, 462; Riis and Schovsbo, ECLs, 2010, 482; Koskinen-Olsson, Collective Management, 2010, 293; Axhamn and Guibault, Cross-border ECL, 2011, 51; US Copyright Office, Mass Digitization, 2015, 82, 103; Foged, Danish licences, 2015, 17; Guibault, Copyright, 2002, 23; Geiger, The Role, 2007, 11; Ficsor, Collective, 2016, 62–63.

2422 See discussion on the term compensation in Ch. 4.1.2 and on compensation for exceptions under the InfoSoc Directive in 4.2.1.

2423 Rognstad, Avtalelisenser, 2004, 155 and Rydning, Extended, 2010, 79; see also von Lewinski, Mandatory, 2004, 9.

2424 Rydning, Extended, 2010, 78–80. See discussion on the subject in Ch. 5.4.2.

2425 See Ch. 4.1.1 on the terminology.

2426 Kur, Of Oceans 2008, 301.

2427 See discussion in Ch. 4.1.3.

2428 See discussion in Ch. 11.4.2.2.

611. Finally, when comparing exceptions with the ECL system it is worth remembering that exceptions and limitations affect all rightholders, whereas the restriction inherent in ECL provisions and agreements only affects the outsiders' rights.[2429] It is unclear how far reaching exceptions can be without upsetting the balance the three-step test is supposed to maintain. For the reasons given above, exceptions as a means to facilitate online cross-border use by libraries might be too prescriptive and at the same time "lack the flexibility to provide solutions adapted to the needs of particular users and the specificities of particular sectors while fully respecting copyright."[2430] Thus to me it seems that for the purpose of enabling cross-border online use by libraries the ECL system is a better tool than mandatory exceptions.

612. Next and last in this chapter, I will look at whether a single European copyright would solve the problems of online cross-border use for libraries.

9.6. SINGLE EUROPEAN COPYRIGHT

613. Unified European Copyright could be realised in a variety of forms; it could consist of a general guideline for a European copyright code, based on current legislation; or an optional copyright code, coexisting alongside national legislation, as is already the case in the area of trademarks and design; or it could take the shape of a uniform copyright title that would supercede national copyright legislation.[2431] A general guideline would not substantially change the current legislative framework and would thus not necessarily change anything with regard to cross-border online use for libraries.[2432] A co-existing optional copyright code would not simplify questions of territoriality and might in fact further complicate the issue, mainly due to the fact that copyright is established without any requirements for registration or other formalities, unlike industrial intellectual property rights. Hence I will only discuss here the single European copyright title, which would supercede national copyright legislation, at least in some areas deemed to be essential for the functioning of a digital single market, such as the basic economic rights and limitations and exceptions to those.[2433]

2429 Trumpke, Exklusivität, 2015, 334.

2430 This quote is taken slightly out of context as it is from a Commission Press Release in connection with the MoU on out-of-commerce works and why they opted for an MoU rather than legislation, cf. <http://europa.eu/rapid/press-release_MEMO-11-619_en.htm?locale=en>, last viewed 15 July 2017. However, it captures the essence of why exceptions may not be suitable.

2431 COM(2011) 287 final, IPR Strategy, 2011, 11; COM(2011) 427/4, Audiovisual works, 2011, 13; Silke von Lewinski, 'Copyright in a Borderless Online Environment: EU Cross-Border Licensing of Rights' in Johan Axhamn (ed), *Copyright in a Borderless Online Environment* (2012) 108; Hugenholtz, Copyright, 2012, 204; Trumpke, Exklusivität, 2015, 669–671.

2432 Trumpke, Exklusivität, 2015, 673.

2433 Hugenholtz and others, Recasting, 2006, 219–220.

614. A unified European copyright title could solve many of the issues this research is tackling. It would mean that an agreement between a CMO and a national library to make works of their members available online would be effective in the whole of EU. However, such a unitary title would not necessarily regulate every aspect of copyright.[2434] A unified title in itself would not solve the situation for digital libraries wishing to put in-copyright works online with cross-border effect with regard to outsiders. In order to solve the issue of outsiders such a title would have to include either exceptions allowing libraries to make in-copyright works available, e.g. out-of-commerce works, or an ECL provision, or at least provide for the EU-wide applicability of current national ECL provisions.

615. In the proposed European Copyright Code drafted by the Wittem Project group[2435] there is no specific exception or limitation to the making available right for libraries or other cultural heritage institutions. Chapter 5 of the Wittem Copyright Code sets out provisions on limitations. Art. 5.3 deals with uses permitted to promote i.a. cultural objectives. There is an explicit limitation for "non-commercial archiving" but none for making works available. In a footnote to this provision a reference is made to Art. 5(2)(c) of the InfoSoc Directive. Furthermore it is stated in the footnote that it is "understood that the exception only covers reproductions made in order to preserve documents, but not any subsequent commercial exploitation of the works that have been archived." It is possible that this formulation opens up for a non-commercial online use in combination with the suggested Art. 5.5 named "Further limitations", which provides for a limited fair use clause for any "other use that is comparable to the uses enumerated" under Article 5. However, in my view this possibility does not provide for enough legal certainty and clarity for digital libraries wishing to put in-copyright works online, especially where cross-border effect is concerned.

616. Supporters of a single European copyright title consider that Art. 118 TFEU[2436] leaves room for the EU to enact such a title, noting that such titles already exist in other IP areas.[2437] Such a title would solve many of the problems for the internal market with regard to products and services with copyright content[2438] and would imply greater legal certainty for rightholders and users.[2439] However, opponents claim that a unitary title would put Member

2434 Ramalho, Conceptualising, 2014, 185; Hugenholtz and others, Recasting, 2006, 220.

2435 Hereafter the Wittem Copyright Code, cf. Wittem Project, European Copyright Code, 2010, *op.cit.*

2436 Art. 118 TFEU, introduced with the Treaty of Lisbon, which entered into force 2009, allows the EU to create European intellectual property rights, cf. C-414/11 *Daiichi Sankyo Co. Ltd and Sanofi-Aventis Deutschland GmbH v DEMO Anonymos Viomichaniki kai Emporiki Etairia Farmakon* ECLI:EU:C:2013:520, CJEU, 18 July 2013.

2437 See discussion and references on the applicability of Art. 118 TFEU for copyright in Ch. 11.4.1.

2438 Eechoud and others, Harmonizing, 2009, 316–317.

2439 Geiger and others, Reaction of CEIPI, 2015, 24.

States' ability to shape their own individual cultural policy at risk and would lead to confusion and complications rather than simplifying the situation. In particular, many publishers and producers have highlighted the need to license content per territory.[2440] Furthermore, an important effect of a unified European copyright title could mean the demise of national CMOs, as their current functioning is essentially based on the territoriality principle.[2441]

617. The possibility of a unified copyright title has until recently been considered a remote possibility.[2442] However, discussion on the establishment of such a title has become more prominent in recent years. Thus the Commission undertook in the IPR Strategy of 2011 to examine the creation of a European copyright code which could be based on a codification of existing EU copyright directives, where there might be a need to go beyond current harmonisation, as well as investigating the feasibility of creating a "unitary" copyright title.[2443]

The Commission has since taken a firm stand on the desirability of a single copyright title and has announced a single copyright code and title as a long-term target.[2444] This approach is also supported by the European Parliament[2445] so the possibility of a unified copyright title might not be so remote. However, as mentioned above a unified copyright title will not in itself solve the issue of online cross-border use of in-copyright works by libraries. There will still be a need for an explicit exception or solution based on licensing, as under an ECL system. In the meantime other solutions, less far-reaching, for cross-border use will have to be adopted. I maintain that such a solution is to be found in the ECL system.

9.7. CONCLUSION

618. None of the legal approaches discussed above, with the possible exception of the legal presumption of mandates, seem to offer a problem-free solution to online cross-border use which is superior to the ECL system. Mandatory collective management as well as mandatory exceptions and limitations would encroach to a greater extent than the ECL system upon the exclusive rights of

---

2440 European Commission, Report on the responses, 2014, 90–91; von Lewinski, Copyright, 2012, 108–109.

2441 Hugenholtz and others, Recasting, 2006, 220–221; Trumpke, Exklusivität, 2015, 673–674.

2442 Axhamn and Guibault, Cross-border ECL, 2011, 61; European Commission, Report on the responses, 2014, 89–91.

2443 COM(2011) 287 final, IPR Strategy, 2011, 11; COM(2011) 427/4, Audiovisual works, 2011, 13.

2444 COM(2015) 626 final, Towards, 2015, 12.

2445 European Parliament, Resolution 2015 on the InfoSoc Directive, 2015, item 26; European Parliament, Reda Draft Report 2015, 5. The resolution calls on the Commission to study the impact of a Single Copyright Title whereas the Draft Report called for the introduction of a Single Copyright Title, see discussion and criticism in Christophe Geiger and others, Reaction of the CEIPI to the Resolution, 2015, 2.

rightholders, in the latter all rightholders and in the former outsiders. The multi-territorial licences under the CMO Directive do not deal with the issue of outsiders and thus do not solve the transaction cost in regard to these. This is an important aspect as, firstly, rightholders of works in libraries are not as well organised as rightholders in the music field and, secondly, there are more orphan works in the literary field than in the music field. Finally, a unified copyright title, even if adopted in the near future, which seems unlikely, does not automatically solve the issue of outsiders; it would either have to contain an exception for libraries or legal support for collective licensing to cover the issue of outsider.

619. It is my view that the ECL system offers the best arrangement for enabling libraries to use digital technology to increase European access to the cultural heritage contained in their collections. The ECL system is the optimal solution because of its inherent flexibility and the fact that ECL agreements are negotiated by stakeholders. What is more, it combines flexibility with adequate safeguards. This seems to have been the conclusion of the EU Commission as reflected in their approach to the use of out-of-commerce works in cultural heritage institutions in the DSM proposal.[2446] However, the ECL system does not automatically provide for the perfect solution, i.a. as it relies on the agreement of parties. If no agreement is reached the use will not be enabled.[2447] Nevertheless, under the current legal structure and absent a unified copyright title I conclude that national ECL agreements, with regard to national works in the collection of national libraries, are the best tool to provide for use of in-copyright works with cross-border effect. In the next chapter I will discuss in detail the requirements such agreements and the underlying legislation must fulfil if they are to be compatible with international norms.

2446 COM(2016) 593 final, Proposal, 2016, Art. 7–9.

2447 Cf. discussion in Ch. 5.2.2 and 11.1.1.

CHAPTER 10

ECLS FOR ONLINE CROSS-BORDER USE BY LIBRARIES AND THE INTERNATIONAL LEGAL FRAMEWORK

...it is imperative to give legal acts an interpretation which takes into account developments in technology, markets and behaviour and not to fix such acts in the past by adopting too rigid an interpretation.[2448]

620. In his forceful opinion in the VOB case Advocate General Szpunar states that judicial interpretation has to meet "...the needs of contemporary society and make it possible to reconcile the various interests at stake" while being consistent with the EU's international obligations and principles underlying EU legislation in the field of copyright.[2449] His conclusion in the specific case was adopted by the CJEU[2450] and thus the court has accepted that a "dynamic" or "evolving" interpretation may be necessary "particularly in fields where technological progress has a profound effect, such as copyright."[2451]

621. In my view ECL agreements are an ideal tool for helping libraries to adapt to technological progress and in particular to operate in a digital environment. A "dynamic" or "evolving" interpretation could indeed allow for the cross-border use by national libraries through national ECL agreements under current EU legislation. Such an interpretation would meet the needs of contemporary society and reconcile the interests of various stakeholders. My views rest on the following line of reasoning set out in more detail earlier in the thesis: the extension effect in ECL provisions constitutes an exception to the outsiders' exclusive rights that must fulfil the three-step test[2452]; once these conditions are met, because the ECL system as a whole is a hybrid structure, the extension effect can be qualified as a presumed legal mandate for the relevant CMO and accordingly the system can be perceived as an arrangement concerning the management of rights with regards to outsiders.[2453] A national

2448 C-174/15 – VOB, AG opinion, par. 27.
2449 Ibid, par. 23.
2450 C-174/15 – VOB, *op. cit.*
2451 C-174/15 – VOB, AG opinion, par. 28.
2452 See discussion in Ch. 6.1 and 6.2.
2453 See discussion in Ch. 6.3.1.

ECL agreement could in this manner be looked upon as a contract that binds all relevant rightholders established, on the one hand, on voluntary mandates for the relevant use from their members of the CMO and, on the other hand, on a legal presumption of legal mandate with regard to the outsiders' rights, if international norms are fulfilled. Use by libraries under such an agreement could thus be seen as based on contractual obligations. Hence courts in other EU Member States[2454], deciding on a dispute regarding the entitlement of use under such an agreement, could apply the Rome I Regulation when determining the applicable laws. This would presumably in most cases lead to the law of the country where the ECL agreement originates.[2455] Accordingly I submit that if a national legislation has ECL provisions and if the CMOs negotiating the ECLs have a mandate covering the EEA area[2456] then such national agreements could have cross-border effect.

Such an interpretation would support the main aim of the EU with regard to access to the cultural heritage through libraries and other cultural heritage institutions, as well as the flexibility of copyright in the digital age. The EU has a strong political commitment to digital libraries and digitization of the cultural heritage of Europe[2457] and the Commission is well aware of the need of libraries and other cultural heritage institutions for "a clearer framework and a level playing field regardless of the Member State in which they are based."[2458]

The legitimacy of an ECL solution for cross-border use of in-copyright works in the collections of libraries is further bolstered by the fact that the system of ECLs offers a solution that would benefit the majority of rightholders, both members of the relevant CMO who have authorised it to conclude agreements with libraries for cross-border use and also outsiders. In fact the main justification for the system is that the extension effect enables use that would otherwise not be legally practicable.[2459] The economic interests of the outsiders are safeguarded[2460] and hence the interference with their exclusive rights is not disproportionate in the light of the interests of the larger group of relevant rightholders, i.e. members of the CMO, and in the light of the public interest objective attained by the solution i.e. as enabling libraries to fulfil their purpose in the digital age and provide access to end-users, the general public. Such agreements could fulfil international requirements, such as the three-step test, as I elaborate on below.

2454 Potentially this could be applied by courts worldwide, but no further attempt will be made to interpret the situation with regard to applicable laws, except within the EU where the Rome I Regulation applies.

2455 See discussion in Ch. 8.4.2.1.

2456 See discussion in Ch. 10.1.2.

2457 See discussion and references in Ch. 2.4.

2458 SWD(2015) 100 final, A Digital Single Market Strategy, 2015, 30; COM(2015) 626 final, Towards, 2015, 6–8.

2459 See discussion in Ch. 5.1.1, 5.1.2, 5.3.3, 6.2.3.2, and 9.1.2.

2460 See discussion in Ch. 5.4 and further in Ch. 10.3.

622. In the following I will assess the compatibility of a national ECL agreement enabling cross-border online use for libraries with the current international legal framework, where there is no national or EU provision on the cross-border applicability of ECL agreements. I will carry out the assessment by looking at the main elements of an ECL system: first, the requirements made of the CMO negotiating an ECL agreement; second, the extension effect which determines the field and scope of application for an ECL agreement; and, third, safeguard measures for outsiders. I will evaluate in particular whether these requirements need to be different for ECL agreements with cross-border use than for ECL agreements for national use.

10.1. REQUIREMENTS OF THE CMO

623. The legitimacy and functionality of the ECL system rest on the requirements of the CMO negotiating an ECL agreement. Key requirements are sufficient representativeness in the relevant field and mandates from members. Underlying requirements include a well-functioning CMO regime with good governance and transparency, as will be further elaborated on here below.

10.1.1. REPRESENTATIVENESS

624. It is central to the rationale of the ECL system that the relevant CMO is presumed to be representative of the interest of the non-members as well as of its members. A CMO is presumed to fulfil that requirement if it is representative of a substantial number of rightholders in the same field of works and use via mandates.[2461] Thus one of the criticisms of the Google Settlement Agreement was the lack of representative CMOs to negotiate such a deal.[2462] However, the criterion for how the requirement of representativeness is fulfilled is not clear-cut in any of the present ECL systems within Europe.[2463] Here I will look at whether the representativeness requirement would need to be any different for cross-border online use under an ECL agreement.

625. The representativeness requirement always relates to a specific territory.[2464] Accordingly, for CMOs to be eligible to negotiate an ECL agreement under ECL provisions in the Nordic countries, they must represent a substantial number of authors of the type of works used in the country

2461 See discussion and references in Ch. 5.2.1.
2462 See Ch. 2.3.1.
2463 Guibault, Cultural, 2015, 178–179. See discussion in Ch. 5.2.1 and 7.2-.7.4.
2464 Trumpke, Exklusivität, 2015, 661.

concerned. An underlying assumption is that the relevant CMO has the mandate from its members to negotiate the uses of works that an ECL provision covers.[2465] The definition of a CMO under the CMO Directive encompasses both CMOs mandated by rightholders directly as well as CMOs mandated by law.[2466] However, a legislative mandate on its own is not sufficient for a collective agreement to be considered an arrangement concerning management[2467], which is of importance for the potential cross-border use. Thus it is an important part of the ECL requirement of representativeness that it is based on direct mandates from rightholders.

626. Rightholders of literary works, the mainstay of library collections, are generally well represented by CMOs in Europe.[2468] The CMOs that may be best suited to negotiate ECL agreements for use by libraries are the reproduction rights organisations (RROs) that manage rights of both authors and publishers of text and image based works. With the advent of digital technology RRO's have ventured into licensing digital uses.[2469] According to IFRRO, the international non-governmental organisation representing RROs, there are RROs in all EU Member States except Cyprus, Estonia and Malta. The EFTA-EEA Member States also have RROs, although Lichtenstein's rightholders' rights are managed by Swiss RROs.[2470] This requirement of representativeness should include all relevant rightholders. Thus if derivative rightholders, such as publishers, hold rights in a meaningful part of the works used under an ECL agreement, it would be important for the compatibility of such an agreement with international norms that the relevant CMO was in fact representative of a substantial part of those rightholders.[2471]

627. However, modern libraries can be host to all types of in-copyright works[2472] in addition to literary works, and these may not always be as well represented by CMOs.[2473] Thus there may not be one CMO that fully represents all works that the library would like to use.[2474] Even so, if ECL agreements became the norm for cross-border online use for all types of works contained in libraries or other cultural heritage institutions, this would probably encourage

2465 See discussion in Ch. 5.2.1 and 7.2–7.4.
2466 Art. 3(a) COM Directive; Guibault and van Gompel, Collective, 2016, 143.
2467 C-301/15 – Soulier, par. 52; C-301/15 – Soulier, AG opinion, par. 57.
2468 SWD(2016) 301 final, IA Part I, 2016, 67, 132–133; Kyst, Aftalelicens, 2009, 52.
2469 Koskinen-Olsson, Collective, 2005,; Tarja Koskinen-Olsson and Lowe, Educational Material, 2012, 8, 32, 43–44, 55–56, 63; Koskinen-Olsson and Sigurðardóttir, Collective, 2016, 246.
2470 See <www.ifrro.org/rro>, accessed 16 July 2017.
2471 See discussion in Ch. 6.2.3.2.
2472 See discussion in Ch. 2.1.
2473 SWD(2016) 301 final, IA Part I, 2016, 67, 133; Samuelson, Comments, 2015, 5–7.
2474 Van Gompel and Hugenholtz, The Orphan, 2010, 65 ff.; Kerremans, Janssen and Valcke, Collective solutions, 2011, 646, 649; Oostveen and Guibault, IPR issues, 2013, 27; Kyst, Aftalelicens, 2009, 51.

the establishment of an umbrella CMO for that purpose.[2475] The CMO Directive seems to expect such a development.[2476]

628. So-called grey literature, i.e. documents, leaflets and other ephemeral material that is created and distributed outside the formal channels of publishers, is a specific problem with regard to the representativeness requirement. The same applies for unpublished works that fall under copyright protection, often without the author being aware of the fact, such as private letters and photographs. The creators may often not see themselves as authors or may not belong to a CMO[2477] and there is no identification system in place for such works.[2478] Thus it could be difficult to use ECLs for collections that mainly contain such works, unless it were decided that they fell within the category of literary works in general (or visual works for the photographs) and the relevant CMOs would be deemed representative.[2479]

629. It is interesting to note that, in the preparatory documents for the general ECL legislative provision in Sweden, it is stated that an ECL agreement can never be limited to the use of orphan works, as the requirement of representativeness could not be fulfilled under such circumstances.[2480] In Finland there were deliberations on a proposal to complement ECL provisions to enable CMOs to license orphan works after a "reasonable effort" to find rightholders. In the event, the proposal was never put forward, probably in part due to the question of sufficient representativeness.[2481] This is in reality more of a theoretical problem as most cases of mass use of works by libraries concerns a combination of orphan works and works of known rightholders.[2482] It is precisely for such a mixture of works that ECL agreements work well, as they eliminate the arduous work for users, such as libraries, of identifying each and every rightholder.

630. Securing representation of foreign rightholders by a national CMO is normally done through reciprocity agreements.[2483] However, it is not always simple

2475 Riis, Rognstad and Schovsbo, Collective Agreements, 2016, 67; Guibault, Collective, 2014, 787; IPO, Government, 2014, 1, fn. 1; Koskinen-Olsson and Sigurðardóttir, Collective, 2016, 244–247; Vuopala, Extended, 2013, 15; Bulayenko, Permissibility, 2016, 66.

2476 Cf. Art. 39 CMO Directive; Guibault, Collective, 2014, 787. This may, however, be more likely to happen in Europe where there is a culture of pre-existing CMOs than e.g. in the USA, cf. Ginsburg and Besek, Comments, 2015, 7; Samuelson, Comments, 2015, 3–4.

2477 In fact they may not qualify for membership, as often there is a requirement of publication in order to become a member of a CMO.

2478 Vuopala, Extended, 2013, 32; Deazley and Stobo, Archives, 2013, 48; Firth and Preira, Exceptions for Libraries, 2016, 28–29.

2479 Vuopala, Extended, 2013, 36.

2480 Prop. 2012/13:141, Regeringens proposition, 2013, 57.

2481 Liedes, Memorandum, 2010, 12–14; Vuopala, Extended, 2013, 35–36.

2482 See discussion in Ch. 5.2.1.1.

2483 See discussion in Ch. 5.1.1.

to achieve sufficient representation of foreign righholders as discussed above.[2484] That is one reason why it seems prudent to limit cross-border effect of national ECL agreements to national publications as will be discussed further below.

10.1.2. MANDATES

631. There is a direct correlation between the mandate that CMOs are granted by their members[2485] and the possible scope of use of works under the extended effect of an ECL agreement which binds the outsider.[2486] The possible scope under an ECL agreement that is concluded on the basis of a specific ECL provision is limited by the provision as well as the mandate, but under a general ECL provision the scope of the CMO mandate is the only outer limit.[2487]

632. The extended effect only comes into force once the CMO has negotiated a licence on behalf of its members with a user.[2488] Such a licence agreement must be consistent with the mandate granted by the members to the CMO both with regard to uses and territory. Thus in order for ECL agreements to enable libraries to make in-copyright works available online with cross-border effect, the relevant CMO would need a mandate from its members to license the making available right in the relevant territories.[2489] Traditionally authors and publishers assign the worldwide administration of their rights to published works to their national CMO.[2490] However, it is not always clear whether digital rights have been assigned to CMOs, in particular with regard to older works.[2491] Nevertheless, under the ECL system, as long as a representative number of members have clearly assigned the digital rights to the relevant CMO, the potential lack of clarity with regard to the digital rights of other members is not a problem, as it will be covered by the extension effect in the same way as for outsiders.

633. The central importance of mandates granted by rightholders, explicitly or implicitly, is made clear by the judgement in the Soulier case. A legislative

---

2484 See discussion in Ch. 5.2.1 and 5.2.3; Guibault, Cultural, 2015, 189; Boulanger and others, Assessing, 2014, 19.

2485 See Art. 5(7) CMO Directive, which stipulates that a rightholder must grant a CMO specific consent for each of the rights that the CMO manages. See discussion on that provision in Ch. 6.3.3.

2486 Sterling, World Copyright Law, 2015, 629–630; Guibault, Cultural, 2015, 179.

2487 Cf. discussion in Ch. 5.3 and 5.3.2.

2488 See Ch. 5.3.

2489 ALAI, Opinion ECL, 2016, 4, 5.

2490 SWD(2015) 100 final, A Digital Single Market Strategy, 2015, 27; Schierholz, Collective Management in Europe, 2010, 1154–1155; Axhamn and Guibault, Cross-border ECL, 2011, 21; Tryggvadóttir, Digital libraries, 2014, 317. With regard to music rightholders see Langus, Neven and Poukens, Economic, 2014, 100–101.

2491 Guibault, Cultural, 2015, 179–180.

mandate does not suffice on its own, even if the CMO represents a large majority of rightholders.[2492] In my view there is an important difference between the French legislation and the ECL system with regard to mandates. Under the French legislation rightholders had not given the relevant CMO a mandate for the particular use that the legislation covered. Instead the CMO's mandate was statutory.[2493] Under the ECL system, however, the CMO must have an explicit mandate from rightholders for use in territories relevant to the ECL agreement.

10.1.3. GOOD GOVERNANCE AND GOVERNMENTAL AUTHORISATION

634. Good governance and effective management are important requirements for the eligibility of a CMO to negotiate and manage an ECL licence.[2494] The relevant CMOs must have the capacity to manage the rights of outsiders effectively. The ability of managing the rights of outsiders is not only determined by the representativeness of the CMO but also by how well the CMO is run with regard to factors such as distribution of remuneration and transparency. This is especially important with regard to cross-border effect.[2495] The CMO Directive, once implemented in all Member States, will be a helpful support in this respect[2496] and will harmonise the requirements for good governance of CMOs across the EU and the EEA.[2497]

635. A related question is whether a system of governmental authorisation is essential to guaranteeing good governance. The CMO Directive stresses the need for effective monitoring of CMOs and their adherence to good governance.[2498] However, it is neutral with regard to the question of authorisation; hence Member States may make authorisation a requirement for ECL agreements as

2492 C-301/15 – Soulier, par. 29–45. See discussion of the case in Ch. 11.2.
2493 See discussion on the French legislation in Ch. 7.2.1.
2494 ALAI, Opinion ECL, 2016, 4. See discussion in Ch. 5.2.
2495 Riis and Schovsbo, ECLs, 2010, 495–498.
2496 It is, however, interesting that the Commission did not seem to have much faith in this, as one of the objections to employing ECLs as a solution for multi-territorial licences for on-line music was that significant discrepancies would persist in local CMOs and that there was no guarantee that they would be transparent, well governed and apply existing rules, cf. SWD(2012) 204 final, Impact Assessment, 2012, 172, 189. I disagree with this pessimistic outlook on the effect of EU harmonisation under the CMO Directive.
2497 Guibault and van Gompel, Collective, 2016, 174; ALAI, Opinion ECL, 2016, 4; IPO, Government, 2014, 7; COM(2016) 593 final, Proposal, 2016, Rectital (24).
2498 Art. 33–38 and Recitals (49)-(51) CMO Directive; Frank Gotzen, 'Multi-territorial licences between judge and legislator. From the "CISAC" cases to Directive 2014/26', 2014, (No 241), Revue Internationale du Droit d'Auteur, 94–161, 140–142.

long as such an authorisation provision is compatible with EU legislation.[2499] The main argument for having an authorisation system is that it provides legal certainty and enables control of the system. Not requiring authorisation, on the other hand, makes the system more flexible.[2500] The Swedish system works well without an authorisation system. Still, in countries with less of a tradition of CMO's an authorisation system might be of more importance.

10.1.4. TRANSPARENCY

636. Sufficient transparency is particularly important for ECL agreements[2501] because of their binding effect for outside rightholders.[2502] This is reflected in the 2011 MoU on out-of-commerce works[2503] which obliges the relevant CMO to "make its best efforts" to alert outside rightholders to the agreement in accordance with procedures negotiated by the parties. Furthermore, the MoU stipulates that a:

> ...digital library project shall be widely publicised so that all stakeholders whose rights and interests might be affected can decide whether or not to participate in the project in full knowledge of its scope; and communication to rightholders shall be made sufficiently in advance of any scanning or use.[2504]

Such transparency measures are essential to enable outsiders to make use of safeguard measures implemented for them, such as opt-outs and individual remuneration.[2505] This is even more important for digital and cross-border use.[2506]

637. The French legislation on out-of-commerce books[2507] under scrutiny in the Soulier case stipulated that "the most appropriate publicity measures" should be laid down in a decree to ensure that rightholders were as well informed as possible about the system and their option to opt-out.[2508] The decree adopted on the basis of the legislation specified that such publicity measures should contain an information campaign initiated by the Ministry of Culture and the relevant CMO and rightholder organisation, which should include online presentations

2499 Guibault, Collective, 2014, 785; Ficsor, Collective Management, 2016, 217–218. See discussion on the issue in Ch. 5.2.1.3, 5.2.3 and 6.3.4.

2500 Tryggvadóttir, Digital libraries, 2014, 324; Rognstad, Avtalelisens, 2012, 629.

2501 Janssens and Tryggvadóttir, Facilitating, 2015, 90; Axhamn and Guibault, Solving Europeana's mass-digitization issues through Extended Collective Licensing?, 2011, 516; ALAI, Opinion ECL, 2016, 4.

2502 See discussion on transparency in Ch. 5.4.4.

2503 See discussion on the MoU in Ch. 7.1.

2504 Principles 2(2) and 2(4) MoU.

2505 Tryggvadóttir, Digital libraries, 2014, 324.

2506 Strowel, The European, 2011, 669; ALAI, Opinion ECL, 2016, 4.

2507 See discussion on the legislation in Ch. 7.2.1.

2508 Art. 134-7 FCIP.

and mailing operations, adverts in the national press and on news websites.[2509] These constitute fairly extensive transparency measures. Nevertheless, the CJEU concluded that the legislation did not provide a mechanism that ensured that authors were actually and individually informed so that they could take a decision on whether they wanted to opt-out or not. Thus an implicit consent of rightholders could not be said to be established for use under the French legislation[2510], at least not for commercial use.[2511] However, as discussed below, the French legislation established a system fundamentally different from the system of ECLs, where none of the rightholders had mandated the CMO to negotiate the digital uses allowed under the legislation. Thus the CJEU mainly considered whether the transparency measures sufficed to establish implicit consent by rightholders for the use in question, as no exceptions were applicable for such use nor did the collective management in question qualify as an arrangement of management of rights[2512], which can facilitate use based on exceptions that fall outside of the exhaustive list in Art. 5 of the InfoSoc Directive. I propose that such transparency measures are different in nature from the transparency efforts aimed at enabling outsiders to take advantage of safeguard measures, such as opt-out and individual remuneration, under an ECL system that qualifies as an arrangement for the management of rights.[2513]

638. The CMO Directive stipulates firmer and more consistent rules of transparency not only for CMOs[2514] but also for users[2515] who are not acting in the capacity of a consumer[2516], which is an "absolute novelty" in EU copyright legislation.[2517] Transparency is also important for users, such as libraries, not least if ECL agreements allow for cross-border use. Thus ECL agreements between national libraries and a national CMO for making works available online should be made public so that users in other countries are able to familiarise themselves with the terms of use.[2518] This is what the Norwegian National Library and the German National Library already do with regard to their collective agreements for making works available.[2519]

639. The information that users should provide must be "necessary" for the collection of remuneration and its distribution and should be limited to what

2509 Decree No 2013-182; C-301/15 – Soulier, par. 16.
2510 Ibid, par. 43.
2511 Ibid, par. 44.
2512 See discussion in Ch. 6.3.1.
2513 See further discussion on the issue in Ch. 10.3.4, 10.3.5 and 11.2.1.
2514 Art. 18–22 CMO Directive.
2515 Art. 17 and Recital (33) CMO Directive.
2516 See definition in Art. 3(k) CMO Directive.
2517 Guibault, Collective, 2014, 754; Guibault and van Gompel, Collective, 2016, 155–156.
2518 Guibault, Cultural, 2015, 190.
2519 Cf. Ch. 5.3.1.4 and 7.2.

is "reasonable" and at the users' disposal.[2520] Information provided by libraries about their actual use under an ECL agreement would be beneficial for the CMO and an important contribution to ensuring the distribution of remuneration to rightholders. Thus the Norwegian Bokhylla ECL agreement obliges the Norwegian National Library to make arrangements, as far as possible, for the relevant CMO to have access to statistics for the material made available under the agreement.[2521]

640. Regrettably, the CMO Directive does not require a CMO to inform the general public or entities not in a contractual relationship with the CMO, on which works a CMO manages. This means that a CMO is not obliged to inform a library, unless they have an agreement with the CMO, whether it represents works that are in the library's collection. Such information is important for digital libraries contemplating obtaining an ECL for the use of works in their collections or if they are performing a diligent search for use of works under the Orphan Works Directive.[2522]

641. However, privacy issues must not be forgotten with regard to transparency and available information. Thus one of the main justifications for the private copy exception has been that monitoring home-copying would entail an unacceptable invasion of privacy.[2523] Hence the CMO Directive states[2524] that the processing of personal data carried out within the framework of the Directive shall be subject to the General Data Protection Regulation.[2525] This applies to information on rightholders, members, users and any other individual that the CMO may be processing.[2526] This can affect which use and user information it is possible to process in relation to works used under an ECL agreement.

642. Another issue related to transparency is the need for a centralised portal for information regarding ECL agreements with cross-border effect, both for rightholders and users. The DSM proposal stipulates that a single online portal should make all the relevant information accessible for rightholders, to

---

2520 Recital (33) CMO Directive; S. van Gompel, 'Directive 2014/26/EU on collective management of copyright and related rights and multi-territorial licensing of rights in musical works for online use in the internal market' in Thomas Dreier and P. Berndt Hugenholtz (eds), *Concise European Copyright Law* (2 edn, Wolters Kluwer, 2016) 595; Guibault and van Gompel, Collective, 2016, 155.

2521 Art. 18 Bokhylla Agreement.

2522 COMMUNIA, Policy paper on proposed Directive on collective management of copyright, 2013, 3; Guibault, Collective, 2014, 761–762; Guibault and van Gompel, Collective, 2016, 156.

2523 Guibault, Contracts, 2000, 134; Ricketson and Ginsburg, International, 2006, 782.

2524 Art. 42 and Recital (52) CMO Directive.

2525 Cf. Art. 94 of Regulation (EU) 2016/679 of the European Parliament and of the Council of 27 April 2016 on the protection of natural persons with regard to the processing of personal data and on the free movement of such data, and repealing Directive 95/46/EC (GDPR).

2526 Van Gompel, Directive 2014/26/EU, 2016, 624.

enable them to identify and object to the use of their out-of-commerce works for a six-month period before any use, and during the whole duration of the relevant licence.[2527] In the light of the fact that cultural heritage institutions in all Member States will be able to use works in accordance with the licence[2528] it seems logical that the agreement would also be made accessible in the same portal, so that their terms would be readily accessible for those users. Moreover, for the same reason information about opt-outs also belongs in such a portal.[2529]

10.1.5. EVALUATION

643. The representativeness of the CMO, both for national and cross-border use, must be extensive enough to legitimise the application of the ECL agreement to outsiders. The representativeness must also secure broad enough coverage of works in the field to minimise the likelihood of opt-outs by outsiders and thus create more legal certainty for users.[2530] At the same time, the requirement of representativeness may not become so cumbersome that it stifles the possibility of entering into an agreement. This would be the risk if the requirement were to be applied strictly in relation to the actual works the ECL agreement covers. If stakeholders are required to identify rightholders of each and every work that could be used under an agreement in order for the requirement to be fulfilled, then this would come fairly close to the controversial diligent search requirement under the Orphan Works Directive.[2531] Hence it is important that the representativeness requirement is flexible and that it is accepted that it can vary in relation to different categories of works.[2532]

644. Furthermore, mandates from rightholders for all types of ECL agreements must expressly reflect the scope of use, both with regard to works and territory. This is of paramount importance for national ECL agreements that enable cross-border use.

645. The same applies to transparency measures. However, it is important to distinguish between transparency measures required to establish a tacit consent of rightholders in general under State mandated collective management, such as at issue in the Soulier case, and transparency measures deemed necessary to inform outsiders under an ECL agreement of the existence of the agreement.

2527 COM(2016) 593 final, Proposal, 2016, Art. 8(2).
2528 Ibid, Art. 8(1).
2529 ALAI, Opinion ECL, 2016, 7.
2530 Guibault, Cultural, 2015, 177.
2531 See discussion in Ch. 4.2.3.4, 4.2.4.2 and Ch. 7.3.3 on the stringent representation requirement in the UK ECL legislation.
2532 Prop. 69 L, Proposisjon, 2015, 29.

646. The best way to secure transparency of ECL agreements with a cross-border element is to make them available online, at least on the websites of the relevant users, as the Norwegian National Library does with regard to its Bokhylla agreement. Even better would be the publication of such agreements on a centralised European portal. However, establishing such a centralised portal would be difficult without EU legislation.

647. Governmental authorisation of CMOs, based on clear rules of procedure[2533], helps to create a more efficient clearance system and supports the legitimacy of ECLs, especially in the international context[2534], which is an important consideration in relation to the cross-border effect of ECLs. Thus I strongly support governmental authorisation of CMOs, in particular for ECL agreements enabling cross-border use.

648. I am of the opinion that the representativeness requirement must be the same for ECL agreements for national and cross-border use. However, it is difficult for national CMOs to achieve sufficient representativeness with regard to foreign rightholders[2535] regardless of whether the use is for national or cross-border use. Given the potentially greater economic impact of online cross-border on outsiders' rights, my view is that ECL agreements granting libraries the right to enable cross-border online use should be limited to national works, as discussed further below.

649. Next I will discuss whether the field and scope of use under ECL agreements for libraries affects their compatibility with the international framework.

10.2. FIELD AND SCOPE OF USE

650. The second key element of the ECL system is the set of provisions to determine the field and scope of use under the extension effect.[2536] Limitations I see as necessary regarding the field and scope of national ECL agreements for online cross-border use by libraries to fulfil international norms are, first, that the agreements should only concern works that are permanently in the libraries collections[2537] and, second, that they should only apply to national works. This

[2533] One commentator on the proposed ECL system in the USA suggests that applications by CMOs for authorisations should be made public, so that anyone could raise concerns about their representativeness or ability to manage ECL agreements, cf. Samuelson, Comments, 2015, 9.

[2534] Tryggvadóttir, Digital libraries, 2014, 324.

[2535] See discussion in Ch. 5.2.1 and 5.2.3.

[2536] See Ch. 5.3.

[2537] As is proposed in COM(2016) 593 final, Proposal, 2016, Art. 7(1). This is also the principle, albeit not as clear, in the Orphan Works Directive, cf. Art. 1(2) and 6(1); Janssens and

second requirement is a twist on the country of origin principle.[2538] It will be further discussed below as well as the question whether ECLs with cross-border effect should only be applicable to published works or also to works made available in another manner and to non-published works. There are several other aspects of the field and scope of use which may affect the compatibility of an ECL agreement with international norms, such as the age of works, commercial availability of the works, the commercial aspect of enabled use and the question of whether only the viewing of works should be allowed in cross-border situations or also the downloading of copies. Below I will elaborate on these issues, beginning with national works versus foreign works.

10.2.1. NATIONAL WORKS

651. I propose that ECL agreements for libraries based on national legislation should only have cross-border effect for national works of the country where the ECL agreement is negotiated. National works in this respect would be works with a certain connection to the country where the ECL agreement is sought, such as publication[2539] in the country concerned or, in the case of unpublished works, where the author is a national.[2540] There are several reasons for this position. Firstly, one of the main objections to using ECL agreements for cross-border use is the weak position of foreign outside rightholders.[2541] Secondly, if ECL agreements encompass works of foreign origin, the group of outsiders can easily outnumber members of a national CMO eligible to negotiate under an ECL provision, which may affect the representativeness requirement.[2542]

652. Although one of the benefits of the Nordic ECL system is that it enables national CMOs to license a foreign repertoire, even where reciprocal representation agreements may not be available[2543], I argue that this only applies for use within the national territory of the relevant CMO. The danger of cross-border online use of works of foreign outsiders based on national agreements became evident a few years back when several Russian websites, such as AllofMP3, which became well-know at the time, started to sell copyrighted

Tryggvadóttir, Facilitating, 2015, 43. The MoU on out-of-commerce works also seems to have this limitation, although its Principle 1(1) might indicate that it was sufficient that the work was contained in any relevant cultural heritage institution.

2538 Guibault, Cultural, 2015, 187–190. See discussion on the Berne Convention principle of country of origin in Ch. 8.1 and on the country of origin approach in Ch. 8.2.2.3.

2539 See discussion on the terms publication and published in Ch. 10.2.2.

2540 The limitation of national works could be further specified, e.g. to exclude translations, cf. SWD(2016) 301 final, IA Part I, 2016, 70.

2541 Triaille and others, Study, 2013, 306. See further discussion and references in Ch. 6.2.1.

2542 Trumpke, The Extended, 2012, 286; Rognstad, Avtalelisenser, 2004, 157.

2543 See e.g. Gervais, Collective Management, 2001, 41; Ficsor, Collective, 2016, 66.

music at a very low price with no territorial restrictions. The websites seemed to be legal within Russia but it was almost impossible for foreign rightholders to opt-out or receive remuneration for the use of their work. This was due to loopholes in the Russian copyright act, enabling CMOs to authorise extensive use of works of outsiders, national and foreign, and insufficient control and regulations of CMOs in Russia at the time. Even though the legislative situation within Russia at the time was very different from the well-regulated ECL systems in the Nordic countries, the situation highlights the dangers and difficulties that can arise in such situations.[2544]

653. The main challenge to the cross-border application of ECLs is that national CMOs do not necessarily represent foreign rightholders sufficiently[2545], despite reciprocal agreements. In particular, it is difficult to make sure that foreign rightholders can in practice make use of safeguard measures for outsiders, such as claiming individual remuneration and opt-out. The situation is different with regard to national outsiders at least where there is sufficient transparency in the dealings of CMOs. Wide publication of ECL agreements and projects based on them should be sufficient to alert national outsiders to the fact that their works might fall under an ECL agreement and hence give them a more realistic opportunity either to claim remuneration for their work or to opt-out. Thus I suggest that if an ECL agreement is limited to works first published in, or with sufficient connections to the country where the ECL is granted[2546], it can have cross-border effect without a specific EU provision to that effect. An example of this approach is the Finnish ECL agreement for the Finnish National Gallery[2547] and the German National Library Project[2548], the latter, however, based on presumption of mandate rather than ECLs.

Thus, limiting ECL agreements to national works will, first, make it easier to ensure that the representativeness requirements are fulfilled[2549]; second, it should be easier for outsiders, who frequently would be residing in the country of origin of the work, to safeguard their interests as well as making it easier for CMOs to find and remunerate outsiders of national works of the country of the CMO[2550]; and finally, it should lessen duplication in digitisation efforts of the

---

2544 See Sergey Budylin and Yulia Osipova, 'Is AllofMP3 Legal? Non-Contractual Licensing Under Russian Copyright Law', 2007, (1), Journal of High Technology Law, 1–17; Trumpke, Exklusivität, 2015, 620–623, 630.

2545 See discussion in Ch. 5.4.5, 5.5 and 6.2.1.

2546 See Ch. 10.2.1.

2547 See Ch. 5.3.1.2, par. 319–321.

2548 See Ch. 7.4, par. 513.

2549 See discussion in Ch. 5.2.1 and Ch. 10.1.1, as well as Riis, Rognstad and Schovsbo, Collective Agreements, 2016, 66; Guibault, Cultural, 2015, 189; Karnell, Outsiders, 1991, 435; Riis and Schovsbo, ECLs in Action, 2012, 949–950; Boulanger and others, Assessing, 2014, 19.

2550 Trumpke, Exklusivität, 2015, 688; Tryggvadóttir, Digital libraries, 2014, 324; Axhamn and Guibault, Cross-border ECL, 2011, 35; SOU 2010:24, Avtalad upphovsrätt, 2010, 229–230;

cultural heritage in different Member States and thus help achieve economies of scale which is a consistent goal of the EU legislator.[2551]

654. This limitation is in line with the approach taken in the Orphan Works Directive and the MoU on out-of-commerce works[2552], as well as the original DSM proposal for the solution on out-of-commerce works.[2553]

655. The next question to be considered is whether ECL agreements with cross-border effect should only cover published works in the traditional sense or also works made available by rightholders, as well as unpublished works.

10.2.2. PUBLISHED VERSUS UNPUBLISHED WORKS

656. The meaning of the term "published" varies between countries. Under the Berne Convention the term is limited to the publication and the consequent distribution of tangible copies of works that are published with the consent of their authors.[2554] However, in German speaking and the Nordic countries the term "published" is used for works that have been made legally available or accessible, and is not limited to publication of tangible copies; it includes making works available or accessible under the communication to the public right, including making them available online.[2555] The question then arises whether, for the purpose of ECL agreements enabling libraries to make works available online with cross-border effect, the term national works should include both works published in the country concerned in the meaning of the Berne Convention as well as works made legally available in another way. In my view it should be possible for ECL agreements to cover all works made legally available. Indeed, it is important that this is so as, increasingly, works are made available exclusively in ways that do not fulfil the Berne Convention criteria for publication.[2556] Such works will become an ever-increasing part of our cultural heritage.

Strowel, The European, 2011, 669.

2551 Guibault, Cultural, 2015, 187, 189; 2011/711/EU, Recommendation, 2011, item 4; Recital (15) OWD: Triaille and others, Study, 2013, 283.

2552 See discussion on the Orphan Works Directive in Ch. 4.2.3 and on the MoU in Ch. 7.1. See also Guibault, Cultural, 2015, 187 ff.; Trumpke, Exklusivität, 2015, 654–656.

2553 Art. 7(4) DSM proposal; SWD(2016) 301 final, IA Part I, 2016, 70–71. See discussion in Ch. 11.3.1.2 on the state of the proposal in this regard at the time of writing at the end of May 2018.

2554 Cf. Art. 3(3) BC; Dreier, Berne, 2016, 24.

2555 See e.g. Art. 6(2) GCA and Art. 8 DCA; See also discussion in Ch. 5.3.3; Michel M. Walter, 'Term Directive' in Michel M. Walter and Silke von Lewinski (eds), *European Copyright Law, A Commentary* (Oxford University Press, 2010) 510–512.

2556 Triaille and others, Study, 2013, 47, cf. fn. 89. See also discussion in Ch. 8.1.

657. The Orphan Works Directive attempts to address the issue by providing that the Directive is applicable to works that have never been published or broadcast but have been made publicly accessible[2557] by a beneficiary institution under the Directive[2558] with the consent of the rightholder or if "it is reasonable to assume that the rightholder would not oppose the uses".[2559] There is a strong moral right dimension to the provision and it may be difficult to determine when it is applicable in practice.[2560] A similar moral right criteria is to be found in the general ECL provisions in Norway and Sweden, which contain a general ban on letting works fall under an ECL agreement under the provisions if there is reason to believe the rightholder would oppose such use.[2561] This would apply to all works, published or unpublished.[2562]

658. Another question is whether ECL agreements enabling libraries to make works available online with cross-border effect should include works that have never been made available in any way, with or without the consent of the author, e.g. private letters of authors donated to a library by their heirs or unpublished manuscripts of poems or other works. Such works may often represent significant examples of the cultural heritage.[2563] Yet, it is a sensitive issue to allow the communication to the public of such works, in particular allowing the online use with cross-border effect, as it may never have been the intention of the author to have the work made available. Furthermore, exceptions often only apply to works that have been made available. This could mean that works not made available by their authors and thus not applicable for use under an exception would become so because of use made under an ECL agreement.[2564] Thus it may be prudent to place some limits on including works that have not been made available with the consent of the authors, as is done in the Orphan Works Directive. The proposed solution for out-of-commerce works in the DSM proposal neither addresses these questions nor defines the term "published".[2565]

659. The next question I will discuss is whether the age of works should have an effect on the international compatibility of ECL agreements for cross-border use.

2557 Presumably in this context it is by giving access to such works on the premises of the relevant institution.
2558 See Ch. 4.2.3.1.
2559 Art. 1(3) and Recital (12) OWD; see also discussion and references in Ch. 4.2.3.3.
2560 Ibid.
2561 Art. 42h SCA and Art. 36(2) NCA, cf. also Prop. 69 L, Proposisjon, 2015, 24, 61.
2562 See discussion in Ch. 5.4.3.3.
2563 See discussion in Ch. 5.3.3.
2564 See discussion in Ch. 5.3.1.5.
2565 See discussion in Ch. 11.3.1.2.

10.2.3. AGE OF WORKS

660. The age of works has a significant effect on their commercial return and their commercial availability. It has been estimated that literary works provide returns for between 1.4 and 5 years on average. Three quarters of original titles are retired after a year and by 2 years, 90 per cent of originals are out-of-commerce.[2566] Thus it is potentially easier for stakeholders to reach an ECL agreement for the making available online by libraries of in-copyright works for older works, as they are of less economic importance for the rightholders.[2567] Older works, whether out-of-commerce or not, often hold important cultural, scientific, educational, historical and entertainment value.[2568] At the same time, there is no readily available market place for facilitating online or digital access to out-of-commerce books; hence there is a greater need for a solution for these than for in-commerce works.[2569] Moreover, ECL agreements covering commercially available works might either be too expensive for non-commercial users such as libraries or there might be too many opt-outs, which would undermine the arrangement.[2570] Finally, the short commercial lifespan of works has been used as an argument for price discrimination based on territoriality[2571], which would be difficult to combine with agreements enabling online cross-border use. Thus, out-of-commerce works would seem to be a more appropriate subject for ECL agreements for cross-border online use, especially if remuneration was based on a single tariff. Furthermore, limiting ECL agreements enabling cross-border use to out-of-commerce works might make such agreements more compatible with international norms.[2572]

661. On the other hand, limiting ECLs to out-of-commerce books could diminish the research and educational value of the digital resources that the system is intended to reinforce.[2573] The situation is further complicated by the blurring of the status of books as in- or out-of-commerce through the print-on-demand possibility.[2574] Thus such a limitation could additionally hamper the system's efficiency goals in that it would require the user or the CMO to

2566 Australian Government Productivity Commission, Intellectual Property Arrangements; Draft Report, 2016, 114, 155; SWD(2016) 301 final, IA Part I, 2016, 65.

2567 In Slovakia in December 2015, the practice under an ECL agreement on the use of out-of-commerce for the national library was that monographs and periodicals published before 2013 were considered out-of-commerce cf. European Commission, Report, 2016, 39.

2568 SWD(2016) 301 final, IA Part I, 2016, 65.

2569 US Copyright Office, Mass Digitization, 2015, 86.

2570 Ginsburg and Besek, Comments, 2015, 3–4; Samuelson, Comments, 2015, 7–8; Band, The Long, 2009, 262.

2571 Langus, Neven and Poukens, Economic, 2014, 64, 72, 86, 119.

2572 Ringnalda, Orphan Works, 2011, 10–11.

2573 US Copyright Office, Mass Digitization, 2015, 86.

2574 Ginsburg and Besek, Comments, 2015, 4.

determine the commercial status of every work in a collection in order to exclude those works that are commercially available.[2575] This issue could, however, be solved by limiting the agreement to works created, published or made available before a certain time, as done in the Norwegian Bokhylla project, i.e. have a certain cut-off date. This approach seems to be widely accepted by stakeholders given the limited number of opt-outs under the project.[2576] This seemed to be the solution that the Commission favoured in the original DSM proposal where it was proposed that requirements for determining the out-of-commerce works should not "extend beyond what is necessary and reasonable and do not preclude the possibility to determine the out-of-commerce status of a collection as a whole, when it is reasonable to presume that all works or other subject-matter in the collection are out of commerce."[2577]

662. Even so, I maintain that it should be left to the negotiating parties, who have expert market knowledge, to negotiate a structure that suits them and the project at hand. Thus I would submit that the coverage of ECL provisions for online library use, whether at national or EU level, should not be limited to either out-of-commerce works or works made legally available before a certain cut-off date. Having said this, the commercial availability of works covered by an ECL agreement could affect the compatibility of the agreement with the three-step test, in particular if the remuneration were below market value. This would have to be evaluated on a case-by-case basis.

663. Next I will discuss the necessity for and nature of limitations to the scope of use under a national ECL agreement for the online cross-border use of works by libraries.

10.2.4. THE EXCLUSIVE RIGHTS

664. ECL agreements enabling online cross-border use by libraries must, like ECL agreements for national use, address the scope of use with regard to both the exclusive communication to the public right and the reproduction right.[2578]

665. It seems obvious that all necessary reproduction acts for online use should be included in an ECL agreement for online cross-border use by

---

2575 Tryggvadóttir, Digital libraries, 2014, 324–325; Janssens and Tryggvadóttir, Facilitating, 2015, 92–93; Janssens and Tryggvadóttir, Orphan, 2016, 207; US Copyright Office, Mass Digitization, 2015, 86.

2576 See Ch. 5.3.1.4.

2577 COM(2016) 593 final, Proposal, 2016, 26. See discussion in Ch. 11.3.2 on the state of the proposal regarding this issue at the time of writing at the end of May 2018.

2578 See Ch. 3 for discussion on the exclusive right in online use.

libraries. Nevertheless, when analysing the process several question arise with regard to the scope of reproduction to be licensed in such agreements. They relate in particular to the interplay with exceptions mandated or allowed under the InfoSoc Directive that may cover some of the necessary acts, such as the reproduction exception for cultural heritage institutions, cf. Art. 5(2)(c)[2579], the mandatory exception for temporary copies under Art. 5(1)[2580] and the private copy exception, cf. Art. 5(2)(b).

666. For the digitisation of works to be used online by libraries it is interesting to note that the Norwegian Bokhylla ECL agreement[2581] stipulates that the Norwegian National Library can make available the "digital storage copies" that the Library produces under the preservation exception in the Norwegian Copyright Act.[2582] In the same manner, the Danish ECL agreements for online use by libraries authorised under the general ECL provision expressly state that the digitisation of works is not covered by the licence, as the necessary digitisation falls under the preservation exception in the Danish Copyright Act.[2583] This is also the case in the Finnish ECL agreement for the Finnish National Gallery.[2584] Thus Nordic ECL agreements providing for online use exclude the act of digitisation because it is covered under the Nordic preservation exceptions.[2585]

667. The DSM proposal, on the other hand, seems to assume that the act of digitisation should be included in a licence for the online use of out-of-commerce works.[2586] The proposal also contains a provision for a mandatory preservation exception for cultural heritage institutions[2587], which would be in addition to the provision in Art. 5(2)(c) of the InfoSoc Directive. The originally proposed provision underlined that the exception should be for the "sole" purpose of preservation. This wording might have hindered the Nordic approach of using the preservation exception for the digitisation part of online use under an ECL licence. However, the word "sole" has now been removed from the proposal, which may give a broader scope for interpretation in this regard.[2588] Furthermore, it might also be possible to use the provision

2579 See discussion in Ch. 4.2.2.1 and 4.2.4.1.1.1.
2580 See discussion on the exception in Ch. 3.1.2.
2581 See discussion on the Bokhylla Agreement (BA) in Ch. 5.3.1.4.
2582 Art. 3 BA, cf. Art. 16 NCA and Art. 1-3(3) of FOR 21.12.2001 no. 1563.
2583 Art. 16 DCA and Ch. 5.3.2.1.
2584 See discussion on the project in Ch. 5.3.1.2.
2585 See also discussion in Ch. 4.2.4.1.1.1.
2586 COM(2016) 593 final, Proposal, 2016, Art. 7(1), see, however, the Council of the European Union agreed negotiation mandate: 2016/0280 (COD) 9134/18, Agreed negotiation mandate, 2018, Art. 7(1) which uses the term reproduction instead of digitisation.
2587 COM(2016) 593 final, Proposal, 2016, Art. 5, 17(12)(c), Recital (18)-(21).
2588 See discussion in Ch. 4.2.4.1.1.1.

in Art. 5(2)(c) of the InfoSoc Directive on specific acts of reproduction that are not for direct or indirect economic or commercial advantage, as was the conclusion in the TU Darmstadt case in relation to the making available under Art. 5(3)(n) of the InfoSoc Directive.[2589] If that use was "specific" enough, use by libraries for the purpose of making works available online with cross-border effect might also be specific enough, especially if it was for out-of-commerce works.

In my view, it seems logical and sensible that if a digital copy exist for preservation purposes it should be possible to license its use under an ECL agreement, as is done in the Nordic countries, in particular because the technological process of digitising analogue copies is expensive and requiring such work to be duplicated would be a waste of resources. If no such copies exist it should be possible to make them for the purpose of the ECL agreement under the reproduction provision in Art. 5(2)(c) of the InfoSoc Directive.

668. Temporary copies in online transmission fall under the mandatory exception of Art. 5(1) in the InfoSoc Directive.[2590] This includes online viewing and thus neither libraries nor end-users would be liable for the reproduction inherent in the online viewing of such works, as demonstrated in the PRCA case.[2591]

669. Permanent copies on the other hand will require the rightholders' authorisation, unless they fall under an exception in national legislation.[2592] The non-mandatory private copying exception, cf. Art. 5(2)(b) of the InfoSoc Directive would presumably cover downloading. However, although present in most Member States, this exception is not harmonised, in particular not with regard to remuneration for private use.[2593] National libraries might be willing to pay remuneration for the making available right and the inherent cross-border use for online use, in an effort to give access to the European cultural heritage. However, increasing the remuneration to make downloading possible for end-users might be deemed unnecessary. Thus the Norwegian Bokhylla project is limited to viewing only of in-copyright works.[2594]

670. If ECL agreements for cross-border online use by libraries were limited to national works, as suggested above[2595], rightholders would to a large extent be residents of the country where the agreements were concluded. Seeking

2589 C-117/13 – TU Darmstadt, par. 17 and 49.
2590 C-360/13 – PRCA par. 61–63. See Ch. 3.1.2.
2591 Ibid, *supra*.
2592 Triaille and others, Study, 2013, 119; Axhamn and Guibault, Cross-border ECL, 2011, 67.
2593 Janssens, The Issue of Exceptions, 2009, 331; Westkamp, Study, 2007, 16–22.
2594 See Ch. 5.3.1.4.
2595 See Ch. 10.2.1.

remuneration for private copying abroad made possible under a national ECL agreement, would be difficult and cumbersome. Such private copying would normally constitute "small" uses generating small amounts of remuneration, which may not be economically viable to distribute abroad.[2596] Downloading and printing are at the same time more far-reaching encroachments on the economic interest of rightholders, members and outsiders alike, than is required by the public interest of giving access to the cultural heritage. This is partly reflected by the fact that the InfoSoc Directive does not oblige Member States to ensure the actual use of the private reproduction exception in Art. 5(2)b); Art. 6(4)(2) of the Directive allows Member States to take measures to ensure that technological measures do not hinder the use of the private reproduction exception but does not make such measures mandatory. Thus, in my view, limiting the use to the making available right and its inherent temporary reproduction would make ECL agreements with cross-border effect more compatible with international norms.[2597] Nevertheless, it is conceivable that national libraries and national CMOs on behalf of rightholders could reach an agreement on remuneration for such use that would be mutually beneficial and thus compatible with the international framework. Thus this might also be an issue best left to the stakeholders to negotiate.

671. The question arises whether the making available of, for example, Norwegian literary works in a country other than Norway should be seen as communication to the public, given that there are relatively few Norwegian speakers outside of Norway. In my view such would still be considered "public" given the CJEU's broad definition of the term.[2598] A related question is whether websites with works in a specific language could be seen as "targeted" to the public[2599] in a country with a different language. Again my view is that as the reasoning behind making such works available cross-border is to enable European access to European culture, all of Europe has to be seen as the "targeted" public. However, the number of Norwegian speakers or readers abroad should affect the remuneration for such online use.[2600] New technology, such as Google translate, may in future enable better enjoyment of works in foreign languages of those who do not master the relevant language, but currently it is too rudimentary to justify that remuneration should take non-Norwegian speakers into account. The same would apply to other language communities.[2601]

2596 See discussion on remuneration in Ch. 5.4.2 and 5.4.5.
2597 Tryggvadóttir, Digital libraries, 2014, 325.
2598 See discussion in Ch. 3.2.3.
2599 See e.g. C-173/11, Football Dataco II, par. 37 and discussion on the targeting approach in Ch. 3.2.2.2 and 8.2.2.2.
2600 See discussion on remuneration for cross-border use in Ch. 10.3.2.1.
2601 Trumpke, Exklusivität, 2015, 698.

10.2.5. COMMERCIAL VERSUS NON-COMMERCIAL USE

672. Most uses by public libraries and other cultural heritage institutions are for non-commercial purposes. However, clear demarcation of where the boundaries between commercial and non-commercial activities lie becomes more problematic when public libraries cooperate with private institutions, such as in digitisation projects.[2602] Given that such co-operation is highly recommended by the EU[2603] it is worth considering whether the question of commercial uses should not simply be left to the parties to negotiate. None of the Nordic ECL provisions are expressly limited to non-commercial use.[2604] If the negotiated use allowed for commercial use it would be reflected in the remuneration.[2605] In this connection it is worth keeping in mind that for many rightholders, such as academic and scientific authors and their publishers, the primary markets for their works are non-commercial.[2606] This also underlines the difficulty in establishing what commercial and non-commercial uses are. Thus I maintain this issue should be left to the negotiating parties.

10.2.6. EVALUATION

673. In order to comply with international norms, national ECL agreements for online cross-border use by libraries should be limited in their field and scope to national works, comprising national publications and works made legally available in other ways. This limitation would constitute the main difference in requirements for ECL agreements for cross-border use as compared to ECL agreements solely for use within the national borders of the ECL issuing country. Other issues, such as the age of works, commercial availability, commercial or non-commercial use and even the down-loading possibility should be left for stakeholders to negotiate. These latter issues could affect the compatibility of a particular ECL agreement with international norms; however, given the public mission purpose of libraries and assuming that a representative number of rightholders had negotiated the use and the relevant remuneration, such agreements would most likely pass the three-step test.

674. Limiting the scope of ECL agreements with cross-border effect to national works should be a workable solution which would cater for the interest both of rightholders and users, including libraries. The main aim of providing cross-border online access to the collections or part of the collections of libraries is to

---

2602 European Commission, Report on the responses, 2014, 41.

2603 Comité des Sages, The New Renaissance, 2011, 37–41; Recitals (21) and (22) OWD.

2604 See Ch. 5.3.1.

2605 Guibault, Cultural, 2015, 184–185; similarly Derclaye (ed) Copyright and Cultural Heritage, 2010, 239.

2606 IFRRO, U.S. Public Consultation: "Mass Digitization Pilot Program", 2015,.

give access to the cultural heritage. National libraries are the main custodians of each country's cultural heritage and thus ECL agreements on the use of national publications online without territorial limitations, at least within Europe, would help to make each country's national heritage available both nationally and regionally. This approach is also in line with several EU initiatives.[2607] Last but not least, limiting the cross-border effect of ECL agreements to national works would to a large extent eliminate the criticism of the country of origin approach with regard to the making available right, i.e. that it would detrimentally affect rightholders who are not also rightholders in the country of origin.[2608]

675. In my view, if the online use of an unpublished work or a work not made available at all is permitted under a national ECL agreement, as is possible in all of the Nordic countries, it should also be possible to include such works in an ECL agreement for online cross-border use. It seems reasonable, provided there is an opt-out possibility, to allow libraries to determine whether the unpublished work is of such cultural value that it merits being digitised and made available.[2609] At the same time it might be prudent to stipulate that such works will not be used under an ECL agreement for cross-border use if there is a specific reason to believe that the author would oppose such use, as stipulated in the Orphan Works Directive and the Norwegian and Swedish Copyright Acts.[2610] Although this provision has a subjective element that may be hard to determine[2611] it signals that care must be taken with regard to moral rights of such works. Furthermore, care would have to be taken to observe agreements or instructions regarding the use of such documents given by their donors, if available.[2612]

676. Last but not least is the discussion on the third main element of an ECL system: safeguard measures for outsiders. In the following discussion I will assess whether such safeguards need specific features for ECL agreements enabling libraries to use in-copyright works online with cross-border effect.

10.3. SAFEGUARD MEASURES

677. The most important safeguard measures for outsiders in the ECL system are, first, guarantee of equal treatment, second, the possibility of individual

2607 Recital (1) MoU on out-of-commerce works; Art. 3(3) OWD; COM(2016) 593 final, Proposal, 2016, Art. 7(4).

2608 Axhamn and Guibault, Cross-border ECL, 2011, 66. See discussion and further references in Ch. 8.2.3.

2609 See Ch. 5.3.3.

2610 Art. 1(3) OWD; Art. Art. 42h SCA and Art. 36(2) NCA.

2611 See discussion in Ch. 4.2.3.3.

2612 Such instructions in a contract between those who donate or place such works in a library or archive, and the relevant institution, or in a document accompanying such gifts or donations.

remuneration if the distribution of remuneration under the ECL agreement is collective, and third, the possibility of an opt-out.[2613]

10.3.1. EQUAL TREATMENT

678. The equal treatment of members and non-members is a fundamental requirement for the legitimacy of any ECL agreement. The CMO Directive underlines the principle of non-discrimination in the case of CMOs' management of rights of non-members under a representation agreement.[2614] That principle should be equally applicable to non-members whose right a CMO manages under a legal provision.

679. The CMO Directive stipulates minimum rights that CMOs must provide for outsiders.[2615] However, the Directive does not sufficiently underline the role of CMOs as trustees of the rights it administers for outsiders, whether under an ECL agreement or for other reasons.[2616] This could have been achieved by adding a provision stating the obligation of CMOs to treat such outsiders in the same way as their members in relevant instances, such as with regard to distribution of remuneration. With such a provision the principle of non-discrimination of members and non-members would have been better supported in the CMO Directive. The DSM proposal, however, expressly underlines that the requirement for equal treatment of all rightholders must be guaranteed in relation to the terms of a licence with extension effect or with presumed mandate for outsiders.[2617]

680. The high membership "thresholds" or qualifications required for becoming a member of CMOs can contribute to an increased number of outsiders.[2618] Membership should be facilitated as far as possible, as even with provisions on equal treatment of members and outsiders, treatment is sometimes not "equal" in practice.[2619] Concerns and criticism during the legislative process of the CMO Directive of over-strict membership requirements of CMOs led to the adoption of a provision in its Art. 5(2) which obliges CMOs to accept rightholders as members unless there are objectively justified reasons against it.[2620]

2613 See Ch. 5.4.
2614 Art. 14 and Recital (30) CMO Directive, see Guibault, Collective, 2014, 745–747.
2615 Art. 7 and Recital (21) CMO Directive, cf. Ibid, 728. This was not so in the original proposal for the Directive, which was criticised, cf. Drexl and others, Comments, 2013, 15–16.
2616 Drexl and others, Comments, 2013, 15.
2617 COM(2016) 593 final, Proposal, 2016, Art. 7(1)(b).
2618 Drexl and others, Comments, 2013, 15, 22.
2619 Ficsor, Collective Management, 2010, 73; Ficsor, Collective, 2016, 78–79; Axhamn and Guibault, Cross-border ECL, 2011, 46; Riis and Schovsbo, ECLs, 2010, 492; Bulayenko, Permissibility, 2016, 66. See also Ch. 6.2.1 with regard to foreign rightholders.
2620 Guibault, Collective, 2014, 724.

681. The criticism of inequality in practice has been aimed particularly at the issue of remuneration for outsiders as discussed next.

10.3.2. REMUNERATION

682. The issue of remuneration is a central concern with any licensing scheme, individual, collective or extended. One obstacle to using ECLs for orphan works, identified by the European Commission was the negotiated remuneration, which the Commission deemed to be prohibitive, based on information on remuneration in the Norwegian Bookhylla agreement.[2621] The conclusions drawn by the Commission were sharply criticised by the EFTA EEA States. They emphasised that remuneration under ECL agreements is always decided in negotiations between stakeholders and thus the Bokhylla agreement only reflected the situation in that particular case.[2622] This issue seems to be precisely what Recital (32) of the CMO Directive is aimed at, i.e. underlining that CMOs should have the flexibility to negotiate new digital uses without the risk that the terms of those licences could be used as a precedent for determining the terms for other uses.

683. If an ECL agreement includes cross-border use, such as in making works available online, the remuneration must take that into account.[2623] The provision in Recital (17) of the Satellite and Cable Directive would seem a prudent guide on how the level of payment should be ascertained, i.e. that all aspects of the use should be considered "such as the actual audience, the potential audience and the language version." It is possible that the negotiated level of payment for rightholders would be lower than if it were negotiated for use in each of the receiving countries.[2624] That may be because the enlarged geographical area may in fact not mean a correlating increase in the commercial value for the rightholder[2625], i.e. a larger area may not necessarily lead to a corresponding increase in use. Furthermore, the market value of national cultural heritage

---

2621 SEC(2011) 615 final, Impact Assessment, 2011, 27–28; Ringnalda, Orphan Works, 2011, 10; Samuelson, Comments, 2015, 13.

2622 Cf. the EEA EFTA Comment on the Commission proposal *for a Directive of the European* Parliament and of the Council on certain permit*ted uses of Orphan Works, (COM* (2011) 289), *Ref. 1110018, 7 December 2011,* available at <www.efta.int/EEA/news/EEA-EFTA-States-comment-proposed-directive-orphan-works-1097>, last viewed 17 July 2017; Janssens and Tryggvadóttir, Facilitating, 2015, 91; Guibault, Cultural, 2015, 184; Guibault, Report, 2015, 15.

2623 See e.g. Recital (17) Satellite and Cable Directive; C-192/04, Lagardère,; discussion of the Lagardére case in Triaille and others, Study, 2013, 53–54; C-462/09 – Stichting de Thuiskopie, par. 30–40; ALAI, Opinion ECL, 2016, 4.

2624 Axhamn and Guibault, Cross-border ECL, 2011, 64; Dreier, Satellite and Cable Directive, 2010, 429.

2625 Axhamn and Guibault, Cross-border ECL, 2011, 63–64.

content may be quite limited in Member States other than the country of origin of the content.[2626] Certainly, the administrative cost for both parties would be lower because the cost of negotiating in each country would be avoided.

684. Because of the hybrid nature of the ECL system[2627], the question arises of whether the remuneration for potential cross-border use can be determined in the country where the ECL agreement is negotiated in the absence of a specific EU provision to that effect. In the Lagardére case the CJEU concluded that the single equitable remuneration due under Art. 8(2) of the Rental and Lending Directive had to be decided by each of the Member States where the terrestrial transmitters were located. It was also for each Member State to determine what constitute the relevant criteria for such remuneration, using assessments of the use of a commercial phonogram in trade and criteria retained in Recital (17) of the Satellite and Cable Directive.[2628] This would suggest that the answer to the question of whether remuneration could be decided in the country of the national ECL agreement would be in the negative. However, this strict territorial interpretation in the Lagardére case might not apply to other directives.[2629] The case concerned a specific provision for the use of specific works, i.e. phonograms. There is no such specific provision with regard to remuneration for specific use under ECL agreements or in any other way, in the Infosoc Directive.

I submit that remuneration for the use of national works by national cultural heritage institutions through making them available online without territorial limitations can be determined in the country where the ECL agreement is negotiated for the whole potential and actual audience. This seems to be supported by the Stichting de Thuiskopie case regarding the effect of the territoriality of copyright in relation to the fair compensation due under Directive 2001/29.[2630] The Court's conclusion was that national norms can have extraterritorial application in order to safeguard rightholders' compensation.[2631] Furthermore, the Court implied that fair compensation does not have to be paid in one Member State if it has already been paid in another Member State.[2632]

685. All the Nordic ECL provisions stipulate that equal remuneration shall be guaranteed to members and non-members alike, regardless of nationality.[2633] However, several actual practices are to the disadvantage of foreign rightholders,

---

2626 Ibid, 66–67.
2627 See discussion in Ch. 6.1.2 and Ch. 6.3.1.
2628 C-192/04, Lagardère, par. 54–55.
2629 Triaille and others, Study, 2013, 53–54.
2630 C-462/09 – AG opinion in Stichting de Thuiskopie, par. 38.
2631 C-462/09 – Stichting de Thuiskopie, par. 30–40.
2632 Ibid, par. 12, 40; in fact stated in the AG opinion, cf. C-462/09 – AG opinion in Stichting de Thuiskopie, par. 55.
2633 See discussion in Ch. 5.4.2 and 5.4.5.

whether they be members of a sister CMO or foreign outsiders; these include the distribution of unclaimed remuneration exclusively to members of the national CMO, no pay-out of remuneration below a certain amount and deductions for collective purposes.[2634] This is a further argument for limiting ECL agreements that enable cross-border online use to national works.

10.3.2.1. The amount

686. The specific subject matter of intellectual property is to ensure rightholders' ability to commercially market or make available their protected subject matter through licences for remuneration. This does not mean, however, that the rightholder is entitled to claim the highest possible remuneration but "only appropriate remuneration for each use of the protected subject-matter."[2635]

This is reflected in EU legislation.[2636] Thus Art. 16(2) of the CMO Directive stipulates that the remuneration for licences shall be "reasonable in relation to, inter alia, the economic value of the use of the rights in trade, taking into account the nature and scope of the use of the work". This criterion is, however, difficult to apply in practice.[2637] As mentioned above, when determining the amount, the criterion in Recital (17) of the Satellite and Cable Directive would be of guidance: the actual and potential audience and the language version. The language version would affect how receptive the audience was.[2638] Furthermore, if works are out-of-commerce, as large parts of the collections in libraries are[2639], it seems evident that remuneration for use of such works would reflect that fact.[2640] As an example, some ECL agreements under the general Danish ECL provision forego any remuneration in specific instances where there is no substantive economic value at stake.[2641]

687. The hybrid nature of the extension effect of the ECL system is in particular demonstrated by the fact that the remuneration is negotiated by the CMO which represents a substantial number of rightholders in the relevant area of the ECL

2634 Riis and Schovsbo, ECLs, 2010, 490–492; Axhamn and Guibault, Cross-border ECL, 2011, 45, 55. See also discussion in Ch. 5.4.2, 5.4.5 and 6.2.1.

2635 Joined cases C-403/08 and C-429/08 – Premier League, par. 104–117, 146. See discussion in Ch. 8.3.1.

2636 E.g. the term "appropriate reward" in Recital (10) InfoSoc Directive and "adequate income" in Recital (5) Rental and Lending Directive.

2637 Guibault, Collective, 2014, 750–751.

2638 C-117/15 Reha Training, par. 50.

2639 Guibault, Cultural, 2015, 189.

2640 Ginsburg, Berne-Forbidden, 2016, 762; Ringnalda, Orphan Works, 2011, 11.

2641 Riis, Rognstad and Schovsbo, Collective Agreements, 2016, 63. An example is an ECL agreement on the reproduction of CD's and DVD's done on behalf of handicapped individuals, see <http://kum.dk/fileadmin/KUM/Documents/Kulturpolitik/Ophavsret/Aftalelicensgodkendelser/Generelle_aftalelicenser/Copydan_AVU-medier_Danske_Handicaporganisationer.pdf>, last viewed 10 November 2016.

agreement. Because of the stronger bargaining power of the CMO compared to individual licensing[2642] the remuneration that is negotiated is presumed to be reasonable, both for members and outsiders.

688. Given the hybrid nature of the ECL system with regard to the extension effect, the issue of reasonable remuneration for outsiders under ECL agreements and compatibility with international norms also relates to the discussion on fair compensation[2643] for use under exceptions. The fair compensation provided for under the Orphan Works Directive[2644] is thus of interest for this study, in particular the guidance in Recital (18) of the Directive. There it is stated that:

> For the purposes of determining the possible level of fair compensation, due account should be taken, inter alia, of Member States' cultural promotion objectives, of the non-commercial nature of the use made by the organisations in question in order to achieve aims related to their public-interest missions, such as promoting learning and disseminating culture, and of the possible harm to rightholders.

689. With regard to libraries it is also interesting to consider the discussion on remuneration for public lending under current Art. 6(1) of the Rental and Lending Directive. In the VEWA case the Court underlined that lending does not have a direct or indirect economic or commercial character.[2645] Thus the Court concluded that

> ...the use of a protected work in the event of public lending cannot be assessed in the light of its value in trade. Consequently, the amount of the remuneration will necessarily be less than that which corresponds to equitable remuneration or may even be fixed on a flat-rate basis in order to compensate for the act of making available all the protected works concerned.[2646]

Accordingly it can be assumed that when assessing whether remuneration for outsiders under an ECL agreement supports the compatibility of the extension effect with international norms, the public mission purpose of libraries to give access to the cultural heritage should be taken note of, as well as the non-commercial nature of the use. However, in order to be in line with international conventions the remuneration must still provide authors, members of the CMO and outsiders alike, with an "adequate income" and not be purely symbolic.[2647] Furthermore, the system for remuneration must be effective.[2648]

2642 See discussion and references in Ch. 5.1.1, 5.4.2 and 5.4.5.
2643 See discussion on the term in Ch. 4.1.2, 4.2.1, 4.2.2.1 and 4.2.2.2.
2644 Art. 6(5) OWD. See discussion in Ch. 4.2.3.6.
2645 Cf. Art. 2(1)(b) Rental and Lending Directive.
2646 C-271/10 – VEWA, Par. 33.
2647 Ibid, par. 33–34.
2648 See with regard to the efficiency of private copying levy system C-521/11 – Amazon.com, par. 31–36.

690. How to determine what is appropriate depends on circumstances. In the SENA case the Court was asked for the criteria to determine 'equitable remuneration' within the meaning of Article 8(2) of the Rental and Lending Directive. The Court concluded that it was not its role to lay down such criteria but rather to guide national courts in how to assess whether national criteria were consistent with EU law. In the Court's opinion the provision in Art. 8(2) did not preclude:

> ...a model for calculating what constitutes equitable remuneration for performing artists and phonogram producers that operates by reference to variable and fixed factors, such as the number of hours of phonograms broadcast, the viewing and listening densities achieved by the radio and television broadcasters represented by the broadcast organisation, the tariffs fixed by agreement in the field of performance rights and broadcast rights in respect of musical works protected by copyright, the tariffs set by the public broadcast organisations in the Member States bordering on the Member State concerned, and the amounts paid by commercial stations, provided that that model is such as to enable a proper balance to be achieved between the interests of performing artists and producers in obtaining remuneration for the broadcast of a particular phonogram, and the interests of third parties in being able to broadcast the phonogram on terms that are reasonable, and that it does not contravene any principle of Community law.[2649]

This seems applicable for determining reasonable remuneration for use under ECL agreements. Thus a fair balance of rights and interest between the different categories of rightholders and users of protected works, also underlined in Recital (31) of the InfoSoc Directive must be safeguarded also with regard to remuneration.[2650]

691. There are different ways to calculate remuneration for online cross-border use; one is to base it on the actual use by end-users, another is to base it on expected use by end-users and the social value of such use[2651] and yet another would be a mixture of remuneration per work and per use.[2652] The Norwegian Bokhylla project uses a price per page made available per year[2653], regardless of actual use, while in the out-of-commerce licensing service of the German National Library the price is a one-time fee per book made available, which varies depending on the age of the book.[2654]

692. An ECL system, which is based on free negotiations between stakeholders, should be an optimal solution for deciding on an appropriate reward. However,

2649 C-245/00 – SENA, par. 39–46.
2650 C-462/09 – Stichting de Thuiskopie, par. 25.
2651 Guibault, Cultural, 2015, 183–184.
2652 US Copyright Office, Mass Digitization, 2015, 94–96.
2653 See Ch. 5.3.1.4.
2654 See Ch. 7.4.

there must be a balance in the negotiating power of the parties[2655] and there may need to be a procedure and a forum for appeal if parties cannot agree.[2656]

10.3.2.2. Individual remuneration

693. One important safeguard measure for outsiders under the Nordic ECL system is that they are, at least in theory, entitled to receive individual remuneration, even if the ECL agreement has negotiated remuneration that will be distributed collectively to members.[2657] It can be difficult for foreign rightholders to receive remuneration for the use of their works under an ECL agreement in another country, and this is in particular true with regard to collective distribution of remuneration.[2658] Even the possibility of receiving individual remuneration does not change that much in practice for this group of outsiders as they may not know about the use under an ECL agreement in another country. This is another reason for limiting ECL agreements with cross-border effect to national works.

694. One would assume that digital use of works should facilitate the individual remuneration in general in collective licensing.[2659] Libraries that scan works for digital use will register those works and this information can easily be forwarded to CMOs. This is relatively easy to do with books, where the rightholders are mostly indicated.[2660] However, identifying embedded works, such as drawings and photos in books, can present much greater challenges. Another problematic area is unpublished works, such as private letters and photographs, and grey literature, i.e. works produced outside of commercial publishing.[2661] Identifying rightholders to such material can be very difficult indeed.

Thus indicating each and every rightholder or work, for remuneration purposes, can become a considerable burden for users such as libraries and raises a question of whether requiring such information is "reasonable, necessary and at the users' disposal".[2662] For practical reasons and in order to safeguard the efficiency of the ECL systems, collective distribution may be preferred or a mixture of individual and collective distribution as is done under the Norwegian Bokhylla project.[2663] Nevertheless, digital use, such as

---

2655 See Ch. 11.1.3.
2656 See Ch. 5.2.2.
2657 See discussion in Ch. 5.4.2.
2658 See discussion in Ch. 5.4.2, 5.4.5 and 6.2.1.
2659 Sterling, World Copyright Law, 2015, 629–630.
2660 However, such works can also easily become orphan, e.g. when authors have passed away and publishers gone out of business with no available information about successors in title.
2661 Vuopala, Extended, 2013, 32; Deazley and Stobo, Archives, 2013, 48. See also Ch. 10.1.1 and 10.2.2.
2662 Recital (33) CMO Directive; van Gompel, Directive 2014/26/EU, 2016, 595.
2663 See discussion on the Bokhylla project and the distribution method in Ch. 5.3.1.4. Along similar lines Ginsburg and Besek, Comments, 2015, 7.

making works available online by libraries will make it far more practical for outsiders to prove the use of their works, even if the library does not identify each and every work. An outsider can simply go online and find the work. Where the remuneration which the library pays is per page per year, as under the Norwegian Bokhylla agreement, the individual remuneration would be easy to work out.

695. Last but not least, there is the safeguard of an opt-out possibility, discussed next.

10.3.3. OPT-OUT

696. An ECL agreement enabling libraries to use works from their collections online with cross-border effect within Europe would, in my view, have to be supplemented with a viable and easy to use opt-out[2664] possibility. Making works available online can affect the possibilities of further economic exploitation of the work. Thus although it would be presumed that the CMO would negotiate appropriate economic safeguards, such as limiting the agreement to older works which are more likely to be out of commerce, there will still need to be the extra safeguard of an individual opt-out. An opt-out possibility *per se* does not replace the need for a prior express or implicit consent of authors for the use of their work[2665], and thus does not automatically make an ECL agreement compatible with international norms. Nevertheless, even if an ECL agreement fulfils international norms for exceptions with regard to the outsiders' right without opt-out, an opt-out option is still a vital tool to secure the proportionality[2666] of the inherent exception of the extension effect on outsiders.[2667] Outsiders should be able to opt-out *a priori* and at all other times for all their works, as it can be burdensome for them to opt-out in each instance.[2668] This seems to be suggested as a possibility in the DSM proposal, which states that rightholders may "at any time" object to their works being subject to an ECL licence or another collective licence by presumed mandate.[2669]

2664 See discussion on opt-outs in Ch. 5.4.3.

2665 Trumpke, The Extended, 2012, 281; C-301/15 – Soulier, AG opinion, par. 40.

2666 Cf. Art. 52(1) EU Charter. See discussion in Ch. 11.4.3.2.

2667 As argued earlier the hybrid nature of the extension effect of the ECL system is to be understood as a mixture of exception on the outsiders' right and an arrangement of management of rights; if the ECL agreement fulfils international norms, in particular the three-step test, the extension effect can be seen a legally presumed mandate and the ECL agreement also an arrangement of management of the rights of outsiders, cf. Ch. 6.1.2 and 6.3.1.

2668 Band, The Long, 2009, 252.

2669 COM(2016) 593 final, Proposal, 2016, Art. 7(1)(c).

697. It is essential that the opt-out option for non-members is viable. This is even more the case with ECL agreements that would allow for cross-border use. Thus the provision in the DSM proposal that all information about works that a proposed ECL agreement with cross-border effect would cover should be made accessible in a single portal is of great significance.[2670] Such a portal could help rightholders to discover whether their works are to be used under an ECL agreement enabling a cross-border use and alert them to the possibility to opt-out. However, as is underlined in the proposal with regard to the out-of-commerce status[2671], it is important that the requirements for making the relevant information available in the portal are feasible and practicable.

698. Although the opt-out is an essential safeguard for rightholders, it raises a number of problems. It can be difficult to establish a clear and simple procedure for outsiders to opt-out and guarantee at the same time that users of ECL licences have a simple way of verifying which works have been opted-out.[2672] Too high a rate of opt-outs will affect the efficiency of the system as a whole and diminish legal certainty for users. This eventuality is less likely if an ECL agreement concerns an area where individual licensing is impractical.[2673] The requirement of representativeness further reduces the likelihood of opt-outs.[2674] This seems to be the case for current library projects under ECLs and ECL-type solutions where opt-outs, although available, are not commonly used.[2675]

Technology is also providing solutions for identifying and registering online uses of works used under ECL agreements. This could make the administration of opt-outs more practically feasible and diminish their negative effects on the ECL solution. This is especially true for works in libraries as cataloguing collections is an important part of their existence.[2676]

10.3.4. TRANSPARENCY

699. Transparency is of crucial importance for the safeguard measures to be effective. If outsiders are not aware of the ECL agreement they cannot make use of the safeguard clauses. Unfortunately, it seems that the CMO Directive has not paid enough attention to the issue of outsiders in their provision on transparency. Art. 21 stipulates that CMOs shall publish on their website information on

2670 Ibid, Art. 8. See now Art. 8a in 2016/0280 (COD) 9134/18, Agreed negotiation mandate, 2018, 49.
2671 COM(2016) 593 final, Proposal, 2016, Art. 7(2).
2672 IPO, Government, 2014, 28–29.
2673 Ficsor, Collective, 2016, 68.
2674 Guibault, Cultural, 2015, 177.
2675 See discussion in Ch. 5.3.1.4 and 7.4.
2676 Tryggvadóttir, Digital libraries, 2014, 325; Rydning, Extended, 2010, 87.

standard licensing contracts and tariffs and Art. 18 specifies which information CMOs must provide to rightholders. Presumably Art. 18 would be interpreted in such a way that CMOs are obliged to provide information to outside rightholders if they asked but this would require some effort on behalf of the outsider. No provision, however, obliges CMOs to announce in general which agreements they have entered into[2677] in a way that enables outsiders to discover whether their works might be covered. Furthermore, although the CMO Directive has detailed provisions on how to distribute amounts due to rightholders[2678] which most likely would apply to outside rightholders in the case of an ECL agreement[2679], these rules relate only to situations where there is individual remuneration for use. It is precisely when there is collective distribution of remuneration that outsiders need to know that their works are being used under an ECL agreement, so that they can either seek individual remuneration or opt-out.

700. It can be difficult for outsiders to know which ECL agreements have been concluded and with whom, and hence difficult to make use of their opt-out right. In the Nordic countries outsiders can notify the relevant CMO in advance that they do not want to have their work used under an ECL agreement.[2680] The process, however, seems somewhat complicated for the outsider who wishes to find out about possible agreements that would cover his or her work, both with regard to claiming individual remuneration and to using his or her opt-out possibility. Obliging CMOs to notify, e.g. on their websites, that an ECL agreement on a certain use has been concluded together with relevant information should not be too onerous and would enable outsiders to claim compensation or to opt-out. This could of course be negotiated in the agreement itself but an explicit transparency provision in the ECL provision would be better. Of course discretion would need to be used in providing public information on ECL agreements in order to protect the negotiating power of the CMO and thus the interest of rightholders, both members and outsiders.[2681]

701. Thus I am of the opinion that there should be explicit provisions in the copyright acts on widely accessible transparency measures to safeguard the outsider's right, especially in the absence of a public authorisation system. This

2677 See here for comparison Art. 29(2) CMO Directive on the obligation of a CMO to inform its members of representation agreements for multi-territorial licensing.

2678 Cf. Art. 13 CMO Directive.

2679 This is not stipulated in Art. 7(1) CMO Directive, which regulates which information CMOs must provide to outsiders. However, it seems obvious that if the agreement covers the works of an outside rightholder, the CMO should be obliged to provide such information. This seems also evident in the light of Art. 3(c) COM Directive, which stipulates that the term "rightholder" includes those who are entitled to a share of the rights revenue by agreement for the exploitation of rights or by law.

2680 Prop. 2012/13:141, Regeringens proposition, 2013, 58.

2681 Drexl and others, Comments, 2013, 24–25.

seems to be provided for in the DSM proposal for the use of out-of-commerce works for cultural heritage institutions, which includes provisions for publicity measures of licences under the solution, in particular with regard to outsiders, that must be applied for "a reasonable period of time" before any works are used under such an agreement.[2682]

10.3.5. EVALUATION

702. The safeguard clauses for outsiders under an ECL agreement for cross-border use must be the same as under an ECL agreement for national use. At the same time, the remuneration must reflect the potential increased use that online cross-border use might incur. Individual remuneration should be the general rule for cross-border online use by libraries and increasingly there should be technology to enable this.[2683] Still, until such technology has become cost-efficient enough, a mixture of individual and collective remuneration may have to continue. Nevertheless, outsiders should still have the option of individual remuneration in such cases. The opt-out option is indispensable for outsiders in ECL agreements enabling cross-border online use by libraries. Such an option must be easy to trigger and keep track of. This would be best achieved through a centralised portal. However, such a portal might be difficult to establish without specific EU legislation.

10.4. CONCLUSION

703. In this chapter I have analysed which requirements ECL agreements with cross-border effect would have to fulfil in order to be compatible with international norms, especially the three-step test. This is important because as argued earlier[2684], the hybrid nature of the ECL system entails that for areas of use that pass the three-step test the limitation aspect of the system with regard to outsiders' rights shifts towards being perceived as a presumed mandate and in those cases ECL agreements could be seen as an arrangement of management of rights for outsiders.

Current national ECL provisions and agreements for libraries allowing them i.a. to give online access to in-copyright works in their collections seem in general to be compatible with international norms and fulfil the three-step test[2685], at least for national use.[2686] An important element of their compatibility is the public interest of enabling access to the cultural heritage. My conclusion is

2682 COM(2016) 593 final, Proposal, 2016, Art. 7(3). See Ch. 11.3.1.4 and 11.3.2.4.
2683 Tryggvadóttir, Digital libraries, 2014, 325; Rydning, Extended, 2010, 87.
2684 See Ch. 6.1.2 and 6.3.1.
2685 See Ch. 4.1.3 on the three-step-test.
2686 See discussion in Ch. 6.2.3.

that the same applies for national ECL agreements for cross-border online use for libraries in Europe if the requirements, outlined in this chapter, are fulfilled. Such an interpretation would take technological developments into account and meet the needs of contemporary society as well as being a tool to reconcile the varying interests of stakeholders. In fact some of the argumentation put forward by Advocate General Spunzar in the VOB case for why e-lending under the public lending derogation fulfilled the three-step test[2687] is applicable for why national ECL agreements by libraries for online cross-border use should fulfil the test. First, with regard to the first step, the use is always specified in an agreement which is negotiated between a representative CMO and the library. The only beneficiaries are non-profit libraries and thus the ECL agreement pursues a legitimate aim in the public interest, i.e. facilitating access to culture. Second, with regard to the second step, as the use is negotiated by a CMO that is representative of a substantial number of all relevant rightholders, it can be presumed not to conflict with the normal exploitation of works. The extension effect, in particular, enables use that otherwise would remain legally unsupported. This would be to the detriment of all concerned: to the general public in Europe, who would not have digital access to the European cultural heritage, to rightholders, both members and outsiders, who would miss out on remuneration for use, and for libraries, which would be unable to carry out their purpose of giving access to the cultural heritage in the digital age. Thus it can be said that the exception, which the extension effect imposes on outsiders, "pursues a legitimate objective in the public interest that cannot be restricted to areas" untouched by economic activities, as Advocate General Spunzar concluded with regard to public lending.[2688] Third, with regard to the third step, as already mentioned, rightholders, both members and outsiders, can be said to be better off under the ECL agreement, as they receive remuneration for use otherwise not enabled.

704. However, as already stated, this interpretation is dependent on such agreements fulfilling the requirements outlined in this chapter. Those requirements are to a large extent the same as for ECL agreements for national use. However, there are some aspects of the requirements that need to be reinforced and adapted to the fact that the agreements allow for cross-border use.

First, for cross-border use under ECL agreements the requirement of representativeness entails that the CMO must have mandates from a substantial number of rightholders for cross-border use, covering the relevant territories. The requirement of good governance and transparency is even more important for cross-border use. Thus a centralised portal where all relevant information

---

2687 C-174/15 – VOB, AG opinion, par. 63–78.

2688 Ibid, par. 70.

on such agreements was accessible would be an important feature for users, i.e. European libraries, and rightholders alike. Governmental authorisation of CMOs for the negotiation of ECL agreements with cross-border use would furthermore, be a helpful tool to secure good governance.

Second, the scope and field of national ECL agreements enabling libraries to use works online with cross-border effect should in my view be limited to national works. That is because it is harder to safeguard the interest of foreign rightholders, whether members of foreign CMOs or outsiders, even when there are reciprocity agreements with foreign CMOs. Other issues regarding the field and scope of use under cross-border enabling ECL agreements could be left to stakeholders to determine, just as with ECL agreements for national use. These would include potential limitations on the age of works, such as a certain cut-off date, commercial availability of the works, the commercial versus non-commercial use of works under the agreement or the possibility for end-users to download copies. Furthermore, it should be underlined that some uses that entail making works available online may fall under exceptions harmonised by the InfoSoc Directive, such as the temporary reproductions necessary for any online activity, cf. Art. 5(1), as well as the making of digital copies, which could be done under current Art. 5(2)(c).

Finally, the safeguard measures for outsiders would have to be the same as under ECL agreements for national use. However, as online cross-border use is an even more significant intervention in the exclusive rights of outsiders, than online use within national borders, the fulfilment of safeguard clauses is even more important. First and foremost, the remuneration must reflect the potential increased use due to wider territorial application. Second, every effort should be made to ensure the remuneration is distributed individually to all rightholders, but in any event that outsiders are entitled to individual remuneration. Finally, it is crucial that outsiders have a viable opt-out option and that transparency and information about that possibility and the use of opt-outs is easily accessible and available, both to rightholders and users. This would be best achieved through a central online portal.

705. If these requirements are properly fulfilled I maintain that national ECL agreements for libraries enabling cross-border online use could be seen to conform to international norms, such as the three-step test. As explained earlier, the hybrid nature of the ECL system entails that for areas of uses that pass the three-step test the limitation of or exception to the outsiders' rights aspect of the system gives way to becoming a legal presumption of mandate for those rights.[2689] Thus ECL agreements that pass the three-step test are to be seen as arrangements of management of rights also with regard to outsiders in

[2689] Ch. 6.1.

the understanding of recital (18) of the InfoSoc Directive.[2690] This conclusion in turn could justify the treatment of ECL agreements as contracts negotiated by the relevant CMO on the basis of a mixture of voluntary mandates of members and legal presumed mandates with regard to outsiders. Consequently, in the event of a dispute regarding online cross-border use under an ECL agreement, convincing arguments could be mustered for the application of the Rome I Regulation to determine applicable laws.[2691] In this respect it is worth underlining that, as argued above, only ECL agreements for the cross-border use of national works would be considered to fulfil international norms in this regard. Yet, this solution lacks legal certainty, due to the application of EU rules on jurisdiction in online infringement cases and the uncertainty about applicable laws in cases of litigation by an outsider whose work an ECL agreement with cross-border effect would cover in a country other than that where the ECL agreement originates.[2692] Sufficient legal certainty will not be established until either the CJEU is asked to decide on the issue or EU legislation is adopted. Furthermore, establishing a centralised portal for information regarding ECL agreements with cross-border effect would be difficult without EU legislation to that effect. The DSM proposal contains a step in that direction with its proposal for an ECL solution for the cross-border use of out-of-commerce works. In the next chapter I will analyse that proposal further. Finally, the question remains whether national ECL agreements enabling cross-border use are consistent with the EU's other aims with regard to copyright, namely legal certainty, a high level of protection,' an appropriate reward to authors and other rightholders for the use of their work, as well as a fair balance of rights and interest between rightholders and users. In the next chapter I will look at these issues specifically.

2690 Ch. 6.3.1.
2691 See discussion in Ch. 8.4.2.1.
2692 Cf. Ch. 8.2.2, 8.3.1 and 8.4.

CHAPTER 11

ECLS FOR ONLINE CROSS-BORDER USE BY LIBRARIES AND THE EU'S LEGAL FRAMEWORK

Cultural heritage is a valuable asset in the knowledge based world, an important resource for the European culture industry and a catalyst for creativity, as well as an important driver of growth and the creation of jobs.[2693]

706. The importance of improved access to the European cultural heritage is undisputed. Thus the EU strategy is to optimise, "by means of the internet, the economic and cultural potential of Europe's cultural heritage" in full respect of copyright and related rights.[2694] I maintain that the hybrid system of ECL[2695] fits well with this strategy and has the potential to optimise and improve the access to in-copyright works in libraries and other cultural heritage institutions.

707. I have previously concluded that the system of ECLs, based on the Nordic model, is consistent with the EU's legislative framework.[2696] However, that discussion concerned national use under ECL agreements, not cross-border use. Here I will scrutinise specifically the compatibility of a national ECL solution for cross-border online use for libraries with EU legislation and with the EU's broader objectives with regard to copyright. I will furthermore discuss the Soulier case and its potential effect on library projects enabled through collective management with legislative support outside of France, the measures proposed in the DSM proposal for the cross-border licensing of out-of-commerce works for cultural heritage institutions and, finally, the competence of the EU to take action.

2693 Klass and Rupp, EUROPEANA… 2014, 947.

2694 See e.g. COM (2007) 242, European agenda for culture 2007, 2007, 8–9; 2011/711/EU, Recommendation, 2011, *op.cit.*; 2006/585/EC, Recommendation, 2006, *op.cit.*; COM(2015) 626 final, Towards, 2015, 2.

2695 See discussion in Ch. 6.1.2 and 6.3.1.

2696 See Ch.6.3.

11.1. THE EU'S OBJECTIVES WITH REGARD TO COPYRIGHT

708. In addition to complying with the international frameworks, EU objectives with regard to copyright can be identified as seeking to ensure the following: legal certainty[2697], a high level of protection[2698], an appropriate reward to authors and other rightholders for the use of their work[2699], as well as a fair balance of rights and interest between rightholders and users.[2700]

11.1.1. LEGAL CERTAINTY

709. Legal certainty is of paramount interest for the good functioning of the digital single market. It has been suggested that using the system of ECL will not confer enough legal certainty, i.a. because of the opt-out possibility.[2701] However, the number of opt-outs will depend on the agreement negotiated by the relevant CMO and user. If the CMO is representative enough of the rightholders whose rights are being negotiated it is likely that the agreement will reflect the willingness of outside rightholders as well. Furthermore, the requirement that the agreement is in an area of use where it is impracticable to negotiate individually, which is in fact the main justification for the ECL system[2702], and is the case with mass use of any type of works in the collections of libraries, further reduces the likelihood of opt-outs.[2703] Finally, another factor diminishing the number of opt-outs would be the limiting of ECL agreements to the use of either out-of-commerce works or to works published before a certain time, i.e. not demanding proof of their commercial availability or lack thereof, but relying on the fact that older works in general are of less commercial interest than newer works.[2704]

710. It is interesting to note in this respect that the Finnish ECL agreement for the National Gallery[2705] includes a clause under which the representative CMO undertakes to work actively to ensure that outside authors or other holders of

---

2697 Recitals (4), (6), (21) and (25) InfoSoc Directive.

2698 Recitals (4) and (9) InfoSoc Directive; COM(2015) 626 final, Towards, 2015, 2; see also i.a. C-306/05, SGAE; C-301/15 – Soulier, AG opinion, par. 34.

2699 Recital (10) InfoSoc Directive; see also i.a. C-306/05, SGAE, par. 36; C-301/15 – Soulier, AG opinion, par. 34.

2700 Recitals (31) and (40) InfoSoc Directive; COM(2015) 626 final, Towards, 2015, 2.

2701 NOU 1988:22, Endringer i åndverksloven m.v., 1988, 40; Ot. prp. nr. 46, Endringer, 2005, 51; Rydning, Extended, 2010, 86; SWD(2012) 204 final, Impact Assessment, 2012, 49, 51, 170–174, 190–191.

2702 See discussion in 5.1.1, 5.1.2, 5.3.3, 6.2.3.2, 9.1.2 and Ch. 10.

2703 Guibault, Cultural, 2015, 177; Ficsor, Collective, 2016, 68. See discussion in Ch. 10.3.3.

2704 See discussion and references in Ch. 10.2.3.

2705 See discussion in Ch. 5.3.1.2.

their rights do not prohibit the use of works of art.[2706] Nevertheless, the opt-out possibility remains an important safeguard for the outsiders' right and must be a real option.[2707] In my view the opt-out possibility under ECL agreements is no more prejudicial to legal certainty than the fact that under the CMO Directive all rightholders must have the right to terminate their mandates to a CMO for all rights or a group of rights or types of works.[2708]

711. Another problem highlighted with regard to ECLs is that they are typically limited in time, whereas libraries and other cultural heritage institutions usually wish to make their works available indefinitely.[2709] This is probably not a major issue however. In the Nordic countries time limited agreements are usually automatically renewable[2710], unless one of the parties terminates them. If parties have agreed on all terms, it is unlikely that the agreement would be terminated other than in exceptional circumstances.

712. A further criticism is that although the system of ECL has the advantage of a tailored solution that fits users' needs, it may also result in restrictive agreements or no agreement at all.[2711] If the negotiating parties do not reach an agreement there is no effective way to ensure that ECLs are concluded, as obligatory conflict resolution would make the system more akin to an exception with regard to all rightholders, both members of the CMO and outsiders.[2712] Fears about the monopolistic tendencies of CMOs have long persisted.[2713] At the same time, refusal to grant a licence, even if it is the act of an undertaking holding a dominant position, cannot in itself constitute abuse of a dominant position.[2714] In my view, this is more a theoretical problem. It seems likely that CMOs and libraries would conclude adequate ECL agreements; first, because a large portion of works from the collections of libraries are out-of-commerce, thus an agreement would provide rightholders with some additional income, even if small, which they would not receive otherwise; second, the political weight given to achieving access to the European cultural heritage should persuade rightholders that negotiating use is preferable to becoming subject to a potential exception for such use which would affect all rightholders, members of the CMO and outsiders alike.[2715]

2706 Point 9 of the Agreement.

2707 See Ch. 10.3.4.

2708 Art. 5(4) CMO Directive.

2709 Boulanger and others, Assessing, 2014, 19.

2710 See e.g. discussion in Ch. 5.3.2.1.

2711 COM(2008) 466, Green paper, 2008, 16; Riis and Schovsbo, ECLs in Action, 2012, 950.

2712 Rydning, Extended, 2010, 103. See discussion in Ch. 5.2.2.

2713 Ricketson, Berne Convention, 1987, 522.

2714 *Radio Telefis Eireann (RTE) and Independent Television Publications Ltd (ITP) v Commission of the European Communities* ECLI:EU:C:1995:98, CJEU, 6 April 1995 par. 49.

2715 Guibault, Cultural, 2015, 191.

713. My research for this publication leads me to the conclusion that an ECL agreement for online use with cross-border effect between a national library and a national CMO for national publications could reduce to a large extent legal and business uncertainty in practical terms. Stakeholders would only need to conform to the national legislation[2716] of the country of their residence, whose legal and business framework they are likely to know. Nevertheless, the legal status of the cross-border effect of the ECL solution remains to be clarified. Although I hold that national ECL agreements could have such an effect on condition that they fulfil international norms as argued above, this is not legally certain.[2717] The CJEU has not been asked to rule on the issue. Many libraries would be reluctant to invest time and effort in negotiating an ECL agreement with explicit online cross-border effect without legal certainty in this respect. Given all this, EU legislation clarifying the cross-border effect would be important.

11.1.2. HIGH LEVEL OF PROTECTION, INCLUDING APPROPRIATE REWARD TO RIGHTHOLDERS

714. A high level of protection for rightholders is intended to "ensure the maintenance and development of creativity".[2718] According to the InfoSoc Directive a high level of protection is linked to remuneration, as in order for authors to continue their creativity they need an appropriate reward for their work.[2719] As the terms of an ECL agreement are negotiated by stakeholders, the ECL system provides for a solution which combines a high level of protection for rightholders with flexible access for users. Normally an individual rightholder would not be able to obtain a better economic deal than negotiated by the CMO, for the particular use under the relevant ECL agreement.[2720] Even though rightholders may have other commercial interests that might not be compatible with online cross-border use by libraries, these interests should be protected by the opt-out possibility. The opt-out possibility also secures the proportionality principle in relation to outsiders. Thus the ECL system seems to fulfil the conditions set out in Recital (22) of the InfoSoc Directive that support for the dissemination of culture should not be achieved by sacrificing strict protection of rightholders.

715. An additional advantage of the ECL system is that it provides for lower transaction costs.[2721] This is an important component of a high level of protection as transaction costs impact on remuneration to rightholders.

2716 Langus, Neven and Poukens, Economic, 2014, 102.
2717 Ch. 9.1.2 and 10.4.
2718 Recital (9) InfoSoc Directive.
2719 Recital (10) InfoSoc Directive; C-462/09 – Stichting de Thuiskopie, par. 32.
2720 See discussion and references in Ch. 5.1.1, 5.4.2, 5.4.4 and 10.3.2.1.
2721 See discussion on transaction costs in Ch. 2.2.1.

Collective management in general, and ECL agreements in particular, provide an efficient way to lower transaction costs, especially where the value of individual rights may be low compared to transaction costs and where it is difficult or even impossible in advance to predict which rights may be required.[2722] The transaction costs for libraries are particularly high because of the sheer number of works, many of little individual value, the number of rightholders and legal uncertainty.[2723] This is even truer for cross-border uses.[2724] Thus an ECL solution enabling the online cross-border use would lower transaction costs for libraries, which should result in higher remuneration to rightholders.

11.1.3. BALANCE BETWEEN RIGHTHOLDERS AND USERS

716. The importance of balance between rightholders and users is highlighted in the 2015 copyright strategy, which states that all its objectives address the "needs of rightholders and users of copyright-protected content alike".[2725]

717. The ECL system offers flexibility not present in exceptions or limitations, allowing users and rightholders to seek a balance through negotiation of relevant aspects of use and remuneration. It thus benefits both parties. The benefit for rightholders is that their bargaining power is stronger when there is room for negotiations. Negotiations on scope of use and reward are usually not possible under exceptions or limitations.[2726] The benefit for users is that, once an agreement is reached, they can use the relevant works without having to worry about liability. The CMO, which is better equipped for such purposes, deals with all claims as well as identifying rightholders and distributing remuneration.[2727] Furthermore, having fixed remuneration for the use creates a more stable and predictable environment for users, such as libraries, to operate in.[2728]

718. Even so, the interests of different rightholders may differ. Thus authors sometimes may prefer remuneration rights for secondary uses rather than full

---

2722 See discussion and references in Ch. 5.1.

2723 Guibault, Cultural, 2015, 173; Boulanger and others, Assessing, 2014, 13–14, 17, 20; Axhamn and Guibault, Cross-border ECL, 2011, 70; COM(2007) 836 final, Creative Content Online, 2008, 23; Langus, Neven and Poukens, Economic, 2014, 2; Triaille and others, Study, 2013, 303.

2724 Langus, Neven and Poukens, Economic, 2014, 101–102.

2725 COM(2015) 626 final, Towards, 2015, 2.

2726 Handke, Collective, 2014, 180–181; Schønning, Ophavsretsloven, 6th ed., 2016, 495; Axhamn and Guibault, Cross-border ECL, 2011, 51; Koskinen-Olsson, Collective Management, 2010, 291; Geiger, The Role, 2007, 11–12; von Lewinski, Mandatory, 2004, 8–9; Lewinski, Collectivism, 2012, 124; Verronen, Extended, 2002, 1148; Axhamn, Exceptions, 2013, 178; Schovsbo, The necessity to collectivize, 2012, 177; Foged, Danish licences, 2015, 17; US Copyright Office, Mass Digitization, 2015, 82, 103.

2727 See e.g. Ringnalda, Orphan Works, 2011, 9–11.

2728 Boulanger and others, Assessing, 2014, 19.

exclusive rights, which are often transferred to derivative rightholders, such as publishers.[2729] Such remuneration rights are sometimes only afforded to authors, cf. e.g. Art. 6 of the Rental and Lending Directive that allows for an exception to the lending right "provided that at least authors obtain a remuneration for such lending" as highlighted in the VOB case.[2730] This is a highly controversial area as it can have important practical consequences[2731], not least after the decision in the Hewlett-Packard case, where the CJEU came to the conclusion that, as publishers were not among those reproduction rightholders mentioned in Art. 2 of the InfoSoc Directive, it was not permissible for Member States to allocate a portion of the compensation due under Art. 5(2)(a) and Art. 5(2)(b) to publishers.[2732] The Commission attempts to reverse the effects of the judgement in the DSM proposal.[2733]

719. The interests of authors and users often coincide.[2734] Thus authors may be more willing than publishers to enter into an ECL agreement for cross-border online use with libraries, as authors would see any remuneration from this source as an additional income, whereas publishers may see the online use as potential competition with their contractual rights. However, the opt-out possibility should protect any incompatible commercial interest.

720. The balance of power between negotiating parties, i.e. libraries and the CMO, is not necessarily equal. Rightholders have the exclusive right to prohibit use and the increased bargaining power of rightholders concentrated in a CMO[2735] can be used to demand unreasonable terms and dues.[2736] CMOs are organised and versed in negotiations for the use of in-copyright works, whereas

---

2729 Kur, Of Oceans 2008, 300–301; Geiger and others, Declaration, 2010, 119; von Lewinski, Mandatory, 2004, 8–9.

2730 C-174/15 – VOB, AG opinion, par. 17, 34.

2731 See e.g. Bechtold, Directive 2001/29/EC, 2016, 436.

2732 C-572/13 – Hewlett-Packard, par. 44–49. On 12 May 2017 the Court of Appeal of Brussels ruled in favour of Reprobel in a lawsuit against Hewlett Packard Belgium following the CJEU decision. The Court of Appeal concluded that the remuneration of publishers in the framework of reprography is legitimate and that it did not affect the authors' own compensation, cf. <https://www.ifrro.org/content/reprobel-wins-national-lawsuit-against-hp-belgium>, last viewed 10 June 2017.

2733 Art. 12 and Recital (36). See e.g European Copyright Society, General Opinion on the EU Copyright Reform Package, 2017, 6–7, which is critical of the attempt, and IFRRO, *IFRRO Position on the Proposal for a Directive on Copyright in the Digital Single Market*, (8 May 2017) 4, which supports the provision.

2734 Kur, Of Oceans 2008, 341.

2735 See Ch. 5.1.1.

2736 Rognstad, Avtalelisenser, 2004, 158; Rydning, Extended, 2010, 71–72; Koskinen-Olsson, Collective Management, 2010, 293; Guibault and van Gompel, Collective, 2016, 154; Xalabarder, Digital Libraries, 2010, 243, 248; Bet. 1981/912, Licenskonstruktioner, 1981, 66–67, 69–70. Thus for authors collective negotiation can be more beneficial than individual negotiating, cf. von Lewinski, Mandatory, 2004, 8–9.

libraries and other cultural heritage institutions are not practiced in negotiating with CMOs.[2737] For this reason, among others[2738], the Commission in 2011 suggested it would be too complex for libraries to acquire extended collective licences for the use of orphan works.[2739] However, given the right incentives, libraries and other cultural heritage institutions could combine their efforts in negotiations with CMOs[2740] and become negotiating partners with equivalent clout. Thus overall, the ECL solution could actually contribute to maintaining the balance between rightholders and users.

11.1.4. EVALUATION

721. National ECL agreements can create legal certainty, provide for a high level of protection for rightholders and provide for the correct balance between the interests of stakeholders in online cross-border situations. Legal certainty is provided for both rightholders and users, such as libraries, through the agreement, which covers scope, uses and remuneration. The content of the agreement is adapted to the needs of both rightholders and users, as it is the result of negotiations between them. The opt-out is a necessary safety valve which might reduce legal certainty, but no more than is the case with collective agreements in general. However, cultural heritage institutions may have to collaborate with each other to ensure they are an equal negotiating partner. Furthermore, the legal clarity of the solution is somewhat diffused because of inconclusive rules on which applicable laws would apply in cross-border disputes. I argue that the hybrid nature of the ECL system is such that for ECL agreements that fulfil international norms the extension effect of the system can be qualified as, or equated to, a legally presumed mandate with regard to outsiders and thus also be seen as an arrangement of management of rights for them. This, may then lead to the conclusion that such ECL agreements are contracts in the understanding of the Rome I Regulations, which would enable cross-border effect of the agreements.[2741] However, this is not legally certain. Apart from this lack of clarity, my conclusion is that the use of ECLs for online use with cross-border effect by libraries is compatible with the EU's legal framework and its objectives for copyright, as well as being in line with the EU's strategy for digital libraries and access to the cultural heritage.

722. The question is whether the Soulier case, discussed next, has implications for any of the above conclusions.

2737 Kerremans, Janssen and Valcke, Collective solutions, 2011, 645, 648; Guibault, Collective, 2014, 750; European Commission, Report on the responses, 2014, 43, 59.

2738 See Ch. 6.3.2.

2739 SEC(2011) 615 final, Impact Assessment, 2011, 27.

2740 US Copyright Office, Mass Digitization, 2015, 94.

2741 See e.g. Ch. 8.4.2.1.

11.2. THE SOULIER CASE

723. In November 2016, the CJEU concluded that the French legislation on the digital exploitation of out-of commerce books of March 2012[2742] was inconsistent with Art. 2(a) and 3(1) of the InfoSoc Directive.[2743] The Court concluded that any use of a work protected under those provisions requires the prior consent of rightholders, unless subject to exceptions in Art. 5. Such prior consent could be explicit or implicit. However, implicit consent required that authors are "actually and individually" informed about the envisaged use of their works, at least for commercial use in a digital format.[2744] The French out-of-commerce legislation stipulates that "the most appropriate publicity measures" shall be laid down in a decree to ensure that rightholders are as well informed as possible about the system and their option to opt-out.[2745] The decree adopted specified that such publicity measures should include an information campaign initiated by the Ministry of Culture and the relevant CMO and rightholders organisation, which should include online presentations and mailing operations, adverts in the national press and on news websites.[2746] These measures constitute fairly extensive transparency procedures; nevertheless, the Court concluded that the legislation did not provide a mechanism that ensured that authors were actually and individually informed, so that they could take a decision on whether to opt-out or not[2747] and was thus inconsistent with the InfoSoc Directive.

724. The conclusion of the CJEU in the Soulier case regarding the French legislation for out-of-commerce books might be seen as raising questions on the validity of all arrangements for managing certain rights that are based on collective licensing with legislative support, such as ECLs.[2748] If that were the case, the basis for the smooth operation of the copyright system in Europe in many areas could be subject to considerable uncertainty. Thus it is important to analyse the judgement and its possible bearing on ECL agreements for libraries.

725. It should first be observed that the French initiative goes a step beyond the ECL system, as it does not require the designated CMO to be representative of the rightholders whose rights it could manage under the legislation on out-of-commerce books. There was no requirement in the legislation that members

---

2742 See discussion on the legislation in Ch. 7.2.1.
2743 C-301/15 – Soulier, par. 52.
2744 Ibid, 35–44.
2745 Art. 134-7 FCIP.
2746 Decree No 2013-182; C-301/15 – Soulier, par. 16.
2747 Ibid, par. 43.
2748 Sganga, The eloquent, 2017, 330; Eleonora Rosati, 'The CJEU decision in Soulier: what does it mean for laws other than the French one on out-of-print books?' (2016) <www.ipkat.com/> accessed 19 November 2016; Nérisson, Opinion, Kluwer Copyright Blog, *op.cit.*

mandate the CMO to manage the specific rights or uses under the legislation. Instead the mandate to manage the rights and uses emanates directly from the State. Accordingly, the French legislation and system is more akin to mandatory collective management, rather than being voluntary collective management, which the MoU on out-of-commerce works[2749] advocates.[2750] The fact that the French legislation offers opt-out possibilities distinguishes it from "normal" mandatory collective management.[2751] However, the *a priori* opt-out is limited in time and the *a posteriori* opt-out is conditional for authors, who must prove that they hold the digital rights alone.[2752] The CJEU in particular criticised the fact that the author's opt-out is dependant either on a mutual agreement with the publisher or on proving that another party was not holder of other rights in the work.[2753]

726. Furthermore, the French legislation also departs from an ECL system in the sense that it is not based on an extended effect or blanket licences; rather the CMO licenses on a work-by-work basis.[2754] Thus it covers use that is in fact possible to license individually. Another important observation is that the French law, unlike the MoU on out-of-commerce works, is not primarily aimed at offering libraries or other cultural heritage institutions the possibility to digitise and make available out-of-commerce books, as it is publishers who have to be first offered exclusive licences to do so, for commercial exploitation.[2755]

727. I maintain that these differences are fundamental, as I will further elaborate on in this chapter, beginning with the question of rightholders' mandates and then discussing the need for proportionality of collective management with legislative support.

11.2.1. ARRANGEMENTS FOR MANAGEMENT OF RIGHTS AND THE CONSENT OF RIGHTHOLDERS

728. I propose that in order for a mechanism of collective management with legislative support to be considered an arrangement concerning the management of rights in the meaning of Recital (18) of the InfoSoc Directive, the requirement of representativeness must be fulfilled. That requirement, essential

2749 See discussion on the MoU in Ch. 7.1.
2750 Triaille and others, Study, 2013, 305; Bulayenko, Permissibility, 2016, 51, 53, 59; Sganga, The eloquent, 2017, 324, 327. This was also the finding in C-301/15 – Soulier, AG opinion, par. 62–64.
2751 Bulayenko, Permissibility, 2016, 59–60.
2752 See discussion in Ch. 7.2.1, par. 487.
2753 C-301/15 – Soulier, par. 46–51.
2754 Ginsburg, Fair Use, 2014, 1429; US Copyright Office, Mass Digitization, 2015, 27; Samuelson, Comments, 2015, 10–11; Bulayenko, Permissibility, 2016, 56.
2755 Triaille and others, Study, 2013, 279–280; Ginsburg, Fair Use, 2014, 1426–1428; Guibault, Cultural, 2015, 184; C-301/15 – Soulier, AG opinion, par. 53; Sganga, The eloquent, 2017, 326.

to the ECL system, presupposes that the members of the CMO have given an explicit mandate for the uses that an ECL agreement can cover.[2756] The French legislation was not based on mandates from rightholders for the digitisation of out-of-commerce books, only on a legislative mandate.

729. It was submitted in the Soulier case that the legislation concerned only an "arrangement for managing certain rights", which the InfoSoc Directive did not preclude Member States from establishing.[2757] However, Advocate General Wathelet stated that such management of rights could only be taken into consideration if holders of those exclusive rights had authorised a management organisation to manage their rights.[2758] He underlined that there was no question of voluntary agreement in the French legislation at issue.[2759] In my opinion Advocate General Wathelet's comments do not exclude that an ECL agreement, where the representativeness requirement is fulfilled, would constitute arrangements concerning the management of rights compatible with the InfosSoc Directive, not least as ECLs are specifically mentioned in Recital (18) of the Directive. Such an ECL agreement would be considered a voluntary agreement in the sense of the MoU and the Orphan Works Directive.[2760]

730. The final decision in the Soulier case does not explicitly discuss Recital (18) of the InfoSoc Directive. The Court concluded that the broad protection afforded by Art. 2(a) and Art. 3(1) covers both the enjoyment and exercise of those rights, which requires prior consent to any use of in-copyright work.[2761] The Court states that such consent can be explicit and implicit. However, in order to have an implicit consent, authors must be "actually and individually" informed prior to the use, in particular when dealing with out-of-commerce works. This requirement was not deemed to be met in the French legislation.[2762]

731. Transparency measures requiring that each rightholder, especially each outsider, is "actually and individually" informed are difficult if not impossible to design in any collective licensing scheme for mass uses with legislative support.[2763] This requirement, indeed, seems to go beyond what is required in the

---

2756 See discussion in Ch. 5.2.1, 10.1.1 and 10.1.2.

2757 Cf. Recital (18) InfoSoc Directive.

2758 C-301/15 – Soulier, AG opinion, par. 54–61.

2759 Ibid, par. 64.

2760 Principle No. 1 MoU; Recital (4) and (24) OWD; Recital (12) CMO Directive; Sganga, The eloquent, 2017, 329.

2761 C-301/15 – Soulier, par. 29–34.

2762 Ibid, par. 43–45.

2763 Recital (22) DSMP; Sganga, The eloquent, 2017, 328. See also discussion on the issue in Ch. 10.1.4.

CMO Directive for ensuring that remuneration is distributed to rightholders.[2764] One of the main goals of all collective licensing and, in particular for ECLs, is the reduction of transaction costs.[2765] Requiring that each and every outside rightholder is "actually and individually" informed contradicts that rationale.[2766] Still, the practical impact of the case rests on whether it is possible to distinguish the arrangement in the French legislation from arrangements concerning the management of rights under Recital (18) of the InfoSoc Directive. I maintain it should be, for the reasons mentioned above, at least for ECL agreements. The impact of recitals is not fully settled. The wording of the relevant provisions examined in the Soulier case, i.e. Art. 2(a) and Art. 3(1), does not explicitly exclude the application of ECLs. Thus, I am of the opinion that the ECL system is compatible with the InfoSoc Directive.[2767] Otherwise the Recital would be meaningless.

732. Support can be found in the CMO Directive for the view that individual prior consent is not mandatory for non-members in collective licensing projects with legislative support, where these can be considered arrangements concerning management of rights under the InfoSoc Directive. Recital (12) of the CMO Directive states that, although the Directive applies to all CMOs, it does not interfere with arrangements concerning the management of rights in the Member States, such as the extended effect of an agreement between a representative collective management organisation and a user. This is reflected in the wording of Art. 5(7) of the CMO Directive, which clarifies that the requirement of specific consent to each and every right is with regard to collective management on the basis of a mandate, and does not affect situations where CMOs manage rights under legislation, such as the rights of outsiders under an ECL agreement.[2768]

11.2.2. THE FRENCH LEGISLATION AND PROPORTIONALITY

733. I maintain that the French legislation on the digital exploitation of out-of-commerce books does not fulfil the requirement of proportionality.[2769] Firstly, the mechanism under the French legislation is based on the CMO first offering an exclusive licence of individual works to the "original" print publishers.[2770] Thus

2764 See in particular Art. 13(3) CMO Directive.
2765 See Ch. 5.1.
2766 Sganga, The eloquent, 2017, 330.
2767 See discussion and references in Ch. 6.3.1.
2768 See references and discussion on Recital (12) and Art. 5(7) CMO Directive in Ch. 6.3.3.
2769 Art. 5(4) TEU; Art. 52(1) EU Charter and discussion in Ch. 11.4.3.2.
2770 Art. 134-5(3) FCIP.

there is no requirement, as for ECL agreements that the solution is only for uses that are either difficult or impractical to license individually.[2771] The essence of the "enjoyment and exercise" of copyright in books is the publishing of books. Hence giving others exclusive licence to do so, even if they have prior print publishing rights in the book, seems to be a disproportionally wide limitation, which might have problems passing the three-step test. Furthermore, as the beneficiaries of the exclusive licence would be private commercial entities, the public interest element of making the cultural heritage accessible, which I see as an important argument for ECL agreements for libraries, is more limited in the French legislation.

734. Secondly, the opt-out possibility, although present, is flawed, and thus not capable of providing the necessary relief of proportionality for the solution. An opt-out possibility, properly construed, should help any arrangement for the management of rights to fulfil the EU proportionality principle.[2772] However, the fact that under the French legislation authors, in order to opt-out, either have to do so jointly with the publisher or prove that they alone hold rights to the work constitutes a formality inconsistent with the Berne Convention.[2773] This limitation of the opt-out meant that the legislation afforded publishers stronger rights than authors.

735. Thirdly, the situation that the French legislation was attempting to address, namely the lack of digital access to out-of-commerce works, could have been addressed in a proportionally less invasive way, either by limiting it to even older books and non-commercial use, as in Germany[2774], or by limiting the beneficiaries to public cultural institutions, such as libraries, for non-commercial aims, as in the Norwegian Bokhylla project.[2775]

11.2.3. EVALUATION

736. The French legislation clearly got the balance of interest between stakeholders wrong and exceeded the parameters provided under the InfoSoc Directive. However, it would be unfortunate if the judgement were seen as potentially affecting all arrangements of management of rights.[2776] I maintain the arrangement under the French legislation is distinct from other forms of management that would be

---

2771 See discussion in 5.1.1, 5.1.2, 5.3.3, 6.2.3.2, 9.1.2, Ch. 10 and Ch. 11.1.1.

2772 Cf. Art. 52(1) EU Charter. See discussion on the principle in Ch. 11.4.3.2.

2773 Art. 5(2) Berne Convention. The opt-out possibility is not a Berne-forbidden formality in itself, see discussion in Ch. 6.2.2.

2774 See discussion in Ch. 7.4.

2775 See discussion in Ch. 5.3.1.4.

2776 Sganga, The eloquent, 2017, 330; Rosati, The CJEU decision in Soulier, 2016; Nérisson, Opinion, Kluwer Copyright Blog, *op.cit.*

compatible with the InfoSoc Directive. Certainly, if the decision in the Soulier case is taken to be applicable to all legally supported collective management, such as the ECL system and presumed management, it would create havoc for the smooth running of copyright and the use of in-copyright works in many areas in Europe. Such a situation would certainly necessitate EU legislation.[2777] Thus, and as argued above, the Soulier decision should only be regarded as applicable to the particular situation in France. In fact the conclusion of the CJEU in the Soulier case could be seen to imply that there may be a stronger possibility for voluntary collective agreements with legislative support to fare differently than the arrangement under the French legislation. That would be conditional, however, on the arrangement being based on clear mandates to the CMO from a substantial number of rightholders and unrestricted opt-out possibilities.

737. In the next sub-section I will discuss the DSM proposal for the use of out-of-commerce works by cultural heritage institutions.

11.3. THE DSM PROPOSAL FOR THE USE OF OUT-OF-COMMERCE WORKS BY CULTURAL HERITAGE INSTITUTIONS

738. Despite the 2011 Recommendation[2778] and the 2011 MoU on out-of-commerce works[2779] national solutions for the online use of in-copyright works for cultural heritage institutions were slow to materialise, and those that were implemented did not provide for cross-border use.[2780] Hence, in 2016 the Commission proposed a solution with cross-border effect for the use of out-of-commerce works by cultural heritage institutions.[2781] The proposed solution is to oblige Member States to put in place legal mechanisms to extend collective licensing to non-members and explicitly state that cultural heritage institutions in all other Member States may use the works in accordance with the terms of the licence. The Commission has thus significantly changed its view with regard to ECLs, which it had previously rejected for EU legislation.[2782]

739. The aim of the proposed solution is to facilitate the digitisation and dissemination of out-of-commerce works, as well as being conducive to reduced

[2777] Hinted at in C-301/15 – Soulier, par. 45.
[2778] 2011/711/EU, Recommendation, 2011, *op.cit.*
[2779] See discussion on the MoU in Ch. 7.1.
[2780] SWD(2016) 301 final, IA Part I, 2016, 65–69.
[2781] COM(2016) 593 final, Proposal, 2016, Art. 7–9.
[2782] ECLs were considered in the preparatory state for the solution of orphan works under the OWC and for the multi-territorial licences for online music for the CMO Directive. However, ECLs were rejected for both, cf. discussion and references in Ch. 6.3.2 and Ch. 9.4.

transaction costs.[2783] The DSM proposal remains very controversial[2784] and at the time of writing[2785] still has not been adopted having undergone several changes in the legislative process. Nevertheless, it is important to analyse the proposed mechanism for out-of commerce works as put forward as well as the amendments already made to the proposal.[2786]

11.3.1. THE PROPOSED SOLUTION

740. Member States shall provide that non-exclusive collective licences[2787] for non-commercial purposes for a cultural heritage institution for the use of out-of-commerce but in-copyright works permanently in their collections may be extended to non-members of the relevant CMO under certain conditions.[2788] Cultural heritage institutions in all other Member States are then permitted to use the works in accordance with the terms of the licence.[2789] Below I will look at the proposal in further detail as well as relevant changes that have been adopted.[2790]

11.3.1.1. Beneficiaries

741. Beneficiaries under the proposal are cultural heritage institutions, which are a publicly accessible library or museum, an archive or a film or audio heritage institution.[2791] This list is narrower than the list of beneficiaries under the Orphan Works Directive. It is not expressly stated that the institutions must be established in a Member State, but that must be an underlying requirement.[2792] Furthermore, the proposal does not define what a publicly accessible institution is, nor does it specify that the institutions must have a public-interest mission.[2793] However, cultural heritage institutions can be presumed to have a public interest mission, in particular if they are publicly accessible.

2783 SWD(2016) 301 final, IA Part I, 2016, 71, 76–79.

2784 Nearly 1000 amendments had been tabled in the Committee on Legal Affairs, responsible for the file in the European Parliament (EP) by April 2017, cf. EP JURI, Draft, 2017, *op.cit.*

2785 End of May 2018.

2786 The newest version at the time of writing being the agreed mandate of 25th of May 2018 for the presidency of the Council to start negotiations with the European Parliament, cf. 2016/0280 (COD) 9134/18, Agreed negotiation mandate, 2018, *op.cit.*

2787 Below the term licences and agreement will be used interchangeably.

2788 Art. 7(1) and Recital (23) DSMP.

2789 Art. 8(1) DSMP.

2790 As of end of May 2018.

2791 Art. 2(3) DSMP. In the Parliament process it has been proposed to extend beneficiaries to educational institutions, research organisations and public-service broadcasting organisations, cf. EP JURI, Draft, 2017, 25; EP IMCO, Opinion, 2017, 28.

2792 See EP JURI, Draft, 2017, 25.

2793 See discussion and references on the issue in Ch. 4.2.2.1 and Ch. 4.2.3.2.

11.3.1.2. *Works*

742. Any type of in-copyright but out-of-commerce works can be licensed under the proposed mechanism.[2794] However, the works must be permanently in the collection of the relevant institution, i.e. works that are owned or permanently held by the relevant institutions.[2795]

743. Works are considered to be out-of-commerce when:

> ...the whole work or other subject-matter, in all its translations, versions and manifestations, is not available to the public through customary channels of commerce and cannot be reasonably expected to become so.

Member States shall, in consultation with stakeholders, ensure that requirements for determining which works are out-of-commerce are necessary and reasonable. In particular, it is emphasised that such requirements should not exclude the possibility that a collection as a whole be presumed to be out-of-commerce.[2796] This wording in the original proposal seemed to open for the possibility that, instead of an active search for the commercial status of works being necessary, it could be decided that all works before a certain time would be considered out-of-commerce.[2797] However, the wording has been slightly amended in later versions of the proposal with the effect that more emphasis seems to be put on a determination being made of the commercial status of the works. The wording "reasonable effort" is still highlighted but with several caveats.[2798]

744. The situation is further complicated as unlike in the originally proposed solution[2799] the mechanism in the Council agreed negotiating mandate is not limited to works first published in the country where the licence is sought. In the original proposal it was proposed that collective licences covering use of works of outsiders must be applied for through CMOs that were representative in the Member States where the works were first published, broadcast or where the producers of audio-visual or cinematographic works had their headquarters. If none of these could be determined, the relevant point of attachment would be the site of the cultural heritage institution in question.[2800] It was expressly stated that the mechanism would not be applicable to works of third-country nationals, with the exception of works that had applicable points of attachment to the country where the licence is issued, such as works published in translation

2794 Art. 7(1) and Recital (25) DSMP; SWD(2016) 301 final, IA Part I, 2016, 71, 79.
2795 Recital (25) DSMP.
2796 Art. 7(2) DSMP.
2797 See discussion in Ch. 10.2.3.
2798 2016/0280 (COD) 9134/18, Agreed negotiation mandate, 2018, Art. 7(2) and Recitals (25) and (25a).
2799 SWD(2016) 301 final, IA Part I, 2016, 70–71.
2800 Art. 7(4) DSMP.

in the relevant country.[2801] However, in the newest version of the proposal, at the time of writing[2802], it is proposed that licences apply to all works in the relevant cultural institutions in the EU Member States, except works that have their origin in a third country, unless the relevant EU CMO is sufficiently representative of that third country.[2803]

745. The mechanism is not explicitly limited to published or broadcast works. Nevertheless, this limitation seemed to be assumed in the original proposal which stated that licences should be sought from CMOs that are representative for the Member State where a work had been published or broadcast.[2804] This limitation was also indicated in preparatory works.[2805] A similar implication is to be found in Art. 7(5) of the Council agreed negotiation mandate. However, in Recital (25) of the same document it is expressly stated that the licences can include works that have never been commercially available, including unpublished works.[2806] Neither the original DSM proposal nor the Council agreed negotiation mandate define published works. Thus Member States can presumably use their own approach in this regard, i.e. apply the solution to published works in the Berne Convention sense or let the term cover works legally made available, even if not in tangible forms.[2807] However, if it is clear that the proposed mechanism will cover unpublished works, such a definition might be irrelevant.

11.3.1.3. Uses

746. The proposed solution will enable the relevant cultural heritage institutions to reproduce, distribute, communicate to the public or make available works that are in their collections.[2808] However, all these uses must be for non-commercial purposes. Still, as under the Orphan Works Directive[2809], the institutions can generate reasonable revenues in order to cover the costs of the licence and the costs of digitising and disseminating the works and other subject matter covered by the licence.[2810]

2801 Art. 7(5) and Recital (26) DSMP.
2802 End of May 2018.
2803 2016/0280 (COD) 9134/18, Agreed negotiation mandate, 2018, Art. 7(4) and (5), Recital (25) and (25a).
2804 Cf. Art. 7(4) DSMP.
2805 The intention seems to have been to limit the licences to published works, cf. SWD(2016) 301 final, IA Part I, 2016, 70–71.
2806 The CULT Committee of the European Parliament had proposed that an exception should be added for the reproduction and dissemination for non-commercial purposes, including across borders, of works that were never intended for commercial use, cf. EP CULT, Draft, 2017, 17, 45.
2807 See discussion in Ch. 10.2.2.
2808 Art. 7(1) DSMP which used the term digitise instead of the term "reproduce" now found in the Council agreed negotiation mandate.
2809 Art. 6(2) OWD, cf. Ch. 4.2.3.7.
2810 Recital (27) DSMP.

11.3.1.4. Cross-border effect

747. The cross-border effect of the solution is provided for in Art. 8. In the original DSM proposal Art. 8 specified that cultural heritage institutions holding a collective licence which applied to outsiders in accordance with Art. 7, could use the works in conformity with the terms of the licence in all Member States.[2811] In the Council agreed negotiation mandate of May 2018 it is proposed in Art. 8 that a licence granted in accordance with Art. 7 may allow the use of the out-of-commerce works by cultural heritage institution in any other Member State. However, before a work is used in a cross-border context, information about the work and the opt-out possibility must be made publicly accessible in a single online portal managed by EUIPO.[2812] In the original DSM proposal the obligation to make this information available in the online portal was only mandatory with regard to works which will be used cross-border[2813] whereas this distinction is not as clear in the Council agreed negotiation mandate for the proposal.[2814]

748. These transparency rules are designed to protect the interests of all rightholders. However, it is not stipulated who is responsible for making this information available to the EUIPO portal. It will also be important to ensure that this transparency requirement does not stifle digitisation efforts before they start. This could be the case if prior identification of each and every work falling under the collective licence were required 6 months before the start of the project. The proposed wording "information that allows for identification of the work"[2815] and now "information for the purpose of the identification"[2816] is presumably meant to prevent that possibility. However, one way to approach this requirement would be to limit projects to national level in the initial stage while the works were digitised, e.g. through national ECLs, and then later to make them applicable for cross-border use under the proposed mechanism. It is regrettable that the proposed solution omits to make mandatory the provision of information on opt-outs through the EUIPO portal, as that would be useful for both users and rightholders.[2817]

11.3.2. THE CONDITIONS FOR THE EXTENSION EFFECT

749. The collective management agreements under the proposed solution can be made binding on outsiders either by extension or by presumed representation.

2811 Art. 8(1) DSMP.

2812 European Union Intellectual Property Office, cf. Ch. 4.2.3.4, par. 201; Art. 8(3) and Recital (28) DSMP, Art. 8a(1) and Recital (28).

2813 Art. 8(2) DSMP.

2814 Art. 8a(1) of the Council agreed negotiation mandate for the proposal.

2815 Cf. Art. 8(2) DSMP.

2816 Art. 8a(1) of the Council agreed negotiation mandate for the proposal.

2817 See discussion in Ch. 5.4.5.

The extension or presumption of representation of outsiders will only apply to non-exclusive licences.[2818] Furthermore, there are certain conditions that must be fulfilled: first, the relevant CMO must be representative in the category of works and the rights which are the subject of the licence; second, equal treatment must be guaranteed to all rightholders the licence extends to, i.e. both members and non-members and presumably also to different kinds of rightholders, such as authors and publishers; and third, all rightholders must be able to opt-out of the licence, both with regard to the out-of-commerce status of their works[2819] and the application of the licence to their works.[2820] Additionally, there are requirements for publicity measures[2821] and for stakeholder dialogue to ensure the relevance and usability of the system.[2822]

11.3.2.1. A representative CMO

750. CMOs that conclude licences which will be extended to outsiders must be "sufficiently representative of rightholders in the relevant type of works or other subject-matter and of the rights which are the subject of the licence".[2823] This representativeness requirement seems to be more in line with the requirements of the Nordic ECL system than the more stringent requirements under the UK ECL system.[2824] The interpretation of the term "sufficiently representative" will need to be determined. However, it is underlined in the recitals of the Council agreed negotiation mandate that Member States should have flexibility in determining the requirements of CMO's representativeness in this regard. Furthermore it is up to Member States to set rules when there is more than one CMO that fulfils requirements for representativeness.[2825]

751. One concern in designing the proposed mechanism in the original proposal seems to have been that the requirements for use of the provisions should not become too burdensome, perhaps in light of the experience with the Orphan Works Directive. This can be seen in the provision in Art. 7(2) of the original proposal, where it was stated that Member States shall ensure, in consultation with stakeholders, that requirements for determining whether

---

2818 Art. 7(1) and Recital (23) DSMP.
2819 The possibility of objecting to the commercial status of the work is no longer mentioned in Art. 7.(1) of the Council agreed negotiation mandate for the proposal.
2820 Art. 7(1)(a)-(c) DSMP.
2821 Art. 7(3) DSMP, see now Art. 8a(1) of the Council agreed negotiation mandate for the proposal.
2822 Art. 9 DSMP.
2823 Art. 7(1)(a) of the Council agreed negotiation mandate for the proposal. The wording in the original proposal was slightly different, using "broadly" instead of "significantly" and "in the category of works" instead of "in the relevant type of works", cf. Art. 7(1)(a) DSMP.
2824 See discussion in Ch. 5.2.1, Ch. 7.3.3, Ch. 10.1.1 and Ch. 10.1.5.
2825 Recital (23) of the Council agreed negotiation mandate for the proposal.

works can be licensed under ECLs or presumption of mandate should not go beyond what is "necessary and reasonable". This wording is still to be found in Art. 7(2) of the Council agreed negotiation mandate for the proposal although in a slightly differently constructed provision. Furthermore, in Art. 9, the Member States should ensure regular stakeholder dialogue with the aim of fostering the relevance and usability of the mechanism.

752. The EU out-of-commerce proposal is silent on both the issue of authorisation and mediation. This should leave the Member States free to legislate on those issues.

11.3.2.2. Equal treatment

753. The second condition for the extension effect is that all rightholders be guaranteed equal treatment in relation to the terms of the licence.[2826] This presumably refers mainly to the equal treatment of members and non-members. However, in the light of the general principle of fair balance between different types of rightholders under the CMO Directive[2827], which is to be left intact by the DSM proposal[2828], this condition should also apply to the relationship between different groups of rightholders.

754. The proposed solution contains no specific provisions on remuneration. However, the requirement of equal treatment should not prevent the additional safeguard requirement in the Nordic legislation that outsiders should be guaranteed the right to individual remuneration, if remuneration should be collectively distributed.[2829] On the other hand it may be questioned whether the UK possibility for outsiders to claim a different (higher) remuneration, even in cases of individual remuneration, would be considered equal treatment under the proposed EU solution.

11.3.2.3. Opt-out

755. The third condition for the extension effect is that all rightholders, i.e. not only outsiders, have the right to opt-out of an agreement with extension effect.[2830] In the original proposal the possibility of opt-out related both to the out-of-commerce status of a work and to the application of the licence to the works of a rightholder but in the Council agreed negotiation mandate for the

2826 Art. 7(1)(b) DSMP.
2827 E.g. Art. 6(3) CMO Directive.
2828 Art. 1(2) DSMP.
2829 See discussion in Ch. 5.4.2 and Ch. 10.3.2.2.
2830 Art. 7(1)(c) and Recital (24) DSMP, unchanged in the Council agreed negotiation mandate for the proposal.

proposal there is only opt-out with regard to the latter. This requirement for opt-out seems to confirm my view that the right to opt-out is essential for ECL agreements that allow for cross-border use, at least for outsiders.[2831] The opt-out right seems to be both *a priori* and *a posteriori*, with no limitation as to when the rightholder can opt-out.[2832] In order to make the opt-out a viable option there are a number of obligatory publicity requirements, discussed next.

11.3.2.4. Transparency

756. In the original DSM proposal Member States were obliged to provide appropriate publicity under two provisions, Art. 7(2) and Art. 8(2). Art. 7(2) required publicity on: first, the out-of-commerce status of works; second, the licence, in particular as applying to outsiders; and third, the opt-out possibility. These transparency measures had to be publicly available for a reasonable time before use of works under the licence commences.[2833] Art. 8(2) provided for publicity obligations on information to be made available in the EUIPO portal, at least six months before any cross-border use of works under the proposed licensing mechanism.[2834] In the Council agreed negotiation mandate for the proposal all publicity requirements have been combined in Art. 8a(1) and have to be publicly accessible for a minimum of six months before any use of works under the proposed licencing mechanism. Furthermore, it is underlined in Recital (28) i.f. in the Council agreed negotiation mandate that publicity measures should be effective without the need to inform each rightholder individually, surely a reference to the Soulier case.[2835]

There is no obligation to provide information about works that have been opted-out, which is an important omission, especially for cross-border uses.

11.3.2.5. Stakeholders dialogue

757. Finally, Member States shall consult stakeholders and encourage stakeholder dialogue on a sector-specific basis "... to foster the relevance and usability of the licensing mechanisms ... ensure the effectiveness of the safeguards for rightholders ...".[2836]

No further guidelines are provided for how the stakeholder dialogue should be organised, thus giving Member States considerable freedom in implementing this provision.

2831 See Ch. 10.3.4.

2832 This understanding is now confirmed in Recital (24) of the Council agreed negotiation mandate for the proposal.

2833 Art. 7(3) and Recital (28) DSMP.

2834 Ch. 8(2) DSMP.

2835 C-301/15 – Soulier, cf. Ch. 11.2.

2836 Art. 9 and Recital (25) i.f. of the Council agreed negotiation mandate for the proposal.

11.3.3. EVALUATION

758. The proposed solution for the use by cultural heritage institutions of out-of-commerce works is clearly compatible with the Nordic ECL system. It has a wider application than the MoU on out-of-commerce works, as it applies to all types of works and provides legal certainty for cross-border use. However, the proposed solution is more limited in scope than the Nordic ECL provisions that are relevant for libraries. First, it only applies to non-commercial use. Second, it only applies to out-of-commerce works, although this can be defined in a flexible way. Third, all rightholders shall have a right to opt-out.

759. The proposed solution in the DSM proposal contains most of the safeguard elements I consider necessary to ensure that online cross-border use by libraries through a national ECL agreement passes the three-step test with regard to the outsiders' right. The only missing element is that the proposed mechanism is no longer limited to the licencing of the use of national works, as it was in the original proposal, but is to be available to all works originating from EU Member States that are permanently in a collection of a relevant EU cultural heritage institution.[2837] I presume that this amendment to the original proposal is to make the mechanism more effective, as cultural heritage institutions would not have to ascertain whether a work was national or not. However, as the mechanism cannot be used for works from third countries, unless the CMO in the relevant Member State is sufficiently representative of rightholders of that third country, there will still have to be a selection and an assessment of the origin of works.

As I have argued, not limiting the ECLs with cross-border effect to national works of the Member State where the cultural heritage institution is established may put foreign outsiders at a disadvantage with regard to receiving remuneration, especially those that are not members of any CMO, but possibly also those that are members of a sister CMO in another Member State.[2838] This can be so even in the case of reciprocal representation agreements with sister CMOs in other Member States. However, it is possible the proposed transparency requirement will be sufficient to counterbalance this danger within the EU. Another risk resulting from not limiting cross-border ECL agreements to national works may be an unnecessary duplication of digitisation efforts as some works will be in the permanent collection of cultural heritage institutions in many Member States. Still that may also be avoided to some extent with cross-border cooperation between the relevant cultural heritage institutions. Finally, even if the mechanism can be used for all works with sufficient connection to any EU Member States, it is still possible that the actual agreements may be limited to national works.

[2837] See Ch. 10.

[2838] See Ch. 10.2.1.

760. It is interesting to note that the term "exception" is not used in the provisions on the use of out-of-commerce works by cultural heritage institutions under the proposed mechanism. However, as will be briefly discussed below, the newer versions of the proposal contain a provision on national ECLs for use within national territories of Member States. In that proposed provision there seems to be a reference that the extension effect is to be seen as an exception.[2839] This seems to support my thesis on the hybrid nature of the ECLs with regard to outsiders.[2840]

761. The fact that the proposal has wider application, i.e. applies to more cultural heritage institutions[2841] than just libraries and to both presumed mandate of management and ECLs[2842], makes no fundamental difference to my thesis, and indeed, is an improvement. The fact that it has a narrower field of application than Nordic ECL provisions for libraries, i.e. the proposed solution is limited to out-of-commerce works and to non-commercial use[2843], raises no significant issues either, especially if the requirements for establishing what constitutes out-of-commerce work are flexible.[2844] Nevertheless, I still maintain that there should be more room for stakeholders to negotiate: they are the experts on the needs of the relevant institutions and on the state of the market for the works.[2845] The main importance of the solution for out-of-commerce works in the DSM proposal, if adopted, is that it would oblige Member States that provide for collective licences for the use of out-of-commerce works by cultural heritage institutions, to extend such licences to outsiders and, most importantly, would provide for the legal certainty of the cross-border effect of such licences. Thus it should increase the online availability of culturally important in-copyright works.

762. My general view of the proposal is that it is a positive and necessary step in the right direction. This is in particular so in the light of the recent decision in the Soulier case.[2846] Nevertheless, some questions remain with regard to the licensing of out-of-commerce works and these will need to be resolved if the solution in the DSM proposal is adopted as proposed. One question concerns

2839 Cf. Art. 9a(2) and (4) of the Council agreed negotiation mandate for the proposal. This was particularly prominent in the Consolidated Presidency compromise proposal of October 2017, cf. 2016/0280 (COD) 13842/17, Proposal for a Directive of the European Parliament and of the Council on copyright in the Digital Single Market – Consolidated Presidency compromise proposal, 2017, Art. 9a(4).
2840 Cf. Recital (18) InfoSoc Directive. See discussion in Ch. 6.3.1, Ch. 8.4.2.1 and Ch. 9.1.
2841 Cf. Art. 2(3) DSMP.
2842 Cf. Art. 7(1) and Recital (21) DSMP.
2843 Cf. Art. 7(1) and (2) DSMP.
2844 See discussion in Ch. 11.3.1.2.
2845 See discussion in Ch. 10.2.6.
2846 C-301/15 – Soulier, cf. Ch. 11.2.

how the requirement that CMOs are sufficiently representative of rightholders is to be assessed. The terminology might be seen as an attempt to avoid the complicated proof of representativeness that may be hindering the UK ECL system from getting off the ground and an effort to adopt the pragmatic practice and interpretation of the Nordic countries.[2847] However, in the Council agreed negotiation mandate for the proposal it is stated that the Member States should have flexibility in determining the requirement for representativeness.[2848] Another question, regarding unpublished works and the proposed licensing mechanism, seems to have been answered by an amendment to the proposal making it clear in a recital that the mechanism can be used to license non-published works and works that have never been made public.[2849] Such works can be culturally important.[2850] A further question, not yet answered, is whether, after the adoption of the mechanism, online use can still be restricted geographically, as is the case under the Norwegian Bokhylla project. Finally, there is the question of whether the proposal will exclude the option of national ECL agreements enabling cross-border online use in other areas or for wider use than under the proposed solution. Many have voiced concern that the DSM proposal may in fact narrow the scope for ECLs in general.[2851] These issues may be sufficiently addressed in a new proposed provision on collective licencing with an extended effect[2852], which I will discuss in the next subchapter.

11.3.4. THE DSM PROPOSAL ON COLLECTIVE LICENSING WITH AN EXTENDED EFFECT

763. A new specific provision on collective licensing with an extended effect was added to the DSM proposal in the Council Consolidated Presidency compromise proposal of 30th of October 2017[2853], presumably in response to the concerns voiced by various stakeholders from the Nordic countries and IFFRO.[2854] This new provision remains in the Council agreed negotiating mandate, albeit with a slightly adjusted wording. According to the provision, ECLs in Member

2847 See discussion in Ch. 5.2.1, Ch. 7.3.3, Ch. 10.1.1 and Ch. 10.1.5.

2848 Recital (23) of the Council agreed negotiation mandate for the proposal.

2849 See Recital (25) of the Council agreed negotiation mandate for the proposal and discussion in Ch. 11.3.1.2.

2850 See discussion in Ch. 10.2.2 and the proposed amendment for an exception for the use of works never intended for commercial use, cf. EP CULT, Draft, 2017, 17, 45.

2851 IFRRO, Position paper, 2017, 1; Nordic RRO's position regarding the Commission's proposal for a new copyright directive, 21 April 2017.

2852 Art. 9a of the Council agreed negotiation mandate for the proposal.

2853 2016/0280 (COD) 13842/17, Proposal for a Directive of the European Parliament and of the Council on copyright in the Digital Single Market – Consolidated Presidency compromise proposal, 2017, Art. 9a.

2854 IFRRO, Position paper, 2017, 1; Nordic RRO's position regarding the Commission's proposal for a new copyright directive, 21 April 2017.

States are expressly permitted "as far as the use within their national territory is concerned" and as long as Member States ensure that they are

> ... only applied within well-defined areas of use where obtaining authorisations from rightholders on an individual basis is typically onerous and impractical to a degree that makes the required licensing transaction unlikely due to the nature of the use or of the types of works or other subject-matter concerned and that such mechanism safeguards the legitimate interests of rightholders.[2855]

There have to be specific safeguard measures: first, the relevant CMO must be sufficiently representative of the rightholders, works and uses under an ECL agreement, on the basis of mandates from rightholders[2856]; second, equal treatment must be guaranteed to all rightholders in relation to the terms of the licence; third, outside rightholders must be able to opt-out, easily and effectively, at any time from the licensing mechanism; and finally, appropriate publicity measures must be undertaken to raise the awareness of rightholders of the possibility of an ECL licence that might apply to their works and of their right to opt-out of such licences. These measures must be implemented in a reasonable time prior to any use under such a license. However, it is expressly mentioned that in order for such publicity measures to be effective it is not necessary to inform each and every rightholder individually.[2857]

764. There is an interesting provision in sub-paragraph (4) of the relevant Article 9a on collective licensing with an extended effect which states that the Article is "without prejudice to the application of collective licensing mechanisms with an extended effect in conformity with other provisions of Union law, including those which allow exceptions or limitations, and shall not apply to mandatory collective management of rights." Obviously this is intended to maintain the instances in EU legislation that provide for mandatory collective management of rights, where there is no opt-out possibility.[2858] The question that arises is what other collective licensing mechanism with an extended effect would this provision be referring to. Recital (28d) clarifies that such mechanisms may include extended collective licensing, legal mandate and presumptions of representation, as well as the ECL stipulated in Art. 3 of the Satellite and Cable Directive. Thus it seems clear that the Nordic ECL provisions where there is no opt-out possibility[2859] but which could still be considered to be in conformity with EU law and international obligations would be included. In Recital (28a) it is furthermore underlined that

[2855] 2016/0280 (COD) 9134/18, Agreed negotiation mandate, 2018, Art. 9a (1) and (2), Recital (28e).

[2856] See also Recital (28g) i.f. which states that the "ability to operate a licence under these mechanisms should also be limited to organisations which are either owned or controlled by their right holder members or which operate on a not for profit basis, regulated by national law implementing Directive 2014/26/EU."

[2857] 2016/0280 (COD) 9134/18, Agreed negotiation mandate, 2018, Art. 9a (3) and Recital (28f).

[2858] See Recital (28d) and discussion in Ch. 9.3.

[2859] See discussion in Ch. 5.4.3.

the provisions in the proposed Directive on the use of out-of-commerce works by cultural heritage institutions should be without prejudice to the use of such works or other subject-matter under exceptions or limitations provided for in EU law or under other licences with an extended effect, where such licensing is not based on the out-of-commerce status of the covered works or other subject matter.

765. The final paragraphs of this new Article 9a stipulate that Member States must inform the Commission when and how they provide for ECL legislation[2860] as well as providing for an obligation on the Commission to report by end of year 2020 on the use of ECLs in accordance with the Article. The report must, if appropriate, be accompanied by a legal proposal for cross-border applicability of such mechanisms.[2861]

766. It is interesting to note that in the original wording of this new provision there was a requirement that the proposed mechanism in this general provision on ECLs was only to be "applied in certain special cases which do not conflict with a normal exploitation of the work or other subject-matter and do not unreasonably prejudice the legitimate interests of the rightholders."[2862] This reference to the three-step test is not expressly maintained in the current version of the proposal. However, in Recital (28d) it is stated that Member States should have the flexibility to introduce licensing mechanism schemes with extended effect "in full respect of Union law and their international obligations related to copyright." This may be an indirect reference to the three-step test.

767. This new provision in Article 9a of the proposed DSM Directive should be a sufficient guarantee for the Nordic countries that the Nordic ECL system will not be adversely affected by the proposed mechanism for out-of-commerce works in cultural heritage institutions.[2863] However, it still remains to be seen when the proposal will be adopted and what the final version of the text will be. Now that the EU Council has adopted an agreed negotiating mandate the next step lies with the European Parliament. The Legal Affairs Committee of the European Parliament, responsible for the matter has not issued its final report on the DSM proposal. However, the proposal is on the Joint Declaration of 2018 on the EU's legislative priorities.[2864] Until the proposal is finally adopted it is hard to further analyse its effect on the ECL system.

2860 2016/0280 (COD) 9134/18, Agreed negotiation mandate, 2018, Art. 9a (5); Recital (28h).

2861 Ibid, Art. 9a(6); Recital (28h).

2862 2016/0280 (COD) 13842/17, Proposal for a Directive of the European Parliament and of the Council on copyright in the Digital Single Market – Consolidated Presidency compromise proposal, 2017, Art. 9a(4).

2863 Another matter is how and whether the exception proposed in Art. 4 on the use of works in cross-border teaching activities will affect the current ECL licensing in the Nordic countries in the area of education, but that will not be further discussed here.

2864 Cf. <www.europarl.europa.eu/oeil/popups/thematicnote.do?id=2063000&l=en>, last viewed 3 June 2018.

768. Next I will discuss the EU's competence for legislation in regard to the cross-border effect of national ECL agreements.

11.4. COMPETENCE OF THE EU TO TAKE ACTION

769. EU competence in legislative matters is based on the EU Treaties. However, the EU can only act within its limits of competence in order to attain the objectives set in the Treaties.[2865] Moreover, EU legislation must conform to the principles of subsidiarity and proportionality.[2866] Furthermore, EU legislation must take certain integration clauses in the Treaty into account, i.e. specific provisions in the Treaties that require the integration of particular horizontal policy interests in other policies. Here I will discuss these issues as well as discussing the choice of instruments and approach.

11.4.1. PROVISIONS ON COMPETENCE

770. There are no specific competence provisions for the EU in copyright matters[2867] The EU can have exclusive, shared or supportive competence.[2868] Some aspects of copyright fall under the area of common commercial policy[2869], which falls under the exclusive competence of the EU, cf. Art. 3(e) TFEU. However, most matters relating to copyright affect the internal market where the EU has shared competence with Member States, cf. Art. 4 (2) (a) TFEU. Shared competence entails that Member States can only act if the EU has not exercised or has decided not to exercise its competence, cf. Art. 2(2) TFEU. Finally, in cultural matters, where copyright also belongs, the EU has only supportive competence, cf. Art. 6(c) TFEU.[2870]

771. Traditionally the EU's legislative initiatives have been based on the need to build an internal market[2871], where it is considered to have the strongest competence.[2872] Art. 114 TFEU, which empowers the EU to adopt measures to achieve the objectives of the good functioning of the internal market and ensure the free movement of i.a. services[2873], has thus commonly been the basis for legal action in the field of copyright. This is also the case for the DSM proposal.[2874]

2865 Cf. Art. 5(2) TEU.
2866 Cf. Art. 5(1) TEU.
2867 Ramalho, Conceptualising, 2014, 178.
2868 Art. 2 TFEU.
2869 Art. 207(1) TFEU.
2870 Ramalho, Conceptualising, 2014, 179–181; Tryggvadóttir, Balancing of interests, 2015, 663–664.
2871 See e.g. COM(2015) 626 final, Towards, 2015, 2.
2872 Ramalho, Conceptualising, 2014, 181.
2873 Cf. Art. 26 TFEU.
2874 COM(2016) 593 final, Proposal, 2016, 4.

772. Art. 118 TFEU allows the EU to create "European intellectual property rights to provide uniform protection of intellectual property rights throughout the Union and for the setting up of centralised Union-wide authorisation, coordination and supervision arrangements". This is now widely considered to pave the way for a unified copyright title[2875], although that may not have been the intention of the legislators. During the drafting of Art. 118 TFEU a Finnish proposal clarifying that the Article also applied to copyright was rejected with the reasoning that the Article was limited to industrial intellectual property, such as patents and trademarks.[2876] This change of view seems to indicate, first, that institutional memory can be short-lived, second, that the term "Intellectual Property" has evolved in the last few years and, finally, that the climate has become more favourable for the introduction of a unified copyright title, at least in some main areas of copyright, despite possible difficulties with regard to the interplay with national laws and rights.[2877]

11.4.2. THE OBJECTIVES OF THE EU TREATIES

773. A key goal of the EU is the establishment of an internal market[2878] and the promotion of EU values.[2879] This includes several objectives as set out in the Treaties. Of importance here is the free movement of goods and services[2880], respect for fundamental rights[2881] and the Union's "rich cultural and linguistic diversity", and the duty to ensure the enhancement and protection of Europe's cultural heritage.[2882, 2883]

774. Providing for EU-wide access to national cultural heritages contributes to the establishment of a single market, as the objective of a single internal market also implies access to the cultural heritage. Such access is one way to safeguard the cultural and linguistic diversity of European cultural goods. The objective of respecting fundamental rights provides normative content to internal market legislation. This implies a balance between fundamental rights, such as the interest of the individual right owner and the public interest.[2884] Thus legislation

2875 European Commission, Report on the responses, 2014, 91; European Parliament, Reda Draft Report 2015, 10; Hugenholtz, Copyright, 2012, 203; Ramalho, Conceptualising, 2014, 184–185; Geiger and others, Reaction of CEIPI, 2015, 9.

2876 Cf. e-mail communication, dated 27 October 2015, from Jukka Liedes, a Finnish expert that participated in the drafting of Art. 118 TFEU; von Lewinski, Copyright, 2012, 108–109.

2877 See discussion in Ch. 9.6.

2878 Cf. Art. 3(3) TEU.

2879 Cf. Art. 3(1) TEU.

2880 Cf. Art. 26(2) TFEU.

2881 Cf. Art. 3(3) TEU and Art. 51(1) EU Charter.

2882 Cf. Art. 3(3) i.f. TEU.

2883 Ramalho, Conceptualising, 2014, 187–190.

2884 Ibid, 189.

providing publicly accessible digital libraries with the means to make the European cultural heritage available to end users certainly meets these objectives, in particular as it concurrently safeguards the rightholders' economic interest.

11.4.3. THE PRINCIPLES OF SUBSIDIARITY AND PROPORTIONALITY

11.4.3.1. Subsidiarity

775. For areas of shared competence the principle of subsidiarity means that the EU may intervene only if it is capable of acting more effectively than the Member States.[2885] Thus it needs to be established that the EU can better attain the objectives than the Member States and create an efficiency gain above a certain minimum level.[2886]

776. As making works available online is essentially a cross-border activity, it seems self-evident that EU legislation should be more effective than legislation in individual Member States.[2887] I have argued above that it is possible for national ECL agreements to have cross-border applicability under certain circumstances, but in order to create sufficient legal certainty EU legislation would be preferable.[2888]

777. Introducing ECLs for libraries and other cultural heritage institutions at the European level might be seen as contradictory to the subsidiarity principle. Cultural matters fall under the competence of Member States and the EU can only intervene to support, coordinate or complement the actions of Member States.[2889] However, access to the European cultural heritage is an issue for the digital single market.[2890] Internal market issues are under the shared competence of the EU and the Member States.[2891] The question is whether the initiative by the EU means that the room for national solutions in this specific area will decrease and be limited within the framework of the proposed mechanism. It seems to be clear from the text of Art. 2(2) TFEU and Protocol on the exercise of shared competence[2892] that the competence is only limited with regard to the specific

2885 Art. 5(3) TEU.

2886 Ramalho, Conceptualising, 2014, 190; N.W. Barber, 'The limited modesty of subsidiarity', 2005, (3), European Law Journal, 308–325, 311–312; Tryggvadóttir, Balancing of interests, 2015, 664.

2887 COM(2016) 593 final, Proposal, 2016, 5; COM(2016) 289 final, Proposal, 2016, 4; COM(2015) 627, Proposal, 2015, 4.

2888 Ch. 9.1.2 and Ch. 10.

2889 Art. 6 TFEU.

2890 COM(2015) 192 final, Communication, 2015, 6–8; COM(2015) 626 final, Towards, 2015, 3–6; COM(2016) 593 final, Proposal, 2016, 3–4.

2891 Art. 4 (2) (a) TFEU.

2892 Art. 2(2) TFEU; Protocol No 25 to the Treaties, sole Article.

act in question and thus does not cover the whole area.[2893] This now seems to be confirmed in the proposed legislation in the new Article 9a.[2894]

11.4.3.2. Proportionality

778. The principle of proportionality requires that legislative action shall not exceed what is necessary to achieve the objectives of the Treaty.[2895] This requires that legislative actions be evaluated with regard to three criteria, first, suitability, second, necessity, and third, proportionality in the sense of balancing of the interests at stake.[2896]

779. Regarding the first criteria, EU legislation is well suited to achieving the dissemination of the cultural heritage and to making it accessible for the public at large, which are the objectives of both the Union and libraries. EU action is also necessary as, despite the possibility that national ECL agreements might have cross-border effect, this has not provided libraries or other cultural heritage institutions with sufficient legal certainty to enable them to start making their collections available online without geographical limitations. There are exceptions, notably the ECL agreement for the Finnish National Gallery, which expressly allows for unlimited online availability, and the German agreement based on the legislation for out-of-commerce works, where it is clear from the agreement that it is meant for online cross-border use, in particular in regard to Europeana.[2897] Finally, as the ECL system is aimed at safeguarding both the interest of rightholders and users, EU legislation enabling ECL agreements would potentially improve the balance between those two groups in Europe. However, it can be questioned whether it is necessary to limit the mechanism to out-of-commerce works and for non-commercial use, for example, or whether leaving those issues to be negotiated by stakeholders might have been more appropriate and more efficient.[2898]

780. Finally, it is important that proportionality is observed under the ECL solution with regard to the inherent limitation[2899] on the outsider's right under the system. Thus even if an ECL agreement fulfils international norms for exceptions with regard to the outsiders' right without opt-out, an opt-out option is still a vital tool to secure the proportionality of the solution with regard to outsiders in most instances.

2893 Ramalho, Conceptualising, 2014, 180.
2894 See Ch. 11.3.4.
2895 Art. 5(4) TEU.
2896 Ramalho, Conceptualising, 2014, 191–192; Jan H. Jans, 'Proportionality Revisited', 2000, (3), Legal Issues of Economic Integration, 239–265, 243–249.
2897 See Ch. 5.3.1.2, par 318–320 and Ch. 7.4, par. 502–506.
2898 See discussion in Ch. 10.2.6.
2899 Cf. Art. 52(1) EU Charter.

11.4.4. RELEVANT INTEGRATION CLAUSES

781. For copyright the main relevant integration clauses that EU legislation must take into account relate to culture, consumer protection and the competitiveness of the Union's industries.[2900]

782. The first integration clause to consider is on culture, which stipulates that the EU "shall contribute to the flowering of the cultures of the Member States, while respecting their national and regional diversity and at the same time bringing the common cultural heritage to the fore."[2901] Neither the term culture[2902] nor cultural diversity is defined in the Treaty.[2903] It is implied that the term "cultural diversity" refers to protection of national cultures of Member States.[2904] However, the same provision highlights that national cultures can be respected while at the same time the common European culture can be brought to "the fore".[2905] Furthermore, the definition of cultural diversity in the UNESCO Convention on the Protection and Promotion of the Diversity of Cultural Expression[2906], to which the EU is a party, implies that cultural diversity relates to authors, producers, disseminating intermediaries and users alike.[2907] An EU provision enabling the European cross-border effect would be attempting to safeguard the interests of all those stakeholders. Hence such legislation would be in conformity with the integration clause on cultural diversity.

783. The second integration clause to consider with regard to copyright legislation relates to consumer protection.[2908] Consumer protection is high on the agenda of EU policies. Although the terms "consumer" and "user" are not interchangeable[2909] and indeed, it is important to distinguish between them for legal certainty and clarity[2910], there is a significant overlap between the two, which makes consumer protection important in copyright.[2911] Thus end-users of

---

2900 Ramalho, Conceptualising, 2014, 192–196.

2901 Art. 167(4) TFEU.

2902 COM (2007) 242, European agenda for culture 2007, 2007, 3; Klass and Rupp, EUROPEANA… 2014, 947; Blake, On defining, 2000, 67–68.

2903 Ramalho, Conceptualising, 2014, 192.

2904 Art. 167(1) TFEU.

2905 Ramalho, Conceptualising, 2014, 192–193; COM(2007) 242 final, *Communication from the Commission to the European Parliament, the Council, the European Economic and Social Committee and the Committee of the Regions on a European agenda for culture in a globalizing world*, (10 May 2007) Section 3.1.

2906 Cf. Art. 4(1) of the UNESCO Convention.

2907 Ramalho, Conceptualising, 2014, 193.

2908 Arts. 12 and 169 TFEU.

2909 Ramalho, Conceptualising, 2014, 194. See on the term 'user' in fn. 35.

2910 Christophe Geiger and others, Reaction of the CEIPI to the Resolution, 2015, 6.

2911 Ramalho, Conceptualising, 2014, 194; Marco B.M. Loos and others, *Analysis of the applicable legal frameworks and suggestions for the contours of a model system of consumer protection in relation to digital content contracts*, (1 June 2011) 17–19; Yochai Benkler, 'From consumers

works under copyright are mostly private persons and as such consumers. Hence consumer protection can be said to be taken into account in copyright legislation when access for users is facilitated, as is the case in legislation providing for the cross-border effect of ECL agreements for cultural heritage institutions.

784. The third relevant integration clause for copyright on competitiveness of the Union's industries[2912] neither defines competitiveness nor which instruments should be used to achieve it.[2913] This integration clause can be seen as less important for libraries and other cultural heritage institutions than for commercial stakeholders in the creative industries.[2914] Nevertheless, competition issues such as the correction of market failure and the provision of a level playing field are important for public and non-commercial players like libraries or other cultural heritage institutions.[2915] The proposed mechanism in the DSM proposal for the use of out-of-commerce works aims to reinforce the legal certainty of the cross-border applicability of collective agreements with legislative support.

785. Thus the conclusion is that an ECL solution aimed at enabling cross-border online use by libraries and other cultural heritage institutions is in line with the specific integration clauses relevant for copyright.

11.4.5. CHOICE OF INSTRUMENT

786. The non-binding instruments for the digitisation and online accessibility of the cultural heritage, i.e. the 2011 Recommendation[2916] and the 2011 MoU on out-of-commerce works[2917] were not able to sufficiently support the legal certainty of cross-border online use of works from cultural heritage institutions.[2918] Such legal certainty would be best achieved through binding instruments, such as the Commission has now put forward in its DSM proposal with the solution for the use of out-of-commerce works for cultural heritage institutions. The Commission has chosen the route of a Directive for the solution. This choice of instrument means that the Member States will have some flexibility in implementing the provision.[2919] However, there can be a downside to that flexibility. First, some legal uncertainty may remain if implementation

---

to users: shifting the deeper structures of regulation toward sustainable commons and user access', 2000, (3), Federal Communications Law Journal, 561–579, 562.

2912 Art. 173(3) TFEU.
2913 Ramalho, Conceptualising, 2014, 194–195.
2914 COM(2015) 626 final, Towards, 2015, 3.
2915 Ramalho, Conceptualising, 2014, 194–195.
2916 2011/711/EU, Recommendation, 2011, *op.cit.*
2917 *Op.cit.* in Ch. 7.1.
2918 SWD(2016) 301 final, IA Part I, 2016, 65–69.
2919 COM(2016) 593 final, Proposal, 2016, 6.

varies significantly between Members States, and, second, the implementation phase could take a long time.[2920] However, it has been suggested that an EU provision for the cross-border applicability of ECL agreements, based on the country of origin approach, might in principle not have to be implemented as such, as the rights would be cleared for use for the whole territory as soon as the national ECL agreement was reached at a national level and came into force.[2921]

787. Another choice of instrument would be a Regulation. A Regulation would confer the most legal certainty and not require national legislation, as it would directly apply in all Member States. The reasoning put forward in the proposed legislation on addressing geo-blocking through Regulation could be argued to apply in this situation *mutatis mutandis*, which is that only "a Regulation ensures the degree of clarity, uniformity and legal certainty which is necessary in order to enable customers to fully benefit from those rules".[2922] However, the choice by the Commission was rationalised as adequate as it relates, and in some instances modifies existing Directives.[2923] Furthermore, a Directive may better adhere to the principle of subsidiarity than a Regulation in this instance.

11.4.6. CHOICE OF APPROACH

788. The Commission has opted for the country of origin approach in its proposal for the use of out-of-commerce works by cultural heritage institutions.[2924] This means that libraries and other cultural heritage institutions will only have to negotiate an agreement in the country where they are situated. This will simplify the licensing process for cross-border online use. In the original proposal the approach was tied to the use of national works which I have argued would help safeguard the interest of outsiders, as it should be simpler for the CMO to identify and contact national outsiders in order to inform them and distribute remuneration. Similarly, it should be easier for outsiders to make use of the necessary safeguard provisions of opting-out or claiming individual remuneration (if applicable).[2925] I further argued, that the combination of the country of origin approach with limitation to national works for the cross-border use of national cultural heritage institutions would pre-empt the main

2920 As an example the implementaion of the OWD was not achieved in all Member States until four years after the adoption of the Directive, cf. discussion in Ch. 4.2.3.8. The CMO Directive was still not implemented in 5 Member States, one year after the deadline for implementation and three years after the adoption of the Directive, cf. <http://eur-lex.europa.eu/legal-content/EN/NIM/?uri=CELEX:32014L0026&qid=1497474584721>, last viewed 18 July 2017.

2921 Guibault, Cultural, 2015, 191.

2922 COM(2016) 289 final, Proposal, 2016, Recital (33).

2923 COM(2016) 593 final, Proposal, 2016, 6.

2924 Art. 8(1) DSMP.

2925 See discussion in Ch. 10.2.1 and Ch. 10.2.6.

criticism of the country of origin approach for digital cross-border use, which is the difficulty of establishing one single point of origin for digital transmissions, as well as the danger of forum shopping.[2926] Under the proposed mechanism in the original proposal neither of these criticisms would have been valid, as the point of origin would be (as it still is) the cultural heritage institution, and forum shopping would not have been possible as licences with cross-border effect would only be with regard to national works from the forum of the relevant cultural heritage institution. However, as explained above, in the current EU Council agreed negotiation mandate the solution is no longer tied to national works of the relevant cultural heritage institution but can cover works from all Member States which are in the permanent collection of any EU cultural heritage institution. Excluded are works from third countries, unless the relevant CMO is deemed to be sufficiently representative of relevant rightholders from that country.[2927] This change in the proposal text may be based on the view that the proposed transparency requirement in the Directive's suggested mechanism for out-of-commerce works will be sufficient to counterbalance this danger.[2928] Furthermore, the new CMO Directive may also strengthen EU CMO's governance and transparency and thus the issues of foreign outsiders within EU might be better handled than before. It remains to be seen how this will work in reality in this regard if the Directive is adopted in its present form.

789. This issue aside, the proposed solution for the licensing mechanism for out-of-commerce works in cultural heritage institutions will benefit end-users or consumers, as the simplified licensing process should lead to increased content online and better access to the European cultural heritage. Finally, it will benefit rightholders, both members of the relevant CMO and outsiders, as they should receive appropriate remuneration for use that would otherwise be too complicated to license. Thus the provisions in the DSM proposal, if adopted, would be positive for all stakeholders and confer as much legal certainty as possible, while the principle of territoriality of copyright still prevails within the EU and EEA area.

11.4.7. EVALUATION

790. The EU is well within its competence to propose the legislation to secure legal certainty of the extension effect of collective licences for cultural heritage institutions. The proposed solution contains the necessary requirements for ECL agreements for the cross-border online use to be compatible with international norms. The EU proposal is more limited with

2926 See discussion in Ch. 8.2.2.3 and Ch. 8.2.3.

2927 See discussion in Ch. 11.3.1.2.

2928 See Ch. 11.3.3.

regard to certain aspects than I consider necessary, such as the fact that it only applies to out-of-commerce works, and only to non commercial use. In my view this should be left to stakeholders to decide. Nevertheless, the proposal, if adopted, will be an important step towards improving access to the European cultural heritage.

11.5. CONCLUSION

791. The hybrid system of ECL for online cross-border use by libraries conforms very well with the EU legal framework for copyright, in particular with its aims and objectives to enable the dissemination of the cultural heritage by libraries by "specific contracts or licences". The use of national ECL agreements for enabling online cross-border use of EU in-copyright works creates legal certainty for stakeholders, a high level of protection for rightholders, flexibility for users and a balance of interest between rightholders and users.[2929]

792. The decision on the Soulier case established that not all national collective arrangements are compatible with EU legislation, in particular the InfoSoc Directive. However, the French legislation for out-of-commerce books can be clearly distinguished from the ECL solution, mainly because in the latter there is a requirement for a clear mandate from a substantial number of rightholders.[2930]

793. This conclusion supports in my view that national ECL agreements could enable cross-border effect without specific EU legislation to that effect. However, they would need to fulfil certain conditions relating to the requirements of the relevant CMO, the field of scope of the use negotiated and finally, the relevant safeguard measures. If these conditions were fulfilled an ECL agreement for cross-border use would fulfil international norms.[2931] As the hybrid ECL system seems to be considered to be an arrangement concerning the management of rights within the EU[2932], ECL agreements could be seen as contracts, based on a mixture of voluntary mandates and legal mandates. Thus disputes regarding uses under the agreements presumably should be settled under the Rome I Regulation on contractual obligations, which would in most cases mean that applicable laws would be the law of where the ECL agreement was negotiated. This would probably mean that the cross-border effect would be deemed legal under the national law of the ECL agreement.[2933]

2929 See Ch. 11.1.
2930 Ch. 11.2.
2931 Ch. 10.
2932 Ch. 6.3.1.
2933 Ch. 8.4.2.1.

Recent case law from the CJEU appears to favour a teleological interpretation of the EU legislation in the area of copyright[2934], which supports this conclusion. In the words of Advocate General Spunzar, which could be taken to apply to this issue as well:

> Such an interpretation would not only be in the public interest of access to science and culture, it would also be in the interests of authors. At the same time, it would in no way be contrary to the wording or general structure of the legal texts in force. On the contrary, only an interpretation of that kind will enable those legal texts fully to fulfil the function assigned them by the legislature, which is to adapt the law of copyright to the realities of the information society.[2935]

Nevertheless, legal certainty with regard to cross-border use remains an important argument in favour of specific EU legislation.

794. Thus it is to be welcomed that the EU has now proposed a mechanism for the use of out-of-commerce works by cultural heritage institutions. As observed above, the EU is well within its competence to put forward such a solution.[2936] This proposal will be helpful in eliminating the legal uncertainty surrounding the ability of national ECL agreements to enable cross-border use.[2937] However, it is narrower in scope than Nordic ECL provisions for libraries and the general ECL provisions.[2938] I maintain that there should be room for more flexibility for stakeholders to negotiate the field and scope of national ECL agreements enabling cross-border online use and still be within international norms.[2939] Nevertheless, the proposed solution is a welcome and important contribution to improving cross-border access to the European cultural heritage.

2934 See e.g. C-174/15 – VOB, par. 51; C-174/15 – VOB, AG opinion, par. 23–29.
2935 C-174/15 – VOB, AG opinion, par. 79.
2936 Ch. 11.4.
2937 Ch. 11.3.1.4.
2938 Ch. 5.3.
2939 Ch. 10 3.

CHAPTER 12
CONCLUSION

It should be stressed that it is highly unlikely that one single solution can be applied for all types of works, domains and territories. The pragmatic approach is to adopt a flexible and innovative perspective, select and even "pick and mix" appropriate solutions adapted to a specific rights clearance situation.[2940]

795. Libraries play an important role in society as custodians of the cultural heritage. It must therefore be a matter of public policy to ensure that libraries can continue to fulfil that traditional role in the modern world and that they adapt as smoothly as possible to the digital reality of today. Establishing an environment in which libraries are able to make works from their collections available online with cross-border effect would be a significant contribution to this endeavour. While copyright is not the only issue that libraries must resolve as they become digital, others being budgetary[2941] rather than legal[2942], copyright is obviously a key consideration in the digital use of in-copyright works by libraries. In this work I have focused on how copyright affects the ability of libraries to put in-copyright works online with cross-border effect within Europe[2943], and how issues arising can be resolved. I have in particular focused on the system of extended collective licences as developed in the Nordic countries as a model to resolve these issues, at least within Europe.

796. I assert that extended collective licensing constitutes a flexible solution; it maintains the necessary balance between rightholders and users of in-copyright works and can offer legal certainty for cross-border online use by libraries of in-copyright works from their collections, thus facilitating increased access to the European cultural heritage. This proposition is analysed throughout this work.

After a short general introduction[2944], where I set out the subject, I discuss, in Part I, the role of libraries in the digital age and mass use by libraries, and

2940 Axhamn and Guibault, Cross-border ECL, 2011, v.

2941 See discussion in Ch. 2.2.2.

2942 2011/711/EU, Recommendation, 2011, recital (9); Derclaye (ed) Copyright and Cultural Heritage, 2010, 233–234; European Commission, Report, 2016, 7; Borghi and Karapapa, Copyright and Mass Digitization, 2013, 104.

2943 Distinct from e-lending, consultation on the premises of libraries or through closed networks, which usually does not include cross-border use.

2944 See Ch. 1.

how these are affected by copyright, also covering the Google Book project, which brought the digitisation of books to the world's attention, and European developments with regard to digital libraries.[2945] I analyse the exclusive rights involved in online use and demonstrate that the interaction is unclear between two applicable exclusive rights, i.e. the reproduction right and the communication to the public right, more precisely the making available right. More importantly, neither the communication right nor the making available right is clearly defined in international treaties or national legislation. Particularly unclear is where and how to localise the making available right, which in turn makes it difficult to assess the cross-border implications of online use by libraries of in-copyright works.[2946] Finally in Part I, I discuss the exceptions to the exclusive rights relevant for libraries. My conclusion is that current exceptions under the EU legislative framework for copyright are not sufficiently effective instruments to enable online cross-border use by libraries.[2947]

797. In Part II of the work, I begin by describing the Nordic ECL system in general and its operation with regard to libraries in particular.[2948] I then analyse the compatibility of the ECL system with international and EU legal norms.[2949] The ECL system was adopted as a pragmatic solution without clear legal definition. As the system has evolved the legal theory on its nature has also developed, not least in order to adapt to the fact of the exhaustive list of exceptions in the InfoSoc Directive. My conclusion is that the extension effect of the ECL provision constitutes an exception to the outsider's exclusive rights and as such must fulfil international norms, such as the three-step test. Nevertheless, as demonstrated, because of the hybrid nature of the ECL system, in ECL agreements for uses that fulfil international norms, in particular the three-step test, the exception impact of the extension effect recedes in favour of a legal presumption of mandate from outsiders thus making it possible to see the extension effect of the system as an arrangement of management of rights.[2950] At the same time, my analysis of the three-step test and the ECL system lead me to conclude that most ECL agreements, in particular for libraries, under the Nordic ECL provisions, do fulfil international norms.[2951] I argue that this determination of the hybrid nature of the extension effect of the ECL system is compatible with recital (18) of the InfoSoc, and can explain how to resolve the dichotomy of the inherent exception of the ECL system with regard to

---

2945 See Ch. 2.
2946 See Ch. 3.
2947 See Ch. 4.
2948 See Ch. 5.
2949 See Ch. 6.
2950 See Ch. 6.1.2.
2951 See Ch. 6.2.

outsiders and the management part of the same system; ECL agreements that fulfil the three-step test are to be perceived as an arrangement of management of rights and thus they fall outside the exhaustive list of exceptions under the InfoSoc Directive. From a theoretical point of view this may be described as a legal fiction, but for practical purposes it has worked, and from a normative perspective it should be encouraged as it provides for a flexible solution where the interest of stakeholders can be taken into account, both rightholders, members of the CMO and outsiders alike, and users[2952] Part II ends with a description of collective management arrangements in other European countries together with a brief account of legislative developments outside Europe.[2953]

798. In Part III, I discuss the effect of territoriality on online use of in-copyright works in general and within the EU, and the interplay of the principles of territoriality and private international law. I argue that if ECLs which fulfil international norms are considered arrangements concerning the management of rights under EU legislation, ECL agreements could be considered contracts with regard to the extension effect. That reasoning could in turn lead to the conclusion that applicable laws in a cross-border dispute regarding use of works under an ECL agreement should be determined under the Rome I Regulation on contractual obligations. This would in most instances result in the applicable law being the law where the ECL agreement originates, which presumably would result in the use under the ECL agreement being considered as authorised in the country of reception.[2954] However, this is not a legally certain outcome as it would be national courts in each country that would determine the applicable laws. Such a question would presumably be put to the CJEU to resolve. Thus EU legislation would be preferable to give legal certainty to cross-border applicability of ECL agreements.[2955] I then look at a number of legislative options for enabling online access with cross-border effect for European libraries. I conclude that ECLs, and possibly the to some extent similar system of presumed mandate, provide the most flexibility for users, as well as adequate safeguards for outsiders, and thus should be the preferred option for cross-border licences for libraries.[2956] Subsequently, I identify the features essential in ECL agreements for online use with cross-border effect by libraries, if they are to fulfil international norms. These essential features include requirements made of the CMO, such as representativeness; requirements with regard to the field and scope of use, most crucially, that such agreements should be limited to national works; and finally, safeguard measures for outsiders, such

2952 See Ch. 6.3.1.
2953 See Ch. 7.
2954 See Ch. 8, especially Ch. 8.4.2.1.
2955 Ch. 8.5.
2956 Ch. 9.

as equal treatment and opt-out options.[2957] Finally, I analyse the compatibility of such ECL agreements with the EU legal framework, concluding that the ECL system is consistent with the EU's objectives with regard to copyright. In the analysis I reflect on the Soulier case, the proposal for the use of out-of-commerce works by cultural heritage institutions in the DSM proposal, and the competence of the EU to take action with regard to the issue.[2958]

799. My conclusion is that, even without EU legislation, Nordic type ECL provisions for libraries (or cultural heritage institutions in general) could provide a sound legal basis for ECL agreements to allow online use with cross-border effect, at least within Europe, and which could conform to international norms such as the three-step test.[2959] Examples already exist in the form of the Finnish National Gallery project[2960] and, although not based on ECLs but rather on presumed mandate, in the German Framework Agreement for the use of out-of-commerce books.[2961]

800. The ECL system provides for a solution which addresses the need to make in-copyright works available in a way that affords flexibility and legal certainty to users, such as libraries, and is at the same time not unacceptably intrusive on the exclusive right of the outside rightholder. This balance is achieved through the negotiation of the ECL agreement between the stakeholders. The rightholders' interest, both members' and outsiders', should be adequately protected by the relevant CMO, given the stronger negotiating power of CMOs compared to the individual rightholder and assuming adequate representativeness by the CMO.[2962] Thus it is a pragmatic solution based on a hybrid system that can secure a leap from an exception effect with regard to outsiders to a system considered an arrangement of management of outsiders' rights, for ECL agreements that enable uses that pass international norms. I argue that the social benefit of disseminating the cultural heritage and preserving cultural diversity in Europe by making national culture available and accessible, at least within Europe, compensates for the loss by the outsider of the right to determine fully in those instances how his or her right is managed. It should also be remembered that the ECL system benefits members of the CMO who, through the agreement, receive remuneration for uses that might not have occurred if the agreement had not been extended to outsiders. Hence the solution is in the interest of all rightholders, who are remunerated,

2957 Ch. 10.
2958 Ch. 11.
2959 See Ch. 10–11.
2960 See Ch. 5.3.1.
2961 See Ch. 7.4.
2962 See Ch. 5.1.

of the cultural and creative sector in general through the increased access, and thus in the public interest.[2963] The solution is consistent with the EU approach of flexible tools to stimulate the development and exploitation of creative content[2964], as well as with the aim of providing libraries with "a clearer framework and a level playing field regardless of the Member State in which they are based".[2965]

801. It is my conclusion therefore, that a solution based on the system of ECL agreements would address the needs both of digital libraries and rightholders. Nevertheless, there remain some issues to be settled. These issues, however, are not all limited to the ECL system as such and relate more to the nature of solutions based on negotiations. Negotiations allow for flexibility but reduce the predictability of the outcome. Consequently, one of the main strengths of the ECL system, the fact that ECL agreements are negotiated and thus provide for flexibility, is also one of its weaknesses when it comes to enabling uses deemed to be in the public interest, as an ECL agreement cannot be forced on parties that fail to conclude a deal.[2966] Hence it has been claimed that a mandatory exception would afford more legal certainty to all parties involved in digitisation and the making available online of the cultural heritage.[2967] It certainly can be argued that a mandatory exception would better suit the purposes of libraries. However, exceptions that allow enough flexibility for libraries may be too restrictive for rightholders.[2968] The following arguments can be put forward against using exceptions: first, making works available online is not a fundamental objective of the EU[2969] and therefore an exception for the online use by libraries or other cultural heritage institutions might not conform with the principle of subsidiarity and proportionality, whereas an ECL agreement would.[2970] Second, it would be difficult to craft an exception broad enough to fully serve the interest of all libraries and yet narrow enough not to encroach on the interest of rightholders. If the balance were to tip too far in favour of libraries, an exception might become incompatible with the three-step test.[2971] If the exception provided for safeguard clauses, such as compensation, limited its application to out-of-commerce works and provided for opt-out possibility for rightholders, all tools that might help an exception conform to

2963 Cf. e.g. Recital (4) MoU for out-of-commerce works, Recital (3) CMO Directive.

2964 Recitals (2), (4), (5) and (8) InfoSoc Directive.

2965 SWD(2015) 100 final, A Digital Single Market Strategy, 2015, 30; COM(2015) 626 final, Towards, 2015, 6–8.

2966 See discussion in Ch. 5.2.4 and 11.1.1, see also Trumpke, Exklusivität, 2015, 525–526; Rognstad, Avtalelisenser, 2004, 158.

2967 Guibault, Cultural, 2015, 187.

2968 See discussion and references in Ch. 9.5.

2969 Ibid.

2970 See discussion in Ch. 11.4.3.2.

2971 See general discussion on the three-step test in Ch. 4.1.3.

the proportionality principle and help it pass the three-step test[2972], it might become too complicated to execute in practice. Such provisions would create considerable practical problems, incurring transaction costs and entailing complicated regulations on to determine the level of compensation, who would determine the out-of-commerce status and where rightholders could opt-out. Finally, it must not be forgotten that an exception will affect the exclusive rights of all rightholders, whereas under an ECL agreement the extension effect is only with regard to outsiders.[2973] It is therefore my contention that ECL agreements provide the optimal solution, providing the necessary flexibility, as stakeholders themselves can agree on the scope and extent of use within the framework set out in this research.

802. I have concentrated on the ECL solution in the European context. European initiatives such as Europeana would benefit from the online availability of national works under ECL agreements, as their access model is based on linking to European cultural heritage institutions. However, Europeana gives worldwide access, which may create some challenges for the applicability of national ECL agreements. Given the potential increased remuneration to rightholders that online use with cross-border effect might generate and which the libraries would have to shoulder, it might be prudent to limit such cross-border use to within the EU/EEA area. In any case, more research is needed to establish whether national ECL agreements could also enable worldwide online use.

803. Despite my conclusion that national ECL agreements can, under present circumstances, enable cross-border online use for libraries, at least within Europe, there remains legal uncertainty around the issue of cross-border applicability. Thus EU legislation explicitly providing for cross-border effect of ECLs would be helpful. This seems to be the intention of the Commission with its proposed solution for use of out-of-commerce works in the DSM proposal.[2974] The proposed solution is, however, in some respects more limited than the Nordic ECL provisions relevant for libraries and other cultural heritage institutions. The Nordic ECL provisions provide flexibility to stakeholders to determine

---

2972 As proposed e.g. by the European Parliament Committees, IMCO and ITRE, in their Opinions to the Committee on Legal Affairs, responsible for the file in the European Parliament, cf. EP IMCO, Opinion, 2017, 4, 37–38; EP ITRE, *Opinion of the Committee on Industry, Research and Energy for the Committee on Legal Affairs on the proposal for a directive of the European Parliament and of the Council on copyright in the Digital Single Market (COM(2016)0593 – C8-0383/2016 – 2016/0280(COD))*, (12 July 2017) 26. A Discussion Paper from the 4th Europeana Licensing Workshop in Luxembourg, 26th and 27th of November 2015 also suggested an exception for the use, i.a. making available online, of out-of-commerce works with an opt-out option.

2973 See discussion and references in Ch. 9.5.

2974 See Ch. 11.3.

issues such as the commercial or non-commercial purposes of use, or whether agreements should be limited to the use of works made after a certain cut-off date or based on their commercial availability. Such flexibility is important in my view and could also be accommodated within the norms of the international and EU legal frameworks, if the basic safeguard measures discussed above[2975] were guaranteed. This begs the question whether the Commission proposal, if adopted, will circumscribe the potential for national solutions with cross-border effect for such institutions.[2976] This concern has, however, now been made redundant with the new provision on collective licensing with an extension effect in Article 9a.[2977] A different approach would have been a very unfortunate outcome.

804. Broadening access to creative content online within Europe will not be facilitated by one single approach.[2978] The same holds true for online use by libraries, as reflected in the quotation at the beginning of this chapter.[2979] Libraries may have to rely on a blend of legal solutions to make works from their collections available online. Indeed, although ECL agreements are in my view the primary tool for enabling online use by libraries with cross-border effect, exceptions should play an important facilitating role as well. First, if a library holds digital copies that have been produced legally under an exception, be it for preservation purposes under a new exception[2980] or the current reproduction exception in Art. 5(2)(c) of the InfoSoc Directive, it should be possible to license such copies for other legal uses, such as for making the works available online under an ECL agreement. Otherwise, libraries might have to digitise the same work more than once, a regrettable waste of resources and at odds with the aim of the EU legislator to ensure economies of scale.[2981] Second, there may be a need for an exception for archive material or grey material, such as private documents or other works never made publicly available, as the requirement for representativeness under the ECL system might be difficult to establish for these types of work.[2982] However, as noted above, the newest version of the DSM proposal now assumes the proposed mechanism for licensing out-of-commerce works for use by cultural heritage institutions could also be used for unpublished

2975 See Ch. 10.
2976 Ramalho, Conceptualising, 2014, 180.
2977 See Ch. 11.3.4.
2978 See also European Parliament, Resolution, 2015, item 10; COM(2015) 626 final, Towards, 2015, 5; see also Rosén, The Nordic ECL Model, 2012, 85.
2979 Janssens and Tryggvadóttir, Facilitating, 2015, 94.
2980 See Art. 5 DSM proposal and discussion in Ch. 4.2.4.1.1.1 and 10.2.4.
2981 Guibault, Cultural, 2015, 187, 189; 2011/711/EU, Recommendation, 2011, item 4; recital (15) OWD: Triaille and others, Study, 2013, 283.
2982 See discussion in Ch. 10.1.1 and 10.2.2. See e.g. Firth and Preira, Exceptions for Libraries, 2016, 28. In the European Parliament the CULT Committee has proposed such an exception, cf. EP CULT, Draft, 2017, 17, 45.

works.[2983] Third, it should be borne in mind that although the Orphan Works Directive will not enable any large-scale use of works, it can be used for some well-defined projects. Finally, libraries may need to turn to individual licensing in some instances. For example, it is unlikely that ECL agreements would ever cover works that are highly commercial, be they old classics still in copyright or new works; nor would an exception to that effect be likely to pass the three-step test. Thus, if a library saw it to be within its remit to make such works available online with cross-border effect, the library would need to negotiate individual licences.

805. Whether the ECL system will become a worldwide phenomenon[2984] is uncertain at this stage; at the same time, it seems highly likely that it will become an EU standard. This is to be welcomed as an important step in securing wider access to the European cultural heritage in the digital age. EU legislation to underpin the ECL system would provide legal certainty on the issue of the cross-border applicability of ECL agreements for libraries. Nevertheless, I maintain that, even without such legislation, ECL agreements fulfilling the requirements set out in this work can already enable such online cross-border use. Such an interpretation would be in the public interest of access to science and culture; it would be in the interests of rightholders, who could be remunerated for use of works that would otherwise be difficult to arrange, and finally, libraries would be assisted in fulfilling their important and traditional role in the digital environment. Such an interpretation would, to use the words of Advocate General Spunzar, "adapt the law of copyright to the realities of the information society."[2985]

[2983] 2016/0280 (COD) 9134/18, Agreed negotiation mandate, 2018, Recital (25) and discussion in Ch. 11.3.1.2.

[2984] Rydén, Are digital, 2016, 17.

[2985] C-174/15 – VOB, AG opinion, par. 79.

BIBLIOGRAPHY

CASE LAW

CJEU: JUDGEMENTS IN A CHRONOLOGICAL ORDER

2017

14 June 2017, C-610/15, Stichting Brein v Ziggo BV and XS4All Internet BV, ECLI:EU:C:2017:456

26 April 2017, C-527/15, Stichting Brein v Jack Frederik Wullems, ECLI:EU:C:2017:300

2016

16 November 2016, C-301/15, Marc Soulier, Sara Doke v Ministre de la Culture et de la Communication, Premier ministre, ECLI:EU:C:2016:878

10 November 2016, C-174/15, Vereniging Openbare Bibliotheken v Stichting Leenrecht, ECLI:EU:C:2016:856

8 September 2016, C-160/15, GS Media BV v Sanoma Media Netherlands BV, Playboy Enterprises International Inc., Britt Geertruida Dekker, ECLI:EU:C:2016:644

31 May 2016, C-117/15, Reha Training Gesellschaft für Sport- und Unfallrehabilitation mbH v Gesellschaft für musikalische Aufführungs- und mechanische Vervielfältigungsrechte (GEMA), ECLI:EU:C:2016:379

2015

19 November 2015, C-325/14, SBS Belgium NV v Belgische Vereniging van Auteurs, Componisten en Uitgevers (SABAM), ECLI:EU:C:2015:764

12 November 2015, C-572/13,Hewlett-Packard Belgium SPRL v Reprobel SCRL, ECLI:EU:C:2015:750

26 March 2015, C-279/13, C More Entertainment AB v Linus Sandberg, ECLI:EU:C:2015:199

5 March 2015, C-463/12, Copydan Båndkopi v Nokia Danmark A/S, ECLI:EU:C:2015:144

22 January 2015, C-441/13, Pez Hejduk v EnergieAgentur.NRW GmbH., ECLI:EU:C:2015:28,

22 January 2015, C-419/13, Art & Allposters International BV v Stichting Pictoright, ECLI:EU:C:2015:27

2014

21 October 2014, C-348/13, BestWater International GmbH v Michael Mebes and Stefan Potsch, ECLI:EU:C:2014:2315

13 October 2014, Joined cases C-431/09 and C-432/09, Airfield NV and Canal Digitaal BV v Belgische Vereniging van Auteurs, Componisten en Uitgevers CVBA (Sabam) (C-431/09) and Airfield NV v Agicoa Belgium BVBA (C-432/09), ECLI:EU:C:2011:648

11 September 2014, C-117/13, Technische Universität Darmstadt v. Eugen Ulmer KG, ECLI:EU:C:2014:2196

3 September 2014, C-201/13, Johan Deckmyn and Vrijheidsfonds VZW v Helena Vandersteen and Others, ECLI:EU:C:2014:2132

5 June 2014, C-360/12, Coty Germany GmbH v First Note Perfumes NV, ECLI:EU:C:2014:1318

5 June 2014, C-360/13, Public Relations Consultants Association Ltd (PRCA) v Newspaper Licensing Agency Ltd and Others, ECLI:EU:C:2014:1195

10 April 2014, C-435/12, ACI Adam BV and Others v Stichting de Thuiskopie and Stichting Onderhandelingen Thuiskopie vergoeding, ECLI:EU:C:2014:254 1

27 March 2014, C-314/12, UPC Telekabel Wien GmbH v Constantin Film Verleih GmbH and Wega Filmproduktionsgesellschaft mbH, ECLI:EU:C:2014:192

27 February 2014, C-351/12, Ochranný svaz autorský pro práva k dílům hudebním, o.s. (OSA) v Léčebné lázně Mariánské Lázně a. s., ECLI:EU:C:2014:110

13 February 2014, C-466/12, Nils Svensson, Sten Sjögren, Madelaine Sahlman, Pia Gadd v Retriever Sverige AB, ECLI:EU:C:2014:76

2013

3 October 2013, C-170/12, Peter Pinckney v KDG Mediatech AG, ECLI:EU:C:2013:635

18 July 2013, C-414/11, Daiichi Sankyo Co. Ltd and Sanofi-Aventis Deutschland GmbH v DEMO Anonymos Viomichaniki kai Emporiki Etairia Farmakon, ECLI:EU:C:2013:520

11 July 2013, C-521/11, Amazon.com International Sales Inc. and Others v Austro-Mechana Gesellschaft zur Wahrnehmung mechanisch-musikalischer Urheberrechte Gesellschaft mbH, ECLI:EU:C:2013:515

7 March 2013, C-607/11, ITV Broadcasting Ltd and Others v TVCatchup Ltd., ECLI:EU:C:2013:147

7 March 2013, C-145/10, Eva-Maria Painer v Standard VerlagsGmbH and Others, ECLI:EU:C:2013:138

2012

18 October 2012, C-173/11, Football Dataco Ltd, The Scottish Premier League Ltd, The Scottish Football League, PA Sport UK Ltd v Sportradar GmbH and Sportradar AG, ECLI:EU:C:2012:642

3 July 2012, C-128/11, UsedSoft GmbH v Oracle International Corp., ECLI:EU:C:2012:407

21 June 2012, C-5/11, Criminal proceedings against Titus Alexander Jochen Donner, ECLI:EU:C:2012:370

26 April 2012, C-510/10, DR and TV2 Danmark A/S v NCB – Nordisk Copyright Bureau, ECLI:EU:C:2012:244

19 April 2012, C-461/10, Bonnier Audio AB and Others v Perfect Communication Sweden AB, ECLI:EU:C:2012:219

19 April 2012, C-523/10, Wintersteiger AG v Products 4U Sondermaschinenbau GmbH, ECLI:EU:C:2012:220,

15 March 2012, C-162/10, Phonographic Performance (Ireland) Limited v Ireland and Attorney General, ECLI:EU:C:2012:141

15 March 2012, C-135/10, SCF Consorzio Fonografici v Marco Del Corso, ECLI:EU:C:2012:140

16 February 2012, C-360/10, Belgische Vereniging van Auteurs, Componisten en Uitgevers CVBA (SABAM) v Netlog NV, ECLI:EU:C:2012:85

9 February 2012, C-277/10, Martin Luksan v Petrus van der Let, ECLI:EU:C:2012:65

17 January 2012, C-302/10, Infopaq International A/S v Danske Dagblades Forening, ECLI:EU:C:2012:16

2011

24 November 2011, C-70/10, Scarlet Extended SA v Société belge des auteurs, compositeurs et éditeurs SCRL (SABAM), ECLI:EU:C:2011:771

4 October 2011, Joined cases C-403/08 and C-429/08, Football Association Premier League Ltd and Others v QC Leisure and Others; Karen Murphy v Media Protection Services Ltd, ECLI:EU:C:2011:631

12 July 2011, C-324/09, L'Oréal SA and Others v eBay International AG and Others, ECLI:EU:C:2011:474,

30 June 2011, C-271/10, Vereniging van Educatieve en Wetenschappelijke Auteurs (VEWA) v Belgische Staat, ECLI:EU:C:2011:442

16 June 2011, C-462/09, Stichting de Thuiskopie v Opus Supplies Deutschland GmbH and Others, ECLI:EU:C:2011:397

2010

7 December 2010, Joined Cases C-585/08 and C-144/09, Peter Pammer v Reederei Karl Schlüter GmbH & Co KG (C-585/08), and Hotel Alpenhof GesmbH v Oliver Heller (C-144/09), ECLI:EU:C:2010:740

21 October 2010, C-467/08, Padawan SL v Sociedad General de Autores y Editores de España (SGAE), ECLI:EU:C:2010:620,

2009

16 July 2009, C-5/08, Infopaq International A/S v Danske Dagblades Forening, ECLI:EU:C:2009:465,

16 July 2009, C-124/08, Hauptzollamt Bremen v J. E. Tyson Parketthandel GmbH hanse j., ECLI:EU:C:2009:229,

23 April 2009, C-533/07, Falco Privatstiftung and Thomas Rabitsch v Gisela Weller-Lindhorst, ECLI:EU:C:2009:257,

19 February 2009, C-557/07, LSG-Gesellschaft zur Wahrnehmung von Leistungsschutzrechten GmbH v Tele2 Telecommunication GmbH, ECLI:EU:C:2009:107

2008

11 December 2008, C-52/07, Kanal 5 Ltd, TV 4 AB v Föreningen Svenska Tonsättares Internationella Musikbyrå (STIM), ECLI:EU:C:2008:703

17 April 2008, C-456/06, Peek & Cloppenburg KG v Cassina SpA, ECLI:EU:C:2008:232

29 January 2008, C-275/06, Productores de Música de España (Promusicae) v Telefónica de España SAU, ECLI:EU:C:2008:54

2006

7 December 2006, C-306/05, Sociedad General de Autores y Editores de España (SGAE) v Rafael Hoteles SA., ECLI:EU:C:2006:764

2005

14 July 2005, C-192/04, Lagardère Active Broadcast v. SPRE & GVL, ECLI:EU:C:2005:475

30 June 2005, C-28/04, Tod's SpA and Tod's France SARL v Heyraud SA, ECLI:EU:C:2005:418

2 June 2005, C-89/04, Mediakabel BV v Commissariaat voor de Media, ECLI:EU:C:2005:348

2003

6 February 2003, C-245/00, Stichting ter Exploitatie van Naburige Rechten (SENA) v Nederlandse Omroep Stichting (NOS), ECLI:EU:C:2003:68

1995

6 April 1995, C-241/91 P, Radio Telefis Eireann (RTE) and Independent Television Publications Ltd (ITP) v Commission of the European Communities, ECLI:EU:C:1995:98

7 March 1995, C-68/93, Fiona Shevill, Ixora Trading Inc., Chequepoint SARL and Chequepoint International Ltd v Presse Alliance SA, ECLI:EU:C:1995:61

1993

20 October 1993, C-92/92, Phil Collins v Imtrat Handelsgesellschaft mbH and Patricia Im- und Export Verwaltungsgesellschaft mbH and Leif Emanuel Kraul v EMI Electrola GmbH., ECLI:EU:C:1993:847

1982

6 October 1982, C-262/81, Coditel SA, Compagnie générale pour la diffusion de la télévision, and others v Ciné-Vog Films SA and others, ECLI:EU:C:1982:334

1980

18 March 1980, C-62/79, SA Compagnie générale pour la diffusion de la télévision, Coditel, and others v Ciné Vog Films and others, ECR 1980 881, ECLI:EU:C:1980:84

1971

8 June 1971, C-78/70, Deutsche Grammophon Gesellschaft mbH v Metro-SB-Großmärkte GmbH & Co. KG., ECLI:EU:C:1971:59

CJEU: JUDGEMENTS IN ALPHABETICAL ORDER BY NAME OF PARTIES

ACI Adam BV and Others v Stichting de Thuiskopie and Stichting Onderhandelingen Thuiskopie vergoeding, C-435/12, ECLI:EU:C:2014:254 l, 10 April 2014

Airfield NV and Canal Digitaal BV v Belgische Vereniging van Auteurs, Componisten en Uitgevers CVBA (Sabam) (C-431/09) and Airfield NV v Agicoa Belgium BVBA (C-432/09), Joined cases C-431/09 and C-432/09, ECLI:EU:C:2011:648, 13 October 2014

Amazon.com International Sales Inc. and Others v Austro-Mechana Gesellschaft zur Wahrnehmung mechanisch-musikalischer Urheberrechte Gesellschaft mbH, C-521/11 ECLI:EU:C:2013:515, 11 July 2013

Art & Allposters International BV v Stichting Pictoright, C-419/13, ECLI:EU:C:2015:27, 22 January 2015

Belgische Vereniging van Auteurs, Componisten en Uitgevers CVBA (SABAM) v Netlog NV, C-360/10, ECLI:EU:C:2012:85, 16 February 2012

BestWater International GmbH v Michael Mebes and Stefan Potsch, C-348/13, ECLI:EU:C:2014:2315, 21 October 2014

Bonnier Audio AB and Others v Perfect Communication Sweden AB, C-461/10, ECLI:EU:C:2012:219, 19 April 2012

Hauptzollamt Bremen v J. E. Tyson Parketthandel GmbH hanse j., C-124/08, ECLI:EU:C:2009:229, 16 July 2009

C More Entertainment AB v Linus Sandberg, C-279/13, ECLI:EU:C:2015:199, 26 March 2015

Technische Universität Darmstadt v. Eugen Ulmer KG, Case C-117/13, ECLI:EU:C:2014:2196, 11 September 2014

Coditel SA, Compagnie générale pour la diffusion de la télévision, and others v Ciné-Vog Films SA and others, C-262/81, ECLI:EU:C:1982:334, 6 October 1982

Copydan Båndkopi v Nokia Danmark A/S, C-463/12, ECLI:EU:C:2015:144, 5 March 2015

Coty Germany GmbH v First Note Perfumes NV, C-360/12, ECLI:EU:C:2014:1318, 5 June 2014

Criminal proceedings against Titus Alexander Jochen Donner, C-5/11, ECLI:EU:C:2012:370, 21 June 2012

Daiichi Sankyo Co. Ltd and Sanofi-Aventis Deutschland GmbH v DEMO Anonymos Viomichaniki kai Emporiki Etairia Farmakon, C-414/11, ECLI:EU:C:2013:520, 18 July 2013

Deutsche Grammophon Gesellschaft mbH v Metro-SB-Großmärkte GmbH & Co. KG., C-78/70, ECLI:EU:C:1971:59, 8 June 1971

DR and TV2 Danmark A/S v NCB – Nordisk Copyright Bureau, C-510/10, ECLI:EU:C:2012:244, 26 April 2012

Eva-Maria Painer v Standard VerlagsGmbH and Others, C-145/10, ECLI:EU:C:2013:138, 7 March 2013

Falco Privatstiftung and Thomas Rabitsch v Gisela Weller-Lindhorst, C-533/07, ECLI:EU:C:2009:257, 23 April 2009

Fiona Shevill, Ixora Trading Inc., Chequepoint SARL and Chequepoint International Ltd v Presse Alliance SA, C-68/93, ECLI:EU:C:1995:61, 7 March 1995

Football Association Premier League Ltd and Others v QC Leisure and Others; Karen Murphy v Media Protection Services Ltd, Joined cases C-403/08 and C-429/08, ECLI:EU:C:2011:631, 4 October 2011

Football Dataco Ltd, The Scottish Premier League Ltd, The Scottish Football League, PA Sport UK Ltd v Sportradar GmbH and Sportradar AG, C-173/11, ECLI:EU:C:2012:642

GS Media BV v Sanoma Media Netherlands BV, Playboy Enterprises International Inc., Britt Geertruida Dekker, C-160/15, ECLI:EU:C:2016:644, 8 September 2016

Hewlett-Packard Belgium SPRL v Reprobel SCRL, C-572/13, ECLI:EU:C:2015:750, 12 November 2015

Infopaq International A/S v Danske Dagblades Forening, C-5/08, ECLI:EU:C:2009:465, 16 July 2009

Infopaq International A/S v Danske Dagblades Forening, C-302/10, ECLI:EU:C:2012:16, 17 January 2012

ITV Broadcasting Ltd and Others v TVCatchup Ltd., C-607/11, ECLI:EU:C:2013:147, 7 March 2013

Johan Deckmyn and Vrijheidsfonds VZW v Helena Vandersteen and Others, C-201/13, ECLI:EU:C:2014:2132, 3 September 2014

Kanal 5 Ltd, TV 4 AB v Föreningen Svenska Tonsättares Internationella Musikbyrå (STIM), C-52/07, ECLI:EU:C:2008:703, 11 December 2008

L'Oréal SA and Others v eBay International AG and Others, C-324/09, ECLI:EU:C:2011:474, 12 July 2011

Lagardère Active Broadcast v. SPRE & GVL, C-192/04, ECLI:EU:C:2005:475, 14 July 2005

LSG-Gesellschaft zur Wahrnehmung von Leistungsschutzrechten GmbH v Tele2 Telecommunication GmbH, C-557/07, ECLI:EU:C:2009:107, 19 February 2009

Marc Soulier, Sara Doke v Ministre de la Culture et de la Communication, Premier ministre, C-301/15, ECLI:EU:C:2016:878, 16 November 2016

Martin Luksan v Petrus van der Let, C-277/10, ECLI:EU:C:2012:65, 9 February 2012

Mediakabel BV v Commissariaat voor de Media, C-89/04, ECLI:EU:C:2005:348, 2 June 2005

Nils Svensson, Sten Sjögren, Madelaine Sahlman, Pia Gadd v Retriever Sverige AB, C-466/12, ECLI:EU:C:2014:76, 13 February 2014

Ochranný svaz autorský pro práva k dílům hudebním, o.s. (OSA) v Léčebné lázně Mariánské Lázně a. s., C-351/12, ECLI:EU:C:2014:110, 27 February 2014

Padawan SL v Sociedad General de Autores y Editores de España (SGAE), C-467/08, ECLI:EU:C:2010:620, 21 October 2010
Peek & Cloppenburg KG v Cassina SpA, C-456/06, ECLI:EU:C:2008:232, 17 April 2008
Peter Pammer v Reederei Karl Schlüter GmbH & Co KG (C-585/08), and Hotel Alpenhof GesmbH v Oliver Heller (C-144/09), Joined Cases C-585/08 and C-144/09, ECLI:EU:C:2010:740, 7 December 2010
Peter Pinckney v KDG Mediatech AG, C-170/12, ECLI:EU:C:2013:635, 3 October 2013
Pez Hejduk v EnergieAgentur.NRW GmbH., C-441/13, ECLI:EU:C:2015:28, 22 January 2015
Phil Collins v Imtrat Handelsgesellschaft mbH and Patricia Im- und Export Verwaltungsgesellschaft mbH and Leif Emanuel Kraul v EMI Electrola GmbH., C-92/92, ECLI:EU:C:1993:847, 20 October 1993
Phonographic Performance (Ireland) Limited v Ireland and Attorney General, C-162/10 ECLI:EU:C:2012:141, 15 March 2012
Productores de Música de España (Promusicae) v Telefónica de España SAU, C-275/06, ECLI:EU:C:2008:54, 29 January 2008
Public Relations Consultants Association Ltd (PRCA) v Newspaper Licensing Agency Ltd and Others, C-360/13, ECLI:EU:C:2014:1195, 5 June 2014
Radio Telefis Eireann (RTE) and Independent Television Publications Ltd (ITP) v Commission of the European Communities, C-241/91 P, ECLI:EU:C:1995:98, 6 April 1995
Reha Training Gesellschaft für Sport- und Unfallrehabilitation mbH v Gesellschaft für musikalische Aufführungs- und mechanische Vervielfältigungsrechte (GEMA), C-117/15, ECLI:EU:C:2016:379, 31 May 2016
SA Compagnie générale pour la diffusion de la télévision, Coditel, and others v Ciné Vog Films and others, C-62/79, ECR 1980 881, ECLI:EU:C:1980:84, 18 March 1980
SBS Belgium NV v Belgische Vereniging van Auteurs, Componisten en Uitgevers (SABAM), C-325/14, ECLI:EU:C:2015:764, 19 November 2015
Scarlet Extended SA v Société belge des auteurs, compositeurs et éditeurs SCRL (SABAM), C-70/10, ECLI:EU:C:2011:771, 24 November 2011
SCF Consorzio Fonografici v Marco Del Corso, C-135/10, ECLI:EU:C:2012:140, 15 March 2012
Sociedad General de Autores y Editores de España (SGAE) v Rafael Hoteles SA., C-306/05, ECLI:EU:C:2006:764, 7 December 2006
Stichting Brein v Jack Frederik Wullems, C-527/15, ECLI:EU:C:2017:300, 26 April 2017
Stichting Brein v Ziggo BV and XS4All Internet BV, C-610/15, ECLI:EU:C:2017:456, 14 June 2017
Stichting de Thuiskopie v Opus Supplies Deutschland GmbH and Others, C-462/09, ECLI:EU:C:2011:397, 16 June 2011
Stichting ter Exploitatie van Naburige Rechten (SENA) v Nederlandse Omroep Stichting (NOS), C-245/00, ECLI:EU:C:2003:68, 6 February 2003
Tod's SpA and Tod's France SARL v Heyraud SA, C-28/04, ECLI:EU:C:2005:418, 30 June 2005
UPC Telekabel Wien GmbH v Constantin Film Verleih GmbH and Wega Filmproduktionsgesellschaft mbH C-314/12 ECLI:EU:C:2014:192, 27 March 2014
UsedSoft GmbH v Oracle International Corp., C-128/11, ECLI:EU:C:2012:407, 3 July 2012
Vereniging Openbare Bibliotheken v Stichting Leenrecht, C-174/15, ECLI:EU:C:2016:856, 10 November 2016

Vereniging van Educatieve en Wetenschappelijke Auteurs (VEWA) v Belgische Staat, C-271/10, ECLI:EU:C:2011:442, 30 June 2011
Wintersteiger AG v Products 4U Sondermaschinenbau GmbH, C-523/10, ECLI:EU:C:2012:220, 19 April 2012

CJEU: OPINIONS OF ADVOCATE GENERALS

Coty Germany GmbH v First Note Perfumes NV, C-360/12, ECLI:EU:C:2013:764, 21 November 2013
Criminal proceedings against Titus Donner, C-5/11, ECLI:EU:C:2012:195, 29 March 2012
Football Association Premier League Ltd and Others v QC Leisure and Others; Karen Murphy v Media Protection Services Ltd, Joined cases C-403/08 and C-429/08, ECLI:EU:C:2011:43
Football Dataco Ltd, The Scottish Premier League Ltd, The Scottish Football League, PA Sport UK Ltd v Sportradar GmbH and Sportradar AG, Case C-173/11, ECLI:EU:C:2012:377, 3 February 2011
Marc Soulier, Sara Doke v Ministre de la Culture et de la Communication, Premier ministre, C-301/15, ECLI:EU:C:2016:536, 7 July 2016
Ochranný svaz autorský pro práva k dílům hudebním, o.s. (OSA) v Léčebné lázně Mariánské Lázně a. s., C-351/12, ECLI:EU:C:2013:749, 14 November 2013
Peter Pinckney v KDG Mediatech AG, C-170/12, ECLI:EU:C:2013:635, 13 June 2013
Pez Hejduk v EnergieAgentur.NRW GmbH., C-441/13, ECLI:EU:C:2014:2212, 11 September 2014
Stichting de Thuiskopie v Opus Supplies Deutschland GmbH and Others, C-462/09, ECLI:EU:C:2011:397, 10 March 2011
Vereniging Openbare Bibliotheken v Stichting Leenrecht, C-174/15, ECLI:EU:C:2016:459, 16 June 2016

Germany

Joseph Beuys Werke, I ZR 24/92 IIC 1995, 26(4), 573–578 (German Federal Court of Justice (BGH))

Sweden

Bildkonst Upphovsrätt i Sverige (BUS) v. Konstnärernas Intresseförening för droit de suite upphovsrätt í Sverige, DUR NJA 2000 s 445 (Supreme Court (Högsta Domstolen))

USA

USDC SDNY

Authors Guild v. Google Inc., Amended Settlement Agreement, Case No 05 CV 8136-DC

Authors Guild v. Google, Inc., Class Action Complaint, No 05 CV 8136
Authors Guild, Inc. v. Google Inc., Amended Settlement Agreement, Case No 05 CV 8136-JES
Authors Guild, Inc. v. Google Inc., Opinion on ASA Case No 05 CV 8136-JES
Authors Guild, Inc. v. Google Inc., Settlement Agreement Case No 05 CV 8136-JES
The Authors Guild v Hathitrust, 11 CV 6351 (HB)
The Authors Guild v. HathiTrust, (Settlement) 11 Civ 6351 (NRB)
The Authors Guild, Inc. et al v. Google Inc., 05 Civ 8136
McGraw Hill Cos. v. Google Inc., Complaint, No 05 CV 8881

USCA for the Second Circuit

Authors Guild v. HathiTrust 12–4547-cv
Authors Guild, Inc. v. Google Inc. 13–4829-cv

Supreme Court of the United States

Campbell v. Acuff-Rose Music, Inc. 510 US 569 (1994)

LITERATURE

Agate J, 'Jurisdiction in the Context of internet Publication' 2012 Journal of Intellectual Property Law & Practice 241–243

Aplin T, 'A global digital register for the preservation and access to cultural heritage: problems, challenges and possibilities' in Derclaye E (ed), *Copyright and Cultural Heritage; Preservation and Access to Works in a Digital World* (Edward Elgar 2010) 3–27

Argyri Panezi, 'Legal challenges for online digital libraries' (Internet, Law & Politics; A Decade of Transformations, Barcelona, Spain 2014)

Arnold R and Rosati E, 'Are National Courts the Addressees of the InfoSoc Three-Step Test?' 2015 Journal of Intellectual Property Law & Practice 741–749

Axhamn J and Guibault L, 'Solving Europeana's mass-digitization issues through Extended Collective Licensing?' 2011 NIR 509

Axhamn J and Guibault L, *Cross-border extended collective licensing: a solution to online dissemination of Europe's cultural heritage?* (IVIR 2011)

Axhamn J, 'Exceptions, limitations and collective management of rights as vehicles for access to information' in Beldiman D (ed), *Access to Information and Knowledge 21st Century Challenges in Intellectual Property and Knowledge Governance: 21st Century Challenges in Intellectual Property and Knowledge Governance* (Edward Elgar 2013)

Baker D and Evans W, 'Digital Libraries economics: the environment' in Baker D and Evans W (eds), *Digital library economics: an academic perspective* (Chandos 2009)

Band J, 'The Long and Winding Road to the Google Books Settlement' 2009 Review of Intellectual Property Law 227–329

Band J, *User Guide to the Marrakesh Treaty* (The Library Copyright Alliance 2013)

Barber NW, 'The limited modesty of subsidiarity' 2005 European Law Journal 308–325

Bechtold S, 'Directive 2001/29/EC – Information Society Directive' in Dreier T and Hugenholtz PB (eds), *Concise European Copyright Law* (2 edn, Wolters Kluwer 2016)

Belder L, 'Friends or foes? Two ways of thinking on the relation between the tasks of cultural heritage institutions and the protection of copyright' in Derclaye E (ed), *Copyright and Cultural Heritage; Preservation and Access to Works in a Digital World* (Edward Elgar 2010)

Benkler Y, 'From consumers to users: shifting the deeper structures of regulation toward sustainable commons and user access' 2000 Federal Communications Law Journal 561–579

Bently L, 'Harmonization by Stealth: The Role of the ECJ' (CRID/Ivir Conference, Ten Years after the EU Directive on Copyright in the Information Society: Locking Back and Looking Forward, Brussels 2012)

Berger C, 'Aktuelle Entwicklungen im Urheberrechts – Der EuGH bestimmt die Richtung' 2012 ZUM 353–432

Bergström S, '"Program för upphovsrätten", originally published in Rättsvetenskapliga studier ägnade minnet av Phillips Hult, Acta Universitatis Upsaliensis, Studia Iuridica Upsaliensia 2, Uppsala 1960, 58–83', 2011 NIR 143

Besek JM, 'The development of digital libraries in the United States' in Bently L, Suthersanen U and Torremans P (eds), *Global Copyright; Three Hundred Years since the Statute of Anne, from 1709 to Cyberspace* (Edward Elgar 2010)

Blake J, 'On defining the cultural heritage' 2000 International and Comparative Law Quarterly 61–85

Borghi M and Karapapa S, *Copyright and Mass Digitization* (OUP 2013)

Borghi M, Erickson K and Favale M, 'With Enough Eyeballs All Searches Are Diligent: Mobilizing the Crowd in Copyright Clearance for Mass Digitization' 2016 Chicago-Kent Journal of Intellectual Property 135–166

Boulanger J and others, *Assessing the economic impacts of adapting certain limitations and exceptions to copyright and related rights in the EU – Analysis of specific policy options* (CRA 2014)

Brindley L, Dame, 'Foreword, Digital Libraries economics: an introduction' in Baker D and Evans W (eds), *Digital library economics: an academic perspective* (Chandos 2009)

Brindley L, Dame, 'Phoenixes in the internet era – the changing role of libraries' in Bently L, Suthersanen U and Torremans P (eds), *Global Copyright: Three Hundred Years Since the Statute of Anne, from 1709 to Cyberspace* (2nd edn, Edward Elgar 2010)

Budylin S and Osipova Y, 'Is AllofMP3 Legal? Non-Contractual Licensing Under Russian Copyright Law' 2007 Journal of High Technology Law 1–17

Bulayenko O, 'Permissibility of Non-Voluntary Collective Management of Copyright under EU Law – The Case of the French Law on Out-of-Commerce Books' 2016 JIPITEC 51–68

Canat J-F, Guibault L and Logeais E, *Study on copyright limitations and exceptions for museums* (WIPO 2015)

Carr R, 'A history of digital library economics' in Baker D and Evans W (eds), *Digital library economics: an academic perspective* (Chandos 2009)

Carroll MW, 'Creative Commons and the New Intermediaries' 2006 Michigan State Law Review 45–65

Christiansen HL, 'The Nordic licensing systems – extended collective agreement licensing' 1991 EIPR 346–349

Christie AF, 'Maximising Permissible Exceptions to Intellectual Property Rights' in Kur A and Mizaras V (eds), *The Structure of Intellectual Property Law: Can One Size Fit All?* (Edward Elgar 2011)

Christophe Geiger and others, *Reaction of the CEIPI to the Resolution on the Implementation of Directive 2001/29/EC on the Harmonisation of Copyright in the Information Society adopted by the European Parliament on the 9th July 2015* (CEIPI 2015)

Crews K, *Study on Copyright Limitations and Exceptions for Libraries and Archives* (WIPO 2008)

Crews K, *Study on Copyright Limitations and Exceptions for Libraries and Archives* (WIPO 2014)

Deazley R and Stobo V, *Archives and Copyright: Risk and Reform* (Archives and Copyright, 2013)

Delos, *The DELOS Digital Library Reference Model Foundations for Digital Libraries* (2007)

Depreeuw S and Hubin J-B, *Study on the making available right and its relationship with the reproduction right in cross-border digital transmissions* (De Wolf&Partners 2014)

Derclaye E (ed) *Copyright and Cultural Heritage; preservation and access to works in a digital world* (Edward Elgar 2010)

Derclaye E, 'The Database Directive' in Stamatoudi I and Torremans P (eds), *EU Copyright Law; A Commentary* (Edward Elgar 2014)

Dinwoodie GB, 'Conflicts and International Copyright Litigation: The Role of International Norms' in Basedow J and others (eds), *Intellectual Property in the Conflict of Laws* (2005)

Dreier T and Hugenholtz PB (eds), *Concise European Copyright Law* (1 edn, Kluwer Law International 2006)

Dreier T and Hugenholtz PB, 'Agreement on Trade-Related Aspects of Intellectual Property Rights (TRIPS)' in Dreier T and Hugenholtz PB (eds), *Concise European Copyright Law* (2 edn, Wolters Kluwer 2016)

Dreier T and others, 'Museen, Bibliotheken und Archive in der Europäischen Union; Plädoyer für die Schaffung des notwendigen urheberrechtlichen Freiraums' 2012 ZUM 273–281

Dreier T, 'Berne Convention for the Protection of Literary and Artistic Works' in Dreier T and Hugenholtz PB (eds), *Concise European Copyright Law* (2 edn, Wolters Kluwer 2016)

Dreier T, 'Satellite and Cable Directive' in Walter MM and von Lewinski S (eds), *European Copyright Law, A Commentary* (Oxford University Press 2010)

Drexl J and others, *Comments of the Max Planck Institute for Intellectual Property and Competition Law on the Proposal for a Directive of the European Parliament and of the Council on collective management of copyright and related rights and multi-territorial licensing of rights in musical works for online uses in the internal market, 11.7.2012, COM(2012) 372/2* (Max Planck Institute 2013)

Drexl J, 'Competition in the field of collective management: preferring "creative competition" to allocative efficiency in European copyright law' in Torremans P (ed), *Copyright Law A Handbook of Contemporary Research* (Edward Elgar 2008)

Dryden J, 'Copyright Exceptions: an archivist's perspective' 2017, (4), WIPO Magazine, 16–19

Durantaye Kdl, 'Orphan works: A comparative and international perspective' in Gervais DJ (ed), *International Intellectual Property; A Handbook of Contemporary Research* (Edward Elgar 2015)

Dusollier S and Colin C, 'Peer-to-Peer File Sharing and Copyright: What Could Be the Role of Collective Management?' 2011 Colum JL & Arts 809–835

Dusollier S, *Scoping Study on Copyright and Related Rights and the Public Domain,* (*WIPO* 2010)

Dworkin G, 'Exceptions to copyright exclusivity: Article 9(2) (Berne) and Article 13 (TRIPS): what is fair use in the new international order' in Hansen HC (ed), *International Intellectual Property Law and Policy*, vol 4 (2000)

Eechoud Mv and others, *Harmonizing European Copyright Law: The Challenges of Better Lawmaking* (Kluwer Law International 2009)

Egloff W, 'Extended Collective Licenses – ein Modell auch für die Schweiz?' 2014 sic! Zeitschrift für Immaterialgüter-, Informations- und Wettbewerbsrecht 671–686

Einarsson Á, *Hagræn áhrif ritlistar (E. The economic effect of penmanship)* (Háskólinn á Bifröst 2014)

European Max Planck Group on Conflict of Laws in Intellectual Property, *Conflict of Laws in Intellectual Property: The CLIP Principles and Commentary* (Oxford University Press 2013)

Fauvarque-Cosson B and Mazeaud D (eds), *European Contract Law – Materials for a Common Frame of Reference: Terminology, Guiding Principles, Model Rules* (Sellier 2008)

Favale M, Kretschmer M and Torremans P, 'Is there a EU copyright jurisprudence? An empirical analysis of the workings of the European Court of Justice ' 2016 Modern Law Review 31–75

Favale M, Schroff S and Bertoni A, *Requirements for Diligent Search in the United Kingdom, the Netherlands, and Italy* (EnDOW 2016)

Fawcett J and Torremans P, *Intellectual Property and Private International Law* (Oxford University Press 2011)

Ficsor M, 'Collective Management and Multi-territorial Licensing: Key Issues of the Transposition of Directive 2014/26/EU' in Stamatoudi I (ed), *New Developments in EU and International Copyright Law* (Wolters Kluwer 2016)

Ficsor M, 'Collective Management of Copyright and Related Rights from the Viewpoint of International Norms and the Acquis Communautaire' in Gervais D (ed), *Collective management of Copyright and Related Rights* (2 edn, Kluwer Law International 2010)

Ficsor M, 'Collective Rights Management from the Viewpoint of International Treaties, with Special Attention to the EU 'Acquis'' in Gervais D (ed), *Collective Management of Copyright and Related Rights* (3 edn, Wolters Kluwer 2016)

Ficsor M, 'The Right of Communication (and Making Available) to the Public in the Light of the Case Law of the Court of Justice of the E.U.' in Stamatoudi I (ed), *Copyright and the Digital Agenda for Europe: Current Challenges for the Future* (Sakkoulas Publications 2015)

Ficsor M, *Guide to the copyright and related rights treaties administered by WIPO and glossary of copyright and related rights terms* (WIPO 2003)

Ficsor M, *The Law of Copyright and the Internet; The 1996 WIPO Treaties, their Interpretation and Implementation* (Oxford University Press 2002)

Firth A and Preira B, 'Exceptions for Libraries and Archives' in Stamatoudi IA (ed), *New Developments in EU and International Copyright Law* (Wolters Kluwer 2016)

Foged T, 'Danish Licences for Europe' 2015 EIPR 15–21

Geiger C and others, 'Declaration: A Balanced Interpretation of the "Three-Step Test" in Copyright Law' 2010 JIPITEC 119–122

Geiger C and others, 'The Information Society Directive' in Stamatoudi I and Torremans P (eds), *EU Copyright Law; A Commentary* (Edward Elgar 2014)

Geiger C and others, *Reaction of CEIPI to the Resolution on the Implementation of Directive 2001/29/EC on the Harmonisation of Copyright in the Information Society adopted by the European Parliament on the 9th July 2015* (CEIPI 2015)

Geiger C, 'Copyright and Free Access to Information: For a Fair Balance of Interests in a Globalised World' 2006 EIPR 366–373

Geiger C, 'Promoting Creativity through Copyright Limitations: Reflections on the Concept of Exclusivity in Copyright Law' 2010 Vanderbilt Journal of Entertainment and Technology Law 515–548

Geiger C, 'The Role of the Three-step Test in the Adaption of Copyright law to the Information Society' 2007 UNESCO e-Copyright Bulletin 1–21

Geiger C, Gervais D and Senftleben MRF, 'Understanding the "three-step test" ' in Gervais D (ed), *International Intellectual Property: A Handbook of Contemporary Research* (Edward Elgar 2015)

Gendreau Y, 'What's in a Name? Extended Collective Licences in Canada' in Karnell G (ed), *Liber Amicorum Jan Rosén* (eddy.se ab 2016)

Gera M, 'Extended collective licensing under the new Slovak Copyright Act' 2016 Journal of Intellectual Property Law & Practice 170–171

Gervais D, 'Collective Management of Copyright: Theory and Practice in the Digital Age' in Gervais D (ed), *Collective Management of Copyright and Related Rights* (3 edn, Wolters Kluwer 2016)

Gervais D, 'Collective Mangement of Copyright: Theory and Practice in the Digital Age' in Gervais D (ed), *Collective management of Copyright and Related Rights* (2nd edn, Kluwer Law International 2010)

Gervais D, 'Extended Collective Licensing: A Significant Contribution to International Copyright Law and Policy' in Karnell G (ed), *Liber Amicorum Jan Rosén* (eddy.se ab 2016)

Gervais D, *Application of an Extended Collective Licensing Regime in Canada: Principles and Issues Related to Implementation* (University of Ottawa 2003)

Gervais D, *Collective Management of Copyright and Neighbouring Rights in Canada: An International Perspective* (The Department of Canadian Heritage 2001)

Ginsburg J and Treppoz E, *International Copyright Law: U.S. and EU Perspectives; Text and Cases* (Edward Elgar 2015)

Ginsburg J, '"With Untired Spirits and Formal Constancy": Berne-Compatibility of Formal Declaratory Measures to Enhance Title-Searching ' 2013 Berkeley Technology Law Journal 1583–1622

Ginsburg J, 'A Tale of Two Copyrights: Literary Property in Revolutionary France and America' in Sherman B and Strowel A (eds), *Of Authors and Origins* (Clarendon Press 1994)

Ginsburg J, 'Berne-Forbidden Formalities and Mass Digitization' 2016 Boston University Law Review 745–775

Ginsburg J, 'Fair Use for Free, or Permitted-but-paid' 2014 Berkeley Technology Law Journal 1383–1446

Ginsburg J, 'The (New?) Right of Making Avalable to the Public' 2004 Columbia Law and Economics Working Paper No 481 1–12

Ginsburg J, 'Toward Supranational Copyright Law? The WTO Panel Decision and the "Three-step-Test" for Copyright Exceptions' 2001 The Center for Law and Economic Studies, Working Paper No 181, Columbia University Public Law & Legal Theory, Research Paper Series

Ginsburg J, "Une chose publique'? The author's domain and the public domain in early British, French and US copyright law' in Torremans P (ed), *Copyright Law: A Handbook of Contemporary Research* (Edward Elgar 2007)

Ginsburg JC and Sirinelli P, 'Google Book Search: Les enjeux internationaux pour le droit d'auteur ' 2010 La Semaine Juridique Edition Générale 486

Ginsburg JC, 'Berne Without Borders: Geographic Indiscretion and Digital Communications (The Stephen Stewart Memorial Lecture 2001)' 2002 IPQ

Ginsburg JC, *Internet publication and U.S. copyright imperialism (ALAI: USA report)* (2011)

Goldstein P and Hugenholtz B, *International Copyright; Principles, Law, and Practice* (2 edn, Oxford University Press 2010)

Goldstein P and Hugenholtz B, *International Copyright; Principles, Law, and Practice* (3 edn, Oxford University Press 2013)

Gomard B, Pedersen HVG and Ørgaard A, *Almindelig kotraktsret* (3 edn, 2009)

Gorman RA, Ginsburg JC and Reese RA, *Copyright; Cases and Materials* (8 edn, Foundation Press 2011)

Gotzen F, 'Copyright in Europe: quo vadis?' 2007 Revue Internationale du Droit d'Auteur 2–89

Gotzen F, 'Multi-territorial licences between judge and legislator. From the "CISAC" cases to Directive 2014/26' 2014 Revue Internationale du Droit d'Auteur 94–161

Graeme B. Dinwoodie, 'Developing a Private International Intellectual Property Law: The Demise of Territoriality?' 2009 William & Mary L Rev 711–800

Griffiths J, 'Unsticking the centre-piece–The liberation of European copyright law?' 2010 JIPITEC 87–95

Guibault L and Hugenholtz PB, *Study on the conditions applicable to contracts relating to intellectual property in the European Union* (IVIR 2002)

Guibault L and others, *Study on the Implementation and Effect in Member States' Laws of Directive 2001/29/EC on the Harmonisation of Certain Aspects of Copyright and Related Rights in The Information Society. Part I; The Impact of Directive 2001/29/EC on Online Business Models* (IVIR 2007)

Guibault L and Quintais JP, 'Copyright, technology and the exploitation of audiovisual works in the EU' in *The Influence of New Technologies on Copyright, IRIS plus 2014-4* (2014) 7–22

Guibault L and van Gompel S, 'Collective Management in the European Union' in Gervais D (ed), *Collective Management of Copyright and Related Rights* (3 edn, Wolters Kluwer 2016)

Guibault L, 'Collective Rights Management Directive' in Stamatoudi I and Torremans P (eds), *EU Copyright Law; A Commentary* (Edward Elgar 2014)

Guibault L, 'Contracts and Copyright Exemptions' in Hugenholtz PB (ed), *Copyright and Electronic Commerce, Legal Aspect of Electronic Copyright Management* (Wolters Kluwer 2000)

Guibault L, 'Copyright Limitations and Contracts. An Analysis of the Contractual Overridability of Limitations on Copyright' (University of Amsterdam, PhD, 2002)

Guibault L, 'Cultural Heritage Online? Settle It in the Country of Origin of the Work' 2015 JIPITEC 173–191

Guibault L, 'Evaluating Directive 2001/29/EC in the Light of Digital Public Domain' in Melanie Dulong de Rosnay and Juan Carlos De Martin (eds), *The Digital Public Domain: Foundations for an Open Culture* (Open Book Publishers 2008)

Guibault L, 'Orphan Works Directive' in Dreier T and Hugenholtz PB (eds), *Concise European Copyright Law* (2 edn, Wolters Kluwer 2016)

Guibault L, 'The nature and scope of limitations and exceptions to copyright and neighbouring rights with regard to general interest missions for the transmission of knowledge: prospects for their adaptation to the digital environment' 2003 e-Copyright Bulletin 1–45

Guibault L, 'Why cherry-picking never leads to harmonisation: The case of limitations on copyright under Directive 2001/29/EC' 2010 JIPITEC 55–66

Guibault L, *D5.4: Report on the effectiveness of licensing systems for clearing content for Europeana use* (Europeana 2015)

Handke C and Towse R, 'Economics of Copyright Collecting Societies' 2007 IIC 937–957

Handke C, 'Collective Administration' in Watt R (ed), *Handbook on the Economics of Copyright: A Guide for Students and Teachers* (Edward Elgar 2014)

Hilty RM and others, *Stellungsname des Max-Planck-Institut für Immaterialgüter- und Wettbewerbsrecht zur Anfrage des Bundesministeriums der Justiz vom 6. Juli 2011; Zum Richtlinienvorschlag der Europäischen Kommission über bestimmte zulässige Formen der Nutzung verwaister Werke, KOM(2011)289* (Max Planck Institute 2011)

Hugenholtz and others, *Extended collective licensing: panacee voor massadigitalisering? Onderzoek in opdracht van het Ministerie van OCW* (IVIR 2014)

Hugenholtz B and Okediji RL, *Conceiving an international instrument on limitations and exceptions to copyright* (IVIR 2008)

Hugenholtz B and others, *The Recasting of Copyright & Related Rights for the Knowledge Economy; final report* (IVIR 2006)

Hugenholtz B, 'Copyright without frontiers: the problem of territoriality in European copyright law ' in Derclaye E (ed), *Research Handbook on the Future of EU Copyright* (Edward Elgar 2009)

Hugenholtz B, 'Harmonization or Unification of EU Copyright Law' in Axhamn J (ed), *Copyright in a Borderless Online Environment* (Norstedts Juridik 2012)

Hugenholtz B, 'The Dutch case for flexibility' in Hugenholtz B and Hargeaves I (eds), *Intellectual Property and Innovation* (2012)

Hugenholtz PB and Senftleben MRF, *Fair Use in Europe. In Search of Flexibilities* (IViR 2011)

Hugenholtz PB and van Velze, 'Communication to a new public? Three reasons why EU copyright law can do without a "new public"' 2016 IIC 797–815

Husovec M, 'Comment on "Pinckney"' 2014 IIC 370–374

Iglesias M, 'Digital libraries: any step forward?' 2008 Auteurs & Média 345–363

Jans JH, 'Proportionality Revisited' 2000 Legal Issues of Economic Integration 239–265

Janssens M-C and Tryggvadóttir R 'Orphan works, out-of-commerce works and making the European cultural heritage available: 'are we nearly there yet'?' in Stamatoudi I (ed), *New Developments in EU and International Copyright Law* (Wolters Kluwer 2016)

Janssens M-C and Tryggvadóttir R, 'Facilitating access to orphan and out-of-commerce works to make Europe's cultural resources available to the broader public' in Stamatoudi I (ed), *Copyright and the Digital Agenda for Europe: Current Challenges for the Future* (Sakkoulas Publications 2015)

Janssens M-C, "'If your books are not online, they are invisible' Gütenberg versus Google, Kritische kijk op de 'Google Books Settlement'" 2010 TORB 206–222

Janssens M-C, 'The Issue of Exceptions: Reshaping the Keys to the Gates in the Territory of Literary, Musical and Artistic Creation' in Derclaye E (ed), *Research Handbook On The Future Of EU Copyright* (Edward Elgar 2009)

Janssens M-C, 'The notion of the work and its place in the massive flow of information' 2001 NIR 87–108

Janssens M-C, 'The Software Directive' in Stamatoudi I and Torremans P (eds), *EU Copyright Law; A Commentary* (Edward Elgar 2014)

Karapapa S, 'The requirement for a "new public" in EU copyright law' 2017 European Law Review 63–81

Karnell G, 'Extended Collective License Systems, Provisions, Agreements and Clauses – A Nordic Copyright Invention with an International Future? ' in *Essays in honour of George Koumantos* (2004)

Karnell G, 'Outsiders' Rights: A Dilemma for Collective Administration of Authors' Rights in a Present and Enlarged European Community' 1991 EIPR 430–435

Karnell G, 'The Swedish implementation of the European Infosoc-Directive' 2006 RIDA 161–233

Keller P, Guibault L and Pfeiffer P, 'Discussion Paper' (4th Europeana Licensing Workshop, Luxembourg 2015)

Kerremans R, Janssen K and Valcke P, 'Collective solutions for cultural collections online: Search and select!' 2011 Journal of Intellectual Property Law & Practice 638–650

Klass N and Rupp H, 'EUROPEANA, ARROW and Orphan Works: Bringing Europe's Cultural Heritage Online' in Stamatoudi I and Torremans P (eds), *EU Copyright Law; A Commentary* (Edward Elgar 2014)

Klimpel P, *Copyright Law, Practice and Fiction: Rights clearance for cultural heritage in the digital age with examples from the audiovisual sector* (National Library Luxembourg/ Europeana 2013)

Kono T (ed) *Intellectual Property and Private International Law: Comparative Perspectives* (Hart 2012)

Koskinen-Olsson T and Lowe N, *Management of Copyright and Related Rights; Module 1: General aspects of collective management* (WIPO 2012)

Koskinen-Olsson T and Sigurðardóttir V, 'Collective Management in the Nordic Countries' in Gervais D (ed), *Collective Management of Copyright and Related Rights* (3 edn, Wolters Kluwer 2016)

Koskinen-Olsson T, 'Collective Management in the Nordic Countries' in Gervais D (ed), *Collective Management of Copyright and Related Rights* (2 edn, Kluwer Law International 2010)

Koskinen-Olsson T, *Collective management in reprography* (WIPO/IFRRO 2005)

Kretschmer M and et al., 'The European Commission's public consultation on the review of EU copyright rules: a response by the CREATe Centre' 2014 EIPR 547–553

Kur A and Schovsbo J, 'Expropriation or fair game for all? The gradual dismantling of the IP exclusivity paradigm' in *Max Planck Institute for Intellectual Property, Competition & Tax Law Research Paper Series No 09-14* (2009)

Kur A, 'Limitations and Exceptions Under the Three-Step-Test – How Much Room to Walk the Middle Ground?' in Kur A (ed), *Intellectual Property Rights In A Fair World Trade System; Proposals for Reform of TRIPS* (Edward Elgar 2011)

Kur A, 'Of Oceans, Islands, and Inland Water – How Much Room for Exceptions and Limitations Under the Three-Step Test?' 2008 Richmond Journal of Global Law & Business 287–350

Kyst M, 'Aftalelicens – Quo Vadis?' 2009 NIR 44–55

Lando O and Beale H, *Principles of European Contract Law: Parts I and II* (Kluwer Law International 1999)

Langus G, Neven D and Poukens S, *Economic Analysis of the Territoriality of the Making Available Right in the EU* (Charles River Associates 2014)

Law D, 'Digital library economics: aspects and prospects' in Baker D and Evans W (eds), *Digital library economics: an academic perspective* (Chandos 2009)

Liedes J, *Memorandum on the Extended Collective Licence* (Digitisation of Cultural Material, Digital Libraries and Copyright, Madrid, Spain 2010)

Lipinski TA, 'Toward a Functional Understanding of Fair Use in U.S. Copyright Law' 2011 Annual Review of Information Science and Technology 523–621

Loos MBM and others, *Analysis of the applicable legal frameworks and suggestions for the contours of a model system of consumer protection in relation to digital content contracts* (University of Amsterdam 2011)

Lucas A, 'Applicable law in copyright infringement cases in the digital environment' 2005 e-Copyright Bulletin 1–14

Matulionyte R, 'Cross-Border Collective Management and Principle of Territoriality: Problems and Possible Solutions in the EU' 2009 The Journal of World Intellectual Property 467–497

Matulionyte R, 'Enforcing Copyright Infringement Online; In Search of Balanced Private International Rules' 2015 JIPITEC 132–145

Matulionyte R, 'Law Applicable To Copyright Infringements in the ALI and CLIP Proposals: A Rebalance of Interests Needed?' 2011 JIPITEC 26–36

Matulionyte R, *Law Applicable To Copyright: A Comparison of the ALI and CLIP Proposals* (Edward Elgar 2011)

Mendis D and Stobo V, 'Extended Collective Licensing in the UK – One Year On: A Review of the Law and a Look Ahead to the Future' 2016 EIPR 208–220

Moscoso A, 'Cross-Border Issues in Collective Management' 2011 Columbia Journal of Law & the Arts 651–656

Nérisson S, 'The Rental and Lending Rights Directive' in Stamatoudi I and Torremans P (eds), *EU Copyright Law; A Commentary* (Edward Elgar 2014)

Nyh T, 'Rättighetsklarering vid film- och TV-utnyttjanden; TV- och sat/cab direktivens genomslag i praktiken' 1996 NIR 191–195

Ohly A, 'Choice of Law in the Digital Environment – Problems and Possible Solutions' in Drexl J and Kur A (eds), *Intellectual Property and Private International Law – Heading for the Future* (Hart 2005)

Ohly A, 'Economic rights' in Derclaye E (ed), *Research Handbook on the Future of EU Copyright* (Edward Elgar 2009)

Olsson H, *Copyright: Svensk och internationell upphovsrätt* (7 edn, Norstedts Juridik 2006) 3

Olsson H, *Upphovsrättslagstiftningen: En kommentar* (2 edn, Norstedts Gula Bibliotek 2006)

Oostveen MAA and Guibault L, *Summary report on IPR issues faced by Europeana and its partners* (Europeana 2013)

Otero García-Castrillón C, 'Choice of law in IP: rounding off territoriality' in Torremans P (ed), *Research Handbook on Cross-border Enforcement of Intellectual Property* (Edward Elgar 2014)

Padfield T, 'Preserving and accessing our cultural heritage – issues for cultural sector institutions: archives, libraries, museums and galleries' in Derclaye E (ed), *Copyright and Cultural Heritage; Preservation and Access to Works in a Digital World* (Edward Elgar 2010)

Peifer K-N, 'Das Territorialitatsprinzip im Europaischen Gemeinschaftsrecht vor dem Hintergrund der technischen Entwicklungen' 2006 ZUM 1–8

Peters M, 'The amended Google Book Settlement: Judge Chin's decision' 2011 WIPO Magazine 9–11

Peukert A, 'Individual, Multiple and Collective Ownership of Intellectual Property Rights – Which Impact on Exclusivity?' in Kur A and Mizaras V (eds), *The Structure of Intellectual Property Law: Can One Size Fit All?* (Edward Elgar 2011)

Peukert A, 'Territoriality and Extraterritoriality in Intellectual Property Law' in Handl G and Zekoll J (eds), *Beyond Territoriality: Transnational Legal Authority in an Age of Globalization, Queen Mary Studies in International Law* (Brill Academic Publishing 2011)

Poole N, *The Cost of Digitising Europe's Cultural Heritage: A Report for the Comité des Sages of the European Commission* (2010)

Ramalho A, 'Conceptualising the European Union's Competence in Copyright – What Can the EU Do?' 2014 IIC 178–200

Reinbothe J and Von Lewinski S, *The WIPO Treaties on Copyright* (2 edn, Oxford University Press 2015)

Reinbothe J, 'Collective Management in Germany' in Gervais D (ed), *Collective Management of Copyright and Related Rights* (2 edn, Kluwer Law International 2010)

Ricketson S and Ginsburg J, 'The Berne Convention: Historical and institutional aspects' in Gervais D (ed), *International Intellectual Property: A Handbook of Contemporary Research* (Edward Elgar 2015)

Ricketson S and Ginsburg JC, *International Copyright and Neighbouring Rights – the Berne Convention and Beyond* (2 edn, Oxford 2006)

Ricketson S, *The Berne Convention for the protection of Literary and Artistic Works: 1886–1986* (Kluwer Law International 1987)

Ricketson S, *The three-step test, deemed quantities, libraries, and closed exceptions* (Centre for Copyright Studies 2003)

Ricketson S, *WIPO Study on Limitations and Exceptions of Copyright and Related Rights in the Digital Environment* (WIPO 2008)

Ricketson S, *WIPO Study on Limitations and Exceptions of Copyright and Related Rights in the Digital Environment* (WIPO 2003)

Ricolfi M, 'Individual and collective management of copyright in a digital environment' in Torremans P (ed), *Copyright Law A Handbook of Contemporary Research* (Edward Elgar 2008)

Rightscom, *The Economic and Social Impact of the Public Domain: Executive Summary Report* (2010)

Riis T and Schovsbo J, 'Extended Collective Licenses and the Nordic Experience: It's a Hybrid but is it a VOLVO or a Lemon?' 2010 Columbia Journal of Law and the Arts 471–498

Riis T and Schovsbo J, 'Extended Collective Licenses in Action' 2012 International Review of Intellectual Property And Competition Law (IIC) 930–950

Riis T, 'Collecting societies, competition and the Services Directive' 2011 Journal of Intellectual Property Law & Practice 482–493

Riis T, Rognstad O-A and Schovsbo JH, 'Collective Agreements for the Clearance of Copyrights: The Case of Collective Management and Extended Collective Licenses' in Riis T (ed), *User 8 Generated Law: Re-Constructing Intellectual Property Law in a Knowledge Society* (Edward Elgar 2016)

Ringnalda A, 'Orphan Works, Mass Rights Clearance, and Online Libraries: The Flaws of the Draft Orphan Works Directive and Extended Collective Licensing as a Solution' 2011 Medien und Recht International 3–11

Rognstad O-A, 'Avtalelisens som nordisk løsningmodell – Noen refleksjoner, særlig knyttet til avtalelisensens legitimitet i utlandet' 2012 NIR 620–632

Rognstad O-A, 'Avtalelisenser' 2004 Nordiskt Immateriellt Rättsskydd (NIR) 151–159

Rognstad O-A, 'Konsumpsjon og digitale overføringer; Et forslag til en alternativ løsningsmodell' in Andersen MB, Heide-Jørgensen C and Schovsbo J (eds), *Festskrift til Mogens Koktvedgaard* (Juris- og Økonomfobundets Forlag 2003)

Rognstad O-A, *Opphavsrett* (Universitetsforlaget 2009)

Rosati E, 'GS Media and Its Implications for the Construction of the Right of Communication to the Public within EU Copyright Architecture' 2017 Common Market Law Review 1221–1242

Rosati E, 'Judge-made EU Copyright Harmonisation: The Case of Originality' (The European University Institute 2012)

Rosati E, 'The Orphan Works Directive, or throwing a stone and hiding the hand' 2013 Journal of Intellectual Property Law & Practice 303–310

Rosati E, 'The Orphan Works Provisions of the ERR Act: Are They Compatible with UK and EU Laws?' 2013 EIPR 724–740

Rosén J, 'Copyright Contracts – EU Solutions or National Concern? A Swedish Proposal to Amend the Copyright Act on Individual and Collective Contracts' in Lidgard HH (ed), *National Developments in the Intersection of IPR and Competition Law: From Maglite to Pirate Bay* (2011)

Rosén J, 'How Much Communciation to the Publis is "Communication to the Public?"' in Stamatoudi IA (ed), *New Developments in EU and International Copyright Law* (Wolters Kluwer 2016)

Rosén J, 'The Nordic Extended Collective Licensing Model as a Mechanism for Simplified Rights Clearance for Legitimate Online Services' in Axhamn J (ed), *Copyright in a Borderless Online Environment* (Norstedts Juridik 2012)

Rosén J, 'The Satellite and Cable Directive' in Stamatoudi I and Torremans P (eds), *EU Copyright Law; A Commentary* (Edward Elgar 2014)

Rydén J, 'Are digital national libraries a vision or a utopia?' 2016 Lov&Data 14–17

Rydning C, 'Extended collective licenses: the compatibility of the Nordic solution with the international conventions and EC law' (Oslo University 2010)

Samuelson P, 'Google Book Search and the future of Books in Cyberspace' 2010 Minnesota Law Review 1308–1374

Samuelson P, 'Legislative Alternatives to the Google Book Settlement' 2011 Colum JL & Arts 697–729

Schierholz A, 'Collective Management in Europe – Practice and Legal Framework' in Walter MM and von Lewinski S (eds), *European Copyright Law, A Commentary* (Oxford University Press 2010)

Schlesinger M, 'Legal issues in peer-to-peer file sharing, focusing on the making available right' in Strowel A (ed), *Peer-to-peer file sharing and secondary liability in copyright law* (Edward Elgar 2009)

Schønning P, *Ophavsretsloven med kommentarer* (2nd edn, GadJura, Thomson Information A/S 1998)

Schønning P, *Ophavsretsloven med kommentarer* (3rd edn, Forlaget Thomson 2003)

Schønning P, *Ophavsretsloven med kommentarer* (5th edn, Thomson Reuters 2011)

Schønning P, *Ophavsretsloven med kommentarer* (6th edn, Karnov Group 2016)

Schovsbo J, 'The necessity to collectivize copyright – and the dangers thereof' in Rosén J (ed), *Individualism and Collectiveness in Intellectual Property Law* (Edward Elgar 2012)

Senftleben MRF, 'How to Overcome the Normal Exploitation Obstacle: Opt-Out Formalities, Embargo Periods, and the International Three-Step Test' 2014 Berkeley Technology Law Journal Commentaries

Senftleben MRF, 'Overprotection and Protection Overlaps in Intellectual Property Law – the Need for Horizontal Fair Use Defences' in Kur A and Mizaras V (eds), *The Structure of Intellectual Property Law; Can One Size Fit All?* (Edward Elgar 2011)

Senftleben MRF, 'The International Three-Step Test: A Model Provision for EC Fair Use Legislation' 2010 JIPITEC 67–82

Senftleben MRF, 'WIPO Copyright Treaty (WCT)' in Dreier T and Hugenholtz PB (eds), *Concise European Copyright Law* (2 edn, Wolters Kluwer 2016)

Senftleben MRF, *Copyright, Limitations and the Three-Step-Test* (Kluwer Law International 2004)

Sganga C, 'The eloquent silence of Soulier and Doke and its critical implications for EU copyright law' 2017 Journal of Intellectual Property Law & Practice 321–330

Shaughnessy TW, 'Digital Information and the Library: Planning and Policy Issues' in Lee S (ed), *Economics of Digital Information: Collection, Storage and Delivery* (Haworth Press 1997)

Sirinelli P, *Exceptions and Limitations on Copyright and Neighboring Rights* (WIPO 1999)

Skarstein VM, 'The Bookshelf: digitisation and access to copyright items in Norway' 2010 Program 48–58

Sterling JAL, *World Copyright Law* (2nd edn, Thomson Sweet and Maxwell 2003)

Sterling JAL, *World Copyright Law* (Cook T ed, 4 edn, 2015)

Stobo V, Deazley R and Anderson IG, *Copyright & Risk: Scoping the Wellcome Digital Library Project* (CREATe Working Paper No10, 2013)

Stratton B, *Seeking New Landscapes: A rights clearance study in the context of mass digitisation of 140 books published between 1870 and 2010* (British Library 2011)

Strowel A, 'Droit d'auteur and Copyright: Between History and Nature' in Sherman B and Strowel A (eds), *Of Authors and Origins* (Clarendon Press 1994)

Strowel A, 'Google books: quel futur pour l'accès aux livres? Une bibliothèque universelle en devenir ou une future galerie commerciale? ' 2010 Auteurs & Media 1–7

Strowel A, 'The European "Extended Collective Licensing" Model' 2011 Colum JL & Arts 665–669

Suthersanen U and Frabboni MM, 'The Orphan Works Directive' in Stamatoudi I and Torremans P (eds), *EU Copyright Law A Commentary* (Edward Elgar 2014)

Sykes J, 'Hybrid library management' in Baker D and Evans W (eds), *Digital library economics: an academic perspective* (Chandos 2009)

Talke A, 'Verwaiste und vergriffene Werke – Kommt das 20. Jahrhundert endlich in die Digitale Bibliothek?' 2013 LIBREAS Library Ideas 131–144

Torremans P, 'Archiving exceptions: where are we and where do we need to go?' in Derclaye E (ed), *Copyright and Cultural Heritage; Preservation and Access to Works in a Digital World* (Edward Elgar 2010)

Torremans P, 'Copyright Territoriality in a Borderless Online Environment' in Axhamn J (ed), *Copyright in a Borderless Online Environment* (Norstedts Juridik 2012)

Torremans P, 'Intellectual property and the EU rules on private international law: match or mismatch?' in Stamatoudi I and Torremans P (eds), *EU Copyright Law; A Commentary* (Edward Elgar 2014)

Torremans P, 'Jurisdiction in Intellectual Property Cases' in Torremans P (ed), *Research Handbook on Cross-border Enforcement of Intellectual Property* (Edward Elgar 2014)

Torremans P, 'Private International Law Issues on the Internet' in Stamatoudi IA (ed), *New Developments in EU and International Copyright Law* (Wolters Kluwer 2016)

Torremans P, *Choice of law in EU copyright directives* (Derclaye E ed, Edward Elgar 2009)

Treppoz E, 'Commentary on Regulation No. 864/2007 (Rome II)' in Cottier T and Veron P (eds), *Concise International and European IP Law* (Wolters Kluwer 2014)

Triaille J-P and others, 'Preliminary studies to the future EU Copyright review: about (some) exclusive rights and (some) exceptions' 2015 Auteurs & Média 147–157

Triaille J-P and others, *Study on the Application of Directive 2001/29/EC on Copyright and Related Rights in the Information Society (The "InfoSoc Directive")* (2013)

Trimble M, 'Advancing national intellectual property policies in a transnational context' 2015 Maryland Law Revue 203–257

Trimble M, 'The Marrakesh Puzzle' 2014 IIC – International Review of Intellectual Property and Competition Law 768–795

Trumpke F, 'Exklusivität und Kollectivierung: Das skandinavische Modell der Erweiterten Kollektiven Lizenz (Extended Collective Licensing)' (Nomos, PhD, 2015)

Trumpke F, 'The Extended Collective License – A Matter of Exclusivity?' 2012 NIR 264–294

Tryggvadóttir R, 'Balancing of interests and cross-border use: Room for Nordic co-operation?' 2015 NIR 652–665

Tryggvadóttir R, 'Digital libraries, the Nordic system of extended collective licenses and cross-border use' 2014 Auteurs & Media 314–325

Tryggvadóttir R, 'Heimildir (bóka)safna til eintakagerðar og dreifingar á efni sem lýtur höfundarétti (e. What permission do libraries and museums have to make copies of and distribute works that fall under copyright protection)' in *Ragnarsbók* (Hið íslenska bókmenntafélag 2009)

van Eechoud M, 'Alternatives to the Lex Protectionis as the Choice-of-Law Rule for Initial Ownership of Copyright' in Drexl J and Kur A (eds), *Intellectual Property and Private International Law, IIC Studies vol 24* (2005)

van Eechoud M, *Choice of Law in Copyright and Related Rights, Alternatives to the Lex Protectionis* (Wolters Kluwer 2003)

van Gompel S and Hugenholtz PB, 'The Orphan Works Problem: The Copyright Conundrum of Digitizing Large-Scale Audiovisual Archives, and How to Solve It' 2010 Popular Communication – The International Journal of Media and Culture 61–71

van Gompel S, 'Directive 2014/26/EU on collective management of copyright and related rights and multi-territorial licensing of rights in musical works for online use in the internal market' in Dreier T and Hugenholtz PB (eds), *Concise European Copyright Law* (2 edn, Wolters Kluwer 2016)

van Gompel S, 'Unlocking the Potential of Pre-Existing Content: How to Address the Issue of Orphan Works in Europe?' 2007 International Review of Industrial Property and Competition Law (IIC) 669–702

Verronen V, 'Extended Collective Licence in Finland: A Legal Instrument for Balancing the Rights of the Author with the Interests of the User' 2002 Journal of the Copright Society of the USA 1143–1160

Vilanka O, 'Rough Justice or Zero Tolerance? – Reassessing the Nature of Copyright in Light of Collective Licensing (Part I)' in *In Search of New IP Regime* (2010)

von Hielmcrone H, 'Orphan works. The Danish solution: Extended collective licensing' 2008 EBLIDA News 1–2

von Lewinski S and Walter MM, 'Information Society Directive' in Walter MM and von Lewinski S (eds), *European Copyright Law, A Commentary* (Oxford University Press 2010)

von Lewinski S, 'Certain Legal Problems Related to the Making Available of Literary and Artistic Works and other Protected Subject Matter through Digital Networks' 2005 UNESCO e-copyright Bulletin 1–14

von Lewinski S, 'Collectivism and its Role in the Frame of Individual Contracts' in Rosén J (ed), *Individualism and Collectiveness in Intellectual Property Law* (Edward Elgar 2012)

von Lewinski S, 'Copyright in a Borderless Online Environment: EU Cross-Border Licensing of Rights' in Axhamn J (ed), *Copyright in a Borderless Online Environment* (Norstedts Juridik 2012)

von Lewinski S, 'Mandatory Collective Administration of Exclusive Rights – a Case Study on its Compatibility with International and EC Copyright Law' 2004 UNESCO e-Copyright Bulletin 1–14

von Lewinski S, 'Recent Developments of German Author's Rights Law – Part I' 2015 Auteurs & Média 158–169

von Lewinski S, 'Rental and Lending Rights Directive' in Walter MM and von Lewinski S (eds), *European Copyright Law, A Commentary* (Oxford University Press 2010)

von Lewinski S, *International Copyright Law and Policy,* (Oxford University Press 2008)

Von Lohmann F, 'Google on what is driving creativity and innovation in the digital economy' 2016 WIPO Magazine 26–28

Vuopala A, *Assessment of the Orphan works issue and Costs for Rights Clearance* (DG Information Society and Media 2010)

Vuopala A, *Extended Collective Licensing – A solution for facilitating licensing of works through Europeana, including orphans?* (Finnish Copyright Society 2013)

Walker DM, *The Oxford Companion to Law* (Oxford University Press 1980)

Walter MM and von Lewinski S (eds), *European Copyright Law, A Commentary* (Oxford University Press 2010)

Walter MM, 'Term Directive' in Walter MM and von Lewinski S (eds), *European Copyright Law, A Commentary* (Oxford University Press 2010)

Wang J, 'Should China adopt an extended licensing system to facilitate collective copyright administration: preliminary thoughts' 2010 EIPR 283–289

Westkamp G, 'Copyright Reform and Necessary Flexibilities' 2014 IIC 497–499

Westkamp G, *Study on the Implementation and Effect in Member States' Laws of Directive 2001/29/EC on the Harmonisation of Certain Aspects of Copyright and Related Rights in The Information Society. Part II; The Implementation of Directive 2001/29/EC in the Member States* (Queen Mary Intellectual Property Research Institute 2007)

White B, 'Guaranteeing Access to Knowledge: The Role of Libraries' 2012 WIPO Magazine 15–18

WIPO, *Berne Convention Centenary 1886–1986* (the International Bureau of Intellectual Property 1986)

WIPO, *Guide to the Berne Convention, WIPO publication No. 615(E)* (WIPO 1978)

WIPO, *WIPO Glossary of Terms of the Law of Copyright and Neighboring Rights* (WIPO 1980)

WIPO, *WIPO Intellectual Property Handbook: Policy, Law and Use* (WIPO 2004)

Wittem Project, *European Copyright Code* (deLex 2010)

Xalabarder R, 'Digital Libraries in the current legal and educational environment: Towards a remunerated compulsory license or limitation?' in Bently L, Suthersanen U and Torremans P (eds), *Global Copyright – Three Hundred Years since the Statute of Anne: From 1710 to Cyberspace* (Edward Elgar 2010)

Xalabarder R, 'Jurisdiction and Applicable Law issues for the protection of moral rights online' in Brison F and others (eds), *Moral Rights Aspects in New Forms of Use* (ALAI 2014)

DOCUMENTS AND REPORTS

AUSTRALIA

ALRC, Copyright and the Digital Economy (ALRC Report 122) (2013)
ALRC, Copyright and the Digital Economy: Discussion Paper (2013)
Australian Government Productivity Commission, Intellectual Property Arrangements; Draft Report (2016)

EU COMMISSION

COM(88) 172 final, Green Paper on Copyright and the Challenge of Technology – Copyright Issues Requiring Immediate Action (1988)
COM(91) 276 final, Proposal for a Council Directive on the coordination of certain rules concerning copyright and neighbouring rights applicable to satellite broadcasting and cable retransmission. (1991)
COM(95) 382 final, Green Paper: Copyright and Related Rights in the Information Society (1995)
COM(96) 568 final, Communication from the Commission; Follow-up to the Green Paper on Copyright and Related Rights in the Information Society (1996)
COM(97) 628 final, Proposal for a European Parliament and Council Directive on the harmonization of certain aspects of copyright and related rights in the Information Society (1997)
COM(2002) 430 Final, Report from the European Commission on the application of Council Directive 93/83/EEC on the coordination of certain rules concerning copyright and rights related to copyright applicable to satellite broadcasting and cable retransmission (2002)
COM(2003) 427 final, Proposal for a Regulation of the European Parliament and of the Council on the law applicable to non-contractual obligations (Rome II) (2003)
COM(2004) 261 final, Communication from the Commission to the Council, the European Parliament and the European Economic and Social Committee on the Management of Copyright and Related Rights in the Internal Market (2004)
COM(2005) 465, Communication from the Commission to the European Parliament, the Council, the European Economic and Social Committee and the Committee of the Regions on i2010: Digital Libraries (2005)
COM(2007) 242 final, Communication from the Commission to the European Parliament, the Council, the European Economic and Social Committee and the Committee of the Regions on a European agenda for culture in a globalizing world (2007)
COM(2007) 836 final, Communication from the Commission to the European Parliament, the Council, the European Economic and Social Committee and the Committee of the Regions on Creative Content Online in the Single Market (COM(2007) 836 final, 2008)
COM(2008) 466, Green Paper; Copyright in the Knowledge Economy (2008)

COM(2008) 513 final, Communication from the Commission to the European Parliament, the Council, the European Economic and Social Committee and the Committee of the Regions on Europe's cultural heritage at the click of a mouse: Progress on the digitisation and online accessibility of cultural material and digital preservation across the EU (2008)

COM(2009) 440 final, Communication from the Commission to the European Parliament, the Council, the European Economic and Social Committee and the Committee of the Regions: Europeana – next steps (2009)

COM(2009) 532 final, Communication from the Commission: Copyright in the Knowledge Economy (2009)

COM(2010) 245 final/2, Communication from the Commission to the European Parliament, the Council, the European Economic and Social Committee and the Committee of the Regions: A Digital Agenda for Europe (2010)

COM(2011) 287 final, Communication from the Commission to the European Parliament, the Council, the European Economic and Social Committee and the Committee of the Regions; A Single Market for Intellectual Property Rights boosting creativity and innovation to provide economic growth, high quality jobs and first class products and services in Europe (2011)

COM(2011) 289 final, Proposal for a Directive of the European Parliament and of the Council on certain permitted uses of orphan works (2011)

COM(2011) 427/4, GREEN PAPER on the online distribution of audiovisual works in the European Union: opportunities and challenges towards a digital single market (2011)

COM(2012) 372/2, Proposal for a Directive of the European Parliament and of the Council on collective management of copyright and related rights and multi-territorial licensing of rights in musical works for online uses in the internal market (2012)

COM(2015) 192 final, Communication from the Commission to the European Parliament, the Council, the European Economic and Social Committee and the Committee of the Regions; A Digital Single Market Strategy for Europe (2015)

COM(2015) 626 final, Communication from the Commission to the European Parliament, the Council, the European Economic and Social Committee and the Committee of the Regions; Towards a modern, more European copyright framework (2015)

COM(2015) 627, Proposal for a Regulation of the European Parliament and of the Council on ensuring the cross-border portability of online content services in the internal market (2015)

COM(2016) 289 final, Proposal for a Regulation of the European Parliament and of the Council on addressing geo-blocking and other forms of discrimination based on customers' nationality, place of residence or place of establishment within the internal market and amending Regulation (EC) No 2006/2004 and Directive 2009/22/EC (2016)

COM(2016) 593 final, Proposal for a Directive of the European Parliament and of the Council on copyright in the Digital Single Market (2016)

COM(2016) 594 final, Proposal for a Regulation of the European Parliament and of the Council laying down rules on the exercise of copyright and related rights applicable to certain online transmissions of broadcasting organisations and retransmissions of television and radio programmes (2016)

COM(2016) 595 final, Proposal for a Regulation of the European Parliament and of the Council on the cross-border exchange between the Union and third countries of accessible format copies of certain works and other subject-matter protected by copyright and related rights for the benefit of persons who are blind, visually impaired or otherwise print disabled (2016)

COM(2016) 596 final, Proposal for a Directive of the European Parliament and of the Councilon on certain permitted uses of works and other subject-matter protected by copyright and related rights for the benefit of persons who are blind, visually impaired or otherwise print disabled and amending Directive 2001/29/EC on the harmonisation of certain aspects of copyright and related rights in the information society (2016)

Comité des Sages, Summary Record of the Public Hearing of the Comité des Sages on: "Bringing Europe's cultural heritage online" (2010)

Comité des Sages, The New Renaissance (2011)

Commission Working Paper, IIIID/1294/79-EN, The Need for a European Trade Mark System. Competence of the European Community to Create One (1979)

DG Internal Market and Services, Public Consultation on the review of the EU copyright rules (2013)

Directorate-General for Internal Market and Services, Handbook on implementation of the Services Directive (2007)

European Commission, Summary Minutes of the 1st meeting of the High Level Expert Group on Digital Libraries (2006)

European Commission, Cultural heritage: Digitisation, online accessibility and digital preservation. Report on the Implementation of Commission Recommendation 2011/711/EU, 2011–2013 (2014)

European Commission, Report on the responses to the Public Consultation on the Review of the EU Copyright Rules (2014)

European Commission, Cultural heritage: Digitisation, online accessibility and digital preservation. Report on the Implementation of Commission Recommendation 2011/711/EU, 2013–2015 (2016)

SEC(2006) 1075, Commission Recommendation on the digitisation and online accessibility of cultural material and digital preservation – Impact assessment (2006)

SEC(2007) 1556, Commission staff working document: Report to the Council, the European Parliament and the Economic and Social Committee on the application of Directive 2001/29/EC on the harmonisation of certain aspects of copyright and related rights in the information society (2007)

SEC(2007) 1710, Commission Staff Working Document accompanying the Communication from the Commission to the European Parliament, the Council, the European Economic and Social Committee and the Committee of the Regions on Creative Content Online in the Single Market (2008)

SEC(2011) 615 final, Impact Assessment on the Cross-Border Online Access to Orphan Works; Commission Staff Working accompanying the document Proposal for a Directive of the European Parliament and of the Council on certain permitted uses of orphan works (2011)

SEC(2011) 1274, Commission staff working paper accompanying the document Commission Recommendation on the digitisation and online accessibility of cultural material and digital preservation, (2011)

SWD(2012) 204 final, Impact Assessment accompanying the document Proposal for a Directive of the European Parliament and of the Council on collective management of copyright and related rights and multi-territorial licensing of rights in musical works for online uses in the internal market (2012)

SEC(2012) 680, Debat d'orientation sur le contenu dans l'economie numerique – Note de cadrage diffusée sous l'autorité de M. le PRESIDENT (2012)

SWD(2015) 100 final, Commission Staff Working Document: A Digital Single Market Strategy for Europe – Analysis and Evidence, accompanying the document: Communication from the Commission to the European Parliament, the Council, the European Economic and Social Committee and the Committee of the Regions; A Digital Single Market Strategy for Europe (2015)

SWD(2016) 301 final, Commission staff working document: Impact Assessment on the modernisation of EU copyright rules, Part I (2016)

SWD(2016) 301 final, Commission staff working document: Impact Assessment on the modernisation of EU copyright rules, Part III (2016)

SWD(2016) 308 final, Commission Staff Working Document: Evaluation of the Council Directive 93/83/EEC on the coordination of certain rules concerning copyright and rights related to copyright applicable to satellite broadcasting and cable retransmission (2016)

2005/737/EC, Commission recommendation of 18 May 2005 on collective cross-border management of copyright and related rights for legitimate online music services (2005)

2006/585/EC, Commission Recommendation on the digitisation and online accessibility of cultural material and digital preservation (OJ L 236/28, 2006)

2011/711/EU, Commission Recommendation on the digitisation and online accessibility of cultural material and digital preservation (OJ L 283/39, 2011)

HLG – Copyright Subgroup, Final Report on Digital Preservation, Orphan Works and Out-of-Print Works (2008)

HLG, Final Report: "Digital Libraries: Challenges and Recommendations for the Future" (2009)

COUNCIL OF THE EUROPEAN UNION

Council, Proposal for a Directive of the European Parliament and of the Council on certain permitted uses of orphan works – Presidency compromise proposal (15190/11 PI 125 AUDIO 45 CULT 75 CODEC 1624, 2011)

Council, 'Council conclusions on the digitisation and online accessibility of cultural material and digital preservation' (3164th Education, Youth, Culture and Sport Council meeting 10 and 11 May 2012)

Council, Proposal for a Directive of the European Parliament and of the Council on collective management of copyright and related rights and multi-territorial licensing of rights in musical works for online uses in the internal market – Presidency compromise proposal (2013)

2016/0280 (COD) 13842/17, Proposal for a Directive of the European Parliament and of the Council on copyright in the Digital Single Market – Consolidated Presidency compromise proposal (2017)
2016/0280 (COD) 7450/18, Proposal for a Directive of the European Parliament and of the Council on copyright in the Digital Single Market – Consolidated Presidency compromise proposal (2018)
2016/0280 (COD) 9134/18, Proposal for a Directive of the European Parliament and of the Council on copyright in the Digital Single Market – Agreed negotiation mandate (2018)

EFTA

Standing Committee of the EFTA States, Subcommittee I on the Free Movement of Goods: EEA EFTA Comment on the Commission proposal for a Directive of the European Parliament and of the Council on collective management of copyright and related rights and multi-territorial licensing of rights in musical works for online uses in the internal market, (COM (2012) 372) (2013)

EUROPEAN PARLIAMENT

Committee on Legal Affairs, Draft Report on the implementation of Directive 2001/29/EC of the European Parliament and of the Council of 22 May 2001 on the harmonisation of certain aspects of copyright and related rights in the information society (2014/2256(INI)) (2015)
European Parliament, Resolution of 9 July 2015 on the implementation of Directive 2001/29/EC of the European Parliament and of the Council of 22 May 2001 on the harmonisation of certain aspects of copyright and related rights in the information society (2014/2256(INI)) (2015)
EP CULT, Draft Opinion of the Committee on Culture and Education for the Committee on Legal Affairs on the proposal for a directive of the European Parliament and of the Council on copyright in the Digital Single Market (COM(2016)0593 – C8-0383/2016 – 2016/0280(COD)) (2017)
EP IMCO, Opinion of the Committee on the Internal Market and Consumer Protection for the Committee on Legal Affairs on the proposal for a directive of the European Parliament and of the Council on copyright in the Digital Single Market (COM(2016)0593 – C8-0383/2016 – 2016/0280(COD)) (2017)
EP ITRE, Opinion of the Committee on Industry, Research and Energy for the Committee on Legal Affairs on the proposal for a directive of the European Parliament and of the Council on copyright in the Digital Single Market (COM(2016)0593 – C8-0383/2016 – 2016/0280(COD)) (2017)
EP JURI, Draft Report on the proposal for a directive of the European Parliament and of the Council on copyright in the Digital Single Market (COM(2016)0593 – C8-0383/2016 – 2016/0280(COD)) (2017)
Madiega T, Cross-border portability of online content services; EPRS Briefing, EU Legislation in Progress (2017)

EUIPO

OHIM presentation for the Copyright Contact Committee 5 June 2013, *Setting up of single EU Orphan Works database* (2013)
OHIM Orphan Works User Interfaces, *Prototype Version 2.0* (2014)

EUROPEAN UNION

Joint Practical Guide of the European Parliament, the Council and the Commission for persons involved in the drafting of European Union legislation (2014)
The Council and the European Commission, eEurope 2002 – An Information Society for All, Action Plan (2000)

NON-GOVERNMENTAL ORGANISATIONS

ALAI, Orphan works – compatibility of the draft Directive with the international norms (2012)
ALAI, Report and Opinion on the making available and communication to the public in the internet environment – focus on linking techniques on the Internet (2013)
ALAI, Opinion on the on the criterion "New Public", developed by the Court of Justice of the European Union (CJEU), put in the context of making available and communication to the public (2014)
ALAI, Opinion on the cross-border effect of licences granted for digitization and communication of out-of-commerce works by cultural heritage institutions under a regime of Extended Collective Licences (ECL) (2016)
EBU, Modern copyright for digital media; E.B.U. Policy Paper (2010)
Europeana, We transform the world with culture: Europeana Strategy 2015–2020 (2014)
European Copyright Society, 'Opinion on the Reference to the CJEU in Case C-466/12 Svensson' (2013)
European Copyright Society, 'Opinion on the Judgment of the CJEU in Case C-201/13 Deckmyn' (2014)
European Copyright Society, Answer to the EC Consultation on the review of the EU copyright rules (2014)
European Copyright Society, Response to the European Commission's Public Consultation on the Review of the EU Satellite and Cable Directive (2015)
European Copyright Society, General Opinion on the EU Copyright Reform Package (2017)
IFLA, Treaty Proposal on Limitations and Exceptions for Libraries and Archives (2013)
IFLA, Guidelines for Audiovisual and Multimedia Materials in Libraries and other Institutions (2004)
IFRRO, 'Principles for Bilateral Agreements' (2006) <www.ifrro.org/node/1115> accessed 6 January 2017
IFRRO, 'Sample Bilateral Agreement – Type A' <www.ifrro.org/node/1116> accessed 6 January 2017

IFRRO, 'Sample Bilateral Agreement – Type B' <www.ifrro.org/node/1118> accessed 6 January 2017

IFRRO, IFRRO Position on the Proposal for a Directive on Copyright in the Digital Single Market (2017)

IFRRO, IFRRO position paper on the proposal for a Directive on Collective Management of copyright and related rights and multi-territorial licensing of rights in musical works for online uses in the internal market (2012)

IFRRO, U.S. Public Consultation: "Mass Digitization Pilot Program" (2015)

KEA European Affairs, Audiovisual Orphan Works in Europe – national survey; Report prepared for the British Film Institute (BFI) (2011)

Norwegian National Library, Response to the Public Consultation on the review of the EU copyright rules (2013)

UCL, Information behaviour of the researcher of the future, a ciber briefing paper, Study conducted for the JISC and the British Library (2008)

NORDIC OFFICIAL DOCUMENTS

NOU 1988:22, Endringer i åndverksloven m.v. (1988)

Denmark

2007/2 LSF 58, Forslag til Lov om ændring af ophavsretsloven (Overdragelse af ophavsret og digitalisering af kulturarven m.v.) (2008)

Bet. 1981/912, Licenskonstruktioner og fotokopiering (1981)

Bet. nr. 1197/1990, Revision af ophavsretslovgivningen; Slutbetænkning fra udvalget vedrørende revision af ophavsretslovgivningen (1990) Folketingstidende 1984–1985 TA, Bind II, Lovforslag nr. L 113 (1984)

Folketingstidende 1994–1995 TA, Lovforslag nr. L 119 (1995)

Lovforslag nr. L 123 2014, Folketinget 2013–14. Forslag til Lov til ændring af ophavsretsloven (Visse tilladte anvendelser af forældreløse værker og ændring af aftalelicensbestemmelsen vedrørende kabelviderspredning) (2014)

Lovforslag nr. L 37, Forslag til lov om ændring af ophavsretsloven. (Databaser, digital eksemplarfremstilling til undervisningsbrug m.v., gengivelse af kunstværker m.v.) (1998)

Lovforslag nr. L 141, Forslag til lov om ændring af ophavsretsloven (Digital eksemplarfremstilling til personlig brug, aftalelicens m.v.) (2001)

Lovforslag nr. L 19, Lov til ændring af ophavsretsloven: Gennemførelse af infosoc-direktivet og nye aftalelicenser m.v. (2002)

Tillæg A, Folketingstidende 1959–60, Forslag til Lov om ophavsretten til litterære og kunstneriske værker (sp 2567 ff, 1960)

Finland

RP 28/2004 rd, Grundlagsutskottets Utlåtande: Regeringens proposition med förslag till lagar om ändring av upphovsrättslagen och 49 kap. strafflagen, GrUU 7/2005 rd, (2004)

RP 181/2014 rd, Regeringens proposition med förslag till ändring av upphovsrättslagen (2014)

Norway

Kulturdepartementet, Høringsnotat, Endringer i åndverkloven (2014)
Ot. prp. nr. 15, Om lov om endringer i åndsverkloven m m (1994)
Ot. prp. nr. 46, Om lov om endringer i åndsverkloven m.m. (2005)
Ot.prp. nr. 46 (2004–2005), Om lov om endringer i åndsverkloven m.m. (2005)
Prop. 69 L, Proposisjon til Stortinget (forslag til lovvedtak): Endringer i åndsverkloven (gjennomføring av EUs hitteverkdirektiv og innføring av generell avtalelisens mv.) (2015)
St.meld. nr. 24, Nasjonal strategi for digital bevaring og formidling av kulturarv (2008–2009) (2009)

Sweden

Ds 2003:35, Upphovsrätten i informationssamhället – genomförande av direktiv 2001/29/EG, m.m. (2003)
Prop. 1979/80:132, Regeringens proposition 1979/80:132 om ändring i uppbovsrättslagen (1960:729), m. m. (1980)
Prop. 1992/93:214, Regeringens proposition om ändringar i upphovsrättslagen (1993)
Prop. 2004/05:110, Regeringens proposition: Upphovsrätten i informationssamhället – genomförande av direktiv 2001/29/EG m.m. (2005)
Prop. 2010/2011:33, Återanvändning av upphovsrättsligt skyddat material i radio och tv (2010)
Prop. 2012/13:141, Regeringens proposition: Förbättrade möjligheter till licensiering af upphovsrätt (2013)
Proposition 1985/86:146, Om vidaresändning av radio- och TV-program (1986)
SOU 2011:32, En ny upphovsrättslag; Slutbetänkande af Upphovsrättsutredningen (2011)
SOU 1990:30, Översyn af upphovsrättslagstiftningen (1990)
SOU 2010:24, Avtalad upphovsrätt: Delbetänkande af Upphovsrättsutredningen (2010)

UK DOCUMENTS

Department for Culture Media and Sport, *Empower, Inform, Enrich* (2009)
Gowers A, *Gowers Review of Intellectual Property* (2006)
Hargreaves I, *Digital Opportunity; A Review of Intellectual Property and Growth* (2011)
IPO, *@the way ahead; A Strategy for Copyright in the Digital Age* (2009)
IPO, *Extended Collective Licensing (ECL): Guidance for relevant licensing bodies applying to run ECL schemes* (2016)
IPO, *Extending the benefits of collective licensing; Consultation on the UK's new extended collective licensing scheme* (2013)
IPO, *Factsheet – Orphan Works Licensing Scheme and Extented Collective Licensing* (2014)
IPO, *Government response to the technical consultation on draft secondary legislation for extended collective licensing (ECL) schemes* (2014)

USA

Ginsburg JC and Besek JM, Copyright Office Notice of Inquiry and Request for Comments on the Topic of Facilitating Access to Copyrighted Works for the Blind or Other Persons with Disabilities, 74 Fed. Reg. 52,507 (2009) (2009)
Ginsburg JC and Besek JM, Comments Pursuant to Notice of Inquiry on Mass Digitzation Piolt Program, 80 Fed. Reg. 32614 (June 9, 2015) (2015)
Library of Congress and others, International Study on the Impact of Copyright Law on Digital Preservation (2008)
Rydén J, Comments in response to the June 9, 2015, Notice of Inquiry regarding Mass Digitization (2015)
Samuelson P, Comments in response to the June 9, 2015, Notice of Inquiry regarding Mass Digitization (2015)
The Section 108 Study Group, The Section 108 Study Group Report (2008)
US Copyright Office, Legal Issues in Mass Digitization: A Preliminary Analysis and Dicussion Document (2011)
US Copyright Office, Orphan Works and Mass Digitization (2015)

WIPO

WIPO, Records of the intellectual property conference of Stockholm (1967) (1971)
WIPO, Prepatory Document for the Second Session of the Committee of Expert on a Possible Protocol to the Berne Convention for the Protection of Literary and Artistic Works (1992)
WIPO CRNR/DC/4, Basic Proposal for the Substantive Provisions of the Treaty on Certain Questions Concerning the Protection of Literary and Artistic Works to be Considered by the Diplomatic Conference (1996)
WIPO SCCR/22/12, Draft WIPO Treaty on Exceptions and Limitations for the Persons with Disabilities, Educational and Research Institutions, Libraries and Archives: Proposal by the African Group (2011)
WIPO SCCR/29/4, Consolidation of proposed texts contained in document SCCR/26/3 (2014)
WT/DS160/R, Panel Report, United States – Section 110(5) of the US Copyright Act (2000)

WEBSITES AND BLOGS

Angelopoulos C, 2017, CJEU Decision on Ziggo: The Pirate Bay Communicates Works to the Public, Kluwer Copyright Blog accessed 1 July 2017
Boyd J, 'IFRRO submits comments on proposed Orphan Works Directive' (*IFRRO*, 01.09.2011) <www.ifrro.org/content/ifrro-submits-comments-proposed-orphan-works-directive-0> accessed 15 December 2016
Boyd J, 20.09.2011, Stakeholders sign ground-breaking MoU on Out of Commerce Works, IFRRO accessed 11 July 2017

COMMUNIA, 'Policy paper on proposed Directive on collective management of copyright' (2013) <www.communia-association.org/2013/01/07/communia-policy-paper-on-proposed-directive-on-collective-management-of-copyright/> accessed 16 July 2017

Cox KL, Association of Research Libraries Issue Brief: Second Circuit Court of Appeals Affirms Fair Use in Google Books Case< www.arl.org> (2015), accessed 22 July 2017

Depreeuw S, 2015, Publication: The variable scope of the exclusive economic rights in copyright, Kluwer Copyright Blog, accessed 1 July 2017

DLF, 'A working definition of digital library' (1998) <http://old.diglib.org/about/dldefinition.htm > accessed 9 December 2015

EFTA Secretariat, 'Vivid Discussions at EFTA's Copyright Seminar' (2010) <www.efta.int/eea/eea-news/2010–09–30-efta-copyright-seminar> accessed 7 July 2017

Ficsor M, 2013, Commentary on the Marrakesh Treaty on Accessible Format Copies for the Visually Impaired, Copyright See-Saw accessed, accessed 12 July 2017

Ficsor M, 2014, Svensson: honest attempt at establishing due balance concerning the use of hyperlinks – spoiled by the erroneous "new public" theory, Copyright See-Saw, accessed 2 July 2017

Giersberg D, '"Not Cloud-Cuckoo-Land" – The German Digital Library' (Goethe Institute, 2009) <www.goethe.de/wis/bib/dib/en5421919.htm> accessed 03.10.2011

Google, 'Google Checks Out Library Books' (Google, 14.12.2004) <www.google.com/press/pressrel/print_library.html> accessed 30 June 2017 31

Guibault L, 2012, Are European orphans about to be freed?, Kluwer Copyright Blog, Last accessed 4 July 2017

Guibault L, 2012, France solves its XXe century book problem!, Kluwer Copyright Blog, accessed 11 July 2017

Husovec M and Gera M, 2016, Slovakia adopts a new Copyright Act: It's a Mixed Bag – Part II, Kluwer Copyright Blog, accessed 26 September 2016

Jasserand C, 2011, Will out-of-commerce books soon be managed by a collective management society in France?, Kluwer Copyright Blog, accessed 11 July 2017

Mariscal P, 2017, The Ten Commandments of Communication to the Public: A Brief Review of CJEU Case-law, Kluwer Copyright Blog, accessed 22 July 2017

Mendis D and Stobo V, 2014, UK: Extended Collective Licensing, Kluwer Copyright Blog, accessed 11 July 2017

National Library of Sweden, 'Remote access across borders' (2015) <www.kb.se/english/about/news/Making-the-material-available-through-streaming-via-the-Internet-/> accessed 7 July 2017

Nérisson S, 2016, Opinion of AG Wathelet in the Soulier and Doke case (C-301/15): Licensing exclusive rights requires express prior consent of the author; opt-out doesn't help, Kluwer Copyright Blog, accessed 11 July 2017 2

Nordemann JB, 2016, Communication to the public in copyright law – the German struggle with the CJEU concept, Kluwer Copyright Blog, accessed 23 January 2017

Rosati E, 'The CJEU decision in Soulier: what does it mean for laws other than the French one on out-of-print books?' (2016) <www.ipkat.com/> accessed 19 November 2016

Rosén J, 2014, What happened to Svensson and his friends after the CJEU decision?, The IPKat Weblog, accessed 2 July 2017

Rosenberg S, 'How Google book search got lost' <https://www.wired.com/2017/04/how-google-book-search-got-lost/>, accessed 30 June 2017

Samuelson P, 'Google Books is not a library' *Huffington Post* (18 March 2010) <www.huffingtonpost.com/pamela-samuelson/google-books-is-not-a-lib_b_317518.html> accessed 29 June 2017

Somers J, 'Torching the Modern-Day Library of Alexandria' The Atlantic <https://www.theatlantic.com/technology/archive/2017/04/the-tragedy-of-google-books/523320/>, accessed 30 June 2017

Spitz B, 2013, Jurisdiction in EU copyright cases: accessibility of a website is a criterion, Kluwer Copyright Blog, accessed 13 July 2017

Strowel A, 2010, Bokhylla.no, the Norwegian bookshelf: a model?, IPdigIT, accessed 7 July 2017

WIP0, Making International IP Law: an interview with Francis Gurry, <www.wipo.int/wipo_magazine/en/2014/05/article_0001.html>, (2014), accessed 22 July 2017

Wu T, 'What Ever Happened to Google Books?' The New Yorker <www.newyorker.com/business/currency/what-ever-happened-to-google-books>, accessed 30 June 2017

KU Leuven Centre for IT & IP Law

The KU Leuven Centre for IT & IP Law Series brings together the results of research activities of the Centre for IT & IP Law. The central research themes of the series concern the legal and ethical aspects of information technology, innovation and intellectual property.

Each book in the series focuses on the essential developments in the current legal framework, necessitated by the rapid evolution of technology in various fields, such as government, media, health care, informatics, digital economy, banking, transport and culture. The research is characterised by an interdisciplinary approach, constantly cross-fertilising legal, technical, economic, ethical and socio-cultural perspectives.

Books are published in English, Dutch and/or French.

www.ingramcontent.com/pod-product-compliance
Ingram Content Group UK Ltd.
Pitfield, Milton Keynes, MK11 3LW, UK
UKHW051846100926
8556IPUK00005B/475

9 781780 686745